More Praise for *The Handbook of Dispute Resolution*

"*The Handbook of Dispute Resolution* is a gold mine of insights and sound advice on all stages of dealing with conflict, from choosing the right process to implementing the settlement agreement. It is a wonderful stimulus to new thinking. Anyone concerned with conflict, whether as participant, third party, advisor, or observer, needs to know this material."
—*Joseph Stanford*, former Canadian Ambassador to Israel and High Commissioner to Cyprus

"*The Handbook of Dispute Resolution* has something for everyone interested in conflict, its prevention, and most importantly, its resolution. The clever arrangement into four distinct sections with treatments by prominent professors and experienced practitioners offers much to advocates, academicians, human resources and risk managers, or neutrals. It is a first-look resource for either novices or advanced practitioners of ADR."
—*Robert A. Creo*, founding president and fellow, International Academy of Mediators

"A must-read for mediators, negotiators, and other dispute resolvers. Moffitt and Bordone bring together ADR's finest to advance our understanding of conflict and its resolution in this well-crafted collection."
—*Charles P. Doran*, executive director, Mediation Works Incorporated

"Moffitt and Bordone have skillfully assembled a basket of gems—each chapter contains fresh insights, cogently presented, brilliantly polished, from the best, the brightest, and the most creative thinkers in the field of conflict management and dispute resolution. This is a must-read handbook for both scholars and practitioners."
—*David Hoffman*, chair, the ABA Section of Dispute Resolution; founder, Boston Law Collaborative, LLC

The Handbook of Dispute Resolution

The Handbook of
Dispute Resolution

Michael L. Moffitt and Robert C. Bordone
Editors

A Publication of the Program on Negotiation
at Harvard Law School

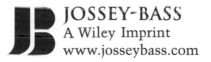

JOSSEY-BASS
A Wiley Imprint
www.josseybass.com

Published by Jossey-Bass
A Wiley Imprint
989 Market Street, San Francisco, CA 94103-1741   www.josseybass.com

Jossey-Bass books and products are available through most bookstores. To contact Jossey-Bass directly, call our Customer Care Department within the U.S. at 800-956-7739, outside the U.S. at 317-572-3986, or fax 317-572-4002.

Jossey-Bass also publishes its books in a variety of electronic formats. Some content that appears in print may not be available in electronic books.

The dialogue from *Curb Your Enthusiasm* in Chapter Ten is from episode number 15, "The Thong" on HBO: Larry David, Jeff Garlin, Gavin Polone, Executive Producers, 2001. Reprinted with permission of HBO.

Library of Congress Cataloging-in-Publication Data

The handbook of dispute resolution / edited by Michael L. Moffitt, Robert C. Bordone.—1st ed.
    p. cm.
  Includes bibliographical references and index.
  ISBN-13 978-0-7879-7538-8 (alk. paper)
  ISBN-10 0-7879-7538-9 (alk. paper)
  1. Dispute resolution (Law)—United States.   I. Moffitt, Michael L., date.
II. Bordone, Robert C., date.
  KF9084.H36 2005
  347.73'9—dc22

                                                                    2005000721

Printed in the United States of America
FIRST EDITION
HB Printing   10 9 8 7 6 5 4 3 2 1

CONTENTS

To Sander Elizabeth and Spencer Emilee,
with hopes that your generation will handle disputes
more wisely than ours does.

M.L.M.

To Mom and Dad, with love and thanks.

R.C.B.

PREFACE

This book was inspired by the remarkable work of scholars and practitioners in a broad range of disciplines, all of whom have been seeking answers to critical questions about how people can best deal with their differences.

Two questions guided us as we crafted the table of contents for this book: What topics are most important to cover in an overview of dispute resolution? And what questions about dispute resolution are most important to answer at this moment in time? With these questions in mind, we solicited specific contributions from colleagues who we thought were well-situated to answer them. To our delight and amazement, we received overwhelming support and cooperation from our contributors.

The Handbook of Dispute Resolution therefore brings together a diverse collection of dispute resolution scholars who have never before appeared within the same volume. That they were each willing to contribute a chapter speaks volumes about their devotion to the field, their generosity, and their leadership. Some of the chapters in this book represent the first time that certain authors have synthesized years of their own work into a manageable form. Other chapters provide insight into the very cutting edge of current thinking in dispute resolution. Some chapters are written by the most prominent names in our field, and some are written by those who appear most likely to lead the next generation of dispute resolution scholars. The two of us have long wished that such a collection existed, and through the efforts of many, it now does.

Every contribution to this book builds on the works of a remarkable set of scholars, practitioners, and innovators—people who engaged in dispute resolution research, theory, and practice at a time when the concept of "dispute resolution" as an organizing concept for disparate disciplinary inquiries was unknown. The two of us did not have the opportunity to know or work with some of the earliest pioneers in this field, though we continue to be inspired by the words of figures such as Mary Parker Follett and Lon Fuller. We *have* been blessed to have had the opportunity to learn from, to work with, and to be inspired by some of the figures who have most shaped the modern understanding of dispute resolution—the prominent names in the field. These include not only many of the contributors to this volume, but also Chris Argyris, Roger Fisher, Christopher Honeyman, Bob Mnookin, Howard Raiffa, Len Riskin, Nancy Rogers, Jeff Rubin, Jim Sebenius, Michael Wheeler, and Bill Ury. To these people, we (personally and on behalf of the field generally) extend our heartfelt thanks.

This book would not have been possible without the pathbreaking work of those before us who created the institutions that have allowed work on dispute resolution to thrive. Some of the relevant institutions are conspicuous—centers and programs at major universities, for example. The forces behind them are less formal, but nonetheless important—deans, department chairs, and faculties who have supported work in this still-not-entirely-established field. Not all of those who contribute to the successes of a project like this one receive the attention they deserve.

Two institutions supporting work in dispute resolution deserve specific mention regarding this project. First, the Program on Negotiation at Harvard Law School (PON). Both of us received our initial professional training through PON. Michael has maintained his affiliation with PON in various capacities ever since he began working there as a first-year law student. Bob continues his full-time affiliation at PON as a faculty member at Harvard Law School and as the deputy director of the Harvard Negotiation Research Project, one of PON's nine interdisciplinary research centers. The Program on Negotiation is a remarkable place with tremendous energy, talent, and promise. It draws an extraordinary collection of scholars, practitioners, and students together, creating opportunities for precisely the kinds of cross-disciplinary fertilization on which our field (and this book) depend. PON provided logistical, institutional, and significant financial support for this project. Quite simply, without PON, this project would never have gotten off the ground.

Second, the Appropriate Dispute Resolution Program at the University of Oregon deserves very special mention. The University of Oregon—where Michael now teaches—has taken enormous and rapid strides to develop a top-notch ADR program, and the school's support for this project can barely be overstated. The dean of the law school provided research stipends and teaching leave to support the creation of this book. The Walker-Weiner Endowed Research Fund at the University of Oregon provided additional financial support for the project. And the faculty of Oregon, through formal faculty colloquia and through informal consultation, has provided invaluable advice on ways to improve the book.

As with most significant endeavors, the efforts that made this book as impressive as it is took place largely behind the scenes. A group of talented and dedicated research assistants were integral to the quality of this volume. Fourteen of our law students spent a total of *several thousand* hours helping to research and to polish these chapters. Every single author in this book owes a debt of gratitude to these students for the many ways in which they helped to make the chapters clearer and cleaner. To David Baharvar, Benjamin Clark, Elizabeth Conklin Dority, Jeremy Dickman, Katherine DeVore, Megan Evans, Pamela Hardy, Gina Hambrick, Robyn Kali Bacon, Christopher Ledford, Mimi Luong, Adam Motenko, Jeffrey Sagalewicz, and Jennifer Welch, we extend our most sincere thanks. We also received generous and skilled support from Jill Forcier, from Florrie Darwin, and from our Jossey-Bass copyeditor, David Horne. You are true professionals, and you should be proud of this collection.

We would like to extend our special thanks to our teacher, mentor, and colleague, Frank Sander of Harvard Law School. Frank first suggested to us the possibility that the two of us might work to create a book like this. Throughout our work together, he graciously offered his services as a sounding board, consultant, and adviser. We are grateful for his professional mentorship, his friendship, and most immediately, for his help with this project.

Finally, we again thank the authors who contributed chapters to this book. No single individual—no matter how well-educated, no matter how experienced—could have produced a volume as rich as this one. We are grateful to have had this opportunity to work with you, and we look forward to continuing to learn with you in the years to come.

Michael L. Moffitt and Robert C. Bordone

CHAPTER ONE

Perspectives on Dispute Resolution

An Introduction

Michael L. Moffitt and Robert C. Bordone

D isputes are a reality of modern life. Each of us has our own perspectives, our own interests, our own resources, our own aspirations, and our own fears. It is no wonder, then, that as we run into each other, we sometimes find ourselves in disagreement about what has happened or about what ought to happen. We each have times when we feel others have hurt us, and we each have times when we are moved to act against real or perceived injustices.

That disputes arise is not remarkable. What is remarkable is the extraordinary variety of ways in which people choose to deal with these differences when they arise. It is this diversity of experiences and approaches that makes the study of dispute resolution so rich, so rewarding, and sometimes so frustrating.

Most people involved in disputes do not enjoy the experience. For many of us, disputes are emotionally draining. Disputes take up time and mental energy. Disputes distract us from the things we would rather be doing. Disputes force us into contact with others—often with others who would not make our list of preferred people with whom to spend time. Dealing with disputes often costs us resources. In short, those caught in a dispute generally view resolution as an attractive goal (assuming the resolution is on some favorable term).

Similarly, society generally treats disputes as costly occurrences—ones that should be avoided if possible, and ones that should be addressed quickly when they cannot be avoided. Society tends to view disputes as threats to the preservation of order. We collectively prefer neighborhoods not to be in strife. We prefer for commerce to flow without the interruptions posed by disputes. We generally prefer for individuals and for groups to live their lives without having disputes tear at the relationships that bind us as a society.

Yet, not all disputes are necessarily bad. Sociologist Laura Nader has suggested that disputes are a helpful vehicle for casting light onto that which is wrong with the status quo.[1] If all disputes are avoided or suppressed, society might ignore wrongs, might perpetuate injustice, and might leave the aggrieved uncompensated. At the macro level, therefore, in a world in which injustice and the abuse of power still exist, disputes can play a useful function as agents of change.

Still, despite the capacity for disputes to function as vehicles for positive social change, most of us experience disputes as burdensome. After all, apart from the macro level, we live our lives at home, where disputes with our partners are emotionally costly. We live our lives at work, where disagreements with our bosses risk damaging our self-images and our financial well-being. We live our lives in our neighborhoods, where disputes can transform mutually supportive networks into cold and unwelcoming factions. Most of us live lives in which it would be nice to have better ways to resolve disputes.

WHAT WE MEAN BY *DISPUTE RESOLUTION*

In a book explicitly focused on dispute resolution, it is only reasonable to expect some clarity about what is meant by the terms *dispute* and *resolution*. Yet the interdisciplinary nature of this undertaking produces more disagreements (disputes?) than clarity on this question. For purposes of this book, we suggest that readers consider dispute resolution in its broadest, most inclusive sense. It would be a shame to have wisdom from one or more disciplines screened out of our inquiry because of a narrow filter on what is "relevant."

Disputes and Conflicts

Are *disputes* and *conflicts* the same thing? Some scholars use the terms interchangeably,[2] while others see important differences between the two.[3] Part of this derives from disciplinary differences. Social scientists are more likely to study "conflicts," while those with legal training may focus on "disputes."[4] Neither discipline has settled on a single definition of either term, however. In the *Dictionary of Conflict Resolution,* for example, the definition of the term *conflict* occupies more than twenty paragraphs, even without considering its many compound usages.[5]

If there is a difference between popular uses of the terms *dispute* and *conflict,* it might roughly be described as one of magnitude. Most observers would intuitively say that a border war is a conflict, and an argument with a hot dog vendor is a dispute. Conflicts are often seen as broader (involving more people), deeper (extending beyond surface issues into questions of value, identity, fear, or need), and more systematic (reaching beyond a single interaction or claim). Yet such line drawing in real life is rarely so obvious.

Even more important, we are not convinced that the work of precisely differentiating between disputes and conflicts merits the effort. No body of knowledge or advice should hinge on whether the condition being described falls into the category of dispute or conflict. We do not interest ourselves with questions about what labels observers put on the dynamics they study, but instead focus on what insights observers have to offer about the people experiencing the problem, their views of the problem, and the processes by which they are seeking to resolve their differences. Throughout most of this book, we and the contributing authors describe disputants, dispute contexts, and dispute resolution processes. We hope that those readers trained in disciplines that are most accustomed to treating questions of conflict will join us in looking past terminological differences.

Even beyond questions of definitional boundaries, one often sees disagreement about how best to describe a dispute. Disputants may differ in the *timeline* they use to describe a set of circumstances underlying a dispute. Figuring out who has the most legitimate claim or who is at fault can depend on when one begins the story. ("The project is late because you committed us to an unrealistic deadline without consulting me" versus "If you had managed your workload better last month, we would have been done with the project on time.") Disputants may differ in the *characters* they would include in the list of relevant participants or decision makers. ("This has nothing to do with him; leave him out of this.") Disputants sometimes use different *labels* for each other. The other person may be an opponent, an adversary, a counterpart, or a partner, for example. Disputants may have different visions of the *scope* of the dispute. For example, each may have a different view of which facts, feelings, issues, and concerns are relevant and appropriate to be included in the description of the dispute.

"Resolution" and Other Elusive Notions

In a simple dispute, the concept of resolution may be perfectly clear. I bump into you, causing you some injury. We talk about how I can make amends for having caused you pain, and we agree that I will make a particular payment in exchange for you releasing me from any further responsibility. I pay you, and you release me. Perhaps this resolves all aspects of the dispute. Or perhaps this payment leaves other issues "unresolved," such as emotions or the effects of the injury or the settlement on parties who were not part of our agreement. Still, in a simple dispute such as this, it is possible to imagine that we might address these other issues as well. When the dispute in question becomes more complex, however, so does the concept of resolution.

The language of resolution implies a level of finality that is only occasionally a realistic condition. Sometimes a dispute is so simple that it is possible to describe a dispute as fully and finally resolved in all senses—legal, emotional, financial, relational, logistical, and so on. A consumer has a complaint about a product and wants to return it. After some discussion, the merchant refunds the consumer's purchase price. Perhaps this dispute can be accurately described as resolved.

Particularly in complex circumstances, however, "resolution" is not a single event—assuming resolution is even possible. At what point in a piece of institutional reform litigation (such as that which led to school desegregation) is the dispute "resolved"? Even legal scholars—those who tend to have the narrowest definition of resolution—would agree that such a dispute is not fully resolved at the moment a court enters a consent decree. Years of supervised implementation remain, making the idea of resolution slippery. When is a collective bargaining dispute resolved? In one sense, the dispute is resolved when a new contract is signed. Yet management and labor will continue to work with one another on an ongoing basis for years. Aspects of the dispute that resulted in the current contract will undoubtedly carry forward, coloring the way the two sides interact between the time when this contract is ratified and the next set of bargaining begins.

Resolution is a tricky notion. One of the editors of this book used to work with a nonprofit consulting firm called Conflict Management Group. In the field, particularly outside of the United States, the name of the firm was the cause of such surprise and concern that the editor occasionally used the acronym CMG to ward off uncomfortable conversations. In some contexts, it was the word *conflict* in the name that caused concern among clients. The editor was once told, "We have no conflict here," by a commander of a military unit in a breakaway republic in the former Soviet Union. His statement was perhaps technically accurate, since the area under his command was in a state of fragile ceasefire. His assertion that the circumstances did not constitute "conflict" reflected not only superficial linguistic differences but also deeply held differences in assumptions about the implications of being in a conflict. Other clients seemed to view the idea of "managing" conflict as bizarre. The firm's name reflected an approach to addressing broad-scale problems of public concern. Rather than aim for a single moment of resolution, the theory behind many of CMG's interventions was that it was better to envision an ongoing stream of disagreements to be managed. One does not "resolve" a marriage or a partnership. In any ongoing relationship (between spouses, business partners, neighbors, professional colleagues), people will have differences, and therefore they will have disputes. That no dispute exists today does not ensure that no dispute will exist next year. The sign of a healthy, productive relationship is not necessarily an absence of disputes but rather the skill with which disputes are addressed.

DISPUTE RESOLUTION: A TOPIC FOR ALL

Given the widespread interest in improving the ways in which we handle disputes, it is not surprising that scholars in many different disciplines have examined the question of dispute resolution. From these disciplinary perspectives, we have learned much about the ways in which people fight and about the ways in which people most effectively deal with their fights.

Those whose primary discipline is law have contributed to our understanding of the disputing process. The law provides the backdrop against which much of dispute resolution takes place. Each party to a dispute may view resorting to court as its alternative to voluntary resolution. If two businesses disputing over an alleged breach of contract do not resolve the matter themselves, it is likely that at least one business will call upon the power of the state, through the mechanism of the law, to resolve the dispute. The legal system is, in many ways, society's most heavily subsidized dispute resolution mechanism.[6] It is no surprise, therefore, that those who have spent their careers studying the law have helpful observations about the ways in which people resolve disputes.

Psychology also offers an invaluable lens on the disputing process. To understand fully what occurs in the context of a dispute, one must understand something of what it means to be human. Disputes raise questions of perceptions. Disputes heighten the importance of emotions. Disputes may threaten certain aspects of the disputants' identities. Any effort at resolving disputes necessarily involves a complex pattern of communication and meaning making, about which those trained in psychology are well situated to offer helpful observations.

Ethicists have a unique and important perspective on the processes of disputing and of resolving disputes. Most disputes have some normative component—whether it is explicit or not. An employee argues that he or she should have received a different assignment from his or her boss. The argument might turn entirely on a question of law (Does the contract entitle the employee to the assignment?) or of psychology (What impact does the boss's decision have on the employee's morale and on how future actions by the boss will be interpreted?). Yet one of the important, unspoken aspects of the conversation between the boss and the employee may be an implicit argument about whether the boss's behavior was condemnable. Invoking the normative argument on the micro level (who was right in this context) raises the stakes considerably in a dispute. Ethics may constrain the behavior of disputants at the micro level; ethics may provide guidance on the normative questions of entitlement in a given dispute; and ethics may teach us something about the larger enterprise in which disputants are engaged.

Economists, mathematicians, and game theorists also offer a significant perspective on the disputing process. Formal analytics can provide clarity in contexts of enormous complexity, when multiple parties are involved, when multiple interests are in play, or when multiple options or issues face the disputants. Even if no individual actor in a dispute behaves in a perfectly rational manner, it is important for those charged with resolving disputes to understand the incentive structures within which disputants operate. The elegance of mathematical models can provide insight not only on the question of whether resolution is possible, but also on the important question of how one can maximize the benefits each of the disputants receives from potential solutions.

This list is not exhaustive. Indeed, a scan of almost any curriculum in any department on a university campus yields disciplinary perspectives with critical insights to offer to those who care about dispute resolution. Sociologists and anthropologists contribute important observations on disputes. A careful examination of different societies' mechanisms for resolving disputes offers us a window not only into societal differences but also into the nature of disputes and that which might be possible. Historians provide invaluable context for understanding the behaviors of those in disputes. Scholars of journalism have long understood the important role(s) of the media in shaping the views of those in disputes. Scientists recognize patterns in the ways in which broad-scale scientific disputes have been resolved in the past. Political scientists have long studied the effects of various structures within which policy disputes are raised and resolved. Theologians offer insight into religious approaches to the management of differences. The history of world religions provides examples of how various faith traditions resolve their disagreements both internally and with other faith traditions that have different or at times even incompatible beliefs. Even literature is filled with vivid and telling stories of the human condition—virtually always accentuated by the introduction (and resolution) of some dispute or conflict.

THE BLESSINGS AND CHALLENGES OF INTERDISCIPLINARY INQUIRY INTO DISPUTE RESOLUTION

Having this many different scholars from this many different disciplines working on the question of dispute resolution is enormously helpful. Interdisciplinary work has provided more and better tools, frameworks, and language for describing disputes. Without the capacity to do high-quality observation of that which exists, it is difficult to imagine how we could develop any sort of useful prescriptions. Without these interdisciplinary perspectives, none of us would understand dispute resolution as well as we do.

Furthermore, interdisciplinary work has increased the quantity and quality of prescriptive strategies. A strategy for dealing with disputes that might be immediately obvious to one discipline might not occur to those in another. The psychologist sees an opportunity to heal emotional scars. The economist sees an opportunity for mutually beneficial trades. The lawyer sees an opportunity for the joint development of norms of behavior. The political scientist sees a way to structure decision making to maximize legitimacy. The communications specialist sees an opportunity to give narrative voice to a perspective that is too often silenced. We who focus on dispute resolution would not be as good at what we do, were it not for the contributions of different disciplines.

Interdisciplinary work also presents important opportunities and tools for assessing how various approaches are working. Not all advice is equally useful, and each discipline has important strengths—and important shortcomings—in its ability to monitor the real-world usefulness of the prescriptions it offers. Interdisciplinary examination of dispute resolution processes strengthens our understandings of those processes.

This interdisciplinary attention to dispute resolution builds on itself. What was perhaps once a spin-off topic of interest for one or more of the disciplines is now beginning to show signs of disciplinary independence. Students can now study the disputing process in programs explicitly aimed at dispute and conflict resolution at both the undergraduate and graduate level at a number of institutions.

Having sung the praises of interdisciplinary work, it is important to acknowledge the limitations and challenges it presents. Any interdisciplinary work, on any topic, is challenging. Each discipline speaks its own language. Practitioners in every field are busy, and most are less reflective than they would prefer to be. Scholars tend to narrow the focus of their work dramatically (in order to say something new and noteworthy to those who are already in the discipline), and as a result, even when they do offer prescriptive advice, they offer it to an increasingly narrow audience. In short, in interdisciplinary fields like dispute resolution, progress—to the extent that one can measure such a thing—often comes in fits and starts, unlike the steady progression of ideas one might see in an exploration captured entirely by a single discipline.

WHAT IS NEEDED

The back and forth between disciplines creates a need simultaneously for at least three important activities: cutting-edge work, interdisciplinary exchanges, and synthesis.

We need cutting-edge work. Typically, cutting-edge work takes place within a single discipline. An advanced experiment sheds light on a relevant psychological phenomenon, previously misunderstood. A mathematical model finds a new application in the analysis of a complex set of incentives. A persuasive new articulation of the philosophical underpinnings of some aspect of the endeavor reaches the community of ethicists. A comparative study reveals important behavioral differences among people acting under various legal constraints. Any of these would contribute to the understanding of dispute resolution—even though the primary findings or work would likely be meaningful only to those already in the discipline. Such advances are critical to improving how we deal with disputes.

We also need interdisciplinary exchanges. No discipline holds a monopoly on the understanding of dispute resolution. Many different voices have something to offer, and yet most scholars and most practitioners spend most of their time talking only with those who have a similar practice or similar educational training. We need psychologists who are interested in dispute resolution to go to lunch with lawyers who are interested in dispute resolution. We need game theorists and political scientists to teach a joint class on dispute resolution. We need therapists and economists to co-mediate disputes in the field. Cross-fertilization is critical to improving how we deal with disputes.

Finally, we need synthesis. We need opportunities to step back and take account of what we have figured out—or at least hypothesized—so far. Practitioners need to have ways to take stock of their current practices, to compare them with developing theories. Scholars need to have ways to see the larger picture(s) being developed by the body of work in their fields and in others. Policymakers need to have more unified bodies of information on which to base their decisions. None of us, no matter how well-intending, no matter how well-read, no matter how disciplinarily nimble, can keep up with everything happening in all of the relevant fields. Moments of synthesis are, therefore, critical to improving our understanding of dispute resolution.

WHAT THIS BOOK OFFERS

This book offers examples of all three activities necessary for interdisciplinary progress. Some of the chapters in this book represent cutting-edge work by some of the leaders in the field. Some of the chapters in this book are written as a product of cross-disciplinary fertilization. The entirety of this collection aims to serve the purpose of synthesis.

One of the challenges of talking about dispute resolution is that each practitioner or scholar seems to have a framework of his or her own for describing the phenomena of disputing and dispute resolution. That we cannot even agree on how to organize our observations—much less agree on the substance of those observations or what meaning to make out of them—illustrates some of the challenges of the previously described interdisciplinary work.

Without any illusion that this is the only way one might organize materials on dispute resolution, we offer the following organizing framework for the materials in this book: we seek to understand *disputants*—the actors who engage in the disagreements that form the basis of our study; we seek to understand *disputes* and *dispute contexts*—the substantive issues in disputes and the circumstances in which the disputes often arise; we seek to understand the *processes* by which disputants seek to address their circumstances; and we seek to understand the *emerging issues* related to the intersection of these three perspectives.

Understanding Disputants

Disputes involve real people—even when the titular parties are organizations. As a result, the complexities of human existence color (or cloud, perhaps, depending on your perspective) the interactions in any dispute context. Disputants differ in all of the ways that humans differ. To understand dispute resolution, therefore, we must come to understand how disputants view themselves, view the dispute, and view each other.

In Part One of this book, we offer eight chapters aimed at clarifying some aspects of the human experience of dispute resolution. Are there "personality" differences that influence the way disputants act in and understand dispute resolution processes? Are there predictable ways in which disputants deviate from pure rationality in the context of disputes? What roles can emotions play in the context of a dispute? In what ways do the individual identities of disputants affect the way they perceive and are perceived? In what ways does the relationship between the parties hold promise—or peril—for disputants? How do the cultures of the parties affect the bargaining dynamics between them? What might we learn by examining the disputing process through a gender lens? And how is it that two people can witness the same thing and make such significantly different meaning out of it?

In short, Part One invites readers to consider the ways in which the individual disputants shape the prospects for resolution.

Understanding Disputes and Dispute Contexts

Disputants act differently in different contexts and in different disputes. To assess a dispute accurately, therefore, we need an understanding of how the disputants view the issues in contention. Even that, however, is not enough. Disputes virtually never take place in a vacuum or in such isolation that they can be wholly separated from the rest of the disputants' lives. To appreciate the prospects for resolution, therefore, we must also understand the broader conditions in which the disputants view the dispute.

Part Two offers seven chapters aimed at shedding light on the different ways disputants might understand their circumstances. Can disputants recognize the opportunities they have to create value through an innovative settlement? What effects do agents play in the disputing process? How can disputants use the process of quantification to aid their decision making in dispute contexts? What effects does it have on disputants when multiple options are on the table simultaneously? In what ways does the organizational setting in which the dispute is occurring affect the behavior of the disputants? What ethical questions does the dispute raise? What legal constraints operate on the disputants as they consider various strategies?

In short, Part Two invites readers to consider the myriad ways in which the same person would act differently, depending on the dispute he or she faces.

Understanding Dispute Resolution Processes

How do disputants go from recognizing the parameters of a dispute to resolving it? The answer, of course, depends on the dispute resolution process(es) they employ. To understand fully the choices before a disputant, we must understand not only the disputant and how he or she views the dispute but also the range of different process choices he or she perceives.

Part Three offers seven chapters providing a detailed look at a variety of different dispute resolution processes. What are the dynamics between disputants when they negotiate—and what should those dynamics be? What role(s) can mediators play? In what ways do those roles differ from those of arbitrators? How do consensus-building processes differ from other forms of dispute resolution? Under what circumstances might litigation be a wise and appropriate forum for resolving a dispute? What effects do integrated conflict management systems, now prevalent in many organizational settings, have on disputants? What lessons can organizational leaders derive from the dispute resolution literature as they adopt informal dispute resolution processes? And how can disputants best choose from among the variety of dispute resolution processes available?

In short, Part Three examines the range of processes generally available to disputants in their efforts at resolution—recognizing that not all processes are created equal.

Emerging Issues in Dispute Resolution

Part Four offers seven chapters exploring some of the emerging issues and new directions for dispute resolution. How will the still-emerging world of cyberspace affect disputants in the future? How will the sweep toward globalization affect the legal regimes and processes we employ to resolve transborder disputes? What opportunities exist to introduce principles of reconciliation and forgiveness into existing systems of dispute resolution? What opportunities and challenges face those who seek to educate youth about dispute resolution? What changes should we expect as dispute resolution becomes more institutionalized and as dispute resolution practitioners face the prospect of professionalization? And with the increase in human knowledge and the growing demand for better, more efficient dispute resolution processes, what are the challenges and opportunities that dispute resolution faces as a field in the years ahead?

In short, Part Four examines the broad trends in dispute resolution, with an eye toward some of the issues that are likely to be central to disputants, practitioners, and scholars.

OUR PERSPECTIVE ON DISPUTE RESOLUTION

As the editors of this book, we are committed to the idea that dispute resolution is a fascinating and critically important area of study and practice.

Some in the field, including some of this volume's contributors, advocate for particular dispute resolution processes over all others. We are modestly more agnostic, believing that there is no particular method of resolving disputes that is consistently superior to any other. Disputants, disputes, and dispute contexts are too complex to permit any universal declarations. Some disputes would best be settled one way. Others should be resolved by another method. Perhaps some ought to be left unresolved—at least initially. We are persuaded, however, that in all but the rarest of circumstances, the use of force is ill advised—a blunt, inelegant, and all-too-often-tragic way to address disputes. Almost without exception, the use of force represents some combination of a failure of skill, a failure of will, or a dearth of creativity on the part of one or more of the disputants.

Without being imperialists of any particular approach to dispute resolution, therefore, we are imperialists about the study of dispute resolution. Whatever approach one concludes is best, whatever perspective one holds about the matter in dispute, whatever role one might play in the context of a dispute, learning more about dispute resolution is useful. This book aims to help in that process.

Notes

1. For a concise articulation of Nader's concerns, see her description of the rise of a "harmony ideology" in L. Nader, "Controlling Processes in the Practice of Law: Hierarchy and Pacification in the Movement to Re-Form Dispute Ideology," *Ohio State Journal on Dispute Resolution*, 1993, 9, 1–25.

2. "In its more common use, *conflict* refers narrowly to a disagreement, the expression or manifestation of a state of incompatibility. . . . When used in this manner, conflict is synonymous with dispute" (Yarn, D. H. [ed.]. *Dictionary of Conflict Resolution*. San Francisco: Jossey-Bass, 1999, p. 114).

3. For example, John Burton suggests that "'Disputes' involve negotiable interests, while 'conflicts' are concerned with issues that are not negotiable, issues that relate to ontological human needs that cannot be compromised" (Burton, J. W. "Conflict Resolution as a Political Philosophy." In D. Sandole and

H. van der Merwe [eds.], *Conflict Resolution Theory and Practice: Integration and Application*. Manchester and New York: Manchester University Press, 1993). We understand Burton's suggestion that conflicts may involve more deeply held beliefs, though we do not share his characterization that conflicts, by definition, include nonnegotiable issues.

4. For more on the evolution of various disciplines' understandings of dispute resolution, see Menkel-Meadow, Chapter Two, this volume.

5. See Yarn, *Dictionary of Conflict Resolution*, 1999, pp. 113–117.

6. We acknowledge that one might view the military as the most expensive dispute resolution mechanism underwritten by society. For the reasons we describe later in the chapter, we are so convinced that resort to force deserves separate treatment from all other dispute resolution processes that we largely omit its mention throughout this book.

CHAPTER TWO

Roots and Inspirations

A Brief History of the Foundations of Dispute Resolution

Carrie Menkel-Meadow

The skillful management of conflicts [is] among the highest of human skills.
—Stuart Hampshire[1]

Disputes are as old as humankind. Dispute resolution is probably just a bit younger. Whether the first disputants settled their own disputes with direct party negotiation, with violence, or with the assistance of a third party for conciliation, mediation, arbitration, or adjudication remains a question for anthropologists and historians to study and debate.[2] Disputing has always been individualistic and dyadic (it takes only two to make a dispute) and communal or group based. Modern dispute resolution theory and practice focus on differences in the types of disputes, the number of disputants, the location of the dispute, the use of third parties, and other factors to analyze what processes might be appropriate for addressing particular disputes.

To illuminate the full dimensions of dispute "handling" (not all disputes are "resolved"), this chapter traces the multidisciplinary roots and origins of the field of dispute resolution. Conceived of as an applied social science, the field of dispute resolution draws its intellectual and practical roots from sources as varied as anthropology, sociology, social psychology, cognitive psychology, economics, political science, game theory, international relations, law, and peace studies.[3] Today's scholars, students, and practitioners of dispute resolution may train in any of these constituent fields or, more recently, in a few specialized programs of conflict resolution study.

As a field, dispute resolution is both a discipline of theory (about how conflicts develop, escalate, and are or are not resolved) and of practice.[4] It is a field particularly attuned to developing and testing "theories-in-use."[5] How can one usefully and ethically apply concepts, principles, and propositions to the pragmatic resolution of conflicts and the betterment of human relations? At its most aspirational, dispute resolution is a sensibility or mind-set about how human beings should approach each other to solve problems, creatively engage with each other to improve current conditions, deal with divergent expectations and objectives, and prevent wasteful, unproductive, and violent interactions. At its most pragmatic, dispute resolution processes offer instrumental techniques and tools for dealing with conflict, resolving disputes, and effectively forming new relationships and transactions. This chapter will briefly review both the intellectual and institutionalized practice history of the field of dispute resolution.

EARLY HISTORY: DESCRIPTIONS OF THE FIELD AND FOUNDATIONAL THEORIES

The social sciences now include a field called "conflict resolution," whereas modern legal studies more often describe the field as "dispute resolution."[6] The different terms signal an important distinction between the two approaches.

Nineteenth-century founders of the field of sociology, including Emile Durkheim, Georg Simmel, and Karl Marx, looked at widespread social and political conflicts and sought to understand their origins, trajectories, and impacts on the larger society. Early on, tensions developed about whether conflict was beneficial for social change,[7] whether it should be managed for social stability,[8] or whether it was simply a normal part of human existence.[9] These intellectual tensions remain with us today. Seen as a social phenomenon, conflict exists at many different levels—individual, familial, group, or nation-state. Indeed, as social psychologists have noted, conflict can also be intrapersonal or intrapsychic. Within a single human being one can find conflicts linked to diverging perceptions, values, attitudes, or behavioral choices.

In law and legal studies, the unit of analysis has been the dispute, or "case"—an activated conflict in which someone has experienced a wrong and "named it, blamed someone or [some] entity and claimed against them" in a formal way.[10] This activation process often plays out in a binary or polarized format of plaintiff and defendant, or complainant and respondent. Seeing a dispute as a separate, self-contained unit of social interaction, requiring some form of formal or legal intervention, is different from seeing a dispute as located in a more socially enmeshed world of multiple parties, interconnected issues, and social and relational history.

Thus the very nomenclature or definition of the relevant unit of analysis tells us something about how a conflict or dispute might be handled, treated, or resolved. For the most part, social scientists have focused on the embeddedness of disputes in larger fields or patterns of conflict and social relations, while lawyers and other dispute resolution professionals have focused on the concrete nature of particular disputes, suggesting use of particular techniques for dispute settlement or other resolution.

Socio-legal scholars who are both lawyers and anthropologists have bridged these disciplines by studying disputes in a broader social context, looking at how cases are socially constructed, labeled, and enacted.[11] Scholars and practitioners of the school of "legal realism" were similarly attracted to looking at how disputes were formed and dealt with in particular settings, and so created a "jurisprudence of dispute resolution" and its institutions.[12]

Together, the insights of these different approaches to studying conflict resolution have given us some basic propositions about the field, what some call a canon of dispute resolution.[13] Within these approaches, some have aimed to provide a taxonomy for analyzing conflict. Others have sought to link description and prescription.[14] Some have focused on the "constructive" and "destructive" aspects of conflicts.[15] Still others have aimed to describe the institutionalized processes best suited to deal with particular kinds of disputes.[16]

Modern theory development, research programs, and practice protocols are derived from a body of knowledge developed by our intellectual mothers and fathers. Mary Parker Follett, a cross-disciplinary pioneer, administrative and organizational scientist, and labor-management consultant in the early part of the twentieth century, was trained as a political scientist and worked as a social worker. Follett analyzed conflict as having one of three forms of resolution: domination, compromise, or integration. In domination, one disputant controls the outcome by force or other superior power (for example, economic or status-hierarchy). In compromise, both parties meet in the middle, often giving up what they really value. Only in integration, where both parties' needs, wants, and objectives are met, is conflict used productively—often by finding a new option or expanding resources so that all disputants can have the most of what they need without unnecessary harm to the other. Follett saw friction as a positive force, a way of identifying true interests and searching for better solutions:

> As conflict—difference—is here in the world, as we cannot avoid it, we should, I think, use it. Instead of condemning it, we should set it to work for us. Why not? What does the mechanical engineer do with friction? Of course, his chief job is to eliminate friction, but it is true that he also capitalizes friction. The transmission of power by belts depends on friction between the belt and the pulley. . . . The music of the violin we get by friction. . . . We talk of the friction of the mind on mind as a good thing. So it is in business too, we have to know when to try to eliminate friction and when to try to capitalize it, when to see what work we can make it do. That is what I wish to consider here, whether we can set conflict to work and make it *do* something for us.[17]

Follett describes an encounter she had in the Harvard library when one patron wanted to open a nearby window in order to have air circulation, but Follett wanted no draft. Illustrating an integrative solution to conflict, the two agreed to open a window in a nearby room instead. In another version of this integrative story, two sisters arguing over a single orange learn that one wants the fruit to eat, the other the zest for cooking. From my own life, I liked the icing; my brother, the cake; so cutting the cake horizontally, rather than vertically, maximized our satisfaction.

Follett's optimism with respect to human problem solving allowed her to see the possibility of agreements in highly conflictual settings, such as labor-management relations, social welfare, and business administration. She also taught practical and creative devices for realizing her optimistic aims. When people appeared to be having disputes about deep value differences, Follett suggested disaggregating issues and claims to make intractable problems more manageable. In other contexts, when the heart of the conflict was unnecessarily obscured by miscellaneous minor claims, she argued in favor of aggregating issues. Much of our current knowledge of integrative bargaining, now applied to labor-management relations[18] and problem-solving and principled negotiation,[19] is derived from Follett's work in the early years of the past century. Follett not only focused on particular dispute resolution processes and techniques but was also interested in how substantive solutions to problems could be creatively designed.

EVOLVING UNDERSTANDINGS OF DISPUTE RESOLUTION IN HISTORICAL CONTEXT

The intellectual founders of our field made contributions to our knowledge from their primary disciplines and particular historical moments.

As the labor movement, the Depression, the New Deal, the run-up to World War II, and the war itself challenged the ability of many of society's conventional domestic and international institutions of dispute resolution to resolve, prevent, or handle disputes, skepticism about both formal institutions and doctrinal law forged a new legal philosophy known as legal realism. Legal realists were skeptical that doctrine and the rule of law alone could adequately deal with social, economic, and political problems. At the same time, legal realists had an optimistic side, believing that legal institutions, when studied and reformed in context, could be used in programs of social engineering to deal adequately with many significant human problems, including social welfare, economic competition, and resource allocation, as well as more individualized disputes and conflicts. Out of the study of "law in action," a number of legal realists developed new bodies of law (such as the Uniform Commercial Code) more responsive to actual practices and recognized a greater diversity of legal institutions that could manage an increased variety of legal disputes.

Sociologists and social psychologists such as Lewis Coser, Kurt Lewin, and Morton Deutsch examined the social functions of conflicts during times of great conflict (the 1940s and 1960s) and perhaps false consensus (the 1950s). Theorist Morton Deutsch distinguished between veridical conflict (real conflict over scarce resources) and displaced, latent, misattributed, false, or contingent conflicts (those that could be managed by correct human diagnosis and reframed thinking, perception, or resource manipulation). He also identified two default perspectives on conflict styles: competition and cooperation.[20] More recently, this model has been expanded to include five "modes" of conflict resolution: competition, accommodation, avoidance, compromise, and collaboration.[21]

Game theorists modeling strategic interactions between two polarized negotiators during the Cold War began a productive research and theoretical program of examining human strategic interaction under conditions of uncertainty.[22] This research assumed zero-sum and life-threatening disputes with little trust and little honest communication between the parties. It has influenced international dispute resolution in both theory and practice, and encouraged assumptions of hostility, scarcity, and bipolarism.

By examining the functional attributes of different institutions, Harvard Law professor and labor arbitrator Lon Fuller became an eloquent spokesperson for the "moral integrity" of different dispute institutions and helped forge yet another school of thought, the Legal Process approach of the 1950s. Fuller, now known to some as "the jurisprudent of ADR," elaborated the defining principles of the uses, for different purposes, of mediation, arbitration, adjudication, legislation, voting, and other principles of "institutional dispute settlement." Fuller asserted that each dispute process has its own particular functional integrity and its own morality. Under his view of each process, mediation is best used when the parties are enmeshed in ongoing relationships (such as in families or in workplaces) and need to be "reoriented to each other"[23] more than having a decision made or a law crafted for them. Arbitration is best used when the parties have crafted rules of their own, such as in collective bargaining agreements or commercial contracts, and need help enforcing their own privately arrived at rules of conduct. Adjudication is necessary only when an authoritative and public decision of legal interpretation is required by the parties or by the larger society. In Fuller's understanding, there are clear differences among the various dispute processes: how facts are found, the role of precedent, who the third party neutral might be, the most opportune time for use of the process, what parties should be involved, and who should be bound or affected by the outcome of a particular dispute resolution process.

Fuller believed firmly in what we today call "process pluralism," while also believing that each process had its own purposes and should not be mixed with other processes:

> Mediation and arbitration have distinct purposes and hence distinct moralities. The morality of mediation lies in optimum settlement, a settlement in which each party gives up what he values less, in return for what he values more. The morality of arbitration lies in a decision according to the law of the contract. The procedures appropriate for mediation are those most likely to uncover that pattern of adjustment which will most nearly meet the interests of both parties. The procedures appropriate for arbitration are those which most securely guarantee each of the parties a meaningful chance to present arguments and proofs for a decision in his favor. Thus, private consultations with parties, generally wholly improper on the part of the arbitrator, are an indispensable tool of mediation.[24]

Fuller was concerned that the roles of mediator, arbitrator, and adjudicator not be mixed because of these separate moralities. Mediators might know the parties well and have separate meetings with them to improve internal and interpersonal relations. Arbitrators and adjudicators should have more neutrality and arms-length distance from the parties because they work with repeat parties having disputes under the same contracts, though arbitrators might be experts in a field or part of a particular industry. In his view, adjudication requires strong adversary presentation of two contested views for the right outcome to emerge from the "suspension between two opposing interpretations."[25] Among legal realists, Fuller was not alone in seeing that each process has its own functional and structural separateness. Others who studied and practiced arbitration saw such processes as allowing self-governance in appropriate circumstances, such as when repeat players in particular industries trust each other more than "outsiders" such as formal courts, judges, and juries.[26]

In times of expanding legal rights and economic prosperity, modern theorists have offered more positive notions of "expanded pies," "value creation," "interdependence," and "joint gain" in using dispute resolution productively to meet the underlying needs and interests of parties, with or without the help of facilitating neutrals or representative agents.[27] Following the optimistic turn of dispute resolution theory to problem solving, another rich body of research developed to explore such barriers to productive conflict resolution as cognitive distortions, ineffective strategic behaviors, and impediments to human communication and coordination.[28] Game theory, as further elaborated in the 1980s, gave way to the study of how cooperation and altruism could take hold and remain robust in repeat interactions of game players.[29] Some economists, mathematicians, psychologists, and lawyers began to explore how conflicts could be used to spark more creative solutions by focusing on analytic approaches (the "science" of dispute resolution). Others explored more "artistic" and behavioral approaches to creative problem solving.[30]

MODERN HISTORY: PROCESS PLURALISM AND MULTIPLE PURPOSES

In 1976, at the Roscoe Pound Conference on the Causes of Popular Dissatisfaction with the Administration of Justice, Harvard Law Professor Frank Sander delivered a speech titled "Varieties of Dispute Processing."[31] He described his vision of a courthouse in which not all cases would proceed through the doorway (literal and figurative) leading to litigation. Instead, the "multidoor" courthouse would direct cases to proceed through a variety of other processes, including mediation, arbitration, conciliation, fact finding, or ombuds services, depending on the nature of the case. This is the major event often credited as "the Big Bang" of modern dispute resolution theory and practice.

Sander's vision attracted attention from two different social forces. The first consisted of a group of judges, led by then Supreme Court Chief Justice Warren Burger,[32] who believed there were too many cases in the courts and who sought diversionary processes and institutions to reduce court dockets and achieve greater judicial efficiency. For members of this group, the "quantitative" or "efficiency" aspects of dispute processing were most significant. The second group attracted to Sander's comments was a more amorphous social movement, inspired by political empowerment movements in the 1960s. Members of this community sought greater party control and participation in dispute resolution, less professionalization of dispute resolution processes, and more tailored solutions to both individual and group problems and grievances.

The notion that particular forms of dispute processing were appropriate for particular kinds of legal, political, social, and economic problem solving reflected an emerging intellectual school, derived from the Legal Process school of the 1950s, called "Process Pluralism." Adherents of this view also believed that particular structures evolve to meet functional needs.[33] This strand of thinking continues to this day as we attempt to "fit the forum to the fuss"[34] and assign particular kinds of disputes to appropriate processes. At the same time, the development of new forms of dispute resolution, combining and hybridizing the primary forms of negotiation, mediation, arbitration, and adjudication, raises important questions about the moral and functional integrity of these new forms.

MODERN APPLICATIONS OF DISPUTE RESOLUTION THEORY

Sander's speech gave birth to the concept of the "multidoor courthouse," and courts and other agencies received funding from the American Bar Association and eventually from both the federal and local governments to begin experimentation with a variety of different processes. These included Neighborhood

Justice Centers (in part inspired by earlier work done in community mediation by the Justice Department's Community Relations Service, dealing with racial conflict in the 1960s),[35] Community Board mediation in San Francisco,[36] and court-annexed programs of mediation, arbitration, and other hybrid forms of case management (early neutral evaluators in courts, summary jury trials, and med-arb (mediation and arbitration conducted together).

Though Sander's ideas were applied primarily in the public sector, to courts and court adjuncts or local agencies receiving government funds, other applications of these ideas developed at about the same time in the private sector. In 1979 the Center for Public Resources was founded by a group of general counsels of leading Fortune 500 corporations to explore more efficient ways for major corporations to deal with their growing legal expenses and transaction costs in disputing both with each other and with customers and consumers. At about the same time, the half-century-old American Arbitration Association, which had been delivering private arbitration services in commercial dealings, construction disputes, and employment matters, broadened its services to include the more flexible mediation process, which developed to incorporate the teachings of modern problem-solving negotiation theory.[37] The first mini-trial, a private, mixed-negotiation, -mediation, and -arbitration procedure in a major patent-infringement case, was held in 1977.[38] It was heralded as an adaptive multiprocess, party-designed procedure that allowed underlying business interests, not technical legal issues, to structure the agreement to all parties' satisfaction and with great financial savings for both the courts and the parties.

In a public version of such an adapted process, the first summary jury trial was pioneered by federal district judge Thomas Lambros in the early 1980s, who had a large docket of mass tort cases and developed a new process within the courts to aid settlement. A panel of regular jurors heard shortened presentations of evidence and arguments in contested liability cases and rendered what was an advisory verdict used to facilitate the parties' negotiation after giving them a more realistic view of their case valuation expectations.[39] This process was used in both federal and state courts to help parties assess divergent legal expectations and encourage more realistic settlements.

Not all were motivated by the aim of rapid or efficient case processing. The community mediation movement sought to return dispute resolution and community problem solving to the communities in which disputes were located. The movement encouraged self-empowerment, antiprofessionalism, and multicultural and multiracial cooperation as means of increasing democratic participation at the local level and reducing violence and intergroup tensions.[40] Those in the community mediation movement were often grassroots organizers and political progressives who sought party participation. Because they depended on private foundations and public money, however, some were later accused of cooptation by establishment institutions.

In another arena, during the 1970s, divorce and family mediation flourished. Both lawyers and psychologists sought better ways of resolving the pain of divorce, especially when parents continued relationships with each other to raise their children. Divorce and family mediation professionals, probably more than other practitioners in the field, were able to craft a multidisciplinary profession with members from a variety of primary disciplines—social work, psychology, law, medicine, and even accounting. Divorce mediation in the private sector encouraged relationship healing, collaborative decision making, and improved family communication. It was subsequently captured (or according to some, coopted) by the public sector in many states. Some states, beginning with California in the early 1980s, began to mandate family mediation or conciliation, often in short, limited sessions, before divorce would be granted.[41] The family mediation movement, in turn, gave birth to a movement called "collaborative law," in which lawyers specialize in negotiated and mediated divorce settlements and often refuse to use more adversarial litigation techniques.[42]

Family disputes were not the only ones to receive particularized attention from dispute resolution practitioners. Even before the 1976 Pound conference, both arbitration (in collective bargaining grievances) and mediation (in federally mandated labor disputes) had been used in labor matters for decades without those processes migrating to other areas of legal disputes. By the 1980s the use of commercial arbitration, first in business-to-business disputes and then, most controversially, in consumer-to-business disputes, led to the use of mandatory arbitration clauses in a wide range of contracts, including employment, health care, banking, and most consumer transactions. Somewhat contradictorily, as businesses began to look to more flexible means of dispute resolution (including mediation and hybrid processes) for themselves, they began to impose, through unbargained-for contractual terms, more rigid, mandatory, and less rights-based processes on consumers. The shift from voluntary and self-deterministic processes to compulsory and mandatory processes unbargained for in contracts marks what may be the most troubling issue in modern dispute resolution.[43]

Coming from both social work and law, a number of reformers in the community mediation movement in the late 1980s proposed an alternative form of criminal justice—one based on restorative justice. The process associated with this movement is most commonly called "victim offender mediation."[44] This form of dispute resolution was derived both from traditional mediation principles and from traditional cultures. The ideas and norms informing such practices included healing for injured victims, acknowledgment of and responsibility for wrongdoing by perpetrators, and community participation and healing. Restorative justice offers remedies that are more restitutionary and reparative than the punitive sanctions of courts.[45]

The impulses behind the restorative justice movement have also inspired new forms of postconflict intranational and nation-state justice.[46] Truth and reconciliation commissions have been formed on many continents to deal with serious political violence and civil war. Beginning in the 1990s, the belief that "truth" and confession can lead to healing and reconciliation has influenced a variety of new alternative justice models in Africa, South America, and Eastern Europe. Whether these alternative institutions have been successful in such places as South Africa, Rwanda, Sierra Leone, Guatemala, and Argentina is now being seriously debated by participants in and scholars of these processes.[47]

In the 1990s the increasing rapidity of human interactions, through computer-assisted communication and negotiations in such areas as intellectual property, international contracts, and complex construction, fostered development of specialized dispute resolution processes. Disputes about domain names on the Internet were handled by several private providers though arbitration on the Internet itself. The Internet auction site eBay adopted one of the first successful online forms of dispute settlement, using procedures from SquareTrade.com.[48] And, in one of the most creative reformulations of dispute processes, the Army Corps of Engineers, working with private contractors, developed a predispute ADR-like process of "partnering," in which all parties to a complex construction project met in retreat settings to develop relationships and establish procedures for preventively dealing with disputes and conflicts before the construction began.[49]

Dispute resolution ideas and processes were also creatively introduced into other domains, inspired by the intellectual work in negotiation and mediation that suggested that better solutions would emerge from greater participation by all stakeholders in a dispute. Expanding from the traditional model of mediation with two disputants, the field of public policy facilitation or consensus building adapted dispute resolution techniques for guided meeting management and alternative political processes. These processes aimed to improve group decision making and achieve greater legitimacy when public policies were stalled in polarized political battles.[50] In the legal arena, a creative administrative lawyer suggested that the new negotiation theories be applied to administrative rule making in the federal government, both to encourage more creative regulatory solutions and to avoid costly post-hoc litigation challenges.[51] The new process, negotiated rule making, or "reg-neg," was formally approved in federal law after successful experimentation and now is used at both national and state levels, despite ongoing controversies about whether it delivers all it promises.[52] Consensus-building processes, inviting all those potentially affected by government action to negotiate outcomes together, have now been used in such areas as airport and waste siting, environmental and other land-use disputes, budget allocations, community and racial disputes, local charter processes, and intergovernmental relations.

Modern ombuds are an adaptation of an old form, the Swedish ombudsman—a mediator between citizens and governments. Ombuds promoted the use of organizational counselors, mediators, and monitors of government, university, and corporate activities to address internal disputes. These ombuds dealt with internal patterns of disputes and conflicts (such as pay equity, discrimination, and bad management) and in some cases interfaced with outsiders in conflict with organizations. The modern ombuds role is another hybrid, because it vests in one person or staff the roles of dispute counselor, adviser, mediator, and sometimes advocate.[53] This idea is one based on process expertise—knowledge of conflict and disputing processes, as well as deep knowledge of organizational culture.

EMERGING PROFESSIONALIZATION
AND INSTITUTIONALIZATION

With the use of increasingly tailored and complex levels of dispute processing among coworkers, repeat players, contractors, and strangers, the practice has moved toward professionalization. Practitioners have developed professional associations such as the Society for Professionals in Dispute Resolution (recently renamed the Association for Conflict Resolution) and the American Bar Association's Section on Dispute Resolution. A new field, called "Dispute System Design,"[54] developed to help parties craft a menu or tiered system of dispute processes tailored for particular organizations or dispute types, especially in settings of repetitive disputes or complex legal disputes. Several new organizations were formed, such as JAMS (Judicial, Arbitration and Mediation Services) (primarily retired judges) and ENDISPUTE (lawyers and social scientists) to advise parties on dispute design and provide third party neutral services.

The institutionalization of various forms of mediation and facilitated negotiation followed from the practical "theory" offered by a convergence of disciplinary perspectives in the 1980s. This emerging theory focused on negotiation for creative problem solving, rather than on "winning." It also encouraged mediation, on the theory that a third party might ensure that negotiations were as efficient and creative as possible. The Program on Negotiation (PON) was founded at Harvard Law School in 1983, Stanford University organized the interdisciplinary Stanford Center on Conflict and Negotiation (SCCN), and the William and Flora Hewlett Foundation began to fund university "theory centers" in conflict resolution as an outgrowth of its funding for creative environmental problem solving. As the theory centers encouraged the interdisciplinary study of conflict processes, the Hewlett Foundation began to fund practical applications of this work in community programs, courts, and a variety of substantive areas such as health care disputes and racial and ethnic conflict. Many of the theory centers and more practical institutions also began offering extensive training programs in interest-based negotiation, conflict resolution skills, mediation, communication, facilitation, and similar processes to both professional and lay groups in the hopes that cultural diffusion would occur at cognitive, behavioral, and organizational levels.

THE LEGITIMACY OF DISPUTE RESOLUTION PROCESSES

From the beginning of the modern period of creative experimentation, many different—often competing—objectives were offered in justification of new procedures. Cost and time savings, efficiency, reduced caseloads, and similar concerns with the economic aspects of procedures were often juxtaposed against processes, such as mediation, that were intended to dig deeper into parties' real, not legalized, needs, interests, motivations, and desires, and search creatively for joint-gain solutions or new relationships. Such processes, for example, psychologically based or innovative business solutions, might actually take more time, involve more parties, and could—and sometimes did—increase costs and involve more professionals. Thus, even from the beginning of the development of alternatives to courts in the 1970s, these new processes were plagued with a variety of alternative rationales, some of them in conflict with each other.

As these dispute resolution processes began to develop more legitimacy, and as they were used more frequently in both the public and private sector, they were criticized on a variety of fronts for "privatizing justice,"[55] disempowering women and minorities,[56] and, ironically, for increasing state intervention in private lives.[57] Recently, the transmission of these problem-solving tools to a variety of groups, nations, nongovernmental organizations (NGOs), and others outside of the United States has also brought criticism for "exporting" American-style processes to radically different cultures and legal systems.[58] In response, many believe that the animating values and practices of dispute resolution offer a potential lingua franca, because their flexible forms and creativity allow processes to be designed and techniques to be used to meet the needs of different populations and problems. Whether a formal legal system, or even the rule of law at some rudimentary level of legitimacy, is necessary to support a more open dispute resolution culture is one of the interesting questions for the future.

DIRECTIONS AND CHALLENGES FOR THE FUTURE

There have been major developments in both dispute resolution theory and practice in the past three decades, offering a wide variety of processes and techniques to apply for different kinds of disputes and with different kinds of parties. At the most abstract levels of theory development, dispute resolution scholars are collecting their knowledge to see if they can articulate a canon of dispute resolution.[59] Theorists are also examining whether fundamental propositions about dispute resolution change as the number of disputants increases.[60] One of the most exciting developments in the field is dispute resolution theorists' and practitioners' work with those arguing for more participatory and democratic deliberation in our large, diverse, and increasingly contentious societies. Inspired by the political and social philosophies of Jurgen Habermas[61] and Stuart Hampshire,[62] which suggested conditions under which political decisions are considered legitimate by citizens (under "ideal speech conditions," when each side can "hear and persuade the other") and more concrete applications of deliberative democracy in highly contested areas,[63] dispute resolution practitioners and theorists are now engaged with political theorists and policymakers to apply this work in broader contexts.

All of the constituent processes continue to profit from university and interdisciplinary center research agendas. These agendas include exploring the impact of race and gender on negotiation and mediation processes,[64] the role of particular third-party interventions in mediation,[65] the effectiveness and robustness of negotiated or mediated agreements,[66] and, increasingly, the role of psychological and emotional states in individual and group dispute interactions.[67] Bridging issues in both domestic and international dispute resolution, the question of how culture is operationalized and used in dispute processes has been debated vigorously among those who see the postmodern fluidity of cultural affinities and self-definitions, and others who see more reified or static categories.[68]

At least two important challenges confront the practical side of the field— evaluation and professionalization. In the decades that dispute resolution has successfully been employed in a variety of locations, supporting foundations, governments, users, and critics of dispute resolution demand that the field prove its effectiveness. The demand to evaluate often causes the conflation of the quantitative and qualitative claims made on behalf of dispute resolution. One multiyear and multimillion dollar study of the use of some dispute resolution techniques in the courts failed conclusively to establish whether lower costs or time savings resulted when mediation, early neutral evaluation, and other devices were used in formal litigation venues.[69] But many other studies, often using both quantitative and qualitative measures, have demonstrated program and process effectiveness. For example, one study found that lawyers forced to use mediation in court programs were more likely to recommend mediation in their own later cases.[70] Combining quantitative measures of efficiency with qualitative assessments of solutions, user satisfaction, and, in organizational settings, changes in "conflict culture or competence," would be a productive path for the field to take. However, efficiency may be inconsistent with finding quality solutions to disputes and developing meaningful communication between parties. Metrics in human relations fields will always be problematic.

As the field of dispute resolution has matured, it has become professional-ized and institutionalized. This worries some people who chose the field for its party participation, deprofessionalization and communitarian values, as well as its process flexibility. Students of professionalization will say, however, that the field's trajectory is normal—new fields of knowledge and practice seek to pro-fessionalize themselves with codes of ethics,[71] professional associations, cre-dentialing, licensing, and standards out of both positive and more self-interested motives. Our expertise is valuable and does tell us how to facilitate and medi-ate difficult human situations. This knowledge and its uses can often be codi-fied.[72] The danger to avoid is ossification. Similarly, success breeds repetition in the reproduction of court programs, training programs, organizational "inte-grated dispute resolution systems,"[73] and routine "opening statements" in medi-ation. Experts seek to meet and share their knowledge in professional associations that then may try to capture and control the economic market for services. In this, dispute resolution as a field is not alone.

What makes dispute resolution different as a field, however, is its continu-ing aspiration to make the world a better place by seeking modes of communi-cation to resolve unproductive conflict, to seek creative and efficient solutions to disputes, to prevent and reduce violence, to encourage reconciliation and peace where there has been violence, and, most important, to encourage every human being to approach every other one in the spirit of shared problem solving and respect for mutual existence. These are lofty aspirations, and at the beginning of the twenty-first century they seem almost naive. The Realpolitikers seem to have won the current day of polarization,[74] ethnic and civil wars, and "clashes of civilizations."[75] Yet the field of dispute resolution continues to expand, train-ing millions of lawyers, business people, schoolchildren, community activists, military personnel, psychologists, social workers, and architects to look for com-mon ground of mutual existence, not settle for bad compromises, and continue to look for high-quality solutions to difficult problems.

There is a great need for more theories-in-use to be developed and tested in the crucibles of individual, familial, commercial, professional, legal, economic, political, and international disputes. And there is a great need to learn who is using these theories and approaches, and to what effect.

Notes

1. S. Hampshire, *Justice Is Conflict* (Princeton: Princeton University Press, 2000), p. 35.

2. See M. Shapiro, *Courts: A Comparative and Political Analysis* (Chicago: University of Chicago Press, 1981); and J. S. Auerbach, *Justice Without Law? Resolving Disputes Without Lawyers* (New York: Oxford Press, 1983).

3. See, for example, L. Kriesberg, *Constructive Conflicts from Escalation to Resolution* (Lanham, Md.: Rowman & Littlefield, 1998); and H. Miall, O. Ramsbotham, and T. Woodhouse, *Contemporary Conflict Resolution* (Cambridge, U.K.: Polity Press, 1999).

4. See D. G. Pruitt and S. H. Kim, *Social Conflict: Escalation, Stalemate, and Settlement* (Boston: McGraw-Hill, 2004); and C. Menkel-Meadow, "From Legal Disputes to Conflict Resolution and Human Problem Solving: Legal Dispute Resolution in a Multi-Disciplinary Context," in C. Menkel-Meadow, *Dispute Processing and Conflict Resolution: Theory, Practice and Policy* (Burlington, Vt.: Ashgate, 2003).

5. See C. Argyris and D. A. Schön, *Theory in Practice* (San Francisco: Jossey-Bass, 1974).

6. See M. Deutsch and P. Coleman (eds.), *The Handbook of Conflict Resolution: Theory and Practice* (San Francisco: Jossey-Bass, 2000).

7. See L. Coser, *The Functions of Social Conflict* (New York: Free Press, 1956).

8. See E. Durkheim, *The Division of Labor in Society* (New York: Free Press, 1984).

9. See G. Simmel, *Conflict and the Web of Intergroup Affiliations* (New York: Free Press, 1955).

10. W.L.F. Felstiner, R. Abel, and A. Sarat, "The Emergence and Transformation of Disputes: Naming, Blaming, Claiming . . . ," *Law & Society Review*, 1980–81, *15*, pp. 635–637.

11. See, for example, K. Llewelyn and E. A. Hoebel, *The Cheyenne Way: Conflict and Case Law in Primitive Jurisprudence* (Norman, Okla.: University of Oklahoma Press, 1941); R. Abel, "A Comparative Theory of Dispute Institutions in Society," *Law & Society Review*, 1973, *8*, 217–347; and L. Nader and H. Todd, *The Disputing Process: Law in Ten Societies* (New York: Columbia University Press, 1978).

12. See C. Menkel-Meadow, "Mothers and Fathers of Invention: The Intellectual Founders of ADR," *Ohio St. Journal on Dispute Resolution*, 2000, *16*, 4, 13; and C. Menkel-Meadow and M. Wheeler, *What's Fair: Ethics for Negotiators* (San Francisco: Jossey-Bass, 2004).

13. See M. Deutsch, "Cooperation and Conflict: A Personal Perspective on the History of the Social Psychological Study of Conflict Resolution," in M. A. West, D. Tjosvold, and K. G. Smith (eds.), *International Handbook of Organizational Teamwork and Cooperative Working* (Chicester, U.K. and Hoboken, N.J.: John Wiley & Sons, Inc., 2003); and Marquette Law Review, *Symposium: The Emerging Interdisciplinary Canon of Negotiation, Marquette Law Review*, 2004, *87*, 637–902.

14. See, for example, H. Raiffa, *The Art and Science of Negotiation* (Cambridge, Mass.: Belknap Press of Harvard University Press, 1982).

15. See, for example, M. Deutsch, *The Resolution of Conflict: Constructive and Destructive Processes* (New Haven, Conn.: Yale University Press, 1973).

16. See, for example, L. L. Fuller, *The Principles of Social Order: Selected Essays of Lon L. Fuller* (Oxford and Portland, Ore.: Hart Publishing, 1981 [rev. ed., K. I. Winston (ed.),

2001]); and F.E.A. Sander and S. B. Goldberg, "Fitting the Forum to the Fuss: A User-Friendly Guide to Selecting an ADR Procedure," *Negotiation Journal*, 1994, *10*, 49–68.

17. M. P. Follett, "Constructive Conflict," in P. Graham (ed.), *Mary Parker Follett: Prophet of Management: A Celebration of Writings from the 1920s* (Boston: Harvard Business School Press, 1996), pp. 67–68.

18. See R. E. Walton and R. B. McKersie, *A Behavioral Theory of Labor Negotiations* (New York: McGraw-Hill, 1965).

19. See R. Fisher, W. Ury, and B. Patton, *Getting to YES: Negotiating Agreement Without Giving In* (2nd ed.) (New York: Penguin, 1991).

20. See M. Deutsch, *The Resolution of Conflict: Constructive and Destructive Processes* (New Haven, Conn.: Yale University Press, 1973).

21. See K. Thomas, "Conflict and Conflict Management," In M. D. Dunnette (ed.), *Handbook of Industrial and Organizational Psychology* (Chicago: Rand McNally, 1976).

22. See, for example, T. C. Schelling, *The Strategy of Conflict* (Cambridge, Mass.: Harvard University Press, 1960).

23. L. L. Fuller, "Mediation: Its Forms and Functions," *Southern California Law Review*, 1971, *44*, 325.

24. L. L. Fuller, "Collective Bargaining and the Arbitrator," in M. L. Kahn (ed.), *Collective Bargaining and the Arbitrator's Role: Proceedings of the Fifteenth Annual Meeting of the National Academy of Arbitrators* (Washington, D.C.: BNA, Inc., 1962), pp. 29–30.

25. L. L. Fuller, "The Forms and Limits of Adjudication," *Harvard Law Review*, 1978, *92*, p. 383.

26. See, for example, S. Mentschikoff, "Commercial Arbitration," *Columbia Law Review*, 1961, *61*, 846–869.

27. See D. A. Lax and J. K. Sebenius, *The Manager as Negotiator: Bargaining for Cooperation and Competitive Gain* (New York: Free Press, 1986); R. H. Mnookin, S. Peppet, and A. S. Tulumello, *Beyond Winning: Negotiating to Create Value in Deals and Disputes* (Cambridge, Mass.: Belknap Press of Harvard University Press, 2000); and R. H. Mnookin and L. E. Susskind, *Negotiating on Behalf of Others: Advice to Lawyers, Business Executives, Sports Agents, Diplomats, Politicians, and Everybody Else* (Thousand Oaks, Calif.: Sage, 1999).

28. See K. Arrow, R. H. Mnookin, L. Ross, L., A. Tversky, and R. Wilson, *Barriers to Conflict Resolution* (New York: W. W. Norton, 1995).

29. See, for example, R. Axelrod, *The Evolution of Cooperation* (New York: Basic Books, 1984).

30. See, for example, S. J. Brams and A. D. Taylor, *Fair Division: From Cake Cutting to Dispute Resolution* (Cambridge, Mass.: Cambridge University Press, 1996); B. Nalebuff and I. Ayres, *Why Not? How to Use Everyday Ingenuity to Solve Problems Big and Small* (Boston: Harvard Business School Press, 2003); and

C. Menkel-Meadow, "Aha? Is Creativity Possible in Legal Problem Solving and Teachable in Legal Education?" *Harvard Negotiation Law Review*, 2001, *6*, 97–144.

31. F.E.A. Sander, "Varieties of Dispute Processing," *Federal Rules Decisions*, 1976, *77*, 111–123.

32. See W. E. Burger, "Isn't There a Better Way?" *American Bar Association Journal*, 1982, *68*, 274–276.

33. See, for example, H. M. Hart Jr. and A. M. Sacks, *The Legal Process: Basic Problems in the Making and Application of Law* (1958 tent. ed., W. N. Eskridge Jr. and P. P. Frickey [eds.]) (Westbury, N.Y.: The Foundation Press, 1994).

34. See Sander and Goldberg, "Fitting the Forum to the Fuss," 1994.

35. See C. B. Harrington, *Shadow Justice: The Ideology and Institutionalization of Alternatives to Courts* (Westport, Conn.: Greenwood Press, 1985).

36. See S. Merry and N. Milner (eds.), *The Possibility of Popular Justice: A Case Study of American Community Justice* (Ann Arbor, Mich.: University of Michigan Press, 1993).

37. See C. Menkel-Meadow, "Toward Another View of Legal Negotiation: The Structure of Problem Solving," *UCLA Law Review*, 1984, *31*, 754–782; and Mnookin, Peppet, and Tulumell, *Beyond Winning*, 2000.

38. See E. D. Green, "CPR Legal Program Mini-Trial Handbook," in Center for Public Resources, *Corporate Dispute Management* (New York: Matthew Bender, 1982).

39. See J. Alfini, "Summary Jury Trials in State and Federal Courts: A Comparative Analysis of the Perceptions of Participating Lawyers," *Ohio State Journal of Dispute Resolution*, 1989, *4*, 213–234.

40. See R. Shonholtz, "Neighborhood Justice Systems: Work, Structure, and Guiding Principles," *Mediation Quarterly*, 1984, *5*, 3–30.

41. See T. Grillo, "The Mediation Alternative: Process Dangers for Women," *Yale Law Journal*, 1991, *100*, 1545–1560.

42. See P. H. Tesler, *Collaborative Law* (Chicago: ABA Press, 2001).

43. See Menkel-Meadow, "Mothers and Fathers of Invention," 2000; and J. Sternlight, "Is Binding Arbitration a Form of ADR? An Argument That the Term ADR Has Begun to Outlive Its Usefulness," *Journal of Dispute Resolution*, 2000, 97–112.

44. See M. Umbreit, *The Handbook of Victim-Offender Mediation* (San Francisco: Jossey-Bass, 2000).

45. See S. Tickell and K. Akester, *Restorative Justice: The Way Ahead* (London: Justice, 2004).

46. See M. Minow, *Between Vengeance and Forgiveness: Facing History After Genocide and Mass Violence* (Boston: Beacon Press, 1998).

47. See, for example, D. Dyzenhaus, *Judging the Judges, Judging Ourselves: Truth, Reconciliation and the Apartheid Legal Order* (Chicago: Northwestern University Press, 1998); J. E. Stromseth (ed.), *Accountability for Atrocities: National and International Responses* (Ardsley, N.Y.: Transnational Publishing, 2003);

R. G. Helmick and R. L. Petersen, *Forgiveness and Reconciliation: Religion, Public Policy and Conflict Transformation* (Radnor, Pa.: Templeton Foundation, 2001); and T. Kelsall, "Truth, Lies, Ritual: Preliminary Reflections on the Truth and Reconciliation Commission in Sierra Leone," unpublished manuscript, University of New Castle on Tyne, U.K., 2004.

48. See E. Katsh and J. Rifkin, *Online Dispute Resolution: Resolving Conflicts in Cyberspace* (San Francisco: Jossey-Bass, 2001).

49. See F. Carr, K. Hurtado, C. Lancaster, C. Markert, and P. Tucker, *Partnering in Construction: A Practical Guide to Project Success* (Chicago: ABA Press, 1999).

50. See L. Susskind, S. McKearnan, and J. Larmer-Thomas, *The Consensus Building Handbook: A Comprehensive Guide to Reaching Agreement* (Thousand Oaks, Calif.: Sage Publications, 1999); and S. L. Carpenter and W.J.D. Kennedy, *Managing Public Disputes* (San Francisco: Jossey-Bass, 2001).

51. See P. Harter, "Negotiating Regulations: A Cure for the Malaise," *Georgetown Law Journal*, 1982, *71*, 1–118.

52. See J. Freeman, "Collaborative Governance in the Administrative State," *UCLA Law Review*, 1997, *45*, 1–98.

53. See H. Gadlin (ed.), "The Many Different and Complex Roles Played by Ombudsmen in Dispute Resolution: Special Issue on Ombudsmen," *Negotiation Journal*, 2000, *16*, 35–114.

54. See W. Ury, J. Brett, and S. Goldberg, *Getting Disputes Resolved* (San Francisco: Jossey-Bass, 1988).

55. See O. Fiss, "Against Settlement," *Yale Law Journal*, 1984, *93*, 1073–1090.

56. See Grillo, "The Mediation Alternative," 1991; and R. Delgado, C. Dunn, P. Brown, H. Lee, and D. Hubbert, "Fairness and Formality: Minimizing the Risk of Prejudice in Alternative Dispute Resolution," *Wisconsin Law Review*, 1985, pp. 1359–1391.

57. See R. Abel, "The Contradictions of Informal Justice," in R. Abel (ed.), *The Politics of Informal Justice: The American Experience* (New York: Academic Press, 1982).

58. See L. Nader and E. Grande, "Current Illusions and Delusions About Conflict Management—In Africa and Elsewhere," *Law & Society Inquiry*, 2002, *27*, 573–594; and C. Menkel-Meadow, "Correspondences and Contradictions in International and Domestic Conflict Resolution: Lessons from General Theory and Various Contexts," *Journal of Dispute Resolution*, 2003, pp. 319–352.

59. See, for example, Marquette Law Review, *Symposium*, 2004.

60. See H. Raiffa, J. Richardson, and D. Metcalfe, *Negotiation Analysis: The Science and Art of Collaborative Decision Making* (Cambridge, Mass.: Belknap Press of Harvard University Press, 2002).

61. See J. Habermas, *The Theory of Communicative Action*, Vols. 1 and 2 (Boston: Beacon Press, 1984).

62. See Hampshire, *Justice Is Conflict*, 2000.

63. See A. Guttman and D. Thompson, *Democracy and Disagreement* (Cambridge, Mass.: Belknap Press of Harvard University Press, 1996).

64. See I. Ayres, "Fair Driving: Gender and Race Discrimination in Retail Car Negotiations," *Harvard Law Review,* 1991, *104,* 817–872; and G. LaFree and C. Rack, "The Effects of Participants' Ethnicity and Gender on Monetary Outcomes in Mediated and Adjudicated Cases," *Law & Society Review,* 1996, *30,* 767–797.

65. See R. B. Bush and J. P. Folberg, *The Promise of Mediation: Responding to Conflict Through Empowerment and Reconciliation* (San Francisco: Jossey-Bass, 1994).

66. See K. Kressel, D. J. Pruitt, and associates, *Mediation Research* (San Francisco: Jossey-Bass, 1989).

67. See K. Leary (special ed.), "Critical Moments in Negotiation: Special Issue," *Negotiation Journal,* 2004, *20,* 143–376.

68. See K. Avruch, *Culture and Conflict Resolution* (Washington, D.C.: United States Institute of Peace Press, 1998); and J. M. Brett, *Negotiating Globally* (San Francisco: Jossey Bass, 2001).

69. See J. Kakalik, T. Dunworth, L. Hill, D. McCaffrey, M. Oshiro, N. Pace, and M. Vaiana, *An Evaluation of Mediation and Early Neutral Evaluation Under the Civil Justice Reform Act* (Santa Monica, Calif.: RAND Institute of Justice, 1996).

70. See R. L. Wissler, "The Effects of Mandatory Mediation: Empirical Research on the Experience of Small Claims and Common Pleas Courts," *Willamette Law Review,* 1997, *33,* 565–579.

71. See Menkel-Meadow and Wheeler, *What's Fair,* 2004.

72. See C. Menkel Meadow, "The Lawyer as Consensus Builder: Ethics for a New Practice," *Tennessee Law Review,* 2002, *70,* 63–119.

73. See D. B. Lipsky, R. L. Seeber, and R. Fincher, *Emerging Systems for Managing Workplace Conflict* (San Francisco: Jossey Bass, 2004).

74. See D. Tannen, *The Argument Culture: Moving From Debate to Dialogue* (New York: Random House, 1998).

75. See S. P. Huntington, *The Clash of Civilizations and the Remaking of the World Order* (New York: Touchstone Press, 1996).

PART ONE

UNDERSTANDING DISPUTANTS

CHAPTER THREE

"I See a Pattern Here and the Pattern Is You"

Personality and Dispute Resolution

Sheila Heen and John Richardson

*There are two kinds of people in the world: those who believe there
are two kinds of people in the world, and those who don't.*
—Robert Benchley

Anyone who has more than one child knows that differences in personality are real. The firstborn may be quiet, eager to please, and shy in new situations. His sister comes along and is an extravert—smiling early and befriending strangers as a toddler. These traits may remain constant throughout life as the firstborn becomes a writer and his sister makes friends easily and often as a college student, professional, and retiree.

Intuitively, we know that there are differences between individuals. Your spouse is agreeable, your brother irascible, your coworker weepy, and your neighbor hyperrational.

The hard question is this: Are there ways to describe the differences in people's personalities that can be useful in conducting or advising negotiations? After all, negotiation is all about dealing with people, getting along with them, and persuading them. Shouldn't knowing how people are different (and what to do about it) be an integral part of negotiation theory and strategy?

One would think so. And yet, the intersection of dispute resolution and personality is a tangle of confusion and contradiction. It is not unexplored territory—scholars have tried to find answers. And it is interesting—there is fascinating work going on and much speculation about what is being learned. Yet there are few clear, satisfying answers to the questions that interest dispute resolution professionals most: Are particular personalities better negotiators?

The authors determined authorship order by coin toss.

Should I negotiate differently with different personalities? And what about when the people and their problematic personalities really are the problem?

WHY LOOK AT DISPUTE RESOLUTION AND PERSONALITY?

Before we get lost in the muddle, it would be wise to stop and ask what is motivating us. What explains our interest? And what is our purpose? What do we—as dispute resolution professionals interested in personality—hope to achieve?

What Draws Our Interest?

Human beings have always gravitated toward ways to simplify the messy business of understanding other human beings. From the signs of the zodiac to the latest quiz in *Cosmopolitan*, systems that classify human beings have always been popular. Some of them are quite entertaining—such as Freud's division of personalities into oral, anal, phallic, or genital.[1] Trying to divide your friends into those groups can be amusing.

Personality also provides a soothing explanation for our own negotiation failures. Why did we reach impasse? Because the personalities at the table made progress impossible. Or why did I not try something different when things got heated? A different approach may have helped, but that "just wouldn't be me."

What Do We Hope to Achieve with This Inquiry?

Perhaps understanding personality can help focus our learning. It might highlight our blind spots, illuminate our own complex behaviors, and remind us of responses that come less naturally. This is perhaps the most promising use of personality instruments and research.

Businesses often use personality analysis to make personnel choices or build teams. The same line of thinking could apply to alternative dispute resolution. Perhaps there are certain "kinds" of people who would make good negotiators or mediators, or who would be a good match with particular kinds of parties or counterparts. We would love to have a simple taxonomy of traits that could help us size up counterparts quickly and accurately. If we could identify another's personality traits, different tactical advice might follow. Perhaps one negotiation strategy works best with introverts, and another with extraverts.[2]

The bottom line is that there is very little evidence that a particular personality profile or trait can be accurately identified or can accurately predict behavior in disputes. Nor can it assist us in reliable decision making in choosing personnel or strategy. By one estimate, less than 10 percent of behavior can be explained by personality profiles,[3] and knowing someone's personality profile has no power to predict his or her future behavior. Indeed, as two scholars who examined the question of personality and negotiation concluded, "From what is known now, it does not appear that there is any single personality type or characteristic that is directly and clearly linked to success in negotiation."[4]

WHAT DOES THE PERSONALITY FIELD OFFER?

Personality is a hard field to get a handle on. There is more disagreement than agreement among social scientists about what "personality" is, what variables best describe the differences between people, and whether and how it can be measured. Psychologists, organizational behaviorists, economists, negotiation researchers, neurologists, and geneticists have all gotten into the act, each contributing different approaches to capturing the essence of personality.

No single chapter could cover the entire field of personality—more than twenty-five-hundred personality profiling instruments are currently in use.[5] In addition to using systems that attempt to capture a cohesive personality profile, some researchers investigate the impact of individual traits: risk-taking propensity, perceived locus of control, cognitive ability, tolerance of ambiguity, propensity to trust, cooperativeness or agreeableness, ethicality, authoritarianism, concern for others versus concern for self, equity concerns, degree of self-monitoring, and emotional intelligence. Some of these traits are included in some of the profiling instruments, others are ignored entirely.

In this chapter, we confine ourselves to touching on a couple of representative personality-profiling instruments. We have chosen two instruments because they are the most popular and relied on in the business world (in which Myers-Briggs is commonplace) and in the academy (in which the Big Five is emerging as the dominant taxonomy in psychology). These two instruments were also developed differently—Myers-Briggs was created deductively, while the Big Five system is an inductive discovery.

For those who want a quick (and admittedly incomplete) look, we have included a section titled "Six Questions People Ask About Personality and Dispute Resolution" at the end of the chapter.

The Most Popular Personality Instrument: Myers-Briggs

Of all the personality instruments, the best known and most widely referred to is the Myers-Briggs Type Indicator. It is administered over two million times each year and is used by eighty-nine companies in the Fortune 100[6] and by the U.S. military. Thousands of research studies, journal articles, and dissertations have focused on it. It is used in couples counseling, family therapy, team building, and career counseling.

The MBTI was developed by the mother-daughter team of Katharine C. Briggs and Isabel Briggs Myers in the 1950s. The test is based on three personality axes hypothesized by Carl Jung: introverted or extraverted, sensing or intuiting, and thinking or feeling. To these, Myers added a fourth: perceiving or judging. These axes describe the ways people gain and process information.[7]

Introverted or Extraverted? The first axis concerns one's appetite for social contact. Extraverts are thought to be energized by other people, experience, and activity. They rely on their environment for stimulation and guidance. In one research experiment, participants were asked to think about past experiences that triggered strong emotions. Participants who were extraverts most frequently described social experiences such as being chosen most popular counselor at a church camp.[8]

Introverts are focused inward. They are interested in the clarity of concepts, ideas, and recollected experience. Introverts enjoy solitude and privacy. While their extraverted colleagues process their thinking aloud, introverts prefer to think things through before talking about them.[9] Asked about emotional memories, introverts more often described solitary experiences or individual achievements, such as shooting their first rabbit at age ten or graduating from junior college.[10]

Sondra VanSant suggests that a mismatch between introverts and extraverts may cause friction in the negotiation process. She suggests that when tensions arise, an extravert may want to address the issue immediately, while an introvert wants to go away and think things through. The extravert may feel that the introvert is avoiding the issue, while the introvert experiences the extravert as confrontational.[11]

Sensing or Intuiting? The second axis focuses on selecting information—what we pay attention to and what we retain. Those who prefer *sensing* are thought to focus on the concrete, the current, and the tangible, and they absorb information sequentially. When asked to describe an apple, sensing types will write down its physical characteristics: red, round, stemmed, or juicy. They are often detail oriented, and so might describe a conflict chronologically in terms of what exactly was said or done when and by whom.

Intuiting folks are more likely to describe an apple by listing associations: The Big Apple, an apple a day keeps the doctor away, or Sleeping Beauty. They look for patterns, see implications, and focus on the ideas behind the realities. They are more abstract thinkers.

What are the implications for conflict? While the sensing types are asking lots of questions to gather concrete facts, their intuitive counterparts get impatient—thinking that the sensing types cannot see the forest for the trees. Intuiting types make arguments based on general issues or analogies; the sensing types get frustrated when intuiting types suggest things that are inconsistent with the facts, or that are not practical or realistic. Don Peters suggests that intuiting individuals may be more comfortable with the fluid process of problem-solving negotiation, while sensing types may gravitate toward a structured, step-by-step process such as litigation. Lisle Baker posits that intuiting types may be better at appreciating the possibility that a judicial resolution may not be favorable to them and that a mediated solution offers a way to shape their future.[12]

Thinking or Feeling? The thinking or feeling preference describes how people judge the information they have—the criteria they prefer for making decisions. Those who score high on the thinking end of the scale prefer to make decisions on the basis of general standards. They will look to the language of the contract, to precedents, or to notions of fairness. For thinkers, conflict is inevitable in relationships because people will disagree over principles, and in the end, fairness is more important than how people feel. In contrast, feelers consider how the decision will affect them or someone they care about. Disharmony is difficult for feelers, and they may avoid stating their real concerns for fear of creating ill will.

Differences here may breed conflict: Thinkers want to look for the "right" answer and apply it to everyone. Feelers want to explore everyone's ideas and find individual solutions that work for people. Feelers are apt to think that the "truth" is not cut and dried. Thinkers believe that a problem can be clearly defined and evidence gathered—and that from that evidence, a correct solution will emerge for what everyone should do. Lisle Baker suggests that thinking types may view feelers as irrational, inconsistent, and illogical, while feelers view thinkers as cold and uncaring.[13] This might suggest that one could try to persuade a feeler by offering to satisfy his or her interests, while a thinker might respond to objective criteria.

Judging or Perceiving? The last MBTI dimension focuses on a need for structure and closure versus a preference for flexibility and keeping options open. If exposed to a new activity, someone scoring high on perceiving might observe the situation for some time, while judging counterparts jump in to take action.

In a conflict, judging types may take the information presented and reach conclusions quickly, while their perceiving colleagues tend to want more information or to consider a broader range of solutions before deciding. Frustrations between the two arise when the judging type gets impatient for closure, seeing the perceivers as flaky and indecisive. The judger may even view the perceiver as having reneged on a "deal" the perceiver considered possible and the judger considered done. Perceivers may see judgers as rigid and overly controlling. Perceivers may feel a discussion has only begun while their judging counterparts are already impatient to finish.

Caveats, Complications, and Concerns with the MBTI

We have been describing the Myers-Briggs system as though its dimensions, categories, and implications were established facts. While the instrument can be a tool for stimulating reflection and discussion, it has important limitations.

Reliability Problems. When it comes to empirical accuracy, Myers-Briggs is a lightning rod for criticism. As many as 47 percent of people who take the MBTI a second time get a different profile outcome.[14] Taking the indicator at different times of the day may change outcomes—it seems you can be a morning senser and an afternoon intuiter, for example.[15] Yet most MBTI advocates claim that you remain "your type" for life, and that differences in results suggest your true type was simply obscured by social stereotypes or your own confusion.

Proponents point to the thousands of studies and articles published about the MBTI. But scratch the surface of the studies and you find that many of the results are anecdotal observations made by instructors, mediators, or students. You will also find that many of those studies are concerned with "exploring applications for the test, not with proving or refuting its basic legitimacy."[16]

Little Ability to Predict Behavior. One of the purposes behind knowing someone's profile would be to anticipate how he or she might behave in a negotiation. Yet the MBTI describes *general preferences* rather than consistent modes of operation. For instance, someone who prefers to come to conclusions quickly and move on (judging) will sometimes hold his or her conclusions open to gather more information (perceiving). Knowing someone's tendency does not mean you can predict how that person will behave in a particular circumstance. There is little evidence that the MBTI can successfully predict behavior or job success.[17]

The MBTI Axes May Not Be Opposed. The MBTI assumes that the characteristics that are paired are perfectly negatively correlated: that being more of a thinker means being less of a feeler. This might not be true. Some pairs may be orthogonal, that is, each half is actually something quite independent of the other half. For example, the second axis pairs intuitives and sensers. To use the terms of Chris Argyris and his Action Science school of thought, this means being good either at formulating conclusions high on the ladder of inference or at gathering data at the bottom of the ladder of inference.[18] Our observations would suggest that you can (and should aim to) be strong on both ends. There are people who are weak on both ends as well.

The Academy's Breakdown: The Big Five

While the MBTI dominates the business world, the so-called Big Five has become the dominant personality taxonomy in experimental psychology, consistently reproduced in statistical analyses of personality measures. Rather than being derived deductively, the Big Five factors were discovered through inductive analysis of large-scale, controlled studies. Its advocates say that the Big Five system was found, not invented, and thus has empirical validity that the MBTI lacks.[19]

Understanding the Methodology. Myers-Briggs was developed deductively. Myers began with Jung's idea that a handful of differences exist, and she then created questions that collected data correlated to that theory.

In contrast, the Big Five system was found by taking the data from personality tests and using factor analysis to figure out underlying constructs. For example, imagine a personality test that has a hundred questions on it, such as "At a party, I like to talk to people I don't know: strongly agree, agree, neutral, disagree, strongly disagree."

We could say that your personality is reflected in your set of one hundred answers. But one hundred variables are too many to keep straight and work with. So we take your test result, and the test results of hundreds of other people, and run them through a statistical program that groups the questions together according to how often people give similar answers to them. So if the people who say "I always balance my checkbook" also tend to say "I am never late for meetings" then the program would group these together and call them part of a hidden or latent variable—an unseen "factor."

According to the emerging consensus among psychologists and social scientists who have done data reduction on personality measures, a handful of factors consistently turn up as significant. One analyst produced six factors, and another four.[20] But most psychologists studying the question come up with the same five (hence the name). Different researchers have assigned different labels to the factors, but they are conventionally listed as: (1) extraversion; (2) agreeableness; (3) conscientiousness; (4) emotional stability; and (5) openness to experience.[21]

Although a computer running factor analysis will break a large set of measures down into a few factors, a human analyst must decide what the underlying personality trait really is. What is it that causes people who balance their checkbooks to also be on time? The trait underlying balanced checkbooks and punctuality is usually labeled conscientiousness but has also been called will to achieve, self-control, task interest, dependability, superego strength, prudence, and thinking introversion.[22] Because of this, the Big Five factors are sometimes described as "bundles" of traits that produce particular behavior.

Each of these bundles (described below) may have something to do with dispute resolution.

Extraversion. On this factor, the Big Five and the MBTI overlap. The concept of extraversion within each instrument is roughly the same: extraverts like meeting and spending time with others, introverts are happier to be alone. Other traits such as assertiveness, sociability, energy, activity, and ambition seem to bundle with extraversion.

A little research has been done on the impact of Big Five extraversion or introversion on disputes or negotiation outcomes. Barry and Friedman's 1998 study on laboratory simulations found that high extraversion had a negative effect on a negotiator's distributive outcomes, and no effect on joint integrative outcomes.[23] Yet in a meta-analysis of published research, Barrick and Mount found that extraversion is positively correlated with success in sales and in managerial positions.[24] While not specifically related to negotiation, we might expect that an ability to form relationships and persuade is a crucial part of both types of jobs. Or it could be that the extravert's energy and activity simply helps him or her get more done.

Agreeableness. Agreeableness might be described as the willingness to please and be pleased. Some have called it social conformity and friendliness, and it is associated with people who are forgiving, tolerant, and trusting.

Such people might be more likely to cooperate in prisoner's dilemmas and social dilemmas—for example, they might volunteer to share information first in the hope that the counterpart will reciprocate. They might also form deeper, more committed relationships over time (distinct from extraverts' ability to make initial contacts). These negotiators might also agree too quickly, and Barry and Friedman's laboratory study found that agreeability tended to reduce individuals' distributive outcomes.[25]

Conscientiousness. High scores on conscientiousness represent care and diligence. This factor has been connected with dependability, organization, and "planfullness."

We might expect that conscientious negotiators would do thorough preparation before the negotiation begins and thus be likely to outperform the average population. Yet the research is split on this question. Barrick and Mount found that conscientiousness does seem to predict success in a wide variety of fields, including professionals, salespeople, and police.[26] Similarly, Lynch and Evans polled prosecutors about the defense attorneys they considered to be the best negotiators.[27] The D.A.s in the study rated the top defense negotiators as especially high on conscientiousness, suggesting it may be an asset for getting better outcomes for clients. Yet Barry and Friedman found no correlation between conscientiousness and higher distributive or integrative outcomes.[28]

Emotional Stability. This factor is sometimes known by its reverse: neuroticism. Those high in neuroticism are easily angered and slow to calm down, frequently worried, and insecure. Such negotiators might have a harder time forming relationships and might attempt to avoid negotiation altogether. Those high in emotional stability are calm and collected, and they get their bearings quickly after a setback. A "stable" negotiator would keep cool, not get distracted, and not take things personally.

One can imagine why emotional stability might be an asset for a negotiator who needs to weather the ups and downs of a dispute. Yet little research has been done to test a correlation. Lynch and Evans's study did identify emotional stability as the most significant trait cited by prosecutors asked to describe what made the defense attorneys they negotiated against so effective.[29] Of course, the prosecutors might have been merely describing what they liked most about their adversaries, not what might get better outcomes for defense clients.

Openness to Experience. Openness is associated with creativity and imagination. It may serve as an aid to creative problem solving and integration. It might also be associated with curiosity and the ability to listen attentively. It indicates a willingness to try new things and so may correlate with higher risk tolerance.

The impact on dispute resolution is again unclear. Lynch and Evans's study is the only one that shows a link between creativity (which they connect to openness to experience) and defense attorney effectiveness in obtaining outcomes for defendants.

Caveats, Complications, and Concerns with the Big Five

While the Big Five taxonomy has come to preeminence in personality psychology, it is not without problems. Lewis Goldberg and Gerard Saucier suggest that these factors may not translate well across languages and cultures, and that they may be more reliable in individualistic cultures than in collectivist ones.[30] Studies have produced different factors in the personalities of Italians and Hungarians, and seven factors in Hebrew and Tagalog speakers.[31] On the other hand, some researchers have replicated the five-factor structure in a study of Japanese subjects.[32]

The most telling criticism of the Big Five is that it simplifies personality down to categories that are too broad to be meaningful. Each of the factors includes a bundle of behaviors and traits, and so produces, at best, a crude snapshot of a person. As Scott Meier of the State University of New York observed, "The Big Five makes me think of being up in a spaceship, looking down at the planet below and seeing five continents. That's useful to know, but once you're back on Earth, it won't help you find your way home."[33]

IS PERSONALITY THE RIGHT PLACE TO LOOK FOR ADVICE?

The literature on personality and negotiation includes a lot of fascinating and provoking ideas. But what is the big picture advice? What is the useful takeaway for negotiation practitioners?

We do not think there is one.

It is common even for scholars who concentrate on personality to say that the whole field is a mess with no firm conclusions to be drawn: "the overall conclusion . . . is that the validity of personality as a predictor of job performance is quite low."[34] The same applies to the narrower topic of personality and dispute resolution. But why?

Too Complicated for a Good Theory

To be useful, a theory needs two virtues: comprehensiveness and parsimony.[35] It needs to accurately describe the things we see in the real world, but in few enough terms that our minds can easily work with the theory. Research in neuroscience seems to indicate that people can keep and work with about seven items in their heads at one time.[36] No model of personality comprehensively describes people in so few terms.

Take the Big Five, for example. The first factor, extraversion, combines concepts such as being strong-willed and social. Those traits seem to often go together, yet you probably know someone who is stubborn and driven, but somewhat solitary. How does this affect negotiation research? We saw earlier that extraversion seems to get in the way of distributive success. Is this because extraverts value relationships and are willing to pay a monetary price to protect them? The extraversion factor also bundles attributes related to stubbornness. Maybe single-minded extraverts do poorly because they don't quickly change tactics in response to new information. Without measuring each independently and testing them in studies, we do not know.

It was this kind of problem that led Hogan to break down extraversion into sociability and ambition. Better comprehensiveness, at a cost to parsimony. But wait, extraversion also includes energy and activity—so much so that some call this factor surgency. Should it be broken down into three? You could do the same thing with each of the Big Five. But then you would have the Big Fifteen. Too many. Personality theory is trapped between the Scylla of comprehensiveness and the Charybdis of parsimony.

If figuring out how to slice and splice personality were not bad enough, we have the problem of figuring out how much of a person's visible behavior is due to her or his personality and how much is due to circumstances. There is a perennial debate between dispositionalists (those who think personality controls our behavior) and situationalists (who say circumstances do). We do know that people tend to be highly reactive in negotiation and often modify their behavior to respond to the perceived behavior of the counterpart. That might make negotiation a "strong situation," that is, one that is likely to minimize the effects of personality.

"Just Take a Moment and Fill Out This Form"

Even if we knew what personality was and could separate it from the context, there is a terrible problem of accurately identifying a given person's personality. Most personality measures rely on self-reports. The "results" are just a summary of your own opinions about yourself. So it's not surprising that people report that an instrument is right on target: "Wow, how did that test know me so well?" Yet the limits on our ability to accurately perceive our own behavior have been consistently demonstrated. A person's view of him- or herself often contradicts the perceptions of those around him or her.

Moreover, when people describe themselves, we run into the problem of "social desirability." It is clearly "better" to be emotionally stable, conscientious, and open to experience than it is to be neurotic, careless, and closed-minded. Even if I am trying to be honest, my answers will be skewed because I like to think of myself as smarter or better than I am.[37]

On top of that, people often try to manipulate others' impressions of them— and personality instruments can be easily manipulated. When subjects were instructed to "fake good" in one study, subjects were able to lower their neuroticism score and raise their extraversion score.[38] Another study found that among people actually hired, 88 percent of them had intentionally elevated their conscientiousness score.[39] You can imagine why. If a potential employer asks whether you hand in your work on time, most people know that "yes" is the right answer.

There is unintentional misperception to consider as well. Lee Ross and others have documented our tendency to attribute bad intentions, and bad character, to people who cause us frustration or grief.[40] And perhaps the most important piece of research to consider in thinking about personality in negotiation is this: when asked to rate a counterpart's degree of agreeableness and emotional stability (neuroticism), bargainers consistently rated people with low-value alternative offers as more agreeable. People with high alternative offers were perceived to be less agreeable. And people with risky alternative offers were taken to be less emotionally stable.[41] We simply should not trust our own estimates of others' personalities, let alone make any decisions or predictions based on them.

The Conclusion?

Should we keep looking or should we give up on personality as a topic within negotiation studies? Despite our reservations about many of the personality instruments, we think the best bet for learning about tendencies in disputes may yet come from the personality field.

The inadequacy of current personality profiles in predicting success on the job has spawned a different sort of tool for sizing up job applicants: The Assessment Center. The Assessment Center has its roots in World War II, when the predecessor to the CIA (the OSS) hired Harvard personality researcher Henry Murray to help select men suited to be spies. Murray created situations in which recruits would perform tasks similar to the work of spies while being watched and evaluated. After the war Douglas Bray picked up the idea and created Assessment Centers for evaluating corporate job applicants, initially for AT&T.

Applicants report to an Assessment Center, where they are asked to role play and handle job-relevant tasks such as running a team meeting, responding to a telephone complaint, or negotiating with a vendor. AT&T found Bray's evaluations as much as 50 percent more accurate than other predictors of success on the job. Today 44 percent of federal, state, and local governments, 62 percent of fire and police departments, and thousands of private companies use Assessment Centers to size up people.[42]

If you want to learn more about your counterparts, your colleagues, your failures, and yourself, learn to watch how each of you actually negotiate or respond in a dispute. These real-world observations provide the best data you can get.

SIX QUESTIONS PEOPLE ASK ABOUT PERSONALITY AND DISPUTE RESOLUTION

1. *Is there really such a thing as personality differences?*

It certainly seems so. Whether hard-wired by genes or chemical mix, prompted by experience, or influenced by the context, two people in a similar situation will often respond differently. This may be particularly so in the pressurized context of a dispute.

Personality researchers attempt to identify and isolate traits that are consistent across situations and different between individuals. This is where things get tricky. Human beings are complex enough, and adaptable enough, that defining and tracking traits, particularly through the dynamic process of negotiation, has proven very difficult.

2. *Are there particular personality traits that give people better outcomes?*

With the exception of cognitive ability (more is better), there is no strong answer in the current research. Although you can find small-scale studies suggesting this or that trait is helpful, you can also find studies that say it does not improve outcomes.

3. *Okay, so should I negotiate differently with different personality types?*

The biggest obstacle to setting your negotiation strategy based on the other person's personality is figuring out what it is. Because people act differently in different situations, researchers have found that people consistently misperceive the personality traits of those with whom they negotiate or are in dispute.

The best advice is to be aware of your own tendencies, have a broad repertoire of approaches and strategies, and be able to engage difficulties constructively as they come up. Pay attention to particular behavior you see, rather than trying to globalize how the other person "is." And if one approach doesn't seem to be working, try another.

4. *Isn't it true that some disputes are hopeless because people's personalities just aren't going to change?*

It is certainly true that there are limits to what can change, and that some differences between people are harder to reconcile than others. And there are definitely limits to *your* ability to change *the other person's* personality.

Yet the impulse to throw up our hands and attribute the problem to the other person's personality flaws is a dangerous one. It blames the other person for the dispute, blinding us to our own contributions to the problem. It may also encourage us to give up on a relationship or dispute too easily or too quickly, when finding a way to work together with less frustration remains possible.

In addition, there are at least three paths forward that personality finger-pointing ignores. Remember that human beings' *behavior* can often change without a grand *personality* change. You might shift the context—offering a private caucus or written channel of communication, for example. You can try to influence the other person's behavior by influencing the story he or she tells about what's going on. Or you might try changing your contribution to the dynamic between you. The other person is reacting both to you and to his or her own experiences, tendencies, and stories, and that's a complex enough set of factors to suggest that progress is possible.

Finally, do not underestimate people's ability to change over time. As a person ages, encounters different life experiences, and makes the transition to new phases in life (where he or she may feel more secure or happier, or have more room for reflection for example), his or her traits and tendencies evolve. You may find that your personality gradually moves into a different era, one you would not have predicted from where you stand now.

5. *Why is personality profiling so popular, if it's so inconclusive?*

People love to talk about themselves. And they especially love to talk about other people. Personality profiling also fits our interest in simplifying the world and the infinitely complex relationships in it. Researchers have long documented the effects of the fundamental attribution error, where we believe we know why people act the way they do, and tend to attribute especially bad behavior to their problematic personality.

People are so complicated that we can't really describe them with few enough variables to meet our needs for parsimony. People can only keep about seven items in their head at one time, before they go into cognitive overload. So they make up something that they can handle in their heads, whether or not it is accurate.

6. *So why pay attention to personality at all?*

The fields of personality and negotiation are both relatively young. Our ability to map interaction in negotiation and dispute resolution, and to recommend paths of influence, is in its infancy. And our ability to isolate traits and trace them through complex interaction is still maturing.

Still, familiarity with common differences between individuals is useful. It reminds us that not every approach to influence works with every person. It can help us generate diagnostic hypotheses about why a negotiation is in trouble ("Ah! We may proceed to closure at different paces"), and come up with prescriptive advice to try out. It may also help us be more forgiving of others' seemingly crazy behavior if we can spot it as a difference in the way the two of us see and respond to the world.

Familiarity with personality differences can also be a self-reflection and coaching tool for yourself. It can help you identify and work on behavior that doesn't come naturally to you. It can also help you explain your behavior to others: "I've learned that I'm not very comfortable making commitments before I have a chance to think things through. Can you give me the weekend and we'll nail this down on Monday?" Becoming familiar with some of the traits that affect your ability to mediate, negotiate, or respond well to disputes can help you become more aware of the situations that bring out these traits, and other choices you might make.

Notes

1. See R. M. Ryckman, *Theories of Personality* (Belmont, Calif.: Thomson/ Wadsworth), 2004.

2. Although many Big Five theorists use the spelling *extrovert,* they are not all consistent. The Myers-Briggs foundation seems to use *extravert,* and this is the more common spelling we found in MBTI research, hence our choice to use throughout for the sake of consistency.

3. W. Mischel, *Personality and Assessment* (Mahwah, N.J.: Lawrence Erlbaum Associates, 1996), p. 38, cited in A. M. Paul, *The Cult of Personality* (New York: Free Press, 2004).

4. R. Lewicki and J. Litterer, *Negotiation* (Homewood, Ill.: Irwin, 1985), p. 276, cited in L. Thompson, "Negotiation Behavior and Outcomes: Empirical Evidence and Theoretical Issues," *Psychological Bulletin,* 1990, *108*(3), 515–532.

5. Paul, *The Cult of Personality,* 2004, p. xiv.

6. Paul, *The Cult of Personality,* 2004, p. xiii.

7. The description in the text of the MBTI draws primarily from L. Baker, "Using Insights About Perceptions and Judgment from Myers-Briggs Type Indicator Instrument as an Aid to Mediation," *Harvard Negotiation Law Review,* 2004, *9,* 115–185, including Baker's interview with Judge John W. Kennedy Jr., presiding justice, San Bernardino County Trial Courts (January 10, 2003); I. Myers, M. H. McCaulley, N. L. Quenk, and A. L. Hammer, *MBTI Manual* (Palo Alto, Calif.: Consulting Psychologists Press, 1998); D. Peters, "Forever Jung: Psychological Type Theory, The Myers-Briggs Type Indicator and Learning Negotiation," *Drake Law Review,* 1993, *42,* 1–121; S. S. VanSant, *Wired for Conflict* (Gainesville, Fla.: Center for Applications of Psychological Type, 2003); S. S. VanSant and D. Payne, *Psychological Type in Schools: Applications for Educators* (Gainesville, Fla.: Center for Applications of Psychological Type, 1995); T. F. Penderghast, "Resolving Conflict with Type," *Bulletin of Psychological Type,* 1996, *19*(4), 29–30; and J. Barkai, "Psychological Types and Negotiations: Conflicts and Solutions as Suggested by the Myers-Briggs Classification," unpublished manuscript, November 1989.

8. See R. Carlson, "Studies in Jungian Typology: II. Representations of the Personal World," *Journal of Personality and Social Psychology,* 1980, *38,* 801–810, cited in Ryckman, *Theories of Personality,* 2004. Carlson's study specifically contrasted "extraverted feelers" with "introverted thinkers," two common combinations.

9. Myers, McCaulley, Quenk, and Hammer, *MBTI Manual,* 1998. p. 26.

10. Carlson, "Studies in Jungian Typology," 1980, p. 96.

11. S. VanSant, *Wired for Conflict,* pp. 16–17.

12. Peters, "Forever Jung," 1993, pp. 33–34; and Baker, "Using Insights . . . ," 2004, p. 131, n53, citing Judge John W. Kennedy Jr., presiding justice, San Bernardino County Trial Courts, from a telephone interview (Jan. 10, 2003).

13. Baker, "Using Insights . . . ," 2004, p. 139.

14. Paul, *The Cult of Personality,* 2004, p. 133.

15. A. S. Westman and F. M. Canter, "Diurnal Changes on the Myers-Briggs Type Indicator: A Pilot Study," *Psychological Reports,* April 1984, p. 133.

16. Paul, *The Cult of Personality,* 2004, p. 133.

17. D. Druckman and R. A. Bjork (eds.), *In the Mind's Eye: Enhancing Human Performance.* Washington, D.C.: National Academy Press, 1991, pp. 95–101, cited in Paul, *The Cult of Personality,* 2004, p. 134.

18. See Stone and Heen, Chapter Ten of this volume.

19. ". . . [R]esearchers agree that there are five robust factors of personality . . . which can serve as a meaningful taxonomy for classifying personality attributes" (Barrick, M. R., and Mount, M. K. "The Big Five Personality Dimensions and Job Performance: A Meta-Analysis." *Personnel Psychology,* 1991, *44,* p. 3). See also J. Digman, "Personality Structure: Emergence of the Five-Factor Model," *Annual Review of Psychology,* 1990, *41,* 417–440; and L. Goldberg, "The Development of Markers of the Big-Five Factor Structure," *Psychological Assessment,* 1992, *4,* 26–42.

20. See R. Hogan, *Hogan Personality Inventory* (Minneapolis: National Computer Systems, 1986). Hogan gets six by dividing Extraversion into Sociability and Ambition (H. Eysenck, *The Structure of Human Personality.* New York: Praeger, 1970). Also see A. Tellengen, "Structures of Mood and Personality and Their Relevance to Assessing Anxiety with an Emphasis on Self-Report," in A. Tuma and J. Master (eds.), *Anxiety and Anxiety Disorders* (Hillsdale, N J.: Erlbaum, 1985), pp. 687–706.

21. See W. T. Norman, "Toward an Adequate Taxonomy of Personality Attributes: Replicated Factor Structure in Peer Nomination Personality Ratings," *Journal of Abnormal & Social Psychology,* 1963, *66,* 574–583.

22. A helpful chart of the labels historically applied to all of the factors can be found in Digman, "Personality Structure," 1990, p. 423.

23. See B. Barry and R. Friedman, "Bargainer Characteristics in Distributive and Integrative Negotiation," *Journal of Personality and Social Psychology,* 1998, *74,* 345–359.

24. Barrick and Mount, "The Big Five Personality Dimensions and Job Performance," 1991, p. 19.

25. Barry and Friedman, "Bargainer Characteristics in Distributive and Integrative Negotiation," 1998, pp. 345–359.

26. Barrick and Mount, "The Big Five Personality Dimensions and Job Performance," 1991, p. 19.

27. See D. R. Lynch and D. T. Evans, "Attributes of Highly Effective Criminal Defense Negotiators," *Journal of Criminal Justice,* 2002, *30,* 387–396. Lynch and Evans's methodology did not allow them to evaluate the statistical significance of their findings, since they did not compare their sample with any control group. Interestingly, their factor analysis of district attorneys' descriptions of criminal defense lawyers found six factors somewhat different from the ordinary five.

28. See Barry and Friedman, "Bargainer Characteristics in Distributive and Integrative Negotiation," 1998, pp. 345–359.

29. See Lynch and Evans, "Attributes of Highly Effective Criminal Defense Negotiators," 2002, pp. 387–396.

30. See H. C. Triandis and E. M. Suh, "Cultural Influences on Personality," *Annual Review of Psychology,* 2002.

31. See G. Saucier and L. R. Goldberg, "Lexical Studies of Indigenous Personality Factors: Premises, Products, and Prospects," *Journal of Personality,* 2001, *69*(6), 847–879.

32. M. Bond, H. Nakazato, and D. Shiraishi, "Universality and Distinctiveness in Dimensions of Japanese Person Perception," *Journal of Cross-Cultural Psychology,* 1975, *6,* p. 193.

33. Paul, *The Cult of Personality,* 2004, p. 197, citing interview on May 2, 2003.

34. Barrick and Mount, "The Big Five Personality Dimensions and Job Performance," 1991, p. 1.

35. See D. Whetten, "What Constitutes a Theoretical Contribution?" *Academy of Management Review,* 1989, *14,* 490–495.

36. Technically, the number is seven, plus or minus two. J. LeDoux, *Synaptic Self: How Our Brains Become Who We Are* (New York: Penguin Putnam, 2002), p. 177, cited in S. Johnson, *Mind Wide Open: Your Brain and the Neuroscience of Everyday Life* (New York: Scribner, 2004), pp. 91–92.

37. Bertram Forer first demonstrated what was later dubbed the "Barnum effect" when in 1949 he administered a personality test and handed back individual results. The results were actually identical, lifted from an astrology book. Participants were asked to rate the accuracy of their results on a scale of 0 (poor) to 5 (perfect). Forer's subjects gave their reports an average rating of 4.2; more than 40 percent gave them a perfect 5 (Forer, B. R. "The Fallacy of Personal Validation: A Classroom Demonstration of Gullibility." *Journal of Abnormal and Social Psychology,* 1949, *44,* 118–123).

38. See M. R. Bagby and M. B. Marshall, "Positive Impression Management and Its Influence on the Revised NEO Personality Inventory: A Comparison of Analog and

Differential Prevalence Group Designs," *Psychological Assessment,* 2003, *15*(3), 333–339, cited in Paul, *The Cult of Personality,* 2004.

39. See J. G. Rosse, M. D. Stetcher, J. L. Miller, and R. A. Levin, "The Impact of Response Distortion on Pre-employment Personality Testing and Hiring Decisions," *Journal of Applied Psychology,* 1998, *83,* 634–644, cited in Paul, *The Cult of Personality,* 2004.

40. See L. D. Ross, "The Intuitive Psychologist and His Shortcomings: Distortions in the Attribution Process," in L. Berkowitz (ed.), *Advances in Experimental Social Psychology,* Vol. 10 (New York: Random House, 1977); and D. Stone, B. Patton, and S. Heen, *Difficult Conversations: How to Discuss What Matters Most* (New York: Penguin, 1999), describing our tendency to ascribe negative intentions to others, based on their impact on us.

41. M. W. Morris, R. P. Larrick, and S. K. Su, "Misperceiving Negotiation Counter-parts: When Situationally Determined Bargaining Behaviors Are Attributed to Personality Traits," *Journal of Personality and Social Psychology,* 1999, *77,* p. 57.

42. Douglas Bray and William Byham's company, DDI, is credited with assessing fifteen million people in seventy countries and has annual revenues of $100 million (Paul, *The Cult of Personality,* 2004, p. 95).

CHAPTER FOUR

The Decision Perspective to Negotiation

Max H. Bazerman and Katie Shonk

*T*he Art and Science of Negotiation, Howard Raiffa's landmark 1982 book,
introduced what is now commonly known as the decision perspective to
negotiation. Raiffa highlighted the element of negotiation that may be most
susceptible to improvement—human decision making. In this chapter, we provide an overview of the rising influence of this perspective in the field, articulate its goals, and present seven of its concrete findings.

Starting in the 1980s, business schools, influenced by the cognitive revolu-
tion in psychology, began to recognize ways in which the expanding body of
behavioral decision research might inform decision making in organizations.
One important application was the topic of negotiation. Academically, the combination of negotiation and decision-making research provided an alternative
to game theory, the dominant view of the time that assumed fully rational actors.
The combination also made a conceptual link between descriptive and
prescriptive research. Prior to this time, the descriptive-prescriptive distinction
had separated researchers into noncommunicating camps. Behavioral researchers
(for example, psychologists, sociologists, and anthropologists) focused on
describing how people *actually* make decisions, whereas more analytic fields
such as economics and decision analysis prescribed how people *ought* to make
decisions.

Raiffa's work represented a conceptual breakthrough for several reasons. First,
Raiffa explicitly acknowledged the importance of developing accurate descriptions

of one's negotiation counterpart, rather than assuming the counterpart to be fully rational. Raiffa uses the term "rational" to refer to negotiation behaviors that maximize the expected usefulness of outcomes to a negotiator. Second, Raiffa's recognition that negotiators need advice implicitly suggested that negotiators do not follow purely rational strategies. Most important, Raiffa opened a dialogue between prescriptive and descriptive researchers by suggesting that negotiators need descriptive advice to anticipate their counterparts' behavior and prescriptive advice to overcome their own decision biases. Specifically, he advocated an integrated "asymmetrically prescriptive/descriptive" approach to negotiation.[1] The approach is "asymmetric" in that it provides advice to individual negotiators, rather than to all parties in a negotiation. The approach aims to predict the behavior of a negotiator's counterparts (hence the label "descriptive") and to develop appropriate strategies to deal with those behaviors (resulting in "prescriptive" advice).

To address some of the questions posed by Raiffa's work, Bazerman and Neale and their colleagues introduced behavioral decision research to the realm of negotiation.[2] This work asks, "If the negotiator and his or her counterpart do not act rationally, what systematic departures from rationality can be predicted? What are the errors that the focal actor is likely to make?" Prescriptive models have provided this descriptive research with a useful benchmark: optimality, or perfect rationality, against which actual performance can be compared and improved. In fact, many would argue that the growth and expansion of behavioral decision research is due in part to the usefulness of performance standards based on such optimality.[3] Behavioral decision theory has identified a number of specific deviations from rationality that can be expected in negotiations.

This chapter provides an overview of seven cognitive biases that affect most negotiators:

1. The assumption that negotiations are necessarily fixed-sum, which leads negotiators to miss opportunities for mutually beneficial trade-offs[4]

2. Self-serving, or egocentric, interpretations of fairness[5]

3. Overconfidence about the likelihood of attaining favorable outcomes[6]

4. Escalation of commitment to a previously selected course of action when it is no longer the best alternative[7]

5. Overlooking the value of considering the cognitive perspective of one's counterpart[8]

6. Overweighting vivid information[9]

7. Focusing too narrowly on information relevant to the negotiation[10]

By understanding these biases, negotiators can anticipate these errors in their counterparts and take steps to avoid making these mistakes themselves. In addition, an understanding of these common errors can aid third parties who seek to help negotiators overcome these cognitive traps.

THE MYTHICAL FIXED PIE

As they approach the negotiating table, people often assume that their task is to divide up a fixed pie of resources. Researchers have described this tendency to view competitive situations as purely win-lose as the "mythical-fixed-pie" mind-set. The widespread belief in a fixed pie likely springs from negotiators' experiences with vivid types of competition that *are* purely distributive, such as sporting events, university admissions, and some types of corporate promotion systems. In fact, purely distributive negotiations are the small minority in the real world. What might initially appear to be a cut-and-dried negotiation between a buyer and seller over price, for example, could in fact expand to incorporate issues such as service, financing, delivery, long-term contracts, and so on. Wise negotiators recognize opportunities to enlarge the pie of value by making mutually beneficial trade-offs among a variety of issues.

Most people fail to recognize complexity as an asset in negotiation. Too often, their focus on dividing up a fixed pie leads them to make unnecessary compromises and concessions. In one of Thompson's studies, participants conducted a negotiation simulation involving eight issues.[11] Of those eight issues, two were entirely compatible—participants on both sides had exactly the same preferences. Despite the fact that no conflict existed regarding these two issues, 39 percent of negotiation pairs disagreed on their preferred outcome for at least one of the two issues. Those pairs that did agree erroneously believed that they had "beaten" the other side on that issue. Negotiators who approach the table with an overly competitive stance are likely to miss out on mutually beneficial trade-offs and to be unrealistically confident in their bargaining abilities.

The mythical-fixed-pie mind-set also causes negotiators to downplay the concessions their counterparts make. In a Cold War–era study, Ross and Stillinger found that 56 percent of participants who were told that an arms reduction proposal originated with Mikhail Gorbachev (as, in fact, it did) thought that the proposal dramatically favored the Soviet Union, 28 percent thought it favored both the United States and the Soviets equally, and only 16 percent thought it favored the United States.[12] When participants were (incorrectly) told that Ronald Reagan had initiated the proposal, 45 percent thought it benefited both sides equally, 27 percent thought it favored the Soviet Union, and 27 percent thought it favored the United States. People tend to view terms and concessions proposed by an adversary with suspicion—an obvious hindrance to outcomes that benefit both sides.

Following Raiffa's emphasis on prescription, researchers have moved beyond description to identify a number of strategies negotiators can employ to move beyond the fixed-pie mind-set and improve their outcomes at the bargaining table.[13] First, negotiators can build trust by sharing information. Being clear and honest about how much they care about each issue is the most direct way for negotiators to create value. Second, they must learn to ask the other side lots of questions. When a counterpart is being cagey, listening closely to what he or she does say and asking questions that will draw out new information is important. Third, negotiators should consider making multiple offers at the same time. By putting two or more offers on the table simultaneously, a negotiator can learn a great deal about the other side's preferences based on which offer he or she finds most appealing. Finally, "post-settlement settlements" can enlarge the pie. After reaching agreement, parties may realize that additional value remains on the table. In such cases, Raiffa recommends that they launch a post-settlement settlement process by hiring a third party to help them find an even better agreement. The process entails little risk, as either side reserves the right to veto any new settlement and revert to the originally agreed upon terms.[14]

EGOCENTRISM

Another barrier to optimal resolution in negotiation is "egocentrism," the widely documented tendency for our perceptions and expectations to be biased in a self-serving manner.[15] When people are confronted with identical information, their role in a given situation tends to color the way they interpret that information. Specifically, people tend first to settle on a certain interpretation or outcome that would benefit them, then justify this preference on the basis of fairness. As we all struggle to view ourselves in the best possible light, we downplay certain qualities that affect our judgment and heighten the importance of others.

Imagine that a divorcing couple has agreed to divide their shared assets as fairly and peacefully as possible. While each spouse may intend to be fair, it is highly unlikely that the total of their two claims will add up to 100 percent of the assets. Instead, one might ask for 60 percent, while the other tries to claim 70 percent. Egocentrism causes both parties to believe that they deserve more of the resources than a neutral adviser would judge.

In one experiment, Bazerman and Neale observed widespread egocentrism in a labor-management simulation.[16] Pairs of students who failed to reach agreement in the simulated dispute were instructed to submit their final offers—one offer apiece—to an arbitrator, who would choose one of the two offers. The students were then asked to estimate the odds that the arbitrator would choose their offer over that of their counterpart. Of course, on average, only 50 percent of the offers could be accepted. Yet the typical negotiator felt that his or her offer had a 68 percent chance of being selected by the arbitrator.

When egocentrism causes negotiators to believe that they will "win," they are less likely to work with their counterparts to craft mutually beneficial solutions. Another significant danger of egocentrism is its tendency to spiral out of control. If one side demands more than what the other side deems "fair," mutual distrust and suspicion are likely.

Egocentrism can escalate when an outcome will benefit not only the focal negotiator but also a group or organization with which he or she is affiliated. Negotiators are less likely to be labeled greedy and self-serving if they make an exorbitant claim for their family, department, or company than if they make that same claim for themselves.

Researchers have applied the concept of egocentrism to "social dilemmas" in which numerous parties are fighting over a shared resource. Gerrett Hardin's "tragedy of the commons" describes the dilemma faced by a group of herdsmen grazing their cattle in a common pasture.[17] A given herdsman may be tempted to raise his profits by increasing the size of his herd. Yet he knows that if everyone does this, the surplus of cattle will eventually destroy the pasture. As a group, the herdsmen should be motivated to limit the number of cattle to a sustainable level. But egocentrism can cause the herdsman to focus only on the arguments in favor of his own overgrazing, ignoring the perspective of other herdsmen.

Egocentrism is evident in thorny real-world environmental dilemmas. In a simulation based on the fish-overharvesting crisis in the northeastern United States, four parties representing various fishing interests claimed more than 100 percent of the resource.[18] In this simulation, each of the parties has different interests. These differences allow for egocentric interpretations of who deserves what percent of the harvest. Each party ends up with self-serving assessments, and the greater the degree to which the assessments are self-serving, the greater the overharvesting in this simulation.

The famous philosopher John Rawls recommends a solution to egocentrism—make decisions under a "veil of ignorance," as if you don't know your role in a given negotiation.[19] Another way to reduce bias is to examine the other side's perspective as thoroughly as possible. For example, in one study, coauthors of academic articles involving three or more authors who thought individually about each other's contributions claimed less credit for themselves than similar coauthors who were simply asked what percentage of the credit they deserved.[20]

OVERCONFIDENCE

A bias related to egocentrism is the common tendency for decision makers to be overconfident in their judgments and, specifically, for negotiators to be overconfident regarding what they will obtain in a negotiation. Overconfidence leads to unrealistic expectations of success in many areas of life, including negotiation. Tversky and Kahneman explain overconfidence in terms of the failure of most negotiators to adjust sufficiently away from their initial anchors.[21] When entering a negotiation, parties hold fast to what they initially believe to be true and, in the process, overlook the full range of possible outcomes. Overconfidence appears consistently in studies of professionals ranging from military officers to auditors to CIA agents.[22] In short, overconfidence plagues decision making in virtually all settings.

A particularly pernicious bias, overconfidence can actually increase our reliance on other cognitive biases by blinding us to our errors. Even worse, overconfidence is likely to spike in moderate and difficult negotiations. Imagine that you are the chief legal counsel for a company that is facing a multimillion-dollar lawsuit. You believe that you have a 90 percent chance of winning the case in court. Should you recommend that the firm's management reject an out-of-court settlement? Would your answer change if you learn that, if you lose the case, your company will go out of business? You may decide that you are less than comfortable with your 90 percent estimate. Bankruptcy, layoffs, and loss of personal credibility are all likely to result when negotiators in high-stakes situations are overconfident regarding their chances of success.

As with egocentrism, the key to reducing negotiator overconfidence is objectivity. Fortunately, training about the existence of overconfidence can go a long way toward increasing negotiator objectivity, as Bazerman and Neale have documented.[23] In one of their studies, two groups of negotiators, one trained to recognize the dangerous effects of overconfidence and another untrained, engaged in a final-offer arbitration process similar to the one described in the previous section. As compared to the trained negotiators, the untrained negotiators were unreasonably confident in their judgments and much less likely to make compromises prior to arbitration. Aside from training, other strategies for adjusting one's confidence and improving negotiation outcomes include enlisting the aid of a mediator and closely monitoring one's own mistakes.

ESCALATION OF COMMITMENT

Whether negotiators are grappling with a labor strike, a custody battle, or a merger, or participating in an auction, they are likely to escalate irrationally their commitment to a previously chosen course of action that may have long since outlived its usefulness.

Here are some of the preconceptions that lead negotiators to fall victim to escalation:

1. Viewing a negotiation as a competition. A competitive spirit can blind negotiators to their true goals and keep them from getting what they really want.

2. Making extreme demands. Negotiators who take a strong public stance at the beginning of talks are unlikely to consider concessions later on, even when concessions would benefit them.

3. Overlooking the other party's position. When they disregard the other side's perspective, negotiators are likely to become overly optimistic about their chances of success.

4. Overweighting past investments. The pressure of sunk costs can lead negotiators to make unwise future plans.

The pressure of sunk costs, which causes us to overweight past investments, is an especially strong determinant of irrational escalation of commitment.[24] Most people understand the abstract principle that the amount of resources they have invested in the past should have little effect on their next move. Nonetheless, past anchors and investments dramatically influence how negotiators behave in the present. For example, in one study, homebuyers and sellers who were asked to appraise a property were affected by the price originally paid by the seller.[25] The purchase price had no effect on how buyers and sellers assessed the property's value. However, it did affect buyers' and sellers' bid expectations and reservation price (the price at which they preferred to walk away rather than to enter or continue the negotiation). The predictable result is that the sunk cost of a purchase price causes home sellers to set an inappropriately high asking price, which can lead them into an escalatory trap as their house sits empty for months.

Competition also triggers irrational escalation of commitment. In 1994, decades of acrimony between Major League Baseball players and team owners culminated in a strike. The season was cancelled; that year, the owners lost approximately $375 million, while the players lost their salaries, status, and bargaining power. During the strike, researchers Sebenius and Wheeler put forth a novel solution: continue with the baseball season, but set aside player pay and team revenues.[26] Once a resolution was reached, the funds could be distributed. The two theorized that the promise of this money would motivate both sides to compromise. A smart idea, but the team owners and players rejected it. Too concerned with "winning," both sides escalated commitment to their chosen courses of action. The team owners actually reveled in the cancellation of the 1994 World Series, disregarding the fact that they were celebrating the loss of millions and millions of dollars.

Negotiators can avoid destructive bidding wars by considering the other side's position, ignoring sunk costs, seeking outside help, and discouraging others from escalating. Anticipating how a counterpart might react to a firm position or hard-nosed offer is always a good idea. Will he or she agree to compromise or dig in deeper? Negotiators should seek to avoid extracting bold statements from the other side, for fear that one's counterpart will later feel the escalatory trap and refuse to compromise. When USAir put itself up for sale in 1995, Robert Crandall, then the chairman of American Airlines, sought to avoid what he predicted would be a mutually destructive bidding war between his company and United Airlines. In an open letter to American's employees, Crandall revealed that American would not be the first to make a bid for USAir. Crandall's thinly veiled message to United: "Don't make a bid, or we'll both end up losing lots of money." The tactic worked; neither company bid on USAir in 1995. As Crandall recognized, sometimes the best way to avoid an escalatory spiral is to stay out of the game entirely.[27]

OVERLOOKING A COUNTERPART'S PERSPECTIVE

Imagine that you are a faculty member at an Ivy League university and the head of your department's faculty search committee. You brought in five new Ph.D. recipients for interviews and talks. One candidate, Susan, emerged as the clear front runner. She presented a fascinating dissertation, had an excellent reputation as a teacher, and impressed almost everyone in your department with her intelligence and friendly personality. During her visit, Susan revealed to you that she had recently interviewed with a number of other top universities. After conferring with your department, you arrange a meeting with your dean and make the case for an unusually high salary and benefits offer. Though skeptical at first, the dean eventually comes around to your point of view. That afternoon, you call Susan and make her the offer. To your surprise, she accepts it on the spot.

As you hang up the phone, do you feel lucky that you have so easily persuaded a star to join your department, or worried that perhaps Susan is not as much of a prize as she seems? If you are like most people, you might feel a bit uneasy. After all, you do not know for sure whether she had any other offers on the table.

The "winner's curse" describes this paradox of winning a prize, then realizing that the other side's acceptance has given you some disappointing information about the value of that prize. The winner's curse is likely to emerge in negotiations in which two conditions exist. First, a winner is susceptible to feeling cursed when his or her gain depends on the other side's acceptance. After all, when is the other side most likely to accept a bid? Under conditions undesirable to the bidder and favorable to the seller—a connection negotiators often fail to make. Second, the winner's curse can occur when the focal negotiator has access to less information than his or her counterpart. In the scenario described above, the job candidate clearly had more information about her bargaining position than did the hiring professor. Before you present an offer to a counterpart, consider the conditions in which your counterpart would accept that offer. Now, if you assume that those conditions are true, does your offer still make sense?

The winner's curse has proven difficult for negotiators to overcome. One group of researchers found that a group of M.B.A. students was unable to apply lessons about how to avoid the winner's curse to specific situations.[28] Clearly, negotiators must remain on their guard. When preparing to make an offer, they should consider how they would feel if their counterpart accepted it immediately. Thrilled? Uneasy? Next, they should think about what an acceptance might say about the value of the item. If the focal negotiator is at an informational handicap, she or he may need to adjust her or his bid or stay out of the game entirely. Seeking out an unbiased opinion from an expert, such as a mechanic or home inspector, can help alleviate the information disadvantage.

OVERWEIGHTING VIVIDNESS

Examine our faculty job search story from the candidate's perspective. Suppose that Susan actually did receive job offers from a number of schools, none of which offered as much prestige or income as your university. Susan, who had felt for a while that her life was balanced too much toward work and not enough toward fun, wondered whether the pressure to research and publish would allow her time for a social life and recreation. But the salary you offered her, along with the promise of a stimulating environment, provoked her to accept the offer on the spot. Her dissertation adviser was proud, and her cohorts were envious.

Two years later, Susan is overworked, lonely, and miserable. She has published a few papers in good journals, but doesn't feel she has the energy to keep up the pace necessary to win tenure at such a competitive school. Too busy working, she rarely sees her old friends and hasn't had time to make many new ones. "What was I thinking?" she asks herself in her darkest moments. Secretly, she plots her escape. She interviews with a less prestigious school in her favorite city in the Pacific Northwest, and she receives a nice offer. Susan can scarcely disguise her relief when she informs you that she is quitting the rat race.

As all negotiators do at times, Susan fell victim to the "vividness bias"—the tendency to overweight vivid qualities (such as school prestige) surrounding a decision and underweight less flashy issues (such as free time) that could have the greatest impact on one's personal happiness. Vivid information is more likely than dull but equally relevant information to influence juries, negotiators, and other decision makers. In one simulation, juries were almost twice as likely to side with a particular party when the arguments presented in that side's favor were vivid than when the arguments presented were dull.[29] Similarly, a labor-management collective bargaining study on the effects of vividness found that the outcomes negotiators were willing to accept were influenced by the vividness of various costs.[30] For example, negotiators were less willing to reach agreement and more likely to turn to arbitration when the costs of reaching a suboptimal settlement were highlighted. Many of us are subjected to the effects of vivid data when buying a new car. By painting a vivid picture of breakdowns and expensive repairs, the salesperson exploits our fears in the hope that we will take the bait and opt for an overpriced extended warranty.

While it can be quite difficult to see beyond vivid data, researchers have come up with a few techniques for lessening its power. First, negotiators need to recognize vividness as a likely source of bias; vivid claims should be examined thoroughly, with a healthy skepticism. Second, prenegotiation preparation can limit the effects of vividness. When negotiators determine their goals ahead of time and stay focused on these goals during the process, they will be better equipped to resist the manipulations of the other side. Susan, for example, should have thought long and hard about her immediate and long-term goals before beginning her job search. If she had, she might have limited her search to less rigorous schools. Finally, negotiators should consider when to use vividness to their own advantage—while being careful not to violate the law or their own ethical codes. When the potential exists to improve outcomes for both sides, vivid data and visuals can punch up an otherwise dull presentation and win over others to the cause.

ERRORS IN FOCUS

The previous section asserted that staying focused on one's goals is important in negotiation. Indeed, we can all think of instances when intense focus has helped us succeed, whether in a job interview, with a test, or in our personal lives. A healthy coping mechanism, focus allows us to absorb important data and respond in creative ways.

Yet an overly narrow focus can be too much of a good thing. Schkade and Kahneman coined the term "focusing illusion" to describe the tendency for decision makers to attend to only a portion of available and relevant information, to overweight that information in their decisions, and to underweight equally relevant information.[31] In particular, focusing can cause us to overlook long-term considerations in favor of immediate desires, to attend too closely to obvious environmental cues and disregard more subtle factors, and to concentrate too much on ourselves and too little on others.

When people assess life satisfaction, salient factors often receive too much weight.[32] For instance, even though Californians and Midwesterners report very similar levels of life satisfaction, when study participants in these locales were asked to rate the life satisfaction of someone similar to them who lived in the other location, both groups rated Californians as being more satisfied with their lives than Midwesterners. In fact, location did not significantly affect the experienced life satisfaction of Californians or Midwesterners. When people are asked about the other location, they focus on an obvious difference—climate— and ignore the importance of other life events.

In *The Art and Science of Negotiation,* Raiffa pointed out that negotiators often run into trouble by focusing too closely on their negotiating counterpart.[33] When we focus on our counterpart's unique interests, we are likely to disregard the needs of the group or organization he or she represents. Negotiators must learn to broaden their perspective by considering all of the decision makers involved, examining how their views may differ, and determining what steps must be taken to reach a mutually beneficial agreement.

On a related note, there is a widespread tendency to succumb to "reference group neglect," the failure to focus on the quality of one's competition.[34] For instance, managers often focus too narrowly on their own company's skills and products while overlooking the quality products put out by their marketplace competitors. The result? Many high-quality products are launched to great fanfare, only to be beat out by a competitor's better-quality or lower-priced product. Negotiators and other decision makers benefit from broadening their focus to encompass the entire competitive landscape.

Don Moore created a straightforward negotiation between a buyer and seller.[35] Both sides were informed that one of them was subject to a deadline for completing the negotiation. Notably, both sides tended to think that the negotiator facing the deadline was at a disadvantage. In fact, of course, the deadline affected both sides equally—they *both* had to beat the clock.

How can negotiators retain the focus necessary to complete difficult, specific tasks while remaining attentive to peripheral information? First, they should recognize that short-term concerns are likely to propel their discussions at the expense of long-term concerns. Taking time out to consider the long-term implications of a decision, concession, or agreement is always a wise move. Second, negotiators must accept that they approach the table with a limited field of vision. One way to broaden focus is, quite obviously, to put together a negotiating team and listen closely to each other's unique perspectives. Finally, parties must accept that adhering closely to a tight agenda is not always a virtue in negotiation. Innovative trade-offs are likely to arise when negotiators remain open to discovering and talking about new, value-creating issues.

CONCLUSIONS

The behavioral decision perspective has offered negotiators a set of concrete tools that they can use to better anticipate their counterparts' behavior and to audit their own behavior. This research perspective has strong cognitive roots, as evidenced by its focus on how the mind can fool even the most sophisticated of negotiators. More recently, the decision perspective has shown how social and emotional variables affect negotiation.[36] Relationships, concerns for fairness, attribution and construal processes, motivated illusions, and feelings are among the most critical social-psychological variables in this literature. In addition, developing research is considering how negotiators subjectively understand the negotiation process.[37] This work examines how mental models affect negotiation; how concerns about ethics, fairness, and values define the rules of the game being played; how the selection of a communication medium has an impact on the way the game is played; how cross-cultural issues in perception and behavior affect the game; and how negotiators organize and simplify their understandings of the game when more than two actors are involved. Collectively, these research streams demonstrate that the decision perspective remains a vibrant aspect of our understanding of negotiation.

A key motivation that drives negotiation research is practical relevance, evidenced by the fact that most negotiation research is conducted in professional schools rather than in disciplinary departments. The decision perspective to negotiation will preserve this practical relevance by helping us understand, predict, and give advice to a focal negotiator, including advice on how to anticipate the behavior of others. At the rocky start of this new millennium, understanding and managing conflict appears to be a more important goal than ever before. While we cannot make conflict disappear, we can use our understanding of the human mind to minimize its adverse impact.

Notes

1. See H. Raiffa, *The Art and Science of Negotiation* (Cambridge, Mass.: Belknap Press of Harvard University Press, 1982).

2. See, for example, M. H. Bazerman and M. A. Neale, *Negotiating Rationally* (New York: Free Press, 1992); M. A. Neale and M. H. Bazerman, *Cognition and Rationality in Negotiation* (New York: Free Press, 1991); M. H. Bazerman, *Judgment in Managerial Decision Making* (6th ed.) (New York: John Wiley & Sons, 2005), M. H. Bazerman, J. R. Curhan, D. A. Moore, and K. L. Valley, "Negotiation," *Annual Review of Psychology*, 2000, *51*, 279–314; L. Thompson, "Negotiation Behavior and Outcomes: Empirical Evidence and Theoretical Issues," *Psychological Bulletin*, 1990, *108*(3), 515–532; and L. Thompson, *The Mind and Heart of the Negotiator* (2nd ed.) (Upper Saddle River, N.J.: Prentice Hall, 2001).

3. See D. Kahneman, P. Slovic, and A. Tversky, *Judgment Under Uncertainty: Heuristics and Biases* (New York: Cambridge University Press, 1982); and Bazerman, *Judgment in Managerial Decision Making*, 2005.

4. See M. H. Bazerman, T. Magliozzi, and M. A. Neale, "Integrative Bargaining in a Competitive Market," *Organizational Behavior & Human Decision Processes*, 1985, *35*(3), 294–313.

5. See L. Babcock and G. Loewenstein, "Explaining Bargaining Impasse: The Role of Self-Serving Biases," *The Journal of Economic Perspectives,* 1997, *11*(1), 109–126.

6. See Bazerman and Neale, *Negotiating Rationally,* 1992.

7. See M. H. Bazerman and M. A. Neale, "Heuristics in Negotiation: Limitations to Effective Dispute Resolution," in M. H. Bazerman and R. Lewicki (eds.), *Negotiating in Organizations* (Beverly Hills, Calif.: Sage Publications, 1983); and K. A. Diekmann, A. E. Tenbrunsel, P. P. Shah, H. A. Schroth, and M. H. Bazerman, "The Descriptive and Prescriptive Use of Previous Purchase Price in Negotiations," *Organizational Behavior & Human Decision Processes,* 1996, *66*(2), 179–191.

8. See W. F. Samuelson and M. H. Bazerman, "The Winner's Curse in Bilateral Negotiations," in V. Smith (ed.), *Research in Experimental Economics,* Vol. 3 (Greenwich, Conn.: JAI Press, 1985), pp. 105–137; and M. H. Bazerman and J. S. Carroll, "Negotiator Cognition," in B. Staw and L. L. Cummings (eds.), *Research in Organizational Behavior,* Vol. 9 (Greenwich, Conn.: JAI Press, 1987), pp. 247–288.

9. See M. A. Neale, "The Effects of Negotiation and Arbitration Cost Salience on Bargainer Behavior: The Role of the Arbitrator and Constituency on Negotiator Judgment," *Organizational Behavior & Human Decision Processes,* 1984, *34*(1), 97–111; and M. H. Bazerman, J. R. Curhan, and D. A. Moore, "The Death and Rebirth of the Social Psychology of Negotiation," in M. Clark and G. Fletcher (eds.), *Blackwell Handbook of Social Psychology* (Cambridge, Mass.: Blackwell, 2000).

10. See M. H. Bazerman and D. Chugh, "Focusing in Negotiation," in L. Thompson (ed.), *Frontiers of Social Psychology: Negotiations* (New York: Psychological Press, forthcoming); and M. H. Bazerman, "A Decision Perspective on Negotiation and Conflict Resolution," in M. H. Bazerman (ed.), *Negotiation, Decision Making, and Conflict Resolution,* Vol. 1 (Northampton, Mass.: Edward Elgar Publishing, 2004).

11. See Thompson, *The Mind and Heart of the Negotiator,* 2001.

12. See L. Ross and C. Stillinger, "Barriers to Conflict Resolution," *Negotiation Journal,* 1991, *7*(4), 389–404.

13. See, for example, Bazerman, *Judgment in Managerial Decision Making,* forthcoming.

14. See H. Raiffa, "Post-Settlement Settlements," *Negotiation Journal,* 1985, *1,* 9–12.

15. See M. H. Bazerman and M. A. Neale, "Improving Negotiation Effectiveness Under Final Offer Arbitration: The Role of Selection and Training," *Journal of Applied Psychology,* 1982, *67*(5), 543–548; and Babcock and Lowenstein, "Explaining Bargaining Impasse," 1997.

16. See Bazerman and Neale, "Improving Negotiation Effectiveness Under Final Offer Arbitration," 1982.

17. G. Hardin, "The Tragedy of the Commons," *Science,* 1968, *162,* 1243–1248.

18. See K. A. Wade-Benzoni, A. E. Tenbrunsel, and M. H. Bazerman, "Egocentric Interpretations of Fairness in Asymmetric, Environmental Social Dilemmas: Explaining Harvesting Behavior and the Role of Communication," *Organizational Behavior & Human Decision Processes,* 1996, *67*(2), 111–126.

19. See J. Rawls, *A Theory of Justice* (Cambridge, Mass.: Harvard University Press, 1971).

20. See E. Caruso, N. Epley, and M. H. Bazerman, "The Good, the Bad, and the Ugly of Perspective Taking in Groups," unpublished paper, Harvard Business School, 2004.

21. See A. Tversky and D. Kahneman, "Judgment Under Uncertainty: Heuristics and Biases," *Science,* 1974, *185*(4157), 1124–1131.

22. See Bazerman, *Judgment in Managerial Decision Making,* 2005.

23. See Bazerman and Neale, "Improving Negotiation Effectiveness Under Final Offer Arbitration," 1982; and Bazerman and Neale, *Negotiating Rationally,* 1992.

24. See, for example, B. M. Staw, "Knee-Deep in the Big Muddy: A Study of Escalating Commitment to a Chosen Course of Action," *Organizational Behavior & Human Decision Processes,* 1976, *16*(1), 27–44.

25. See Diekmann, Tenbrunsel, Shah, Schroth, and Bazerman, "The Descriptive and Prescriptive Use of Previous Purchase Price in Negotiations," 1996.

26. See J. K. Sebenius and M. Wheeler, "Let the Game Continue," *The New York Times,* Oct. 30, 1994, Sec. 3, p. 9.

27. *Chicago Tribune,* November 10, 1995, p. B1.

28. See S. B. Ball, M. H. Bazerman, and J. S. Carroll, "An Evaluation of Learning in the Bilateral Winner's Curse," *Organizational Behavior & Human Decision Processes,* 1991, *48*(1), 1–22.

29. See M. G. Wilson, G. B. Northcraft, and M. A. Neale, "Information Competition and Vividness Effects in On-line Judgments," *Organizational Behavior & Human Decision Processes,* 1989, *44*(1), 132–139.

30. See Neale, "The Effects of Negotiation and Arbitration Cost Salience on Bargainer Behavior," 1984.

31. See D. A. Schkade and D. Kahneman, "Does Living in California Make People Happy? A Focusing Illusion in Judgments of Life Satisfaction." *Psychological Science,* 1998, *9*(5), 340–346.

32. See Schkade and Kahneman, "Does Living in California Make People Happy?" 1998.

33. See Raiffa, *The Art and Science of Negotiation,* 1982.

34. See C. Camerer and D. Lovallo, "Overconfidence and Excess Entry: An Experimental Approach," *The American Economic Review,* 1999, *89,* 306–318.

35. See D. A. Moore, "The Unexpected Benefits of Final Deadlines in Negotiation," *Journal of Experimental Social Psychology* (forthcoming).

36. See Bazerman, Curhan, and Moore, "The Death and Rebirth of the Social Psychology of Negotiation," 2000.

37. See, for example, Bazerman, Curhan, Moore, and Valley, "Negotiation," 2000.

CHAPTER FIVE

Enemies, Allies, and Emotions

The Power of Positive Emotions in Negotiation

Daniel L. Shapiro

In 1991, a man named Cyril Ramaphosa received an invitation from a friend to join him for a weekend of fly fishing. Cyril loves to fly fish. He readily agreed to the invitation. Three hours into their road trip, Cyril's host informed him that Roelf Meyer and his family would be joining them for lunch on Saturday.

These events would be of little interest to most people, if not for the fact that Cyril Ramaphosa was South Africa's chief negotiator for the African National Congress and Roelf Meyer was the Deputy Minister of Constitutional Affairs for the then-ruling National Party. Two weeks later, these two men would be negotiating some of the most contentious issues involved in the transition to a multiracial, democratic South Africa.

On that Saturday afternoon in 1991, however, Roelf asked Cyril to teach his sons and him how to fly fish. They were in the outback of South Africa, far away from the politics of everyday life. They had an enjoyable several hours until Roelf miscast. A hook stuck in his hand. He looked up at Cyril and asked, "What do you do now?"

"Let's go see my wife," Cyril said. "She's a nurse."

Cyril's wife attempted to disengage the hook, but without success.

Cyril knew what had to be done. He gave Roelf a big glass of brandy and said, "OK. Drink this. Look away, and trust me." He pushed the hook through Roelf's hand and got it out.

Approximately two weeks later, these two men found themselves on opposite sides of some key negotiation issues. Over the years, the National Party had imprisoned a number of political resisters to apartheid, including African National Congress leader Nelson Mandela and many of his colleagues. By 1991, many of those prisoners were released—but not all of them.

The National Party was willing to release the political prisoners in return for an explicit end to the African National Congress's armed struggle. The African National Congress wanted the prisoners released, but refused to consent to a quid pro quo. The purpose of its armed struggle was to have the political prisoners released, and it would not cease that struggle until the prisoners were, in fact, released. Essentially, the African National Congress's message was: Once political prisoners are released, then we will cease our armed struggle.

The National Party was faced with a choice: Should it cease negotiating with the African National Congress and face continued armed resistance? Or should it release the prisoners and trust that the African National Congress would live up to its word and stop its armed struggle?

Roelf leaned forward over a table and whispered in Cyril's ear, "I hear you saying, 'Trust me.'"

"Exactly," Cyril replied.

Roelf ordered release of the prisoners, and one week later the African National Congress announced an end to its armed struggle.[1]

Whether in negotiation of large-scale political issues or of everyday conflicts between colleagues or spouses, emotions have the potential to impede or facilitate a wise agreement. Tension like that between the pro-apartheid government and the anti-apartheid African National Congress can act as a major barrier to agreement. Distrust, fear, and suspicion may create a climate of animosity and paranoia. Yet the emotions that bond people—such as the friendly affection and enthusiasm between Cyril Ramaphosa and Roelf Meyer—can help facilitate peaceful agreement between divided individuals or groups.

In this chapter, I argue that negotiators neither can get rid of emotions nor should they try. I describe two important negotiating goals: *affective satisfaction* (the extent to which negotiators are happy with how they felt in a negotiation) and *instrumental satisfaction* (the extent to which negotiators believe their substantive goals and desires are met in a negotiation). I then review evidence suggesting that emotions can be used to reach each of these negotiating goals. Finally, I describe *how* a negotiator can act constructively on *relational identity concerns*,[2] thus stimulating positive emotions in a negotiation and, in turn, bringing one closer to one's negotiating goals.

WHAT IS AN EMOTION?

Although people often have a good sense of what emotions are, defining them is not as easy.[3] Researchers and philosophers have proposed hundreds of definitions.[4] For purposes of this paper, I define an emotion not as a distinct biological entity but rather as an "emotional syndrome," a constellation of common characteristics with none defining its essence.[5] Symptoms of an emotion that often occur together include a distinct facial expression, a unique subjective feeling, a pattern of physiological arousal, and a readiness to act in ways that promote one's well-being.[6] For example, the emotion of anger may include a hostile glare, an "explosive" feeling in one's body, heightened physiological arousal, and a readiness to attack the person perceived to be blameworthy for an offense.[7]

GET RID OF EMOTIONS? WE CAN'T

Imagine you are working late one night at the office. A junior colleague knocks on your door. You invite him in. He looks nervous.

"What's on your mind?" you ask.

"I need your advice."

"Sure. What's up?"

"Tomorrow morning, for the first time, I'm going to be the lead negotiator for our team. I'm really nervous about this. It's a complicated case, and I've prepped for weeks now. But I'm not sure how to deal with the emotions in the negotiation—mine or theirs. What's your advice?"

I sometimes pose this hypothetical question to groups I am training in negotiation. I ask the workshop participants to take a moment and write down what advice they would give to this young colleague. Whether the participants are diplomats, politicians, lawyers, or business people, a majority of participants typically respond, "I'd tell my young colleague: 'Don't get emotional,'" or something similar. They explain that the young colleague should not worry. Rather than get emotional, he should keep a straight face and stay "rational." He should focus on the substantive issues. Participants in my workshops tend to see emotions as an impediment to good negotiating.

Their advice is neither helpful nor humanly possible. Emotions are unavoidable. As human beings, we cannot extract emotions from our interactions. We are in a state of "perpetual emotion,"[8] always experiencing some affective state or another. We may feel any of a long list of emotions, whether boredom, excitement, fear, sadness, surprise, disgust, confusion, interest, or nostalgia. The causes and effects of emotions are often unavoidable.

Causes of Emotions in a Negotiator

Emotions can be stimulated in a multitude of ways. There are, of course, neurological, biological, and genetic factors that contribute to the excitation of emotions.[9] People with bipolar disorder, for example, find that their mood fluctuates between episodes of extreme excitement and extreme depression. It is likely that a combination of genes, acting together, contribute to this disorder.[10]

During a negotiation, there are a limited number of actions we can take to reduce the negative impact of neurological, biological, and genetic triggers on our behavior. If we know that our mood sours when we are hungry or tired, we can be sure to eat and get a good night's rest before negotiating. But these actions cannot redress moment-to-moment obstacles that arise in the negotiation, and we usually do not have control over these variables in the other negotiator. We can suggest when to break for lunch or quit working for the day. But we cannot force our counterpart to eat or sleep at our command. Therefore, it is advantageous to consider three "social variables" that stimulate emotions. We can affect these variables in the moment and independent of the other party, and such action can affect the emotions of each party.

The *context* surrounding negotiators elicits emotions. The junior negotiator charged with leadership of his team may feel a surge of anxiety upon walking into the other team's office. The context of negotiating in the other team's office may heighten his feelings of insecurity. If the actual meeting becomes tense, he may suggest that they continue conversation in a more informal context such as over lunch, or he may call for a short coffee break to reduce rising tensions.

Emotions also may be stimulated by *our own thoughts and feelings.* We may think, "I forgot to prepare the financial reports for today's meeting!" Anxiety then appears in full force. To calm such emotions, we can "talk back" to ourselves, telling ourselves, "Forgetting to do the memo is not the end of the world. Just let everyone know it won't happen again."

A final, related trigger of emotions is how we *interpret the actions of the other negotiator toward us.* If, for example, the other says to us, "Oh, I thought you went to private school instead of to a relatively unremarkable state institution," we may take offense—and feel emotions such as anger or frustration. A simple reinterpretation of the situation can change our emotions, such as if we hypothesize that he or she feels insecure in status and is trying to "prove" his or her competence.

Effects of Emotions on a Negotiator

Emotions have an impact on us in four ways. First, emotions affect our *physiology.* When we are angry, our heart rate increases and we sweat more than when we are calm. If we are fearful, blood rushes to our arms and legs, an evolutionary response that can help us escape from a potentially dangerous situation. When impassioned, our heart rate increases and we may sweat. Harrer and Harrer monitored the heart rate of the famous conductor Herbert von Karajan. On landing his private jet at Salzburg Airport, his heart rate rose. It increased further when he was instructed to make an emergency takeoff just after landing. And it rose even more while he conducted passages of Beethoven's "Leonora Overture No. 3."[11]

Second, emotions affect our *cognition.* When we are frustrated, we tend to think negative thoughts.[12] When we are happy, we are more likely to think positive thoughts. Strong emotions also tend to narrow the scope of our thinking.

When we are angry at someone, it is hard to think about anything or anyone other than that person. We experience tunnel vision.

Third, emotions have an associated *action tendency*.[13] An action tendency is a proclivity to behave in a particular kind of way. An emotion readies us for changes in the way we interact with our environment.[14] When angry, we may want to attack the other person, whether through words or action. When embarrassed, we may want to hide our faces and ourselves from others. In this sense, an action tendency does not "cause" us to act in any one way or another. Rather, it prepares us for a particular activity. If a negotiator demeans you and you feel angry, you may experience an action tendency to attack the other person or insult her or him back. Though your action tendency prepares you to strike out at the other, you may decide not to act on it.

Fourth, emotions affect a negotiator's *subjective feeling*. Each of us experiences the sensation of emotions in a unique way. For some of us, the feeling of anxiety may be experienced as a "knot in the stomach," while for others it may be "butterflies" or a feeling of tightness in the shoulders. The subjective experience is our personal, physical feeling of the emotion.

The Two-Way Interaction Between Effects and Causes of Emotions

Each of the four effects of emotion—physiology, cognition, action tendency, and subjective feeling—is also a possible cause of emotion. The more you think negative thoughts, the more likely you will feel sad.[15] The happier you feel, the more positive your thoughts will be.[16] Thus, each effect of emotion is also a possible stimulant of emotion and a part of the actual emotional experience.

EMOTIONS CAN HELP US REACH NEGOTIATION GOALS

For a negotiator, emotions can be a source of strength or vulnerability. They affect our ability to reach two important goals: affective satisfaction and instrumental satisfaction. Negotiators who deal effectively with emotions increase their ability to reach each of these goals.

Two Goals of a Negotiation

The first goal, *affective satisfaction*, focuses on your general level of satisfaction with the emotions you experience during the negotiation.[17] To what extent do you feel satisfied with your emotional experience during the negotiation? Affective satisfaction is a measure of your meta-emotions, which are your feelings about your feelings.[18] If the other party insults you to such a degree that you boil with anger and storm out of the room, you may later admit that the interaction left you feeling affective dissatisfaction. If, conversely, the other party treated you with due deference, you may have negotiated with enthusiasm and later recognized your sense of affective satisfaction.

When a third party is involved—whether an agent, mediator, or facilitator—affective satisfaction is perhaps most important for the principal parties, who are responsible for committing to and sustaining the terms of agreement. However, affective satisfaction is also important for the agent, because positive emotions can facilitate creative thinking, a good working relationship, and other factors that are helpful for joint problem solving.[19]

The second goal, *instrumental satisfaction,* measures the extent to which substantive work requirements are fulfilled.[20] If South African negotiators Cyril Ramaphosa and Roelf Meyer walked away from their negotiations with buckets of good feelings but few new ideas about how to deal effectively with their issues, the meeting might be considered an affective success but an instrumental failure.

'Til Death Do Us Part: Positive Emotions Aid Affective Satisfaction

The valence of an emotion—whether it is positive or negative—has an impact on the extent to which a negotiator reaches his or her goals. Positive emotions are those that feel pleasant, whereas negative emotions are those that feel unpleasant.[21] Positive emotions often help us feel more affective satisfaction than do negative ones.

Negative Emotions Reduce Affective Satisfaction. How we deal with emotions can have a tremendous impact on our affective satisfaction in a negotiation. For evidence that this is true, one needs look no further than to the research of John Gottman, a professor from the University of Washington in Seattle. He studies some of the most challenging negotiations on earth—those between a husband and wife.

Couples enter his "love lab," where they are asked to discuss a topic of chronic conflict, such as family finances, the distribution of household chores, divergences over drinking or smoking habits, or relations with in-laws. While the couple interacts, sensors monitor their heart rate and blood pressure. A video camera records their facial expressions, noting the slightest grimace or smirk. After the interaction, a researcher meets privately with each spouse, and they view the video of the marital interaction. The spouse then discloses his or her personal thoughts and feelings experienced during the interaction.

Through a sophisticated method of statistical analysis, Gottman can take fifteen minutes of the interaction between husband and wife and predict, with more than 90 percent accuracy, which couples will remain married and which will divorce within a few years.[22] Gottman has found that four ineffective behaviors are predictive of divorce:[23]

- *Criticism* of the other's character (for example, "You're late again. Why do you only think of yourself?")

- Expressions of *contempt* (for example, rolling one's eyes while the other speaks)

- *Counterattack* (for example, "I may not always get to the house chores on time, but I'm not nearly as lazy as *you*!")

- *Stonewalling* (for example, hiding behind the newspaper while ignoring the other's bid to talk)

Each of these four behaviors stimulates negative emotions. Over time, these negative emotions can accumulate into a general sense of affective dissatisfaction with the relationship, which can motivate divorce.

Another line of research looks into the question of whether or not *expressing* negative emotions leads to affective satisfaction. Is venting a good thing? One school of thought argues that venting helps us overcome negative emotions. It suggests that people are like a boiling kettle: we need to let out steam before our emotions get too hot. Otherwise we will explode, yelling at colleagues, displacing anger onto innocent family members, or doing something else that we later will regret. In contrast, a second school of thought argues that venting reinforces our current negative emotions. According to this school, as we spill out our hatred about "that jerk" or "that crabby coworker," we harden our negative feelings about the other person, sometimes to the extent that we feel self-righteous. As a result, we become *more* distressed, not less.

There is evidence that each school of thought has some truth. The confusion stems from the fact that the expression of negative emotions is both a *sign of distress* and a *possible means of coping with that distress.*[24] Expressing negative emotions is adaptive to the degree that it helps deal with the distress. At one end of the spectrum, imagine a situation in which a negotiator decides not to make a big deal out of her counterpart's demeaning remarks toward her, but to ensure that her resentment does not spill into her future interactions with the counterpart, she discusses her anger in private with a colleague. She comes to some sense of understanding that her counterpart may not have meant harm by his statements. Contrast that with a situation in which a negotiator rants and raves at another negotiator who says something disrespectful.[25] The negotiator may intend to get things "out into the open" in order to "clear the air," but such venting heightens relational tension. Thus, expressing negative emotions, if not done carefully, runs a serious risk of reducing our affective satisfaction and that of the other.

Positive Emotions Generate Affective Satisfaction. The flipside of Gottman's findings on divorce is that enlisting positive emotions into a negotiation can contribute to affective satisfaction. In fact, Gottman has been able to quantify the ratio that differentiates happy couples from unhappy ones. A couple is more likely to divorce if the ratio of their positive to negative interactions dips below five to one. That means that even in stable, happy relationships, people still complain. Yet for every criticism or negative comment, there are at least five appreciative statements. Over time, these positive interactions create a reservoir of positive emotions, which offsets the negative impact of hurt feelings.

Positive Emotions Tend to Aid Instrumental Goals

For most of us, we do not negotiate just to feel good. We have substantive interests, and we want to have them satisfied. Emotions can help us reach our instrumental goals. But should we try to stimulate positive or negative emotions? While there is a useful place for both, the scales tip toward the positive.

Negative Emotions: For One-Time, Distributive Deals. You want to sell your 1993 Toyota. It has been a part of your "family" for many years, but you are ready for a new car. A man responds to the ad you placed in the local paper: "1993 Toyota for sale. $2000." The man arrives at your home, examines the car, and offers you $200, one-tenth of your asking price. Will expressing outrage at his offer scare him into giving you a concession, or will it harden him against your interests? If three conditions are met, the strong expression of negative emotions—whether anger, guilt, embarrassment, or the like—can enhance a negotiator's outcomes.

First, strongly expressing negative emotions can enhance an outcome if a good relationship with the other side is unimportant to reaching your instrumental and affective goals. In terms of instrumental satisfaction, intimidating or threatening another may improve your substantive interests if you have no need or interest in a positive long-term relationship with the other side. In the markets of Morocco, for example, a traveler might act outraged at the seller's high price for a candle. Anger can let the other know the gravity of your demands and your genuine willingness to walk away from the agreement. However, scaring or "guilting" the other to make concessions can affect an ongoing relationship. If others feel mistreated by you, they will be less motivated to work with you. And when cooperation is necessary, it may be given begrudgingly, if at all.

A negotiator's affective satisfaction must also be unaffected by the relationship quality. If a negotiator's own values, morals, or ethics are inconsistent with the action of coercion, the negotiated outcome may be instrumentally satisfying but not affectively rewarding. For example, coercing the other party may help you reach your monetary goals, but at a cost to your own emotional well-being. Thus, when judging the importance of a relationship, a negotiator should consider both the instrumental and affective consequences of disregarding the relationship quality.

The second condition upon which emotional coercion can be a workable strategy is if the negotiated issues are zero-sum. For example, anger can be an effective strategy in persuading others to concede to your demands *if* the issues at hand are purely distributive in nature. More for one party means less for the other. In this circumstance, strategic advantage rests with the party who is better able to cause the other to feel fear, impotency, or indebtedness.

Research offers evidence to support the short-term benefits of anger expression in a zero-sum, one-time negotiation. In a recent study, participants acted as sellers who bargained via computer simulation with a buyer over the price, warranty, and service contract of a cell phone.[26] Participants were unaware that, in reality, there was no buyer, but rather a computer program that made offers and counteroffers. After some of the rounds, the buyers received information about the sellers' emotions, such as "This offer makes me really angry" or "I am happy with this offer." Participants evaluated the seller's offer and intentions, then adjusted their demands to try to reach an agreement. Results of the study confirmed that bargainers make lower demands and larger concessions with an angry customer than with a happy one.

The design of this buyer-seller study arguably met each of the basic conditions within which expressing strong negative emotions yields higher instrumental gains. The phone deal was assumedly a one-time transaction, so the seller presumably had little reason to care about the long-term relationship with the other party. The transaction occurred without any face-to-face contact, further reducing either's care for a long-term relationship. And each of the two issues was quantifiable and zero-sum. A better price or longer warranty for one comes at a greater cost for the other.

The third condition upon which emotional coercion can be a workable strategy is if the other negotiator has a weak BATNA (Best Alternative To a Negotiated Agreement).[27] It is much more effective for you to influence another when you and they both know that their BATNA is weak. The two of you share a clear understanding that, if agreement is not reached, the cost for them is high. Moreover, if you have a strong BATNA, that further advances your negotiating power.

Positive Emotions: Because There's Usually More to a Negotiation Than Just Distribution. Positive emotions, just like negative ones, can be used to reach instrumental goals. However, the circumstances for their optimal use are different. Positive emotions are best stimulated when two conditions are met:

1. *The Relationship Is Important.* Many negotiators undervalue the importance of relationships in a negotiation. With a good relationship, two negotiators may feel freer to share information, trust one another, communicate their interests, understand the interests of the other, and brainstorm about possible agreements for mutual gain.[28]

Furthermore, in an ongoing relationship, how you treat the other *now* may affect their decision about how to treat *you* in the future.[29] If you deceive them and they find out, they may be less likely to trust your word in the future. Perhaps more troubling, they may assume that you have established a norm that deception is acceptable—and follow your lead.

2. *The Issues Involve Opportunities to Create and Distribute Value.* Positive emotions are most helpful when a situation involves not only distributive issues but also the potential for creating options that meet each side's interests. Compared to those in a neutral mood, negotiators in a positive mood reach more optimally integrative outcomes and use less aggressive tactics.[30] Positive emotions elicit problem solving, creative brainstorming of ideas, and empathy for the perspective of the other parties.[31]

Whereas a zero-sum negotiation excludes creative thinking, more complex circumstances allow parties to think about ways of addressing their quantitative and qualitative interests. Rather than assuming that issues such as security and status are purely distributive, a negotiator in a positive mood is more likely to realize that such issues can be enhanced for each party.[32] Two neighboring, disputing countries need not argue over security as though more for one means less for the other. Through creative problem solving, they may be able to create ways for both countries to have a high degree of security.

Positive emotions can improve parties' ability to distribute value in the negotiation. Parties can work side-by-side in designing a process that each deems fair for distributing the value that has been created. Hence, each party has some control over the process for distributing the value that has been jointly created.

On Balance, Negative Emotions Are Risky Business

While negative emotions can help a negotiator reach his or her goals, the risks involved preclude their use as a wise general strategy.

Negative Emotions Can Get in the Way of Clear Thinking. Stimulating negative emotions can come at a heavy price.[33] Anger and other negative emotions are linked to inaccurate judgments and reduced concern for the other parties' preferences.[34] Negative emotions may lead us to act in ways that are counter to our own instrumental goals. We may reject an ultimatum that is superior to our alternatives,[35] or we may replace our original instrumental goals with new goals focused on attacking the person who triggered our anger.[36] For example, two companies meet for months and discuss the details of merging. Only weeks before the merger is to happen, Nancy and John, the chief executive officers, meet to discuss details. John senses that Nancy does not value the culture of his organization. He feels insulted, because *he* spent the last five years of his life primarily building his company's culture. Nancy does not back down from her critique, which angers John to the extent that he calls off the whole deal, despite the financial benefits to each company.

Furthermore, if we stimulate negative emotions in the other, we put ourselves at risk of "catching" those negative emotions, just as one can catch a cold from being around a sneezing friend. Emotions are contagious, especially when intense. Our mood may deteriorate to the point that we become emotionally hijacked.[37] Thinking takes a backseat to emotions, and we risk engaging in behavior we will later regret.

Positive emotions rarely run these same risks. While we want to check that we are not being manipulated by positive emotions, few negotiators complain that their negotiations are being sidetracked because people are "too happy." Nevertheless, before committing to a decision, we do want to draw on information supplied by our reasoning and our emotions. Otherwise, negotiators risk making an inefficient exchange of items due to their affinity for one another and consequently failing to maximize value-creating opportunities.[38]

Most Negotiations Involve Conditions Aided by Positive Emotions, Not Negative Ones. Good relations between colleagues are increasingly important in many contexts. Diplomats, politicians, lawyers, academics, and organizational workers often interact with a small, stable network of colleagues.[39] Whereas organizations traditionally have been hierarchically structured, many are now introducing team-based work. Employees increasingly negotiate with colleagues rather than having decisions made by superordinates. By building good relationships, employees improve their ability to deal well with interpersonal differences.[40]

Negotiators easily can fall for the trap of thinking that a negotiation is a one-time, zero-sum interaction, even when there are possibilities for value creation and relationship building.[41] For example, let us return to the study of the participants acting as sellers of the price, warranty, and service contract of a cell phone.[42] The external validity of the study can be called into question. In a real-life transaction, the buyer and seller would be wise to recognize their shared strategic incentive to care about their long-term relationship. What happens, for example, if the phone breaks? A strong relationship between the buyer and seller might improve the efficiency with which the problem is dealt. Rather than each party threatening the other, they may be able to efficiently and amicably problem-solve their differences, perhaps by having the buyer's phone replaced with a new or refurbished one. The buyer gets a functional phone, and the seller's reputation and customer relations are enhanced.

Given the risks of negative emotions and the benefits of positive ones, the best general advice for a negotiator is to stimulate positive emotions in oneself and in those with whom one negotiates.

To Stimulate Positive Emotions, Focus on Relational Identity Concerns

Some people assume that emotions "happen to them." They are passive recipients of the internal ebbs and flows of their emotions. They have no control over whether they feel happy, sad, nervous, or enthusiastic.

This assumption is wrong.

You Can Stimulate Emotions in Yourself and Others. While it is true that emotions can result from biological or physiological changes in our bodies, scientific research now makes it clear that *we* have a great deal of power to affect the emotions we feel. We can induce emotions in ourselves and in others.[43]

The successful car salesperson has known about the power of emotions for a long time. You walk to the car lot, and immediately he builds rapport with you, tells you a joke, and tries to personalize the conversation. He is trying to *get you in a good mood.* He is a mood inducer. Without being aware of what is happening, you may be the victim of his emotional manipulation.

"You have kids?" he asks.

"Yes," you answer.

"Me, too. This is a great car for the kids. Comfortable. Safe."

If you do not stay aware of your emotions, you may feel unduly persuaded by the salesperson's opinion. He has kids, and so do you. You assume that you must share the same incentive: to protect the safety of children. But it also may be the case that the salesperson has an incentive to sell the car as quickly as possible to make room for next year's models. You would be wise to consider upon what objective data his opinion is based. How does the safety or comfort of this car compare statistically with that of other similar cars? With awareness of your emotions and his incentives, you can listen to the opinion of the car salesperson, use what information he offers as data, and search out additional data from which to make a wise decision.

The Power of Relational Identity Concerns. Emotions are not simply reactions to a particular behavior or situation. They often serve a forward-looking communicative function: they give others (and ourselves) a signal about our likely intentions. A negotiator who expresses anger may be communicating the message "Take my concerns seriously or else I'm walking away from this negotiation—even if it's to my substantive detriment!" The look of fear on a colleague's face may signal "Help me! Protect me from being crushed by the other party!"[44]

During a negotiation, many of our concerns are about our perceived identity in relation to the other party. Is the other treating us the way we expect or desire to be treated? I refer to this category of concerns as *relational identity concerns*.[45] They are "concerns" because we experience a felt desire to have them satisfied. They are "identity concerns" because the concerns focus on our desire to maintain a positive sense of self. And they are "relational identity concerns" because in different relationships, the degree of satisfaction required to address these concerns varies. For example, a negotiator may have little need to "have things my way" in marital decisions. At work, that same negotiator may desire a great deal of autonomy over decisions being made, asserting his or her opinion strongly on virtually every issue.

Two factors have consistently converged as essential to understanding and measuring interpersonal behavior.[46] While these concerns are known by many different names with subtly different meanings,[47] I term these two dimensions "autonomy" and "affiliation."[48]

Autonomy is the freedom to act without the imposition of others. Negotiators' behavior can be considered autonomous when they act in accordance with internalized, personally accepted principles and not in response to coercion or pressure from others.[49]

A negotiator's initial concern for autonomy often arises early in the negotiation process. Who proposes the agenda? Who initiates conversation? Who listens, who talks, and who interrupts? To what extent does each party consult the other before making decisions?

Affiliation is the interpersonal closeness or distance that one party feels toward another. To what extent do parties feel a sense of connection, bonding, and "us-ness"? Do parties work side-by-side as a team, or do they sit across the table from one another as adversaries? Who feels included? Who does not?

You can stimulate positive emotions from the outset of a negotiation by constructively addressing people's relational identity concerns. If you respect these relational identity concerns—ensuring that you and others receive an appropriate degree of autonomy and affiliation—then positive emotions can result.

For example, rather than *telling* the other party your demands, you may respect the party's autonomy by asking his or her advice on the issues facing each of you.[50] You might build affiliation with your counterpart by getting his or her recommendations on how the two of you could work jointly to deal with your differences. These types of actions will tend to stimulate enthusiasm and cooperation in you and in others. Joint work will become more efficient, more effective, and more amicable than if you haggle as adversaries over the issues facing each of you.[51]

APPLYING THE RELATIONAL IDENTITY CONCERNS FRAMEWORK: BACK TO SOUTH AFRICA

With the relational identity concerns framework in mind, let us revisit the situation between Cyril Ramaphosa and Roelf Meyer, the leaders who helped to negotiate many of the contentious issues regarding transition to a multiracial, democratic South Africa. During their meeting in the outback of South Africa, only two weeks prior to their negotiations, what did they say and do to address each other's relational identity concerns, thereby enlisting positive emotions?

They built affiliation in several ways. First, Cyril and Roelf jointly engaged in the activity of fly fishing. Their shared experience of trying to catch fish became a basis for their assumption that they could function well as a team. Second, their meeting took place in the outback of South Africa, far away from the eyes and ears of constituents who might disapprove of these two men meeting under such cordial circumstances. They could converse candidly without fear of ostracizing themselves from their constituents. Thus, each man got to know the other on a personal level and could assess the other's integrity and trustworthiness. Third, Cyril treated Roelf like family. After Roelf got the hook stuck in his hand, Cyril called his wife for support. This action demonstrated Cyril's care for Roelf. Cyril did not want to see Roelf in pain. Cyril's action enhanced the felt affiliation between the two of them.

Each man also respected the autonomy of the other. There was no presumption that, because Roelf was white or a member of the ruling party, Cyril *must* teach him how to fly fish. He did not demand that Cyril teach him. The request came in the form of a friendly inquiry. Roelf *asked* Cyril to teach him how to fly fish, thus allowing each man to preserve his autonomy.

Roelf and Cyril also enlisted positive emotions in one another by relinquishing some of their own autonomy to the other. This was a courageous move of trust and vulnerability. For example, Roelf willingly relinquished some of his autonomy by allowing Cyril to force the fish hook through his hand. Roelf trusted that Cyril would not abuse his expanded autonomy, and Cyril did not let him down. It was this same dynamic of trust that Roelf and Cyril replicated at the negotiation table during their critical negotiations. Roelf had to decide whether or not to release African National Congress prisoners in hope that the African National Congress would stop its armed struggle a week later. Roelf whispered in Cyril's ear, "I hear you saying, 'Trust me.'" Cyril and Roelf had an implicit understanding that each would stand true to his word and would not impinge upon the other's autonomy. The prisoners were released one week later.

SUMMARY

In this chapter, I proposed that emotions are an essential, irreplaceable ingredient in any negotiation. Getting rid of emotions is not possible and not desirable. Positive emotions can be used to help us reach our instrumental and affective goals in a negotiation. We can stimulate positive emotions in negotiators by dealing constructively with people's relational identity concerns, specifically for autonomy and affiliation.

Notes

1. This story was told by Cyril Ramaphosa to Bruce Patton at a workshop given by the Harvard Negotiation Project in 1991, available at the Harvard Negotiation Project Website, forthcoming.

2. See D. L. Shapiro, "Negotiating Emotions," *Conflict Resolution Quarterly*, 2002, *20*(1), 67–82.

3. See B. Fehr and J. A. Russell, "Concept of Emotion Viewed from a Prototype Perspective," *Journal of Experimental Psychology: General,* 1984, *113,* 464–486.

4. For a recent set of definitions, see J. Van Brakel, "Emotions: A Cross-Cultural Perspective on Forms of Life," in W. M. Wentworth and J. Ryan (eds.), *Social Perspectives on Emotion,* Vol. 2 (Greenwich, Conn.: JAI Press, 1994).

5. See J. R. Averill, "Emotions Unbecoming and Becoming," in P. Ekman and R. J. Davidson (eds.), *The Nature of Emotions: Fundamental Questions* (New York: Oxford University Press, 1994).

6. See R. R. Cornelius, *The Science of Emotion: Research and Tradition in the Psychology of Emotions* (Upper Saddle River, N.J.: Prentice Hall, 1996); and N. H. Frijda, *The Emotions* (Cambridge, U.K.: Cambridge University Press, 1986).

7. See R. S. Lazarus, *Emotion and Adaptation* (New York: Oxford University Press, 1991).

8. See D. L. Shapiro, "Negotiation Residuals: The Impact of Affective Satisfaction on Long-Term Relationship Quality," *Program on Negotiation Papers,* no. 00–3 (Cambridge, Mass.: Program on Negotiation Books, 2000).

9. See N. R. Carlson, *Physiology of Behavior* (8th ed.) (Boston: Pearson, 2004).

10. See S. E. Hymen, "Introduction to the Complex Genetics of Mental Disorders," *Biological Psychiatry,* 1999, *45*(5), 518–521.

11. See G. Harrer and H. Harrer, "Music, Emotion, and Autonomic Function." In M. Critchley and R. A. Henson (eds.), *Music and the Brain* (London, U.K.: Heinemann, 1977), pp. 202–215.

12. See A. Ellis, "Rational Emotive Behavior Therapy," in R. Corsini and D. Wedding (eds.), *Current Psychotherapies* (6th ed.) (Itasca, Ill.: F. E. Peacock, 2000).

13. See Frijda, *The Emotions,* 1986.

14. See N. H. Frijda, "Emotions and Hedonic Experience," in D. Kahneman, E. Diener, and N. Schwarz, *Well-Being: The Foundations of Hedonic Psychology* (New York: Russell Sage Foundation, 1999), p. 197.

15. See Ellis, "Rational Emotive Behavior Therapy," 2000.

16. See Ellis, "Rational Emotive Behavior Therapy," 2000.

17. See Shapiro, *Negotiation Residuals,* 2000. The concepts of affective and instrumental satisfaction are similar to the concepts of procedural and distributive justice; see N. A. Welsh, "Perceptions of Fairness in Negotiation," *Marquette Law Review,* 2004, *87,* 753–767.

18. See J. M. Gottman, L. F. Katz, and C. Hooven, *Meta-Emotion: How Families Communicate Emotionally* (Hillsdale, N.J.: Erlbaum, 1997).

19. See A. N. Isen, "Positive Affect and Decision Making," in J. M. Haviland-Jones and A. G. Johnson (eds.), *Handbook of Emotions* (New York: Guilford Press, 2000).

20. See Shapiro, *Negotiation Residuals,* 2000.

21. See D. Watson and A. Tellegen, "Toward a Consensual Structure of Mood," *Psychological Bulletin,* 1985, *98,* 219–235.

22. See J. Gottman and N. Silver, *Why Marriages Succeed or Fail: What You Can Learn from the Breakthrough Research to Make Your Marriage Last* (New York: Fireside, 1994); and J. M. Gottman and R. W. Levenson, "The Timing of Divorce: Predicting When a Couple Will Divorce over a 14-Year Period," *Journal of Marriage and the Family*, 2000, *62*, 737–745.

23. See Gottman and Silver, *Why Marriages Succeed or Fail*, 1994.

24. See E. Kennedy-Moore and J. C. Watson, *Expressing Emotion* (New York: Guilford Press, 1999).

25. See L. Thompson, V. H. Medvec, V. Seiden, and S. Kopelman, "Poker Face, Smiley Face, and Rant 'n' Rave: Myths and Realities About Emotion in Negotiation," in M. Hogg and S. Tinsdale (eds.), *Blackwell Handbook in Social Psychology, Vol. 3: Group Processes* (Cambridge, Mass.: Blackwell, 2000).

26. See G. A. van Kleef, C.K.W. De Dreu, and A.S.R. Manstead, "The Interpersonal Effects of Anger and Happiness in Negotiations," *Journal of Personality and Social Psychology*, 2004, *86*(1), 57–76.

27. See R. Fisher, W. Ury, and B. Patton, *Getting to YES: Negotiating Agreement Without Giving In* (2nd ed.) (Boston: Penguin, 1991).

28. See R. Fisher and S. Brown, *Getting Together: Building Relationships as We Negotiate* (Boston: Penguin, 1988).

29. See R. M. Axelrod, *The Evolution of Cooperation* (New York: Basic Books, 1984).

30. See P. J. Carnevale and A. M. Isen, "The Influence of Positive Affect and Visual Access on the Discovery of Integrative Solutions in Bilateral Negotiation," *Organizational Behavior and Human Decision Processes*, 1986, *37*(1), 1–13.

31. See Isen, "Positive Affect and Decision Making," 2000.

32. See B. L. Frederickson, "The Role of Positive Emotions in Positive Psychology: The Broaden-and-Build Theory of Positive Emotions," *American Psychologist*, 2001, *56*, 218–226.

33. Shapiro, "Negotiating Emotions," 2002, p. 70.

34. See K. G. Allred, J. S. Mallozzi, F. Matsui, and C. P. Raia, "The Influence of Anger and Compassion on Negotiation Performance," *Organizational Behavior and Human Decision Processes*, 1997, *70*(3), 175–187.

35. See M. H. Bazerman, J. Curhan, and D. Moore, "The Death and Rebirth of the Social Psychology of Negotiations," in G. Fletcher and M. Clark (eds.), *Blackwell Handbook of Social Psychology* (Cambridge, U.K.: Blackwell, 2000); and M. M. Pillutla and J. K. Murnighan, "Unfairness, Anger, and Spite: Emotional Rejections of Ultimatum Offers," *Organizational Behavior and Human Decision Processes*, 1997, *68*(3), 208–224.

36. See J. P. Daly, "The Effects of Anger on Negotiations over Mergers and Acquisitions," *Negotiation Journal*, 1997, *7*(1), 31–39.

37. See D. Goleman, *Emotional Intelligence* (New York: Bantam Books, 1995).

38. See J. R. Curhan, M. A. Neale, L. D. Ross, and J. Rosencranz-Engelmann, "The O. Henry Effect: The Impact of Relational Norms on Negotiation Outcomes," AoM Conflict Management Division 2002 Mtgs. No. 14092, 2004, available at [http://ssrn.com/abstract=321448].

39. See Shapiro, "Negotiating Emotions," 2002.

40. See Fisher and Brown, *Getting Together*, 1988.

41. See M. H. Bazerman and M. A. Neale, *Negotiating Rationally* (New York: Free Press, 1985).

42. See van Kleef, De Dreu, and Manstead, "The Interpersonal Effects of Anger and Happiness in Negotiations," 2004.

43. See A. M. Isen, T. Shalker, M. Clark, and L. Karp, "Affect Accessibility of Material in Memory and Behavior: A Cognitive Loop?" *Journal of Personality and Social Psychology*, 1978, *36*, 1–12; K. Kraiger, R. S. Billings, and A. M. Isen, "The Influence of Positive Affective States on Task Perceptions and Satisfaction," *Organizational Behavior and Human Decision Processes*, 1989, *44*, 12–25; and Carnevale and Isen, "The Influence of Positive Affect and Visual Access on the Discovery of Integrative Solutions in Bilateral Negotiation," 1986.

44. See B. Parkingson, *Ideas and Realities of Emotion* (New York: Routledge, 1995).

45. See Shapiro, "Negotiating Emotions," 2002.

46. See J. S. Wiggins, "Agency and Communion as Conceptual Coordinates for the Understanding and Measurement of Interpersonal Behavior," in W. M. Grove and D. Ciccetti, *Thinking Clearly About Psychology: Personality and Psychopathology*, Vol. 2 (Minneapolis: University of Minnesota Press, 1991).

47. See A. Angyal, *Foundations for a Science of Personality* (Cambridge, Mass.: Harvard University Press, 1941); D. Bakan, *The Duality of Human Existence: Isolation and Communion in Western Man* (Boston: Beacon Press, 1966); S. L. Bem, "The Measurement of Psychological Androgyny," *Journal of Consulting and Clinical Psychology*, 1974, *42*, 155–162; J. Benjafield and E. Carson, "A Historico-developmental Analysis of the Circumplex Model of Trait Descriptive Terms," *Canadian Journal of Behavioural Science*, 1986, *17*(4), 339–345; E. L. Deci and R. M. Ryan, *Intrinsic Motivation and Self-Determination in Human Behavior* (New York: Plenum Press, 1985); C. Gilligan, *In a Different Voice* (Cambridge, Mass.: Harvard University Press, 1982); and Wiggins, "Agency and Communion as Conceptual Coordinates for the Understanding and Measurement of Interpersonal Behavior," 1991.

48. See Shapiro, "Negotiating Emotions," 2002.

49. See J. R. Averill and E. P. Nunley, *Voyages of the Heart: Living an Emotionally Creative Life* (New York: Free Press, 1992).

50. See Fisher and Brown, *Getting Together*, 1988.

51. See Fisher, Ury, and Patton, *Getting to YES*, 1991; and A. Schneider, "Shattering Negotiation Myths: Empirical Evidence on the Effectiveness of Negotiation Style," *Harvard Negotiation Law Review*, 2002, *7*, 143–233.

CHAPTER SIX

Relationship Dynamics in Disputes

Replacing Contention with Cooperation

Keith G. Allred

E very conflict can escalate out of control. Fueled by contention and suspicion, escalating conflicts consume enormous amounts of time, energy, and money while rarely yielding satisfactory resolutions. Alternatively, most conflicts can be resolved to mutual satisfaction without the costs of escalation, particularly when trust and cooperation are prominent.

Understanding the triggers of cooperative or contentious dynamics in disputes is critical. These dynamics affect not only the cost of the dispute and the prospects of sound resolution but also the health of the relationships within which the conflict occurs. The dynamics of a dispute influence the ability of the parties to interact with each other productively in the future. That future relationship is often more important to the parties than the outcome of any particular dispute.

Social psychologists have identified triggers of cooperative and contentious dynamics. In recent research, I have investigated these triggers through the experiences of hundreds of executives in government and business. I asked these executives to invite between four and ten colleagues to rate them on their ability to employ or avoid the triggers of the cooperative or contentious dynamics identified by previous research. Known as 360 degree or multirater feedback, this research identified those triggers that are the most powerful predictors of the ability to maintain productive ongoing relationships in the context of a dispute. I review these findings here.[1]

VICIOUS CYCLE TRIGGERS

Biases that lead us to exaggerate other people's hostility and unreasonableness trigger vicious cycles of suspicion and conflict escalation. These exaggerated perceptions prompt us to respond with negative behaviors of our own. Although based in misperceptions, our hostile responses can create self-fulfilling prophecies. Those on the other side are likely to respond to our hostile behavior with negative behavior of their own. Then, taking the other side's genuinely hostile response as confirmation of our earlier misperceptions, we fail to recognize that our own actions created exactly what we feared. My research indicates that four such biases—naïve realism, the confirmatory bias, and the accuser and excuser biases—are particularly potent triggers of these kinds of vicious cycles. A fifth bias—the lone moderate effect—which could not be examined using the multi-rater method in my study, has also proven in other research to be a powerful trigger of vicious cycles.

Naïve Realism

My research indicates that *naïve realism*—the assumption that most people make that their view of the world is the way the world "really" is—is an especially powerful trigger of vicious cycle conflicts. Naïve realism has three aspects.[2] First, when confronting a problem or question, we typically think that we are reasonable and objective. Second, we assume that anyone looking at the same evidence would draw the same conclusions we do. Third, when others reach different conclusions, we suspect that they are unreasonable or driven by suspect motives.

This last inference triggers the vicious cycle. The perceived unreasonableness of the other side suggests a need for extreme measures on our own part. As a consequence, we feel justified in taking actions we would otherwise consider to be excessively hostile. In cycles of conflict, these perceptions are often painfully symmetric. Yet we are usually unaware that the other side is just as convinced of our obstinacy as we are of theirs. As each side escalates accordingly, costs mount, the prospects of sound resolution dim, and relationships deteriorate.

The Confirmatory Bias

The *confirmatory bias*—the tendency to seek out information that verifies our pre-existing beliefs and to ignore or find flaws with disconfirming information—is a second powerful trigger of vicious cycles of conflict. The destructive power of the confirmatory bias is the result of a counterintuitive reality—providing the same information to two opposing parties can actually further polarize their beliefs.

Lord, Ross, and Lepper studied the polarizing effects of the confirmatory bias by examining the views of activists on both sides of the capital punishment debate.[3] The researchers administered a questionnaire to the activists to measure the degree of difference in their opinions on the topic. Then, they asked the activists to read two articles from law journals, one in favor of capital punishment and one opposed. Experts had previously chosen the articles as having equally compelling evidence and logic. The researchers then measured the activists' views again. They found that the pro–capital punishment activists were even more in favor of capital punishment and the anti–capital punishment activists were even more against it than they had been before reading the same information. Viewing the information through the distorted lens of the confirmatory bias, each side sought out evidence to support their opinions and found it. Each side also looked for faults in the article that challenged their own views. They found these, too.

Because each side is unaware of his or her own confirmatory bias and thinks that he or she is being reasonable and objective, he or she is surprised by the other side's inability to see the "facts." As with naïve realism, each tends to conclude that, given the other side's refusal to see the facts, extreme measures will be needed to deal with this evident unreasonableness. Once again, as each remains unaware that he or she is perceived to be just as unreasonable by the other side, a vicious cycle of polarization ensues.

Accuser and Excuser Biases

A third trigger of vicious cycles stems from the combined effect of two biases—the accuser and excuser biases—that influence the way in which we assign responsibility for harmful behavior.[4] As attribution theory and cognitive appraisal theories of emotion suggest, it is not only what other people do to us that drives our response to them, but why we think they did it.[5] Suppose that Katherine and David are colleagues at work. Katherine is asked to lead a project. As she puts together her project team, she does not give David the assignment he wants. David will make a judgment about whether Katherine is personally responsible for this. If David thinks that Katherine passed him over for the assignment because company policy prevented her from giving it to him, he will not hold her personally responsible and the event will pose little difficulty for the relationship. If, however, David thinks that Katherine passed him over because she is prejudiced against him, then he will hold her personally responsible. When David holds Katherine responsible for her harmful behavior, it arouses his anger toward her. His anger, in turn, elicits an impulse to retaliate. This causal chain, by which we move from blame to anger to retaliation, equips us with a way of detecting and then deterring hostility by punishing it.

While based in an adaptive logic, angry retaliation is a crude instrument that typically does more harm than good. Angry retaliation proves to be ineffective, in part, because it leads people to miss opportunities to find mutually beneficial solutions to problems. My colleagues and I conducted an experiment in which each participant was assigned to negotiate the terms of a job contract with another participant.[6] The situation that they negotiated included a potential solution that created value for both sides. Half of the pairs were made angry at each other and the other half were not. We found that the negotiators who were angry with each other discovered the value creating solution less frequently than did those who were not angry with each other. Rather than seeking to find solutions that benefited themselves and the other side, the angry negotiators were looking for vengeance.

Angry retaliation also proves to be counterproductive because we tend to be biased in the way we assign blame. My colleagues and I conducted research that identified an *accuser bias:* when someone does something that causes us harm, we tend to hold that person excessively responsible.[7] We readily bring to mind factors within the person's control that might explain his or her behavior and tend to ignore or dismiss factors beyond his or her control that might explain that behavior. For example, when David judges Katherine's decision to pass him over for the assignment, he will tend to focus on her prejudice against him while underemphasizing or ignoring factors beyond her control, such as company policy. David's judgment, thus exaggerating Katherine's responsibility, will tend to elicit an excessively angry and retaliatory response from him.

While it is easy to understand how excessively angry and retaliatory responses can lead to vicious cycles, the effects of the accuser bias are actually exacerbated by an opposite bias. Our research found that when we are the one who behaves in a way that harms someone else, we tend to fall victim to an *excuser bias.* We focus on factors beyond our control that explain away our own behavior while tending to ignore factors within our control.[8] When Katherine judges her own actions, she will readily bring to mind the company policy that prevented her from giving the assignment to David. She will focus on this policy even if she could have given David the assignment if she had really wanted to do so. Katherine is also likely to underestimate the role played by the prejudice she feels toward David.

The pernicious interplay of the accuser bias and excuser bias can fuel vicious cycles of conflict, as seen in Figure 6.1.[9] When David interprets Katherine's behavior through the distorted lens of the accuser bias, he will likely become angry and retaliate. In a meeting with their common boss, he may criticize work that Katherine did on another project. Because of the excuser bias, Katherine will view his retaliation as unjustified. After all, she thinks that it is not her fault; company policy kept her from giving David the assignment he wanted. As Katherine considers David's "unjustified" retaliation, her own accuser bias will lead her to attribute his retaliatory behavior to something about him, perhaps his hostile personality. She will become angry and counterretaliate. Perhaps she will go to their boss to ask that David be removed from her project entirely, citing his inability to work well with others on the team because of his prickly personality. When David learns of this, it will tend to confirm his earlier view that she is prejudiced against him. His resulting anger and retaliation perpetuates the vicious cycle that has begun.

David's Response

Katherine's Response

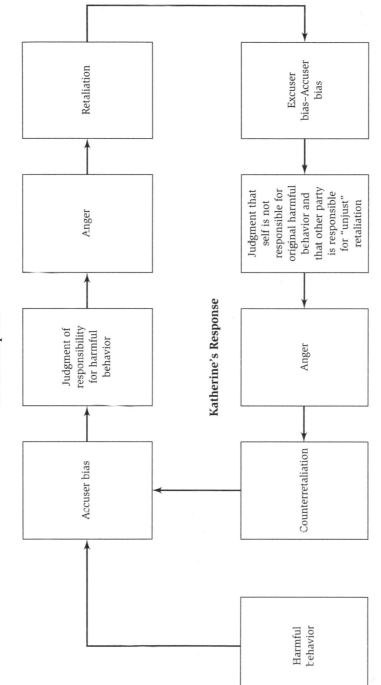

Figure 6.1. The Interplay of the Accuser and Excuser Biases.

In their examination of these dynamics within married couples, Bradbury and Fincham found that this pattern of derogating judgments of responsibility is a strong predictor of marital distress and divorce.[10] Distressed marital couples not only blame each other excessively for harmful behaviors but also discount each other's positive behaviors by attributing them to circumstances beyond their spouses' control. Accordingly, these relationships are marked by negative emotions and retaliatory behaviors that tend to perpetuate themselves.

In their examination of satisfied marital couples, Bradbury and Fincham found that such couples experience not only an absence of derogating attributional biases but a reversal of them. Satisfied spouses tend to assume, to an inaccurate degree, that when their partners do something that has a negative effect, there must be some extenuating circumstances to explain it. They also tend to credit their spouses for behavior that has a positive effect and feel grateful to them, even when the behavior was actually unintended. Feeling more gratitude than anger toward each other, these spouses rarely retaliate and often seek to return their partners' perceived favors in a pattern that tends to perpetuate itself.

One of the most interesting aspects about the marital couples that Bradbury and Fincham studied is the extent to which both the negative and positive patterns are self-fulfilling prophecies. In the beginning, the spouses in the stressed marital couples are not so much meaner to each other than are the satisfied marital couples as they are more derogating in the way in which they interpret each other's behavior. However, because they respond to each other's perceived hostility with real hostility, they make what were initially biases become truths. After several rounds of the vicious cycle, they have proved each other right. The distressed marital couples are purposely doing mean things to each other while avoiding doing nice things for each other. Similarly, the satisfied marital couples do not start out being nicer to each other than are the dissatisfied marital couples. However, because they perceive nicer behavior, they respond with nicer behavior. Over time, they make each other's overly rosy view of each other correct. They really are trying to do nice things for each other and to avoid doing mean things for each other. But this is a reality that they have created for themselves.

The vicious cycle fueled by the interplay of the accuser and excuser bias is not restricted to individual-qua-individual relationships such as those between colleagues and spouses. These vicious cycles take hold in relationships between groups of people—management and labor, Republicans and Democrats, or Israelis and Palestinians. In fact, research suggests that these biases are even greater between groups than between individuals.[11]

The Lone Moderate Effect

While these first four biases can trigger vicious cycles at all levels of human relationships—interpersonal to international—Keltner and his colleagues have identified a fifth bias, the *lone moderate effect*, that is unique to relationships between groups of people.[12] The lone moderate effect describes the illusion that individuals have of being the only moderate in a particular controversy. In one of the first studies to identify this bias, Robinson and his colleagues administered a questionnaire to prochoice and prolife activists to measure their opinions about abortion. Then they asked these activists to complete the same questionnaire a second time according to how they thought the average person in the opposite camp would complete it. Finally, they asked the activists to complete the questionnaire a third time according to how they thought the average person in their own camp would complete it. Participants from both groups overestimated the extremity of the other group's views. Perhaps more surprisingly, participants also thought that the average member of their own group had more extreme views than was actually the case. In other words, most people had the illusion that they were one of the only moderates in either group. Similar studies by Robinson and colleagues confirm that this effect is common in relationships between groups.

As a mediator, I have seen the lone moderate effect perpetuate vicious cycles of conflict. In 2000, local government officials in north-central Idaho asked whether I would mediate a dispute they were having with the Nez Perce Tribe. Conflicts over jurisdiction—such as where the sheriff department's jurisdiction ended and the tribal police department's jurisdiction began—had raged for years. As I responded to the local government officials' request by investigating both parties' willingness to enter into mediation, the presence of the lone moderate effect became apparent.

Just as Robinson's research suggests, leaders of both groups overestimated the extremism not only of the other group but also of their own memberships. In fact, my exchanges with the government officials and tribal leaders were strikingly similar. Even as they expressed their willingness to enter into mediation, both warned me of the extremism and unreasonableness of the other side that might forestall mediation efforts. Then, in tones of concern, both acknowledged that the presence of extremists on their own side might derail the process.

Eventually, a colleague and I made a formal mediation proposal. To their mutual surprise, it was approved unanimously by all twenty-three local governments and by all nine members of the Nez Perce Tribal Executive Committee. The mediation produced a document called Memorandum of Understanding that the parties signed in 2002, establishing a framework for dispute resolution and productive relations. Though there have been some bumps along the way, local government and tribal leaders continue to pursue mutually beneficial solutions to their differences. For years, however, the conflict had escalated and they had been prevented from making this sensible progress because leaders on both sides mistakenly thought that they were the only ones who would support such an effort.

The lone moderate effect is a partial explanation for the degree of perceived polarization in U.S. politics. The press and pundits speak continually of a deeply polarized nation, "red states" vs. "blue states," and an escalating "culture war." The increasingly shrill tone of elected officials and talk show participants would seem to make these obvious truisms. However, the empirical evidence clearly shows that the majority of the public is not nearly so polarized.[13] Most Americans agree to a great extent on the major issues of the day and are increasingly disaffected by both major political parties and the tone and leadership that are being offered to them. Today there are as many Independents as Republicans or Democrats, and their number is growing. Still, a misperception can become self-fulfilling prophecy. As the large number of moderate Americans becomes increasingly disaffected by the polarized choices they are offered, fewer vote or otherwise participate in the political process. They thus cede the political playing field to the partisans, who genuinely are more extreme and passionate. As a result, the country does become more polarized, at least with respect to those engaged in the political process.

VIRTUOUS CYCLE TRIGGERS: THE ROLE OF PROCEDURAL JUSTICE

Although there are multiple ways in which our exaggerations of the hostility and unreasonableness of others trigger vicious cycles, there are ways in which our perceptions of others can trigger virtuous cycles of cooperation and trust. My multirater research suggests that the concept of procedural justice is especially important for understanding the perpetuation of such virtuous cycles. For many years, social science research on justice or fairness focused almost exclusively on what is called distributive justice. Distributive justice research investigates the fairness of the outcome of a given decision or process. Specifically, it examines whether benefits and burdens are allocated fairly. For example, distributive justice research examines how people judge the fairness of such things as negotiated settlements, compensation policies of companies, and tax policies of governments.[14] However, thirty years ago, Thibaut and Walker began investigating how people think about the fairness of the procedures that generate outcomes or decisions.[15] Their initial findings were so significant that they inspired a vibrant stream of research that continues to this day, offering significant insights into how to sustain cooperation and trust. As seen in Figure 6.2, procedural justice research can be divided into two categories. One category of research has identified the factors, or antecedents, that lead people to feel that a procedure or interaction was fair. A second category of research has identified the consequences of individuals' perceptions that a process is fair.[16]

Antecedents to Perceptions of Fair Process

Procedural justice research indicates that the most powerful antecedent to our perception that a process has been fair is the perception that we were able

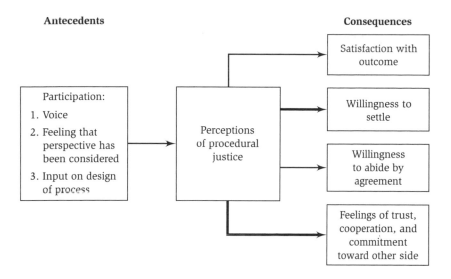

Figure 6.2. Antecedents and Consequences of Procedural Justice.

to participate in that process. The more we feel we were able to participate in a process, the fairer we feel the process was. Procedural justice research identifies three particular forms of participation that are worthy of specific mention. First, we perceive a process to be fairer to the extent that it affords us an opportunity to articulate our perspective on the issues at hand. This form of participation has sometimes been called voice. The second form of participation is closely related. Our sense of fair process increases to the extent that we feel our perspective is actually heard and considered. If we articulate our perspective but no one is listening, our sense of fair process is limited. This does not mean, however, that we have to feel that our perspective was agreed with to feel that the process is fair. We just need to feel that our perspective was given genuine consideration. The third form of participation is participation in the design of the process itself. If we are in a dispute with someone and he or she asks us what we think the process should be to try to resolve it, we will feel the process is fairer whatever the process turns out to be.

Consequences of Perceptions of Fair Process

Perceptions of fair process have powerful consequences, four of which merit particular mention. First, the fairer we feel the process is, the more satisfied we tend to be with the outcome. The extent to which the outcome is our preferred outcome is certainly the more powerful predictor of our satisfaction. However, our perceptions of fair process have a unique effect above and beyond outcome favorability or outcome satisfaction. Research indicates that the more unfavorable the outcome is, the more weight we place on our perception of whether the process was fair in assessing our satisfaction with the outcome. We can feel reasonably satisfied with an unfavorable outcome if we know that the process that generated it was fair.

Second, the fairer we feel a process is, the more willing we are to settle a dispute. This is, again, independent of the favorability of the settlement proposal. In fact, research indicates that feeling that the dispute resolution process was fair has more than twice the influence on willingness to settle than the favorability of the settlement proposal has. Third, the fairer we feel a process is, the more willing we are to abide by the outcome or agreement. We will honor an agreement, even if it is not particularly close to the one we desired or hoped for, to a greater extent if the process that generated it felt fair. Finally, and most important for the health of our ongoing relationships, the more we feel that a given person or institution treats us in a procedurally fair way, the more trust and loyalty we feel toward that person or institution. The extent to which we feel another person or institution treated us fairly has a much more powerful effect on the degree of trust and loyalty we feel toward them than does the favorability of the outcome they offered us.[17]

This last finding deserves particular attention. Imagine that you are faced with a situation in which you have significant interests that are sharply at odds with the interests of someone with whom you have an important ongoing relationship. You may feel that you face a dilemma between standing firm on an issue of great importance to you and damaging a significant relationship or conceding on an important issue for the sake of a significant relationship. Procedural justice research suggests that you will do much more for the ongoing relationship by genuinely listening to and considering the other side's perspective, whether or not you ultimately agree with it, than you will by simply conceding and giving the other side the exact outcome they want. The effects of feeling heard and considered on the quality of the ongoing relationship are truly powerful.

My research confirms the potency of perceptions of fair process. The participants in my study who were rated by their colleagues as being good at listening to and genuinely considering others' perspectives were also rated as being much more effective at maintaining trusting and cooperative relations.

The Dark Sides of Procedural Justice

While the procedural justice literature identifies potent triggers of virtuous cycles, its lessons present potential downsides. First, the implications of procedural justice can be used manipulatively. In a dispute, we might follow a strategy of giving the other side large doses of procedural fairness so that we do not have to concede anything substantively.

Although there is little empirical research on the matter, my experience as a mediator suggests that manipulative uses of procedural justice are on the rise in both the public and private sectors. In the public sector, for example, the National Environmental Policy Act (NEPA) requires extensive opportunity for public input on federal actions that may have an environmental impact. Many participants in these processes report that they feel that government agencies are simply going through the motions of soliciting input without really considering it. The fact that the input process is required by law is probably partly to blame for participants' sense that the agency is not soliciting input out of genuine interest.

An experience of mine in the private sector made the dangers of soliciting input without genuine interest particularly vivid. Leaders of a Fortune 500 aerospace company asked me to help them identify and overcome obstacles to collaboration in their organization. A few years earlier the company had implemented a "quality circle" program aimed at generating employee feedback. When the company failed to respond to any of the employees' concerns, workers were infuriated. As one employee noted: "It was fine that the company didn't care what I thought, but it was truly insulting to ask for my views and then ignore them." There is a simple lesson here. Those who are not prepared to make some modification based on what they learn from the other side should not ask for the other side's perspective.

Second, overly simplistic applications of the principles of procedural justice can actually cause greater polarization in large-scale conflicts involving many different parties. Once again, the example of government decision making under NEPA is instructive. If the Forest Service is developing a new plan for management of a national forest, it is required by NEPA to solicit public input on the options being considered. Public input is typically solicited through public meetings and formal written comments. Of course, participating requires time, money, and effort. Those parties that actively participate tend to be those that have sufficiently vested interests in the question at hand to motivate that participation. Environmentalists; off-highway-vehicle advocates; and timber, mining, and cattle interests tend to be very well represented in public meetings and through formal written comments when the management of a national forest is at stake. However, these groups are not necessarily representative of the broader public, which does not take the time and effort to participate as fully. In fact, the interest groups who do participate tend to hold more extreme views than those of the public at large. The unintended consequence, then, of applying procedural justice principles to these multiparty contexts can be further polarization, not less, because greater voice is given to those with more extreme views.

AVOIDING VICIOUS CYCLES AND PROMOTING VIRTUOUS CYCLES

The research that explores the biases underlying vicious and virtuous cycles suggests both personal practices and formal procedures for increasing the chances of resolving disputes through cooperation and trust and avoiding costly escalation.[18]

Personal Practices for Avoiding Vicious Cycles and Promoting Virtuous Cycles

My multirater feedback research revealed five personal practices that helped executives stay out of vicious cycles and promote virtuous cycles. The first three draw on the procedural justice literature. The first practice is "listening closely to the other party." The second practice is "understanding and appreciating the other party's perspective." The third practice is treating the other party "with consideration and respect" whether or not they agree with the other party. Those executives who were given high marks by their colleagues for these practices were far more successful in maintaining trust and cooperation than were those executives who received low marks on these items. The fourth practice draws on my research on the accuser and excuser bias. The higher participants were rated for "being quick to accept their responsibility for problems that arise and slow to blame them on others," the more successful they were at sustaining cooperation and trust. The fifth practice allowed executives to avoid the pitfalls of naïve realism and confirmatory bias. Those participants who scored higher than average at recognizing that "reasonable and objective people may come to different conclusions than I do" were better able to build trust and cooperation. Those who were rated below average on this item tended to find themselves in cycles of suspicion and contention.

The executives' estimation of their peers' uses of these practices were powerful predictors of those individuals' ability to maintain good relations in the midst of disputes. All together, they accounted for over 70 percent of the variance in ability to maintain trust and cooperation. It is important to note, however, that the executives' ratings of their own use of these practices had very little power to predict how well they did at maintaining relationships. It turns out that we are poor judges of our own abilities in these matters.

Procedures for Avoiding Vicious Cycles and Promoting Virtuous Cycles

In addition to personal practices, the research on triggers of vicious and virtuous cycles suggests two procedures that can be used to help maintain good relationship dynamics among parties to a dispute.

The first, a procedure sometimes known as *mirroring*, is a formal version of active listening and draws on insights from research on procedural justice, naïve realism, and confirmatory bias. There are three steps to this procedure. In the first step, each side explains its perspective to the other side. In the second step, each side mirrors back to the other side what it heard to be the other side's perspective. It is important that neither side editorialize about the other side's perspective or indicate where they disagree with it. Nor is it necessary for either side to indicate where it agrees with the other. The point is simply to provide a descriptively accurate account of the other side's perspective. In the third and final step, each side asks the other side whether the account it provided of the other side's perspective was accurate. If the account was not accurate in any way, the other side is invited to correct the inaccuracies.

Through mirroring, the parties actively look at the dispute from the perspective of the other side. In doing so, they have an opportunity to counteract the influence of naïve realism and the confirmatory bias as they discover that the other side's perspective is not so unreasonable as they may have initially thought. Through mirroring, each side also has an opportunity to demonstrate that it has heard and considered the other side's perspective, thus drawing on the power of procedural justice to prime the pump of cooperative, trusting interactions.

A second procedure is to bring in a neutral third party. The obvious advantage is that, by virtue of being neutral, the third party is not subject to the partisan misperceptions that elicit vicious cycles. The skilled neutral is therefore in a position to help each side overcome those biases. Neutrals, of course, can play a variety of specific roles. A neutral serving as mediator can make sure that the process allows everyone to feel that his or her perspective has been heard and considered. A mediator can also help each side understand that the other side's perspectives or positions are not necessarily the result of a tendency to be unreasonable, extreme, and intentionally hostile. A neutral serving as an arbitrator who offers a nonbinding opinion or as an early neutral evaluator can help each side see merits in the other side's positions as well as weaknesses in its own. In this way, advisory opinions can help counteract the effects of naïve realism and the confirmatory bias.

COOPERATION AND TRUST ARE NOT ENOUGH

It would be much easier to avoid vicious cycles and promote virtuous ones if sustaining cooperation and trust were all we had to worry about. In at least two important respects, however, cooperation and trust are not enough. First, sometimes hostility and unreasonableness are not misperceptions but reality—a reality that requires a serious response. Second, while cooperation and trust will go far toward preventing the enormous costs of conflict escalation, they are no guarantee of finding the most mutually satisfying resolution.

The Need to Detect and Respond to Real Hostility and Unreasonableness

To this point, a reader might conclude that every escalating conflict occurs because otherwise reasonable parties have tied themselves in knots through misperceptions. That would be the wrong conclusion. Unfortunately, hostility and unreasonableness can be all too real. To take one of the most extreme examples in modern history, the Allies were not mistaken to regard Hitler as hostile. No effort to genuinely consider Hitler's perspective, no attempt to consider reasons for his harmful behaviors that fell beyond his control, and no attempt to appreciate the merits of his perspective and the weaknesses of their own would have led the leaders of the allied countries to any conclusion other than that he was a hostile, evil leader intent on horrendously destructive aggression. The policy of appeasement was ineffective and mistakenly applied the lessons of World War I, which was a conflict that escalated out of control because the parties misperceived and misjudged each other.[19]

Hitler is one of the most extreme examples of the fact that genuine hostility exists in our world. Even in less extreme cases, the fact of real hostility and unreasonableness makes it much more difficult to overcome the biases that lead us to exaggerate them or to see them where they do not exist. Instead of having the luxury of assuming that such perceptions are always misperceptions, we face the challenge of discerning when the hostility is real and when it is not.

Although I know of no research that determines the proportion of conflicts driven by genuine hostility, my reading of the research literature and experience as a mediator lead me to estimate that of every ten seriously escalating conflicts only one involves a party that is fundamentally and genuinely hostile. These are conflicts of the World War II sort. Of the same ten, six or seven involve parties that are not fundamentally hostile or unreasonable. Rather, these parties have made each other so through the self-fulfilling prophecies of vicious cycles. These are conflicts of the World War I type. Finally, I would suggest that the remaining two or three conflicts do not fit easily into either category. These conflicts involve some genuine hostility and unreasonableness exacerbated by biased perceptions. Although at the writing of this chapter not all of the relevant information may be in, the current Iraq War seems a candidate representative of this category. Clearly, Saddam Hussein was a ruthless and evil dictator hostile to his own people and to the United States. It is increasingly apparent, however, that biases, including the confirmatory bias, were at work among officials in the United States and the United Kingdom. These biases led to exaggerations of the threat that Hussein posed beyond his own borders.

The Need to Pursue Joint Gains

Although cooperation and trust can help us avoid the costs of conflict escalation, they offer no guarantee of mutually satisfying resolutions.[20] One problem seems to be that parties who share a high regard for each other can become so concerned about each other's outcomes that they overlook their own best interests. Curhan and associates illustrate this phenomenon with O. Henry's short story "The Gift of the Magi."[21] In this classic tale, a young husband sells a prized watch to buy combs for his wife's beautiful hair, while the wife sells her hair to buy a chain for her husband's watch. The couple might take satisfaction in their mutual commitment and affection. However, similarly self-sacrificing outcomes would be less than ideal in public or private sector disputes. Good will should always be combined with the active pursuit of joint gains.

CONCLUSION

Maintaining productive ongoing relationships in the context of conflict is a skill critical to success in private and professional endeavors. Inevitably, parties to every relationship will face some disagreements or confront somewhat incompatible interests and needs. The important question is how well they will manage those situations. By overcoming the biases that can trigger vicious cycles of suspicion and contention and by employing those practices that trigger virtuous cycles of trust and cooperation, parties can avoid the enormous costs of escalation. They can also increase the chances of value-creating resolutions and, perhaps most important, maintain or even enhance the prospects for dealing with each other productively in the future.

Notes

1. The instrument I developed in conducting this research is the Personal Conflict Profile. My thanks to my research associate Victoria Chiongbian for running the statistical analyses and to dynamicfeedback.com for providing the online administration of the instrument for this research.

2. See R. J. Robinson, D. Keltner, A. Ward, and L. Ross, "Actual Versus Assumed Differences in Construal: 'Naïve Realism' in Intergroup Perception and Conflict," *Journal of Personality and Social Psychology*, 1995, *68*, 404–417.

3. See C. G. Lord, L. Ross, and M. R. Lepper, "Biased Assimilation and Attitude Polarization: The Effects of Prior Theories on Subsequently Considered Evidence," *Journal of Personality and Social Psychology*, 1979, *37*, 2098–2109.

4. See K. G. Allred, "Anger and Retaliation: Toward an Understanding of Impassioned Conflict in Organizations," in R. Lewicki, R. Bies, and B. Sheppard (eds.), *Research on Negotiation in Organizations*, Vol. 7 (Stamford, Conn.: JAI Press, 1999).

5. For an overview of attribution theory in this regard see B. Weiner, *An Attributional Theory of Motivation and Emotion* (New York: Springer-Verlag, 1986). For an overview of cognitive appraisal theories of emotion see N. H. Frijda, "Place of Appraisal in Emotion," *Cognition and Emotion*, 1993, *7*, 357–388.

6. See K. G. Allred, J. S. Mallozzi, F. Matsui, and C. P. Raia, "The Influence of Anger and Compassion on Negotiation Performance," *Organizational Behavior and Human Decision Processes*, 1997, *70*, 175–187.

7. See Allred, "Anger and Retaliation," 1999.

8. See Allred, "Anger and Retaliation," 1999.

9. See K. G. Allred, "Anger and Retaliation in Conflict: The Role of Attribution," in M. Deutsch and P. T. Coleman (eds.), *The Handbook of Conflict Resolution: Theory and Practice* (San Francisco: Jossey-Bass, 2000).

10. See T. N. Bradbury and F. D. Fincham, "Attributions in Marriage: Review and Critique," *Psychological Bulletin*, 1990, *107*, 3–33.

11. See I. Choi and R. E. Nisbett, "Situational Salience and Cultural Differences in the Correspondence Bias and Actor-Observer Bias," *Personality and Social Psychology Bulletin*, 1998, *25*, 949–960.

12. See D. Keltner and R. J. Robinson, "Imagined Ideological Differences in Conflict Escalation and Resolution," *International Journal of Conflict Management*, 1993, *4*, 249–262.

13. For excellent reviews of the empirical evidence, as well as commentary, that the U.S. electorate is not nearly as polarized as portrayed, see M. P. Fiorina, S. J. Abrams, and J. C. Pope, *Culture War? The Myth of a Polarized America* (New York: Pearson Longman, 2005); S. Greenberg, *The Two Americas: Our Current Political Deadlock and How to Break It* (New York: Thomas Dunne, 2004); and A. Wolfe, *One Nation, After All* (New York: Penguin, 1998).

14. See, for example, M. Deutsch, *Distributive Justice: A Social Psychological Perspective* (New Haven, Conn.: Yale University Press, 1985).

15. See J. Thibaut and L. Walker, *Procedural Justice: A Psychological Analysis* (Hillsdale, N.J.: Erlbaum, 1975).

16. For the most comprehensive review of procedural justice research, see E. A. Lind and T. R. Tyler, *The Social Psychology of Procedural Justice* (New York: Plenum Press, 1988).

17. See Lind and Tyler, *The Social Psychology of Procedural Justice*, 1988.

18. Two additional personal practices not amenable to testing through multirater research are suggested by research on triggers of virtuous and vicious cycles. First, Babcock and her colleagues have found that taking time to focus on assessing the weaknesses of our own positions helps us overcome naïve realism and confirmatory bias. Second, the procedural justice research suggests that when we face a dispute with someone, we will tend to garner that person's trust and cooperation if we ask him or her to recommend a process for dealing with the dispute. See L. Babcock, H. S. Farber, C. Fobian, and E. Safir, "Forming Beliefs About Adjudicated Outcomes: Perceptions of Risk and Reservation Values," *International Review of Law and Economics*, 1995, *15*(3), 289–303.

19. See J. S. Nye, *Understanding International Conflicts: An Introduction to Theory and History* (4th ed.) (New York: Longman, 2002).

20. See K. L. McGinn and A. Keros, "Improvisation and the Logic of Exchanges in Embedded Negotiations," *Administrative Science Quarterly*, 2002, *47*, 442–473.

21. See J. R. Curhan, M. A. Neale, L. Ross, and J. Rosencrantz-Engelmann, "The O. Henry Effect: The Impact of Relational Norms on Negotiation Outcomes," submitted for publication, 2004.

CHAPTER SEVEN

Identity, Beliefs, Emotion, and Negotiation Success

Clark Freshman

Identity, beliefs, and emotion can all be unpopular topics. Backlashes against "identity" politics fill both the popular and academic press. It is easy to think of identity as just another roadblock to negotiation. Economists might think of it, as they largely do of emotion, as just another "barrier" to rational settlement. So, too, psychologists often treat beliefs as problems. Popular psychologies, such as neurolinguistic programming, speak often of limiting beliefs,[1] and social psychologists regularly inventory our many mistaken psychological biases.[2] Apart from any more particular criticisms, identity, beliefs, and emotion face skepticism for seeming too soft, either because the concepts themselves are soft or the insights are not particularly useful.

This chapter instead shows that particular identities, beliefs, and emotions affect negotiation in complicated ways, which may be understood through both qualitative and quantitative methods. Some versions of identity, beliefs, and emotion may indeed be dysfunctional and disruptive, but useful versions also exist. The contrast is often between fixed versions of each and flexible versions of each. Our fixed identity—I must do this because this is who I am—can look a lot like just another example of positional bargaining. Indeed, some identities may harden into particularly rigid positions when people equate identity with

I am grateful to Sue Ann Campbell and Barbara Cuadras for their usual excellent help at locating and retrieving many interdisciplinary sources and to Michael Douglas for his careful editing and researching.

moral commands. In times of conflict, with ourselves or with others, many people have come to ask, "What would Jesus do?" (or "What would Buddha do?").[3] This may provide a refreshing counterweight to the sometimes amoral practices of negotiation, and it may at other times exaggerate conflict: "I must do this because this is who I am; if I act differently, I am not merely losing a negotiation, I am betraying myself." And when the identity is linked to a group, then one is betraying one's family, one's nation, one's religion, and so on.

One may view emotions as fixed: a person is not being difficult, he or she is a difficult person; not sad but depressed; not annoyed but a rageaholic. So, too, beliefs may become a part of one's identity: Are you prochoice or are you prolife? rather than What restrictions do you think make sense on reproduction?

A competing notion views identity, emotions, and beliefs not as fixed but rather as a set of forces, sometimes competing and sometimes complementary. According to this view, we do not identify solely by religion or by family but by religion, family, friendship, profession, and many other sources. This chapter reveals the dichotomy of those competing notions. At times my voice is the objective researcher, as you may read in your own capacity. I shift language to invite you to experience, too, your role as an individual negotiating, mediating, and otherwise living in this world.

To illustrate, consider two scenes:

Scene One: Carrie Menkel-Meadow, a contributor to this and many volumes on dispute resolution, gets a call from a colleague on her law faculty. The colleague says someone has a problem, and the colleague thinks that Carrie would want to help. "Why me?" Carrie asks. The simple reply: "Well, you are a woman." Carrie does not like the assumption that she would always want to help any woman, any time, with any grievance. She does not help and does not sound very warm when she tells me about the colleague.

Scene Two: Woody Allen is in bed with a woman. More intimacy seems imminent. Then more people appear—his parents on his side of the bed, her parents on her side of the bed. It is a visual enactment of a common therapeutic insight: when lovers come together, they bring with them all of their family history.[4] So, too, that may partially explain why legal disputes between couples and families become so explosive. The conflicts are not merely between individual family members but in the inner worlds of family members.

The scenes illustrate several important points about identity and negotiation. First, there are two related but distinct aspects of identity. Identity includes the way others identify us (such as seeing us as a woman or as a woman's advocate), and identity also includes how we see ourselves, including the competing claims on how we see ourselves. At one level, the Menkel-Meadow story tells us that the way others perceive our identity may matter. The Woody Allen scene tells us that how we perceive ourselves also matters.

Second, the two scenes exemplify the fixed and fluid understandings of identity. The faculty colleague sees a prominent scholar of dispute resolution, legal ethics, and other areas as a woman; the woman sees herself as more complex. So, too, the Woody Allen example offers a *more* complex picture: there are six competing identities (the two lovers and two parents for each). It also offers a richer possibility, too, of transforming and evolving identities. From the mix, a couple may form. (And, to go a step further, from their encounter, a new child might literally be born!)

At a third level, the scenes highlight how pervasively identity may matter. As with emotion, it is easy to see only intense versions—little seems more intense in our Western culture than sex. Carefully crafted studies of negotiation, however, show that those induced to be in a slightly better mood (by such things as exposure to a funny video or a mildly pleasant scent) perform better than other negotiators in otherwise identical situations.[5]

This chapter shows how even mild differences in beliefs, identities, and emotions matter. The most quantitative research deals with emotion, but it is suggestive of how other mild differences may matter as well. It is not merely in the emotionally extreme world of divorce negotiation that emotion matters. Carrie's story shows that identity may affect much of our everyday life. This may be easier for those outsiders in some sense (by race, gender, sexual orientation, and so on) to appreciate than others. (And some of us privileged in much of our daily lives may find ourselves feeling like outsiders when we negotiate with unfamiliar groups, or in unfamiliar places, or both.) When we fit in completely, our own identity may be invisible, much as we think of some food as "ethnic" because it is different from our familiar food, though we can see that even something as "all-American" as roast beef has its own ethnic roots.[6] In part because different readers themselves experience identity differently, some of the examples that follow may provoke "aha" reactions in some while others may conclude that "identity" is not explaining anything more than individual differences or individual context.

For both emotion and identity, seeing how even mild versions matter is crucial: it is far easier to imagine actually managing mild versions of either than something deeply rooted. As with so many tasks, various outsiders in various times may find shifting how others identify them as relatively hard. A New Yorker in California may ease rapport by dressing differently, but many African Americans believe their skin color marks the way others see them.

Examples may yoke theory to practice for some while others may still dismiss identity as mere politics and rhetoric. The following section of this chapter situates identity, beliefs, and emotion in the worlds of both critical theory and social science. It presents evidence both that identity may matter and that identity may not be fixed. The chapter then examines how identity and beliefs may affect negotiation in more particular ways. It concludes by addressing the question of how we may better manage the complex relationship between beliefs, emotion, and identity. Those who find little value in reading about problems that remain insoluble might start with the final section, which introduces several techniques for better managing beliefs, emotion, and identity.

MANY FLOURS, MANY BREADS: THE COMPETING SOURCES OF IDENTITY AND BELIEF

Many people see identities as fixed. Both popular and academic negotiation trainings use tests designed to identify individuals with certain negotiation "types." Sometimes this involves identifying others with a particular set of identities and beliefs. For example, one seminar claimed that people's body types matched their personalities and negotiation styles. Others promise insight into oneself. Participants answer questions for a few minutes, and the test returns a label of one's negotiation "personality" as if it were his or her single identity. The widely used Thomas-Kilmann conflict styles inventory is one such test.[7] Often, these tests box people in. One otherwise great book on negotiation puts it simply, quoting a Danish proverb that you must bake with the flour you have.[8]

This emphasis on fixed identities runs counter to research from several disciplines, including critical theories such as postmodernism and the social sciences of psychology and economics. It is worth exploring these several methods since some may place greater faith in one method than in another. Also, many may find it more persuasive when several methods point in the same direction— what the philosopher Rawls called an "overlapping consensus."[9]

Adherents of postmodernism might challenge the metaphor of baking a bread with a single "flour." Many speak of postmodern conditions in which people interact with more cultures and have more opportunities to develop different and diverse ideas.[10] This means people may collaborate, problem solve, and resolve conflict in different ways. People may behave one way when they interact in a small legal community, for example, and may behave in other ways in different conditions. People who are relatively cooperative in one-on-one interactions may find themselves more self-confident and more willing to explore collaborative options—or even competitive strategies—in an online environment.[11] So, too, the relative masking of identity by technology may short-circuit the way negotiators might otherwise label each other.

Though postmodern critical theories sound very different, some economic and business perspectives make similar points about the fluidity of identity. Max Bazerman of Harvard Business School, and a contributor to this volume, emphasizes how individuals may sometimes have to negotiate with different versions of themselves at any given point.[12] Others emphasize change over time. Richard

Posner, one of the foremost scholars in the field of law and economics and a prominent federal appeals court judge, emphasizes the problem of future selves: the Richard Posner today may not make the best decisions for the Richard Posner tomorrow because that Richard Posner may have evolved in some way.[13]

Psychological research also complicates the way we identify both ourselves and others. Take competition and cooperation, for example. Where Thomas-Kilmann and other personality tests might divide people into competitors, accommodators, and so on, modern psychology suggests circumstances will bring out different aspects of the same person. One study shows that people given positive feedback on a brief test feel slightly happier and behave more cooperatively than an identical group of people given negative feedback.[14] Indeed, psychologists call the tendency to think others act as they do because of personality—as opposed to different contexts—the *ultimate* attribution error.[15] This insight is not merely Western. Buddhist psychology teaches that there is no fixed personality but rather ever-changing beliefs and feelings sometimes called mind-states.[16]

Although psychological research undermines the traditional tendency to identify ourselves with fixed personality types, it also recognizes how very readily we get stuck in the way we view those unlike ourselves in some way. It is relatively easy to see subtleties in ourselves, such as explaining why we may have acted "out of anger" or otherwise not "been ourselves." When we see negative behavior in others, it's more likely we will identify that as some pervasive trait. However well-intentioned, simple-minded trainings about "diversity" or "cultural competence" may inadvertently reinforce stereotypes.[17] This can include stereotypes of how "they" "always" negotiate. Psychologists do not treat the tendency to overgeneralize about others as some idiosyncratic fault of any of us. Rather, any given set of "us" tends to see any given set of "them" as having more in common with each other than they actually have. Psychologists call this the "outgroup homogeneity effect."[18] If we are American, we know there are many Americans and many negotiation styles, from the used car dealer to the obsequious custom tailor, but we may too quickly accept descriptions of "the" Japanese (or Latin, or European, and so on) negotiation style.

As with many general tendencies, of course, some of us may fall into such generalizing patterns more readily, more often, or more deeply. Academic psychologists have developed sophisticated methods to test automatic and unconscious beliefs about others, such as how quickly we associate "white" with "good" and "black" with "bad."[19]

To complicate matters further, psychological research recognizes how the way people identify each other may involve many different combinations. It would be easy for the woman academic whose colleague asks her to help "another woman" to conclude she was seen as "just another woman." Pioneering research by Rosabeth Kanter on organizations, however, showed that people may have several distinct categories in which to see different women, albeit all of them disempowering in some way. Women could be seen as nurturing "mothers," as insensitive "iron maidens," or as other stereotypes.[20] Perhaps the faculty member in the earlier example thought that one woman would nurture another, or that one woman would avenge another. Other psychological research shows that similar distinct stereotypes may apply to older people.[21] Susan Fiske, a leading scholar on the psychology of discrimination, concludes more generally that characteristics may combine in practically any way to create distinct "subtypes" of different individuals.[22]

This psychological fluidity, as we will see in the final section, is not merely a problem. It is sometimes possible to create new ways for people to see themselves and others that promote cooperation, such as emphasizing certain common identities. This positive aspect of fluid identities is also recognized by some who speak of postmodern conditions.

HOW IDENTITY AFFECTS NEGOTIATION

Identity, beliefs, and emotion may affect negotiation in multiple ways. To begin with, there are the simple effects of how others identify us and how we perceive ourselves. In complicated ways, initial senses of identity may interact with emotion. As we see in this section, how we perceive ourselves may often intensify the negative role of identity, along with negative emotions. As the next section suggests, however, awareness of emotion also offers one path to shift from fixed identities to more fluid and functional identities.

Negotiation and How Others Identify Us

Simply put, research confirms what many minorities fear: various "outsiders," such as women and African Americans, often get worse outcomes in negotiations. At least one careful meta-analysis of many studies involving women and male business students shows that women often get worse outcomes.[23] Do such different outcomes also exist outside simulated negotiation in schools? Ayres found that some outsiders got worse deals from real car dealers as well. He sent out teams of car buyers to test this. They dressed the same; they followed similar bargaining strategies; they answered questions in similar ways. And they got different results. African American men got offers that left four times more profit to dealers than did white men; African American women also did worse. White women did not do worse in a statistically significant sense.[24]

Looking at the pattern of offers and time spent with customers, Ayres argued that the different offers grew out of different beliefs. Salespeople acted as if they thought African American women simply did not like to bargain. When they negotiated with African American men, however, they spent plenty of time bargaining—just with much worse offers. It was as if salespeople took some pleasure in putting African American men in their place, according to Ayres.[25]

How these patterns play out in other negotiations is an important question for future research. In principle, many scholars associated with critical race theory, an important movement in law schools and other disciplines, see discrimination as "societal" and "structural," so one would expect similar patterns of discrimination across society.[26] Ayres's other economic and empirical work has found different results in at least one area: African American men and women and Hispanic men received better jail bond rates than whites.[27] Economic perspectives, such as Ayres's, suggest that patterns of discrimination may vary according to such circumstances as different degrees of information that outsiders may have, as well as perceptions in different circumstances. Different outcomes in different circumstances also fit the psychological perspective on the way individuals may be seen in many subtypes.[28] Seeing women through the mothering subtype perspective may hurt in job negotiations, in which employers may assume women will work less hard or simply accept less pay, but may actually help in other circumstances, such as child custody negotiations.

How Conceptions of Self-Identity May Limit Us

Apart from how others see us, how we see ourselves also affects negotiation. Sometimes we see ourselves as people who must bargain, sometimes we see ourselves as people who cannot bargain—or *ought* not. Recall the controversy over deploying American troops through Turkey to attack Iraq. When reports of a request for compensation arose, some Americans were offended that Turkish leaders would bargain over support. Different perspectives on identity might provide an explanation: some Americans might think it wrong to bargain over what might be seen as a moral issue, at least once some publicity arose. Alternatively, some Turks might have originally thought it necessary to bargain for a concession from the Americans rather than be seen as merely an extension of American will.

This same dynamic is *one* way to understand why individuals, too, may bargain when they do. Bazerman reveals how he and others may sometimes spend time bargaining excessively over an item as if their time had no value.[29] This may seem irrational from an economic view. But an identity analysis suggests that an individual might bargain because he or she identifies as a negotiator and, at some level of consciousness, feels bound to negotiate whenever possible. Psychologists might see this as yet another example of the consistency principle—people may feel that they must be consistent with some identity.[30]

Identity may limit individuals from bargaining in other circumstances as well. Gerald Williams tells the story of an American looking in a shop in Italy.[31] She liked an item, asked the price, and started to pay. The Italian would have none of it and showed her out. Williams explained this as a product of the shopkeeper's personal sense of insult that someone would not pay him the respect of bargaining. Notice as well that identity may have exacerbated the problem: seeing an American treating him in such a way may have exaggerated his fears of personal insult, an insult perceived as not just to himself but to those with whom he identified, be they Italians or shopkeepers or some other identity. Without blaming either the woman or the shopkeeper, we might see that the woman might have wanted to bargain too little and the shopkeeper too much.

Evidence suggests that many may bargain far less than the expected outcomes might justify. The title of one book suggests women often do worse because "women don't ask."[32] When male graduate students get their first academic job, they ask for more (salary, support, and so on) than women often do.[33] But research suggests that men may also negotiate too little in some circumstances. For example, large numbers of men also pass up parental leave policies that cover fathers, for various possible reasons discussed in the following paragraphs.[34] In different contexts, then, different individuals and different groups may find themselves bargaining far more or far less than others might see as appropriate.

We may understand these dynamics in two very different ways. Economists might offer a rational explanation. Women settling for less salary and men turning down the opportunity to care for children may seem irrational if one focuses on the payoff of those individual decisions. Economists, however, might redirect our attention to the way both men and women may try to signal something about themselves. Men and women may turn down leave to "signal" that they are the kind of people who work harder (or, from another perspective, that they will not slack on the "mommy" or "daddy" tracks).[35]

Feminists and other critical perspectives offer a rather different explanation that may be tied to identity. Men may turn down leave lest they be seen as what one state governor has called "girly-men." In some sense, then, women's sense of identity may enable them to take leave—or bargain for additional leave—when men's might not. As in so many other fields, however, outsiders face "double-binds" that insiders do not.[36] Many bosses may simply praise the man who turns down leave as a dedicated professional, but the woman who does the same may look like a "bad mother." And if someone cannot be a good mother, then she may be seen as cold and unreasonable. Men who bargain over wages may seem "savvy," but women may seem too pushy or domineering, too consistent with the iron maiden stereotype.

Sometimes the refusal to bargain, and the role of identity, may remain unconscious, and sometimes it may operate quite consciously. After University of Chicago Professor of Law Mary Anne Case read Ayres's evidence of car-bargaining studies, she did not want to buy a car—even if she might compensate for the bias by adopting different tactics.[37] (Ayres quoted one economist as suggesting women might get better deals by using feminine wiles.[38]) African

American law professor Devon Carbado writes that he could avoid being trailed in record stores (as if he were shoplifting) if he were to hum opera—thereby invoking a status as a "good black."[39] This might seem easy enough, and yet Carbado and others associated with critical race theory rightly note how problematic it may feel to "work identity" in such ways.[40] So, too, economist Ayres thinks it unfair to ask negotiators of some races or genders to adopt more cumbersome tactics to get better negotiation results. As he puts it, "It may be that black and female testers could also have received the price quoted to white males if they had executed twenty push-ups during the course of bargaining. If so, the fact that the white male testers did not have to execute the push-ups to receive the price would clearly constitute discrimination."[41]

Identity, Beliefs, and the Emotional Escalator

Ultimately, negotiations often play out through a network of interrelated identities, beliefs, and emotions. Your identity may entail certain beliefs (for example, people should not treat me differently because I am a woman/man). These beliefs may even include more elaborate scripts, sets of beliefs about how one should negotiate—such as the Italian shopkeeper's.[42] Often beliefs remain unconscious. They may remain what cognitive therapists call automatic thoughts.[43] When another negotiator violates your beliefs, you may experience an emotion, such as anger.[44] (Notice, as you read the shift from "one" to "you," how your identity now may shift from academic researcher or trainer or negotiation student to the more personal experience of your own negotiations.) If we do not understand the relationship between identity, emotion, and beliefs, we get stuck in fixed senses of ourselves, of others, and of negotiations themselves. If we do understand this relationship, then we have multiple possibilities to improve negotiations.

Sometimes emotions from a negotiation introduce or exaggerate the role of identity. Your anger, and the behavior your anger generates, may bring out certain other emotions and behaviors in others. Peter Kramer, the celebrated author of *Listening to Prozac*, notes how such dynamics might play out in a therapist's office: a somewhat shy patient sees a doctor; the doctor asks questions; the shy patient demurs; the doctor asks more; the patient may seem more reticent, or may get angry. In turn, the doctor suspects the patient may be paranoid and may treat him or her more aggressively, thereby making the patient still more defensive and guarded.[45] Negotiations may follow parallel tracks: one woman may think it's best to offer a single, fair price, but the male seller may think it's natural for people to follow a more elaborate dance of offers and counteroffers.[46] The dance becomes a brawl, the man feeling that the woman "doesn't understand" the "give and take" or may be "stubborn." The woman may think the man is trying to take advantage of her. Even if identity did not play any role to begin with, the intensity of emotion may lead one party to start seeing a "naive woman" and the other to see another "angry man."

STRATEGIES FOR MANAGING IDENTITIES, BELIEFS, AND EMOTIONS

This complex network (beliefs, emotions, sensations, and behaviors) offers several possibilities for negotiators to better meet their goals. Just as the problem of identity might be seen from several perspectives (critical theory, psychology, economics) so, too, solutions come from many approaches. These include traditional cognitive strategies as well as less traditional strategies based on emotional awareness and management, including mindfulness and awareness of nonverbal expressions of emotion.

Traditional negotiation theory and training emphasize thinking differently, or what psychologists would call purely *cognitive* strategies. Years of negotiation training rest on ideas that insights will set us free: teach students to be aware of dysfunctional biases such as reactive devaluation,[47] and students will shed the patterns.[48] But research suggests mere awareness may not change the behavior.[49] When negotiation students learn one lesson through a simulation, they often fail to apply the lesson in the next negotiation—unless the instructor makes the analogy quite explicit.[50]

Sometimes individual negotiators may invoke more useful identities to help negotiations. Gilson and Mnookin, for example, suggest that parties might sometimes choose bargaining agents, such as particular lawyers, because they have a reputation for collaborative bargaining.[51] So, too, individual negotiators might invoke a reputation for fairness, or a common membership in some trade, small professional group, or other community. In both ways, individuals may try to invoke one identity rather than other identities that might engender irrational competition or undermine collaborative solutions.

Sometimes cognitive strategies work better with third parties. Much research now makes clear that parties often discount the offers made by other parties. This is the much-studied phenomenon of reactive devaluation.[52] We can also see this as identity and emotion at work: how seriously can we consider an offer from "them"? If you are like most people, you'll value the same offer more if instead a "neutral" mediator suggests it. In other contexts, too, third parties such as mediators may help shape identities to achieve different results. Think again of the different outcomes men and women achieve in negotiation. When business school students were merely told that men and women negotiated differently, women did worse in the negotiations.[53] However, when students were told that they were all successful and skilled business students, men and women negotiated more equally.[54]

Applying this exact intervention may work with many groups of relatively equal parties but may pose problems in other contexts. For example, does it help to tell an abused woman she can bargain well, when in fact she might be best advised to opt out of mediation?

In other ways, though, mediators may help mold the identity of parties. Many family mediators put pictures of children in the middle of the table to remind parties that they are not merely feuding ex-lovers with a tangled past but coparents with a common future. Other mediators work through community organizations that stress other identities, such as mediation provided by Orthodox Jewish organizations, Islamic mediation, and, more recently, mediation through gay and lesbian community centers.[55] Some mainstream mediators stress ideas such as "cultural competence."[56] For some, that competence means sensitivity to things such as the way some Asian families may favor male over female children. The danger, of course, is that third parties may emphasize identities that promote one party over another, or one unrepresented person (a daughter) over another (a son). In today's complex times, when parties may present themselves with many different potential identities—and when mediators may know of many other possibilities (for example, feminist perspectives for women from traditional cultures)—some mediators retreat to a kind of passive neutrality, merely mirroring what the parties say. This so-called neutrality, however, may simply have the effect of preserving older identities, or strengthening the more verbally insistent party.[57]

Instead, active kinds of neutrality may put competing identities on more equal ground.[58] Mediators may identify several ways similar parties may approach similar problems. This gives parties ideas and different kinds of identities to enable choices.[59] The Asian mother who wants equal treatment for a daughter need not see herself as a "rebel" or "eccentric" but instead as a "feminist." She does not stand alone against her community; she stands with a community of women.

EMERGING INTERVENTIONS: EMOTIONAL AWARENESS, MINDFULNESS, AND NONVERBAL COMMUNICATION

Given all the limits to purely cognitive interventions, you might consider other strategies. The more that we see that our identities, beliefs, and emotions are not fixed, the more we will want tools to make us aware of potential shifts. So, too, we will want some tools to try to induce shifts to more enabling identities, beliefs, and emotions.

Emotional Awareness and Simple Emotional Shifts

Consider again the importance of brief emotions. We already saw that very small effects, such as a pleasant sound, a funny video, or a pleasant scent, shift our emotions enough to influence the way we negotiate. Other research also shows that brief changes affect how we categorize and blame others. In one recent study, when people were angry, they were more likely to blame those they had been trained to see as different.[60] This difference could be far milder than the race and gender differences we usually think about. In one recent experiment, for example, participants took a brief test and were told they were either "overestimators" or "underestimators"—not based on the test, as it turns out, but just through random assignment.[61] When some of the participants were induced to be angry, they were more likely to show signs of having unconscious negative stereotypes of the "other" kinds of estimators! Fear of exactly this reaction may partially explain why women and other outsiders may negotiate less: they may fear bargaining will trigger negative emotions in others, and the negative emotion may activate disabling stereotypes.

Given the importance of small emotional shifts, then, the simplest interventions to help with identity and beliefs would be to manage moods in ourselves and others. You might try a simple extension of the basic research: when negotiating or working with others, try to induce a more pleasant environment through sounds, smells, sights, and so on.

Mindfulness

If we could be more aware of the shifting emotions, beliefs, and identities in ourselves and others, such interventions might be more effective. Mindfulness practices may help us notice our own shifts, and may enhance our awareness of nonverbal expression of emotions in ourselves. It may also help us notice emotional shifts in others.

Briefly put, mindfulness involves awareness of moment-by-moment thoughts, physical sensations, emotions, and intentions. That awareness is in a particular way, moment-by-moment, fully accepting and free from judgment.[62] In some sense, mindfulness is also an end goal, like a healthy heart or an appropriate weight. And like those other physical goals, different people may arrive at mindfulness in different ways, much as some people may diet (in any number of ways), others may exercise (also in any number of ways), and others may combine both. So, too, mindfulness might involve sitting and paying attention to passing thoughts, or walking and noticing physical sensations, or stretching in yoga poses and noticing physical and mental changes.

However developed, mindfulness works to manage identity and emotion in three complementary ways. Partly it is a cognitive tool. Mindfulness of our own thoughts lets us know when we are identifying with one or another of our various identities or ways of viewing the world. For example, someone might be aware of particular thoughts, such as thinking, "What would Donald Trump do?" or "What would Jesus do?" Mindfulness of the body also gives us a way of knowing when we are experiencing certain kinds of physical tension—this may be a signal in turn that one is experiencing an emotion—possibly from a sense of identity violation or some belief. We may get angry at a car dealership and, as we reflect on the anger, discover an expectation that—despite so much of what we have heard and seen—somehow the negotiation should go faster, smoother.

Second, mindfulness gives us information on the exact kinds of changes in sounds, scents, food, and others that may affect our own mood. This is important information: studies rest on the generalizations that some changes make most people feel better, but not all. Certain sounds and smells that made most people feel a certain way in studies may not induce that effect in all of us. Mindfulness lets us discover our own individual triggers.

Third, mindfulness practices *may* themselves *sometimes* shift moods and identities. One tool for developing mindfulness is to meditate in particular ways, such as concentrating on one object (one's breath or one's footsteps). One expands to accepting awareness of thoughts, sensations, and so on once one has achieved a certain balance. Research shows such simple meditations have profound physical effects: eight weeks of regular meditation tend to shift brain patterns toward the left part of the brain, a region associated with more happiness and positive emotion.[63] This shift lingers even when one is not actually meditating. Simply put, if you meditate, you may not even need to think to overcome the identity-belief-emotion network; you may simply feel happier and approach problems more flexibly. There is some evidence that you can get some of these automatic benefits from other kinds of meditation as well.[64] Others suggest that mindfulness practices themselves tend to dissolve the identification with ourselves as separate and to promote a sense of connection with others. An important caveat: experienced meditation teachers caution that practices unfold in sometimes unpredictable cycles, so one may sometimes sit in meditation to return to the peace of some pleasant sitting only to discover that the current sitting is not as pleasant, or even unpleasant.[65]

Nonverbal Communication of Emotion in Ourselves and Others

Training in nonverbal awareness of emotion offers another alternative. Paul Ekman's pioneering work on nonverbal expression of emotion has shown that several distinct emotions all involve distinct physical sensations and facial expressions. When you feel contempt, for example, you will tend to smile with only one side of your face.[66] When you are angry, you may feel physical sensations of warmth; your eyelids may draw down, but your eyes will remain open and glare.[67] For those practicing mindfulness meditation, Ekman's teachings provide tools to recognize emotions more quickly and precisely through physical sensations and, of course, a chance to test for yourself whether his research fits your experience.

Learning to see how the rapidly changing expressions of others reveal emotions can be a powerful tool. Over time, for example, one may learn to recognize the very quick facial changes that mark the very beginnings of emotions such as anger. Ongoing research suggests individual patterns differ in how quickly anger arises, but at least some individuals display anger briefly before it escalates fully.[68] If you are mediating a dispute and notice some of the telltale signs of anger, this may be a time to take a break, rather than to press on. As an additional cross-cultural benefit, Ekman's research over decades confirms that these same nonverbal markers reveal emotions not just in American or Western cultures but even in cultures as distant (from most readers of this book) as that of Papua New Guinea.[69]

As with mindfulness, there is a caveat: Ekman often cautions that knowing that someone is experiencing an emotion does not tell us why. If someone you see as your opponent shows contempt with a half smile, it could be contempt for your offer or contempt for himself as he realizes how little he has prepared. But such cautions apply to all information: when someone says, "And that's my final offer," we know it very well might not be.

CONCLUSION: IDENTITY, BELIEFS, EMOTION, AND NEGOTIATOR COMPETENCE

Identity is not about political correctness. Identity, beliefs, and emotion work together to shape our thoughts and actions in negotiations—and our lives. Scientific research now confirms this. This remains particularly true for various outsiders who may face disadvantages in negotiation. It is also true in the many ways that even mild shifts in our identities, beliefs, and emotions may affect how we negotiate. This is both a peril and a potential: the identity-belief-emotion trio often readily shifts for ourselves, and (to some degree) for the way others perceive us. With such insight, we may work to avoid restricting identities, emotions, and beliefs and to develop instead enabling ones in ourselves and in others.

Notes

1. See J. O'Connor and J. Seymour, *Introducing NLP: Psychological Skills for Understanding and Influencing People* (London: Thomson, 1990).

2. See, for example, M. H. Bazerman, *Judgment in Managerial Decisionmaking* (New York: John Wiley & Sons, 1994); and R. H. Mnookin, S. R. Peppet, and A. S. Tulumello, *Beyond Winning: Negotiating to Create Value in Deals and Disputes* (Cambridge, Mass.: Belknap Press of Harvard University Press, 2000).

3. See, for example, F. A. Metcalfe, *What Would Buddha Do? 101 Answers to Life's Daily Dilemmas* (Berkeley, Calif.: Seashore, 1999); N. Harrison, *365 WWJD: Daily*

Answers to What Would Jesus Do? (New York: HarperCollins, 1998); and C. M. Sheldon, G. W. Sheldon, and D. Morris, *In His Steps, What Would Jesus Do?* (New York: Inspirational Press, 1998). See also 1 John 2:6 ("The one who says he resides in God ought himself to walk just as Jesus walked.").

4. See P. D. Kramer, *Should You Leave?* (New York: Scribner, 1997). The scene described is from the movie *Annie Hall,* Woody Allen (director), MGM/UA Studios, 1977.

5. For a review, see C. Freshman, A. Hayes, and G. Feldman, "The Lawyer-Negotiator as Mood Scientist: What We Know and Don't Know About How Mood Relates to Successful Negotiation," *Journal of Dispute Resolution,* 2002, *1,* 1–79. For a recent study of how the very mild differences in emotions affect the success of law students, see C. Freshman, A. Hayes, and G. Feldman, "When 'Not Too Bad' May Not Be Good Enough: A Theoretical and Empirical Exploration of Efficient Emotion and Law Student Success at Grades, Negotiation, and Mental Health," unpublished paper, Faculty of Law, University of Miami, 2004. (Available on request from clark_freshman@post.harvard.edu)

6. See K. W. Crenshaw, "Foreword: Toward a Race-Conscious Pedagogy in Legal Education," *National Black Law Journal,* 1989, *11,* 1–14; see also M. R. Mahoney, "Whiteness and Remedy: Under-Ruling Civil Rights *Inwalker v. City of Mosquite,*" *Cornell Law Review,* 2000, *85*(5), 1309–1357.

7. See G. R. Shell, *Bargaining for Advantage: Negotiation Strategies for Reasonable People* (New York: Viking, 1999).

8. See Shell, *Bargaining for Advantage,* 1999.

9. See J. Rawls, *Political Liberalism* (New York: Columbia University Press, 1993).

10. See, for example, J. Simon, "Inevitable Dependencies: A Comment on Martha A. Fineman, The Neutered Mother, the Sexual Family, and Other Twentieth Century Tragedies," *Columbia Journal of Gender & Law,* 1995, *5,* 152–165; and P. M. Rosenau, *Post-Modernism and the Social Sciences: Insights, Inroads, and Intrusions* (Princeton, N.J.: Princeton University Press, 1992). Paraphrasing Pauline Rosenau, Menkel-Meadow points to the distinction "between more sceptical, nihilistic post-moderns who believe that 'truth' is always partial, transitory, and uncertain, and affirmative postmoderns who instead seek to broaden and increase the methods of knowledge acquisition." See C. Menkel-Meadow, "The Trouble with the Adversary System in a Postmodern, Multicultural World," *William and Mary Law Review,* 1996, *38,* pp. 15–16.

11. Some psychologists note that online communication "allows its users to inflict pain without being forced to see its effect" and may "incite a deeper level of meanness." See A. Harmon, "Internet Gives Teenage Bullies Weapons to Wound from Afar," *New York Times,* Aug. 26, 2004, p. A 1.

12. M. H. Bazerman, *Judgement in Managerial Decision Making* (5th ed.) (New York: John Wiley & Sons, 2002).

13. See R. A. Posner, "Are We One Self or Multiple Selves?" *Legal Theory,* 1997, *3,* 23–27; see also R. A. Posner, *Aging and Old Age* (Chicago: University of Chicago Press, 1995).

14. See J. P. Forgas, "On Feeling Good and Getting Your Way: Mood Effects on Negotiator Cognition and Bargaining Strategies," *Journal of Personality & Social Psychology*, 1998, *74*, 565–577.

15. See L. Ross and R. E. Nisbett, *The Person and the Situation: Perspectives of Social Psychology* (Philadelphia: Temple University Press, 1991).

16. For a relatively easy introduction to this idea, see J. Goldstein, *Insight Meditation: The Path of Freedom* (Boston: Shambhala, 1994).

17. For a survey and criticism, see C. Freshman, "Prevention Perspectives on 'Different' Kinds of Discrimination: From Attacking Different 'Isms' to Promoting Acceptance in Critical Race Theory, Law and Economics, and Empirical Research," *Stanford Law Review*, 2003, *55*, 2293–2347.

18. See C. Freshman, "Whatever Happened to Anti-Semitism? How Social Science Theories Identify Discrimination and Promote Coalitions Between 'Different' Minorities," *Cornell Law Review*, 2000, *85*, 313–442.

19. See, for example, one version of such an implicit association test, Implicit Association Test Corp, Harvard University, 2004 [https://implicit.harvard.edu/implicit/]. For general background on such tests, see also A. G. Greenwald, B. A. Nose, and M. R. Banaji, "Understanding and Using the Implicit Association Test: 1. An Improved Scoring Algorithm." *Journal of Personality and Social Psychology*, 2003, *859*(2), 197–216. On Ayres's recommendation of using the implicit association test in litigation and elsewhere, see I. Ayres, *Pervasive Prejudice? Unconventional Evidence of Race and Gender Discrimination* (Chicago: University of Chicago Press, 2001).

20. See R. M. Kanter, *Men and Women of the Corporation* (New York: Basic Books, 1977).

21. See A.J.C. Cuddy and S. T. Fiske, "Doddering but Dear: Process, Content, and Function in Stereotyping of Older Persons," in T. D. Nelson (ed.), *Ageism: Stereotyping and Prejudice Against Older Persons* (Cambridge, Mass.: MIT Press, 2002).

22. See S. T. Fiske, "Stereotyping, Prejudice, and Discrimination," in D. T. Gilbert, S. T. Fiske, and G. Lindzey (eds.), *The Handbook of Social Psychology*, Vol. 2 (Boston: McGraw-Hill, 1998).

23. See L. J. Kray, L. Thompson, and A. Galinsky, "Battle of the Sexes: Gender Stereotype Confirmation and Reactance in Negotiations," *Journal of Personality & Social Psychology*, 2001, *80*, 942–958.

24. See Ayres, *Pervasive Prejudice?* 2001.

25. See Ayres, *Pervasive Prejudice?* 2001.

26. See F. Valdes, J. M. Culp, and A. P. Harris, "Battles Waged, Won, and Lost: Critical Race Theory at the Turn of the Millennium," in F. Valdes, J. M. Culp, and A. P. Harris (eds.), *Crossroads, Directions, and a New Critical Race Theory* (Philadelphia: Temple University Press, 2002).

27. See Ayres, *Pervasive Prejudice?* 2001.

28. See Fiske, "Stereotyping, Prejudice, Discrimination," 1998.

29. See M. H. Bazerman, *Smart Money Decisions* (New York: John Wiley & Sons, 1999).

30. For a thorough psychological introduction, see R. B. Cialdini, *Influence: How and Why People Agree to Things* (New York: Morrow, 1984); and R. B. Cialdini, *Influence: The Psychology of Persuasion* (New York: Morrow, 1993). For a briefer introduction as applied to negotiators, see Shell, *Bargaining for Advantage,* 1999.

31. See G. R. Williams, "Negotiation as a Healing Process," *Journal of Dispute Resolution,* 1996, *1,* 1–66.

32. See L. Babcock and S. Laschever, *Women Don't Ask: Negotiation and the Gender Divide* (Princeton, N.J.: Princeton University Press, 2003).

33. See Babcock and Laschever, *Women Don't Ask,* 2003.

34. See C. Freshman, "Re-visioning the Dependency Crisis and the Negotiator's Dilemma: Reflections on the Sexual Family and the Mother-Child Dyad." *Law and Social Inquiry,* 1997, *22,* 97–129.

35. See A. M. Spence, *Market Signaling: Informational Transfer in Hiring and Related Screening Processes* (Cambridge, Mass.: Harvard University Press, 1974).

36. See, for example, M. J. Radin, "The Pragmatist and the Feminist," *Southern California Law Review,* 1990, *63,* 1699–1726.

37. See M. A. Case, "Developing a Taste for Not Being Discriminated Against," *Stanford Law Review,* 2003, *55,* 2273–2291.

38. See Ayres, *Pervasive Prejudice?* 2001.

39. D. Carbado, "Straight Out of the Closet: Race, Gender, and Sexual Orientation," in Valdes, Culp, and Harris (eds.), *Crossroads, Directions, and a New Critical Race Theory,* 2002.

40. See C. W. Carbado and M. Gulati, "Working Identity," *Cornell Law Review,* 2000, *85,* 1259–1308.

41. I. Ayres, "Fair Driving: Gender and Race Discrimination in Retail Car Negotiations," *Harvard Law Review,* 1991, 817, 832n45.

42. I use *scripts* here to refer to any set of expectations, including reasonable and functional expectations. Some psychologists, particularly psychoanalysts, use scripts more narrowly to describe maladaptive expectations based on inappropriate past situations that distort how one sees and behaves in the present. See, for example, P. Ekman, *Emotions Revealed: Recognizing Faces and Feelings to Improve Communication and Emotional Life* (New York: Times Books, 2003), p. 41.

43. See A. T. Beck, *Prisoners of Hate: The Cognitive Basis of Anger, Hostility, and Violence* (New York: HarperCollins, 1999).

44. See R. Kumar, "Affect, Cognition, and Decision Making in Negotiation: A Conceptual Integration," in M. A. Rahim, *Managing Conflict: An Interdisciplinary Approach* (New York: Praeger, 1989); and D. Stone, B. Patton, and S. Heen, *Difficult Conversations: How to Discuss What Matters Most* (New York: Viking, 1999).

45. See Kramer, *Should You Leave?* 1997.

46. See D. M. Kolb and J. Williams, *Everyday Negotiation: Navigating the Hidden Agendas in Bargaining* (San Francisco: Jossey-Bass, 2003).

47. "Reactive devaluation" refers to the way most of us value the identical offer less if made by an "opponent" rather than a neutral, like a mediator.

48. See K. J. Arrow, R. H. Mnookin, L. Ross, A. Tversky, and R. Wilson (eds.), *Barriers to Conflict Resolution* (New York: W. W. Norton, 1995).

49. See J. J. Gillespie, L. Thompson, J. Loewenstein, and D. Gentner, "Lessons from Analogical Reasoning in the Teaching of Negotiation," *Negotiation Journal,* October 1999, *15*(4), 363–371.

50. See Gillespie, Thompson, Loewenstein, and Gentner, "Lessons from Analogical Reasoning in the Teaching of Negotiation," 1999.

51. See R. J. Gilson and R. H. Mnookin, "Disputing Through Agents: Cooperation and Conflict Between Lawyers in Litigation," *Columbia Law Review,* 1994, *94,* 509–566.

52. See Arrow, Mnookin, Ross, Tversky, and Wilson (eds.), *Barriers to Conflict Resolution,* 1995. See also R. Korobkin and C. Guthrie, "Heuristics and Biases and the Bargaining Table," *Marquette Law Review,* 2004, *85,* 795–808.

53. See Kray, Thompson, and Galinsky, "Battle of the Sexes," 2001.

54. See Kray, Thompson, and Galinsky, "Battle of the Sexes," 2001.

55. See C. Freshman, "Privatizing Same-Sex 'Marriage' Through Alternative Dispute Resolution: Community-Enhancing Versus Community-Enabling Mediation," *U.C.L.A. Law Review,* 1997, *44,* pp. 1692–1695.

56. See A. Barsky, D. Este, and D. Collins, "Cultural Competence in Family Mediation," *Mediation Quarterly,* 1996, *13*(3), 167–178.

57. For critiques of such neutrality, see Freshman, "Privatizing Same-Sex 'Marriage' Through Alternative Dispute Resolution," 1997. See also J. R. Coben, "Gollum Meet Smeagol: A Schizophrenic Rumination on Mediator Values Beyond Self-Determination and Neutrality," *Cardozo Journal of Conflict Resolution,* 2004, *5*(2), 65–85.

58. See Freshman, "Privatizing Same-Sex 'Marriage' Through Alternative Dispute Resolution," 1997.

59. For a more complete discussion, see Freshman, "Privatizing Same-Sex 'Marriage' Through Alternative Dispute Resolution," 1997.

60. See D. DeSteno, N. Dasgupta, M. Y. Bartlett, and A. Cajdric, "Prejudice from Thin Air: The Effect of Emotion on Automatic Intergroup Attitudes," *Psychological Science,* 2004, *15*(5), 319–324.

61. See DeSteno, Dasgupta, Bartlett, and Cajdric, "Prejudice from Thin Air," 2004.

62. See J. Kabat-Zinn, "Full Catastrophe Living," in J. Kabat-Zinn, *Wherever You Go, There You Are* (New York: Hyperion, 1994).

63. See Health Emotions Research Institute, University of Wisconsin, October 2004. [http://www.healthemotions.org/research/index.html]. See also D. Goleman,

Destructive Emotions: How Can We Overcome Them? A Scientific Dialogue with the Dalai Lama (New York: Bantam Books, 2003).

64. See C. Freshman, A. Hayes, and G. Feldman, "Mindfulness in the Law and ADR: Adapting Meditation to Promote Negotiation Success: A Guide to Varieties and Scientific Support," *Harvard Negotiation Law Review,* 2002, *7,* 67–81.

65. See J. Goldstein, *Insight Meditation* (Boston: Shambhala Books, 2003); and Freshman, Hayes, and Feldman, "Mindfulness in the Law and ADR," 2002.

66. See P. Ekman, *Emotions Revealed* (New York: Times Books, 2003).

67. See Ekman, *Emotions Revealed,* 2003.

68. See P. Ekman, "Emotional Profiles," unpublished manuscript on file with the author, 2003.

69. See Ekman, "Emotional Profiles," 2003.

CHAPTER EIGHT

Cultural Pathways in Negotiation and Conflict Management

Anthony Wanis-St. John

"Centuries before there was any such a thing as a 'Western perspective on conflict resolution,' conflicts were being resolved peacefully. . . . We in the West are only now beginning to formalize an understanding of conflict based on a set of principles that have been known and practiced by people around the world for many years."[1]

Culture has inspired interest on the margins of research on bargaining and problem solving simply because it is fascinating—even to those who do not believe in its relevance. In the context of negotiation, culture presents an intriguing and elusive aggregated set of variables. Despite this sense of general curiosity, our knowledge about culture, negotiation, and conflict management is young and lacks a strong organizing framework. Researchers disagree, for example, on the kind, scope, and duration of impacts that culture has on the negotiation process.

This chapter proposes a framework for organizing the existing streams of literature and research. Within this framework, I advance the argument that, as negotiation theorists and practitioners, we have tended to ascribe either too much or too little to culture. I also argue that we should begin working on an alternative way of considering culture in terms of negotiation: we should begin exploring its possible positive contributions. The chapter describes two important theories that inform the way in which we deal with cultural differences at the negotiation table, debunks some myths about culture and negotiation, and uses this information to offer a tentative template useful for conducting cross-cultural negotiations. The chapter concludes by proposing further directions for research.

When negotiators come from different cultures, we should not assume that culture will necessarily be an obstacle to reaching agreement. Cultural differences present learning opportunities that can potentially enrich the negotiation.

Though not determinative of negotiation outcome, culture should be considered highly *relevant* to the ways in which we manage conflict. Culture can and should be seen as an *enabler* of conflict management practices, rather than as a cause of conflict or an obstacle to negotiation.

DEFINING CULTURE

The word *culture* has a controversial history in the social sciences and has had a variety of meanings over time. These differences in definition have an enormous impact on the way we understand the relevance of culture to human behavior.

Kevin Avruch surveyed the problematic history of the term *culture* and traces its evolution from a term of exclusion and racism to a concept that affirms the moral equivalence among the enormous variety of human groups and their behaviors, norms, and beliefs. Avruch divides culture into two categories: generic and local. *Generic culture* refers to universally held attributes of the species *Homo sapiens sapiens*. *Local culture* refers to "complex systems of meanings created, shared, and transmitted by individuals in particular social groups."[2] This distinction reflects the wider debate in anthropology between particularism and universalism. Particularists (from the tradition of interpretive anthropology) might argue that cultures are so unique and varied that they can only be understood on their own terms, from within their own contexts. A particularist might note, for example, that in some cultures a professor is shown a great amount of deference (students use formal titles to address the professor and may stand when the professor enters a room). In other cultures, teacher and student address each other on a first-name basis, and students may make very few if any gestures of deference. Universalists (rooted in the structuralist anthropology tradition) argue that even such seemingly different "cultural" behaviors are themselves indicators of universal phenomena (the cultural treatment of social rank).[3]

Culture has had at least three major definitional lives.[4] Victorians defined culture as an exclusive quality that some people express in their appreciation of the fine arts, manners, and constrained behavior. Culture later came to be associated with all people, but with qualitative differences; some people's cultures were depicted as civilized, while others were "savage" or "primitive." Most anthropologists and sociologists today understand culture as a universally held, but highly diversified attribute of humans, with moral equivalence among cultures.

Even today definitions of culture are highly varied. Organizational behavior specialists often point to Edgar Schein's argument that culture refers to the "shared mental models that the members of an organization hold and take for granted" and that facilitate its success.[5] Schein does not believe that organizational cultures are any less complex than national cultures. Faure and Sjostedt proposed that culture "is a set of shared and enduring meanings, values and beliefs that characterize national, ethnic, or other groups and orient their behavior."[6] Jeanne M. Brett and colleagues describe culture as "the unique profile of a group with respect to psychology (e.g., values, norms and behaviors) and social institutions (e.g., legal, economic and political structures)."[7]

Despite their differences, proponents of all three definitions agree that culture informs our collective identity and behavior. Culture is a mostly unconscious language.[8] It is multidimensional,[9] encompassing values, habits, norms, and language. Because it is primarily only shared with others who are members of the cultural group, it is usually of limited accessibility in a world of more than six billion people, thus fostering group unity. Further, cultures are dynamic and changing, especially where they come in contact with each other. Contact with those of another culture influences attitudes and behaviors. Culture is a universal human phenomenon, with local distinctiveness. An individual can belong to and be influenced by more than one culture, and can move in and out of cultural affiliations.

NEGOTIATION EMBEDDED IN CULTURE

Cultures, however we define them, can be thought of as pathways that we travel along in life. Much of what we do and see while on our culture path is influenced by the fact that we are on *that particular path.* Sometimes we leave well-known pathways and explore others. Culture also creates behavioral "pathways" that color our information processing and social actions without predetermining them in every instance. Individuals and groups can, after all, challenge assumptions, learn new behaviors, and set aside old ones. Our cultural identity is in this sense a kind of matrix in which conflict and conflict management behaviors can be embedded—but also from which they can escape.

People bargain and negotiate all over the world. And increasingly we do so with people whose values and behaviors are unfamiliar to us. Emigration, global commerce, exile, and tourism are just some of the classic circumstances under which we negotiate with people from other cultures. It comes as no surprise to anthropologists and sociologists that how we resolve our differences depends at least to some extent on macro-level shared group identity characteristics, such as ethnic culture, language, and religious beliefs. Cognitive and social psychologists affirm the roles of emotion, reciprocity, empathy, and assertiveness in the behaviors and processes of negotiation and conflict management. Even the casual observer sees that the range of our emotional expressions, the ways we feel persuaded, and the boundaries of our empathy and assertiveness for others can all be highly influenced by our cultural assumptions and preferences. In my culture, is it acceptable to challenge authority? Do I rely on legal norms, intuition, or practicalities to propose solutions to conflicts? How and when is it OK to share information about my priorities and interests? The answers to these and other questions are profoundly influenced by the cultural references on which the parties to a conflict can call.

"UNIVERSAL" DIMENSIONS OF CULTURE

Cultures, as defined earlier, are a universal phenomenon. All human beings emerge from and belong to some cultural grouping(s). And yet, paradoxically, cultures are the very essence of human uniqueness, permitting us to feel a sense of belonging to one ethnic group and not others (that is, Irish-American but not Mandarin Chinese, French-Canadian but not Bedouin Arab), a sense of belonging that is typically limited to members only.[10]

Cultures have been studied in a number of ways that emphasized either universality or uniqueness. Cultural anthropologists used to study cultures to seek out their unique aspects, rather than any characteristics they might share with other cultures. However, over time critical studies emerged that transcended the universalist-particularist divide in studies of culture by demonstrating how societies in fact confront a common set of problems. Each culture develops its own particular ways of resolving those problems.

Early insights about the universal dimensions of culture—the common challenges human societies confront, but to which they develop unique answers—included relationship to authority, conception of self as individual and as member of society, conception of self in terms of gender characteristics, and socially acceptable methods of dealing with conflict.[11]

Today one of the leading theorists in the field of organizational anthropology is Geert Hofstede, a Dutch researcher, whose work suggests the following set of five *universally present* but *culturally varied* dimensions of human behavior: [12]

Power Distance. *Power distance* refers to the degree to which members of a culture accept greater differences of power between the least and most powerful members of society. I believe it is highly relevant to many negotiation issues, including how negotiators are chosen, who gets to raise problems to be negotiated, the way in which parties are persuaded, the degree of deference shown among parties, and whether a party's members speak as a group or select a single, authoritative spokesperson.

Collectivism Versus Individualism. This dimension of human culture refers to the relative emphasis a society places on meeting individuals' needs over group needs. It thus affects the negotiation issues and goals brought to the table, their prioritization, and the ways in which information about those issues, such as interests, is shared. This dimension also works with power distance to influence the choice, role, and authority of negotiators.[13]

Masculinity Versus Femininity (Assertiveness Versus Modesty). Hofstede writes about a dichotomy in human behavior between modesty and assertiveness (with assertiveness serving essentially as a measure of aggressiveness). However, Hofstede's terminology of this phenomenon is gendered. While I find the identification of social modesty with femininity and the identification of social assertiveness with masculinity somewhat perplexing, Hofstede correctly points out that human cultures place different emphases on modesty and assertiveness and consider them appropriate in vastly different contexts. At the negotiation table, for example, modesty in demands and demeanor can be employed in the expectation of reciprocal modesty, and this could be problematic when not reciprocated or when misinterpreted as detachment from the outcome by a counterpart accustomed to assertiveness in behavior and claiming tactics.

This dichotomy provides a starting point for the cultural expectations of assertiveness at the negotiation table, but it is clearly just a start. Assertiveness, coupled with awareness of one's interests, has become a prescribed approach to interest-based negotiation. At the very least, cultural context should inform us about the impact our modest and assertive behaviors are likely to have on our negotiations. Assertive behaviors can be perceived, correctly or incorrectly, as tactics to claim value, while modest ones may be identified—again, correctly or incorrectly—with tactics to create value at the negotiation table.

Uncertainty Avoidance. *Uncertainty avoidance* describes the extent to which one is comfortable managing situations that present ambiguity. Intolerance of ambiguity can affect one's willingness to negotiate in the first place, since the outcome of a negotiation cannot be foreseen. Even for those who "get to the table," uncertainty avoidance affects such things as process choice, reliance on explicit rules versus creative solutions, the need for general principles versus detailed agreements, the form that commitment takes, the degree of implementation oversight sought by parties, the ability to tolerate deviance from the agreed upon terms, and even practicalities such as types of dispute resolution clauses acceptable to parties.[14] Uncertainty avoidance is a powerful cultural dimension that has received inadequate attention within the cross-cultural negotiation literature.

Long-Term Versus Short-Term Orientation. Hofstede's complex research on long-term versus short-term orientation helped to overcome a decidedly

"Western" bias in prior research on cultural differences. He and his colleagues found that some cultures emphasize short-term goals and gains over the long-term ones, and that other cultures prioritize the long term. Negotiators' behaviors, expectations, and interests, and even their assessment of the issues under consideration, are all affected by the timeframe they consider relevant.

For each of these five dimensions, Hofstede created indices ranking countries (and sometimes culturally similar groups of countries) relative to each other. Despite several shortcomings in his research, his work represents an empirical and highly valid contribution to our understanding of human cultures that permits negotiation research to go beyond the perpetuation of stereotypes.

ETHNORELATIVISM

Hofstede's insights are well complemented by those of Milton Bennett, who proposed that our ability to tolerate human cultural differences can be depicted in developmental stages. Bennett's work stems from the same tradition as that of Erikson, Freud, and others who have portrayed psychological and social growth in stages.[15] Bennett believes that there are six general stages of development in human tolerance, on a continuum from ethnocentrism to ethnorelativism. Ethnocentric stages proceed from the denial of intolerance to defensiveness about differences to the minimization of those differences.

Denial. At the most basic level of ethnocentrism, we remain either totally ignorant of other cultures or cling to the belief that our own culture is the basic template from which others come. We thus deny any intolerance. "Mine is the only culture."

Defense. If we have at least some awareness of other cultures and especially of their different norms, at this stage we tend to believe in the inferiority of others' ways and the superiority of our own. "Mine is the only good culture."

Minimization. In the final stage of ethnocentrism we are still unable to cope with the profound differences among cultures, but no longer feel the need to judge them so negatively. However, in so doing, we tend to incorrectly lump all people together. "We are all basically the same, despite some small differences."

I believe that most of us hover around this third, seemingly innocuous stage of ethnocentrism, in which we cover up cultural differences behind comfortable but universalist declarations of "oneness" because such differences seem difficult to discuss or understand. Much of negotiation research and practice is somewhat ethnocentric. To achieve better cross-cultural competence, we must move beyond this. Bennett's next three stages, his stages of ethnorelativism, proceed from acceptance of differences to adaptation to integration back-and-forth and into-and-out-of cultures.

> *Acceptance.* At the most basic stage of ethnorelativity, we set aside the denial of difference, as well as the tendency to judge it negatively. "Everybody's got their own way of seeing things. The world is a complex place."

> *Adaptation.* In the adaptation stage, we become more skilled at seeing shared realities through different lenses and consequently can make adjustments to our understanding of an action, phenomenon, or idea different from our own. "Part of how I view the world is informed by how others view the world. What makes sense in one context may not make sense in another."

> *Integration.* Finally, we may be able to master the behavior, understandings, and beliefs of multiple cultural realities, and we feel comfortable moving among them. A strong attachment to a single culture gives way to the possibility of belonging to more than one. "How I perceive things and act upon them can change as I move from one cultural context to another."

From a negotiation standpoint, the ability to see negotiation process and substance equally from one's own point of view as well as through the cultural lenses of others would be an ideal skill to have and share.

STRUCTURING KNOWLEDGE ABOUT CULTURE AND NEGOTIATION

Research into the diversity and universality of human cultures has a long, complex, and rich history. Unfortunately, relatively little of that research has explicitly affected thinking about negotiation and conflict management. In part that is because the multidisciplinary field of negotiation and conflict management has divergent research programs that disagree about what makes the world go around, multiple opinions regarding the causes of its revolutions, and divergent methodologies for studying it.[16] But there are two other reasons for culture's lack of integration into the negotiation literature. The field of negotiation and conflict management has long been engaged in relatively fruitless debate about the *relevance* of culture to negotiation. The field has also been characterized by an inability to grasp the full *impact* of culture. I use the term *relevance* simply to describe the extent to which the literature depicts culture as a variable in negotiation along a continuum. I define *impact* specifically in terms of whether culture is portrayed as a motivator of conflict or an enabler of its resolution. Practitioners of cross-cultural conflict management pop up in a wide variety of professions, including managers, cross-cultural counselors, mediators, and human resource specialists. Theorists also emerge from a great diversity of social science disciplines whose methodological differences affect how we pursue the creation of knowledge. We tend to diminish, discount, or ignore propositions from disciplines not our own. We do not have a unified research paradigm that explores the conflict-negotiation-culture nexus. Yet some tentative advances in this field can be claimed.

Through juxtaposition of the questions of relevance and impact, a rich panorama emerges in which we can appreciate four critical assumptions that underlie negotiation theory and practice. First I will consider relevance and impact separately, then together.

The Relevance Debate

The culture question divides most conflict management researchers and practitioners into two groups, those who believe culture is less relevant (or even irrelevant) and those who believe that it plays a substantial role. The less-relevant school represents the majority of negotiation writing, although this is usually not explicitly spelled out. Those who view culture as less relevant commit one of two errors: they fail to take culture into account at all in their analysis, or they believe that they can create laundry lists of things to do or not do that permit the nonmember to succeed in transactions with the "other" culture.

Although one rarely finds outright denials of relevance, there is a tinge of what Henry Kissinger called "crusading universalism"[17] in some strands of the prescriptive literature on negotiation. Negotiation classics such as *Getting to YES, The Art and Science of Negotiation,* or *Negotiating Rationally* analyze conflicts and prescribe negotiation strategies that might work for people who find it relatively easier to come up with creative solutions to shared problems without resorting to higher authority or rigid rules.[18] Not all cultures share these characteristics. Consider the dissonance between this advice and the worlds of those whose societies (in Hofstede's terms) have higher power distance and uncertainty avoidance measures. People all over the world (including me) have flocked to *Getting to YES* for advice, yet the implementation of that advice (such as the methods for exchanging information and interests, or the limitations on separation of people from problems) is heavily influenced by factors that can be attributed to culture. There may in fact be negotiation universals. Well-intentioned but overly standardized conflict management advice—regardless of the cultural assumptions in which it is embedded—may quickly lose some of its value as the cultural context in which it is given shifts.[19] At the very least, we must adapt that advice for the people to whom we are giving it.

Beyond the universalists' near-denial of relevance, culture is sometimes seen as potentially relevant, but mostly as a barrier to successful negotiation and conflict management. Questions from this perspective presuppose failure in negotiation and look to culture as one possible cause of that failure. Did cultural differences help ignite the October 1973 war that pitted Egypt and Syria against Israel?[20] Was culture a factor in the failure of the Greek and Turkish Cypriot leaders to negotiate the reunification of Cyprus under the Annan plan in Spring 2004?[21] These are examples of questions we could ask, if we assume that culture is relevant but potentially problematic.

The methodological weaknesses of researching culture and negotiation were noted by Zartman in a trenchant critique that was really an appeal for more coherence in the way research about culture and negotiation is conducted. Still, Zartman too considered cultural differences to be an impediment to making agreements.[22] Slowly but surely the older debate on relevance of culture is giving way to newer discussions on the *ways* that culture has an impact on our conflict and negotiation behaviors.

The Impact Debate

The impact debate inquires into how culture can be both a cause of conflict or an enabler of negotiation.

Some of those who consider culture a negative factor go so far as to claim that it is a variable in the causes of civilizational conflict—in short, culture is a cause of regional and global war.[23] It should be easy to critique this school of thought, since it requires the analyst to reduce large, complex groups to mindless monoliths. Ultimately, problems of misattribution "perpetuate stereotypes."[24] Problems of human communication—our ability to send and receive messages accurately—are more complex when crossing cultural bridges. But this is different than saying that culture *causes* the conflict. In fact, it would be more truthful to say that cultural ignorance (ethnocentrism) contributes to human miscommunication across cultures, rather than culture itself.

Culture per se is not a cause of conflict. Whites and blacks in the United States, Muslims and Hindus in India, Muslims and Christians in Bosnia, or Hutus and Tutsis in Burundi do not have conflicts because of their cultural affiliations. Rather, they may have conflict over contested rights, resources, custody of holy sites, political power, and myriad other issues. In such conflicts, unscrupulous leaders are able to keep followers motivated by depicting the other groups negatively, based on stereotypes of the other group's culture.

At the very least, negotiation research can now claim to have taken culture more seriously. Various articles point to ways in which culture influences negotiation behavior, and most imply that cultural misunderstanding hurts efforts to reach agreement. For example, Stephen Weiss argued that cross-cultural competence (or lack of it) should help determine if and when one party adapts to the other party's cultural negotiation styles, among other process options.[25] Similarly, Jeanne Brett and her colleagues found no direct links between cultural differences and the parties' abilities to create optimal agreements. Brett nevertheless pointed to the need for negotiators to understand how to implement joint-gains strategies differently, since such behaviors are culturally influenced. Different cultures may have different expectations regarding sharing of information and preferences, ability to deal with multiple issues simultaneously, and the desire to continuously improve an agreement.[26] Such observations are helpful and move us away from seeing cultural differences as obstacles, but they do not quite reach the level of affirming that cultural differences can actually be a source of value creation and an enabler of negotiation.

But can differences among cultures actually be helpful in negotiations? Negotiation theorists have long pointed to the need for differences among parties in order to optimize negotiation outcomes: differences among preferences, priorities, risk probabilities, abilities, and so on.[27] Parties that need and demand exactly the same thing will have a hard time creating value-maximizing deals and solutions. Culture can be one of those differences that help parties build value.

Examples of successful cross-cultural coexistence, even under extreme conflict circumstances, seriously challenge the assumption that culture facilitates conflict. In the corporate sector, one can find examples of successful commercial integrations across both organizational and national cultural differences that defy predictions of failure. Other notable counterexamples include the Neve Shalom/Wahat al-Salaam Village for Jews, Christians, and Muslims in Israel, and the remarkable case of the Rwandan town of Giti, whose leaders and people did not engage in the 1994 genocide, despite having a mixed Hutu-Tutsi population and being in close proximity to the slaughter.[28] Saying that cultural differences cause people to not get along is temptingly simple, but highly inaccurate. Rather, cultural differences are potentially positive aspects of our global existence.

The dimension of how cultural differences can create an opportunity for relationship building, mutual learning, and value creation in negotiations is an area of action research that deserves significant attention. My purpose here is to raise this possibility and question the prior assumptions in negotiation and cultural research, not to argue that this dimension is self-evident or axiomatic. In the age of globalization, it behooves us to look at successful cases of cross-cultural negotiation and conflict management and discover if in fact participants used their cultural differences as a bridge rather than as a barrier.

Putting Impact and Relevance Together

The juxtaposition of impact and relevance assumptions results in four separate ways of looking at culture and negotiation (Figure 8.1). Three of the categories are well represented in practice and theory. A fourth is relatively unexplored.

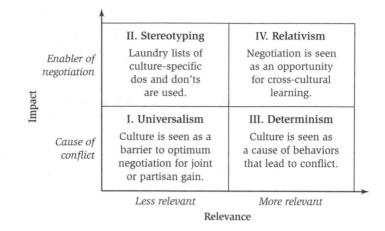

Figure 8.1. Four Ways of Looking at Culture and Negotiation.

Universalism. In quadrant I, culture is less relevant than other variables, except to the extent that it gets in the way of communication, in which case culture is just one more process barrier on the way to agreement. This approach emphasizes aspects of negotiation that seem universal. Consequently, the prescriptive advice it provides is thought to be universally applicable.

Stereotyping. In quadrant II, culture is less relevant than other variables, but there are highly predictable behaviors that nonmembers of a culture can learn in order to "succeed" when interacting with other cultures. ("When negotiating with someone from that culture, you should always . . .") Given the complexities and multiple dimensions of cultures, such an approach does not provide negotiators with much cross-cultural competence.

Determinism. In quadrant III, culture is more relevant, but predetermines the behavior of members and generally leads to interpersonal and social conflict. Here culture is acknowledged as being important to our understanding of conflict; however, its importance is cast in negative terms. Cultures are reduced to monoliths that incline their members to conflict with nonmembers. This approach often relies on and perpetuates stereotypes similar to those in quadrant II, but accords them more weight.

Relativism. In quadrant IV, culture is seen as both an influencing factor in negotiations and a potentially positive opportunity for joint creative problem solving. In this perspective, cultural differences are not to be feared as an obstacle to communication but are seen rather as a learning opportunity. This is the unexplored quadrant of the culture-negotiation encounter. This view can correct stereotypes and adjust prescriptive advice so that it fits with other cultures. As a research paradigm, this approach has the potential to offer us "foreign" strategies for reaching optimal, integrative agreements, or at least teaching us the relative merits of those approaches. It can also help us to understand that cultures need not incline us to conflict with each other. This is important for a globalized world. We must be willing to invest in understanding the cultures with which we are less familiar, and invite others to understand us better too.[29]

Our assumptions should be made explicit and sometimes questioned. And to be somewhat consonant, I do not believe that any single quadrant of assumptions is entirely wrong or right. They just represent, in quadrants I, II, and III, the state of our knowledge of culture and negotiation. Quadrant IV represents my desired state for both knowledge creation and cross-cultural competence.

We should be seeking to learn how different cultures reach agreements and manage conflicts, looking critically at their traditions, best practices, and failures. But we should also be aware that there is a reduced set of universally occurring negotiation dynamics that we must specify for each other when negotiating across cultures. I mean to make a connection between Bennet's ethnorelativity concept described above and the quadrant IV approach to negotiation and culture that I describe here. In this regard, our understanding of culture and negotiation also starts, I suspect, from a point of ethnocentrism, in which "our" beliefs about optimal negotiation strategies and behaviors are thought of as better (consciously or unconsciously). From this we can strive to move toward ethnorelative approaches to negotiation research in which we recognize our own culturally relevant preferences, try to understand others, and build bridges between them.

CROSS-CULTURAL DUE DILIGENCE

Using Hofstede's categories to derive negotiation preferences that vary among cultures, a negotiator can more easily educate others about his or her own preferences and can make adjustments for others. Mediators can more skillfully diagnose the reasons for failed conflict management between the parties. Table 8.1—admittedly a tentative template—may aid in preparing for cross-cultural negotiations and in interpreting other parties' negotiation behavior at the table. Ultimately, it may also aid in creating jointly decided upon "microcultures"[30] that reflect increased comfort and cross-cultural competence among specific negotiators at the table. This is the basis for changing the game from negotiating *against* other cultures, to negotiating *with* them, and using differences of culture to create value in the process and substance of negotiation.

Table 8.1. Cultural Negotiation Preference Template (tentative).

Negotiation Preference Category	Your Culture(s)	My Culture(s)
Process choice: distributive, integrative, mediated, and so on		
Kinds of issues to be negotiated		
Level of detail needed for issue closure		
Exchange of information regarding interests and priorities		
Choice of criteria: precedents, rules, laws, practicalities, and so on		
Choice and level of authority of negotiators		
Intraparty decision making: consensus or hierarchical		
Commitment form		
Implementation ambiguities		
Monitoring and oversight		
Dispute management during implementation		

CULTURE AND NEGOTIATION: BEYOND THE MYTHS

Some assumptions merit a specific challenge. In this section, I address a select number of myths about culture and negotiation.

Cultures Are Complex, Not Monolithic. Culture is a *set* of aggregated variables that are relevant to the practice of conflict management, rather than a single quality that predetermines everything. Further, individuals within a culture can vary considerably. Many people in the world today are the product of more than one culture and can borrow from all of them consciously or unconsciously in their behaviors and attitudes.

Culture Influences Negotiations. Among themselves, people within other cultures may negotiate differently than I do. Skills training and advice provided by people of one cultural context to people in a different cultural context might need some adjustment.

Language Fluency and Immersion Are Not Enough. There is plenty of accumulated experience in the problems of emigration, expatriation for a job, and other dislocations that show that learning a language cannot, in and of itself, provide cross-cultural competency. Language is but one dimension of culture, albeit an important one.

Cultural Awareness Is Not Enough. People who should know better sometimes commit errors and fail to recognize the need to build a bridge among culture-based understandings. Building a bridge to another culture requires more than awareness, it requires empathy with that culture.

Cross-Cultural Competence Is Not a One-Way Street. It is not incumbent on executives or government officials from the United States or anywhere else to be globally competent while others remain comfortably "national." All people who interact with others from different cultures need this skill. Those who interact in potentially confrontational settings with other cultures may need it more.

People Can Learn from Each Other. Cross-cultural communication and negotiation errors are researched as if people are incapable of learning, adapting, and evolving. They are also researched in ways that devalue the ability of the individual to differ from the cultural group to which he or she belongs. Prescriptions for cross-cultural interaction sound flat, rather than dynamic, because they implicitly assume that there is a better way of doing things, and that others should conform to it.

Cultures Are Not Static. People and leaders can change the dynamics of cultural behavior by attaching "new value and meaning" to identities to get "politically induced cultural change" and political mobilization.[31] A group can move from national pride and elitism to a hurt and victimized identity, or vice versa, for example. An exclusive culture can become more tolerant. In postconflict Rwanda, twelve years after the 1993 genocide, cultural identities that were once so easily manipulated by foreign invaders and native citizens are beginning to lose meaning as that country deliberately embarks on a campaign to create a new, inclusive identity.

FUTURE RESEARCH DIRECTIONS

We have much still to learn about culture and negotiation. Several kinds of research merit our attention. On the theory-generation side, we need more deep case studies that focus on one culture and describe in detail how that particular culture manages conflict among its members. We need to explore the failures and successes therein as well. Some of this might contribute to insightful advice in the quadrant II tradition, as long as it goes beyond stereotyping. We continue to need research on the universal aspects of culture and negotiation, and such knowledge probably requires comparative studies that look at numerous and diverse cultures. Such studies can help us determine all the different ways that our cultures facilitate our negotiation behavior. This will help create further quadrant IV knowledge and advice to the extent that we test hypotheses about cross-cultural negotiation in both small and large comparative studies. We currently do not have enough descriptive or prescriptive literature in this regard. Given the ongoing global interactions in all sectors of our lives, such research will no doubt be useful to scholars, to practitioners, and to parties in disputes and deals.

Notes

1. J. Z. Rubin, "Western Perspectives on Conflict Resolution," in P. Salem (ed.), *Conflict Resolution in the Arab World* (Beirut, Lebanon: American University of Beirut, 1997), p. 3.

2. K. Avruch, *Culture and Conflict Resolution* (Washington, D.C.: United States Institute of Peace, 1998), p. 10.

3. Perhaps the best-known structuralist is Claude Levi-Strauss, who pointed to universalist patterns of duality underlying all "superficial" cultural distinctions. The definitive volume synthesizing the literature on the existence of universally expressed human behaviors is D. E. Brown, *Human Universals* (New York: McGraw-Hill, 1991).

4. For a brief, accessible history of the definitions of culture, see Avruch, *Culture and Conflict Resolution,* 1998. Avruch relies on the survey of definitions completed by Kroeber and Kluckhohn, in A. Kroeber and C. Kluckhohn, "Cultures: A Critical Review of Concepts and Definitions," paper of the Peabody Museum, Vol. 47, Harvard University, 1952.

5. E. Schein, *Corporate Culture Survival Guide* (San Francisco: Jossey-Bass, 1999), p. 20.

6. G. O. Faure and G. Sjostedt, "Culture and Negotiation: An Introduction," in G. O. Faure and J. Z. Rubin (eds.), *Culture and Negotiation* (Thousand Oaks, Calif.: Sage, 1993), p. 3.

7. J. Brett and others, "Culture and Joint Gains in Negotiation," *Negotiation Journal,* 1998, *14*(1).

8. See E. T. Hall, *The Silent Language* (New York: Doubleday, 1959).

9. See J. Salacuse, "Ten Ways That Culture Affects Negotiation Style," *Negotiation Journal,* July 1998, *14*(3), pp. 221–240.

10. Although it may be problematic, I equate cultures with ethnicities, rather than with nations or states, given my belief that states and nations are far more "constructed" social entities, sometimes resulting in manipulated identities that serve particular political purposes. See the rich literature on nationalism, ethnicity, and identity for the various sides of this debate: for example, B. Anderson, *Imagined Communities: Reflections on the Origin and Spread of Nationalism* (New York: Verso, 1991); J. Hutchinson and A. D. Smith (eds.), *Nationalism* (Oxford, U.K.: Oxford University Press, 1994); A. D. Smith, *National Identity* (Cambridge, U.K.: Cambridge University Press, 1991); E. J. Hobsbawm, *Nations and Nationalism Since 1780* (Cambridge, U.K.: Cambridge University Press, 1992); and T. H. Eriksen, *Ethnicity and Nationalism: Anthropological Perspectives* (London: Pluto Press, 1993).

11. See A. Inkeles and D. Levinson, "National Character: The Study of Modal Personality and Sociocultural Systems," in G. Lindsey and E. Aronson (eds.), *Handbook of Social Psychology*, Vol. 4 (Reading, Mass.: Addison-Wesley, 1969).

12. See G. Hofstede, *Culture and Organizations: Software of the Mind* (New York: McGraw-Hill, 1997), especially Chapters Two, Three, Four, Five, and Seven.

13. Brett and others asserted that power distance and individualism versus collectivism would play an important role in cross-cultural negotiations. Neither they nor other researchers have placed much emphasis on the other dimensions, which I suspect are highly relevant to culture and negotiation (Brett and others, "Culture and Joint Gains in Negotiation," 1998).

14. In my field research on ADR practices in Latin America, I found that people are more likely to use court-annexed mediation services when mediated agreements have the status of *res judicata:* the agreement is equal to a judicial decision and can be enforced by the same courts the parties are avoiding. See A. Wanis-St. John, "Implementing ADR as an Aspect of Judicial Reform in Transitioning States: Lessons Learned from Practice," *Harvard Negotiation Law Review,* Spring 2000, *5,* pp. 339–381.

15. See M. J. Bennett, "Towards Ethnorelativism," in R. M. Paige (ed.), *Education of the Intercultural Experience* (Yarmouth, Maine: Intercultural Press, 1993).

16. Social psychologists and organizational behaviorists have been more concerned with culture and negotiation, and their experimental research has at least forged ahead where others feared to tread. See, for example, J. L. Graham, A. T. Mintu, and W. Rodgers, "Explorations of Negotiation Behavior in Ten Foreign Cultures Using a Model Developed in the U.S.," *Management Science,* 1994, *14*(1), pp. 72–95; C. Tinsley and J. Brett, "Managing Workplace Conflict," Dispute Resolution Center Working Paper 161, Northwestern University, 1997; K. Leung, "Negotiation and Award Allocation Across Cultures," in P. C. Earley, and M. Erez (eds.), *New Perspectives on International Industrial/Organizational Psychology* (San Francisco: Jossey-Bass, 1997); and Brett and others, "Culture and Joint Gains in Negotiation," 1998. A more case-study approach to culture and negotiation can be found in works such as R. Cohen, *Negotiating Across Cultures: Communication Obstacles in International Diplomacy* (Washington, D.C.: United States Institute of Peace, 1991). See the review essay A. Wanis-St. John, "Thinking Globally, Acting Locally," *Negotiation Journal,* 2003, *19*(3), pp. 389–395, for a summary of the different types of prescriptive negotiation-culture literature.

17. Kissinger was referring to an aspect of political culture that underlies U.S. foreign policymaking; see H. Kissinger, *Diplomacy* (New York: Simon & Schuster, 1994).

18. See R. Fisher, W. Ury, and B. Patton, *Getting to YES: Negotiating Agreement Without Giving In* (2nd ed.) (Boston: Houghton Mifflin, 1991); H. Raiffa, *The Art and Science of Negotiation* (Cambridge, Mass.: Belknap Press of Harvard University Press, 1982); and M. Bazerman and M. Neale, *Negotiating Rationally* (New York: Free Press, 1992).

19. The author himself has been involved in worldwide negotiation consulting from South Asia to South America, and finds universalist approaches to interest-based negotiation to need at least local adaptation.

20. Cohen posed this question; see Cohen, *Negotiating Across Cultures*, 1991.

21. See United Nations. "Comprehensive Settlement of the Cyprus Problem," March 2004. [http://www.cyprus-un-plan.org/]. See also U.N. Secretary General Annan's statement after the failure of negotiations, United Nations. "Unique and Historic Opportunity to Resolve Cyprus Problem Missed, Says Secretary-General After Settlement Plan Rejected," April 26, 2004. [http://www.cyprus-un-plan.org/UNIQUE_AND_HISTORIC_CHANCE_TO_RESOLVE_CYPRUS_PROBLEM_MISSED.pdf].

22. See I. W. Zartman, "A Skeptic's View," In G. O. Faure and J. Z. Rubin (eds.), *Culture and Negotiation* (New York: Sage, 1993).

23. See, for example, the alarmist literature of Huntington and the corpus of responses it generated: S. Huntington, *The Clash of Civilizations* (New York: Simon & Schuster, 1998).

24. See P. R. Kimmel, "Culture and Conflict," in M. Deutsch and P. Coleman (eds.), *Handbook of Conflict Resolution* (San Francisco: Jossey-Bass, 2000).

25. See S. Weiss, "Negotiating with Romans, Pt. I," *Sloan Management Review*, Winter 1994, *35*(2), pp. 51–61; and S. Weiss, "Negotiating with Romans, Pt. II," *Sloan Management Review*, Spring 1994, *35*(3), pp. 85–99.

26. See Brett and others, "Culture and Joint Gains in Negotiation," 1998.

27. For more on the sources of value, see D. Lax and J. Sebenius, "The Manager as Negotiator: The Negotiator's Dilemma: Creating and Claiming Value," in S. Goldberg, F. Sander, and N. Rogers (eds.), *Dispute Resolution* (Boston: Little Brown, 1992); and Moffitt, Chapter Eleven, this volume.

28. See J. Stuecker, "Ethnicity in Rwanda," unpublished graduate thesis, Seton Hall University, 2002; and J. M. Janzen and R. K. Janzen, *Do I Still Have a Life? Voices from the Aftermath of War in Rwanda and Burundi* (publications in Anthropology) (Lawrence, Kan.: University of Kansas, 2000).

29. For examples of quadrant IV literature, see D. Augsberger, *Conflict Mediation Across Cultures* (Louisville, Ky.: Westminster/Knoxville University Press, 1992); D. W. Young, "Prescriptive and Elicitive Approaches to Conflict Resolution: Examples from Papua New Guinea," *Negotiation Journal*, 1998, *14*(3), pp. 211–220; and J. P. Lederach, *Preparing for Peace: Conflict Transformation Across Cultures* (Syracuse, N.Y.: Syracuse University Press, 1995).

30. See Kimmel, "Culture and Conflict," 2000.

31. P. Brass, "Elite Competition and Nation Formation," In J. Hutchinson and A. D. Smith (eds.), *Nationalism* (Oxford, U.K.: Oxford University Press, 1994), p. 87.

CHAPTER NINE

Negotiation Through a Gender Lens

Deborah M. Kolb and Linda L. Putnam

Negotiation is a critical skill in the workplace today. In the not-too-distant past, those who negotiated did so because their jobs required them to bargain over contracts with suppliers, customers, or unions. In other words, negotiation was a skill used primarily by people who did it for a living. Now, changes in the economy and shifts in organizational structures make negotiating a major part of virtually everyone's job. The shifting boundaries between a firm, its suppliers, its customers, and even its competition require more people than ever to both negotiate complex deals and then bargain over their implementation. Within organizations, there has been a shift from hierarchical structures to ones that are more networked and team based. To function in decentralized, self-managed teams, people increasingly find themselves in roles in which their responsibility exceeds their authority. That is, their increased responsibility and span of control often exceeds their authority in the organizational hierarchy. To accomplish their tasks, they will probably need to negotiate with a range of internal and external stakeholders to get their budgets approved, secure commitments for project staffing, and get buy-in on scheduling, among other tasks. Further, the frequency with which people change jobs

Parts of this chapter have been adapted from Kolb, D. M. "Gender and Negotiations." In R. J. Ely, E. G. Foldy, and M. A. Scully (eds.), *Reader in Gender, Work, and Organization*. Malden, Mass.: Blackwell Publishing, 2003.

throughout their careers creates many opportunities to negotiate both conditions and compensation and also to secure funds to support new ventures.

The growing relevance of negotiation in the workplace has increased the educational demand for negotiation skills. A significant field of research, guided by a pragmatic concern for practice, has developed to meet that demand. The field is marked by an interest in empirical research that can be easily translated into prescriptive advice that promises to improve negotiation skills.

Not surprisingly, with practical concerns in mind, questions about gender have arisen. Specifically, researchers have focused primarily on one question: Do men and women negotiate differently? When the research question is posed this way, gender is equated with biological sex and treated as an individual and invariant attribute of identity. Although this research yields some insights about sex difference, there is a limitation to what one can learn about gender and, indeed, about negotiation from this approach. A more fruitful way is to look at gender not as an individual variable but as a social construct that structures and gives meaning to theory and practice in the field of negotiation. A gender lens on negotiation, therefore, not only illuminates a different set of dynamics about gender but also expands the domain of strategic advice that can help all negotiators become more effective at what they do.

GENDER AS THE STUDY OF INDIVIDUAL DIFFERENCE

Gender is one of the most easily measured variables, so it is not surprising that the question "Do men and women negotiate differently?" has dominated the research on gender in negotiations. Indeed, after many years of indifference to the topic, interest in the question has burgeoned. We now know that women don't ask, often let opportunities for negotiation slip by, typically set low goals, concede easily, and let their emotions show, among other factors.[1] Although individual studies on sex differences may produce significant findings, cumulative results across studies are often contradictory. Meta-analyses of these studies have shown only small, statistically significant differences and on just two dimensions. Women tend to be more cooperative than men and tend to receive lower outcomes when money is at issue.[2]

To ask a question about differences between men and women assumes that gender is an essential and stable attribute of individuals. Accounting for these differences requires that there is some basis in biology, socialization, role theory, or entitlements to explain why they exist.[3] The most common argument posits that women emphasize nurturance and support in their relationships because of their social development and the mothering roles they often (or are expected to) play. In contrast, according to this argument, men are groomed for separation and individualism, behaviors presumably more suited to demands of negotiation.[4] Thus women are more likely to treat a negotiation as an event in a long-term relationship, one linked to a larger social context and concerned with fairness and sensitivity to others, while men see it as a one-time event with no direct consequences for future interactions.[5] In laboratory experiments, where most of the gender research has been conducted, the latter perspective yields better results.

Without directly testing for the effects of developmental differences and social roles, these explanations are marshaled after the fact to account for the considerable deficiencies of women when they negotiate, especially when it is for compensation. Studies show that women expect less pay than do men;[6] do not feel the same entitlement to higher salaries as men do;[7] or place less value on pay than on other aspects of their jobs.[8] And these feelings translate into behavior that in turn affects outcomes. Researchers have observed that women demand and accept less in salary negotiations than do men,[9] are less confident and less satisfied with their negotiation performances,[10] and feel lower self-efficacy about their bargaining abilities.[11] Consistently, in this line of research, women are compared negatively to men, who typically approach a negotiation with an offensive orientation of seeing themselves entitled to and requesting a higher salary.[12] Thus, when men outperform women in salary negotiations, the reasons for these differences are often attributed to "problems" that women have.[13]

More recently, research has challenged some of these global findings by taking a more situational approach. In this work, scholars accept that gender differences in negotiation are unlikely to be universal but rather will be "triggered" under certain conditions.[14] In highly ambiguous situations when women are negotiating for themselves, men do outperform women in distributive bargaining. However, these effects disappear when women and men bargain as agents. When women bargain for others, they set higher goals, make higher first offers, and perform better than they do when they negotiate for their own needs.[15] In many instances, they outperform their male counterparts when they bargain for others.[16]

In a field that prides itself on pragmatism, the advice that results from this stream of research is problematic. First, the findings boil down to two—either women are the same as men or different from men (that is, deficient). So the advice is directed only to women; namely, How can women overcome their deficiencies and better equip themselves to negotiate, or how can they strengthen their instrumental orientation to the task?[17] No similar advice exists for men. Second, the advice from this work may itself be gendered and subject to gender stereotypes about sex differences that people use to judge behavior.[18] Thus, to tell women to act in a more self-interested, assertive, or instrumental way assumes that these behaviors are neutral in the sense that men and women can use them with the same effects and same consequences. However, these behaviors when enacted by a woman are likely to be seen differently than they are when men employ them. Assertiveness, self-orientation, and an instrumental focus may backfire against women. This asymmetry in other research arenas has created double binds for women.[19]

Rejecting the deficiency focus of the gender difference research, other scholars seek to show the benefits of a feminine orientation.[20] From this perspective, it is precisely "women's relationship-orientation" that benefits the negotiation process and the agreements it produces. In particular, these scholars argue that a focus on empathy, sensitivity to others, and the ability to manage conflict and collaboration simultaneously is advantageous in negotiations.[21] A feminine approach, one that values relationships, should serve negotiators in integrative or mutual gains approaches, as opposed to zero-sum or distributive negotiations. Indeed, the importance of relationships has been popularized in a number of books.[22] The concept is captured in the *dual concern* model—to do well for oneself, one must also possess a high concern for the interests of the other party.[23] Thus, these models describe the use of skills such as empathy and understanding as central to reaching mutual gains outcomes.[24]

Although considerable evidence exists for the dual concern model, the actual association of these feminine skills with specific outcomes is not well developed.[25] When researchers have tested to see if a "feminine concern" for others is correlated with joint gains for women and men, the findings are not encouraging.[26] It is not enough to care about the other party. For women to achieve high joint gain, in this case profit, they need to be primed to pay more attention to their own needs. Without this priming, they make concessions too easily. For a man, looking out for self yields the highest joint profit without attending to the interests of the other party. This study calls into question the notion of valuing feminine skills. Indeed, it is difficult to separate the advice—pay more attention to self-interest—from traditional ways of looking at gender differences.

Further, even when feminine skills are valorized for their contribution to mutual gains, a subtle translation process occurs. To value the feminine is to appreciate the relational belief system in which such attributes as empathy and caring are rooted.[27] However, these skills are divorced from context and become instrumental means to achieve self-oriented goals.[28] Thus, empathy becomes a way to learn about the other party in order to do well for oneself,[29] and concern for the other party translates into "enlightened self-interest."[30] In other words, these so-called feminine attributes are co-opted to fit into a more masculine approach to negotiation.

Taken together, the gender difference approach that dominates most thinking about gender and negotiations has a distinct theoretical bias that limits its practical utility. The research and the pragmatic advice that derive from this line of work reinforce masculine attributes—enlightened individual self-interest, analytic rationality, objectivity, and instrumentality. Those attributes typically labeled as feminine—empathy, concern for relationships, subjectivity, and emotional expressiveness—remain less valued. While feminine attributes are appreciated, they pale beside the traits associated with masculinity, which are seen as intrinsically tied to success. And advice to follow an androgynous approach ignores the gender schemas that influence how that approach will be viewed.[31]

This approach also fails to account for the gendered contexts within which this research is conducted. Thus in a study that purports to account for relational consequences in negotiation, high-status men in same-sex dyads are more accommodating than high-status women are with their female counterparts.[32] In a business school context, in which women are in the minority, striving to be recognized, it is not surprising that they try to claim as much value as they can. Thus even when context factors are considered, gender continues to be a problem, but only for women. It is not surprising, therefore, that this focus on individual difference which targets only women for improvement would leave the theory and practice of negotiation basically untouched.

GENDER AS A LENS FOR NEGOTIATION THEORY AND PRACTICE

To view negotiation through a gendered lens is to go beyond simple comparisons between men and women and to look more deeply at the gendered nature of negotiation itself and at the roles power and position play in it. This approach draws from recent scholarship that treats gender as an organizing principle of social life.[33] With its roots in a number of postmodern literatures, this perspective questions the apparent neutrality of what constitutes knowledge in a field, and it shows how power shapes certain truths and taken-for-granted assumptions.[34] Using this perspective, we examine the gendered nature of negotiation as a field to explore how theory, research, and norms of practice privilege certain ways of being (that is, the masculine) and marginalize other ways of knowing (that is, the feminine). This point underscores the issue that gender relations always are ones of power. Using this lens, we aim to uncover what has been silenced or ignored in the field. In our own work, the first author elaborates on the *shadow negotiation* rooted in the power and relational dynamics heretofore undertheorized in negotiation.[35] This perspective illuminates three particular areas: the problem of social position, the challenges of maintaining legitimacy in bargaining interactions, and the possibilities of transformative outcomes from negotiations.

Gender and the Problem of Social Position

Several theoretical perspectives dominate the negotiation field: economic decision analysis,[36] social psychology,[37] and cognitive psychology.[38] These perspectives focus on individual actors engaged in transactional dealmaking as either principals or agents. According to this view, actors achieve mutual gains through rational analyses of issues, interests, and options, and through the construction of packages that bridge different positions. The problem with these rather technical models is that they neglect the very social processes that make mutual gains possible. To focus on cognitive factors, such as analytic prowess, errors in judgment, or barriers to an agreement, minimizes how important social positioning is to enacting integrative approaches effectively. Scholars then blame individual deficiencies as the cause of inequitable outcomes, ones that no amount of rationality could actually correct.[39]

A good example of this problem is the concept of bargaining power. Researchers tend to define power as a situational variable, typically manipulated experimentally in laboratory studies.[40] Other scholars have dismissed the role of power altogether, noting that powerful actors do not necessarily achieve the best outcomes.[41] Very little research addresses how one's position in an organization's hierarchy or one's connection to or exclusion from influential networks shapes the choices of bargainers. Most research fails to explore how social positioning influences those choices and imposes constraints on bargainers.

The importance of social positioning is well illustrated in field studies of people who are relative newcomers to management in organizations.[42] In an investigation of salary negotiations, for example, one team of researchers demonstrated that access to social networks through having allies in organizations leads to higher salary outcomes than does lack of access.[43] Thus, people who do not have contacts or friends in organizations are disadvantaged in entry-level salary negotiations. Looking at negotiation through a gender lens highlights the sources and consequences of these power inequities. It suggests that theory and research need to consider the challenges of social positioning, its bases in status or identity, and how it affects the process and outcomes of negotiation.[44] In this way, researchers can address whether differences often attributed to gender have their roots in differential social positioning.[45] By making this shift, research and theory can help any negotiators, and it will not only be women who may be in disadvantageous positions. The framework of *strategic moves*—making value visible, raising the costs of the status quo, enlisting allies, and managing the process—is one structure that helps negotiators in a disadvantaged position enhance their stances at the table.

Gender and Legitimacy in Bargaining Interaction

A gender lens also shifts the focus away from essential characteristics of men and women to the negotiation interaction itself. From this perspective, gender is continually socially constructed, produced and reproduced. In other words, we "do gender" rather than have a gender.[46] "Doing gender" means that in the process of enacting a social practice (such as negotiation), individuals are constantly engaged in constructing identities and social situations in gendered ways. In this way, gender is not an individual characteristic, but both a means and an outcome of the ways parties socially construct negotiation. For example, enacting transactional bargaining, rooted in exchange and commodity values that grow out of a masculine-biased system, socially constructs negotiation in a gendered way.[47] Enacting negotiation as a form of mutual inquiry and learning, in contrast, constructs the process with less of a bias to a masculine system. This approach to gender and negotiation interaction emphasizes the fluidity, flexibility, and variability of gender-related behaviors. The challenge is to understand how parties enact negotiation in a particularly gendered way.

Understanding how people "do gender" in negotiations focuses on the conditions under which gender becomes salient to the interactions. It also highlights how important or relevant gender is to the way the negotiation is enacted.[48] For example, depending on whether the parties see these behaviors as appropriate or comfortable, a person may choose, either consciously or unconsciously, to act in a stereotypically gendered way—males acting competitively or females enacting the role of helper. Negotiators, in other words, have some choice in the degree to which they conform to gender schemas in a negotiation.

Expectations and stereotypes that others hold are other ways in which gender becomes salient in a negotiation. Work on stereotypes in which negotiators are primed with particular gender stereotypes suggests that these expectations have important influences on outcomes.[49] When masculine stereotypes are associated with negotiation effectiveness, men achieve higher payoffs than do women. Complementarily, when bargainers are primed to link negotiation effectiveness with feminine traits, women surpass men in the amount gained from the interaction. This research shows how susceptible parties are to enacting negotiation in a gendered way, when primed to do so.[50] Research on situational determinants of gender demonstrate that people are more likely to "do gender" in certain situations; specifically, in distributive negotiations, under time pressure, when indicators of performance are unclear, and when negotiators are acting on their own behalf.[51]

A gender lens on the bargaining interaction goes further than looking at conditions under which gender becomes salient—it also highlights the microprocesses by which this occurs. The power and positioning of a negotiator are not established permanently at the outset of the bargaining but rather are continually negotiated. This observation means that one party to a negotiation can undermine or delegitimize the other party by making gender, or other aspects of status and identity, salient to the process.[52] Whereas the initiating party may view this action as a strategic move, made without malice, the target may experience it as an attack that undermines the target's position and sense of self. Delegitimizing one of the parties during a negotiation reduces the likelihood of a mutually beneficial outcome, unless the target is able to resist. Research on the microprocesses of negotiation interaction reveals a number of options for how people resist these strategic moves through the use of "turns."[53]

"Turns" are ways that people can respond to the other negotiator's discrediting or undermining actions by shifting the meaning of those behaviors.[54] Having a repertoire of turns—including interrupting the action, naming a challenge, reframing a question, correcting impressions, diverting attention from problems, refocusing on the underlying issue, and even moving physically, helps negotiators manage difficult negotiations.[55] Turning the interaction takes place in the "shadow" of a negotiation. These turns are also ways of resisting gender stereotypes as well as of responding to moves that put a negotiator in a disadvantageous position.[56]

Gender, Interdependence, and Transformative Outcomes

A third way that a gender lens illuminates negotiation dynamics is by examining bargaining as a relational system. Rather than valorizing a woman's concern for relationships as the perspective of gender difference research does, a gender lens focuses on how a relational orientation might influence theory and practice. A feminist view of relationships calls for reframing traditional concepts such as interdependence and bargaining power. Interdependence is clearly the sine qua non of negotiation. Parties need each other to make agreements— a seller needs a buyer; warring countries need each other to have peace. Interdependence, as it has been theorized and applied in practice, is based on an instrumental assumption; namely, that parties need each other primarily to satisfy their individual interests. As a result of this individualistic view, theory and research on how parties construct interdependence are underdeveloped and typically treated as a residue of dependence.

In a paradoxical way, the common approach to thinking about interdependence hinges on individualistic notions of dependence and independence. Growing out of this approach, independence is often viewed as a construct that is aligned with a masculine orientation, while interdependence is treated as a relational construct. Masculine values of enhancing independence are also linked to bargaining power. As parties bargain on the issues at the table, they work out the nature of their dependence on each other.[57] Bargaining power derives from these perceptions of dependence and independence as a function of each party's Best Alternative To a Negotiated Agreement (BATNA). The viability or attractiveness of the other party's walkaway alternative—whether it is to buy another car, to quit, to strike, to sue, to go to war—sets the parameters for perceptions of dependence. As parties endeavor to improve their BATNAs or the perception of their BATNAs, they highlight their independence and minimize their interdependence.[58] These actions may result in a stalemate, which may help parties reach a point of parity, acknowledge their interdependence, and finally push them into a stage of earnest negotiations.[59] From this perspective, parties must be forced to recognize their joint dependence on each other by acknowledging that their fates are intertwined. In effect, interdependence becomes equated with jointly controlling each other's fate.

A second conceptualization of interdependence is through promotive interdependence,[60] or integrative bargaining.[61] This notion is simple and familiar. Through problem solving, parties bargain on issues to meet each other's individual needs and to discover how their interdependence benefits each of them. In essence, the guidelines for mutual gains negotiations—focusing on interests, identifying priorities, trading across differences—promote interdependence. Elsewhere, we label this process as task interdependence to capture its benefits as well as its limitations.[62] Meeting mutual needs is important in negotiation, but it is also short term, based on the immediate achievement of instrumental gain. Failure to find a creative agreement can cause the experience of interdependence to dissipate. Furthermore, it is unclear as to how a problem-solving process carries over into future negotiations, especially when external circumstances change.

A gender lens, in contrast, suggests a different take on interdependence and why it is important. First, interdependence is negotiated. It is not a residual or a byproduct of an agreement. Interdependence is created through the connecting work that negotiators do to appreciate and understand how their fates are intertwined. This perspective envisions parties in conflict not as atomistic and separable entities but rather as connected to each other in multiple ways.[63] Mary Parker Follett put it well when she described how this kind of connection works: "I never react to you but to you-plus-me, or to be more accurate, it is I-plus-you reacting to you-plus-me. That is, in the very process of meeting, we both become something different."[64] Interdependence, in other words, involves change and learning. To connect requires a stance of curiosity, one that recognizes that a person can never fully understand or appreciate the other in the absence of dialogue and mutual inquiry.

In our own research, we have shown how asking questions about the context of the situation, listening for silences, and raising hidden agendas not only enable parties to appreciate the ways that they are interdependent but help them to see their dispute in a new light.[65] This new way of understanding the dispute comes, in part, from gaining new insights about the context of the situation. Circular questioning is one way that parties inquire about the context of the situation. In this approach, a negotiator seeks to understand how his or her actions influence those of the other party. Questions move in a circular fashion from the situation at hand to the context in which the issues and circumstances reside. By asking these kinds of questions, negotiators recognize how their interests and concerns influence each other. Focusing on how each party's action might have influenced the other can yield new understandings of the issues and what is important.[66] Similarly, listening for silences entails hearing what is not spoken. It occurs when a party actively processes what the other person says and inquires about a pause, a qualifier, a hesitation, or a confusing contradiction. Rather than presuming to know what the other person means, listening for silences pushes the negotiator to test out interpretations before acting on them. Finally, negotiators connect through the raising of hidden agendas. Parties always have multiple interests, some of which they articulate (for example, their salary needs, their budgetary requirements), while others remain hidden (for example, their competition over scarce resources, the desire to protect their turf). These hidden agendas are always present and can disrupt negotiations. A proposed solution that meets overt interests will be rejected if it fails to meet hidden interests. Finding language to discuss these issues—be it gender, competition, or some other consequential matter—can open up the negotiation and make it possible for parties to resolve deep as well as surface issues. Obviously, how one introduces these matters is critical. Appreciative moves that invite participation and conversation and ones that preserve the face of the other are more likely to surface hidden agendas that challenge an action.[67]

Through connectedness, new understandings can transform the very nature of a negotiation. Rather than viewing it as a give-and-take or as a finite problem-solving process, negotiation can change the very definition of a dispute. Transformation occurs as parties come to see the issues in a different way.[68] This new dimension moves outside the frames of reference of both parties and situates the problem in a new realm. A dispute over resources and turf, for example, is recast as a structural issue that negatively affects the performance of both parties. Opportunities for transformation emanate from probing, exploring, and being puzzled about the negotiation context. It comes from taking the risk to label a situation differently and to keep the other side's position open to alternative interpretations. Transformation also aims for negotiated settlements, but ones that attend to relational and identity concerns in addition to substantive matters.[69] Parties to a turf dispute join together to negotiate with others to alter the conditions that created the problem in the first place.

CONCLUSION

Traditionally, the study of gender in negotiation has been narrowly conceived as research on sex differences. The results of this work reinforce existing stereotypes and practices. Examining negotiation from a gender lens reveals that focusing on the individual bargainers misses the social and interactive dynamics that characterize negotiation. Attending to these social processes expands the strategic repertoire of what people need to know to be effective bargainers and to see how gendered notions permeate negotiation practice. Furthermore, a gender lens highlights transformative possibilities in negotiation. Developing interdependence through connectedness leads to open inquiry, which in turn can create new understandings about the nature of a dispute. This broader definition of negotiation holds possibilities for transformative outcomes unimagined before the bargaining began.

Notes

1. See L. Babcock and S. Laschever, *Women Don't Ask: Negotiation and the Gender Divide* (Princeton, N.J.: Princeton University Press, 2003).

2. See A. E. Walters, A. Stuhlmacher, and L. Meyer, "Gender and Negotiator Competitiveness: A Meta-analysis," *Organizational Behavior and Human Decision Processes*, 1998, *76*, 1–29.

3. See, for example, B. Major, "From Social Inequality to Personal Entitlement: The Role of Social Comparisons, Legitimacy Appraisals, and Group Membership," *Advances in Experimental Psychology*, 1994, *26*, 293–355; and B. Major, D. McFarlin, and D. Gagnon, "Overworked and Underpaid: On the Nature of Gender Differences in Personal Entitlement," *Journal of Personality and Social Psychology*, 1984, *47*, 1399–1412.

4. See D. M. Kolb and G. Coolidge, "Her Place at the Table," in J. W. Breslin and J. Z. Rubin (eds.), *Negotiation Theory and Practice* (Cambridge, Mass.: Program on Negotiation, Harvard Law School, 1991).

5. See L. Greenhalgh and D. I. Chapman, "Joint Decision-Making: The Inseparability of Relationship and Negotiation," in R. M. Kramer and D. M. Messick (eds.), *Negotiation as a Social Process* (Thousand Oaks, Calif.: Sage, 1995); L. Greenhalgh and R. W. Gilkey, "Our Game, Your Rules: Developing Effective Negotiating Approaches," in L. Moore (ed.), *Not as Far as You Think: The Realities of Working Women* (Lexington, Mass.: Lexington Books, 1986); and J. J. Halpern and J. M. Parks, "Vive la Difference: Differences Between Males and Females in Process and Outcomes in a Low-Conflict Negotiation," *The International Journal of Conflict Management*, 1996, *7*, 45–70.

6. See L. Jackson, P. Gardner, and L. Sullivan, "Explaining Gender Differences in Self-Pay Expectations: Social Comparison Standards and Perceptions of Fair Pay," *Journal of Applied Psychology*, 1992, *77*, 651–663, and D. McFarlin, M. Frone, B. Major, and E. Konar, "Predicting Career-Entry Pay Expectations: The Role of Gender-Based Comparisons," *Journal of Business and Psychology*, 1989, *3*, 331–340.

7. See J. Jost, "An Experimental Replication of the Depressed-Entitled Effect Among Women," *Psychology of Women Quarterly*, 1997, *21*, 387–393; and V. Karman and C. Hartal, "Gender Differences in Anticipated Pay Negotiation Strategies and Outcomes," *Journal of Business and Psychology*, 1994, *9*, 183–197.

8. See S. Desmarais and J. Curtis, "Gender and Perceived Pay Entitlement: Testing for Effects of Experience with Income," *Journal of Personality and Social Psychology*, 1997, *72*, 141–150; and R. J. Ely, *Feminist Critiques of Research on Gender in*

Organizations, working paper no. 6 (Boston: Center for Gender in Organizations, Simmons School of Management, 1999).

9. See S. J. Solnick, "Gender Differences in the Ultimatum Game," *Economic Inquiry,* 2001, *39,* 189–200.

10. See C. Watson and L. R. Hoffman, "Managers as Negotiators: A Test of Power Versus Gender as Predictors of Feelings, Behavior, and Outcome," *Leadership Quarterly,* 1996, *7,* 63–85.

11. See K. Stevens, A. Bavetta, and M. Gist, "Gender Differences in Acquisition of Salary Negotiation Skills: The Role of Goals, Self-Efficacy, and Perceived Control," *Journal of Applied Psychology,* 1993, *78,* 723–735.

12. See L. A. Barron, "Ask and You Shall Receive? Gender Differences in Negotiators' Beliefs About Requests for a Higher Salary," *Human Relations,* 2003, *56,* 635–662.

13. See A. F. Stuhlmacher and A. E. Walters, "Gender Differences in Negotiation Outcomes: A Meta-analysis," *Personnel Psychology,* 1999, *52*(3), 653–667.

14. See H. C. Riley and K. McGinn, *When Does Gender Matter?* (Denver: Academy of Management, 2002); and M. Gelfand, V. S. Major, J. Raver, L. Nishi, and K. O'Brien, "A Dynamic Theory of Gender in Negotiation," unpublished paper, University of Maryland, 2003.

15. See M. E. Wade, "Women and Salary Negotiation: The Costs of Self-Advocacy," *Psychology of Women Quarterly,* 2001, *25,* 65–76.

16. See Babcock and Laschever, *Women Don't Ask,* 2003.

17. See Babcock and Laschever, *Women Don't Ask,* 2003.

18. See V. Valian, *Why So Slow?* (Cambridge, Mass.: MIT Press, 1998).

19. See J. K. Fletcher, *Disappearing Acts* (Cambridge, Mass.: MIT Press, 1999); and J. T. Wood and C. Conrad, "Paradox in the Experiences of Professional Women," *The Western Journal of Speech Communication,* 1983, *47,* 305–322.

20. See, for example, J. K. Fletcher, "Castrating the Feminine Advantage: Feminist Standpoint Research and Management Science," *Journal of Management Inquiry,* 1994, *3,* 74–78; S. Helgeson, *The Female Advantage: Women's Ways of Leadership* (Garden City, N.Y.: Doubleday, 1990); and Gelfand, Major, Raver, Nishi, and O'Brien, "A Dynamic Theory of Gender in Negotiation," 2003.

21. See Kolb and Coolidge, "Her Place at the Table," 1991.

22. See, for example, R. Fisher and S. Brown, *Getting Together* (New York: Penguin, 1987); and W. Ury, *Getting Past No* (New York: Bantam, 1990).

23. See D. G. Pruitt, *Negotiation Behavior* (New York: Academic Press, 1981).

24. See Kolb and Coolidge, "Her Place at the Table," 1991; and R. H. Mnookin, S. R. Peppet, and A. S. Tulumello, *Beyond Winning: Negotiating to Create Value in Deals and Disputes* (Cambridge, Mass.: Belknap Press of Harvard University Press, 2000).

25. See D. G. Pruitt and P. J. Carnevale, *Negotiation in Social Conflict* (Pacific Grove, Calif.: Brooks/Cole, 1993).

26. See P. S. Calhoun and W. P. Smith, "Integrative Bargaining: Does Gender Make a Difference?" *International Journal of Conflict Management,* 1999, *10,* 203–224.

27. See Fletcher, "Castrating the Feminine Advantage," 1994; Fletcher, *Disappearing Acts,* 1999; and Gelfand, Major, Raver, Nishi, and O'Brien, "A Dynamic Theory of Gender in Negotiation," 2003.

28. See D. M. Kolb and L. L. Putnam, "Relational Interdependence," paper presented at the annual meeting of the Academy of Management, Denver, Aug. 7–11, 2002.

29. See Mnookin, Peppet, and Tulumello, *Beyond Winning,* 2000.

30. See J. Z. Rubin, D. Pruitt, and S. H. Kim, *Social Conflict* (New York: McGraw-Hill, 1994).

31. Valian, *Why So Slow?* 1998.

32. See J. Curhan, "Making a Good Impression in Negotiation: Gender Differences in Impression Goals," paper presented at the annual meeting of the Academy of Management, Seattle, Aug. 5–9, 2003.

33. See, for example, J. Acker, "Hierarchies, Jobs, Bodies: A Theory of Gendered Organizations," *Gender and Society,* 1990, *4,* 139–158; Ely, *Feminist Critiques of Research on Gender in Organizations,* 1999; Fletcher, *Disappearing Acts,* 1999; M. Kilduff and A. Mehra, "Postmodernism and Organizational Research," *Academy of Management Review,* 1997, *22,* 453–482; and D. M. Kolb and L. L. Putnam, "Through the Looking Glass: Negotiation Theory Refracted Through the Lens of Gender," in S. Gleason (ed.), *Frontiers in Dispute Resolution in Industrial Relations and Human Resources* (Ann Arbor, Mich.: Michigan State University Press, 1997).

34. See M. Calas and L. Smircich, "From a Woman's Point of View: Feminist Approaches to Organization Studies," in S. R. Clegg, C. Hardy, and W. R. Nord (eds.), *Handbook of Organization Studies* (Thousand Oaks, Calif.: Sage, 1996).

35. See D. M. Kolb and J. Williams, *Everyday Negotiations: Navigating the Hidden Agendas of Bargaining* (San Francisco: Jossey-Bass, 2003); D. M. Kolb and J. Williams, "Breakthrough Bargaining," *Harvard Business Review,* 2001, 87–107; and D. M. Kolb and J. Williams, *The Shadow Negotiation: How Women Can Master the Hidden Agendas that Determine Bargaining Success* (New York: Simon & Schuster, 2000).

36. See H. Raiffa, *The Art and Science of Negotiation* (Cambridge, Mass.: Belknap Press of Harvard University Press, 1982); and D. A. Lax and J. K. Sebenius, *The Manager as Negotiator: Bargaining for Cooperation and Competitive Gain* (New York: The Free Press, 1986).

37. See Rubin, Pruitt, and Kim, *Social Conflict,* 1994; and L. Thompson, *The Mind and Heart of the Negotiator* (Upper Saddle River, N.J.: Prentice Hall, 2001).

38. See, for example, M. A. Neale and M. H. Bazerman, *Cognition and Rationality in Negotiation* (New York: Free Press, 1991).

39. See L. L. Putnam and D. M. Kolb, "Rethinking Negotiation: Feminist Views of Communication and Exchange," in P. M. Buzzanell (ed.), *Rethinking Organizational and Managerial Communication from Feminist Perspectives* (Thousand Oaks, Calif.: Sage, 2000).

40. See S. Bacharach and E. Lawler, *Bargaining* (San Francisco: Jossey-Bass, 1981); and R. Pinkley, M. Neale, and R. Bennett, "The Impact of Alternatives to Settlement in Dyadic Negotiation," *Organization Behavior and Human Performance*, 1994, *80*, 386–402.

41. See Lax and Sebenius, *The Manager as Negotiator*, 1986.

42. See C. Watson, "Gender Versus Power as a Predictor of Negotiation Behavior and Outcomes," *Negotiation Journal*, 1994, *10*, 117–127; and Kolb and Williams, *The Shadow Negotiation*, 2000.

43. See M. L. Seidel, J. T. Polzer, and K. Stewart, "Friends in High Places: The Effects of Social Networks on Discrimination in Salary Negotiations," *Administrative Science Quarterly*, 2000, *45*, 1–27.

44. See Kolb and Williams, "Breakthrough Bargaining," 2001.

45. See, for example, C. A. MacKinnon, *Toward a Feminist Theory of the State* (Cambridge, Mass.: Harvard University Press, 1989); and J. B. Miller, *Toward a New Psychology of Women* (Boston: Beacon Press, 1976).

46. See J. A. Howard and J. Hollander, *Gendered Situations, Gendered Selves* (Thousand Oaks, Calif.: Sage, 1997); and C. West and D. H. Zimmerman, "Doing Gender," *Gender & Society*, 1987, *1*, 125–151.

47. See Putnam and Kolb, "Rethinking Negotiation," 2000.

48. See Riley and McGinn, *When Does Gender Matter?* 2002; and Gelfand, Major, Raver, Nishi, and O'Brien, "A Dynamic Theory of Gender in Negotiation," 2003.

49. See L. J. Kray, L. Thompson, and A. Galinsky, "Battle of the Sexes: Gender Stereotype Confirmation and Reactance in Negotiations," *Journal of Personality and Social Psychology*, 2001, *80*(6), 942–958.

50. See H. C. Riley, "When Does Gender Matter in Negotiations? The Case of Distributive Bargaining," unpublished dissertation, Harvard University, 2001.

51. See Riley and McGinn, *When Does Gender Matter?* 2002; and Gelfand, Major, Raver, Nishi, and O'Brien, "A Dynamic Theory of Gender in Negotiation," 2003.

52. See Kolb and Williams, *The Shadow Negotiation*, 2000; and Kolb and Williams, *Everyday Negotiations*, 2003.

53. See, for example, D. M. Kolb, "Staying in the Game or Changing It: An Analysis of Moves and Turns in Negotiation," *Negotiation Journal*, 2004, *20*(2), 253–268.

54. See E. Goffman, *Interaction Ritual: Essays in Face-to-Face Behavior* (New York: Doubleday/Anchor, 1967).

55. See Kolb, "Staying in the Game or Changing It," 2004; Kolb and Williams, *The Shadow Negotiation*, 2000; and Kolb and Williams, *Everyday Negotiations*, 2003.

56. See S. Gherardi, *Gender, Symbolism, and Organizational Culture* (Thousand Oaks, Calif.: Sage, 1996).

57. See Bacharach and Lawler, *Bargaining*, 1981; and Kolb and Williams, "Breakthrough Bargaining," 2001.

58. See Lax and Sebenius, *The Manager as Negotiator*, 1986.

59. See Rubin, Pruitt, and Kim, *Social Conflict,* 1994.

60. See R. L. Lewicki, D. M. Saunders, J. W. Minton, and B. Barry, *Negotiation* (4th ed.) (Homewood, Ill.: Richard D. Irwin, 2003).

61. See R. E. Walton and R. B. McKersie, *A Behavioral Theory of Labor Negotiations: An Analysis of a Social Interaction System* (New York: McGraw-Hill, 1965).

62. See Putnam and Kolb, "Rethinking Negotiation," 2000.

63. See R. Kegan and L. L. Lahey, *How the Way We Talk Can Change the Way We Work* (San Francisco: Jossey-Bass, 2002).

64. M. P. Follett, "Relating: The Circular Response," in P. Graham (ed.), *Mary Parker Follett: Prophet of Management* (Boston: Harvard Business School Press, 1995), p. 42.

65. See Kolb and Putnam, "Relational Interpendence," 2002; L. L. Putnam, "Transformations and Critical Moments in Negotiations," *Negotiation Journal,* 2004, *20*(2), 269–295; and Kolb and Williams, *Everyday Negotiations,* 2003.

66. See S. Cobb, "Empowerment and Mediation: A Narrative Perspective," *Negotiation Journal,* 1993, *9,* 245–259.

67. See Kolb, "Staying in the Game or Changing It," 2004.

68. See Putnam, "Transformations and Critical Moments in Negotiations," 2004.

69. See Putnam and Kolb, "Rethinking Negotiation," 2000.

CHAPTER TEN

Bone Chips to Dinosaurs

Perceptions, Stories, and Conflict

Douglas Stone and Sheila Heen

In 1787 in Woodbury Creek, New Jersey, a man came upon a complete dinosaur skeleton—the first discovered by human beings. The bones were shown to Dr. Caspar Wistar, the leading American anatomist at the time. After recording the obvious—that they were large—he deemed them to be of little interest. They were stored, and eventually lost.[1] It was not until fifty years later that dinosaurs were officially "discovered."[2]

It is easy to make fun of Dr. Wistar. Even a child could have told that these bones were special, or so one would think. But Wistar was operating under a significant analytic disadvantage: there was no such thing as a dinosaur, no pre-existing category or storyline to fit these bones into. He made sense of them based on what he already knew about the world.

That is a good description of how we all make sense of the world. Far from simply reflecting or recording reality, our minds engage in a complex interplay between what we perceive and what we already know. We take bits and pieces of information, fill in gaps, and make connections between fragments that create meaning and a coherent story. "Out of a few . . . bone chips," notes cognitive psychologist Ulric Neisser, "we remember a dinosaur."[3]

But in a dispute, my dinosaur may look nothing like your dinosaur:

- Rita is shocked and indignant that the hospital staff would question her young daughter's injuries, implying that Rita herself might be responsible. The hospital staff report that Rita was rude and uncooperative with them, and abrupt with her daughter.

- Malcolm is against the proposed Maxi-Mart Mall. He favors the preservation of the current Old Mill Building. Fran, who is no fan of "run-down buildings," supports the new development, citing the added consumer choices and lower prices.

- Arthur and Felix, business partners for a dozen years, are fed up with each other. Arthur says Felix is confrontational and unappreciative of his creative contributions to the company. Felix complains that Arthur avoids conflict and will not account for his time so that Felix can do proper resource planning.

This chapter is about the relationship between the bone chips and the dinosaur. We will look at some of the systematic ways in which our perceptions turn into stories and at some of the predictable ways our stories will diverge in disputes.[4]

COLLECTING BONE CHIPS: DATA AND THE COMPLEXITY OF "WHAT HAPPENED"

If two people are locked in a dispute with each other, how does it come to be that they describe the same situation differently? Broadly, there are two reasons: first, we may be taking in different "bones" or data; and second, we may interpret even the same bones differently.

The first question, then, is why are we taking in different data? There are two factors that contribute to this: "access" and "selection."

Access to Different Pools of Data

In any dispute, each person has access to information that the other person does not. In an organization, for example, where you sit determines what you see. The sales people have information about the effort it takes to bring a client along, the specific demands a particular client has made, the many terms on which they have managed to hold the line, and the kinds of promises that competitors are making.

The legal team has seen all the ways these kinds of deals can go bad, while the engineers wonder why the sales people continue to promise what cannot be built, on a timeline that cannot be met. Meanwhile, executive management worries about how profits will play on Wall Street, and they urge the sales people to be more aggressive in meeting their targets. Each group is aware of information the others are missing, and accordingly, tells different stories about what is going on.

Same Pool, Different Selection

And yet, two people can have different recollections even if they have access to the *same* data, for example, when describing a meeting both attended. This is where things get interesting. Presumably, if there were two video cameras in the same meeting pointed in roughly the same direction, they would record roughly the same thing.

But our brains do not operate like cameras.[5] Instead, we must go through a number of steps to incorporate what we see, hear, and feel into long-term, retrievable memory—the kind of memory that shapes our perceptions of a conflict.

First, we have to decide what to pay attention to and take in. At any given moment, so much data about the world enters our brains through our senses that paying attention to everything would overwhelm us with stimuli. Hence, "a key proficiency of consciousness is not the ability to perceive the external world, but rather the ability to shut so much of it out."[6] The Danish writer Tor Nørretranders calls this selective attention the "user illusion"—we think we see all of the raw data around us, but in fact take in a very small slice of the available information,[7] perhaps as little as one percent of our stimulus field.[8]

Building a Story

Next, we need to encode what we see or hear into memory. We have at least two kinds of memory—*working memory* and *long-term memory.* Working memory enables us to capture information for a short period of time—hearing and retaining a phone number long enough to walk to the next room to dial, for example. It is in full swing during a negotiation or conversation, and keeps us engaged long enough to take a quick note of what the other person is saying and to formulate a response.

Afterward, however, we have a hard time remembering exactly what was said and when. That is because moving something into long-term memory requires us to connect new information with existing knowledge in memory.[9] This means that when we encounter new information, we automatically scan our brains for similar or analogous categories in which to file it.[10] We may "remember dinosaurs," but only if we already know what a dinosaur is. This point is crucial: *human beings are not good at remembering isolated "data" or creating unique files in our heads. We have to find a way to connect the fragments with stories, and to connect a new story with an existing story already on file.* Artificial intelligence researcher Roger Schank puts a fine point on it: "Human memory is story-based, and these stories are the essence of human intelligence."[11] He also points out, "Conversation is no more than responsive story-telling."[12]

Consider an example. If a friend mentions to us, "Maria bumped me in the hall," we do not know how to understand this information. Do we file it under "accidental bumps" or "narrow halls" or "problematic people" or perhaps even "flirting"? In order to make sense of it, we want to know: Who is Maria? Why did she bump our friend? When and where did this happen? Is this the first time or is it typical of her? If our friend does not include this information in her comment, we will likely make it up. Even as you read this, you may have developed a visual image of the "bump" in your mind, and your image is not just pieces of data, it is a little story.

Note, by the way, that your "Maria bumped me" story would be different from the story you might tell if you were told that "I bumped Maria," or "Maria and I bumped into each other," though to a third-party observer, each of these "bumps" might look exactly alike.

Reinforcing Existing Storylines

So we are constantly taking the new fragments and weaving them into the stories we tell about our lives, our conflicts, ourselves, and others. We interpret new situations in light of old experiences ("She's just like that other boss I had") and already-developed life themes ("This is another example of me just trying to get a fair break").

Donald Schön of MIT and Chris Argyris of Harvard Business School created an analytic tool to capture this process by which our brains select data, make inferences from it based on past experiences, and construct conclusions, or stories, about the world. A simplified version of their "Ladder of Inference" is depicted in Figure 10.1.[13]

These conclusions or stories then influence the new data we select as important, and over time our stories become self-reinforcing. It is those things that are important, meaningful, or familiar to us that automatically attract our attention.[14] Once I view my colleagues as incompetent, I then see through this "frame" and notice all the new data of incompetence that follows.[15] I may also be more likely to overlook or dismiss disconfirming data (of competence), because it does not fit into my story, or if I do take it in, I might regard it as an

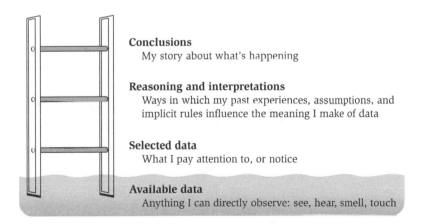

Conclusions
My story about what's happening

Reasoning and interpretations
Ways in which my past experiences, assumptions, and implicit rules influence the meaning I make of data

Selected data
What I pay attention to, or notice

Available data
Anything I can directly observe: see, hear, smell, touch

Figure 10.1. The Ladder of Inference.

Source: D. Stone, B. Patton, and S. Heen, *Difficult Conversations: How to Discuss What Matters Most* (New York: Penguin, 1999). Adapted from an original model created by Chris Argyris and Donald Schön.

exception to the way my colleague really is. Our brains work hard to tell simple stories that are consistent with what we already know, and that protect us from the discomfort of cognitive dissonance.[16]

The Impact of Strong Emotion

To complicate matters, conflict often triggers emotions, which impose their own demands into these busy brain processes. Chemicals such as adrenaline, cortisol, dopamine, serotonin, norepinephrine, and oxytocin create and accompany emotions and profoundly affect our ability to perceive and recall what happens when we are in dispute.[17] We face conflict when something important to us is threatened: a relationship, our self-image, our well-being. The perception of danger triggers two pathways to the brain, one unconscious and one conscious. In a split second—before our rational self is often even aware of it danger signals travel to the amygdala, which causes our adrenal gland to secrete a rush of adrenaline, converting glycogen into energy-rich glucose and sending blood to our extremities to prepare us for sudden movement.[18]

This influences how we perceive what is happening. In this state, the memories we retain are much cruder, containing less complexity and specificity, even while they are particularly vivid and deeply encoded. We miss the subtleties or specifics of what is said because our slower, rational mind—housed in the neocortex—is not in charge. Interestingly, while we have extensive neural pathways that deliver danger information from the amygdala to the neocortex, it seems to be largely a one-way street. There are few paths for delivering rational information from the neocortex to the amygdala.[19]

This is not to say that we cannot become more aware of this process and work around it. It does partly explain why parties in conflict can be particularly reactive, and later recall a very different version of events than their counterpart. This, combined with the leaps of logic made by our rational mind while encoding perceptions into memory, leaves us particularly susceptible to some predictable distortions in our stories.

DINOSAUR ANATOMY 101: STORY ELEMENTS THAT COUNT

We do not turn bone chips into dinosaurs arbitrarily, or with infinite latitude. Our stories bear a predictable relationship to our data, and there are certain story elements that form particularly significant patterns in how our stories are told. Below, we consider three of the more important patterns: characters, causation and blame, and timelines.

The Characters

One of the most common clashes in our stories will be how we describe the characters who reside in them. Our stories about the conflict are filled with heroes and villains, victims and oppressors, protector and child, the overbearing and the underappreciated.

Most people have a sympathetic self-story. We are doing our best, sticking up for what is right, and acting rationally based on what we know. And so as we tell the story of the conflict, we are cast firmly in the role of hero.

Starring: Us as Good Guy Hero. There are a number of reasons why we cast ourselves in the role of hero. The first is what we will call the "private data" phenomenon. I know my own hopes, dreams, problems, feelings, limitations, pressures, coping mechanisms, personal history, and past relationships. I know the backdrop of larger stories I tell myself about who I am in the world—"this is one more thing for this small-town boy to overcome," or "I'm not going to be taken for a sucker *this* time." I know the ways in which the other person's actions caused me harm, inconvenience, confusion, or expense. And I know my own intentions, why I did what I did given the constraints I was under.

This information—so rich and vivid for me—is information that I alone possess. The very information I use to tell my sympathetic self-story is information you do not even have. Similarly, I have little access to the same information about you: what this dispute means to you in the context of your life, what motivated you and what constraints you are under, and how my actions have affected you. If I hear about this at all, it is secondhand, and so the information is bound to be less compelling.[20]

This differential access to information is sometimes called Egocentric Bias by researchers. It produces couples who each claim to be responsible for 80 percent of the housework and only 20 percent of the arguments.[21] We have lots of information about all we take care of around the house, and our good intentions and virtuous conduct when it comes to the fights.

In addition to the private-data phenomenon, each of us has a self-interest in constructing stories that protect our identities as responsible, caring, competent, or good people.[22] Our colleague complains that we dropped the ball on the project. We *know* this is not true because we are not the kind of person who would drop the ball or break a commitment. Preserving our sense of how we see ourselves is so crucial to each of us that we are rarely even willing to consider that someone else's description of what happened might be true.

Against: Them as Bad Guy Villain (or Bumbler at Best). Once we have snagged the role as hero, this leaves only one role for our counterpart—the villain (aka, "the problem," or "that jerk"). And once we cast her or him as overbearing, thoughtless, incompetent, or unkind, we are more likely to notice and encode into memory any new evidence that confirms our view. Called Stereotype Bias, this tendency can fuel the escalation of a conflict, and means that changing our view of the other person as villain can be quite difficult.[23]

This is particularly the case because our story includes not just *what* they are doing, which is bad enough, but it includes *why* they are doing it, which makes things worse. My belief that you hurt me *on purpose* causes me to tell a different story about the situation, and my feelings of anger, hurt, or betrayal increase.

If during a meeting I feel embarrassed based on your comments, I assume that you intended to embarrass me. Now the cognitive trap is set. The more hurt I feel, the more likely I am to describe your action as intentional, calculated to bring about just the sort of embarrassment I now feel.[24] My story is particularly difficult to overturn with disconfirming data, because I do not have access to the private data it turns on—your intentions.

It is a short leap, of course, from "you meant to embarrass me" to "you're a bad person"—malicious, jealous, controlling, or at the very least inexcusably thoughtless.[25] I see you as you are—a villain sent straight from central casting.

It is interesting to consider how my story of me and you is different from your story of me and you. What would we find if we visited each other's stories? Alasdair MacIntyre puts it this way: "Each of us being a main character in his own drama plays subordinate parts in the dramas of others, and each drama constrains the others. In my drama, perhaps, I am Hamlet or Iago or at least the swinehead who may yet become a prince, but to you I am only A Gentleman or at best Second Murderer, while you are my Polonius or my Gravedigger, but your own hero."[26]

Of course, during moments of reflection we know it is not so simple as heroes and villains, but in the context of a difficult dispute, such reflective moments are few. We tell positive stories about ourselves and make negative attributions about others, and before we know it, we are as caught in the flow as the water circling the drain.

Causation and Blame

In a dispute, we do not just want to know *what* went wrong, we want to know *why* it went wrong. Yet despite our interest in causation, we are strikingly bad at creating explanations that capture what is really going on. Gamblers are notorious for their quirky explanations for why things happen. If I play craps and lose, I might explain that I was at a "cold table." If I win, perhaps it is because I finally got around to sending that check to charity, or maybe I was just really "feeling it." Chance, as an explanation, is just not very satisfying.

In the 1960s, neuropsychologists observed the human need to assign causation in work with "split-brain" patients—people who have had the right and left sides of their brain surgically separated to treat intractable epilepsy. Our left hemisphere handles language and symbols, and the right specializes in nonverbal information such as images and spatial relations. Split-brain patients whose right brain was shown the command "walk" got up and walked, without knowledge of the command by the left brain. When they were asked why they were walking, however, their left brains went to work constructing a reason—a story that would connect and explain their behavior. One patient quickly explained he was going to get a soda.[27] To interface with the world, we need to know our own—and others'—intentions and the cause of events. And we prefer a theory that is simply made up to no theory at all.

Conflict situations further obscure our ability to think clearly about cause and effect, and our inaccurate attributions in turn heighten the conflict. There are two key factors in this. First, as systems thinker Peter Senge puts it, "Reality is made up of circles but we see straight lines."[28] The second is that it is hard to see causation when we ourselves are participants in the system.

We See Lines Not Circles. Treating causation as a straight line leads to what some theorists have called the "biased punctuation of conflict."[29] Leigh Thompson describes the tendency succinctly: "An actor, A, perceives the history of conflict with another actor, B, as a sequence of B-A, B-A, B-A, in which the initial hostile or aggressive move was made by B, causing A to engage in defensive and legitimate retaliatory actions. Actor B punctuates the same history of interaction as A-B, A-B, A-B, however, reversing the roles of aggressor and defender."[30]

The true causes of a conflict can more usefully be schematized as a "system" or circle to which each party contributes. As we wrote in *Difficult Conversations:* "[C]ausation is almost always . . . complex. A contribution *system* is present, and that system includes inputs from both people. . . . Whether the batter strikes out or hits a home run is a result of the interaction between the batter and the pitcher. Depending on your perspective, you might focus on the actions of one or the other, but the actions of both are required for the outcome."[31]

The conceptualization of causation as a circle rather than a line nicely sidesteps the question of whether a conflict started with cause A or cause B. In reality, it may be that A and B were simultaneous, or simply that the inputs from each party are too complex to determine. What we do know is that we are locked into a self-reinforcing system, and once stuck, factors such as blame, anger, fear, and image threats set in and make matters worse.[32] The only way out is to uncover the system.

We Don't See Our Own Contribution. A second reason we have trouble with causation is that in disputes we are not observers of the system, we are participants. We cannot see ourselves as others see us, and so our descriptions of the causes of the conflict often lack our own contribution to the problem.

Imagine a conflict in which Alan tells the following story of the cause: "After all I've done for Betty, she doesn't even have the courtesy to call me. She never has time for me because she selfishly pursues whatever makes her happy in the moment. Sure, I was upset with her the other day, but Betty knows I'm a good, caring, and generous person. I wish Betty were the same way."

The story Betty tells is quite different: "Alan is unpredictable and given to bursts of anger. Who knows what irrational thing will trigger him next? I get anxious and hypervigilant around him. I've been trying to keep my distance; it's ruining our working relationship."

We can see what neither Alan nor Betty can—that they are each contributing to the situation. Alan has to make sense of Betty's behavior without a key piece of information: his own contributions to the system of actions and reactions. Betty does the same. Each tells a story that blames the other for the problem, and, unintentionally, these stories perpetuate and heighten the conflict.

Timelines: The Role of the Past and the Future on Today

In addition to different stories of characters and causation, our stories will often have very different timelines—beginnings, key events, and predictions about the future.

Divergent Beginnings. In the mid-1990s, Conflict Management Group was asked to help mediate an ongoing zoning dispute relating to a casino.[33] The parties, who referred to themselves as The Town and The Tribe, were in conflict over the expansion of The Tribe's casino. As part of the diagnostic process, the mediators interviewed people on each side of the conflict, asking each when the conflict began. The Town leaders reported that "this whole thing got started about three years ago when The Tribe quietly entered a petition to put a small parcel of town land into trust."[34]

When the mediators asked The Tribe the same question, its members began this way: "This conflict began in 1636 when white colonists declared war on our people . . ." The Tribe's story began about 360 years earlier than the story told by The Town.

The mediators did not have the sense that either party was being strategic. In fact, it seemed quite the opposite: questions about when the conflict began seemed so obvious to each side that they hardly warranted discussion. It was as if they were being asked, "When were you born?" The question "When was this conflict born?" appeared equally straightforward to both parties.

Differences in perceptions about when and how conflicts start often create tensions of their own. The person who dates the conflict further back in time will often be accused of "living in the past" or "using the past against me." Similarly, the person who feels the conflict is of more recent vintage will often be accused of "ignoring the deeper issues," "pretending the past never happened," or "failing to take responsibility for past actions." While one side views the past as having an indispensable role in the current situation, the other sees it as getting in the way of a better future.

Divergent Views of "Historical Facts." It is also often true that the parties cannot agree on the past at all. What happened, when it happened, and what is most important become central issues in the current dispute.

In the mid-1990s we were involved in a series of "Track II" dialogues between Greek and Turkish Cypriots on the island of Cyprus.[35] The small Mediterranean island was partitioned in 1974, and from that time until the late 1990s people from the two communities had virtually no opportunity to talk across the partition except through these informal dialogues. Religious leaders, journalists, business leaders, educators, and community leaders met periodically in an old hotel that stood stranded in the UN-patrolled buffer zone between the two communities.

To better understand their common history, the facilitators asked each side—the Greek Cypriots and the Turkish Cypriots—to create a timeline of the conflict.[36] On sheets of paper—one per date—each side would list key dates and a brief explanation of what happened. As the facilitators explained the task, participants from both communities protested that the exercise would be a waste of time. "We know the history," they said. "It has been our lives."

Nonetheless, they agreed to play along. Each community picked out perhaps twenty key moments, and then laid them out on the floor on opposite sides of a string timeline. The result was two parallel time lines, one created by Greek Cypriots, one created by Turkish Cypriots. Participants then "walked through history," with each side narrating the key moments.

Both sides were shocked. The initial reaction was often one of distrust: "You could not in good faith think your timeline is accurate. Ours is history. Yours is propaganda."[37] But over time, with intense discussion, most participants came to see the other side's timeline as a genuine expression of how they remembered and understood the key moments from the past.

Consider one of many examples. The Turkish Cypriots listed the late 1960s as a crucial time. They lived in monocommunal enclaves and, by their telling, experienced severe oppression at the hands of the Greeks. The Greeks, remembering it as a time of relative calm, did not list it at all. They had little awareness of the oppression the Turks described. Some of the Turks had experienced the events directly; others knew about them from the stories their parents told. Few Greek Cypriots had any personal involvement in the oppression, and had no reason to pay much attention to what they regarded as the "isolated incidents" about which they had occasionally read. As is common in such conflicts, these omissions went in both directions. The Turkish Cypriots omitted events that were of great importance to the Greek Cypriots as well.

In individual and particularly in group conflicts, these disparate perceptions of history take hold and quickly become "myths." The memory becomes stylized and it begins to stand for something—our strength in victory or courage in defeat, a flagrant example of how evil the other side is, the time we stood up for what was right, and so on. Vlamik Volkan has talked about the concept of "chosen traumas" and "chosen glories" in the context of how we experience national identity and our relationship to enemies.[38] There is no reason to assume that these concepts are limited to the stories we tell about national identities.

Rewriting Recollection. Our stories of the past are not static, but change with each telling. This allows for room for positive change. At the same time, when current tension rises, our story of the past grows darker. A study of four hundred Michigan couples followed them through the first four years of marriage. The couples who grew increasingly unhappy during the four years remembered the earlier years more negatively, even though they expressed being happy at the time.[39] Called Consistency Bias, how you are now in the relationship is often recalled to be how you have always been.

This is closely related to Hindsight Bias: once we know the outcome of a particular event or conflict, that outcome seems inevitable.[40] We remember all the ways in which we "saw it coming" and it was "obvious" what would happen. These distortions in the ways in which we rewrite history mean that finding a more positive solution may require re-rewriting our recollections in significant ways.

BUILDING THE DINOSAUR: THE CRUCIAL ROLE OF FRAMES

We have looked at how we take in data, and at some of the common elements that go into the making of a story. We now take a closer look at some of the processes by which we interpret meaning. There is no generally agreed upon term for these phenomena. They are referred to as mental models,[41] heuristics, partisan perceptions,[42] mindsets, schemas, paradigms, theories, or frames.[43] We will use the word *frames,* because we like the image of someone looking out through the frame of a window—their mind's window—onto the world.

A frame can be something as simple as a label or as complex as a life story. It can be an important memory, wisdom passed on from elders, or an assumption about the world or oneself. It can be an emotion, a prediction, a metaphor, a value, or a rule. Our test for whether something is a frame is a practical one: does knowing someone's frame help explain important aspects of how the person makes sense of the world that would be hard to explain otherwise?

The central role of these frames is reflected in a popular personality test called the Thematic Apperception Test, or TAT. The subject is shown twelve pictures, one at a time, and asked to tell a dramatic story about each picture. For example, the first picture might be of a man in a boat on a lake. One person might tell a story about a rugged individual off on a relaxing trip. Another might tell a story about being abandoned.

Each person's twelve stories are recorded and then combed for recurrent themes, characters, roles, and plots.[44] Often the subject would say that his or her stories were all unique, without unifying threads, and yet the listener can clearly hear recurring roles ("I'm the victim!"), schemas ("Power is what matters"), or assumptions ("People will usually disappoint you"). These themes, or frames as we are calling them, are strong enough and consistent enough to become "perception and experience hardened into personality."[45]

Yet these frames, as powerful as they are for helping us piece the bone fragments together, are unseen and undiscussed. Conflicting frames may be at the heart of a conflict without anyone being aware of either their own frames or the other party's.[46] In the following sections, we uncover a few examples of how they work and what to look for.

Labels

The use of one word instead of another can have a huge impact on how we see the world, and thus, on how we act. Consider the social psychology experiment in which participants played a game in which they could choose either to cooperate or defect. The game was played under two conditions. In the first, the game itself was labeled "The Wall Street Game," while in the second it was labeled "The Community Game." Other than that, the rules of the game were identical. Participants playing the Wall Street Game cooperated one-third of the time. Participants playing the Community Game cooperated two-thirds of the time.[47]

Why did the label have such a strong impact? Because it causes participants to tell themselves a totally different story about what is going on. The game, like life, is full of ambiguities and variables. We resolve those ambiguities and make predictions about the variables based on whatever information we have, no matter how meager. We tell a story, and based on that story, we take action. The small change in frame results in a big impact on behavior.[48]

Metaphors

In their book *Frame Reflection*, Donald Schön and Martin Rein examine the role of metaphors as frames in a dispute.[49] They offer an example of an underlying frame and how it affects how we perceive conflicting facts and arguments. In the early 1960s Americans were talking about the problem of "urban blight" and the need for "urban renewal." Over time the metaphor shifted toward a philosophy that these areas were "natural communities" requiring "attention and care." Schön and Rein describe how the choice of metaphor has an impact on how we see a problem and possible solutions: "Once we are able to see a slum as a blighted area, we know that blight must be removed. . . . The metaphor is one of disease and cure. . . . Once we are able to see the slum as a 'natural community,' then it is also clear what is wrong and what needs doing. We should think twice . . . about dislocating people from their local areas; natural communities should be preserved."[50]

The problem itself is extraordinarily complex. By winning the battle of the metaphors, we set the terms of the debate. The metaphor tells us what is important and what is not, and points us toward resolution. While it is almost impossible to understand complex problems like this without finding ways to simplify them, it is crucial to remember that the metaphor is not the reality.

Linguist George Lakoff offers another interesting example of how metaphors affect perception. Examining the political landscape of the United States in 2004, Lakoff wondered why "the facts" seem to be of so little relevance to people's political views. His answer is that metaphors trump facts. In *Don't Think of an Elephant,* he argues that voters think of the country in terms of a family, and that they see the government as parental figures. Conservatives, he believes, see government through the metaphor of the "strict father," while progressives see government through the metaphor of "nurturing parents." "People think in frames. The strict father and nurturing parent frames each force a certain logic. To be accepted, the truth must fit people's frames. If the facts do not fit a frame, the frame stays and the facts bounce off."[51]

Assumptions and Implicit Rules

We all operate on a set of assumptions and implicit rules about how things should be, what is normal to expect, how people should behave. *Curb Your Enthusiasm,* a TV show on HBO, gets great mileage from writer and star Larry David's ongoing inability to get everyone else in the world to conform to his (very odd) rules.

In one episode, David is at lunch with someone who, at a charity auction, has purchased the right to dine with him (on the show, David plays himself, the wealthy writer and producer of the hit TV show *Seinfeld*). The waiter brings David his lunch first, and the following conversation ensues with his guest:

DAVID: Mind if I start?

GUEST: Oh, he [the waiter] said it will just be a couple minutes.

DAVID: So, you don't want me to start, is that it?

GUEST: It's a couple minutes. You don't mind, do you?

DAVID: I just think it's kind of weird. If you got your food first, I would say go ahead and start. What do I care?

GUEST: I would wait for you to get yours.

DAVID: I really wouldn't want you to wait. I would be uncomfortable if you waited.

GUEST: I feel it would be polite to wait for your food to arrive.

DAVID: Well, I think it's kind of impolite to prevent someone who's hungry from eating.

GUEST: Yeah, but we're supposed to be having lunch together.

DAVID: We *are* having lunch! I don't get what's the difference? Do we have to start at the same time?

GUEST: I don't see why you can't wait two seconds for your cold sandwich. It's not like it's even hot.

DAVID: I don't see what you care if I take a bite of my food. Why does that bother you?

GUEST: Because we're having lunch together.

DAVID: So what!?

GUEST: The two of us.[52]

Nothing much is at stake, here, of course, but even so, the clash of implicit rules creates a conflict, and David ends up feeling victimized by his dinner guest and agitated by his own inability to control the situation.

In the real world, conflicts over implicit rules can wreak serious havoc. Consider a conflict between father and son. The son experiences his father as distant, the father perceives the son to be self-absorbed. Each is reacting to different rules about the expression of emotion, rules that are not uncommon to members of their respective generations.

The father is a member of the "greatest generation," had fought in World War II, and had provided for his family for forty years. He had never sought acknowledgment and never complained. His rule: "Do what is expected of you. There is great honor in getting your job done, quietly and without burdening others with your own emotional needs."

His son's rule is different: "Life is about being in authentic relationship with those you love. You do that by understanding yourself and allowing others in. You say what you need, and try to give others what they need." These rules are not exactly in opposition, but it is not hard to see how they lead to different expectations and behaviors, and quite different interpretations of the behaviors of others.

Rules and assumptions can be narrow ("eat when served" versus "don't eat until everyone is served") or broad and philosophical. Rules often conflict, as in the case of these pairs:

"It's a dog-eat-dog world" versus "people are basically good."

"Conflict is bad" versus "conflict is normal."

"It's important to be liked" versus "It's important to be respected."

Our assumptions can operate as the headline that captures the big picture of the situation and at the same time cuts to the heart of the matter. You might see a conflict as being "a simple matter of patent law and property rights," whereas I might experience the same conflict as being a matter of "David versus Goliath. I'm sticking up for the little guy."

Personal Experiences, Values, and Beliefs

Of course many of our rules and resulting frames come from our experiences in the world. A difficult childhood during which siblings were given favored treatment might lead to a view of life as fundamentally unfair. An extended family in which members "haven't spoken for twenty years" in the wake of disagreement might produce adults who shy away from conflict. Or it might produce adults determined to face conflicts early and often.

A particularly powerful experience can itself be a frame. If we are in conflict about whether to get a dog, I may not be able to get around my memory of having been attacked by a dog as a child. Moments of intense shame or danger as well as moments of joy and euphoria can be particularly powerful frames. I may view a conflict about abortion through the frame of my own experience with abortion. I may see debates about the economy through my memory of my father losing his job when I was a teenager.

Values and beliefs form frames as well. Religious beliefs and group membership—or decided antimembership—shape our views of human nature and the meaning of life.

Understanding other people's stories goes beyond understanding the "facts" or even seeing the current situation from their vantage points. Deeper understanding requires learning about the hidden structures that make up their frames on the world, on the conflict, and on your role in the bigger themes of their lives.

When Emotions Tell the Story

Emotions not only affect data collection and encoding, they also affect our frames. We often conceptualize emotions as "things" people "have." But an emotion can also be thought about as a lens, or even as a storyteller, and can have a powerful impact on how we tell the story of both past and future.

This is particularly true for emotions such as depression or anxiety. Kramer and Hanna refer to the distorting effect as "dysphoric cognitions," and note that these "contribute to various 'negative illusions' about the self and others, including heightened perceptions of vulnerability, perceived loss of control . . . worst-case thinking, and fatalistic rumination about one's prospects for changing the course of events."[53] It is tempting to think of perception purely in terms of cognitive mechanisms, but it is impossible to understand the way someone makes sense of the world without understanding how she or he feels.

FROM BONE CHIPS TO *RAMPAGING* DINOSAURS

So perhaps Ulric Neisser was right—but incomplete. It is not just that out of bone chips, we construct dinosaurs. In fact, we construct whole worlds these dinosaurs inhabit, complete with personalities, intentions, histories, and enemies. Our own storylines, themes, metaphors, and frames are the lenses through which we make reality into *our* reality.[54]

In the end, we may not always be able to develop a new narrative that works for all parties in a dispute, but we can attempt to follow the simple but elegant advice of poet William Carlos Williams: "Their story, yours, and mine—it's what we all carry with us on this trip we take, and we owe it to each other to respect our stories and learn from them."[55]

Notes

1. See B. Bryson, *A Short History of Nearly Everything* (New York: Doubleday, 2002).

2. See E. H. Colbert, *The Great Dinosaur Hunters and Their Discoveries* (New York: Dover, 1984).

3. U. Neisser, *Cognitive Psychology* (New York: Appleton-Century-Crofts, 1967), p. 285.

4. Understanding conflicting "stories" is a key aspect of the theory and practice of what is called "narrative mediation": "Narrative mediation is different from problem-solving approaches. . . . It does not subscribe to the assumption that what people want (which gets them into conflict) stems from the expression of their inner needs or interests. Rather, it starts from the idea that people construct conflict from narrative descriptions of events" (Winslade, J., and Monk, G. *Narrative Mediation: A New Approach to Conflict Resolution.* San Francisco: Jossey-Bass, 2001, p. xi). We wish to thank Sarah Cobb for introducing us to this school of thought.

5. See D. L. Schacter, *Searching for Memory: The Brain, the Mind, and the Past* (New York: Basic Books, 1996).

6. S. Johnson, *Mind Wide Open: Your Brain and the Neuroscience of Everyday Life* (New York: Scribner, 2004), p. 90.

7. T. Nørretranders, *The User Illusion: Cutting Consciousness Down to Size* (New York: Viking/Penguin, 1991), p. 277.

8. L. Thompson, *The Mind and Heart of the Negotiator* (Upper Saddle River, N.J.: Prentice Hall, 1998), p. 104.

9. See Schacter, *Searching for Memory*, 1996.

10. See R. C. Schank, *Coloring Outside the Lines: Raising a Smarter Kid by Breaking All the Rules* (New York: HarperCollins, 2000).

11. R. C. Schank, *Tell Me a Story: Narrative and Intelligence* (Evanston, Ill.: Northwestern University Press, 1990), p. 12.

12. Schank, *Tell Me a Story*, 1990, p. 24.

13. See C. Argyris, R. Putnam, and D. McLain Smith, *Action Science* (San Francisco: Jossey-Bass, 1985), pp. 57–58.

14. See Schacter, *Searching for Memory*, 1996.

15. See J. Z. Rubin, D. G. Pruitt, and S. H. Kim, *Social Conflict: Escalation, Stalemate and Settlement* (New York: McGraw-Hill, 1994).

16. For a discussion of cognitive dissonance, see generally L. Festinger, *A Theory of Cognitive Dissonance* (Palo Alto, Calif.: Stanford University Press, 1957).

17. High status in a group triggers higher serotonin levels (blunting rejection reactions and creating confidence) and lower levels of cortisol (a stress hormone); dopamine is released as a reaction to something unexpected—positive or negative—and "marks" it in memory as important to learn from; pleasure comes from endorphins and norepinephrine; oxytocin produces relaxation in the face of stress. See Johnson, *Mind Wide Open*, 2004.

18. See Johnson, *Mind Wide Open*, 2004.

19. See Johnson, *Mind Wide Open*, 2004. This suggests that our brains are wired for "the fear system to take control in threatening situations while preventing the reign of our conscious, deliberate selves" (pp. 64–65).

20. See D. L. Schacter, *The Seven Sins of Memory: How the Mind Forgets and Remembers* (Boston: Houghton Mifflin, 2001).

21. See M. Ross and F. Sicoly, "Egocentric Biases in Availability and Attribution," *Journal of Personality and Social Psychology*, 1979, *37*, 322–336; and A. Christensen, M. Sullaway, and C. King, "Systematic Error in Behavioral Reports of Dyadic Interaction: Egocentric Bias and Content Effects," *Behavioral Assessment*, 1983, *5*, 129–140.

22. See generally Chapter Six of D. Stone, B. Patton, and S. Heen, *Difficult Conversations: How to Discuss What Matters Most* (New York: Penguin, 1999), on identity and its role in difficult conversations.

23. See Schacter, *The Seven Sins of Memory*, 2001, pp. 153–157.

24. For a helpful discussion of attributions and intentions in conflict settings, see K. G. Allred, "Anger and Retaliation: The Role of Attribution in Conflict," in D. Morton and P. T. Coleman (eds.), *The Handbook of Conflict Resolution* (San Francisco: Jossey-Bass, 2000).

25. Whereas I see my own behavior as being embedded in a complex *situational* context and experience myself as being well meaning in light of that context, I don't

have access to the context that others experience around themselves, and so I attribute their behavior to simple *character* traits. See L. Ross and R. E. Nisbett, *The Person and the Situation: Perspectives of Social Psychology* (New York: McGraw-Hill, 1991).

26. A. MacIntyre, *After Virtue* (2nd ed.) (South Bend, Ind.: University of Notre Dame Press, 2003), pp. 213–214.

27. See Schacter, *The Seven Sins of Memory*, 2001, citing research by Dartmouth neuroscientist Michael Gazzaniga summarized in M. S. Gazzaniga, *The Social Brain: Discovering the Networks of the Mind* (New York: Basic Books, 1985); and M. S. Gazzaniga, "The Split Brain Revisited," *Scientific American*, 1988, 279, 50–55.

28. P. M. Senge, *The Fifth Discipline: The Art and Practice of The Learning Organization* (New York: Doubleday, 1990), p. 73.

29. R. L. Kahn and R. M. Kramer, *Untying the Knot: De-escalatory Processes in International Conflict* (San Francisco: Jossey-Bass, 1990), p. 267.

30. Thompson, *The Mind and Heart of the Negotiator*, 1998, p. 267. See also K. G. Allred, K. Hong, and J. P. Kalt, "Partisan Misperceptions and Conflict Escalation: Survey Evidence from a Tribal/Local Government Conflict," Faculty Research Working Paper Series, JFK School of Government, Harvard University, 2002.

31. Stone, Patton, and Heen, *Difficult Conversations*, 1999, p. 64.

32. See Rubin, Pruitt, and Kim, *Social Conflict*, 1994.

33. We were periodically involved in this mediation. It was headed up by Rob Ricigliano, then a senior consultant with Conflict Management Group. He is now director of the Peace Studies Program at the University of Wisconsin-Milwaukee.

34. Putting land in trust means land is transferred away from the town and the town tax rolls and added to The Tribe's reservation land.

35. The project was developed under the auspices of the Institute for Multi-Track Diplomacy and Conflict Management Group, in association with the Fulbright Commission, the American Embassy in Cyprus, and members of the Harvard Negotiation Project. The authors participated in a number of these workshops in the mid-1990s.

36. Louise Diamond of the Institute for Multi-Track Diplomacy originally led this exercise called "A Walk Through History" (based on an exercise created by Joe Montville). The exercise was repeated more than two dozen times with different groups of Greek and Turkish Cypriots, always with similar outcomes.

37. This reasoning almost perfectly reflects what Ross and Ward call "naïve realism." Ross and Ward posit that we each assume we see the world as it is, and assume that those who claim to see it differently just do not have the facts. When we give them the facts, and they still see it differently, we attribute it to irrationality, stupidity, or bias. See L. Ross and A. Ward, "Naïve Realism in Everyday Life: Implications for Social Conflict and Misunderstanding," in E. S. Reed, E. Turiel, and T. Brown (eds.), *Values and Knowledge* (Mahwah, N.J.: Lawrence Erlbaum, 1996).

38. See generally V. Volkan, *Bloodlines: From Ethnic Pride to Ethnic Terrorism* (New York: Westview Press, 1997).

39. See D. Holmberg and J. G. Homes, "Reconstruction of Relationship Memories: A Mental Models Approach," in N. Schwarz and S. Sudman (eds.), *Autobiographical Memory and the Validity of Retrospective Reports* (New York: Springer-Verlag, 1994).

40. See Schacter, *The Seven Sins of Memory,* 2001.

41. See Senge, *The Fifth Discipline,* 1990.

42. See R. Fisher, E. Kopelman, and A. K. Schneider, *Beyond Machiavelli: Tools for Coping with Conflict* (Cambridge, Mass.: Harvard University Press, 1994).

43. Erving Goffman offers a nice definition of frame: "I assume that definitions of a situation are built up in accordance with principles of organization which govern events—at least social ones—and our subjective involvement in them; frame is the word I use to refer to such of these basic elements as I am able to identity" (Goffman, E. *Frame Analysis: An Essay on the Organization of Experience.* Boston: Northeastern University Press, 1986, pp. 10–11). Goffman, in turn, borrows his theory of frames from G. Bateson, *Steps to an Ecology of Mind* (Chicago: University of Chicago Press, 1972).

44. See A. M. Paul, *The Cult of Personality: How Personality Tests Are Leading Us to Miseducate Our Children, Mismanage Our Companies, and Misunderstand Ourselves* (New York: Free Press, 2004).

45. Family therapist and organizational consultant Jeffrey Kerr of the Family Institute of Cambridge, in conversation on October 5, 2004, in Marlborough, Massachusetts.

46. See O. Nudler, "On Conflicts and Metaphors: Toward an Extended Rationality," in J. W. Burton (ed.), *Conflict: Human Needs Theory* (New York: St. Martin's Press, 1990).

47. See Ross and Ward, "Naïve Realism in Everyday Life," 1996.

48. Related to labeling is our tendency to categorize. We all look out of our windows and impose categories on the world. "Us and them" is an example of a binary category choice that has a significant impact on our stories (Rubin, Pruitt, and Kim, *Social Conflict,* 1994).

49. See D. Schön and M. Rein, *Frame Reflection: Toward the Resolution of Intractable Policy Controversies* (New York: Basic Books, 1994).

50. Schön and Rein, *Frame Reflection,* 1994, p. 27.

51. G. Lakoff, *Don't Think of an Elephant: Know Your Values and Frame the Debate* (White River Junction, Vt.: Chelsea Green Publishing, 2004), p. 17.

52. L. David, "The Thong," *Curb Your Enthusiasm,* Home Box Office, second season, episode five, aired October 21, 2001.

53. R. M. Kramer and B. A. Hanna, "Dysphoric Cognition and Self-Defeating Bargaining Behavior," in D. M. Kolb (ed.), *Negotiation Eclectics* (Cambridge, Mass.: PON Books, 1999), p. 145.

54. The degree to which our stories can be engaged and changed is an area for future research. Clearly, there are situations that are more and less amenable to "re-storying." The more intense the dispute, the more hardened becomes the narrative, as is the case with trauma or depression, or when there is a threat to a basic human need. Default stories are often highly resistant to change, and more work needs to be done to determine what mediators can do to help parties see the world through frames that are both empowering and help to manage conflict.

55. William Carlos Williams, as quoted in R. Coles, *The Call of Stories: Teaching and the Moral Imagination* (Boston: Houghton Mifflin, 1989).

PART TWO

UNDERSTANDING DISPUTES AND DISPUTE CONTEXTS

CHAPTER ELEVEN

Disputes as Opportunities to Create Value

Michael L. Moffitt

Some have suggested that negotiations aimed at resolving disputes might be fundamentally different from dealmaking negotiations.[1] Business ventures, international treaties, and marriage, such observers say, are *deals*—the product of a different kind of interaction. In such contexts, perhaps, opportunities to create value are conspicuous. The parties can craft an efficient and elegant agreement—one that both would prefer to no agreement. Their agreement can capitalize on the parties' joint interests. It can include value-creating trades that build upon the parties' differences, rather than merely divide a finite resource among the parties. Intuitively, these kinds of value-creating endeavors are easier in a dealmaking context.

What this perspective misses is that all interactions involve the potential for disputes. Some disputes relate to past events in the relationship. Who dropped the ball on the marketing plan? Who failed to prevent the environmental damage? Who was supposed to take out the recycling? Other disputes will be more future-oriented. How will we divide the profits? How should we deal with border security? How should we spend Friday night? Disputes and potential disputes are ubiquitous. As a result, even dealmaking takes place in the shadow of the prospect of disputes.

Even if it were empirically demonstrable that more value is captured in dealmaking contexts than in dispute resolution contexts, dividing negotiations into dispute resolution and dealmaking can be unhelpful for negotiators in practice. What the deal-dispute framework suggests is that negotiators who find themselves in a dispute should seek ways to *convert* their context to a deal-making one. The framework calls on negotiators to treat the dispute situation as similar to a dealmaking one by searching for joint opportunities to create value. Perhaps for some negotiators this is a helpful reminder not to ignore the possibility of forward-looking mechanisms for capturing value in disputes.

My concern is that the people who most need to be skilled and aimed at finding value—those who are locked in the most difficult and bitter disputes—are the *most likely* to resist the recharacterization of their dispute as a possible "deal." "Why would I want to think about making another deal with that company? They've already betrayed my trust once." "We do not deal with brutal dictators." "I'm not here to make a deal with that insensitive jerk. I hate him for what he did, and I want him to pay." If value creation is only for dealmaking, then the deal-dispute division risks suggesting to these disputants that they ought not to focus on value creation. And yet they are precisely the parties who would most benefit from such a focus.

A closer look at interactions between people or organizations reveals that differing and conflicting interests are present in virtually all circumstances—even when the parties' relationship bears none of the hallmarks of a dispute. Any two people who spend significant time together quickly discover that not all of their interests are identical or shared. And yet, businesses engage in joint ventures, countries sign treaties, couples marry—and disputants reach resolution.

Disputants need not imagine that to create value they must somehow expend the energy to convert their situation into a dealmaking context. Instead, the challenge for negotiators is to recognize the value-creation opportunities, along with the dispute resolution opportunities, inherent in virtually all interactions. In this chapter, I highlight some troublesome assumptions about value creation in disputes, and I provide illustrations of the most common sources of value creation in dispute contexts. I then offer three pieces of advice to disputants who would seek to create value in the process of resolving their disagreements.

ASSUMPTIONS ABOUT VALUE IN DISPUTES

Much of the language used to describe disputes masks the value creation opportunities inherent in dispute contexts. To the extent that one genuinely considers disputants to be "at war" or "in a battle," for example, the notion of value creation appears almost anathema. Our language does not support easily the idea that both sides might win a battle.[2] Certainly, warfare is not typically described as holding the prospect of mutual benefit. Someone wins and someone loses. The best that the loser can hope for is that the loss brings as little detriment as possible. Even descriptions outside of warfare—for example, speaking of disputes as "contests"—suggest that the interaction between disputants is necessarily zero-sum. A dollar more for me is a dollar less for you. If I get what I want, you do not get what you want.

Though they often do not acknowledge it, some of the foundational models of dispute resolution rest on the assumption that disputes are zero-sum exchanges. In describing a single-issue dispute, many economists' models suggest that each party has a reservation price—a price point at which he or she is indifferent between settling and walking away to his or her Best Alternative To a Negotiated Agreement (BATNA). In a two-party dispute, according to this framework, each side will have a reservation price, whether or not every disputant has consciously fixed one or labeled it as such. These two points may combine to produce a Zone of Possible Agreement (ZOPA) or they may not. If the claimant's reservation price is low (he will take anything above a low number), and the defendant's reservation price is high (she will pay up to a large sum to settle the case), a large ZOPA exists.

For example, in a medical malpractice case, a plaintiff and her lawyer may have determined that any settlement offer above $300,000 would be preferable to going to court. In arriving at that number, they consider the expenses the plaintiff has already incurred, the costs she is likely to incur in the future, the value she places on resolution, the value she places on having her day in court, and so on. They also consider, of course, their estimates of the risks and opportunities of trial. Meanwhile, if the defendant hospital's insurance company has determined that it would pay up to $1 million to avoid litigation, the ZOPA is between $300,000 and $1 million (Figure 11.1).

Some negotiation theorists describe the values within the ZOPA as the "surplus value" available.[3] Economists assume that absent irrationality or an inefficient bargaining process, when there is a ZOPA, each party ought to receive an outcome that is more favorable than his or her BATNA. What remains to be determined in a negotiation is the distribution of that surplus.

In this regard, perhaps, even this simplistic model of bargaining speaks of the possibility of value-capturing. The parties are better off by making an agreement than they would be in the absence of an agreement. This is the least robust meaning of value, however, as the benefit stems only from the *fact* of agreement, rather than from the *terms* of the agreement. An agreement at one

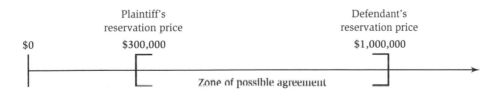

Figure 11.1. Example of a ZOPA.

point in the ZOPA is no more or less value-laden than an agreement at any other point. The only issue is how the value is distributed among the disputants. The ZOPA model, therefore, still assumes a fundamentally zero-sum interaction: more for me is less for you.

The analytic model based on reservation prices is too simplistic, of course, to capture accurately the realities of complex disputes. Most disputes have multiple variables. Even when a dispute is "just about money," there are many potential issues to resolve. Who pays how much? When? In what form? In exchange for what specific release? And so on. Effective negotiators will almost always hunt for ways to make the focus of their negotiations non-zero-sum. In doing so, they reveal ways in which the model based on reservation prices is overly simplistic.

VALUE-CREATION OPPORTUNITIES

Possible benefits beyond zero-sum distributions appear in a variety of forms in negotiated agreements. I refer to the process of discovering and capturing these benefits for the parties during a negotiation as value creation. Scholars have helped to clarify a limited set of conditions in which disputants (or any negotiators) might discover these non-zero-sum settlement opportunities.

Shared Interests

Much of the dispute resolution literature includes the assumption that disputants are motivated by a complex set of interests, even when each party articulates one very simple-sounding position. Assuming that disputants hold multiple interests, it is reasonable to expect that sometimes they will have some interests that are opposed. (You want to pay less, and I want to receive more from you.) Disputants may have other interests that are differing, but not opposing. (I care about a change in policy, and you care about confidentiality.) Finally, it is reasonable to assume that some of the disputants' interests are shared. (You and I both want the project to be completed on time. You would prefer a cleaner environment and so would I. Both divorcing parents want their children to receive a quality education.) Shared interests present the opportunity for crafting arrangements that make both sides better off in a noncompetitive way.

Even in circumstances in which most of the disputants' interests are conspicuously opposed, the disputants may also have shared interests. A group of college seniors are outraged at what they perceive as the college administration's lack of responsiveness to the needs and concerns of female students. They file a lawsuit alleging gender discrimination, demanding a considerable cash payment and a change in specific college policies. The college denies all of the allegations contained in the lawsuit. The students and the college administration do not have identical sets of interests. Yet they have at least some shared interests. The college administration wants to maintain the reputation of the school. It wants to attract high-quality students and to provide students with a first-class education. It wants happy alumni. The soon-to-be-graduates share these interests. The seniors do not want to receive a diploma from a discredited institution that attracts a weaker pool of students, has a soiled reputation, and is unable to provide a top-notch education. Building on their shared interests, the students and the administration might undertake a comprehensive review of policies. They might agree to a process for addressing future issues. They might jointly agree to the allocation of funds to a gender studies program. Disputants will virtually never have identical interests, but focusing on interests in common presents the opportunity to discover mutually attractive settlement options.

Reducing Transaction Costs

Unresolved disputes can be costly. In some cases, the continually growing expenses associated with an unresolved dispute are easy to identify and quantify. As the landlord and tenant fight over who will pay to repair the leaky plumbing, the water bill continues to rise, as does the risk of permanent water damage. In other cases, the costs associated with an ongoing dispute may not be quantifiable, but they are nonetheless real. Two neighbors who are bitter over an unresolved issue about noise may lose sleep because of the stress involved in the dispute. They may also miss out on opportunities to socialize or to share expenses on things like lawn care. Being in a dispute takes a toll. Resolving disputes earlier at least helps to preserve whatever value remains to be captured.

Transaction costs are not just about resolving a dispute sooner, however. To minimize unwanted transaction costs, disputants should also consider carefully the process they choose for resolving their dispute. The process of negotiating can be costly. Negotiating takes time and often creates stress. In many contexts, agents get involved in negotiations, adding further direct expenses. Other dispute resolution mechanisms may have additional direct costs, ranging from mediators' fees, to filing fees in arbitration or in court, to discovery and more.[4] Disputants may be able to structure dispute resolution processes in ways that minimize these expenses. For example, disputants involved in complex litigation might jointly agree on limited discovery, or on a strict timetable for the various stages of the process, or even on a process for resolving the dispute quickly if no agreement is reached by a certain deadline. I know one married couple who decided to set a limit on how long they would argue over the division of household chores. After the expiration of that time, if they had not come to a resolution, they would always do rock-paper-scissors to resolve their dispute. This process occasionally yielded inelegant outcomes, but by cutting off the transaction costs involved in further argument, they captured value—or at least prevented its further destruction.

Reducing Implementation Problems

In some circumstances, the resolution of a dispute is self-executing. One side hands some money to the other side, ending the dispute. Often, though, an agreement requires more complex implementation, raising the prospect of implementation problems. No perfect system of implementation monitoring exists, and disputants therefore face the prospect of moral hazard. Moral hazard is a condition in which one party might act in a way that harms the interests of the other party during implementation, but does so in a way that is difficult for the other party to recognize or prevent.[5] Consider a construction dispute between a homeowner and a contractor. If the two sides consider an agreement that has the contractor rebuilding a structure for a fixed sum, several implementation risks arise. The contractor might not use the highest-quality materials, might not prioritize the job, or might not assign the most competent workers to the project. If the homeowner does not have a sophisticated understanding of construction, he or she has no real chance of spotting defects in the contractor's implementation of the deal. Even if the homeowner had the expertise, monitoring would require time and expense. Anxious about this prospect, the homeowner may pass up an agreement that captures the potential benefit of having the contractor do the rebuilding. If disputants recognize the possibility of moral hazard in implementation, they may be able to structure the agreement to manage those risks and create an acceptable deal for all parties. The homeowner and the contractor might agree to a timeline; they might jointly share the expense of hiring an independent contractor to inspect the site unannounced three times during construction; and the contractor might agree to a penalty clause in the event any defects are found within three years of construction.

Differences in Priorities

In rare circumstances, a dispute is all about one issue—for example, who gets how many dollars. In most disputes, multiple issues are on the table, or lurk somewhere just beneath it. Anytime there are multiple issues, it stands to reason that disputants are likely to value them differently. The plaintiff wants more money, sooner, with greater publicity. The defendant wants to pay less, later, and with less fanfare. Yet each may put different weight on these three issues. For example, the plaintiff may care most about the short-term payout, while the defendant cares most about how the settlement is presented to the public. If the disputants can recognize these differences in relative valuation, they can structure a resolution that captures the value of trading off the issues. The plaintiff gives the defendant the nondisclosure assurances it seeks in exchange for a greater immediate payout.

Differences in Timeframe

People value things differently at different times. Most of us would prefer a dollar today over a dollar next year. Yet we may differ in how much more attractive a dollar today is. Installment contracts and structured payments are the vehicles for capturing value when disputants have different preferences regarding time horizons. If a small business has a short-term cash flow problem, it might offer to settle a dispute with one of its suppliers by promising to pay the supplier a sum well above the nominal amount of the dispute, provided it need not make the payment until two years from now. Assuming the supplier has no short-term need for cash, and that the supplier is confident that it will receive the payment at the proposed time, the offer could be value creating when compared with a straight exchange of dollars today.

Opportunities to create value out of differences in timeframe are not limited to financial exchanges. For example, the issue of cattle grazing near rivers can create considerable disagreement between ranchers and environmental groups. In some areas, disputing parties have discovered that they have different timelines and have crafted value-creating solutions based on those differences. The traditional method of ranching allowed cattle onto large tracts of land, without respect to the season. Because cattle are drawn to water, they would spend much of the spring eating every new plant shoot that came up near the river. Pursuant to an agreement between ranchers and environmentalists in some places, cattle are now fenced out of the areas directly connected to the streams during the spring season. As a result, the plants have a chance to grow to maturity, birds have time to nest, and flowers can go to seed before the cattle are let in. And it turns out that this arrangement not only has had a more beneficial impact on the ecosystem but also has produced greater total forage for the cattle because the plants were able to grow to maturity.[6]

Differences in Prediction

Some disputes hinge not on differing perceptions about what has already happened but rather on differing perceptions about what will happen in the future. A man driving a rental truck runs into a car driven by a woman who was stopped at a stop sign. She has some bruises, but otherwise appears fine. Will the victim develop further injuries later on? If the victim believes that more serious injuries may manifest themselves at a later time, she may demand a high price to settle the claim today for a flat fee. If the truck driver believes that the minor injuries currently visible are all that will result from the accident, he is unlikely to accept such a high demand. The two may be unable to persuade each other about the likelihood of further injuries, but they have the opportunity to craft a contingent agreement, capitalizing on their differing predictions about the future. They could craft a settlement that includes a modest payment for current injuries, medical monitoring for a period of time, and a contingent clause that provides the accident victim with a large payout if future injuries are discovered. Because the victim believes injuries will appear, she will be excited about the prospect of a large payout. Because the driver believes no injuries will occur, he will view his costs to resolve the dispute as relatively modest.[7]

Differences in Risk Tolerance

Some people love taking risks and some try generally to avoid them. In certain circumstances, the stakes are low enough that even those who are generally risk averse can tolerate a risk. In others, most are willing to pay a premium not to bear any risk. Out of this basic dynamic, insurance companies do business, and disputants can find opportunities to create value. For example, two business partners fighting over ownership of a product may eventually decide to send the product to market, rather than have it languish during a protracted ownership dispute. Yet they still must decide on how they will split the uncertain future profits. If one partner has a real need for financial security, while the other is more secure and better able to take on the risk, the two can structure an arrangement in which the less nervous party takes on the risk of the product failing, in exchange for a greater percentage of the profits if the product succeeds.

Disputants' risk tolerances play a role even in cases that proceed to trial. The plaintiff dreams of a lottery-sized payout, and the defendant hopes that the jury will award the plaintiff nothing. Yet each party may fear the "bad" outcome even more than it wants the "good" outcome. If the plaintiff does not receive any award, he or she will be unable to afford ongoing medical care. If the jury hits the defendant with a heavily punitive award, it will send the company into bankruptcy. Even if these two parties are unable to agree to a settlement package before trial, they could form a so-called "high-low" agreement, creating a floor and a ceiling on the plaintiff's eventual recovery. For example, the disputants might agree to a "low" of $500,000 and a "high" of $2 million. Having signed their high-low agreement, the parties would take the case to trial, and the jury would make its award. If the jury award fell below $500,000, the defendant would pay the plaintiff the agreed-upon "low" number of $500,000. If the jury award came in above $2 million, the defendant would pay the plaintiff $2 million. If the jury award fell between the two figures, the jury award would stand as the award. Such high-low agreements can help to create more attractive settlement options than would otherwise be possible in conditions of high risk.

Differences in Capabilities

Disputants rarely enter a dispute with identical skills, resources, and abilities. If they are able to identify the ways in which they have different capabilities, they may be able to craft agreements that capitalize on the combination of their relative strengths and weaknesses. The authors of *Beyond Winning* describe the 1997 dispute between Intel and Digital Equipment Corporation over Intel's alleged misappropriation of Digital's intellectual property when it created a new computer chip. Intel and Digital settled the multimillion dollar claim and counterclaim with a series of agreements that involved the sale of existing manufacturing facilities, the licensing of current technology, and agreements for future work over the coming decade. The disputants were able to capitalize on the resources and capabilities each brought to the table, treating the settlement negotiations much like potential business partners exploring a possible joint venture.[8]

NEGOTIATING BEHAVIOR LEADING TO VALUE CREATION

Understanding the analytic framework for assessing the opportunities for value creation is one important piece of the negotiation puzzle. To translate that analytic understanding into a negotiated agreement that captures the available value, however, also requires negotiators to adopt *behaviors* consistent with the search for value. On that issue, I offer three observations about negotiations aimed at value creation. First, contrary to popular perception, value creation is not simply a matter of cooperation. Indeed, many who view themselves as entirely cooperative never discover value-creating trades. Second, inquiring into each party's interests is important, but the inquiry must extend beyond interests if the eventual deal is to maximize value. Third, the timing and sequence of negotiators' commitments—their agreements to do or not do certain things—affects the likelihood that they will discover value-creating trades.

Not Simply About "Cooperation"

Relying perhaps in part on the prominence of the prisoner's dilemma as a model of bargaining, some negotiation analysts appear to suggest that the road to value creation is simple: the disputants need only to "cooperate." This suggestion is both overstated and understated.

The name for the prisoner's dilemma model of bargaining behavior stems from a hypothetical situation in which investigators have arrested two suspects they believe committed a crime together. The police separate the suspects and independently ask each to implicate the other prisoner. If both suspects maintain their collective innocence (cooperate with each other), each will receive only a small punishment because of the lack of proof. If each suspect implicates the other, both will be convicted and will receive a greater punishment. If one side maintains his innocence, but the other implicates him (by defecting), the prisoner who defects will be rewarded by the police, while the implicated prisoner receives the harshest punishment (see Figure 11.2).

Within the prisoners' dilemma model, each party's payout is a function of its own choice and the choice of its counterpart. The model assumes that each party must choose either to cooperate or to defect, and must make its choice without knowing what the other side will do. The payouts then are determined by the combination of the two parties' choices. In a condition of joint cooperation, each side receives a favorable payout. If both sides defect, each receives a much less attractive payout. Within the prisoner's dilemma model, when only

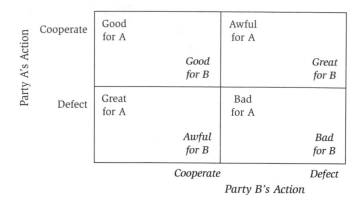

Figure 11.2. A Basic Prisoner's Dilemma Model.

one side defects, that side stands to gain the greatest possible individual payout, while the lone cooperating side receives the least attractive payout.

The prisoner's dilemma model holds two attractive features for theorists wishing to model disputants' bargaining behavior. First, the model captures part of the tension many negotiators experience over issues of cooperation and disclosure. Most negotiators recognize that if both sides fail to disclose important information, the likelihood of solving the problem in a jointly satisfactory manner is greatly reduced. At the same time, most negotiators recognize that unilateral disclosure creates a risk of exploitation. So it is with the prisoner's dilemma. Both might recognize the stable benefits of a good-good payoff, and both fear being the lone cooperator who receives the awful payoff. The second attractive aspect of the prisoner's dilemma is that, with its variable payoffs, the prisoner's dilemma is a model of bargaining that does not assume a fixed pie.[9] There are more total benefits to be divided among the negotiators in a condition of joint cooperation than in a condition of mutual defection. Negotiators receive more or less favorable results based on their behavior and on the behavior of their counterparts, and yet cooperation is not necessarily without risks. In these senses, the prisoner's dilemma is a reasonable model of certain aspects of bargaining.

Nevertheless, the prisoner's dilemma model is limited in its descriptive and prescriptive utility. One obvious drawback is that it assumes only two disputants or participants. While such conditions are clean and easy for economists to analyze, real-world disputes rarely reflect the sterile condition in which only two people are affected by a dispute or its resolution. If one person injures another, many different parties may be affected by the injury or by a proposed resolution. The victim's family, the victim's employer, the injurer's family and employer, insurance companies for the various actors, and possibly society at large may be affected in ways that would be ignored if the only perspectives considered were those of the victim and the injurer.

Even more troubling from the perspective of modeling disputes, the prisoner's dilemma assumes that negotiators have a binary choice: cooperate or defect. This construction of negotiation poses two problems. First, as a descriptive matter, disputing conditions are rarely so straightforward. Much of what a negotiator does is neither purely cooperative nor purely the opposite. When I asked that careful question, was I cooperating or defecting? If I make a forceful, principled argument for my side, does that constitute cooperation or defection? How about when I made a generous counteroffer? Second, even if it were possible to discern cooperation from defection, the model is utterly silent on how it is that real-world negotiators translate "cooperation" into value creation. Only by building on one or more of the value-creating opportunities listed earlier can the two sides reap the rewards of cooperation.

"Focus on Interests" . . . and Then Some

"Focus on interests, not positions" is the hortatory phrase that most succinctly signals one of the foundational premises of much of modern dispute resolution theory. Positions and interests are not the same thing. In *Getting to YES,* the authors illustrate this with the often-recounted story about two sisters fighting over a single orange. Each demands the entire orange without realizing that one wants the fruit to eat and the other wants the peel for baking.[10] Interests, in the usage of modern dispute resolution, are the things that motivate negotiators. Interests are the hopes, fears, concerns, and dreams that shape how disputants will make decisions. Positions are a function of a person's interests. A position is an expression (often in the form of an offer or demand) of what one person believes would satisfy his or her interests.

It is rarely difficult to figure out what a disputant's position is. A representative of a defendant company says, "No payment whatsoever. Not even a dime." What interests might underlie the representative's position? Maybe the company is concerned about the precedent; maybe this is viewed as a matter of principle; maybe it is important not to have any new liability on the books this year; maybe the representative wants to make sure that no money is charged to a particular department; and/or maybe the representative wants to look tough to his or her colleagues. Any of these interests might motivate the representative to advance the "no payment" position. A plaintiff says, "No less than $300,000." What are the plaintiff's interests? The plaintiff may be motivated by principle, by a short-term need for cash, by a long-term need to secure retirement, by a fear of future complications or injuries, or by concerns about public image.

Drawing on the distinction between positions and interests, many have come to embrace "interest-based" approaches to negotiation. In the context of collective bargaining negotiations, for example, the Federal Mediation and Conciliation Service has explicitly encouraged disputants and potential disputants to engage in a process of "interest-based bargaining."[11]

The popular usage of the terms "interests" and "positions" remains impre- cise. One often hears talk in the media (and even at the negotiation table) of each side's "negotiation position." Perhaps these negotiators have consciously chosen to engage in a position-based approach to negotiation—one akin to a haggle. Perhaps it is simply a product of sloppy language usage. Or perhaps the negotiators have never understood the distinction between positions and inter- ests. Despite this continued variation in language, the general prescription to focus on underlying interests is an important part of the prescription for creat- ing value in the context of dispute resolution.

As described earlier, however, opportunities to create value do not stem uniquely from the intersection of the disputants' interests. To be certain, shared interests present an obvious opportunity to create value. Similarly, disputants with differing interests (rather than opposed interests) may discover value- creating trades. Some aspects of value creation, however, hinge on information not normally captured under even the broadest umbrella definitions of "inter- ests." Capitalizing on differences in resources or capabilities, for example, demands information about more than just the parties' interests. Similarly, efforts to minimize transaction costs and avoid moral hazard demand more than mere reference to the parties' interests.

Focusing on interests may be an essential step in negotiating to create value. For disputants to assure themselves that they have discovered the most efficient, value-laden agreement, however, merely focusing on interests is not enough. The disputants should explore each of the possible sources of value—including those that build on information beyond interests.

Avoid Sequential, Piecemeal Commitments

In a process of haggling, in which the parties assume that there is only one issue under discussion and that the interaction is zero-sum, each negotiator is likely to make unilateral, sequential, conditional commitments. "It will take $100,000 to settle this today." "I will not offer you a dime." "Unless you offer at least $80,000, we can just stop talking." "I would pay you a few thousand dollars to get rid of the nuisance of this case." And so on. For a variety of reasons, hag- gling carries considerable risks, yet it is an archetypal process of negotiation. The pros and cons of haggling are discussed in Chapter Eighteen of this book and need not detain us here.

Sequential or piecemeal commitments are more troubling in real-world dis- puting contexts with multiple issues under discussion. Sometimes disputants will aim to "create momentum" by engaging in the dangerous practice of mak- ing sequential commitments. In a negotiation over five issues, for example, negotiators might try to generate momentum by resolving a couple of the "easy" issues first. The union gets what it wants on vacation time, and management gets the revised job descriptions it wants. While this might build momentum and good will, it also greatly increases the risk of impasse or an inefficient final outcome.

Negotiating through a process of sequential commitments creates a greater risk of impasse because the parties may resolve all of the easy issues first. They may pick away at the problem, resolving issues one by one until only one issue remains. The problem is that the issue that remains is likely to be the most contentious issue. What happens then? Each side is likely to perceive itself as having made the majority of the concessions, or for some other reason to be "deserving" of a favorable resolution on the last issue. If the final issue is indivisible, nothing is left except for one side to concede to the other. That is an unattractive position, making it more likely that each side will dig in and demand to receive what it wants on the final issue. Absent strong justifications for a particular resolution on the final issue, the circumstances are likely to lead to one or both sides playing a game of "chicken," which in turn increases the risk of impasse.

Even if sequential commitments produce no impasse, they create a risk of inefficient deals because they block the possibility of issue-swapping later in the negotiation. Maybe the union should have gotten vacation time *and* the job descriptions in exchange for the company getting what it wanted on the issue of pension reform. If the union cares more about the first two issues, and management cares most about the third, it would be inefficient to adopt a negotiating process of sequential commitments because such an approach precludes the possibility of trades across issues.

One model for dealing with the combination of sequential commitments and complex problem solving is the One-Text Process, sometimes called a Single Negotiating Text approach. Within this model of negotiating, a facilitator (either an outside party or one or more of the disputants specifically identified to play this role) surveys each of the disputants to learn of their interests and priorities. Using that information, the facilitator creates a single discussion draft and then solicits feedback on the ways the draft fails to satisfy each party's main interests. It is important that the facilitator not ask any party to commit to the draft or to any part of the draft. Indeed, such commitments are forbidden by the ground rules of the One-Text Process. The facilitator maintains full control over the draft, ensuring that only one draft text is under consideration at any given moment. The facilitator revises the draft, seeks more feedback, and continues to solicit feedback and to revise the text until no further beneficial revisions appear possible. At that point, the facilitator presents the disputants with a single choice: accept the draft in whole or reject it entirely. This method prevents partial commitments and sequential commitments, and neither side is asked for serial concessions. The One-Text Process has been used successfully in many high-stakes international negotiations. For example, the eventual agreement in the Camp David accords was the twenty-third draft created through a similar process.[12] The One-Text Process also has been an important tool for resolving more contained disputes.[13]

CONCLUSION

Disputes are rarely fun. Few enter a dispute with unbridled enthusiasm, thinking, "Oh boy, an opportunity for me to craft a value-creating agreement with my counterpart!"

Yet conceiving of disputes in terms that preclude the discovery of such arrangements can be destructive in a self-fulfilling sense. Those who conceive of disputes as battles are rarely disappointed—within relatively little time, they tend to find their counterparts engaged in battle-like behavior. Those who see the interaction as limited in possibilities will probably engage in strategic behaviors that make it that much harder to discover possibilities.

Even if disputes are not fun, we should be focused on identifying those aspects of disputes that hold the greatest promise for a resolution that captures value.

Notes

1. The first articulation of this division appears in F.E.A. Sander and J. Z. Rubin, "The Janus Quality of Negotiations: Dealmaking and Dispute Settlement," *Negotiation Journal,* 1988, *4,* 109–113.

2. This is true, curiously, even though we are relatively comfortable with the idea that a battle might produce no winners. The concept of Pyrrhic victories suggests that winners may ultimately be losers, and the idea of mutually assured destruction suggests that war in some forms produces only losers. Still, we have no image of war producing only winners.

3. See, for example, Korobkin, Chapter Seventeen in this volume.

4. Dispute resolution processes themselves can create or destroy value. Unless one side sees a distributive opportunity to be gained by creating procedural transaction costs, disputants should prefer more efficient processes over those that are more costly. The costs involved in dispute resolution processes, however, are not always quantifiable. Dispute resolution processes offer disputants vastly different participatory experiences. These different experiences have an impact on disputants' affective satisfaction—the extent to which they are happy with the process by which the dispute was resolved—even if they produce identical substantive outcomes. A litigant has a different experience than does a party to a mediation. Some disputants would prefer to be a litigant because they place a high value on being part of a public hearing in which a determination of rights is pronounced. Other disputants would prefer to be a party to a mediation because they place a high value on autonomy—being able to craft the final terms of the

resolution themselves. For more on affective satisfaction, see Shapiro, Chapter Five in this volume.

5. Mnookin, Peppet, and Tulumello define moral hazard as "[t]he problem created when a contract shifts risk from one party to another party and information asymmetries permit the non-riskbearer to behave adversely under the contract without detection or consequence" (Mnookin, R. H., Peppet, S., and Tulumello, A. S. *Beyond Winning: Negotiating to Create Value in Deals and Disputes.* Cambridge, Mass.: Belknap Press of Harvard University Press, 2000, p. 26). See also M. L. Moffitt, "Contingent Agreements," *Marquette Law Review,* 2004, *87,* 691–696.

6. This description of the issues surrounding the management of riparian systems oversimplifies the matter somewhat of course. Additional considerations include such things as erosion rates, channel gradients, plant species, evapotranspiration, and grazing-fee structures. A concrete example of a successful timeline-based trade similar to that described in the text is the project spearheaded by Wayne Elmore on a stream called Bear Creek in the high desert of Oregon. For more on the research underlying these grazing practices, see B. J. Rhodes, C. B. Marlow, and H. W. Sherwood, "Monitoring Streambank Stability: Grazing Impacts or Stream Variability?" *Montana AgResearch,* Fall 1995, pp. 3–8; D. R. Allen and C. B. Marlow, "Shoot Population Dynamics of Beaked Sedge Following Cattle Grazing," *Journal of Range Management,* January 1994, *47,* 64–69; and R. W. Knight, "Streamside Erosional Response to Animal Grazing Practices on Meadow Creek in Northeastern Oregon," Masters Thesis, Corvallis, Oreg.: Oregon State University, 1978. Materials also available at [http://www.cropinfo.net/riparian.htm].

7. For more on the uses of contingent agreements in crafting settlements, see Moffitt, "Contingent Agreements," 2004.

8. See Mnookin, Peppet, and Tulumello, *Beyond Winning,* 2000.

9. Although the prisoner's dilemma by its nature does not assume a fixed pie, it also does not necessarily assume that conditions of joint cooperation produce the greatest total benefit. If the payoff grid were structured so that cooperation yielded five units of satisfaction to each cooperator, and the cooperate-defect payoff were ten for the defector and one for the lone cooperator, the greatest total "value" would come from a condition of unilateral defection. For more on the challenges of considering efficiency and distributive equity, see H. Raiffa, *The Art and Science of Negotiation: How to Resolve Conflict and Get the Best Out of Bargaining* (Cambridge, Mass.: Belknap Press of Harvard University Press, 1982).

10. See R. Fisher, W. Ury, and B. Patton, *Getting to YES: Negotiating Agreement Without Giving In* (2nd ed.) (New York: Penguin, 1991).

11. See C. Brommer, G. Buckingham, and S. Loeffler, "Cooperative Bargaining Styles at FMCS: A Movement Toward Choices," *Pepperdine Dispute Resolution Law Journal,* 2002, *2,* 465–490. For an interesting account of the introduction of interest-based bargaining into the context of railway labor negotiations, in which the National Mediation Board has jurisdiction, see L. M. Bubala, "Interest-Based Bargaining in the Railway Collective Bargaining Agreements: The Groundbreaking CSXT/UTU Yardmaster Agreement," *Oregon Law Review,* 2004, *82,* 935–977.

12. For more on the One-Text Process or the Single Negotiation Text process and its applications, see Fisher, Ury, and Patton, *Getting to YES*, 1991; and Raiffa, *The Art and Science of Negotiation*, 1982.

13. I have seen the One-Text Process help teachers and school boards reach resolution on collective bargaining agreements, just as I have seen the One-Text Process aid in creating joint plans for parties on opposite sides of a cease-fire line. Disputes and conflicts in many contexts share the characteristics that make the One-Text Process useful.

CHAPTER TWELVE

Six Principles for Using Negotiating Agents to Maximum Advantage

Scott R. Peppet

Often, we do not negotiate for ourselves. Instead, we ask someone to represent us at the bargaining table. Agency—when someone else acts on our behalf—has advantages and disadvantages in negotiation. This chapter explores how agents complicate negotiations and how agents can both benefit and irritate the principals they are supposed to serve.[1] Answering the question of how principals can use agents to maximum advantage in negotiation will both summarize and extend our understanding of agency in negotiation. By "maximum advantage," I do not presuppose that a principal's only desire is to do well for him- or herself at others' expense, nor that negotiation is zero-sum. Instead I mean, simply, how can a principal make best use of a negotiating agent, regardless of that principal's goals or preferred approach to negotiation? To answer this question, this chapter first explores the problems and opportunities inherent in agency, then articulates six guiding principles for using agents in negotiation.

OPPORTUNITIES AND PROBLEMS

We all have many agents working for us at any given moment. You entrust your safety to the pilot of a commercial airliner; you ask a physician to examine and heal you; you elect representatives to govern in the legislature; you hire employees to work for you; you cast votes for corporate officers running enterprises in which you hold stock; you trust the postman to carry your letters to faraway places; you have teachers educating your children; you beg your spouse to confront a frustrating neighbor on your behalf. Agency is a basic fact of life, not an occasional complicating factor. In a modern world, we each delegate to others constantly. This frees us to pursue our own interests and talents while giving us the benefits of others' time and expertise.

Agents provide many advantages and opportunities in negotiation. A negotiating agent—whether a lawyer, a sports agent, or a diplomat—may be able to assert his or her principal's interests more skillfully or forcefully than can the principal. Agents may have special training, such as a legal education, that equips them to argue for or defend a principal. And agents may be able to detach themselves from the emotional throes of a negotiation and gain perspective on the client's long-term interests. This may allow an agent to handle delicate issues that his or her principal might negotiate poorly.

There are also problems inherent in hiring a negotiating agent. Principal-agent theory focuses on three ways in which agents may differ from their principals.[2] First, the agent may have different *preferences* than the principal. For example, the agent may not want to work as hard as the principal wishes him or her to work. Second, agents may have different *incentives* than the principal. They may have a different stake in the outcome, or may receive different rewards, than the principal. Third, an agent may have *information* unavailable to the principal, or vice versa. For example, the principal may not know how hard the agent is working. These divergences between agent and principal give rise to problems relating to monitoring, incentives, coordination, and strategy. The following sections consider each in turn.

The Monitoring Problem: A Primer on Principal-Agent Economics

Principal-agent economics[3] is concerned with situations in which a principal cannot directly observe an agent's actions and the principal cannot completely infer the agent's behavior by observing the outcome of the agent's activities.[4] In other words, the principal depends on the agent, but the principal does not have sufficient information to judge the agent's performance perfectly. In these situations, an agent can take advantage of a principal—and vice versa. The most obvious example occurs when an agent pretends to work harder than he or she is actually working, otherwise known as "shirking." An employee might look busy while typing away at his computer, but he may actually be e-mailing a friend. Similarly, a lawyer negotiating for a client may bill for hours of unnecessary research or work done at a snail's pace.

Shirking can arise in various ways in the negotiation context. A negotiating agent may exaggerate the effort involved in negotiating a deal or dispute or skew her reports about what took place at the bargaining table. She might describe the intransigence of the other side, or how all of her skill and courage were needed to counter the other side's "hard bargaining" behavior. In reality, however, the agent may have faced a cooperative, efficient counterpart who posed no real challenge and demanded no extraordinary efforts.

The threat of an agent shirking or otherwise acting contrary to a principal's interests leads to *agency costs.* These are costs associated with attempting to control one's agent and minimize shirking or other troublesome behavior. For example, an employer may purchase software to monitor e-mail usage or spend time patrolling the halls to catch unwary employees. A client may pore over a lawyer's billing statement or hire a secondary attorney to monitor the first lawyer's performance. A principal may try to monitor the events unfolding in a negotiation by attending negotiation sessions that he or she could otherwise skip.

These attempts to monitor are inevitably imperfect. By definition, agency problems arise in those situations in which one cannot completely oversee an agent's behavior or infer the agent's actions from the outcome he or she produces. In addition, monitoring is expensive. A principal may not have the time, resources, or expertise to police her agent. In negotiation, for example, a principal may be unable to observe her agent once the agent leaves to bargain with the other side.[5] The principal may never know exactly what words the negotiating agent chooses, how the agent's tone affects the negotiation, or whether the agent fully implements the principal's preferred strategy or tactics. There may be no efficient way for a principal or client to monitor her negotiating agent's behavior this closely.

The Incentive Problem: No Perfect Fee Structure

In addition to monitoring, or in its place, a principal may use incentives to control an agent's behavior. Employers, for example, often structure employee compensation to align an employee's incentives with the employer's goals. Imagine that you are hiring an agent to negotiate several sales contracts for your business. If you want the agent to work quickly, you might pay "by the piece"— paying for each contract closed. For example, this is how many cellular phone operators have incentivized salespeople to sign up large numbers of new customers quickly. If you want the agent to work carefully and thoroughly, you might pay him or her by the hour. Or, if you want your agent to maximize the price received in each contract, you might structure a contingency fee that varies according to the negotiated outcome. Many negotiating agents, including lawyers, real estate brokers, investment bankers, and sports agents, work for contingency fees.

Unfortunately, no incentive structure can perfectly align the interests of a principal and an agent.[6] Instead, each structure creates new incentive and monitoring problems. An hourly fee may induce an agent to delay. A flat fee or "by the piece" fee may create undesirable haste or impatience on the part of the agent. A contingency fee may lead to underinvestment of time or effort by the agent if the agent can settle the client's matter quickly and at very little cost for a reasonable amount. Put differently, under a contingency fee an agent may negotiate a mediocre but acceptable solution quickly rather than struggle to achieve an excellent (but more time-intensive) settlement, simply because the agent has only minor marginal gain from pushing for the better deal. In each case, although incentive structures can help to minimize agency costs, they are an imperfect solution.

The Coordination Problem: Communication Is Not Free

Using a negotiating agent introduces a third type of problem: coordinating the agent's actions, goals, and strategies with those of the principal. If a negotiating agent perfectly understands her client's desires, she can negotiate most effectively on her principal's behalf. In reality, of course, an agent does not have all of this information. Even if a principal and an agent have aligned incentives and the desire to work well together (in other words, both are honorable and uninterested in shirking), the principal and agent must still coordinate their roles, responsibilities, and resources to maximum advantage.

This can become quite complicated. Should both principal and agent attend negotiation sessions? If so, who will say what? What role will each play? If not, what is the agent authorized to say or do on the principal's behalf? Does the agent have sufficient information from the principal about the latter's interests and priorities to be able to represent the principal in his absence?

These are particularly complicated questions for those interested in problem-solving, collaborative, or principled negotiation, as opposed to traditional positional or hard-bargaining negotiation. Rather than simply demanding a certain outcome, problem solving requires considering one's interests, needs, resources, and priorities. Problem solving also generally requires weighing considerations of fairness and comparing a proposed negotiated outcome to an available "walk-away" alternative. These tasks, however, are information-intensive. For a negotiating agent to carry out these tasks on a principal's behalf requires that the agent learn a great deal from the principal prior to setting out. What does the principal want? How does the principal reconcile his competing or contradictory interests? What are his relative priorities as between his interests? How does the principal see his walk-away alternative? What are the principal's risk preferences, and what resources and capabilities does he have available to trade?

To equip an agent to problem solve, a principal will have to answer at least some of these questions for his agent. In the absence of such information, a negotiating agent is likely to lack confidence about the principal's interests—and therefore may engage in more traditional forms of hard bargaining rather than in problem solving. And regardless of the principal's preferred approach to a negotiation, using an agent will require information exchange and coordination between the principal and that agent.

The Strategy Problem: Agency Complicates Negotiation Strategy

Hiring a negotiating agent also introduces several strategy problems vis-à-vis a principal's negotiation with the other side by increasing the likelihood of strategic misunderstanding. If a principal negotiates for herself, she can regulate how collaborative or adversarial she wishes to be, and she can monitor the other side's reactions. When she sends an agent to the bargaining table, however, the principal can no longer fine-tune her strategy and tactics. She must trust that the agent will not behave in ways that might be perceived as overly (or insufficiently) aggressive. And she must trust that the agent will recognize when his impact on the other side may be different from what he intended.[7] For example, one common problem is giving the other side the impression that a principal and her agent are using "good cop–bad cop" tactics.[8] Even if this is untrue, the other side may attribute such intentions to them and react accordingly. To further complicate matters, it may be true.

Involving an agent makes possible tactics otherwise unavailable to the principal alone. "Good cop–bad cop" is one such tactic. Authority tactics are another. An agent may reject a counterpart's offer (or threaten to do so) by claiming that his principal has not authorized him to accept such a small settlement. This may be an honest disclosure about the agent's authority, in which case the agent is trying to save the other side time. But the agent may be bluffing—trying to use deception about authority to convince the other side to revise its expectations. Similarly, an agent may try to pressure eleventh-hour concessions out of the other side by claiming that his principal has demanded those concessions in order to authorize a final settlement.

Introducing agents may cause other strategic problems. In some cases two agents simply may not get along. Their relationship may deteriorate during their negotiation as a result of bargaining behavior or strong emotions. They may grow overly suspicious of each other or overly defensive. As a result, their negotiations may become protracted and expensive as their fees mount and the promise of an agreement recedes. Principals may have to intervene in such circumstances. Two CEOs, for example, may decide to take a negotiation "back" from their lawyers because they fear that their attorneys will ruin the deal. In other words, the principals may intervene upon realizing that their agents have become unable to continue representing them effectively. Such a collapse negates the efficiency benefits that agents can provide if they can manage negotiation strategy effectively for their principals.

SIX PRINCIPLES FOR MANAGING AGENCY IN NEGOTIATION

Despite these myriad potential problems, principals regularly hire negotiating agents because of the many benefits agents confer. Agents may have special skills, experience, or information that makes them better able to negotiate than the principal. Agents may simply have more time available than the principal. The point here, however, is that principals and agents must structure their arrangements carefully so as to maximize the advantages of agency and minimize its costs.

Principals must address the potential problems inherent in monitoring, incentives, coordination, and strategy to gain maximum advantage from using an agent. This section organizes possible solutions to these problems in the form of six basic principles or guidelines for managing a negotiating agent. These six are not the only principles one could devise, nor do they apply perfectly to all negotiation contexts. But they do cover the terrain fairly well, and they are aimed at advancing the prescriptive discussion of how agency theory, game theory, and negotiation theory can best help principals and negotiating agents work together. In that vein, they should be thought of as "principles for consideration," not absolute rules.

Principle One: If possible, use agents (and work for principals) whose preferences are known and acceptable to you.

A simple first principle is to use agents, and to work for principals, whom you know or whose reputations you can discover. Agency relationships can easily go awry because of basic differences in orientation, perspective, or ideology. In the legal context, clients can be unpleasantly surprised to discover themselves in a war of attrition when they simply sought legal advice and problem-solving counsel. Conversely, a lawyer may be confronted with a client who demands unsavory tactics or unethical behavior. As a result, just as clients screen their attorneys, lawyers sometimes try to screen potential clients by asking colleagues or friends for information about the client's history.

Finding out about your agent or principal before entering into an agency relationship is wise. Because of both monitoring and incentive-based solutions to agency problems, principals will be best served if they initially choose like-minded agents, and vice versa. In the negotiation context, this means asking about an agent's negotiation approach, experience, and philosophy. Does the agent have a reputation as an adversarial or hard bargainer? Is the principal likely to require deceptive or dishonest tactics? What stance does each take toward the risks inherent in trying to problem solve or collaborate? Do they have similar goals and reputations? These questions are fundamental to establishing a successful principal-agent relationship in the negotiation context.

Principle Two: If possible, use agents (and work for principals) whose preferences are known to the other side.

Negotiation can be roughly analogized to the famous prisoner's dilemma game.[9] If two negotiators collaborate and share information openly (that is, they "cooperate" in the game), they each benefit. Their ability to trust one another often will facilitate finding mutually advantageous or "joint gain" solutions, and they are thus likely to reach more economically beneficial bargaining outcomes than they would if forced to deal with a hard-bargaining counterpart. Conversely, two hard bargainers (or "defectors" in a prisoner's dilemma game) may each suffer. They may engage in difficult and adversarial tactics that increase transaction costs, decrease the odds of settlement, and lessen the chance of finding joint gains.[10]

To the extent that parties can separate honest collaborators from deceptive hard bargainers, collaborators will deal only with other collaborators, thus avoiding the possibility of exploitation and increasing the likelihood of a successful negotiation. Unfortunately, it may be difficult or impossible to be certain about a counterpart's type.

This uncertainty imposes costs. To the extent that a party cannot sort collaborators from hard bargainers, she will enter a negotiation with trepidation. If she treats an undetectable hard bargainer as an honest collaborator, a negotiator may fare badly. As a result, she may choose to protect herself by limiting herself to "safe" strategies that protect against exploitation. She may withhold information about her needs and priorities from the other side, fearing that her counterpart will try to use that information to extract concessions. This can lead to failed negotiations—the negotiating parties may not reach agreement even though an agreement is possible. It may also cause inefficient outcomes—the parties may reach a deal, but it may not be the most economically beneficial deal possible.

Ronald Gilson and Robert Mnookin have proposed an ingenious solution to this problem by analyzing the dynamics of negotiations in the legal context.[11] Although they recognize that many clients, or principals, do not know each other and thus cannot sort hard bargainers from collaborators, they also realize that often an *attorney* does know opposing counsel. In a given city, for example, all of the family lawyers may know each other, and thus two divorce attorneys may be acquainted. As a result, a client can use his or her choice of agent—in this case, choice of lawyer—to *signal* collaborative intent (or an intent to hard bargain) to the other side. If a client hires an attorney with a solid reputation for collaboration, it may facilitate pursuing that approach by indicating the client's preference for collaboration.

This signal is not perfect.[12] But it is certainly better than no signal at all, and worth serious consideration by a principal contemplating hiring a negotiating agent. Whenever possible, Principle Two suggests hiring a well-known agent who can serve as a strong signal of the principal's intentions.[13] Whether hiring a sports agent, diplomat, political representative, or attorney, a principal should consider that agent's reputation and whether it will help to move the negotiation forward. I do not assume that all principals will want to pursue collaborative strategies. Some may want to hire an agent known as a hard bargainer. Regardless of strategy, however, a principal should ensure that his or her agent shares the principal's orientation, strategy preferences, and approach, and that the agent has a reputation in line with the strategic signals that the principal seeks to send.

Principle Three: If possible, change the structure of the negotiation to align the incentives of principal and agent.

As discussed earlier, the incentives of principals and agents may diverge, leading the agent to act contrary to his or her principal's interests. Principals and agents must therefore try to arrange fee structures and other incentives to align their interests. Contingency fees can help. Bonuses for reaching a negotiated agreement also may incentivize a negotiating agent, as may bonuses for achieving certain performance objectives (such as settling for more or less than a given amount, creating certain types of value, or meeting certain of the principal's key interests). The point is that fees can help to minimize incentive divergence between principals and agents.

Principals and agents should also look beyond these basic fee arrangements and ask whether there are ways to change the basic structure of their negotiation for mutual advantage. The effort of the nascent "Collaborative Law" movement to change the traditional adversarial style of lawyers illustrates this process of structural adjustment. To date, Collaborative Law has been used primarily in the family or divorce law context. The basic idea is simple. Both divorcing parties agree to hire self-identified "collaborative lawyers" to handle their case. The lawyers and parties then agree that, so long as each side is represented by a collaborative lawyer, the attorneys will serve their clients *only* during negotiations. In other words, if the attorneys fail to settle the case, they will withdraw.[14] The parties and their lawyers sign limited retention agreements (LRAs) that limit the scope of the lawyer-client relationships and require the lawyers to withdraw if they cannot reach settlement. These agreements explain the lawyers' limited roles and the mandatory mutual withdrawal provisions. In addition, the parties and their lawyers sign a collaborative law participation agreement at the start of their negotiations. This is a contract with the other side that signifies mutual interest in the Collaborative Law process.

Collaborative Law practitioners describe this contractual modification of the traditional lawyer-client relationship, and of the traditional lawyer-lawyer negotiation process, as a huge benefit for all involved. Collaborative Law practice is touted as more cost-effective, more creative, and less damaging to the clients' relationship than traditional adversarial litigation. It has become fashionable in the family law context—there are now at least eighty-seven local and regional Collaborative Law groups in twenty-five states.[15]

Mandatory mutual withdrawal provisions are a clever alteration of the structure of the traditional lawyer-client, principal-agent relationship. If the parties do not settle, the client loses because he or she must expend the costs necessary to find, hire, and train new counsel.[16] This gives the client incentive to be reasonable. The lawyer, meanwhile, will lose the fees that the lawyer would normally receive for litigating the matter. This signals the lawyer's intent to collaborate and reach agreement.

Collaborative Law is a useful example of how a principal-agent relationship can be structured to meet the interests of both the principal and the agent. By signing an LRA, both the lawyer and the client signal an intention to collaborate—to each other, and to the other side. These signals facilitate their working relationship and make it more likely that they will productively negotiate for the principal. To the extent possible, principals and agents should consider such incentive-aligning, game-changing moves.[17]

Principle Four: Share information between principal and agent to the extent necessary to effect the principal's strategy.

As discussed previously, coordinating information exchange between a principal and an agent can pose challenges. How much time should principals spend educating their agents about their interests, priorities, and strategy preferences prior to a negotiation? Educating to the point that the agent is a functional equivalent of the principal is both unrealistic and unwise—such extensive information exchange would take so much time that it would eviscerate the efficiencies of using an agent in the first place. Yet this leaves a principal and agent having to decide how much information to share, and when, to prepare the agent to negotiate on the principal's behalf.

The challenge is that for two agents to negotiate successfully they must understand the strategy preferences of their principals *and* learn sufficient information from those principals to be able to interact without the principals present. In particular, if agents hope to problem solve on their clients' behalf, they must have more and different information than if they simply hope to haggle. To problem solve requires understanding their clients' interests, priorities, risk preferences, and alternatives, as well as their clients' perceptions, emotions, and sense of fairness. To haggle, agents need only to know more basic information such as their clients' bottom line and aspirations.

Thus, Principle Four simply states that principals and agents should structure their information exchange to make it possible for the agent to enact the principal's choice of strategy in the principal's absence. In practice this means that discussion about strategy choice must be explicit, early, and ongoing during the principal-agent relationship. Only if the agent really understands the principal's preferred strategy can the agent know the sorts of questions to ask of the principal and the kind of information to insist upon.

One challenge, of course, is that in many negotiations the principal may not be able to determine beforehand what strategy to use. Strategy selection depends in part on sizing up the other side and how it seems inclined to negotiate. Principle Four thus requires an ongoing conversation between principal and client to coordinate information exchange based on lessons learned during interaction with the other side. If a negotiation seems to have the potential for complex, interest-based problem solving, an agent should probably begin prepared to pursue such avenues at least to some limited degree. The agent can then return to the principal for more information if necessary.

Principle Five: Treat role coordination and authority delegation as an ongoing negotiation, not a one-time event.

Principals often worry about how much authority to delegate to an agent. The problem is obvious—too much and the agent may make unwanted commitments for the principal, too little and the agent's freedom of action may be too restricted to permit a successful negotiation. This is one manifestation of the monitoring, incentive, and coordination problems in the negotiation context. Because principals cannot perfectly trust or monitor agents, they seek to control agents by restricting their agents' authority.

Roger Fisher and Wayne Davis have persuasively argued for a different approach to authority delegation.[18] They advocate for principals and agents to conceive of authority allocation as an ongoing task that proceeds throughout the negotiation process. The question to ask, in other words, is not how *much* authority to delegate, but *when* to delegate authority. At the start of a negotiation, an agent should not have authority to make substantive commitments, but instead should only be able to establish a negotiation process and begin discussion with the other side. As bargaining progresses and both principal and agent learn more about the other side, the negotiation itself, and the agent's performance, the principal should begin to give the agent more leeway. Eventually, assuming that performance satisfies the principal, the agent should be given sufficient authority to negotiate a final settlement package and recommend it to the principal for approval.

One can complicate and challenge this approach.[19] At the same time, it is fundamentally good advice, and a useful revision to the common approach to negotiation authority.

Principle Six: Rely most heavily on an agent when psychological biases or emotional risks cloud the principal's decision making.

Negotiators are often subject to various cognitive and emotional heuristics or "biases" that can prevent rational decision making and thus prevent reaching agreement.[20] Sometimes agents can help. Research on how these cognitive, social, and emotional biases influence agents is still in its infancy, and it is important not to assume that agents are a panacea for these problematic effects. At the same time, some evidence suggests that agents may dampen these biases. At least in some instances, an agent may be less susceptible to these psychological phenomena and thus able to balance out a principal's questionable tendencies. For example, an agent may be less prone than a principal to discount or misconstrue information learned from the other side.[21]

At the very least, principals and agents should be attuned to the ways in which a principal's reasoning may be compromised or his or her thinking affected by psychological biases. If a principal's emotions may cloud her decision making, an agent can and should use his perspective, expertise, and judgment to help the principal reason more clearly. This is a benefit of agency and one way in which principals and agents can structure their relations to maximum advantage.

CONCLUSION

This chapter has introduced principal-agent theory and the opportunities and problems of using negotiating agents. It has also offered some preliminary prescriptive advice for managing agents in negotiation. Agency raises important questions beyond effectiveness and efficiency. The ethical issues raised by agency are particularly interesting, including the reciprocal obligations of principals and agents to each other, when and whether agents are morally responsible for the immoral ends of their principals, and whether agents have any obligation—moral or otherwise—to adopt collaborative negotiating strategies. These aspects of agency are obviously beyond the scope of this chapter. As a beginning, however, the principles articulated here offer some guidance for managing negotiating agents to best effect.

Notes

1. For useful discussions of agency in negotiation, see R. Mnookin and L. E. Susskind (eds.), *Negotiating on Behalf of Others* (Thousand Oaks, Calif.: Sage, 1999); D. Lax and J. Sebenius, "Negotiating Through an Agent," *Journal of Conflict Resolution,* 1991, *35*(3), 474–493; and J. Pratt and R. J. Zeckhauser (eds.), *Principals and Agents: The Structure of Business* (Boston: Harvard Business School Press, 1985).

2. Zeckhauser calls these three elements—preferences, incentives, and information— the "golden triangle." See R. J. Zeckhauser, "Introduction," in R. J. Zeckhauser (ed.), *Strategy and Choice* (Cambridge, Mass.: MIT Press, 1991).

3. See Pratt and Zeckhauser, *Principals and Agents,* 1985; D. Sappington, "Incentives in Principal-Agent Relationships," *Journal of Economic Perspectives,* 1991, *5*(2), 45–66; and Zeckhauser, *Strategy and Choice,* 1991.

4. See K. Arrow, "The Economics of Agency," in J. Pratt and R. Zeckhauser (eds.), *Principals and Agents: The Structure of Business* (Boston: Harvard Business School Press, 1985).

5. See K. Nicolaidis, "Minimizing Agency Costs in Two-Level Games," in R. Mnookin and L. E. Susskind (eds.), *Negotiating on Behalf of Others* (Thousand Oaks, Calif.: Sage, 1999).

6. See R. H. Mnookin, S. R. Peppet, and A. S. Tulumello, *Beyond Winning: Negotiating to Create Value in Deals and Disputes* (Boston: Belknap Press of Harvard University Press, 2000).

7. See D. Stone, B. Patton, and S. Heen, *Difficult Conversations* (New York: Penguin, 1999).

8. See Mnookin, Peppet, and Tulumello, *Beyond Winning,* 2000.

9. See D. Lax and J. Sebenius, *The Manager as Negotiator: Bargaining for Cooperation and Competitive Gain* (New York: Free Press, 1986); R. Korobkin, *Negotiation Theory and Strategy* (New York: Aspen Law and Business, 2002); and S. R. Peppet, "Lawyer's Bargaining Ethics, Contract, and Collaboration: The End of the Legal Profession and the Begininng of Professional Pluralism," *Iowa Law Review,* 2005, *90,* 475.

10. For more on the dynamics of value creation in the context of negotiation, see Moffitt, Chapter Eleven in this volume.

11. See R. Gilson and R. Mnookin, "Disputing Through Agents: Cooperation and Conflict Between Lawyers in Litigation," *Columbia Law Review,* 1994, *94,* 509.

12. See Peppet, "Lawyer's Bargaining Ethics, Contract, and Collaboration," 2005.

13. This obviously simplifies the matter to some extent. In an ideal world, many would want to hire an agent with a collaborative reputation but a secret ability and willingness to exploit the other side. For our purposes here I assume that this is impossible.

14. See D. A. Hoffman and R. S. Pollak, "'Collaborative Law' Looks to Avoid Litigation," *Massachusetts Lawyers Weekly,* 2000, *28,* 1989.

15. See J. Lande, "Evading Evasion: How Protocols Can Improve Civil Case Results," *Alternatives to the High Cost of Litigation,* 2003, *21,* 149–165.

16. See J. Lande, "Possibilities for Collaborative Law: Ethics and Practice of Lawyer Disqualification and Process Control in a New Model of Lawyering," *Ohio State Law Journal,* 2003, *64,* 1315–1384.

17. I do not pretend that such structure changes are easy, nor that they are always successful. For my recent critique of Collaborative Law, see Peppet, "Lawyer's Bargaining Ethics, Contract, and Collaboration," 2005.

18. See R. Fisher and W. Davis, "Authority of an Agent: When Is Less Better?" in R. Mnookin and L. E. Susskind (eds.), *Negotiating on Behalf of Others* (Thousand Oaks, Calif.: Sage, 1999).

19. See M. H. Bazerman, "Rational Authority Allocation to an Agent," in R. Mnookin and L. E. Susskind (eds.), *Negotiating on Behalf of Others* (Thousand Oaks, Calif.: Sage, 1999).

20. For an overview of some of the psychological phenomena that affect negotiators in a variety of contexts, *see* Bazerman and Shonk, Chapter Four in this volume.

21. See R. Birke and C. R. Fox, "Psychological Principles in Negotiating Civil Settlements," *Harvard Negotiation Law Review,* 1999, *4,* 1–58.

CHAPTER THIRTEEN

Finding Settlement with Numbers, Maps, and Trees

Marjorie Corman Aaron

Most parties in a dispute eventually face a decision: whether to settle their dispute upon certain terms or not. Whether negotiating toward settlement directly or with the assistance of counsel and a mediator, parties are best able to make decisions in their own best interest if they understand their alternatives. Those alternatives necessarily include possible outcomes of the litigation process and their anticipated effect, as well as the proffered settlement and its anticipated effect. To this end, decision analysis, or risk analysis,[1] presents an important opportunity for the parties who want to assess the relative values of their alternatives.

This chapter does not suggest that quantitative comparisons of the dollar values of a party's alternatives represent the only wise way to make a decision. An individual party might wisely decide to reject a significant settlement offer for a claim of modest dollar value in favor of the personal, emotional satisfaction of watching the defendant's executives being cross examined, or for the goal of exposing alleged corporate immorality. That might be exactly the right decision, whatever an analysis of the numbers suggests.

However, I believe that *all* parties (and their lawyers) benefit from thoughtful analysis of their alternatives through careful and rigorous consideration of the value and cost to them of settlement options and of the embedded risks and possible outcomes of the litigation process. Settlements are truly informed and voluntary only if the parties choose them with a full understanding of their alternatives.

This chapter assumes the reader is familiar with basic decision or risk analysis in a tree structure. The "how-tos" of decision tree analysis are straightforward and are clearly described in many other texts.[2] My goal is to articulate how decision or risk analysis can assist parties and lawyers in negotiation and dispute settlement.

DECISION TREES AS TOOLS TO PROMOTE PERSPECTIVE

For a lawyer seeking to prepare a client for negotiation or mediation, the process of building a tree focuses the client on each component—the procedural twists, the probabilities and monetary value of possible outcomes—of the client's litigation alternative. The language and process of the discussion around building the tree is less emotional and more methodical than that in many lawyer-client discussions about an impending case, creating distance between the client and his or her case. Discussion takes place in terms of the legal and factual theories that may lead to full or partial summary judgment, and the methodological requirement to place these unpleasant possibilities on the tree functions as part of the exercise, rather than as validation of the other side. This process stands in contrast to more highly charged discussions of why and how the plaintiff was wronged or lines of questioning in deposition. The lawyer must explain to the client exactly why a given motion might result in partial summary judgment versus a complete victory or defeat. Counsel will have to explain the factors that might weigh against a liability verdict and how, even if liability were found, there is a wide range of possible damage awards. Once the possible branches have been drawn, and probability and pay-off estimates made, calculation of the expected monetary value (EMV) focuses the client on one way to think about settlement value.

The world of legal practice is far from perfect. Often, counsel fail to analyze rigorously their clients' cases or fail to discuss their analyses with their clients in a careful, clear, and meaningful way. Counsel may be emotionally and financially invested. Leaving aside the partisan perception bias that often infiltrates counsel's estimated probabilities, even highly regarded counsel sometimes fail to consider systematically the possible outcomes at various stages of the litigation. Most commonly, counsel will have named the highest (or nearly the highest) jury award as the payoff in the event of a liability finding, but will have failed to consider the wider range of possible damages and the probabilities associated with various points in the range.

Building a decision tree provides an opportunity to counter the typical, dangerous tendencies of disputants to oversimplify their decisions. When discussing litigation, some disputants and their lawyers rush quickly through discussions of what might happen at various stages in litigation, as if courts fired off litigation outcomes in rapid, predictable succession, much like a machine pitching base-balls in a batting cage. This is in sharp contrast to the litigation process itself, which takes time and often involves difficult strategic choices at each stage. Building the tree structure forces the participants to slow down and weigh what the reality might be at each step along each branch. It is not glib. It is not done with a dramatic sweep of the arm. The very process of a thorough, thoughtful decision analysis, stopping to ask questions at each node and each branch, may reinforce the choices required in litigation.

CLARIFYING AND CALIBRATING ADJECTIVAL AMBIGUITIES

In preparation for settlement negotiation or mediation, a lawyer might tell his or her client, "I am quite confident that we will survive summary judgment, and I think we will have a very strong case on liability at trial." What does this mean for settlement valuation? Assume that if plaintiff wins at trial, damages in the amount of $250,000 will certainly be recovered. Based upon the adjectives used by the lawyer, would the lawyer and the client be willing to settle the case for $200,000? For $150,000? For $125,000? Of course, it depends on what the lawyer means by "quite confident" and "very strong."

For the past fifteen years, I have used a class exercise involving ten different descriptive phrases that purport to describe the strength of liability in a hypothetical case.[3] These include language such as "highly likely to win on liability," "very strong," "should win," and so forth. Participants are asked to record the percentage numbers they would ascribe to each phrase if they had spoken it with the vocal inflection provided to describe the chances of liability in a case. I then poll the class and derive a range for each descriptive phrase from the participants' highest to lowest recorded percentages. My poll *never* records a range narrower than 15 percent for any descriptive phrase. The typical range is 20 to 30 percent, and some cross over the midpoint. For example, the phrase "very strong on liability" often yields percentages ranging from 65 percent to 90 percent. The phrase "should win" often yields likelihood of liability percentages from 30 percent to 60 percent.

The lawyer-client discussion of percentages required to construct a decision tree often reveals disparities between the way descriptive phrases were intended and the way they were understood. It may also better enable lawyer and client to understand and discuss differing approaches to risk. Imagine a case in which a lawyer has previously stated to his or her client that the case is "quite strong." At the time, if asked, the lawyer might have quantified the "quite strong" chance of winning as 60 percent. The client heard the words "quite strong" and assumed that the lawyer meant an 80 to 90 percent likelihood. On that basis, the client expended significant sums in attorneys fees and is prepared to invest considerably more to prepare the case for trial. To the attorney, based upon his or her attitude toward risk, a 60 percent shot is one worth taking unless the settlement offer on the table becomes much higher. (For purity's sake, we will disregard the attorney's attitude toward fees, or assume that he or she would take the 60 percent shot even if on a contingency fee.) The client may be more risk averse in general, or may need money now—making it difficult to turn down money on the table for a chance of only 60 percent. Perhaps it would take an 80 percent or 90 percent chance for the client to feel comfortable turning down the settlement offered.

A decision tree approach requires candid discussion between lawyer and client about the likelihood of each branch on the tree, each twist in the litigation path. That discussion is *always* worth having. Even if the decision tree is used for nothing more than adding clarity in the conversation of trial alternatives and the client's comfort with attendant levels of risk, the tree has added value.

IT'S EASY TO GET LOST WITHOUT A MAP

For most of us, when trying to follow directions, much less choosing from among alternative routes, looking at a map is far more helpful than an oral recitation. The same is true for client and lawyer faced with a case of any procedural complexity, involving multiple legal theories, evidentiary hurdles, different measures of damages, or ranges of damages calculations. In such a case, without a map, a client may simply be unable to process the available information readily due to the degree of complexity.

In a relatively complex case, creating the decision tree structure enables the parties and counsel to see uncertainties, anticipated twists, and possible outcomes in a way that would not be possible without a visual map. A many-branched tree structure emerging on the white board, legal pad, or computer enables the lawyer and client to see all of the variables that must fall into place to reach a subset of desirable outcomes. When a settlement offer on the table is compared to the prospect of a litigation process that must wind its way through that map, the settlement offer's simplicity and certainty may begin to appear more attractive (or less so, depending on the tree). By mapping and thus clarifying the structure of the litigation alternative, the tree helps the parties and counsel to make their decision, without probability percentages, costs, or payoffs.

THE POWER AND LIMITS OF EXPECTED
MONETARY VALUE CALCULATIONS

When a formal decision tree or risk analysis is performed, all possible outcomes at each step of the litigation process are mapped in a tree structure. Each chance node is followed by the number of branches needed to represent what might happen at that stage. Appropriate probabilities are assigned to each branch based on the parties' and counsel's best judgments. The monetary consequences of each possible outcome—net payoffs or payments, after deduction or addition of costs—are estimated. Depending on the estimated time to trial, that calculation may include discounting to present value. When all of the branches, probabilities, and payoffs are included, the rather dramatic calculation of EMV can be performed. Often, and unfortunately, referred to as the "settlement value," this single numerical result is achieved by multiplying (discounting) the dollar value of the possible outcomes by the probability that each will occur and adding them together. It is a cumulative outcome, weighted by the probabilities of the occurrence of various possible outcomes.

The EMV is an important data point. It suggests that if the case is tried one hundred times, the weighted average of the dollar values of those trial outcomes would be the EMV. If the decision maker were a computer intent upon betting wisely, its settlement-indifference point would be the EMV.

Analysis based on EMV may have only limited power to influence settlement positions. No case will be tried a hundred times. Putting in analytically correct branches, probabilities, and payoffs does not mean that the resulting EMV number will be the outcome in any single trial, much less the trial that is scheduled. Assuming the parties understand this (and they should), some will view the EMV as irrelevant to settling their single case. An EMV calculation also does not consider the parties' or lawyers' attitudes toward risk or their risk tolerance. Consider two cases with an EMV of $50,000. In the first case, one party has a 50 percent chance of winning $100,000 and a 50 percent chance of winning nothing, but paying nothing. In the second case, that party has a 60 percent chance of winning $100,000 and a 20 percent chance of winning nothing and paying nothing, but a 20 percent risk of having to pay $50,000 on a counterclaim. The $50,000 EMV is only part of the settlement picture. Depending on the financial circumstances, risk tolerance, and personal attitudes toward risk of both parties, these cases are likely to settle for quite different amounts. Sophisticated decision analysis can incorporate risk preferences into this calculation as well, but my experience suggests that this level of formal analysis is often unhelpful.[4]

With due deference to its limits, the EMV has strong claims for parties seeking to make prudent financial or business decisions. Many of us act according to a rationale of discounted risk and value. We do not (knowingly or without a gambler's addiction) invest our life savings on a horse race or in junk bonds. If there is a 90 percent chance of torrential rain, we wear rain slickers or carry umbrellas to protect costly shoes and clothing. If the chance of rain is 20 percent and we are wearing jeans and flip flops, we do not necessarily bother with rain gear.

Similarly, when making a financial decision, prudence requires asking, "What are the odds? What will I have to invest? What could I win? What could I lose?"

Investing heavily for a small chance of winning modest gains, or passing up an opportunity to cut losses in the face of a high likelihood of far greater future losses, is generally judged financially imprudent. Building a decision tree in a litigated case and calculating its EMV asks the same question over a sequential series of litigation steps and possible outcomes to determine a prudent settlement amount from a business or financial perspective.

EMOTIONAL ATTACHMENT TO NUMBERS

Many disputing parties recognize that emotion can get in the way of prudent decisions in their own or their corporate entity's best interests. We watch nations engage in politically and economically disastrous decisions as the result of national anger or pride. Unwise escalation and competitive drive lead companies to bid too high in corporate takeover battles. Sports stars reject enormous salary offers out of pride, ego, greed, and sometimes as a result of a distasteful or demeaning negotiation process.

Often, parties to a dispute articulate the desire for a "fair and reasonable" settlement and state their desire to make a sound and rational business or personal financial decision. They are able to recognize that emotions may be barriers to such sound judgment. However, they lack a measure for recognizing what settlement point is objectively fair and what is personally unacceptable capitulation. Assume that a plaintiff is angry with her former employer for her termination, which caused economic and emotional damage. Prior to mediation, she wanted to get at least a million dollars. The defense offered $500,000. Plaintiff's counsel does not think, based upon the progress of the negotiations thus far, that the defense will be convinced to offer anything more than $550,000 plus a bridge to the company's retirement status and eligibility for retirement medical benefits.

Without careful analysis, the plaintiff might feel the $550,000 plus retirement medical offer is insulting and that settling on those terms is giving a victory to the stingy and powerful corporate entity. However, if the plaintiff and her attorney build a decision tree for their case, include their analysis of possible outcomes of pretrial motions as well as their best estimates of probabilities for a range of possible trial (and perhaps appeal) results, and find that the resulting EMV is in the $500,000 range, the plaintiff might feel differently about the offer. While it obviously falls far short of what she had wanted, she may recognize that her original goal was fueled by emotion. The EMV allows her to accept a settlement in the range of the EMV as a sound financial decision in her own best interest, rather than a capitulation.

In performing their analysis, the plaintiff and her attorney should calculate the monetary value (if not the additional peace-of-mind value) of the retirement medical benefit, using reasonable estimates of life expectancy and, at minimum, the amount of the company's annual contribution. After adding the dollar value of the retirement medical benefit to the lump sum portion, the plaintiff may come to see the settlement offer at least as the elusive "fair and reasonable" because it approaches or surpasses the EMV.

POWER OF PROBABILITY DISTRIBUTIONS

For a decision maker, the question is not only what the weighted average of possible outcomes is if the case were tried a hundred times—the question posed in an EMV calculation. Equally important questions are: Of all of the possible ways the case may turn out, how likely is it to turn out the way I'd like? What are the chances that the verdict amount will be greater than a certain threshold? How likely is it to be a disaster? Even if I lose, what are the chances that the loss will be safely within our ability to pay the verdict? A decision tree can provide insight into these questions, but not by "rolling back" the calculations from right to left, as is done when calculating the EMV. When a client or a lawyer wants to view the distribution of possible outcomes and their probabilities, calculations of probabilities flow from left to right. Each probability is multiplied by the next probability along each branch of the tree until you reach the terminal node at the far right. By looking at the array of possible outcomes, which is simply the list of values at the terminal nodes, the lawyer and client can see all of the possible ways (in dollar terms) the case might end and the probability associated with each possible ending.

Figure 13.1 shows how the probability calculations would work in a simple case involving a risk of summary judgment, a plaintiff's claim that could (under various theories and with different juries) generate high-, mid-, or low-level damages, and a counterclaim which, if successful, would generate a well-defined damages amount.

Note that each probability reflected at each possible outcome on the far right is simply the product of all of the probabilities that preceded it from the far left. Thus, from the top, a .8 chance of surviving summary judgment, multiplied by a .7 chance of success at trial, multiplied by a .8 chance that the counterclaim fails, and a .3 chance of a very high damages award—the best result for the plaintiff—has only a 13.4 percent chance of occurring.

The next outcome down on the right, found by following the path from surviving summary judgment (.8), liability finding at trial (.7), failure of the counterclaim (.8), and "mid" damages award (.4), has a 17.9 percent probability. However, if you look to the fourth, fifth, and sixth outcomes down from the top, you find the probabilities of having the counterclaim amount deducted from the liability award. The sum of these three possible outcomes—11.2 percent—is

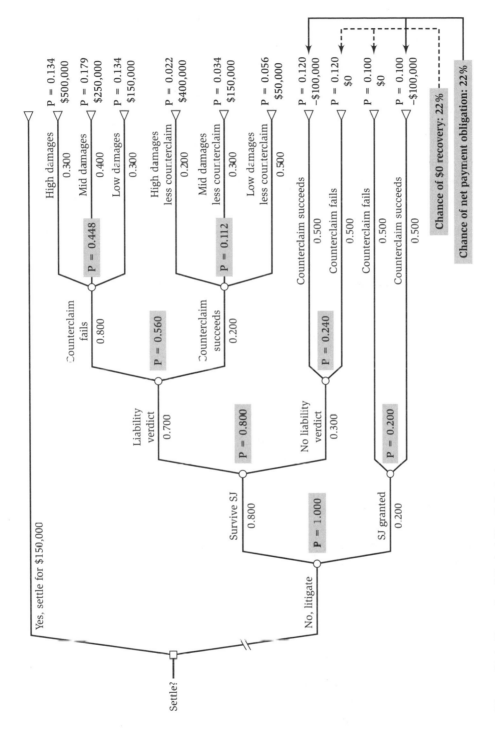

Figure 13.1. Example of Probability Calculations.

seen by looking left to the chance node labeled "counterclaim succeeds." Note that toward the bottom of the tree, along the path of "no liability verdict," the chances of a zero dollar verdict for the plaintiff, with a liability finding on the counterclaim and thus a payment obligation, is 12.0 percent (roughly equivalent to the chances of the plaintiff's "best outcome"). Moreover, if summary judgment were granted against the plaintiff but the counterclaim were to survive summary judgment, the plaintiff would have an additional 10 percent chance of the litigation outcome being a payment obligation. When these probabilities—12 percent and 10 percent—are added, the plaintiff can see that there is a 22 percent chance of an outcome that is a payment obligation on the counterclaims. The tree also shows a 22 percent chance of receiving nothing (but paying nothing to the defendant) by adding the 10 percent chance of summary judgment being granted, but the counterclaim failing, and the 12 percent chance of surviving summary judgment, but the plaintiff losing on liability and on the counterclaim.

The process of multiplying probabilities can easily be followed along each branch to its endpoint. Client and lawyer will be able to see that while their most desired outcomes are present, their likelihood may be outweighed by outcomes in much lower or negative dollar ranges. Seeing these outcomes arrayed and assigned a distribution of probabilities is a powerful reminder that the case will only be tried once, and that any of these results may occur.

COUNTING INTANGIBLES BECAUSE THEY ARE REAL

When constructing the decision tree for a litigation alternative, we often forget to think outside easily quantifiable litigation calculus. When considering the payoffs or endpoints, we add verdict amounts (negative numbers for defendants), dutifully subtract attorneys fees, and perhaps discount to present value. We know that there are other, less tangible but real, costs associated with trial. A relatively simple one is the employee time that will be lost as a result of depositions not yet taken, trial preparation, or attendance in court. Ongoing litigation may also dramatically affect a company or organization by pitting the interests of its associates or staff against each other. The litigation process and its uncertainty cause stress for many; some people may be particularly anxious at the prospect of testifying at trial. These detriments would be calculated as negative value consequences of pursuing the trial alternative. However, where a litigant would find satisfaction in the assertion of power or vindication by forcing the opponent to testify, proceeding to the trial would be credited with additional positive value in the payoff calculation on the far right of the tree, or that amount would be deducted at the end of the settlement branches.

Some parties may be well served by an effort to consider and assign value to some of these consequences. A relatively easy category is lost time. It is fair (and some might say, wise) to ask the question, What are your executives' or other witnesses' time worth? This is particularly straightforward when that time is billed out to clients or within the corporation, as is often true for consultants and engineers. In other industries, precision may not be possible, but a reasonable estimate should be. One could take a single executive's annual compensation and arrive at an approximate hourly rate. In certain business contexts, it is fair to state that hourly time is not the problem, but rather distraction, lost opportunity, and failure to think about the next profitmaking deal. The purpose is not to trump up fake numbers for the purpose of encouraging settlement. The goal of the exercise is to avoid missing real costs that would not be reflected in a lawyer's typical "litigation budget" document.

It is admittedly more difficult to quantify some of the other real, but less tangible or precise, consequences of trial, such as loss of reputation or a stalled career. Still, if the purpose of the tree is to map the full decision's risks and its benefits, these intangibles should be reasonably quantified and fairly counted.

DECISION ANALYSIS AS A TOOL FOR MEDIATORS

In many legal disputes, both parties and often their lawyers firmly believe they will prevail at trial. Both sides claim theirs is the stronger case and see the other side's arguments or evidence as weak. Partisan perception bias is generally recognized to be the culprit[5] when there are no significant asymmetries of information. Particularly for a facilitative mediator, who has committed *not* to provide any neutral evaluation, partisan perception bias presents the most difficult challenge.

To help the parties and counsel to "see reality," facilitative mediators are generally advised to "ask probing questions." The theory is that such questions, albeit posed in a neutral way, will help the parties and counsel identify the weaknesses in their case and strength in the other side's case.[6] As a matter of practice, such "probing questions" are difficult to pose in a neutral way. One party's attorney says, "We will certainly get over summary judgment, and this is a rock-solid case on liability." When the mediator raises an experienced eyebrow and asks, "Do you really think these facts are likely to give rise to a constructive discharge finding? How does your theory deal with evidence of an offer to move your client's office location?" counsel and party are likely to respond defensively. The direct or indirect questioning of counsel's assertion risks creating an impression that the mediator "has taken the other side." The mediator's question goes directly to the heart of the plaintiff's grievance, and the mediator is expressing doubt, raising issues of trust and perceived neutrality.

Parties' assertions of certainty are not, however, hopelessly beyond discussion for mediators. A decision analysis approach can help parties explore assertions without raising the same risk of perceived bias. Consider a case in which a finding of constructive discharge is critical for an award of substantial damages. If the plaintiff were found to have quit, rather than suffered constructive discharge, her damages would be limited to emotional distress from sexual harassment in the form of a hostile work environment while at the company. While discussing and building the decision tree with the mediator, plaintiff's counsel estimated the probability of a constructive discharge finding at 85 percent. Other estimates by the plaintiff's counsel may be somewhat optimistic to the mediator, but the 85 percent on constructive discharge seems wildly inflated, based on evidence discussed in the mediation. Rather than direct a "probing question" straight at this issue, the mediator might say, "Of course all of these probabilities are just estimates. When you say that a probability is 50 percent or 60 percent or 85 percent, you are saying that if the case were to be tried one hundred times, this might happen fifty times, or sixty times, or eighty-five out of a hundred times. But of course, the case will only be tried once. And no one can ever know for certain. When I say that I think I have a very strong argument, I might mean that I think it is a 60 to 70 percent chance. But there is always a range. It is never precise. If I were estimating the probabilities on a case or a particular motion, and I thought it was 70 percent, I certainly wouldn't argue that it was 70 percent and not 68 percent or 65 percent, or 70 percent and not 72 percent and not 75 percent or more. No one can be that precise, especially because the case will only be tried once. What I'd like to do is go back over your numbers. You've estimated 85 percent as the probability that there will be a finding of constructive discharge. I see that means you see it as a strong part of the case. Okay, but what if strong meant 70 percent or even 65 percent? That's still much higher than 50-50. Let's see what will happen to the EMV if you adjust percentages . . ."

In this way, the mediator has not expressed an opinion on the constructive discharge issue but has more generally probed counsel's certainty. The mediator has explored the idea of differing degrees of "strength" and how that may affect EMV, and thus what is a "fair and reasonable" settlement from plaintiff's perspective.

FOR THE MEDIATOR WILLING TO EVALUATE WHEN NECESSARY

Whether evaluative mediation is heretical, antithetical, oxymoronic, or sometimes an essential mediation practice component is not the topic of this chapter. It should be undisputed that many mediators believe evaluation to be entirely appropriate in certain circumstances. Although this chapter does not purport to provide a full range of advice to parties, their lawyers, or their mediators regarding effective techniques for evaluation,[7] the essence of that advice would be this: evaluate the merits of the trial alternative only as necessary to counteract the effect of partisan perception bias. Evaluate (or ask the mediator to evaluate) tactfully, carefully, and late in the process, after the mediator has actively listened to each side's perspective, arguments, theories, and analysis. The inherent danger is that, once the mediator has provided at least one party with a negative evaluation, the mediator may no longer be perceived as neutral. The recipients of the negative evaluation may thereafter assume that any offer carried by the mediator, any negotiation coaching advice, or any suggested term is designed to achieve the other side's settlement number or terms because the mediator favors the other side's case. If that happens, the mediator can no longer function effectively in the neutral's role.

To evaluate and maintain both sides' confidence, the mediator is wise to create as much distance as possible between him or herself and the evaluation provided. If possible, it is also helpful for the mediator to adopt or accept as many of a party's arguments, theories, or assessments and to incorporate them into the neutral analysis. A decision tree approach to a mediator's evaluation enables both, while permitting the use of language with less emotional content. When the mediator adjusts a probability estimate down from 85 percent to 60 percent or 50 percent, he or she does not have to say, "I think your case is weaker." The fact that the discussion and recording of percentage and dollar estimates are physically directed to the drawn decision tree is also helpful. In effect, a decision tree can become an intermediary between the mediator and the evaluation being presented. When an EMV calculation is performed, the mediator can refer to the results of this neutral analysis rather than to his or her view of the strengths and weaknesses. The EMV or decision tree results may then be regarded in the manner of an objective criterion, a neutral, analytical suggestion of a settlement point. The mediator may also choose to offer his or her evaluation in ranges of probability or payoff, resulting in a range of EMVs as possible settlement amounts.

In some cases, using a decision tree may permit the mediator to evaluate selectively and sparingly, adopting or accepting (for the sake of argument) many of the probability and payoff judgments placed on the tree by one side. I refer to this technique as "piggy-backing" because the mediator's evaluation rides the structure and many of the numbers used in one or both sides' trees. When the mediator's evaluation diverges significantly only as to a few branches or payoff estimates, the mediator can engage in discussion only on those issues, explaining why his or her analysis is different. To the extent that the mediator's evaluation adopts one side's judgments and tree, that side has difficulty completely disregarding the EMV result. Most people are not 100 percent confident that they will be right 100 percent of the time. An EMV result derived from their own judgments plus just a few different assessments by an apparently intelligent and neutral mediator can powerfully influence the parties' views of a "fair and reasonable" settlement.

COMPARING ALTERNATIVE PATHS—WHAT WOULD EACH OUTCOME REALLY MEAN?

Becoming entangled in the litigation branches of a decision tree is easy. We become involved in capturing all the possible permutations of the case progression, ensuring that the tree as drawn is a fair and logical map of the litigation, and that the probabilities and payoffs represent careful and experienced judgment and analysis. It can be an intellectually challenging and engrossing task. In a litigation and settlement context, when attorneys are leading the discussion and building the tree, there is a tendency to ignore the fact that litigation is not the only path or branch to follow. Settlement—deciding not to litigate any further—is an entirely different branch or separate tree that is worthy of drawing and valuing.

Looking back from the litigation choice to the settlement choice, and mapping or charting the latter's consequences, are critical and often overlooked steps in making a wise decision. While evaluating the uncertainties associated with trial is important, looking at the decision of whether to litigate or to settle by exploring what will happen if you do settle is equally important. In practice, you can build the tree, or an extensive system of branches, representing the litigation on one flip chart or yellow pad and then list what will happen if the litigation ends. The settlement amount on the table should be listed, but what that amount or the settlement terms would enable the party to do should also be listed. On the plaintiff's side, one might list pay for college, fund a retirement annuity, pay for home health care, purchase a home in a different location. On the defense side, one might list pursue a corporate transaction after removal of the case's cloud on securities filings, purchase replacement equipment, complete a departmental reorganization, protect technical secrets, and so on. The visual juxtaposition and comparison of the choices—settlement versus litigation—facilitates the parties' wise decisions in their own interest. This is, after all, the point.

LIMITS AND RISKS OF QUANTIFICATION

"Garbage in, garbage out" is the phrase often used to denigrate the process of decision analysis. No one should deny that a decision tree is only as good as the thought and analysis that go into it. If the party, lawyer, or mediator constructing the tree has not thought carefully about the possible twists in the litigation process, if they have not researched and analyzed the case law and the factual evidence, and considered whether damages assertions can be proven, the resulting tree will be of no value.

Conversely, "quality ingredients in, quality product out." There is much value for a decision maker in a decision tree that carefully maps the next steps in the litigation and the possible outcome at each step, if the probabilities at each branch are informed by experienced and objective analysis, and the damages or cost figures are supported by evidence and consistent with legal theories of recovery.

Decision analysis necessarily involves quantifying—recording numbers that represent one's judgment about likely outcomes and percentage numbers that represent one's judgment about the likelihood of a particular outcome. Not everything in life can be quantified, nor should it be. The fact that our legal system requires quantification for compensation of bodily injury, disfigurement, pain and suffering, emotional distress, and lost quality of life does not render the quantification exercise less artificial and more valid. While it seems appropriate to record numbers for lost wages, or even estimates of likely jury awards, we might appropriately question the exercise of quantifying the emotional stress associated with going to trial, or the dollar value of watching the corporate higher-ups testify if forced to go to trial. When decision analysis moves into the territory of the intangible, the exercise seems more artificial and an uncomfortable validation of a mercenary ethic or worldview. For these reasons, this author often omits the step discussed earlier in "Counting Intangibles Because They Are Real." I will often list the less tangible positive and negative consequences of a settlement and litigation choices on the relevant easel or legal pad, but do not ask the parties to assign value—except perhaps in terms of lost time.

Finally, the process of decision tree analysis can be fairly criticized for creating an illusion of precision when precision is neither real nor possible. When a lawyer or party states that the chances of a liability verdict in a trial are 70 percent, that percentage number cannot be verified unless the case is indeed to be tried the proverbial one hundred times. Moreover, the lawyer who estimates the probability at 70 percent would be foolish to argue with another lawyer who would put it at 68 percent or 72 percent. No matter how long a span of trial experience, no one would claim to predict the future with such precision. The probability percentages used are simply place holders representing how strong we believe a claim to be and how confident we are that an argument or piece of evidence will convince a trier of fact. The payoff numbers placed at the terminal nodes and the outcome at the far right of the decision tree can be similarly misleading in their precision.[8] When $50,000 is placed at the payoff point of a decision tree as an estimate of a mid-level jury award for emotional distress, the number has no more claim on reality than a lawyer's stated opinion that the mid-level emotional distress award would most likely be in the $40,000 to $60,000 range. For the purposes of the decision tree, picking a number representing one's best estimate of mid-level damages is necessary. The risk is that once percentages and number are recorded, people begin to believe and rely upon these numbers and percentages as if they were precise and entirely accurate. The only antidote is to step back from the tree and to note that each probability and payoff represents an estimate. Ironically, to facilitate wise decisions, after the tree has been painstakingly created and calculated, perhaps it should be blurred just a bit—viewed from some distance through a fuzzy lens.

Notes

1. Many people use the terms *decision analysis, risk analysis, litigation risk analysis,* or *decision tree analysis* interchangeably. For those who value precise terminology, decision analysis might be thought of as broader than risk analysis, for decision analysis looks to decisions over which the parties have control as well as those involving future risk and uncertainty. Decision analysis can be used to analyze the cost of acquiring information, making business decisions such as whether to submit proposals, building a new manufacturing facility, and so on. Thus, a decision tree includes decision nodes, which analyze the consequences of particular decisions, as well as chance nodes, reflecting points at which chance—externally imposed decisions or events—will determine the next outcome. These are the "risk analysis" portion of the tree, as they analyze the probabilities, risks, and costs associated with various possible outcomes. In a typical mediated case, the decision question is whether to settle for a certain amount or litigate. Following the "litigate" decision node are chance nodes, branches, and more chance nodes until the payoff or terminal node is reached. In other words, underlying (or to the right of) the decision problem is the risk analysis. For writings on decision analysis and risk analysis, see H. Raiffa, *The Art and Science of Negotiation* (Cambridge, Mass.: Belknap Press of Harvard University Press, 1982); and J. H. Hammond, R. L. Keeney, and H. Raiffa, *Smart Choices: A Practical Guide to Making Better Life Decisions* (New York: Broadway Books, 2002). For earlier work in this area see H. Raiffa, *Decision Analysis: Introductory Lectures on Choices Under Uncertainty* (Reading, Mass.: Addison-Wesley Publishing Company, 1970); and R. O. Schlaifer, *Analysis of Decisions Under Uncertainty* (New York: McGraw-Hill, 1967). This list of resources does not purport to be exhaustive, as the method is not new and has been described and used in many fields. Marc Victor, president of Litigation Risk Analysis, has authored numerous articles over the past twenty years and is recognized as one of the pioneers in the application of decision analysis to legal disputes and dispute settlement.

2. The following texts also contain clear and readable directions for people who wish to learn the how-tos of decision or risk analysis in a legal context. See M. Aaron and D. P. Hoffer, "Decision Analysis as a Method of Evaluating the Trial Alternative," in D. Golann (ed.), *Mediating Legal Disputes: Effective Strategies for Lawyers and*

Mediators (New York: Little Brown, 1996), for descriptions of how to do the analysis for the resolution of legal disputes; this text was specifically written for mediators and lawyers in dispute resolution. Another entirely practical discussion of how to construct a decision tree is found in M. Aaron, "Decision Analysis as a Method of Evaluating the Trial Alternative," in D. Golann (ed.), *Mediating Legal Disputes: Effective Strategies for Lawyers and Mediators* (New York: Little Brown, 1996). A comprehensive treatment may also be found in D. P. Hoffer, "Decision Analysis as a Mediator's Tool," *Harvard Negotiation Law Review*, 1996, *1*, 113, and in various articles by Marc Victor. When computer assistance will be helpful, this author uses the software called DATA, offered by TreeAge, Inc.

3. The author was introduced to this exercise by her mediation mentors and colleagues Eric Green and Jonathan Marks, founders of the company then known as Endispute, Inc.

4. Factoring risk preferences and attitudes into the decision tree and thus reflecting it in the EMV is technically possible. However, within my practice, I choose not to do this for two reasons. First, thinking about and graphing a risk attitude curve can become quite complex, and I do not want the decision analysis process to become less accessible to the parties or counsel. Second, in my limited experience with this method, people tend to look at the decision tree and EMV that technically include their discounts for risk attitudes and risk intolerance and then say, "Oh, but I have to consider how I feel about the risks." That serves to double count and distort the risk issue. I suggest that practitioners—parties, lawyers, and mediators using this method—separate the data from the parties' feelings about that data. The decision tree is a theoretically nonemotional, analytical representation of the trial alternative. The EMV number that results is a piece of data—the predicted average trial result, weighted by probability. The parties and their attorneys can and should consider carefully how they want to consider the map of the tree and the data point it yields, and how they feel about the risks presented.

5. Partisan perception bias is a well-known psychological phenomenon, extensively documented in psychology. For clear summary treatments, see M. H. Bazerman, *Judgment in Managerial Decision Making* (New York: John Wiley & Sons, 1998). Partisan perception bias was alive and well among law students in Cincinnati, Ohio, in the spring of 2004. In a negotiation course exercise, whether students were assigned the plaintiff's or defense's side of a case simulation led to approximately a 30 percentage point difference in their average estimate of the likelihood of a liability verdict and a ten-fold difference in their estimate of likely damages awards, based upon virtually identical facts.

6. The facilitative mediator asking "probing questions" might also be characterized as a subtle type of evaluation, as it assumes a mediator view of reality and illumination toward that view. The author recognizes that this characterization challenges much of the current writing and that discussion is better deferred to another place and time.

7. See M. Aaron, "Evaluation in Mediation," in D. Golann (ed.), *Mediating Legal Disputes: Effective Strategies for Lawyers and Mediators* (New York: Little Brown, 1996).

8. Particularly in contract cases, the damages recoverable can sometimes be readily and precisely stated, along with statutory interest. If the lawyer is on a contingency fee or a flat fee basis, or has provided a reasonably accurate budget through trial, the tree's payoff numbers can be credited with the virtue of precision.

CHAPTER FOURTEEN

Option Generation

Be Careful What You Ask For . . .

Chris Guthrie

Option generation is central to negotiation theory. From the authors of *Getting to YES,* who argue that "the key to wise decision-making [in negotiation] lies in selecting from a great number and variety of options,"[1] to the authors of *Beyond Winning,* who identify option generation as the key to value creation,[2] option generation "is seen as one of the basic concepts of successful negotiation."[3]

Despite its central role in negotiation theory, option generation "seems to be underrepresented" as a subject of study[4] and "is not a well-understood phenomenon."[5] Negotiation theorists have almost uniformly endorsed it, but in so doing, they have celebrated its virtues without acknowledging its vices.

Option generation surely does have its virtues. To reach agreement, negotiators must consider at least one option, but if they focus narrowly on one option—such as the amount of money that will change hands—they may hit an impasse. Exploring other options may enable them to come to agreements they might not otherwise be able to reach.

Moreover, option generation can lead to *better* agreements because it enables negotiators to use value-creating tactics such as "log-rolling" and "add-ins."[6] Negotiators "logroll" when they engage in mutually beneficial trades based on different values they place on available options.[7] "For example, a new professor just out of graduate school and on the path toward tenure may be more interested in having extra research resources (i.e., laptop computer, research assistants, discretionary funds, etc.) than [in] teaching a particular course. The recruiting school, on the other hand, may be flush with such resources but is in need of having particular courses being taught."[8] By making trade-offs among these options, the new professor and the school can obtain better deals than they would have if they had merely compromised.

Negotiators use "add-ins" when they include options in a deal that are not necessary to the deal but that add value for both sides. "For example, two executives negotiating the licensing rights for a particular product may also negotiate the rights for a second unrelated product. This additional, and unrelated, product is not necessary to close the immediate deal at hand, but it is beneficial because it creates additional value, expanding the size of the pie."[9] Likewise, two litigators negotiating the terms of a sensitive settlement agreement might include a confidentiality clause, thereby making the agreement more attractive to their respective clients.

But option generation also has its vices. Option generation can lead negotiators to defer or avoid decision making altogether.[10] Even if decision aversion is not a problem, option generation can induce negotiators to make irrational decisions that may not reflect their actual preferences.[11] Finally, option generation can lead negotiators to feel worse than they otherwise would about the outcomes they obtain.[12]

Because the virtues of option generation are widely assumed, this chapter focuses its attention on the process's vices. It addresses these vices in the order in which they ordinarily arise in a negotiation setting, focusing first on deferral and avoidance, then on irrational decision making, and finally on negative postnegotiation feelings. The chapter concludes by advising individuals to retain agents (such as lawyers) to help them overcome the vices and capitalize on the virtues of the option-generation process.

DECISION AVERSION

Option generation can make negotiation decision making more difficult. Negotiators who generate options have more to choose from and are sometimes required to make painful trade-offs to select one option over others. Confronted with this difficulty, negotiators may develop an aversion to decision making, prompting them to defer or even avoid deciding altogether.

Deferral

Decision aversion can lead to decision deferral. In one illustrative study of this phenomenon, Amos Tversky and Eldar Shafir asked participants assigned to either a one-option group or a two-option group to imagine that they wanted a CD player and that they passed by a store holding a one-day sale. Participants assigned to the one-option group learned that the store had a popular Sony CD player on sale for $99, which was well below the list price. When asked whether they would buy the CD player or delay decision making to learn more about other models, thirty-four percent indicated that they would delay decision making. Participants assigned to a two-option group learned that the store had the popular Sony CD player on sale for $99 and a top-of-the-line Aiwa CD player on sale for $169, both well below list price. When asked whether they would buy either of the CD players or delay decision making to learn more about other models, forty-six percent, a much larger group, indicated that they would delay decision making.[13] As the number of attractive options increased from one to two, the percentage of participants opting to delay decision making rose by more than thirty five percent. As psychologist Barry Schwartz explains it, "Faced with one attractive option, two-thirds of people were willing to go for it. But faced with two attractive options, only slightly more than half were willing to buy. *Adding the second option created a conflict, forcing a trade-off between price and quality.* Without a compelling reason to go one way or the other, potential consumers passed up the sale altogether. By creating the conflict, this second option made it harder, not easier, to make a choice."[14]

Negotiators who generate their *own* options might feel differently than consumers selecting from among options proposed by a seller. Still, no matter who generates the options, negotiators must make trade-offs to select one option over other available options. These trade-offs can lead to decision deferral. Thus negotiators, much like the hypothetical consumers in the CD player study, may be more likely to defer decision making when confronted with multiple options. In some circumstances, this is reasonable because a delay might allow negotiators to gather useful information about these (or other) available options; in other circumstances, however, delay might preclude the negotiators from reaching a deal. For example, an individual reluctant to negotiate the purchase of a house because she cannot decide among three or four houses might lose out on all of the houses she is considering because other buyers purchase them before she is able to act. Similarly, a disputant unable to select one of several options proposed by his counterpart may find that his counterpart withdraws the proposal in frustration.

Avoidance

Even more troubling than the research on decision *deferral* is the research on decision *avoidance.* This research suggests that negotiators considering multiple options may be less likely than those considering fewer options to select any option at all.

In one powerful illustration of this phenomenon, researchers set up rotating displays of gourmet jams in an upscale grocery store. Customers who approached a display were invited to sample the jams and were given a one-dollar-off coupon on any of twenty-four jams. One display featured six different jams, while the other featured twenty-four different jams. Researchers tracked the percentage of customers who stopped at each display as well as the percentage of customers who subsequently purchased jam. Their results were striking. Customers were more attracted to the larger display but were more likely to buy after stopping at the smaller display. Of the 104 customers who stopped at the smaller display, thirty-one (nearly thirty percent) subsequently purchased a jar of jam; of the 145 customers who stopped at the larger display, only four (roughly three percent) chose to do so.[15] In other words, ninety-seven percent of those who considered the large option set (versus seventy percent of those who considered the smaller option set) opted *not* to choose because choosing from among multiple options can be demotivating.[16]

Like a consumer confronted with multiple product options, a negotiator confronted with a large array of options may be demotivated to choose—opting to avoid negotiation altogether. In some circumstances, of course, a negotiator may feel she has to negotiate because she is attempting to acquire an item she needs; for example, a negotiator whose car breaks down may have to buy another car. In other circumstances, though, she can walk away. In litigation, for example, a negotiator who feels demotivated to choose can opt not to negotiate because a court will resolve the dispute for him.

IRRATIONAL DECISIONS

Assuming negotiators are able to overcome aversion to decision making at the bargaining table, option generation can still cause problems. Namely, it can induce negotiators to make irrational decisions that fail to reflect their underlying preferences.[17] The definition of a "rational" or "irrational" decision is a subject of some dispute.[18] Most researchers agree, however, that a negotiator seeking to decide rationally must assign a subjective value to each option based on its particular properties, rank the options, and then select the one most highly valued.[19] Unfortunately, as the number of options under consideration grows—from one to two, two to three, three to several—making rational decisions becomes more difficult due to three psychological phenomena: option devaluation, context-dependence, and noncompensatory decision making.

Option Devaluation

From a rational perspective, negotiators should be able to value an option based solely on its inherent properties rather than on "comparisons drawn between it and other alternatives."[20] In fact, however, comparisons influence negotiators' assessments by generally decreasing the attractiveness of the options being compared[21] due to a phenomenon called "option devaluation."[22]

Options tend to have both advantages and disadvantages relative to one another, and the process of comparison brings to mind the relative pros and cons of each. People tend to find disadvantages or "losses" more aversive than they find equivalent advantages or "gains" attractive.[23] Because the process of comparison brings to mind the relative advantages and disadvantages of the options under consideration, and because each option's disadvantages are likely to loom larger than its advantages, comparisons tend to decrease the attractiveness of *all* options under consideration.

In one study of this phenomenon, researchers asked prospective consumers to evaluate several consumer goods. The researchers randomly assigned participants to either an isolated condition, in which they indicated the maximum amount they would pay for a single item (for example, a round-trip ticket to fly from the San Francisco Bay Area to a specified destination), or to one of two comparison conditions, in which they indicated the maximum amount they would pay for each of four items of a particular type (for example, flights to four destinations from the San Francisco Bay Area). When the researchers asked participants to indicate the maximum amount they would pay for a round-trip ticket to Los Angeles, participants indicated they were willing to pay an average amount of $130.97; when comparing it to trips to Seattle, Las Vegas, and San Diego, however, participants indicated that they would pay less than $100 for the Los Angeles trip. Similarly, participants were willing to pay $206.27 to fly to Seattle when evaluating that trip on its own; when comparing it to the other destinations, though, participants were unwilling to pay even $140 for the Seattle trip. In general, across various consumer goods, the researchers found that participants evaluated options more favorably when considering them in isolation than when considering them along with others.[24]

Research suggests that this option devaluation phenomenon is also likely to occur in negotiation.[25] Negotiators, like consumers, appear to devalue each available option when comparing it to others that are available. When the other options provide relevant information about the value of the options already under consideration, this is sensible; however, this phenomenon seems to occur even when the additional options do not provide relevant information. This is because the very process of comparison "emphasize[s] the advantages and disadvantages of options under consideration" and "disadvantages are given greater weight than advantages" in the evaluation. Thus, "whenever the options under consideration have both meaningful advantages and meaningful disadvantages, comparisons hurt."[26]

Context Dependence: Contrast and Compromise

From a rational perspective, negotiators who generate a new option for consideration should not alter their relative valuation of options already under consideration unless the new option conveys relevant information about those other options.[27] A person who prefers hamburger over pasta might rationally change his preference to pasta upon learning that veal parmesan is on the menu because the presence of veal parmesan might indicate that the restaurant specializes in Italian food. But a person who prefers hamburger over pasta should not change this preference upon learning that a burrito is also available.[28]

In fact, however, negotiators' assessments of options are often systematically influenced by the availability of an additional option that provides no new information. In other words, negotiators "make context-based inferences about the worth of alternatives whether or not the context provides a valid basis for such inferences."[29] Two types of context-dependence that can induce negotiators to make irrational decisions are "contrast" and "compromise."

Research on contrast suggests that negotiators are likely to evaluate an existing option more favorably when a similar but inferior option is added to the choice set.[30] In one study of this phenomenon, Itamar Simonson and Amos Tversky asked participants to select one of two or three options. Researchers gave participants assigned to a two-option group a choice of either $6 or an elegant Cross pen, while they gave participants assigned to a three-option group a choice of $6, an elegant Cross pen, or a lesser known, unattractive pen. Thirty-six percent of the participants in the two-option group versus forty-six percent of the participants in the three-option group selected the Cross pen. The availability of the inferior pen substantially increased the likelihood that participants would select the superior Cross pen.[31]

In a similar study of decision making in the negotiation context, I asked participants to imagine that they were involved in a dispute with a partner over a painting in their office. The participants learn that they are dissolving their partnership and that the only remaining issue is this painting. I randomly assigned them to either a two-option group or a three-option group. Those in the two-option group learn that their partner proposed two options to resolve the dispute over the painting: (1) the partner keeps it and pays the participant a $20,000 lump sum, or (2) the two partners sell the painting back to the artist for $40,000 and split the proceeds. Like those in the two-option group, the participants in the three-option group could choose either to give the painting to the law partner and pocket a $20,000 lump sum or sell the painting back to the artist and split the proceeds. Additionally, the participants in this group learn that the partner has proposed a third possibility: (3) the partner keeps the painting and pays the participants four annual payments of $5,000 each.

This third option is similar but inferior to the first option. Both of the options require the participants to give the painting to the partner, but those selecting the first option receive an immediate $20,000, while those selecting the third option get $20,000 over four years. This latter option is inferior to the former because of the greater uncertainty associated with receiving all of the funds and because of the time value of money. Although there should be no difference in the participants' preference between options one and two in the two groups, I found that the availability of the third option in the three-option group had a significant impact. In the two-option condition, sixty-five percent of the participants preferred to sell the painting to the artist and thirty-five percent preferred to give it to the partner. In the three-option condition, however, only thirty percent of the participants preferred to sell to the artist, while seventy percent preferred to give it to the partner. For participants assigned to the three-option group, the $20,000 lump sum option appeared more attractive because it was accompanied by a similar, though inferior, option. Participants who would otherwise prefer to sell the painting back to the artist were induced to give the painting to their partner for $20,000. The presence of the third option—payment on an installment plan—significantly increased the attractiveness of the first option—full payment up front.[32]

A second form of context-dependent decision making is "compromise" or "extremeness aversion."[33] Research on this phenomenon suggests that negotiators are likely to evaluate an option more favorably when it appears to be intermediate, rather than extreme, in a choice set. In one illustrative study, Simonson and Tversky asked participants to make a hypothetical decision to purchase a camera. They asked one group of participants to select either a lower-quality, lower-priced camera or a medium-quality, medium-priced camera. They asked another group of participants to choose either of those two cameras or a higher-quality, higher-priced camera. In the former group, half of the participants chose the medium-quality camera; in the latter group, in which the medium-quality camera appeared to be an intermediate option between the other two cameras, nearly three quarters of the participants selected it.[34]

In a similar problem involving negotiation decision making, I asked participants to imagine that they were representing a property-management company in a prospective land deal. The company, the participants learn, is seeking to buy a piece of relatively inexpensive land on which to develop an apartment complex targeting college students. I asked participants assigned to a two-option group to select either BlueAcre (located on an open field seven miles from the university campus and available for $150,000) or RedAcre (located in a residential neighborhood one mile from the university campus and available for $250,000). As with those assigned to the two-option group, I asked participants assigned to a three-option group to choose either BlueAcre or RedAcre. Additionally, participants in the three-option group could select YellowAcre (located in a residential neighborhood one half-mile from campus and available for $580,000).

The presence of YellowAcre in the choice set should not affect a participant's preference for BlueAcre or RedAcre as a rational matter, but it did. I found that forty-four percent of the subjects in the two-option group recommended BlueAcre and fifty-six percent recommended RedAcre. In the three-option group, a much larger percentage of participants, seventy seven percent, preferred RedAcre. For the members of this group, RedAcre appears to have been more attractive because it constituted a compromise option. The presence of an extreme option, YellowAcre, increased RedAcre's attractiveness significantly.[35]

Noncompensatory Decision Making

From a rational perspective, negotiators selecting from among multiple options should use what decision researchers call a "compensatory" strategy. Compensatory decision making involves identifying and evaluating salient attributes of each option and making trade-offs between or among those options. The compensatory strategy is rational because it requires a decision maker to incorporate and weigh all of the available information.[36]

Researchers have found that people often follow a compensatory strategy when making simple decisions, but when confronted with complex decisions involving multiple options, they tend to consider only a fraction of the available information about those options. "When faced with more complex choice problems involving many alternatives, people often adopt simplifying strategies that are much more selective in the use of information. Further, the strategies adopted tend to be noncompensatory, in that excellent values on some attributes cannot compensate for poor values on other attributes."[37]

In one illustrative study, Naresh Malhotra recruited three hundred heads of households to participate in a hypothetical home-purchase study. He randomly assigned participants in his study to one of twenty-five groups, which varied based on the number of options (that is, homes available for purchase) and the number of attributes about which information was provided. He asked each participant to rank the houses under consideration and then compared their ordered lists to their "ideal house" (determined by an optimizing model). He found that participants made much less accurate decisions as the number of options under consideration reached ten or fifteen. Holding the number of attributes constant, seventy percent of the participants selected the "ideal" house when only five houses were under consideration. By contrast, when ten houses were under consideration, forty-eight percent selected the house that most closely approximated their ideal. When twenty-five houses were under consideration, only thirty-seven percent made the "correct" choice.[38]

In a disturbing real-world example of noncompensatory decision making, Judith Hibbard and her colleagues examined how several large companies select health care plans for their employees and dependents. They interviewed thirty-three professional "purchasers" employed by companies located in four regions. On average, each purchaser was responsible for selecting health care plans for nearly one hundred thousand "covered lives." The researchers' findings were not encouraging. Half of the purchasers said it was difficult for them to consider all of the attributes that they should consider in selecting the plans; some admitted that they avoided making any trade-offs between the options; and twelve percent even admitted "that they made their choices on the basis of a single dimension such as cost or geographic access." Only one out of five purchasers appeared to use a compensatory strategy.[39]

Like the hypothetical home purchasers who participated in Malhotra's study and the actual health insurance purchasers who participated in the study conducted by Hibbard and her colleagues, negotiators who generate a sizeable list of options are likely to use noncompensatory rather than compensatory strategies to reach decisions, ignoring available information and avoiding trade-offs. As a consequence, they are less likely to make negotiation decisions that reflect their true preferences.

NEGATIVE AFFECT

Negotiators may also find that option generation increases the likelihood they will experience negative emotional consequences after reaching an agreement. Namely, research suggests that negotiators selecting from more options may experience greater postnegotiation dissatisfaction and regret.

Dissatisfaction

Negotiators who select from among multiple options may ultimately feel less satisfied with the outcomes they obtain. As "the number of options under consideration goes up and the attractive features associated with the rejected alternatives accumulate, the satisfaction derived from the chosen alternative will go down."[40]

In a recent study involving a simulated negotiation, Charles Naquin asked pairs of participants to negotiate a well-known problem called "The New Recruit," in which some play the role of a recruiter and others play a job candidate. The parties attempt to negotiate the terms and conditions of the candidate's prospective employment, including salary, benefits, start date, and so on. Some of the participants negotiated a four-issue version of the problem, while other participants negotiated an eight-issue version of the problem. Naquin found that those who negotiated the eight-issue version obtained objectively better outcomes but expressed much less satisfaction with them. Naquin argues that "negotiators who deal with more issues are likely to have more counterfactual thoughts imagining how the outcome might have been better, and this frustrating comparison between reality and what might have been is likely to result in reduced levels of post-negotiation satisfaction."[41]

Regret

Negotiators who choose from multiple options are also more likely than their counterparts to experience postdecision regret. Regret is often "created by a comparison between the actual outcome and that outcome that would have occurred had the decision maker made a different choice."[42] Indeed, some researchers argue that if a decision maker "cannot compare what is with what would have been, there should be no reason for regret."[43]

Following the completion of a negotiation, a negotiator can more easily contemplate "what would have been" if he actually selected one option over others than if he merely selected the only available option. In the former case, things obviously would have turned out differently if he had made a different choice because the rejected options are so salient.

OVERCOMING THESE VICES

Option generation has potential vices—deterring negotiators from making decisions, inducing irrational decision making, and producing postnegotiation dissatisfaction and regret—but it also has well-known virtues. To capture the virtues of the process without falling prey to its vices, negotiators should consider hiring agents (such as lawyers) to negotiate for them. Agents may help disputants overcome any aversion to negotiation, facilitate rational decision making, and help disputants manage postnegotiation feelings.

Averting Aversion

When confronted with difficult decisions—those involving multiple options, requiring stark trade-offs, and threatening negative emotional consequences—people often want agents to play an active role in their decision making. Medical patients, for example, "commonly prefer to have others make their medical decisions."[44] Research has shown that sixty-four percent of people claim that they would want to make their own treatment decisions if they contracted cancer, but only twelve percent of those who actually contract cancer want to make their own treatment decisions.[45] Likewise, disputants are likely to feel some aversion to deciding when confronted with complicated and emotionally charged negotiation decisions. By hiring agents and giving them broad authority to negotiate on their behalf, disputants can avoid the negative effects of decision aversion.

Facilitating Rationality

Not only do people want their agents to help them with complicated decisions, they also want their agents to make decisions rationally and fully, even though they are often unable to do so themselves. As Robert Cialdini observes, "we often don't take a complex approach to personally important topics, [but] we wish our advisors—our physicians, accountants, lawyers, and brokers—to do precisely that for us."[46]

In four studies involving high-stakes decisions, Barbara Kahn and Jonathan Baron found evidence supporting this proposition. In a study of investment decisions, for instance, they found that sixty-eight percent of their study participants believed a stockbroker should use a rational-decision approach, but only fifty-one percent indicated they would do so themselves. Likewise, in a medical-decision-making study, they found that sixty-one percent of their study participants thought that physicians should use a rational-decision approach, yet only thirty-two percent indicated that they would do so if deciding for themselves. In short, "although subjects were unlikely to use a compensatory rule when making decisions themselves, they were significantly more likely to advocate the use of compensatory decision rules when an agent was to make the decision on their behalf."[47]

Agents such as lawyers are likely to have greater emotional distance from the subject matter of a negotiation. This distance should help them to make more rational recommendations or decisions than would disputants themselves. Moreover, research evidence suggests generally that lawyers are more analytical and rational than most other people.[48] There is even some evidence suggesting that this may be so in settlement negotiations.[49] Thus, lawyer-negotiators are perhaps less likely than the disputants themselves to make irrational decisions in complex negotiations involving multiple options.

Managing Negative Affect

Agents can also help disputants manage any negative feelings arising after the negotiation. First, agents can help clients justify the decisions they make in the negotiation. Research suggests that people seek reasons or justifications for their decisions and that decisions supported by good reasons can attenuate negative affect.[50] Second, agents can help their clients appreciate the ephemeral nature of their feelings of dissatisfaction and regret, explaining that these feelings tend to dissipate markedly in time due to various psychological mechanisms.[51]

CONCLUSION

Option generation has enjoyed a central place in negotiation theory because of its considerable virtues. Unfortunately, however, the process also has its potential vices, including decision aversion, irrationality, and negative affect. By retaining an agent to negotiate on their behalf, disputants can increase the likelihood they will overcome these vices and enjoy the virtues of option generation.

Notes

1. R. Fisher, W. Ury, and B. Patton, *Getting to YES: Negotiating Agreement Without Giving In* (2nd ed.) (Boston: Houghton Mifflin, 1991), p. 66.

2. See R. H. Mnookin, S. R. Peppet, and A. Tulumello, *Beyond Winning: Negotiating to Create Value in Deals and Disputes* (Cambridge, Mass.: Belknap Press of Harvard University Press, 2000).

3. G. Nierenberg, *The Complete Negotiator* (New York: Nierenberg and Zeif Publishers, 1986), p. 194.

4. J. G. Johnson and M. Raab, "Take The First: Option-Generation and Resulting Choices," *Organizational Behavior and Human Decision Processes,* 2003, *91*(2), p. 215.

5. G. Klein, S. Wolf, L. Militello, and C. Zsambox, "Characteristics of Skilled Option Generation in Chess," *Organizational Behavior and Human Decision Processes,* 1995, *62*, p. 63.

6. See C. E. Naquin, "The Agony of Opportunity in Negotiation: Number of Negotiable Issues, Counterfactual Thinking, and Feelings of Satisfaction," *Organizational Behavior and Human Decision Processes,* 2003, *91*(1), 97–107.

7. See L. A. Froman and M. D. Cohen, "Compromise and Logroll: Comparing the Efficiency of Two Bargaining Processes," *Behavioral Science,* 1970, *30*, 180–183.

8. Naquin, "The Agony of Opportunity in Negotiation," 2003, p. 98.

9. Naquin, "The Agony of Opportunity in Negotiation," 2003, p. 98.

10. See S. S. Iyengar and M. R. Lepper, "When Choice Is Demotivating: Can One Desire Too Much of a Good Thing?" *Journal of Personality and Social Psychology,* 2000, *76*, 995–1006.

11. See C. Guthrie, "Panacea or Pandora's Box? The Costs of Options in Negotiation," *Iowa Law Review,* 2003, *88*, 601–653.

12. See Guthrie, "Panacea or Pandora's Box?" 2003; and Naquin, "The Agony of Opportunity in Negotiation," 2003.

13. See A. Tversky and E. Shafir, "Choice Under Conflict: The Dynamics of Deferred Decision," *Psychological Science,* 1992, *3*, 358–361.

14. B. Schwartz, *The Paradox of Choice: Why More Is Less* (New York: HarperCollins, 2004), p. 126.

15. See Iyengar and Lepper, "When Choice Is Demotivating," 2000.

16. See Iyengar and Lepper, "When Choice Is Demotivating," 2000.

17. See Guthrie, "Panacea or Pandora's Box?" 2003.

18. See D. Frisch and R. T. Clemen, "Beyond Expected Utility: Rethinking Behavioral Decision Research," *Psychological Bulletin,* 1994, *116*, 46–54; and G. Gigerenzer, P. M. Todd, and The ABC Research Group, *Simple Heuristics That Make Us Smart* (New York: Oxford University Press, 1999).

19. See J. R. Bettman, M. F. Luce, and J. W. Payne, "Constructive Consumer Choice Processes," *Journal of Consumer Research,* 1998, 25, 187–217.

20. L. Brenner, Y. Rottenstreich, and S. Sood, "Comparison, Grouping, and Preference," *Psychological Science,* 1999, *10*, p. 225.

21. See Brenner, Rottenstreich, and Sood, "Comparison, Grouping, and Preference," 1999.

22. See Guthrie, "Panacea or Pandora's Box?" 2003.

23. See D. Kahneman and A. Tversky, "Prospect Theory: An Analysis of Decision Under Risk," *Econometrica*, 1979, *47*, 263–291.

24. See Brenner, Rottenstreich, and Sood, "Comparison, Grouping, and Preference," 1999.

25. See Guthrie, "Panacea or Pandora's Box?" 2003.

26. Brenner, Rottenstreich, and Sood, "Comparison, Grouping, and Preference," 1999, p. 228.

27. See A. Tversky and I. Simonson, "Context-Dependent Preferences," *Management Science*, 1993, *10*, 1179–1189.

28. This example is based on M. Kelman, Y. Rottenstreich, and A. Tversky, "Context-Dependence in Legal Decision Making," *Journal of Legal Studies*, 1996, *25*, 287–318.

29. I. Simonson and A. Tversky, "Choice in Context: Tradeoff Contrast and Extremeness Aversion," *Journal of Marketing Research*, 1992, *29*, p. 292.

30. See J. Huber, J. Payne, and C. Puto, "Adding Asymmetrically Dominated Alternatives: Violations of Regularity and the Similarity Hypothesis," *Journal of Consumer Research*, 1982, *9*(1), 90–98.

31. See Simonson and Tversky, "Choice in Context," 1992.

32. See Guthrie, "Panacea or Pandora's Box?" 2003.

33. See I. Simonson, "Choice Based on Reasons: The Case of Attraction and Compromise Effects," *Journal of Consumer Research*, 1989, *16*, 158–174.

34. See Simonson and Tversky, "Choice in Context," 1992.

35. See Guthrie, "Panacea or Pandora's Box?" 2003.

36. See Bettman, Luce, and Payne, "Constructive Consumer Choice Processes," 1998; and J. W. Payne, J. R. Bettman, and E. J. Johnson, *The Adaptive Decision Maker* (Cambridge, Mass.: Cambridge University Press, 1993).

37. Payne, Bettman, and Johnson, *The Adaptive Decision Maker*, 1993, p. 2.

38. See N. K. Malhotra, "Information Load and Consumer Decision Making," *Journal of Consumer Research*, 1982, *8*(4), 419–430.

39. See J. H. Hibbard, J. J. Jewett, M. W. Legnini, and M. Tusler, "Choosing a Health Plan: Do Large Employers Use the Data?" *Health Affairs*, 1997, *16*(6), 172–180.

40. Schwartz, *The Paradox of Choice*, 2004, p. 132.

41. Naquin, "The Agony of Opportunity in Negotiation," 2003, p. 98.

42. D. E. Bell, "Reply: Putting a Premium on Regret." *Management Science*, 1985, *31*, p. 117.

43. M. Zeelenberg, J. Beattie, J. Van Der Pligt, and N. K. De Vries, "Consequences of Regret Aversion: Effects of Expected Feedback on Risky Decision Making," *Organizational Behavior and Human Decision Processes*, 1996, *65*, p. 149.

44. A. Gawande, *Complications: A Surgeon's Notes on an Imperfect Science* (New York: Henry Holt and Company, 2002), p. 220.

45. See L. F. Degner and J. A. Sloan, "Decision Making During Serious Illness: What Role Do Patients Really Want to Play?" *Journal of Clinical Epidemiology*, 1992, *45*, 941–950.

46. R. B. Cialdini, *Influence: Science and Practice* (4th ed.) (Boston: Allyn and Bacon, 2001), p. 9.

47. B. E. Kahn and J. Baron, "An Exploratory Study of Choice Rules Favored for High-Stakes Decisions," *Journal of Consumer Psychology*, 1995, *4*(4), p. 325.

48. See Guthrie, "Panacea or Pandora's Box?" 2003.

49. See R. Korobkin and C. Guthrie, "Psychology, Economics, and Settlement: A New Look at the Role of the Lawyer," *Texas Law Review*, 1997, *75*(4), 77–141.

50. See E. Shafir, I. Simonson, and A. Tversky, "Reason-Based Choice," *Cognition*, 1993, *49*, 11–36; and J. J. Inman and M. Zeelenberg, "Regret in Repeat Purchase Versus Switching Decisions: The Attenuating Role of Decision Justifiability," *Journal of Consumer Research*, 2002, *29*(1), 116–128.

51. See Guthrie, "Panacea or Pandora's Box?" 2003.

CHAPTER FIFTEEN

Organizational Influences on Disputants

Corinne Bendersky

The nature of an organization affects the way individuals within the organization handle disputes. In particular, relationships and power distribution can encourage individuals to take either direct or indirect approaches, to use either formal or informal procedures, and to take either collective or individual actions to address conflict.

As an illustration of these dynamics, consider a common scenario within a business organization: a member of the sales department and a member of the product development department are disputing over which of them is responsible for providing and analyzing data to determine why a new product is underperforming in the market. Neither prefers to be the one to produce or share the potentially unflattering information.

Imagine first that this dispute occurs within a large, bureaucratic organization in which jobs are clearly defined and people are promoted through the ranks on the basis of their experience and seniority. Both parties fear that providing the information may hinder opportunities for promotion in the future. Furthermore, neither wants to spend the time it would take to collect, organize, and analyze the data, since it would distract them from their regular tasks. Therefore, the individuals involved might try to avoid responsibility by claiming that the task is not part of their job descriptions. To deal with this problem, their bosses might engage in a formal review of the company's information-sharing policy and decide to amend the policy so that data produced and shared to help assess company performance is explicitly rewarded during performance

233

reviews, regardless of the content. Thus, the individual who ultimately provided the data would not feel threatened or humiliated.

Imagine now that the same dispute arises within a small, entrepreneurial company in which everyone interacts to make decisions regardless of their formal titles and roles in the organization. Each of the parties may be more motivated by the success of the company than by concern over opportunities for promotion, given the small size of the organization. As a result, neither has much incentive to hide the data in the first place, although neither may want to spend the time needed to collect, organize, and analyze it. The individuals might meet together to discuss what data they need to make their decision and debate whose responsibility it is to produce. The individual who ultimately agrees to do it would probably not feel any sense of threat or humiliation, because these discussions are just part of doing his or her job.

Disputing processes (the approaches people take to dealing with conflicts) can be very different depending on the organizational context in which they occur. In the example, the same conflict—determining responsibility for providing and sharing unflattering data—resulted in similar outcomes. The individual who shared the data experienced no threat or humiliation for doing so. The process for arriving at this outcome, however, differed considerably. The large bureaucratic organization used formal policy review and amendment, whereas the smaller, entrepreneurial organization used direct discussion and decision making. This chapter explores the ways in which the nature of relationships and power in an organization affect how individuals pursue different disputing processes within those organizations.[1]

DISPUTING PROCESSES IN ORGANIZATIONS

Organizations are structured systems of individuals and groups working together to meet a common set of goals. Individuals' roles in an organization and the power differences among members largely define the relevant social relationships. In most organizations, people are compensated financially and/or socially as an incentive to work toward achieving the organization's goal. In organizations ranging from for-profit businesses and the military to schools and churches, these incentives and social relationships have important implications for conflicts that occur within their boundaries. This chapter focuses on business organizations, though the observations apply equally to a range of different contexts.

Individuals in organizations may pursue many different kinds of disputing processes. The array of disputing processes in organizations can be categorized according to three dimensions: direct versus indirect, formal versus informal, and individual versus collective (see Table 15.1).

Table 15.1. Dispute Resolution Options in Organizations.

	Formal	Informal
Individual	Direct: Pursuit of established internal dispute resolution process	Direct: Negotiation or managerial mediation
	Indirect: Anonymous complaint to a suggestion board	Indirect: Avoidance or circumvention
Collective	Direct: Strike or collective bargaining	Direct: Peer intervention (for example, team meeting)
	Indirect: Policy review	Indirect: Organizational silence

Direct Versus Indirect Disputing Processes

When an individual or group identifies a specific conflict and attempts to resolve it, they are using *direct* disputing processes. Examples of direct disputing processes include face-to-face negotiations, group discussions, and formal dispute resolution procedures such as arbitration and mediation. Although direct disputing processes in no way imply successful conflict resolution, they do ensure that everyone involved explicitly acknowledges and participates in the resolution effort.

In contrast, parties use *indirect* disputing processes when they decide not to pursue a conflict or address an issue explicitly. One party's conflict resolution efforts may be unrecognized by the other. Indirect disputing processes include both active evasion and passive tolerance. For example, the parties may actively evade the issue and detract attention from the conflict by denying its presence or shifting the focus to another issue. Alternatively, parties may passively tolerate the issue by curtailing interaction with the issue. Indirect disputing processes may also involve efforts by one party to resolve the conflict by circumventing the other disputant, as when someone uses his or her own resources to fix a problem rather than rely on the other party's participation.

Formal Versus Informal Disputing Processes

Many organizations provide their members with some kind of formal dispute resolution process. Perhaps the most vivid examples of formal dispute resolution processes can be found in the context of an organization working within a collective bargaining structure. Most unionized companies use neutral arbitration to address certain disputes. Estimates suggest that roughly half of nonunion workplaces also have formal dispute resolution processes, or at least clear policies that specify the reporting structure and promise some measure of protection from retaliation to complainants.[2] These include alternative dispute resolution systems that may offer mediation, ombuds offices, and peer review panels.[3] These formal dispute resolution processes ensure some level of due process protection for both complainants and respondents. In addition, they create a structure that systemizes dispute resolution to improve fact-finding and reduce biases inherent in a system with power imbalances among the interest groups. The enforcement power of formal dispute resolution deters subsequent violations by holding managers accountable for professional and impartial treatment of their employees. In the example at the outset of this chapter, the managers who initiated a policy review to address the conflict in the large bureaucratic organization relied on a formal (and indirect) mechanism for addressing the dispute. They could have also used a more direct, formal procedure by mediating between the two employees.

Despite the benefits of formal procedures, many disputants fear that using them may damage their reputations or relationships. Indeed, evidence indicates that bringing or responding to a formal complaint may limit subsequent career advancement opportunities.[4] For instance, if a technician files a formal complaint against his supervisor, he risks being excluded from training opportunities that are essential for getting promoted. In addition, other technicians he works with might distrust him and be less willing to share information or even to socialize with him afterwards. Thus, in most organizations, disputants often resolve conflicts informally.

Informal processes include negotiating directly with the other disputant(s), asking other group members or a boss to intervene and informally mediate, and avoiding the conflict or tolerating the situation. Some estimates indicate that, in unionized settings, ten disputes are settled informally for every grievance that is filed formally.[5] One can easily imagine other settings in which this ratio is considerably higher.

One of the benefits of informal processes is that the disputants have complete control over the outcome. Unlike formal avenues, which often culminate in a third party deciding how the conflict should be resolved,[6] informal processes allow the disputants to decide the outcome of their conflict themselves. Informal processes are also more efficient and less costly than formal channels. In the opening example, the individuals resolved the conflict in the entrepreneurial organization by deciding between themselves who should analyze and provide the necessary data. This informal process took far less time and fewer organizational resources than did the formal policy review that was conducted in the bureaucratic organization.

However, since there are no enforcement mechanisms in informal processes, these processes are limited by the willingness of more powerful disputants to participate in good faith. Furthermore, there is no security against negative repercussions, such as retaliation or damaged personal relationships. There is also no recourse if the other party refuses to negotiate. Therefore, disputants who are not confident in their negotiation skills or those who face a conflict with a much more powerful individual may be unwilling to use any direct processes at all, leading them instead to avoid or suppress conflicts.

Individual Versus Collective Disputing Processes

In addition to the direct versus indirect and formal versus informal dimensions, disputants also may choose to address a conflict individually or collectively. When disputants pursue an individual disputing process, they believe that the conflict is their own problem, and assume the risks and responsibility of resolving it. They are unconcerned by how the outcome might implicate or affect anyone besides the individual disputants. An individual approach may involve a third party, such as a mediator who facilitates the dispute resolution process, so long as the disputants' interests are represented individually. Individual disputing processes are most effective when the parties have relatively equal power. This increases the chances that both will participate in good faith and also limits the risks of outright retaliation.

Collective disputing processes involve mobilizing others with similar problems to try to influence a person or entity. Collective action may include unionization, boycotts, social movement demonstrations, petition generation, and team interventions. These processes can generate social power when individual negotiation or organizational power is lacking. While potentially effective, collective disputing processes can be difficult, time consuming, and often risky tasks, compared with individual actions.

EFFECTS OF ORGANIZATIONAL CHARACTERISTICS ON DISPUTING PROCESSES

Individuals may choose to pursue particular disputing processes depending on their own preferred style, the characteristics of the conflict, and the characteristics of the context in which the conflict occurs. This section focuses on how individuals decide what approach to take based on relationships and power in the organization. Although organizational characteristics may not be more important than individuals' styles or characteristics of the conflict, they nevertheless exert an important influence on individuals' decisions.

Relational Networks

Relationships are often determined by people's interdependent roles in the organization. People may not be able to succeed at their job without others' participation and cooperation, making it difficult to avoid someone with whom one is in conflict. Conflicts over relationships, as opposed to tasks, are especially detrimental in organizational settings.[7] Whereas moderate levels of conflict over tasks may enhance productivity by increasing critical analyses of the merits of different options, relationship conflicts hurt productivity by distracting people from their work and decreasing cooperation and goodwill among workgroup members. For example, a boss who challenges his subordinate to provide better data analysis is focusing on the task, and the conflict may improve the quality of the output. A boss who bullies her subordinate by telling him he is incompetent is focusing on a relational issue. This type of conflict will damage the quality of the output. Thus, relationship conflicts in organizations directly and negatively affect performance.

The nature of relational networks (the social ties among one's colleagues) is a key characteristic of organizations that affect disputants' behavior. Groups with tight relational networks (in which most members of the network know and rely on each other) are generally constrained by norms of reciprocal behavior. Members are highly interdependent, information is sufficiently accessible to establish reputations, and members have the ability to mobilize allies to enforce or deter others' behavior. These characteristics make interpersonal conflicts potentially very costly.

When relational networks are loose (few people besides the focal person know or rely on others in the network), one's work output does not depend on the output of other members. Interactions may be specified through formal procedures such as contracts and job descriptions. Therefore, interpersonal conflicts may have little impact on one's work experience or productivity, and are less problematic than when relational ties are tight.[8]

For example, conflicts among nurses on a hospital floor, who must all interact to ensure patient health, can be very costly to the patients, as well as to the specific individuals involved. Nurses may refuse to cover for each other during breaks, withhold information, and try to influence the doctors' opinions of each other. In contrast, conflicts among members of a large sales force may have little impact on each person's ability to sell the product. The lack of interdependencies among the salespeople reduces the potential consequences of interpersonal conflicts.

While the higher cost of relationship conflicts in tight-knit (versus loose-knit) groups is well documented, the effects on disputants' behavior is less clear. Some research suggests that tight relational networks are conducive to informal, direct types of conflict behavior, whereas loose relational networks promote indirect approaches. Tight-knit groups can generate trust and a sense of shared fate, and are likely to confront conflicts directly as a regular part of living in a confined social space. Information spreads rapidly throughout the network in tight-knit groups. As a result, reputations are important and behavior can be monitored, which might generate opportunities for collective interventions. In loose-knit relational networks, however, conflicts may not be confronted as often because there is enough social space for people to avoid one another. Furthermore, there are not as many opportunities to mobilize allies, and actors have sparse knowledge of each other's activities in general, so conflict agreements cannot be monitored.[9]

Alternatively, some research indicates that tight relational networks can generate conformist and exclusionary behavior, which leads to widespread conflict avoidance (in other words, indirect disputing processes) instead of direct approaches. This phenomenon is called "organizational silence."[10] Organizational silence creates the illusion that participants understand the reasoning and thinking underlying the issues facing the group. In reality, their silence reflects a complacency that often leads to suboptimal decision making and slow adaptation to change.[11]

Indirect processes might predominate in tight-knit relational networks when members interpret dissent as disagreement, and therefore as a threat to the group's cohesion. Members might also avoid direct disputing processes in tight-knit networks because relationships are more enduring than in loose-knit groups. Therefore, conflicts may appear to have long-term or widespread consequences that make it more appealing for members to avoid them altogether in order to maintain their places in the social network. Thus, this research suggests that in some instances, tight-knit relational networks can be *less* conducive to direct disputing processes than loose relational networks, and may in fact encourage collective, indirect, informal disputing processes.

Even though relational networks are important factors in organizations that affect individuals' choices about disputing processes, one cannot predict individuals' behaviors based on the nature of relational networks alone. Another important factor to consider when exploring the social dynamics of an organization is the distribution of power within that organization.

Organizational Power Distribution

Organizational power is the ability to access resources, make decisions, and give or withhold rewards to others. Unlike negotiation power, which is primarily a function of one's alternatives to reaching an agreement in a given negotiation,[12] organizational power is stable from one negotiation to the next. In other words, organizational power gives one consistently strong alternatives in repeated negotiations that occur in the organization over time.

Organizational power is a function, in part, of an organization's structure, its culture, or both. Structural power is related to one's formal role or position in the organizational hierarchy. The structural status of managers, supervisors, professionals, or executives, for example, gives them more organizational power than does the structural status of assistants, technicians, or janitors. Cultural power, however, is derived through social norms and shared underlying assumptions about who in the organization deserves organizational power. While cultural power and structural power are often highly correlated, the mechanisms through which they are maintained and reinforced differ considerably. Cultural power is reinforced socially, whereas structural power is reinforced through formal policies and rules. Thus, in an organization in which there are few differences in structural power among members, it is still possible that some members have considerably more cultural power due to social norms of deference and respect. For instance, in their research on creativity, Sutton and Hargadon found that status differences based on technical skill emerged through the brainstorming process and were supported by a culture that encouraged wisdom instead of hierarchical differences.[13]

Power in organizations may be unequally distributed, as in hierarchical bureaucracies, or equally distributed, as in participatory, self-directed teams. When relational networks are tight-knit, unequal power may induce "conformity to a leader's idiosyncratic position, stifling all dissent, skepticism, and cautionary information from the members."[14] With this type of unequal power distribution, individuals with more power can assert their definition of the terms of a conflict situation and its appropriate resolution.[15] Individuals with less power may have little choice but to acquiesce to a superior's preferences, avoid conflicts altogether, or use adversarial processes designed to offset power differences between the individuals involved.

In contrast, when power differences in organizations are relatively small, direct disputing processes are more common. Decision making is often more consultative and participatory in nature, and people feel more comfortable challenging one another's ideas.[16] Effectively managing conflicts may be culturally valued (that is, disagreement is not considered threatening) more when power is equally distributed than when it is unequally distributed, making direct disputing processes less risky.

In summary, interdependent relationships and power dynamics influence individuals' decisions to pursue disputing processes in organizations. In organizations with loose-knit relational networks, conflicts are generally handled indirectly, informally, and individually, regardless of the distribution of power. In organizations with tight-knit relational networks, conflicts are addressed directly, informally, and individually when power is equally distributed. When power is unequally distributed in tight-knit networks, people take actions to minimize their own vulnerability. Many conflicts will be handled indirectly, informally, and individually (as when relational networks are loose). In this situation, when conflicts are addressed directly, it is either done through formal channels or collective actions because both of these direct approaches minimize the threat of retaliation to the low-power individual.

See Table 15.2 for a visual summary of the effects of organizational characteristics on disputing processes.

Table 15.2. The Effects of Organizational Characteristics on Disputing Processes.

	Tight Relational Networks	Loose Relational Networks
Equal Power Distribution	Direct, informal, and individual	Indirect, informal, and individual
Unequal Power Distribution	Indirect, informal, and individual OR direct, formal, and collective	Indirect, informal, and individual

SPECIFIC CHARACTERISTICS AND FUTURE RESEARCH

Many specific organizational characteristics may also affect individuals' disputing processes. Research on organizational influences on disputants' behavior is being pursued in many areas.[17] For instance, the availability of formal dispute resolution options may encourage people to use direct approaches to dealing with conflicts, both formal and informal.[18] People in organizations with formal dispute resolution procedures, extensive negotiation skills training, and neutral facilitators are most likely to use direct disputing procedures. Furthermore, when formal dispute resolution processes are structured like quasijudicial legal procedures, disputants may be inclined to pursue formal, individual resolution options, which would mimic the remediation that a court might provide. Alternatively, when social movement activity (such as identity or diversity support groups) is visible inside organizational boundaries, disputants might be more inclined to pursue collective disputing processes.[19]

Another important mechanism through which organizational characteristics might affect individuals' disputing processes is managerial control systems. Control systems describe the collections of mechanisms "that managers use to direct attention, motivate, and encourage organizational members to act in desired ways to meet an organization's objectives."[20] Individuals working in organizations with particular types of managerial control systems will be more likely to engage in conflict behaviors that are consistent with meeting the organization's overall objectives. In organizations that encourage and reward maximum individual performance, for instance, efficient dispute resolution processes (in other words, direct, informal, and individual) may be most prevalent. In those that are more team oriented and that reward socially desirable behavior, people might tend to avoid dealing directly with conflicts individually, relying on formal collective options instead.[21]

Whether the stakes involved justify engaging in a direct process for resolving a dispute also depends on organizational context. When groups work on complex, nonroutine tasks, then directly debating the strengths and weaknesses of different options can generate better-quality, more creative outputs. However, if the task is very routine, debate will only slow the group down, and conflicts are best handled indirectly.[22] For example, arguing about the best way to file a joint motion for extension of time will not add much value to the product, whereas debating the best design for a new product will generate more creative innovation. In addition, diverse groups make better decisions than do homogeneous groups, but only if the groups effectively use direct disputing processes. When conflicts are suppressed or avoided, diverse groups fail to confront different points of view. As a result, teams without direct disputing processes fail to capture the benefits that a diversity of views can bring to decision making.[23] Thus, when characteristics of the group make conflicts potentially beneficial, encouraging direct disputing processes is extremely important.

The sum total of this research clearly suggests that context matters to disputants, and that their decisions are systematically affected by a variety of organizational characteristics. Disputants' conflict behaviors can best be understood by considering not only the characteristics of the individuals and the conflict they are facing, but also the characteristics of the organizational setting in which those conflicts are taking place.

Notes

1. Although employees often file external claims and lawsuits against their employers, those actions are beyond the scope of this chapter. I will concentrate only on disputing processes that stay within organizational boundaries.

2. See P. Feuille and D. Chachere, "Looking Fair or Being Fair: Remedial Voice Procedures in Nonunion Workplaces," *Journal of Management,* 1995, *21*(1), 27–42.

3. See M. Rowe, "Dispute Resolution in the Non-Union Environment: An Evolution Toward Integrated Systems for Conflict Management?" in S. Gleason (ed.), *Frontiers in Dispute Resolution and Human Resources* (East Lansing, Mich.: Michigan State University Press, 1997); and A.J.S. Colvin, "Institutional Pressures, Human Resource Strategies, and the Rise of Nonunion Dispute Resolution Procedures," *Industrial and Labor Relations Review,* 2003, *56*(3), 375–392.

4. See D. Lewin, "Grievance Procedures in Nonunion Workplaces: An Empirical Analysis of Usage, Dynamics and Outcomes," *Chicago-Kent Law Review,* 1990, *66*(3), 823–844.

5. See D. Lewin and R. S. Peterson, *The Modern Grievance Procedure in the United States* (Westport, Conn.: Quorum, 1988).

6. Formal mediation is an exception.

7. See K. A. Jehn and C. Bendersky, "Intragroup Conflict in Organizations: A Contingency Perspective on the Conflict-Outcome Relationship," in B. Staw and R. Kramer (eds.), *Research in Organizational Behavior* (Greenwich, Conn.: JAI Press, 2003).

8. See C. Morrill, *The Executive Way: Conflict Management in Corporations* (Chicago, Ill.: University of Chicago Press, 1995); and M. Baumgartner, *The Moral Order of a Suburb* (New York: Oxford University Press, 1988).

9. See Morrill, *The Executive Way,* 1995; Baumgartner, *The Moral Order of a Suburb,* 1988; and D. M. Kolb and J. Bartunek, *Hidden Conflict in Organizations: Uncovering Behind-the-Scenes Disputes* (Thousand Oaks, Calif.: Sage, 1992).

10. See I. Janis, "Sources of Error in Strategic Decision Making," in J. Pennings (ed.), *Organizational Strategy and Change* (San Francisco: Jossey-Bass, 1985); E. Morrison and F. Milliken, "Organizational Silence: A Barrier to Change and Development in a Pluralistic World," *Academy of Management Review,* 2000, *25*(4), 706–725; and L. A. Perlow, *When You Say Yes but Mean No: How Silencing Conflict Wrecks Relationships and Companies . . . and What You Can Do About It* (New York: Crown Business, 2003).

11. See B. Uzzi, "Social Structures and Competition in Interfirm Networks: The Paradox Of Embeddedness," *Administrative Science Quarterly,* 1997, *42,* 35–67.

12. See L. Thompson, *The Mind and Heart of the Negotiator* (2nd ed.) (Upper Saddle River, N.J.: Prentice-Hall, 2001).

13. See R. I. Sutton and A. Hargadon, "Brainstorming Groups in Context: Effectiveness in a Product Design Firm," *Administrative Science Quarterly,* 1996, *41*(4), 685–718.

14. Janis, "Sources of Error in Strategic Decision Making," 1985, pp. 168–169.

15. See S. R. Barley, "Contextualizing Conflict: Notes on the Anthropology of Disputes and Negotiations," *Research on Negotiation in Organizations,* 1991, *3,* 165–199.

16. See G. Hofstede, *Cultures and Organizations* (London: McGraw-Hill, 1991).

17. See, for a more comprehensive review, Jehn and Bendersky, "Intragroup Conflict in Organizations," 2003.

18. See C. Bendersky, "Dispute Resolution Systems: A Complementarities Model," *Academy of Management Review,* 2003, *28*(4), 643–655.

19. These research topics are currently being pursued by C. Bendersky and C. Morrill.

20. C. Long, R. Burton, and L. Cardinal, L. "Three Controls Are Better Than One: A Computational Model of Complex Control Systems," *Computational and Mathematical Organization Theory,* 2002, *8,* p. 198.

21. These research topics are currently being pursued by C. Bendersky, C. Long, and C. Morrill.

22. See K. Lovelace, D. Shapiro, and L. Weingart, "Maximizing Cross-Functional New Product Teams' Innovativeness and Constraint Adherence: A Conflict Communications Perspective," *Academy of Management Journal,* 2001, *24*(4), 779–784.

23. See K. A. Jehn, G. Northcraft, and M. A. Neale, "Why Differences Make a Difference: A Field Study of Diversity, Conflict, and Performance in Workgroups," *Administrative Science Quarterly,* 1999, *44,* 741–763.

CHAPTER SIXTEEN

A Taxonomy of Dispute Resolution Ethics

Jonathan R. Cohen

Participants in dispute resolution frequently find themselves confronted with ethical questions. Some questions apply to professionals. For example, if deception in negotiation can be strategically advantageous, might an attorney zealously advocating for her or his client at times be obliged to deceive? Suppose a mediator believes that the agreement being reached is substantively unfair. Should the mediator raise this issue with the disputants? Other questions arise for the disputants themselves. If a person injures another, is not the injurer ethically obliged to apologize and offer amends? Must the injured party then forgive the injurer? Questions also arise at the broad level of social policy. Suppose we cannot effectively sanction all but the most extreme ethical violations. Are discussions of dispute resolution ethics Pollyannaish? Dispute resolution participants also face questions on the personal and practical level. How should one proceed when one has ethical doubts? What should a professional do if, for example, the professional's role clashes with the professional's personal morals?

People have wrestled with some of these issues for centuries. An essay such as this can by no means list, let alone answer, the many, varied questions of dispute resolution ethics. My goal instead is to offer a *taxonomy* to use in thinking about dispute resolution ethics, to provide both an intellectual overview of the field and, simultaneously, a structure to assist practitioners in understanding ethical challenges they and those with whom they work may face. Like most taxonomies, this one is not perfect. The classification scheme is four-part: (1) professional ethics, (2) disputant ethics, (3) social policy, and (4) personal

244

experience. These categories are not fully distinct but rather interrelated, and often a particular ethical question will implicate issues in multiple categories.

PROFESSIONAL ETHICS: ROLES AND RULES

Many participants in dispute resolution enter the conflict as *professionals.* They are not part of the underlying conflict themselves. Rather they come to the conflict in distinct, socially defined roles. Such roles include lawyer, mediator, arbitrator, judge, ombuds, and diplomat. These roles typically have professional rules or codes of ethics that attach to them. For example, in the context of professional practice, the attorney who negotiates may be bound by a variant of the ABA Model Rules of Professional Conduct; the family mediator operates pursuant to the Model Standards of Practice for Family and Divorce Mediation; the arbitrator follows the Revised Code of Ethics for Arbitrators in Commercial Disputes.[1] Hence, when ethical questions arise, the professional who wants to behave appropriately should look toward the applicable ethical standards. For example, can the attorney "puff" during a negotiation, arguing that the claim is worth more than the attorney believes? The Comment to Model Rule 4.1 indicates that the answer is sometimes "yes." Can a mediator break confidentiality? Sections 4 and 6 of the Uniform Mediation Act outline the circumstances in which breaching confidentiality is permitted.

That professionals must know the ethical standards of their field is only the beginning of the inquiry. On many ethical issues the codes are effectively silent, leaving room for professional discretion. Furthermore, not all professionals actually do adhere—or perhaps even should always adhere—to such adopted professional standards.[2] Nevertheless, conscientious practitioners should be aware of the applicable ethical codes. There is a wisdom to this awareness beyond mere compliance. Individual attorneys, mediators, or ombuds need not tackle difficult ethical questions on their own. They may gain guidance—and perhaps save time too—by learning what ethical position their professions have adopted and the reasons it was adopted.

When entering this world of professional ethical codes, it is helpful to keep two basic issues in mind. First, because different approaches to dispute resolution function differently, varied systems of professional ethics have been developed.[3] One might call this *functional variety.* For example, while the process of mediation may have a general ethos of conciliation, the attorney representing a client within it may still be bound by the ethics of zealous advocacy. Different ethics attach, depending on one's function within the process. Being clear about one's professional role and the attendant ethics is therefore essential, though not always easy.

Second, practitioners must recognize the distinction between *aspirational ideals* and *minimum standards* in articulations of ethical norms. Ethics codes do not always clearly define whether they provide noble (but vague and questionably attainable) goals or whether they prescribe floors for sanctionable conduct. For example, ethical codes may call on professionals to be "honest" and pursue what is "just" or "fair." However, only severe departures from these ideals, such as cases of fraud or legally unconscionable agreements, may actually violate the code. Many dishonest statements do not rise to the level of fraud, and many unfair and unjust outcomes are not legally unconscionable. In evaluating both their own behavior and that of their counterparts, it is essential that practitioners be clear about the nature of the applicable ethical standards. For example, even if the negotiating lawyer strives for high levels of candor and honesty, he or she should be aware that the opposing lawyer is technically bound to very low standards. Perhaps our ethics codes will be revised someday to provide greater clarity. Until then, the burden of deciphering these codes rests on the practitioner.

DISPUTANT ETHICS: UNDERLYING MORAL VALUES

Generally speaking, dispute resolution professionals are not the central players in the conflict, though it may be easy for them to lose sight of this fact. The central players are the parties. Accordingly, one should consider ethics questions not solely from the viewpoint of the professional but also from the viewpoints of the parties themselves. This underlying ethical category is "disputant ethics." Perhaps the most basic question from this category is, "When people are in conflict, what *should* they do?" This is not a question of strategy, but one of normative ethics. Much can be learned from the nearly tautological recognition that parties wishing to behave ethically in a conflict should attempt to pursue ethical ends by ethical means. What then are such ends and means?

Perhaps the most salient ethical end for parties in conflict is that of reconciliation—of making peace. All other things equal, most believe that peace is to be preferred to strife. Functionally, peacemaking usually benefits both parties by reducing tension, fostering future relations, permitting commerce, and avoiding violence. Peacemaking also benefits society generally through promoting social order, harmony, and functionality. This is not to say that reconciliation is always an appropriate goal in a conflict. Some may see establishing justice as the central ethical goal, even if doing so entails greater conflict. Others may question whether reconciliation in the face of conflict is even a laudable goal. For example, legal anthropologist Laura Nader has argued against a negative view of conflict *per se,* rather seeing it as an important and irreducible aspect of social existence and transformation, and, conversely, attempts to reconcile, if not suppress, conflict as an effort toward social control and subordination.[4] Nevertheless, most see reconciliation in the face of conflict as not only a praiseworthy human endeavor but an essential one.

Now let us turn to the issue of means. If making peace where there is strife is a central ethical end, what are appropriate means for achieving it? This can be broken into two inquiries: (1) Are certain means ethically inappropriate? The answer is undoubtedly yes. Even in war, all but the most extreme parties would maintain that certain ethical limits apply (for example, regarding the avoidable destruction of innocent life, the treatment of prisoners, and so on). More mundanely, little moral justification exists for lying in legal negotiations.[5] (2) Are certain means ethically laudable? This second inquiry may have the most to teach us. Many approaches to dispute resolution can be seen not only as functional enterprises (that is, they functionally help resolve the dispute) but also as ethical ones. When a court renders a verdict, ideally it does so on a fair basis, namely, through the competent and impartial application of the law. Mediators usually try to foster a respectful form of dialogue in which disputants listen to one another. In propounding "principled negotiation," Fisher, Ury, and Patton suggest that negotiators invoke not just any criteria to reach resolution, but principled criteria.[6] At a basic level, many dispute resolution processes can themselves be seen as ethical enterprises. Rather than parties resolving disputes based on power (for example, through vigilantism), these approaches help the parties to resolve disputes fairly.

A second foundational issue in the domain of disputant ethics stems from apology and forgiveness. Conflict often arises on the heels of injury, whether intentional or accidental. While issues of fault are sometimes unclear (for example, one does not know exactly what caused the accident) and sometimes complex (for example, as when legal and moral fault differ), often they are not. Many injurers know that they are at fault, both legally and morally, for what they have done. How *should* an injurer respond? Though behavior in modern society does not necessarily reflect this conclusion, the moral response to injuring another is to take responsibility. The injurer should usually apologize and seek to make amends, for example, by offering fair compensation for the injury.[7] By contrast, denying responsibility when one is at fault is a profound moral failure. Questions also arise for the injured. If the injurer apologizes and offers fair compensation, is the injured obliged to accept the offerings and forgive the injurer? What if an apology and compensation are not forthcoming? Should the injured "seek justice" by pursuing legal remedies, or should he or she "turn the other cheek"? Observe that questions such as these are at root ones for the disputants, not the professionals. Yet to serve the disputants effectively, professionals must be aware that the disputants may face such basic ethical questions.

SOCIAL POLICY

So far, ethical issues have been examined principally from the viewpoint of an individual—either the professional or the disputant. However, social policy plays an important role as well. Social policy questions are not about personal decisions concerning what is right or wrong. Rather they ask how we should—and perhaps more important, how we can—effectively structure social policy to achieve ethical outcomes in dispute resolution. Following the framework described earlier, I shall first consider social policy questions affecting professional ethics, and then social policy questions affecting disputant ethics.

Perhaps the most salient issue of professional ethics from the social policy perspective is enforcement. What can realistically be accomplished with social policy? Oliver Wendell Holmes once remarked that the law was what the bad man knew it to be.[8] Though law is often described in lofty terms, the realist perspective reflected in Holmes's comment suggests that the issue in practice is what, if any, punishment a lawbreaker will face. A similar realist orientation may be taken to questions of professional ethics.

Encouraging ethical behavior is no simple undertaking. I recall a conversation from roughly a decade ago with Thomas Schelling, then of Harvard's Kennedy School of Government. We were discussing the growth of ethics courses in the curricula of various professional schools (for example, business schools, public policy schools, and so on). He commented (I paraphrase), "If one asks whether these courses can assist people who want to do right in determining what is right, I think these courses have much to offer. If one asks instead whether these courses will motivate students to want to do right in the first place, I am skeptical."

Enforcement of any articulated ethical standard related to dispute resolution will be imperfect. How often are ethical violations detected? Suppose a party lies during a negotiation about having an alternative offer, or suppose a mediator or judge acts with partiality. How will others know a transgression has occurred? Even if the transgression is detected, will sanctions actually ensue? The difficulties of enforcement undoubtedly motivate some of the ethical minimalism found within professional codes. For example, legal ethics codes have long done little more than prohibit fraud—indeed some codes even explicitly permit "puffing." They do so because more stringent standards would be largely unenforceable though, by most accounts, lying in negotiation is morally wrong.[9]

Related to sanctioning are the issues of reputation and market structure. Though official sanctioning of all but the most egregious behavior is rare, reputational effects may deter much unethical conduct. Significant ethical issues also exist at the level of market structure. Different ethical frameworks may distinguish professional approaches to dispute resolution. Put another way, the selection of the dispute resolution mechanism implicitly involves a selection of a set of dispute resolution ethics.[10] If one wants to be adversarial, one may choose a hard-nosed litigator. If one wants to be cooperative, one may seek out a mediator or perhaps a "collaborative lawyer" to help settle the case. The size, shape, and functioning of the professional guilds we create, therefore, influence how ethics are practiced.

Ethical questions of social policy also arise concerning the disputants. How do we teach children to behave when they have disputes? Is the culture we transmit one of closed-minded, adversarial argumentation or one of open-minded, respectful discourse?[11] The structures we put in place to process disputes influence our cultural understanding of appropriate behavior. Observe, for example, that switching from a traditional adjudicative courthouse to a "multidoor" courthouse that includes mediation is both a functional change and also an ethical change, encouraging disputants to speak for themselves (rather than through their lawyers), to listen to one another, and to exercise self-determination.[12]

PERSONAL EXPERIENCE

Personal experience forms the final category of this four-part taxonomy. This category consists of the embodied practice of ethics; that is, ethics on a lived, human level. There is much overlap here with the categories of professional ethics and disputant ethics. What is distinctive is the focus. Often we approach matters of professional and disputant ethics in an intellectual manner. For example, a professional may try to determine whether a particular course of action is permitted, required, or forbidden by professional ethics codes, or a disputant may try to reason about what is the right thing to do. By contrast, this category focuses on the experiential realm of ethical life. The subject here is less about thinking about ethical issues than about how ethical issues *feel* in practice. Consider a few examples.

What should a professional who has ethical doubts do? What should a professional who has made an ethical mistake do? How can professionals avoid making ethical mistakes? For many professionals, the practice of ethics is influenced by their relationships with other professionals. When facing new situations, they seek guidance from mentors. When they have ethical doubts, they seek counsel and support from colleagues. Recall that many dispute resolution professionals function within organizations that affect the ethical choices of their members.[13] Such organizational influences should not, of course, substitute for the exercise of the professional's own conscience. Further, the professional is the one who must ultimately live with his or her own moral choices. The psychological price to a professional of betraying his or her own personal values can be tremendous.[14]

An individual's ethical decision making in a dispute can define who one is. Disputes can bring out either "the best" or "the worst" in people. Just as wars often serve as defining ethical moments in the history of nations, so too disputes can be defining periods in people's lives. There are few more significant measures of a human being than how one treats others, and situations of conflict are critical times for taking that measurement.[15] It is easy to be polite to someone one likes. The real test is interacting with those one dislikes. Disputes challenge us as moral agents. Sometimes that challenge is to forebear (for example, from rudeness and vindictiveness) and sometimes it is to persevere (for example, find the courage to stand up for oneself). What will it feel like to try to forebear or persevere? Will one develop an ulcer or remain calm and serene? When one looks in the mirror, either today or years from now, how will one feel about what one has done?

AN EXAMPLE: RESPONDING TO MEDICAL ERROR

To illustrate the application of this taxonomy, consider an example. Suppose a doctor makes a mistake when treating a patient, resulting in serious adverse medical consequences. Let us consider this four-part taxonomy as a means of structuring our understanding of some of the ethical issues that arise.

For dispute resolution professionals, the most salient ethical challenge may be role clarity: understanding clearly one's professional role and the attendant ethical obligations. On the medical provider's "side" there is a dizzying array of possible professional roles. These include attorney for the physician, attorney for the hospital (or medical organization), and attorney for the insurance company. There may be hospital employees, such as members of risk management teams, mediators, ombuds offices, and even "patient" representatives. There may also be outside professional consultants, such as mediators. Numerous professionals may also become involved on the patient's behalf, including lawyers, clergy, and psychological counselors. In a complex world, role conflicts and confusion can easily arise. Does the lawyer provided by the insurance company fully represent the doctor's interests? Is the hospital-employed mediator or ombuds truly impartial? If the hospital chaplain is paid by the hospital, will that create a conflict in ministering to the patient? The complexities of confidentiality (for example, regarding statements made to attorneys, mediators, physicians, psychologists, and clergy) increase the risk of professional misstep based upon role confusion.

For the disputants themselves, the ethical challenges can be quite poignant. Most salient may be the doctor's (or hospital's) decision whether to remain largely silent about the error (addressing with the patient only future treatment for the new medical condition) or to disclose fully and perhaps even apologize for what occurred. The medical ethics of patient care undoubtedly point toward the latter, but the adversarial air that commonly arises in the context of possible litigation may lead to the former. Relatedly, trust issues arise both for patients and medical providers. A doctor's apology may influence the patient's choice of whether to continue with that physician or seek care elsewhere. Should the doctor's apology—or lack thereof—affect the patient's decision whether to bring a lawsuit?

The lens of social policy brings further ethical issues into view. To address the need for disclosure and apology, several states have recently passed laws requiring either disclosure of serious errors by physicians or exclusion of medical apologies from admissible evidence.[16] Such laws assume that following medical errors most doctors and hospitals remain silent, fearing that, based on the advice of attorneys or insurers, an apology would be used against them in court. Society may have an interest in developing laws that promote open dialogue and ongoing relationships after medical errors rather than adversarial modalities of interaction, such as litigation.

In challenging contexts such as medical error, the experiential level of ethics is likely to be important for both disputants and dispute resolution professionals. Errors can produce a powerful sense of shame, especially for professionals such as physicians who strive for high levels of competency. Admitting an error involves squarely facing that shame. Yet not admitting the error is no easy path either. How would the doctor who remains silent feel looking at him- or herself in the mirror? For patients, questions of how to proceed after the adverse event can tie deeply to their feelings as well. Suppose the physician does not apologize for the mistake but remains silent, and the patient sues seeking financial compensation. Might the patient nevertheless forgive the physician in his or her heart to achieve psychological closure? And how will the patient make such choices, alone or with external aid? Though the ethical decisions to be made may be the same, patients with support from family and friends may be better at handling the sense of vulnerability they may feel and hence better able to make those decisions than patients without such support. For dispute resolution professionals, too, the lived practice can be poignant. For many, spending a day working to resolve a purely financial dispute does not produce the same experience as struggling with issues linked to people's health, and even their lives.

CONCLUSION

Disputes raise a variety of ethical issues for professionals, for disputants, and for society. Frequently these issues are complicated. I have presented a four-part framework for viewing some of the major ethical issues. These lenses are professional ethics, disputant ethics, social policy, and personal experience. By no means does this framework capture all of the ethical issues at stake, but it may help identify some of the major ones. Ethical behavior usually requires awareness. Understanding the type of ethical issue at stake will not by itself resolve ethical challenges, but it can be an important step in that direction.

Notes

1. See, for a collection and analysis of such codes, P. Bernard and B. Garth, *Dispute Resolution Ethics: A Comprehensive Guide* (New York: American Bar Association, 2002).

2. See, for a critique of excessive deference by lawyers to such professional role ethics, D. Luban, *Lawyers and Justice: An Ethical Study* (Princeton, N.J.: Princeton University Press, 1988).

3. See C. Menkel-Meadow, "Ethics in Alternative Dispute Resolution: New Issues, No Answers from the Adversary Conception of Lawyers' Responsibilities," *South Texas Law Review*, 1997, *38*, 407–454; and K. Kovach, "New Wine Requires New Wineskins: Transforming Lawyer Ethics for Effective Representation in a Non-Adversarial Approach to Problem Solving," *Fordham Urban Law Journal*, 2001, *28*, 935–977.

4. See L. Nader, "Controlling Processes in the Practice of Law: Hierarchy and Pacification in the Movement to Re-form Dispute Ideology," *Ohio State Journal on Dispute Resolution*, 1993, *9*, 1–25.

5. See G. Wetlaufer, "The Ethics of Lying in Negotiation," *Iowa Law Review*, 1990, *75*, 1219–1273.

6. See R. Fisher, W. Ury, and B. Patton, *Getting to YES: Negotiating Agreement Without Giving In* (2nd ed.) (New York: Penguin, 1991).

7. See J. Cohen, "Advising Clients to Apologize," *Southern California Law Review*, 1999, *72*, 1009–1069.

8. See O. W. Holmes, "The Path of the Law," *Harvard Law Review*, 1897, *10*, 457–478.

9. See G. Hazard, "The Lawyer's Obligation to Be Trustworthy When Dealing with Opposing Parties," *South Carolina Law Review*, 1981, *33*, 181–196.

10. See S. Peppet, "Contractarian Economics and Mediation Ethics: The Case for Customizing Neutrality Through Contingent Fee Mediation," *Texas Law Review*, 2003, *82*, 227–285.

11. See D. Tannen, *The Argument Culture: Moving from Debate to Dialogue* (New York: Random House, 1998).

12. See C. Menkel-Meadow, "Whose Dispute Is It Anyway? A Philosophical and Democratic Defense of Settlement (in Some Cases)," *Georgetown Law Journal*, 1995, *83*, 2663–2696.

13. See D. Rhode, "Ethical Perspectives on Legal Practice," *Stanford Law Review,* 1985, *37,* 589–652.

14. See S. Daicoff, *Lawyer, Know Thyself* (Washington, D.C.: American Psychological Association, 2004).

15. See J. Cohen, "When People Are the Means: Negotiating with Respect," *Georgetown Journal of Legal Ethics,* 2001, *14,* 739–802.

16. See J. Cohen, "Toward Candor After Medical Error: The First Apology Law," *Harvard Health Policy Review,* 2004, *5,* 21–24.

CHAPTER SEVENTEEN

The Role of Law in Settlement

Russell Korobkin

Litigants often view the choice between seeking an adjudicated outcome of a dispute and settling out of court as one between invoking the public rule of law as a dispute resolution mechanism on one hand and substituting private contract for law on the other. This dichotomy overstates the difference in the role law plays in adjudication and in alternative dispute resolution (ADR). Law significantly affects nonadjudicative settlements in two related but distinct ways. First, the substantive law relevant to the parties' dispute affects out-of-court settlement outcomes because a litigant with a strong case can demand more as a condition of agreeing to a private settlement than can a party with a weaker case. Lawyers are quite familiar with the indirect impact that substantive legal entitlements have on private dispute resolution. Second, the law concerning settlement negotiation behavior and many of the rules governing the adjudication process also influence nominally "private" dispute resolution activities. This less-recognized effect of law on ADR is the subject of this chapter. More specifically, this chapter considers the ways in which these bodies of law create, shape, and constrain the ability of disputants to exercise bargaining power in ADR

The author gratefully acknowledges helpful comments from Andrea Schneider, Kathy Stone, Steve Yeazell, and the editors. J. R. Eppler and Heather Richardson provided excellent research assistance.

processes, which in turn affects both the likelihood that disputes will be settled out of court and the terms of such settlements.

To assess this role of law in ADR, the chapter begins by presenting a brief analytical model of bargaining that explains the process by which lawyers attempt to settle disputes outside of the adjudicatory process. It then considers the extent to which the law of "bargaining behavior" limits misrepresentation and coercion as sources of bargaining power in nonjudicial forums, and the extent to which certain adjudication rules—such as fee-shifting statutes and offer-of-settlement rules, evidentiary restrictions concerning settlement negotiations, and judicial review of some types of settlement agreements—affect disputants' bargaining power outside the courthouse.

BARGAINING POWER AND DISPUTE RESOLUTION

In a simple model of settlement that assumes two disputing parties, the plaintiff compares the possibility of settling her lawsuit through negotiation, mediation, or a related ADR process with the alternative of an adjudicative resolution through the formal legal system. The plaintiff's "reservation point" (RP) is the amount of money, list of nonmonetary provisions of a settlement agreement, or combination of the two to which she would be indifferent between settlement and adjudication. Thus, the plaintiff will prefer to settle the case out of court for any package of provisions that exceeds her RP, and she will prefer to seek adjudication if the most advantageous package of provisions that she can negotiate is inferior to her RP. The defendant's RP is the maximum amount of money or other concessions that he will agree to give as compensation to the plaintiff to settle the dispute short of adjudication. For any amount below the defendant's RP, he believes that he will be better off settling than litigating. For any amount above that RP, he will prefer litigating to settling.[1]

Because a party's RP divides potential settlement agreements that he believes would make him better off than would pursuing adjudication from potential settlement agreements that he believes would make him worse off, litigants determine their RPs—implicitly, if not explicitly—by evaluating what substantive legal entitlements a court would vindicate, along with the differential transaction costs and risk associated with adjudication.[2] Information learned during settlement negotiations can affect this evaluation, causing a party's RP to change, as can some rules of court procedure.

If the plaintiff's RP exceeds the defendant's, no settlement is possible because there is no set of terms that would cause both parties to prefer agreement to adjudication (Figure 17.1).

Figure 17.1. No Settlement Is Possible.

If the defendant's reservation point exceeds the plaintiff's, an out-of-court resolution of the dispute is possible because there are one or more sets of agreement terms that both parties would prefer to adjudication. To reach agreement, however, the parties need to agree on a particular set of settlement terms that lie in the "bargaining zone" between the parties' RPs (Figure 17.2).

Given this view of the potential and limitations of attempts to settle disputes short of adjudication, the extent of a litigant's bargaining power—defined as the ability to convince the opponent to make concessions that she would prefer not to make—depends on two factors: the opponent's estimate of the litigant's RP, and the opponent's own RP. For example, a plaintiff can persuade a defendant to offer a more generous settlement proposal in one of two ways. First, he can convince the defendant that her own RP should be high and, therefore, that a more generous settlement would be preferable to adjudication. Second, he can convince the defendant that his RP is high and, therefore, that less generous offers would fall outside the bargaining zone and meet with rejection. Symmetrically, a defendant can persuade the plaintiff to accept a less generous offer by convincing him either that his RP should be low or that the defendant's RP is low.

The law of settlement affects litigants' bargaining power, and hence the outcomes of ADR processes, both directly and indirectly. Procedural rules governing litigation have a direct impact by affecting the expected benefits and costs to disputants of both out-of-court settlement and adjudication. Rules governing behavior in ADR processes have an indirect impact by affecting the ability of litigants to persuade their adversaries to reassess the adversary's estimates of one or both parties' RPs. The following sections consider how various elements of the law of settlement have these effects.

Figure 17.2. Bargaining Zone Makes Settlement Possible.

THE LAW OF BARGAINING BEHAVIOR

"Most cases . . . settle and courts rarely set aside settlement agreements."[3] Notwithstanding this fact, an agreement to settle a dispute voluntarily is a contract. The negotiation of such an agreement—be it through bilateral negotiation involving only the disputants or through more structured ADR procedures such as mediation—is subject to the same limitations on behavior that the common law provides in any contracting context. In addition, the rules of professional responsibility provide another layer of restrictions on the actions of attorney-negotiators. This section considers the limitations that the law places on bargaining behavior and the effect these limitations have on outcomes of ADR processes.

Affirmative Misrepresentation

Lies, or factual misrepresentations, can create bargaining power in out-of-court settlement negotiations when used by a disputant to convince the opposing party to change his estimate of his own RP or his estimate of the speaker's RP. More specifically, false statements can create power in one of two ways: first, they can change the opponent's perception of his or her substantive legal entitlements in a particular dispute; second, they can change the opponent's perceptions of the speaker's preference for adjudication as compared to settlement.

As an example of the former effect, a plaintiff's lawyer might tell the defendant (or present documentation indicating) that the plaintiff was seriously injured by the defendant's actions when, in fact, the injury was minor. If believed, such a falsehood might cause the defendant to reassess the extent of the legal liability a court would likely find, increase her RP, and thus be willing to offer more generous settlement terms. As an example of the latter effect, the plaintiff's lawyer might tell the defendant that the plaintiff is anxious for his day in court and cannot wait to expose publicly the misdeeds of the defendant, when, in fact, the plaintiff dreads having to testify. If believed, this falsehood might cause the defendant to reassess her estimate of the plaintiff's preference for settlement relative to adjudication, adjust upward her estimate of the plaintiff's RP, and believe that a relatively generous settlement offer will be necessary to avoid adjudication. In either case, the false statement can create bargaining power for the plaintiff, causing the defendant to offer a higher settlement price than she otherwise would. It is little wonder, then, that many lawyers consider "deception . . . the spirit of negotiation,"[4] and some scholars argue that the capacity to mislead is the mark of a successful negotiator.[5]

The laws of contract, tort, and professional responsibility proscribe some affirmative misrepresentations made in the course of bargaining—subjecting the perpetrator to rescission of a resulting agreement and reinstatement of the original lawsuit, a damage award,[6] or professional sanctions—but not other misrepresentations. In general, the common law requires that for a false statement to be actionable it must be "material" and lead to "justified" reliance by the listener.[7] Lawyers may be subject to professional discipline for false statements that are material even if the listening party does not rely on their veracity.[8] In some circumstances, the contours of these rules as applied to the dispute resolution context are clear; in other cases they are murky, leaving unclear the extent to which a lawyer may legally use deception to increase his or her client's bargaining leverage.

Whether the law of bargaining permits a disputant to make false statements designed to convince the opposing party that his or her legal position is less desirable than he or she might otherwise have believed depends on the nature of the statement. Consider a false statement concerning a factual issue that would be relevant to the issue of liability or damages should the dispute reach adjudication. It is sometimes said that false statements of fact are actionable but false statements of opinion are not, but this is not true, strictly speaking. Instead, the legally determinative question is usually whether the statement is of the sort that generates reasonable reliance, with the fact-opinion distinction serving as a rough, but sometimes misleading, proxy for when reliance is justified. A plaintiff's claim that he suffered a broken leg when he collided with the defendant is actionable if false, whereas his claim that he suffered "substantial injury" is probably not actionable. This is not, however, because the latter statement takes the form of the opinion, but rather because a reasonable defendant might rely on the former claim when predicting the expected result of adjudication but would almost certainly investigate the latter claim further before relying on it.[9]

Based on the same principle, the more general false statements are, the more likely they are to be legally permissible. A car dealer may not gain a bargaining advantage by falsely claiming that her car will enjoy eighty miles per gallon of gas mileage, but she may seek advantage by telling the buyer that the car gets "excellent gas mileage," even if she does not believe this to be true. The latter statement will be categorized as "puffing" or "sales talk," on which no reasonable buyer would rely. The same distinction also applies to the context of settlement negotiations. As an example, a court recently considered a plaintiff's complaint that a defendant, who had agreed to provide the plaintiff with breeding chickens as part of a settlement agreement, had falsely claimed that the breeding stock had "very high productive traits." Noting that the alleged statement did "not set forth a concrete representation," the court labeled the claim "commercial puffery" that "cannot form the basis for a fraud claim."[10]

Disputants may be tempted to seek bargaining power not only by misrepresenting facts in a way that would tend to reduce the expected value of adjudication for their adversary but also by misrepresenting the status of the law for the same purpose. This behavior is probably permissible under the common law, on the ground that it is unreasonable for a lawyer to rely on an adversary's interpretation of case law or other legal precedent because precedent is nearly always subject to multiple interpretations. This analysis might not be correct, however, if the adversary is *pro se* (representing himself without an attorney), as courts are traditionally more sympathetic to a bargaining party with inferior knowledge who relies on claims made by a counterpart with greater knowledge or access to information or who holds himself or herself out as particularly knowledgeable about a given topic.[11] State law versions of Model Rule of Professional Conduct 4.1,[12] which prohibits attorneys from making false statements of "material fact *or law* [emphasis added]," create at least a theoretical risk of professional discipline as a consequence of such misstatements, as do local versions of Rule 8.4's more general prohibition of "conduct involving dishonesty, fraud, deceit, or misrepresentation." Bar Association prosecutions for this type of statement made outside of the courtroom setting are quite rare, however.

Bargaining power can be obtained not only by convincing the counterpart that adjudication would be less desirable for him than he might previously have thought, thus convincing him to lower his RP, but also by convincing the counterpart that the speaker's RP is better than the counterpart previously believed. For example, assume that a plaintiff's RP for settling the dispute out of court is $25,000, but she hopes to negotiate a substantially higher settlement amount. The defendant will enjoy substantially more bargaining power if he can convince the plaintiff that he will pay no more than $30,000 to settle the case than if the plaintiff believes that his RP is $100,000. Thus, in this circumstance the defendant stands to profit by convincing the plaintiff that his RP is lower than it actually is.

The law of bargaining permits parties and their attorneys to use some tools to manipulate perceptions of their RPs in this way but proscribes the use of others. As a starting point, it is clear that disputants may attempt to gain bargaining power by lying about their RPs without running afoul of the law. That is, claims about one's own (or one's client's) RP are never actionable, even if they are demonstrably false at the time made, such as when an agent claims less settlement authority than he or she actually has in an attempt to deflect pressure to make a concession.[13]

This rule can be ascribed to bargaining custom: because false statements about one's RP are common, no reasonable negotiator would rely on such claims, which implies that such statements are never material and that reliance on them can never be justified. Model Rule 4.1 reinforces just this position, noting in its comments that "under generally accepted conventions in negotiation . . . a party's intentions as to an acceptable settlement of a claim" do not constitute "material fact[s]."[14] Alternatively, the rule can be justified on the ground that, although a lie concerning one's RP can alter the distribution of the cooperative surplus that results from an out-of-court settlement, it cannot cause the party who believes the false statement to enter into a settlement agreement that is worse than her RP, unlike a false statement concerning the underlying merits of the case. For example, a plaintiff with an RP of $25,000 who accepts a settlement agreement of $30,000 because he believes (incorrectly) that the defendant's RP is $30,000 is better off with an agreement than with no agreement, even if he would not have agreed to that settlement amount had he known that the defendant's actual RP was $100,000.

Although disputants may seek bargaining power by directly misrepresenting their RPs, courts have sometimes taken a dimmer view of a disputant's false claims to have an alternative to adjudication that she does not have, even though this indirectly has the identical affect of making her RP appear better than it actually is. Courts are more likely to proscribe such behavior if the false claim is based on a fact that would be better known to the speaker to than to her adversary. For example, in one recent case, after losing a jury verdict of $243,000, the defendant's attorney attempted to negotiate a settlement of the case for a lesser amount, claiming that his client was on the verge of declaring bankruptcy. Based on this representation, the plaintiff settled for a lower figure. The plaintiff presumably did so because she interpreted the defendant's statement as a claim that its alternative to settlement was to declare bankruptcy rather than to abide by the adjudicated verdict, and that the defendant's RP was therefore below $243,000. When the plaintiff learned that the defendant had $1.4 million in assets and, in fact, was not considering bankruptcy, she asked the court to rescind the settlement agreement and order the defendant to pay the full amount of the court verdict. The trial court held that the defendant's claims of "gloom and doom" constituted an acceptable negotiation technique, but the appellate court disagreed, finding the statements to be misrepresentations that "go beyond the usual hyperbole."[15]

Nondisclosure

Disputants have no general duty to disclose information voluntarily to their negotiation counterparts. This principle of American law dates back nearly two hundred years to *Laidlaw* v. *Organ*. In that case, a tobacco buyer failed to disclose to the seller that the Treaty of Ghent had been signed, ending the War of 1812 and with it the British blockade of American shipping that had depressed the price of the crop. Instead, when the seller asked whether the buyer knew of any information affecting the tobacco's value, the buyer remained silent. Chief Justice John Marshall held that the buyer had no obligation to disclose his private information.[16]

Today, however, Justice Marshall's principle that the failure to disclose information that might reduce one's relative bargaining power is not actionable is riddled with exceptions. When these exceptions are invoked in the settlement context, the law effectively requires negotiators to sacrifice bargaining power by providing information that causes the adversary to determine that her RP is better than she otherwise would have thought or reveals that the speaker's RP is not as strong as the adversary otherwise would have believed. In either case, the disclosure can enable the adversary to capture more of the cooperative surplus than she might otherwise have expected.

When a lawsuit has been filed, the formal discovery process creates disclosure obligations that do not exist in negotiations outside the litigation context. Under the Federal Rules of Civil Procedure, for example, litigating parties are required to disclose certain basic information, including any existing insurance policies that cover the defendant.[17] The Federal Rules impose no duty to disclose nonenumerated categories of information absent a request by the other party, but once such a request is made according to the discovery rules, disclosure then becomes obligatory. The law treats failure to disclose in response to a discovery request the same as an affirmative misrepresentation, subjecting the perpetrator to either rescission of the settlement agreement or money damages[18] as well as to sanctions.[19] Thus, the law's discovery regime, by its very nature, places limits on the ability of a disputant to gain power by simply failing to disclose material information that would add to the strength of his or her opponent's legal position.

Beyond the circumstances in which the formal discovery regime creates disclosure requirements, the law requires disputants and their lawyers to disclose material information that is inconsistent with the implications of their actions, even when they have not made an affirmatively false statement. So, for example, one court found a plaintiff's attorney guilty of misconduct for opposing the defendant's motion to have an autopsy performed on a deceased person and for providing discovery responses that created the impression no autopsy had been performed, without revealing that he had, in fact, already had an autopsy conducted.[20] Another chastised a defendant's lawyer for responding to the plaintiff's discovery requests without revealing that his client was in bankruptcy, which had the effect of making the bankruptcy trustee, rather than the defendant, potentially liable for the plaintiff's injuries, although the plaintiff never inquired as to the whether the defendant had filed for bankruptcy.[21]

Other courts have found actionable nondisclosure when, under the circumstances, the failure of a party to provide truthful information induces a false belief on the part of the adversary, even when the party has not provided any information likely to create the false impression.[22] Thus, courts have found fraud and sanctioned attorneys for continuing to prosecute lawsuits without informing the defendant that the plaintiff had died midway through the litigation.[23] Presumably, this is because failing to divulge this information while carrying on with the suit implies that the plaintiff remains alive, and that information to the contrary might affect the defendant's RP.[24]

The disclosure requirements of the discovery process and of the common law tradition are both arguably applicable when a litigant fails to disclose relevant facts in response to an incomplete or ambiguous discovery request. In this circumstance, it is difficult to discern the precise location of the line separating legal nondisclosure by the responding party and actionable misrepresentation based on the theory that nondisclosure is inconsistent with the affirmative statements made by the responding party as part of the discovery process.

The facts of one difficult attorney-discipline case illustrate the problem.[25] A plaintiff, whose eye was injured by a small object when driving past the defendant's property, believed that he had been struck with a rock kicked into the air by the defendant's lawn mover. To gain information, the plaintiff used the discovery process to present the defendant with a series of interrogatories concerning the alleged lawn mower incident. The plaintiff asked questions about conditions such as who was operating the lawn mower, whether the defendant was aware of anyone who had witnessed the incident, whether the defendant or his insurance company had investigated the accident, whether reports or photographs had been prepared, and so on. The defendant's lawyer responded that the defendant operated the lawn mower and that there was a lawn mower photograph, but that there were no witnesses or reports of the alleged lawn mower incident. The lawyer did not reveal, however, that at the time the plaintiff drove by the defendant's property, the defendant's son had fired a BB gun, and that the defendant's insurance company had investigated and prepared a report concerning a possible injury caused by the gun.

The defendant's lawyer claimed that the plaintiff's sole theory of liability concerned the lawn mower, that all the discovery requests concerned the lawn mower, and that he had no general duty to disclose facts to the plaintiff that would have, effectively, helped the plaintiff's case and thus increased his bargaining power in settlement negotiations. The court's majority disagreed, finding, over a dissent, that the statements in and omissions from the discovery responses were misleading and created impressions that were untrue, resulting in violations of the state equivalents of Model Rules 3.3 and 8.4.[26]

Disclosure of relevant facts is also required of disputants who learn new information that materially contradicts statements previously made, and the failure to provide such information is grounds for rescission of a subsequent agreement, an action for damages, or attorney discipline. The rule applies when the disputant learns that his or her original statement was incorrect and when changed circumstances render a statement that was accurate when made no longer accurate. So, for example, one court held that an action for fraud was appropriate when a witness for the defense made one statement in his deposition then investigated and learned the statement was wrong, but neither he nor the defendant informed the plaintiffs.[27] Another held that a tenant's lawyer who told a landlord that he was holding the tenant's rental payment in his trust account was obligated, after returning the money to the tenant, to inform the landlord that the representation, although truthful when made, was no longer accurate.[28] The federal discovery rules codify this requirement when information is sought through formal discovery, explicitly requiring disputants to amend prior discovery responses when they know the response was incorrect when made or when circumstances change that render the original response no longer true.[29]

The law establishes more extensive disclosure requirements when there is a fiduciary relationship between disputants or an agreement is otherwise not negotiated at arm's length. In negotiating a property agreement as part of a divorce, for example, spouses are required to disclose all assets to one another, and the failure to do so can lead to subsequent rescission or reformation of the agreement.[30] Unfortunately for practitioners, there are no reliable, hard-and-fast rules that delineate the range of relationships that trigger heightened disclosure requirements.

Finally, even when failures to disclose information do not rise to the level of constructive fraud or misrepresentation, courts can rescind settlement agreements based on the doctrine of unilateral mistake when one party knows that the other party is mistaken as to a material fact but makes no effort to correct the mistake.[31] In *Spaulding* v. *Zimmerman,* the plaintiff settled a claim arising from an automobile accident for a relatively small amount, while the defendant knew from its medical inspection that the victim's injuries were much more serious than the plaintiff believed. Although the court determined that the defendant's failure to disclose this information neither constituted fraud nor violated the rules of legal ethics, it nevertheless upheld a lower court's decision to vacate the settlement agreement based on the defendant's knowledge that the plaintiff was mistaken concerning the extent of the injuries.[32]

Predicting when courts will invoke the unilateral mistake doctrine is difficult. In theory, to prevent moral hazard, a unilateral mistake should not make a settlement agreement voidable if the error results from the negligence of the mistaken party.[33] And it is often at least arguably the case that a disputant's unilateral mistake results from its failure to investigate the facts to the extent that a prudent party would. This limitation, however, did not prevent the *Spaulding* court from rescinding the parties' settlement agreement. Nor did it prevent the court in *Stare* v. *Tate* from refusing to enforce a settlement agreement between divorcing spouses as written when the wife's attorney's draft of the agreement contained a computational error (to the husband's benefit) that was recognized by the husband but not disclosed.[34] Not all courts enforce the unilateral mistake rule however, instead finding that, in an arms-length transaction, both sides are responsible for knowing the relevant facts, and neither side has an obligation to correct another's mistake, even if known.[35]

The Mediation Context

Although some ADR scholars have advocated that the rules governing bargaining behavior should be more strict in the context of mediation than in unmediated negotiation, the law of bargaining has yet to develop heightened standards of behavior for disputing parties or their lawyers engaged in mediation or similar noncoercive ADR procedures involving a neutral party.[36] At the same time, courts have declined to impose on lawyers interacting with mediators the arguably more strict duty of candor owed to tribunals under Model Rule of Professional Conduct 3.3[37] than to third parties under Model Rule 4.1.[38]

Ironically, laws in some states designed to strengthen mediation as a dispute resolution process might effectively reduce constraints on using misrepresentation to create bargaining power in that setting. In two recent cases, the California Supreme Court has interpreted that state's mediation confidentiality statute as providing an absolute privilege for statements made in mediation,[39] strongly suggesting that evidence of deceit in the course of a mediation cannot be introduced in court or in disciplinary actions for any reason. Some lower courts in other states have so held explicitly.[40] The consequence is that, in jurisdictions that recognize an absolute mediation privilege, contract and tort law might technically limit the ability of negotiators to use deceit to create bargaining power, while evidence law effectively makes these limitations unenforceable.[41]

Coercion

Just as a disputant may exercise bargaining power by persuading his opponent that her prospects for adjudication are less desirable than she previously believed, he can also weaken his opponent's RP by persuading her that she will suffer negative consequences in addition to the risks of adjudication should she refuse to settle the dispute out of court. The law provides no impediment to a plaintiff warning a defendant of external consequences that might arise from a failure to settle. For example, an injured plaintiff might attempt to persuade the defendant that the publicity accompanying a trial will hurt sales of the product that allegedly injured him or her and that, therefore, the defendant should be willing to offer a settlement amount that exceeds the expected cost of a jury verdict.

Generally speaking, the law also permits a disputant to gain bargaining leverage by threatening that, if an impasse occurs, he or she will take action that will harm the opponent. For example, a plaintiff might threaten to publicize his claim against the defendant to news organizations, thus maximizing the harm suffered by the defendant as a result of pretrial publicity. Alternatively, the defendant might threaten to stop doing business with the plaintiff if the plaintiff proceeds with litigation, thus reducing the overall value of adjudication to the plaintiff, especially if the defendant is a valued supplier. In the vast majority of cases in which a party argues duress as a basis for rescinding a settlement, the courts are unsympathetic, observing that what the claimant labels as "coercion" is merely the garden variety exercise of bargaining power.

Despite its general permissiveness, the law does place limits on the ability of disputants to use threats to gain bargaining power. Some of these limits can be understood as protecting society as a whole from negative externalities from the disputant's decision to settle. For example, it is a long-standing rule that plaintiffs cannot condition their forbearance in bringing criminal charges on the defendant's willingness to settle a civil suit, on the ground that society, not the plaintiff, is the rightful beneficiary of any criminal claim.[42]

Other limits, however, embodied in the legal doctrine of duress, place limits on bargaining behavior for the protection of the target of the coercive conduct. Doctrinally, a contract is voidable on duress grounds if the speaker makes an "improper threat" and the target has "no reasonable alternative" but to accede to that threat.[43] But this statement of the law only raises the question of what threats are improper and what available alternatives are reasonable. In the extreme case, a settlement certainly would be voidable if the defendant threatened the plaintiff's life should he or she decline the settlement proposal. But, while the legal status of such extreme examples are clear, the line between allowable efforts to reduce the other party's RP and actionable duress is difficult to define, in part because there are relatively few published opinions in which courts find actionable duress in the settlement agreement context.

In *Indelicato* v. *Provident Life and Accident Ins. Co.*, an insurance company made monthly disability payments to a claimant for four years before entering an agreement to settle all future liabilities for a lump sum payment. The claimant later challenged the enforceability of the lump sum agreement on the grounds that it was induced by the company's threat to cut off her monthly payments if she would not agree to the settlement. Finding that these allegations stated a valid claim for duress, the court denied the insurer's motion for summary judgment.[44]

In *First Nat'l. Bank of Cincinnati* v. *Pepper*, a company discharged its corporate counsel and a dispute arose over whether the lawyer was owed fees for work previously performed. The lawyer demanded $100,000—far more money than any reasonable estimate of the amount owed—and the company refused to pay. The company then needed a number of its governance documents, still in the hands of the lawyer, in order to finalize a desirable merger with another company. The lawyer refused to return the documents before the company settled the fee dispute and threatened to leave the country for a long vacation if an agreement was not reached quickly. Fearing the loss of the merger opportunity, the company agreed to settle the lawyer's claim for $75,000, effectively realizing that its RP for obtaining the necessary documents and settling the fee dispute was substantially higher than its RP for settling the fee dispute alone and making concessions accordingly. The company later contended that the agreement was voidable on grounds of duress, and the Second Circuit agreed. It reasoned that the lawyer's threat to withhold the documents was improper because he had no reasonable basis for believing he was owed $100,000 (or even $75,000), and that the company's acquiescence was defensible because it reasonably believed that it faced irreparable harm if it did not accede to the attorney's inflated demand in order to secure the repatriation of its documents.[45]

Courts routinely state that improperly coercive tactics are not limited to threats to commit a tort or a crime,[46] but the reported judicial opinions in the settlement context suggest that a threat must at least approach this standard for a court to consider it an improper use of bargaining power. Although the *Indelicato* court offered little analysis, the alleged threat might be considered "improper" because it was arguably one to commit a tort (bad faith breach of insurance contract). The *Pepper* decision could be understood as based on the fact that the attorney had no legal right to withhold the company's governance documents.

The published opinions suggest that if courts determine a threat is improper, they are likely to interpret loosely the requirement that the victim has no reasonable alternative but to acquiesce. The *Indelicato* court found that the plaintiff had no reasonable alternative because a person living on disability insurance payments would likely lack the resources and time to bring a suit to recover benefits wrongly withheld. The *Pepper* court determined that this requirement was met because the victim reasonably believed it had no other alternative even though, in fact, other alternatives might have been available to it. This pattern is not uniform, however. In a recent case, the Seventh Circuit examined with greater scrutiny the options available to a plaintiff and denied a duress claim when the defendant threatened to withhold a signature from a government document that needed to be filed prior to a looming deadline to protect the plaintiff's $5 million tax benefit. The court determined that plaintiff could have pursued a temporary restraining order forcing the defendant to provide the needed signature immediately.[47]

The body of case law suggests that, in general, disputants may generate bargaining power by threatening to take collateral actions to the detriment of their adversary unless the adversary agrees to proposed settlement terms. Threats become impermissible, however, when the threatened action approaches being tortuous or criminal conduct. In such circumstances, there is a serious risk that courts will find the threat impermissible, even without carefully establishing that the threatened action actually would be a tort or a crime, and perhaps with some deference to the plaintiff's determination of whether it had a plausible alternative course of action to acquiescence.

As is true of misrepresentation, claims of coercion are likely to be looked upon more favorably by courts when the complaining party is not represented by counsel. For example, when an Alaska town accused a mechanic in its employ of various transgressions including padding his overtime claims, suspended him without pay, and seized his tools, the mechanic agreed to pay $20,000 to settle the town's claims against him and then challenged the agreement on grounds of duress. In ruling that the mechanic had alleged facts concerning the settlement negotiations that, if proven to a jury, would support a duress claim, the Alaska Supreme Court included whether or not the party challenging the agreement had been represented by counsel (in this case the plaintiff had not) among the factors that it took into account in rendering its decision.[48] Implicit in this ruling is the suggestion that the law permits greater use of bargaining power against represented adversaries than against those who are unrepresented.

ADJUDICATION RULES AND BARGAINING ENTITLEMENTS

The preceding section considered how the law of bargaining behavior can indirectly affect the ability of disputants to settle their cases out-of-court and the terms of those settlements by permitting or prohibiting certain exercises of bargaining power by the disputants. This section demonstrates how procedural rules of litigation—usually not considered relevant to ADR processes—can also have a significant impact on out-of-court settlements by affecting the desirability of litigating for the parties and thus indirectly affecting their RPs in settlement negotiations. Myriad adjudication rules can affect settlement; the rules discussed here are meant to be exemplary rather than exhaustive.

Fee-Shifting Statutes and "Offer of Settlement" Rules

In U.S. jurisdictions, the dominant rule governing the payment of attorneys fees and other litigation costs, often called the "American rule," is that each disputant is responsible for his or her own costs regardless of the outcome. The opposite procedure, often referred to as the "English rule" or "loser pays," requires the losing party to pay the fees and costs of the prevailing party. Notwithstanding the dominance of the American rule, a wide variety of statutes provide that the English rule, or something like it, applies in disputes governed by the statute in question.[49] These statutes affect the RPs of one or both disputants, and they can affect both whether a bargaining zone exists and the distribution of the cooperative surplus between two settling parties. The precise effect of a loser-pays rule in adjudication on settlement outcomes depends on a number of factors.

Assuming a dispute in which each side has a 50 percent chance of prevailing at trial and the parties are risk averse, a loser-pays rule will decrease the plaintiff's RP and increase the defendant's, increasing the chance that a bargaining zone will exist and a settlement will be possible. If both parties are sufficiently optimistic about their adjudication prospects, however, such that their combined probability prediction of prevailing at trial exceeds 100 percent, this optimism effect can potentially swamp risk aversion, and a loser-pays rule could increase the plaintiff's RP (because the plaintiff believes the defendant will probably be forced to pay his attorneys' fees) while reducing the defendant's (because the defendant assumes the plaintiff will have to pay her attorneys' fees). As a result, the existence of a bargaining zone is less likely.

If the defendant has a better chance of prevailing in adjudication than does the plaintiff, a loser-pays statute will reduce the defendant's RP relative to the American rule, because her expected cost of legal fees should the case go to trial is negative. The statute will simultaneously reduce the plaintiff's RP, because his expected cost of legal fees increases. Together, the effects would suggest that a lower settlement price is likely, although the possibility of reaching settlement would not necessarily change. If it is the plaintiff who is likely to prevail, a loser-pays statute will have the opposite effect, shifting the bargaining zone higher relative to what it would be if the American rule were in effect.

Holding all else constant, an asymmetrical loser-pays statute that allows a prevailing plaintiff but not a prevailing defendant to collect attorneys fees increases the plaintiff's and the defendant's RPs, making a higher settlement price likely.

Under an "offer of settlement" rule, a party that makes a formal settlement proposal can recover from the opposing party his or her attorneys' fees and costs incurred after the offer is made if the recipient does not achieve a trial verdict that is superior to the settlement offer. In short, an offer-of-settlement rule resembles a loser-pays rule, except that the prevailing party is identified by comparing the settlement offered to the adjudicated result, and cost shifting begins only after the settlement proposal is made.

Offer-of-settlement rules can have a range of effects on dispute resolution dynamics. First, a settlement proposal made under an offer-of-settlement rule will reduce the RP of a recipient plaintiff (or increase the RP of a recipient defendant), because the offer increases the recipient's expected cost of litigating the case. If litigation is unsuccessful, the recipient will now have to pay a portion of the offering party's costs in addition to all of his or her own. Thus, the act of making an offer of settlement actually creates bargaining power.

Second, offer-of-settlement rules encourage disputants to make settlement proposals earlier in the litigation process than they otherwise might, because cost shifting does not begin until the date the proposal is made. When settlement discussions take place earlier in the litigation process, the difference in cost between private dispute resolution and adjudication is larger, because fewer costs necessary to try the case will have been expended. This, in turn, suggests that the plaintiff's RP will be somewhat lower and the defendant's RP somewhat higher than they would be after more adjudication expenses are incurred, increasing the likelihood that the parties will reach an out-of-court settlement.

The Federal Rules of Civil Procedure and many state court systems employ modified offer-of-settlement rules,[50] but the specific provisions incorporated into many of these dampen the effect that the rules otherwise could be expected to have on ADR dynamics. Federal Rule of Civil Procedure 68 permits defendants but not plaintiffs the power to make offers of settlement,[51] which gives defendants a tool to increase their bargaining power. But the rule provides cost shifting only for "costs"; attorneys fees, usually the largest expense item in litigation, are not covered by the rule unless the substantive statute under which the suit is brought provides for fee shifting,[52] substantially limiting the amount of bargaining power that defendants can generate by making an offer of settlement. At the state level, the details of offer-of-settlement rules vary tremendously. Jurisdictions take different positions as to whether attorneys fees are included,[53] whether expert witness fees are included,[54] and whether both plaintiffs and defendants or only defendants may invoke the rule.[55]

Admissibility of Settlement Discussions

Rules of litigation procedure that limit the admissibility in court of communications made during ADR processes also can effect both whether a bargaining zone exists and, if so, how the cooperative surplus created by a settlement agreement is divided between the disputants. The best example of this is Federal Rule of Evidence 408, which prohibits the admission of evidence of settlement offers and "conduct or statements made in compromise negotiations" offered to prove liability or damages from subsequent adjudicatory proceedings should attempts at ADR fail.[56] The vast majority of state evidence codes contain either identical or similarly worded exclusionary rules.[57]

The primary purpose of these rules is clear: they seek to prevent disputants from using settlement discussions as a tool for gaining a litigation advantage. In so doing, they have the second-order effect of encouraging parties to volunteer information in the course of ADR, including settlement offers, admissions, or even apologies, from which a judge or jury might conceivably infer evidence of liability or of damages. By encouraging the dissemination of information that might otherwise remain private, such rules facilitate disputants' efforts to locate the bargaining zone and reach an out-of-court settlement agreement that falls within it.

Perhaps less obviously, these rules also can be understood as providing disputants with a tool to create bargaining power in the settlement context that otherwise would not exist. For example, recall that a defendant gains bargaining power by convincing a plaintiff to reduce her RP. A conciliatory posture, a generous offer, an admission of liability, an expression of concern for the plaintiff, or even an apology might convince the plaintiff that she need not use adjudication as a punishment. With this motivation, the plaintiff might lower her RP, thus enabling the defendant to strike a settlement deal at a lower price. Without the certainty that such statements cannot be used against him in court should negotiation fail, the fear of subsequent exploitation might prevent the defendant from attempting to employ bargaining power in this way.

The protection provided by the exclusionary rule adopted by most jurisdictions should apply to the mediation setting, as mediation is clearly one specific type of "compromise negotiation" protected by the rule.[58] Some states have enacted additional rules, however, specifying that statements made in media-tion generally, or in certain types of mediation (usually court-sponsored versions), are subject to the same exclusionary rule that covers non-mediated settlement negotiations.[59]

As discussed earlier, some states have created a privilege—rather than just an exclusionary rule—for conduct or statements made in the course of media-tion. Conduct or statements made in settlement negotiations generally do not enjoy such a privilege. It is important to notice that a strictly enforced privilege has quite a different effect on the ability of parties to use settlement negotia-tions to exercise bargaining power. An absolute privilege arguably protects deceit in the mediation context. Federal Rule of Evidence 408 and similar state exclusionary rules do not shield deceit, because statements made in settlement negotiations can be introduced in a subsequent legal action for damages or rescission of a settlement agreement. In such cases, the evidence would not be introduced for the purpose of proving liability or damages in the original cause of action, as the exclusionary rules prohibit.[60]

Judicial Review of Settlement Terms

In most areas of litigation, the disputants' private agreement to settle out of court puts an end to litigation. If a lawsuit has already been filed, the plaintiff simply dismisses his or her claim and, unless one of the parties challenges the enforceability of the agreement, the dispute comes to a close. In some special circumstances, however, the law requires judicial approval of the contents of a private settlement agreement before the parties are permitted to dismiss the suit. One obvious example is the requirement that courts approve criminal plea agreements,[61] but this procedural step applies in the context of some civil disputes as well, either as a mechanism for protecting the disputants themselves against overreaching by their adversary, or as a means of protecting third parties who have an interest in the dispute but no place at the ADR table.

In the divorce context, for example, a judge approves the terms of an out-of-court settlement agreement for the paternalistic purpose of protecting the interests of the parties themselves.[62] The precise rules vary by jurisdiction, but the general principle is that courts must enter divorce decrees, and that they have equitable power to refuse to incorporate into their decrees an agreement entered into by the parties. Some jurisdictions essentially limit this judicial power to cases in which the court finds evidence of negotiating behavior that could give rise to a postcontractual challenge, such as fraud or duress, but others provide judges with more latitude to police the substantive fairness of the negotiated terms.[63]

Judicial approval of lawsuit dismissals is required in class action[64] and share-holder derivative lawsuits[65] to protect parties to the dispute who are not parties to settlement negotiations. Such parties—primarily members of the plaintiff class—may have interests that conflict with those of the lead plaintiffs (or plaintiffs' attorneys) who actually negotiate the terms of out-of-court settlements. The law also mandates judicial approval of consent decrees in which the Justice Department settles antitrust lawsuits against private companies to ensure that the agreements are in "the public interest."[66]

In all of these contexts, law effectively places limits on the ability of disputants to exercise bargaining power in nonjudicial forums, although the doctrines at issue often fail to specify precisely the extent of this constraint. Courts often refuse to enforce divorce agreements that divide assets or future income when one party agrees to accept substantially less than he or she is entitled to under the law, but the precise test is rarely, if ever, articulated.[67] In one attempt to describe the circumstances in which courts should refuse to approve a class action settlement as fair, Judge Richard Posner wrote for the Seventh Circuit that "a settlement is fair to the plaintiffs . . . if it gives them the expected value of their claim if it went to trial net of the costs of trial. . . ."[68] If taken literally, this suggests that class action defendants able to persuade the lead plaintiffs that their claim is less likely to prevail in adjudication than the judge believes, and therefore that the claim has a lower value net of litigation costs than the judge believes, may not be permitted to profit from the bargaining power derived from their persuasiveness. Such a rule places an important limitation on the ability of litigants to exercise bargaining power in settlement negotiations.

CONCLUSION

By using ADR processes to settle disputes out of court, litigants substitute private bargains for public dispute resolution based on substantive rules of law. This fact, however, should not obscure the important role that law plays in the development of those private bargains. Both the law governing bargaining and aspects of the law governing litigation shape the outcomes of settlement agreements by placing limits on the ways in which disputants are permitted to exercise bargaining power against their counterparts.

Notes

1. See R. Korobkin, *Negotiation Theory and Strategy* (New York: Aspen Law and Business, 2002), pp. 1792–1794.

2. For a more complete description, see Korobkin, *Negotiation Theory and Strategy,* 2002, pp. 37–57.

3. *Zamora* v. *Clayborn Contracting Group,* 47 P.3d 1056 (Cal. 2002), p. 1064.

4. W. W. Steele Jr., "Essay: Deceptive Negotiating and High-Toned Morality," *Vanderbilt Law Review,* 1986, *39,* p. 1390.

5. See J. J. White, "Machiavelli and the Bar: Ethical Limitations on Lying in Negotiation," *American Bar Foundation Research Journal,* 1980, 926–928.

6. Most jurisdictions allow the victim of fraud that induces a settlement agreement an election of remedies between rescinding the agreement and reinstating the litigation or suing for damages caused by the fraud, while a minority permit only rescission. See, for example, *Phipps* v. *Winneshiek County,* 593 N.W.2d 143 (Iowa 1999), p. 146.

7. See *Restatement (Second) of Contracts* § 164 (1981); and *Restatement (Second) of Torts* § 525 (1977). When a settlement agreement is incorporated into a court order, rules of civil procedure may also incorporate contract and tort principles concerning the circumstances in which misrepresentation is grounds for rescission of court order and thus of the agreement. See, for example, Massachusetts Rules of Civil Procedure § 60(b)(3) (2004), permitting courts to relieve a party from a final order on grounds of fraud or misrepresentation.

8. Model Rules of Professional Conduct R. 4.1 (2002).

9. See *Sullivan* v. *H. H. Gilbert Management Corp.,* 9 Mass L. Rep. 443 (Mass. 1998), p. 7, refusing to enforce a settlement agreement when the plaintiff's lawyer falsely told the defendant's lawyer during settlement negotiations that the plaintiff was alive.

10. *Nasik Breeding and Research Farm Ltd.* v. *Merck and Co., Inc.,* 165 F. Supp. 2d 514 (S.D.N.Y. 2001), p. 530.

11. See *Ware* v. *State Farm Mutual Auto. Ins. Co.,* 311 P.2d 316 (Kan. 1957), finding actionable fraud when an insurance agent induced a settlement by falsely telling the unrepresented victims that they had no legally valid claim against his client. See also *Vulcan Metals Co. Inc.* v. *Simmons Mfg.,* 248 F. 853 (2d Cir. 1918), explaining that the relative knowledge of the negotiators is a relevant factor in the analysis of a misrepresentation claim.

12. The Model Rules of Professional Conduct, promulgated by the American Bar Association, are not themselves law, but they have been adopted in large part by most states as the law governing lawyers.

13. See *Morta* v. *Korea Ins. Corp.,* 840 F.2d 1452 (9th Cir. 1988), p. 1456 (insurance adjuster falsely claims that $900 was "all he could pay" to settle a claim).

14. Model Rules of Professional Conduct R. 4.1 c.2 (2002).

15. *James* v. *Lifeline Mobile Medics,* 792 N.E.2d 461 (Ill. App. 2003), pp. 465–467.

16. *Laidlaw* v. *Organ,* 15 U.S. 178 (U.S. 1817).

17. Federal Rules of Civil Procedure R. 26(a)(2004).

18. See *Cresswell* v. *Sullivan and Cromwell,* 668 F. Supp. 166 (S.D.N.Y. 1987), holding that intentionally withholding production of documents subject to document request can constitute fraud, giving plaintiff a right to sue for rescission of subsequent agreement or for damages.

19. See *Crowe* v. *Smith,* 151 F.3d 217 (5th Cir. 1998), upholding sanctions against an attorney who gave incorrect discovery responses that he knew at the time were incorrect.

20. *Mississippi Bar* v. *Mathis,* 620 So. 2d 1213 (Miss. 1993), p. 1221.

21. *Kernan v. One Washington Park Urban Renewal Assoc.*, 154 N.J. 437 (N.J. 1997), pp. 459–467.

22. See, for example, *Midwest Commerce Banking Co. v. Elkhart City Centre*, 4 F.3d 521 (7th Cir. 1993), p. 524.

23. *Kentucky Bar Ass'n. v. Geisler*, 938 S.W.2d 578 (Ky. 1997), pp. 578–579 (bar sanction); and *Virzi v. Grand Trunk Warehouse and Cold Storage Co.*, 571 F.Supp. 507 (E.D. Mich. 1983), p. 512 (rescission).

24. See Virginia State Bar Opinion 952 (1987), holding that a lawyer need not reveal the death of a client unless asked but noting that the case might be different if the client's death "would arguably affect the settlement."

25. *Mississippi Bar v. Land*, 653 So. 899 (Miss. 1994).

26. *Mississippi Bar v. Land*, 653 So. 899 (Miss. 1994).

27. *Phipps v. Winneshiek County*, 593 N.W.2d 143 (Iowa 1999).

28. *In re Williams*, 414 Ore. 530 (Ore. 1992), p. 537.

29. Federal Rules of Civil Procedure R. 26(e) (2) (2004). See also *Rozier v. Ford Motor Co.*, 573 F.2d 1332 (5th Cir. 1978), p. 1341.

30. See *In re the Marriage of Burch*, 563 N.E.2d 1049 (Ill. App. 1990), p. 1057 (failure to disclose asset to spouse would constitute fraud); and *Atkins v. Atkins*, 534 N.E.2d 760 (Ind. App. 1989), p. 763 (failure to disclose change in asset value to spouse constitutes constructive fraud).

31. See Restatement (Second) of Contracts § 153 (1981).

32. *Spaulding v. Zimmerman*, 116 N.W.2d 704 (Minn. 1962), p. 710.

33. See *Lowe v. Steinman*, 284 A.D.2d 506 (N.Y. App. 2001), p. 508.

34. *Stare v. Tate*, 98 Cal. Rptr. 264 (Cal. App. 2d. 1971), p. 269. See also *Building Service Employees Pension Trust v. American Building Maintenance Co.*, 828 F.2d 576 (9th Cir. 1987), p. 578; and *Thompson-Arthur Paving Co. v. Lincoln Battleground Associates, Ltd.*, 382 S.E.2d 817 (N.C. App. 1989), p. 822.

35. See *Brown v. County of Genessee*, 872 F.2d 169 (3d. Cir. 1989), pp. 174–175.

36. See generally C. M. Fairman, "Ethics and Collaborative Lawyering: Why Put Old Hats on New Heads?" *Ohio State Journal on Dispute Resolution*, 2003, *18*, 505–528.

37. Model Rules of Professional Conduct R. 3.3 (2002). Although the text of rule 3.3 is substantially similar to the text of rule 4.1, rule 3.3 lacks the qualifying language included in the comments to rule 4.1.

38. See *In re Fee*, 989 P.2d 975 (Ariz. 1995), p. 980, holding that the rule 3.3 duty of candor is owed to a judge acting as a mediator because he is "still a judge." See also J. J. Alfini, "Settlement Ethics and Lawyering in ADR: A Proposal to Revise Rule," *The Northern Illinois University Law Review*, 1999, *19*, 255–272, concluding that mediation does not qualify as a "tribunal" under rule 3.3.

39. *Rojas v. Superior Court*, 15 Cal. Rptr. 3d 643 (Cal. 2004); and *Foxgate Homeowners' Assoc., Inc. v. Bramalea California, Inc.*, 26 Cal. 4th 1 (Cal. 2001).

40. See *Vick v. Waits*, 2002 WL 1163842 (Tex. App. 2002).

41. See P. Robinson, "Centuries of Contract Common Law Can't Be All Wrong: Why the UMA's Exception to Mediation Confidentiality in Enforcement Proceeds Should Be Embraced and Broadened," *Journal of Dispute Resolution*, 2003, 135–173, arguing that the mediation privilege should not be absolute.

42. See United States Code Service title 18, § 4 (2004). Even this rule does not achieve universal acceptance. See *Commission on Legal Ethics of the West Virginia State Bar* v. *Printz*, 416 S.E.2d 720 (W. Va. 1992), p. 726, holding that refraining from seeking criminal prosecution in exchange for an embezzler paying restitution did not violate the rules of professional responsibility.

43. Restatement (Second) of Contracts § 175 (1) (1981).

44. *Indelicato* v. *Provident Life and Accident Ins. Co.*, 1990 U.S. Dist. LEXIS 127592 (S.D.N.Y. 1990), pp. 8–12.

45. *The First Nat'l. Bank of Cincinnati* v. *Pepper*, 547 F.2d 708 (2d. Cir., 1976); and *The First Nat'l. Bank of Cincinnati* v. *Pepper*, 454 F.2d 626 (2d Cir. 1972).

46. See *Veronda* v. *California Dept. of Forestry and Fire Protection*, 2002 WL 1578879 (N.D. Cal. 2002), p. 5.

47. *Professional Service Network* v. *American Alliance Holding Co.*, 238 F.3d 897 (7th Cir. 2001), p. 901.

48. *Helstrom* v. *North Slope Borough*, 797 P.2d 1192 (Alaska 1990), p. 1198.

49. For a catalog of federal statutes that authorize fee shifting, see *American Jurisprudence, Second Edition, Federal Courts*, 32, § 280 (2003).

50. Twenty-nine states provide offer-of-settlement provisions. See L. T. Kidwell, "Annotation, Allowance and Determination of Attorney's Fees Under State Offer of Judgment Rule," *American Law Reports* (5th ed.), 2004, *119*, 121.

51. Federal Rules of Civil Procedure R. 68 (2004).

52. *Marek* v. *Chesny*, 473 U.S. 1 (U.S. 1985), p. 9, holding that "costs" in rule 68 refers to "all costs properly awardable under the relevant substantive statute" giving rise to the suit.

53. A minority of states considers attorneys fees an element of costs for offer-of-settlement rule purposes. See Alaska Statutes § 09.30.065 (2004); and Connecticut General Statutes § 52–192a (2003). Most states, however, along with Federal Rules of Civil Procedure, rule 68, permit a "prevailing party" for purposes of an offer-of-settlement rule to recover attorneys fees if the underlying statute provides for fee shifting. See *Marek* v. *Chesny*, 473 U.S. 1 (U.S. 1985); *Ellison* v. *Green*, 775 So. 2d 831 (Ala. Civ. App. 1994); *Steele* v. *Jensen Instrument Co.*, 59 Cal. App. 4th 326 (2d Dist. 1997); and *Collins* v. *Minnesota School of Bus., Inc.*, 655 N.W.2d 95 (Minn. 1991).

54. The states are split on whether expert witness fees are recoverable under offer-of-settlement provisions. Compare *Bundrick* v. *McAllister*, 2003 Ala. Civ. App. LEXIS 947 (Ala. Civ. App. 2003), finding that costs under Alabama Rules of Civil Procedure rule 54 (2004) do not include expert witness fees, with Arizona Rules of Civil Procedure § 68(d) (2004), permitting expert witness costs.

55. The majority of states follow the provision of the federal rule that permits only defendants to benefit from an offer-of-settlement rule. A minority of states allows either disputant to benefit from the rule. See California Civil Codes § 998 (2004); and Wisconsin Statutes § 807.01 (2003).

56. Federal Rules of Evidence R. 408 (2004). Courts are split on whether a dispute must have progressed to the point that a lawsuit has already been filed for the protections of rule 408 to apply. Compare *Breuer Electric Mfg. Co.* v. *Toronado Systems of America, Inc.*, 687 F.2d 182 (7th Cir. 1982), p. 185 (rule 408 applies to prospective claims), with *Cassino* v. *Reichhold Chemicals*, 817 F.2d 1338 (9th Cir. 1987) (rule 408 applies only to claims that are the subject of litigation).

57. See J. M. McLaughlin and J. B. Weinstein, *Weinstein's Federal Evidence, Vol. 6* (2nd ed.) (New York: M. Bender, 2004), § T-40-T-45 (state-by-state analysis).

58. See *Sheldone* v. *Pennsylvania Turnpike Commission*, 104 F. Supp. 2d 511 (W.D. Penn. 2000), p. 515; and *Vernon* v. *Acton*, 732 N.E.2d 805 (Ind. 2002), p. 809, charting how Indiana explicitly equated mediation and settlement negotiations for the States Evidence Rule 408. See also C. W. Ehrhardt, "Confidentiality, Privilege and Rule 408: The Protection of Mediation Proceedings in Federal Court," *Louisiana Law Review*, 19, *60*, 91–125. The full extent that mediation communications are in fact protected by confidentiality rules, however, remains an unclear area of the law. See generally E. E. Deason, "Predictable Mediation Confidentiality in the U.S. Federal System," *Ohio State Journal on Dispute Resolution*, 2002, *17*, pp. 255–274.

59. See Maine Rules of Evidence (2004, article 4, § 408(b)) ("Evidence of conduct or statements by any party or mediator at a court-sponsored domestic relations mediation session is not admissible for any purpose.")

60. See *Uforma/Shelby Bus. Forms, Inc.* v. *N.L.R.B.*, 111 F.3d 1284 (6th Cir. 1997), pp. 1293–1294.

61. Federal Rules of Criminal Procedure R. 11(e) (2004). Rule 11 requires that the court determine there to be a factual basis for the plea and to provide other procedural safeguards for the defendant, but no additional standard for accepting or denying a plea bargain is defined. See *United States* v. *Bean*, 564 F.2d 700 (5th Cir. 1977), p. 703.

62. See *Sword* v. *Sweet*, 92 P.3d 492 (Idaho 2004), p. 498 (divorce property settlement not enforceable until approved by court). Other examples include the requirement that judges independently review a proposed settlement on a minor's claim to ensure that the settlement is in the minor's best interest (see *Dacanay* v. *Mendoza*, 573 F.2d 1075 (9th Cir. 1978), p. 1078); and that bankruptcy courts approve bankruptcy settlements only after determining that the proposed agreement is "fair and equitable" and in the "best interests of the estate" (see *Connecticut Gen. Life Ins. Co.* v. *Foster Mortgage Corp.*, 68 F.3d 914 (5th Cir. 1995), p. 917).

63. See *Drawdy* v. *Drawdy*, 268 S.E.2d 30 (S.C. 1980) ("it [is] incumbent on the family court . . . to satisfy itself that the agreement is a fair contractual end to the parties' marital claims"); and *Diers* v. *Diers*, 177 N.W.2d 503 (Neb. 1970) (the court must scrutinize divorce settlement agreements to ensure a "fair and equitable result").

64. See *Mars Steel Corp.* v. *Continental Illinois Natl. Bank*, 834 F.2d 677 (7th Cir. 1987), pp. 680–681.

65. See *Bell Atlantic Corp.* v. *Bolger*, 2 F.3d 1304 (3rd Cir. 1993), p. 1311.

66. See *United States* v. *Microsoft Corp.*, 56 F.3d 1448 (D.C. Cir. 1995), p. 1451.

67. See *In re Marriage of Bisque*, 31 P.3d 175 (Col. App. 2001), refusing to enforce a separation agreement that gave the wife 91 percent of the marital property; and *In re Marriage of Sheila A. Johnson*, 790 N.E.2d 91 (Ill.App. 2003.), p. 95, vacating an agreement in which the husband agreed to make monthly payments totaling $340,000 to the wife in exchange for sole ownership of his $100,000 pension.

68. *Mars Steel Corp.* v. *Continental Illinois Natl. Bank*, 834 F.2d 677 (7th Cir. 1987), p. 682.

PART THREE

UNDERSTANDING DISPUTE RESOLUTION PROCESSES

CHAPTER EIGHTEEN

Negotiation

Bruce Patton

Negotiation can be defined as back-and-forth communication designed to reach an agreement between two or more parties with some interests that are shared and others that may conflict or simply be different.[1] As such, negotiation is one of the most basic forms of interaction, intrinsic to any kind of joint action, as well as to problem solving and dispute resolution. It can be verbal or nonverbal, explicit or implicit, direct or through intermediaries, oral or written, face-to-face, ear-to-ear, or by letter or e-mail.

This chapter describes the basic analytic elements of negotiation, uses them to define the goals of negotiation, and briefly discusses the implications of these elements for effective, systematic preparation. It then explores some of the most common approaches and choices in negotiation process, including their strengths and weaknesses, challenges to effective implementation, and guidelines for use. It takes a particularly close look at the "collaborative" approach to negotiation that has been proposed to deal with the complexities of shared, differing, and conflicting interests, including the critiques of that approach that have emerged since the publication of the seminal work *Getting to YES* in 1981.[2]

SEVEN ELEMENTS OF NEGOTIATION

There is no one right way to organize ideas, but some approaches work better than others for specific purposes. In defining a set of core variables or elements of negotiation to be of help to a negotiator, a framework should help us define our goals and prepare effectively to minimize surprises and to identify and take advantage of opportunities. It should also help us appreciate and wisely evaluate the consequences of available process choices. It should be simple enough to remember and robust enough to incorporate any insight or learning we might have about negotiation. And ideally, such a framework should operate at a basic human level underneath cultural or even gender differences, so that the same framework can be used in different contexts.

The seven-elements framework for understanding and analyzing negotiation was developed at the Harvard Negotiation Project to meet these criteria. It is one way to define comprehensively the terrain of negotiation that needs to be understood and managed (whatever procedural tactics or strategies a negotiator might adopt). Each of the seven elements—interests, legitimacy, relationship, alternatives, options, commitments, and communication—is described in the following sections.

Interests

A party's basic needs, wants, and motivations are commonly referred to as its *interests.* For example, a negotiator seeking to settle a dispute might care about getting enough money to cover expenses, not setting a bad precedent, and getting the negotiation over with before leaving for vacation. Interests are the fundamental drivers of negotiation. People negotiate because they are hoping to satisfy their interests better through an agreement than they could otherwise. The measure of success in negotiation is how well your interests are met, which is also the criterion you use to compare and choose among different possible outcomes.

Interests are *not* the same as the positions or demands that people typically stake out and argue for in negotiation. A position is a proposed outcome that represents merely one way among many that issues might be resolved and interests met. For example, a small local magazine ran a disparaging article about an aspiring politician whom they had confused with a convicted felon of the same name and hometown. The politician sued for libel and demanded monetary damages (a position), but the plaintiff's underlying interest was to restore his reputation. When the magazine countered with an offer of a correction and a glowing front-cover biography, the politician accepted, because the offer met the politician's interests better than his own position.

The notion of interests encompasses a wide range of possibilities, from substantive goals such as money, deadlines, or guarantees to emotional desires such as respect, recognition, feeling fairly treated, or even seeing another person happy. One can think in terms of levels of interests, with something like Maslow's basic human needs at the root of a tree of interests that may include a wide range of needs and motivations beyond the purely instrumental.[3]

Often we have multiple interests at stake in a negotiation, some of which may be inconsistent and require setting priorities. For example, we may want to be honest and fair but also not have to admit error. More generally, we want certain things in the short term but also want to maintain leverage for future negotiations (by not expending all of our bargaining chips now) and at the same time not to upset the rules of the game that we rely on (such as no one resorting to violence), even if breaking the rules might improve our immediate return. Much of the challenge of negotiation is in figuring out how best to reconcile such conflicts or whether there are creative solutions that avoid our having to make such tough choices.

Between the parties, interests can be shared (neither of us wants to spend too much time negotiating; both of us want to set a good precedent), differing (I care about net present value; you care about cash flow), or conflicting (price, credit, ownership, who gets the corner office). While negotiation is often assumed to be an adversarial battle focused on conflicting interests, this assumption overlooks two important points. First, some of the most intense conflicts are often fueled by *identical* interests—both parties want to feel fairly treated. Negotiators are often shocked to discover this, which usually leads them to explore why their perceptions of fairness differ. Second, the potential value inherent in shared or differing interests may be as large or larger than the value in dispute. In one commercial litigation, for example, the parties' anger about something that had happened in the past caused them not to realize that, as circumstances had developed, the potential value of a continuing relationship was more than ten times greater than the amount in dispute. When an outsider pointed this out, the parties suddenly found the motivation to find a settlement.

Legitimacy

Fairness or *legitimacy* is one of the most powerful of human motivations, and thus constitutes a special category of interests. It routinely plays a major role in negotiation, too often (and unwisely) overlooked. It is not uncommon for negotiations to fail, for example, not because the option on the table is unacceptable, but because it does not feel fair to one or both parties. In effect, people pay to avoid accepting a solution that feels illegitimate. In experiments, for example, one person is told that he or she has $10 to split with another (unknown) person and that he or she can specify who gets how much but will only get the money if the other person agrees to accept the split (otherwise neither person gets any money). Logically, the second person should be willing to accept any split of the $10, even $9.99 to the splitter and 1¢ for them, but in fact most people would rather get nothing than approve a split that feels too unfair.[4]

Often this interest in legitimacy and feeling fairly treated is the main driver in a dispute, though parties with divergent views on what is fair may fail to realize that beneath their conflicting positions is the same interest. In the Israeli-Palestinian conflict, for example, the perceived legitimacy of where the border is drawn between Israel and a Palestinian state is at least as important as how many acres are on each side. In many business contexts, the issues at stake in any given dispute are less important than the precedent set for future dealings. In a famous example, President Ronald Reagan fired thousands of air traffic controllers for undertaking an illegal strike, even though the controllers had legitimate grievances and replacing them was far more costly than working out a settlement.

Relationship

A third important variable in negotiation is the *relationship* a negotiator has or wants with other parties.[5] This includes the negotiator's relationship both with those across the table and with anyone else who might affect the negotiation or be affected by the negotiator's reputation coming out of it. Having a fond or trusting relationship may make dispute resolution easier, while hostile feelings can make it much harder. Perhaps more important, the conduct and outcome of a negotiation have the potential to either damage or strengthen a relationship in a variety of ways. As a result, the prospect of a dispute can be very stressful in an important ongoing relationship, such as that between a boss and an employee, or between sales and marketing. (Such a prospect should therefore motivate extra attention to the choice of negotiation process.)

Sometimes, as with a family member or a business partner, maintaining a certain kind of relationship may be a much more important interest than the particular substantive issues in dispute. In other contexts, the parties may lack any personal or formal connection but nevertheless face the prospect of on going dealings, including occasional disputes, in which they would prefer to have a way of working things through (a working relationship) that entails lower rather than higher transaction costs (an afternoon of tough negotiation rather than a year of litigation). However, even when there is neither a prior nor likely a future relationship with the other side, a negotiator still has to weigh the impact on the outcome of *this* negotiation of the working relationship between the parties *during* the negotiation. If that relationship becomes heated and hostile, the chances of agreement decline, and the chances of a creative value-maximizing agreement decline precipitously.

Finally, a negotiator also has an ongoing relationship with himself or herself that can influence the conduct of negotiation. Psychological drives to avoid inconsistency ("cognitive dissonance"[6]), to preserve key values that define one's identity,[7] or to "do the right thing" (conscience) may shape a negotiator's choices. For example, a competitive type who believes "I'm someone who wins, no matter what it takes" may operate with few scruples, while someone deeply committed to fairness, to religious values, or to the Golden Rule may proceed quite differently.

Alternatives and BATNA

When we turn to thinking about how a negotiator can satisfy her or his interests, a critical question is what the negotiator could do in the absence of a negotiated agreement. That is, if the negotiation fails, what will each negotiator
do—what are the *alternatives* to agreement or possible "walkaway" courses of
action? By definition, an alternative to agreement must be a course of action
that the negotiator can implement without the consent of the other negotia-
tor(s). In trying to negotiate the resolution of a business dispute, for example,
one party's alternatives might include doing nothing, suing the other party, trying to sell out to a third party, holding a press conference, and so on.

Since a negotiator unable to reach agreement will have to choose one of his
or her various alternatives to pursue, a key question is which one? Among the
various alternative courses of action a negotiator could pursue, which would
best satisfy that negotiator's interests? This alternative is commonly referred to
as the negotiator's Best Alternative To a Negotiated Agreement, or BATNA.[8]

A negotiator always has *some* BATNA, even if he or she has not figured out
what it is or it is not very attractive. For example, in negotiating with a mugger
who puts a gun to your head and demands your money, your BATNA might be
to refuse, to try to fight, or perhaps to do nothing. In many cases, there will
be uncertainty involved in various of your alternatives (such as the outcome of
litigation, for example) that may require probabilistic assessment to calculate
expected values and thereby determine your likely BATNA, but this doesn't
change the concept.

Your counterpart also has a BATNA, as well as perceptions of its relative
attractiveness, one or the other of which you may be able to affect. For example, one law professor confronted by a mugger promoted negotiation by emphasizing the downside of the mugger's BATNA and offering attractive options:
"You don't really want to kill me; I have too many friends in the police department who would come after you. How much do you really need? $20? $50? Why
don't we avoid the need for a felony and just make it an indefinite loan?"

Options

A major reason to negotiate, of course, is to seek an outcome that offers more
value than one's BATNA, enough more to justify the investment of time and
effort in negotiating. *Options* are possible agreements or pieces of a potential
agreement upon which negotiators might possibly agree. Options can include
substantive terms and conditions, procedures, contingencies, even deliberate
omissions or ambiguities—anything parties might agree on that might help to
satisfy their respective interests.

The most basic form of option is a trade. I give you money, you give me a
car. We create value by an exchange of something that I have that I value less

than you do for something you have that I value more than you do. In general, options create value in negotiation by maximizing the satisfaction of shared interests (for example, we pool our efforts and exploit economies of scale) or by exploiting *differences* in interests (such as different capabilities, resources, valuations, risk preferences, time horizons, or predictions). For more detailed information on how to do this, see Chapter Eleven in this volume.

Commitments

Possible options for agreement are one thing. Actual decisions and agreements, even offers and demands, are quite another. A *commitment* is an agreement, demand, offer, or promise by one or more parties, and any formalization of that agreement. Commitment is commonly signaled by words such as "I will offer," "I demand," "We agree," or "I promise not to . . .". Commitments can occur at any point in a negotiation and encompass anything from a minor procedural point (for example, a shared understanding of an agenda) to final and complete agreement, and anything in between (agreement to meet again; agreement on some terms, but not all).

Communication

Finally, there is the *communication* process by which parties discuss and deal with the preceding six elements of negotiation. For example, do they begin by trading commitments or information about interests? Do they approach the process as adversaries or colleagues, beseech or threaten, trade concessions or brainstorm without commitment? Do they focus on advocacy, inquiry, or both? There are myriad ways to approach the process of negotiation, and many have predictable effects on the likely outcomes.

Collectively, these seven elements are one proven and useful way to organize the landscape of negotiation. However, it is not the only possibility, and it subsumes concepts to which others might give greater prominence. For example, some might include "parties" as a fundamental descriptive component of negotiation.[9] In the seven-element model the question of who the parties are is subsumed under interests and left open. We look at our interests and those of others whose interests might enable the most attractive options for us. "Issues" is another concept that can be helpful, as well as how issues are "framed." In this model, issues are seen as more derivative of the parties' interests than an independent element, while framing is an important aspect of legitimacy and communication.[10] "Perceptions,"[11] "doubts,"[12] and "emotional neediness"[13] have also been raised as important concepts. Perceptions are certainly an important aspect of legitimacy and relationship, and perhaps interests as well. Doubts are an important aspect of legitimacy, and emotional neediness a critical aspect of how negotiators assess their interests and communicate about the relative attractiveness of their respective BATNAs. Likewise, aspiration levels undoubtedly play an important role in the outcome of many negotiations, but we can see aspirations as derivative of a negotiator's perceptions of each side's BATNA and the available options. While all of these concepts are potentially useful, we are looking for a core list of variables that is no longer than it needs to be and short enough to remember. As long as additional useful concepts can fit within the core framework, we can meet our objectives without losing the usefulness of having a basic framework.

A very different descriptive framework, however, has been proposed by Robert Mnookin, Scott Peppet, and Andrew Tulumello.[14] They argue that the essential challenges of negotiation are rooted in three "tensions": between creating and distributing value, between empathy and assertiveness, and between the interests of principals and agents. These three tensions are indeed important, and deserving (among other things) of much thought in determining how to conduct a negotiation (or in the case of principals with their agents, a set of linked negotiations). But they do not constitute a set of fundamental variables of negotiation, nor aid on their own in defining the goal of negotiation or a systematic approach to preparing. Indeed, Mnookin, Peppet, and Tulumello actually use the seven elements just described to explain the three tensions and develop advice for dealing with them. Their three tensions are probably better seen as issues to manage in the communication process, rather than as a possible alternative to the seven-elements framework.

DEFINING A GOOD OUTCOME IN NEGOTIATION

It is hard to do anything well if you are unclear on the goal or how to measure progress toward it. So what is the goal of negotiation? Most fundamentally, it is to meet your interests as well as possible, but in any event at least as well as they would be met by your BATNA. (This is an important point, because it means that the goal of negotiation is *not* necessarily agreement. An agreement makes sense only if it is better for you than your BATNA.) For an agreement to be possible and sustainable, it should also meet the other side's interests at least as well as their BATNA, and also any potential spoiler's interests well enough for them not to interfere.

Beyond this core, each of the elements suggests additional criteria of what, everything else being equal, would constitute a better outcome:

- A creative, elegant, no-waste solution that captures as much available value as possible—among the best of possible options[15]
- A legitimate solution—no one feels taken advantage of
- A firm, implementable, and sustainable commitment
- A process that is as efficient as possible, the product of good communication

- A process that helps to build the kind of relationship we want with this or other parties

In any given context there are likely to be trade-offs that need to be made among these various criteria, but this checklist helps us not to overlook any potentially important aspect of our goal.

PREPARING FOR NEGOTIATION

Because differences in context, personalities, knowledge, and skills make every negotiation to some extent unique, there is no one "right" way to negotiate. Moreover, because negotiation is an unpredictable interactive process not wholly within the control of any one party, good preparation should not focus on just one target "script." Instead, a useful method of preparation should help a negotiator to anticipate and deal with any variety of eventualities. Rather like a paratrooper jumping from a plane and unsure exactly where he or she will land, negotiators want to have a good knowledge of the entire negotiation terrain, so that they can readily assess at any given time where they are and the best route toward where they would like to be.

The seven elements of negotiation offer a roadmap for getting prepared in this way. While there may be no one best way to deploy the elements, as core variables in the negotiation process there *is* a standard set of questions one can ask about each of them, the answers to which will help a negotiator assess how best to proceed in any given context. A basic list of such questions is set forth in Figure 18.1.

The seven elements help negotiators use all-too-limited preparation time efficiently and effectively by offering a standard of relevance and importance. Negotiators are often advised, for example, to "know the facts cold." But which facts? There are too many that might potentially be useful, but it is the facts that help us answer the seven-element checklist of questions that are most likely to be relevant. The seven-element checklist also helps us implement other common preparation advice, such as "understand the other side" (think through what their interests might be) or "identify weaknesses" (analyze their alternatives and possible arguments).

NEGOTIATION PROCESSES

A seven-element checklist for defining success in negotiation and for preparing to negotiate is relatively manageable and easy to remember. But juggling seven variables simultaneously in the course of interaction is quite another story. Negotiators face almost limitless possibilities as they consider which elements

Interests

- What are our interests? What might theirs be?
- Are there third parties whose interests should be considered?
- Which interests are *shared*, which are just *different*, and which *conflict*?

Alternatives

- What is our BATNA? What might theirs be?
- Can we improve our BATNA? Can we worsen theirs?
- How could potentially unrealistic expectations be tested?

Options

- What possible agreements or pieces of an agreement might satisfy both sides' interests?
- What are some ways to use differing interests to create value?

Legitimacy

- What external criteria might plausibly be relevant?
- What standards might a judge apply? What "ought" to govern an agreement?
- What will *they* argue? Do we have a good response, one that *accepts* their point, then adds to it?
- What will each of us need to be able to justify an outcome to our constituents?

Commitments

- What is our authority? What is theirs?
- What are some illustrative, well-crafted commitments?
- What would be good products of this meeting?
- What are mechanisms for changing commitments over time? What are mechanisms for resolving disputes?

Relationship

- Which relationships matter? How is each now? How would we like it to be?
- What can *we* do to bridge the gap at low cost and risk? How should we start off?

Communication

- What do we want to learn from them? How can we improve our listening?
- What do we want to communicate? How can we do so most persuasively?
- What are our agenda and plan for the negotiation?
- What negotiation process approach would we like to use?
- How should we handle inevitable disagreements?

Figure 18.1. Systematic Seven-Element Checklist for Preparation.

to emphasize or ignore and how to handle each one. In practice, however, there are a few major archetypal approaches to the process of negotiation at the root of most interactions. Four of the most common are described here.

Positional Bargaining: The Dance of Concessions

The simplest and most common approach is haggling, or *positional bargaining*.[16] One party stakes out a high (or low) opening position (demand or offer) and the other a correspondingly low (or high) one. Then a series of (usually reciprocal) concessions are made until an agreement is reached somewhere in the middle of the opening positions, or no agreement is reached and the parties walk away to pursue their respective BATNAs. "Your lawsuit has no basis in law, but to avoid the costs of litigation we're prepared to offer $50,000." "We'd consider $500,000. Have you seen these pictures of my maimed client?" "Perhaps $100,000." "$300,000." "$200,000 is the most I can offer." "Done."

One explanation for the prevalence of positional bargaining is its simplicity. The focus is primarily on the element of commitment. And one can understand why that might be: since the goal of negotiation is a mutual commitment, it is natural for each party to suggest what they would like that commitment to be. The inevitable gap between the initial proposals focuses the process on whether and where in the middle the parties might agree. Since negotiation is generally not a subject taught in schools and negotiation analysis is a recent field of study, it is hardly surprising that a relatively simple and manageable approach to negotiation is widespread.

In addition to its simplicity, positional bargaining has the advantages that it is universally understood, frequently expected, and concrete. There are also strategic benefits from effectively staking out a favorable position. If you can "anchor" a position effectively, you can shift the other party's aspirations and the likely outcome in a direction favorable to you. Thus much of the lore of bargaining focuses on how to achieve effective anchoring through, for example, lock-in tactics ("My hands are tied," "It's company policy"), stubbornness and stonewalling, apparent sincerity, bullying (outbursts, guilt, psychological pressure), repetition, logic (real or contrived), and misdirection (changing the subject, counterattacks, non sequiturs). Finally, focusing on positions avoids the risk that by revealing information about your interests you invite the other side to hold them hostage. ("Oh, too bad you're interested in *that*. That will cost you.")

However, the simplicity of positional bargaining and its overwhelming focus on commitments has substantial drawbacks. Perhaps most significant, by discouraging the exploration of interests, it makes it difficult to find creative, value-maximizing options. Without knowing the parties' interests, it is hard to find opportunities for joint gain. Moreover, a negotiation climate focused on commitment discourages creativity and brainstorming—you cannot think expansively if you are worried that you will be committed to any idea you consider.

Second, positional bargaining tends to be slow and inefficient. Each party tries to make the smallest concessions possible, and even then only when necessary to avoid a failed negotiation. One way to signal to the other party that you are near the limits of your authority or ability to move is to take longer and longer between smaller and smaller concessions. And because reaching agreement is often perceived unpalatably as "giving in" or "backing down" to the other side, negotiators want to "hold out" as long as possible before doing so. The situation is even worse in multiparty negotiations. The number of arbitrary bilateral bargains required increases geometrically with the number of parties, but because each bilateral result tends to be arbitrary, it is impossible to find a common solution. The usual response is to form coalitions to make the number of parties manageable, but coalitions by their nature find it hard to make the myriad decisions needed to pursue an extended concession strategy.

Third, positional bargaining tends to produce arbitrary "split-the-difference" outcomes that poorly satisfy either party's interest in fairness, are hard to explain to constituents, and do little to set a precedent that reduces the need for additional (time-consuming) negotiation in the future. Consider a personal injury lawsuit. A typically bargained settlement might lead to this report: "We agreed on compensation of $97,500 for the accident." "Why?" "Well, they started at $250,000, we started at $0 and then . . .". Each side wonders, "Could I have gotten more with a better negotiator?" In contrast, consider this report: "Of course they wanted more, but in the end we agreed on the usual standard, absent recklessness or egregious injury, of three times special damages, which comes to . . .". Whether the final number is more or less than the "split-the-difference" result, this outcome is far easier to explain, and each settlement reached using this rule strengthens the precedent for future negotiations.

Finally, positional bargaining tends to promote an adversarial relationship. It tends to focus on the areas of conflict between the parties and establish a distributive "win-lose" frame—who can more skillfully take advantage of whom? Moreover, inevitable perceptual bias leads people to see their own intentions and moves more positively and others' more negatively, often promoting an escalating (and self-fulfilling) cycle of hostility.[17] While such biases exist in all negotiation, they are exacerbated by the incentives to dissemble in positional bargaining about your interests, your BATNA, your authority to commit, and so on. You routinely leave a haggled negotiation wondering what you don't know—whether you were "taken" or at least could have gotten "more." Such feelings can lead to resentment and a determination to exact revenge, or at least to "make it up next time."

Sometimes in an effort to preserve an important relationship or avert conflict, one or both negotiators will adopt a "soft" form of positional bargaining by putting the relationship first, taking reasonable positions, conceding generously, and making offers (versus threats). This can produce agreement quickly, but not necessarily a good agreement, because there has still been little exploration of interests or possible creative options. Moreover, this approach to negotiation encourages the other side to take advantage. If you try to appease the other side and preserve the relationship by making a concession when they get upset, they may indeed calm down—for a while—but they will also learn to get upset if they want a concession.[18] Over time, this can produce a lopsided dynamic that breeds resentment on one side and disrespect on the other, thereby damaging the very relationship it was intended to preserve.

To some extent, these drawbacks of positional bargaining can be overcome with more sophisticated and skillful implementation. Indeed, more skillful and experienced bargainers tend to temper the usual focus on commitments by adding others of the seven elements into the mix, for example using legitimacy arguments to justify positions, empathetic listening to buttress the relationship against the effects of tough positioning, or an interlude of brainstorming rules to explore options without commitment. Used in a genuine search for better outcomes, such skillful behaviors essentially begin to transform bargaining into the alternative archetype of "problem-solving negotiation" described later in this chapter. However, used manipulatively to enhance a competitive negotiation "victory," such efforts may exacerbate the relationship costs of positional bargaining and breed cynicism about the possibility of alternative approaches.

Positional bargaining tends to make the most sense as an approach for two parties with relatively simple, low-stakes issues and little commitment to the relationship, when there is a strong market context limiting the arbitrariness of outcomes (or when there are *no* independent measures of fairness), or when bargaining is well-established or expected or represents a game both sides want to play for fun. Stock markets, for example, are a context in which simple bargaining is efficient and effective. Traditional bazaars are a context in which bargaining is expected, stakes are typically low, market standards may be limited, and there is often an element of game playing.

Favors and Ledgers

A second important process archetype also involves trading commitments, but takes advantage of an ongoing relationship between the parties to produce more creative and value-maximizing outcomes. The basic idea is to agree to a one-sided outcome now—a "favor"—in exchange for a reciprocal favor in the future. Negotiators then keep a "ledger" of who owes whom what. The result is a creative way to "expand the pie" by relaxing the timeframe for trades, which often permits deals and dispute resolutions that otherwise seem impossible.

With varying degrees of formality, favors and ledgers ("logrolling" with a "bank") is common in many ongoing relationships, and ubiquitous in legislative bodies. It is operative, for example, when an alliance partner says, "We've refrained from poaching your accounts, even when we were invited in.

Now it's your turn to do the same." Or your boss says, "I know this is a nasty assignment, but someone's got to do it. We'll make it up to you."

While favors and ledgers has benefits, it also has drawbacks. First, parties need to ensure that they have a shared perception of the size of a favor and a reliable means of recording that, or they risk a serious rupture in the relationship when the creditor party seeks "repayment." More important, there is always a risk that the counterpart will no longer be in power when repayment is desired, and the counterpart's "heirs" may disclaim knowledge or obligation to repay. ("What favor? That deal set a *precedent.*") Finally, like regular positional bargaining, favors and ledgers tends to result in arbitrary outcomes. While these may feel fair overall to the negotiators, they may be very difficult to explain to constituents, and they tend to set no useful precedent. Indeed, one common legislative measure of the "size" of a favor is how far it goes *against* the interests of the legislator's constituents.

Chicken

A third common archetype of negotiation process focuses on alternatives—whose are better, and who can worsen the other's (threats). "Our walkaway is better than yours, and furthermore, we will make yours worse by . . ." This is commonly called the game of *chicken*—"Give in to my demands, or I will kill us both. There will be more mourners at my funeral than at yours and more flowers on my grave." A labor strike or lockout, much litigation, and certain kinds of military action are common examples of this approach in use.

Chicken is typically the unintended end result of an escalation process. It begins with each side frustrated by a lack of progress and blaming the *other* side's stubbornness and unreasonableness. Someone then issues an ultimatum or makes a threat. But the other side, with reciprocal perceptions of unfairness and an equal desire not to "back down" to bullying, responds with a counterultimatum or counterthreat, rather than a concession, starting a cycle of escalation.

Chicken tends to be extremely costly, with significant resources poured into the battle instead of into finding a good outcome. In the end, as with the proverbial teenagers driving their cars straight at each other, both sides may die. This is how Lebanon in 1975 went from being a stable, safe paradise known as "the Miami Beach of the Middle East" to a war-ravaged near-wasteland. Each of two armed factions was confident there would be no civil war, "because we have the ability to destroy this country, and the other side won't risk that."[19]

Playing chicken will sometimes pay off, but it is among the riskiest of negotiation strategies. For the most part, it represents a failure of skill and perspective on the part of negotiators. This is not to say, of course, that a negotiator should never hold firm or refuse to concede. A negotiator may wisely refuse to participate in discrimination or securities fraud, for example, out of principle.

As always, agreement makes sense only if it satisfies a negotiator's interests better than the negotiator's BATNA.

This illustrates an important but subtle distinction between a *threat* and a *warning.* A threat, as in the game of chicken, is not something you intrinsically want to do, but something you might do (or at least threaten to do) to coerce another party to do something you want. In contrast, a warning is a statement offered to educate the other side that your BATNA is better than their current offer (and may involve less pleasant consequences for them than they have anticipated). While a warning *may* influence the other side to change his or her offer, its purpose is primarily to ensure that he or she does not make an unwise choice based on inaccurate assumptions.

The distinction is important because a threat, essentially extortion, is illegitimate, while a warning is not. (This is why recipients will try to construe a warning as a threat—if they succeed, they can try to ignore the threat as "inappropriate.") Consider a simple example. This is a threat: "If you don't meet our demand for a discount on old-style gas lasers, we're going to delay paying our huge outstanding invoice and put your loan repayment at risk." This is a warning: "If we can't reach agreement on a fair discount for gas lasers, it is going to make economic sense for us to create a homegrown substitute component using newer (cheaper and more reliable) semiconductor lasers and stop buying from you. If we do that, it will also make sense for us to sell such a component to others who want it (to spread our costs). Before you decide about a discount, you should probably consider what that might do to demand for the gas lasers you are trying to sell."

Problem-Solving "Circle of Value" Negotiation

As scholars began to subject the negotiation process to more systematic analysis, the drawbacks of positional bargaining became more starkly apparent. The outline of an alternative *problem-solving* approach emerged from a combination of theoretical analysis on the one hand and case studies and extrapolations from (allegedly) atypical negotiations on the other. This approach was first succinctly articulated in *Getting to YES,* and has been elaborated in various ways since. In essence, it argues that (1) negotiators should work together as colleagues to determine whether an agreement is possible that is better for both than no agreement, (2) in doing so they should postpone commitments while exploring how best to maximize and fairly distribute the value of any agreement, and (3) it makes sense for one party to take this approach even if the other does not.

This problem-solving approach is intended to overcome the drawbacks of traditional positional bargaining:

• Rather than focusing on positions, which represent each party's uninformed first thoughts about possible solutions, the problem-solving approach focuses on the parties' underlying interests, looking for ways to maximize the satisfaction of shared interests and create value by "dovetailing" divergent interests.

- Rather than making early commitments and then concessions, which limits creativity and can slow progress, the problem-solving approach explicitly postpones all formal commitments to the end—"Nothing is agreed until everything is agreed." Demands and offers are avoided or sidelined in favor of brainstorming and improving multiple options to create and distribute value. Tentative commitments begin to form informally and gradually strengthen as negotiators become increasingly confident about what options make the most sense. They become firm commitments, usually fairly quickly, only at the end of the negotiation when there is a complete package.

- Rather than arbitrary, split-the-difference results, the problem-solving approach encourages explainable, well-reasoned outcomes that set sustainable precedents. Problem-solving negotiators change the question from what the parties are *willing* to do to what they *should* do based on independent standards and principles of fairness.

- Rather than put the relationship at risk in an adversarial process, the problem-solving approach allows parties to maintain and build their relationship *even as they disagree* by uncoupling the quality of the relationship from the degree of agreement. (This is described as "separating the people from the problem" in *Getting to YES*.) Like two scientists who may disagree about the explanation for a problem neither fully understands, the relationship is maintained by remaining both forcefully candid *and* respectful—explicitly aware of the possibility that it may be your own view (however obvious it may seem and however strongly felt it may be) that is incomplete or even in error. Problem-solving negotiators are prepared to put their views to a fair test. In this way the problem-solving approach avoids a commonly felt need to choose in a negotiation whether you care more about maintaining your relationship with the other side or about achieving a favorable substantive outcome. This is welcome news for those involved in negotiations (among family, with business partners, between nations) in which both substance and relationship are of vital importance.

Mnookin, Peppet, and Tulumello argue that the problem-solving approach also helps manage each of their three tensions. The first tension, between creating and distributing value, is also sometimes called the "negotiator's dilemma,"[20] because to create value requires that negotiators disclose their interests, but disclosing first can put you at a strategic disadvantage in capturing the resulting value. (Labor may care more about a wage increase and management about capping health care costs, permitting a mutually beneficial trade if these preferences are discovered. But if management reveals its preference and labor does not, labor may achieve a proportionately larger wage increase.) The problem-solving approach helps manage the tension between creating and distributing value by fostering a collaborative working relationship that permits gradual and reciprocal disclosure of interests while brainstorming options without commitment, and that helps negotiators address distributional questions side-by-side with objective standards, rather than through adversarial "claiming" and subjective valuation.

Mnookin and others point out that their second tension, between empathy and assertiveness, is widely perceived, but not inescapable—it is an artifact of insufficient skill. The problem-solving approach helps people overcome this tension by postponing commitments and encouraging the exploration of different views, making it easier to empathize without agreeing, and by depersonalizing the discussion, allowing negotiators to assert their views about the problem without it being framed as an attack on their counterpart.

The third tension, between the interests of agents and principals—which are never perfectly aligned and often quite different—is also eased by a more open and collaborative problem-solving approach. Normally this tension produces some mutual distrust and a struggle over the degree of the agent's authority. Principals are often cagey about their interests and BATNA and give their agent rigid instructions about process and limited authority to commit. Predictably, this limits the ability of the negotiators to find optimal solutions. By taking a problem-solving approach, the tension becomes discussable as a challenge to be jointly managed (by using tailored incentives, gradually increasing delegations of authority, and other creative options). This improves both the relationship between agent and principal and the prospects for an optimally satisfying outcome.

The problem-solving method is sometimes called the "circle of value" approach to negotiation,[21] because the core of the process involves negotiators exploring options for creating and distributing value (through an iterative discussion of interests, options, and standards of legitimacy) with a collaborative, side-by-side, problem-solving mentality. This way of working together has to be carefully created and maintained, like a special space or "circle." Negotiators create the circle by managing how they communicate and managing the working relationship that nurtures and is nurtured by that way of interacting. The elements of commitment and BATNA (especially threats) are kept out of the circle (except for alternatives based on legitimate standards, such as a market price, that come into the circle as part of legitimacy). Indeed, commitments and threats "break" the circle. A commitment, even an offer, because of its anchoring effect, creates a strong incentive for the other side to counteranchor. But as soon as they do, the discussion naturally devolves into a dance of concessions, absent a careful effort to re-create the circle by turning commitments back into options and refocusing on brainstorming. ("Paying you $1,000,000 in diamonds is one option. Another might simply be agreeing to continue doing business. But before we decide what makes the most sense, let's figure out what the range of options is and the implications of each.") Likewise, threats (either to go to

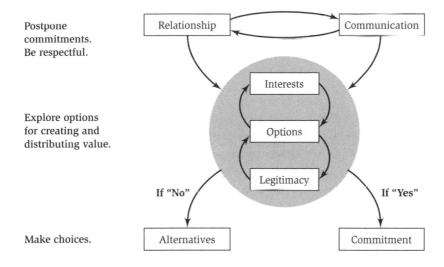

Postpone
commitments.
Be respectful.

Explore options
for creating and
distributing value.

Make choices.

Figure 18.2. The Circle of Value Approach to Negotiation.

Source: Copyright © 1997, 2004 by Vantage Partners, LLC. Based on material © 1991 by Conflict Management, Inc. All rights reserved. Used with permission.

my own "great" BATNA or to make yours more uncomfortable) immediately tend to provoke counterthreats and escalation, effectively ending any efforts or ability to create value. This way of understanding the problem-solving approach is modeled visually in Figure 18.2.

The problem-solving or circle of value approach is most useful for situations in which the stakes are high, relationships or the precedential value of the outcome are important, issues are multiple or complex, or there are many parties. In other words, it applies to most real-world negotiations.

CRITIQUES OF THE PROBLEM-SOLVING APPROACH

Various commentators have offered a range of critiques of the problem-solving approach to negotiation. Four of the most common are discussed here.

It Glosses Over the Hard Facts of Distributive Life

The earliest critique was that the guidelines for problem solving are useful for finding creative, value-enhancing options but ultimately offer little help in coping with the reality of distributive conflict in which interests are opposed. Or, put another way using a traditional dichotomy (inspired by labor negotiations) that divides negotiation into integrative and distributive contexts,[22] problem solving is helpful with the former, but generally not with the latter.[23]

There are several answers to this critique. One is that distributive negotiation has no objective reality. Negotiators always have at least some shared interests, including minimizing the transaction costs of negotiation and finding such value-creating opportunities as may exist, which analysts believe may often be significant, even when parties believe there are none.[24] A heated negotiation between a teachers' union and a school board is an example. The union and the board may see the issues between them as strictly distributive, but miss their shared interest in developing the confidence of the taxpaying public—who determine the size of their shared budget pie—and the mutually disastrous erosion of that support likely to result from mutual attacks. A few critics persist in the argument, inviting us to "assume that only distributive issues remain." But this ignores the fact that the parties still have a shared interest in reaching agreement, if one is possible, because no value can be realized until the deal is done.

A second answer is that even distribution need not be a relentlessly adversarial process. Sometimes this is because the precedent that is set may cut both ways over time. But even when the parties across the table have no ongoing relationship, each party always has an ongoing relationship with themselves and a desire to maintain their identity and self-image. That self-image is likely to include some sense of being fair and "doing right," as well as some sense of being able to do well for yourself or your client. This allows issues of distribution to become another problem to be worked through in a collaborative *and* tough-minded dialogue. While there may still be disagreement about *what* is fair, at the end of the day the parties might choose to use a fair procedure (such as flipping a coin, or even splitting the difference) to resolve remaining disagreement. Or they might seek still greater joint gain by trading off which standard to apply on different issues based on an issue's relative importance to one side or the other.

A third answer is that the problem-solving approach offers very specific and effective advice for achieving a favorable distribution of value. Legitimacy is a very powerful tool for moving the human psyche, and it is much easier to accede to a good argument than to coercion. Reaching agreement requires that *both* sides agree, and seeking to persuade the other side with good arguments can be among the most expeditious routes to that end. Of course there are likely to be multiple conflicting legitimate arguments about what the outcome should be, and the parties may well not agree on which is the "best." They could become positional over principles. But conflicting standards need not be a dead end, any more than they would be for judges analyzing a difficult case. First, the parties can dig deeper for standards and principles with which to distinguish among different standards and for an understanding of how different views and approaches might be reconciled or balanced. Such a process will favor a party that is better prepared, more articulate, and more sincere, all of which are good systemic incentives. Second, if needed, negotiators can resort to fair procedures or trade off whose standard will prevail, as discussed above.

An interesting concrete example of not only the applicability of a problem-solving approach to distributive issues but its superiority involved a company locked in a half-billion-dollar dispute with a foreign government over the renewal of a contract. The contract, negotiated years ago in a notoriously corrupt era, was renewable "under identical terms and conditions at the company's sole option." The current government, believing the contract an obvious product of corruption, refused to renew it, leading to expensive and prolonged litigation. (Interestingly, the company negotiators *also* privately assumed the contract was corrupt, fueling a willingness to make concessions.) Over most of a decade, multiple tentative settlements were reached through haggling, and every one was scuttled by political opposition from one group or another. Indeed, it became apparent that *no* settlement bargained under these conditions could survive the necessary political and regulatory scrutiny needed for approval.

Successful settlement required two fundamental changes. First, it was necessary to show negotiators on both sides that the original contract was actually *not* the result of corruption. Luckily, credible records were available explaining the contract as a creative solution *proposed by the government* to a simple regulatory dilemma (the company needed a contract longer than that allowed by law, except through renewal). It was also possible to show that even today around the world similar contracts are for as long or longer. Second, a new contract had to be negotiated on the merits, so that each term could be explained and justified in terms of current industry standards. No arbitrary haggling could produce a result that would withstand politically motivated scrutiny and garner the full lobbying support of the negotiators on both sides.

Of course many terms were still contentious and many alternative approaches were possible. The negotiators explored, debated, and weighed many options. Especially on the government side, many parties still had entrenched demands and expectations that were not justifiable on the merits. In each case, patient inquiry and advocacy ("Where does that number come from? How would we explain that?"), combined with a firm resolve not to agree to anything arbitrary, eventually produced a coherent and defensible outcome with very substantial monetary gains for each side, one that was then approved without hiccup.

Ultimately, this critique may be more about the willingness and ability of some negotiators to work in a collaborative, problem-solving way than about the ability of that approach to produce good results.

It Takes Two to Tango

A second common critique of the problem-solving approach is that it only works if both sides are committed to it. Of course, to a large extent this is true of any approach to negotiation, so it is not on its own a reason to stick with the status quo. Moreover, there are three good reasons to pursue the problem-solving approach whether or not the other side is like-minded. First, given good preparation and thoughtful prudence, there is no downside. A prepared negotiator knows what can be shared about his or her interests without inviting or enabling extortion. A prudent one insists on incremental and reciprocal disclosure, as well as on not rewarding pressure or agreeing to anything without a good reason. A skillful negotiator can also reframe the other side's commitments as merely options to consider, reinforcing the lack of commitment by putting multiple options on the table, and at the same time counteract any possible anchoring effects of the other's commitments by mentioning reciprocally "extreme" options as possibilities.

Second, there are many benefits to the problem-solving approach, whether or not the other side is in the same mind-set. Looking for shared interests and creative options and postponing commitments makes it more likely that no value-creating opportunities will be overlooked. Offering and asking about principles and standards of fairness not only helps you protect yourself, it ensures that the outcome is shaped by the wisdom of the community—those who have grappled with similar issues in the past.

Finally, to the extent that what ensues is a negotiation (whether tacit or explicit) over how to negotiate, the problem-solving approach will tend to trump by force of logic and legitimacy. Because legitimacy is a basic human driver to which only sociopaths by definition are indifferent, it is easier to remain firm on principle than mere will, and more likely to be persuasive. After all, the other side also wants a successful outcome, and will tend to follow the path of least resistance to get it.

In any event, empirical research contradicts this critique, finding that "enlightened" or educated negotiators tend to be successful in achieving superior outcomes even when negotiating with more traditional negotiators.[25]

Sometimes the Person *Is* the Problem and Can't Be "Separated"

This persistent critique questions the ability of a negotiator to take a collaborative, "side by side" stance when the other negotiator's behavior and role in the relationship is itself the issue. The response given in *Getting to YES* is that you can separate the behavior from the person's character and address the behavior side-by-side, which has the advantage of assuming in a potentially self-fulfilling way that others are capable of changing their behavior.[26] By maintaining a respectful stance, you create the psychological safety to change (the other is a good person who was simply unaware of his or her impact) and the incentive to do so (keeping your respect).[27]

This response is helpful as far as it goes, but is perhaps inadequate in two ways. First, it does not address the fact that behavioral change can also sometimes be negotiated with a forcefully judgmental stance that is not at all collaborative. The military, for example, has occasionally been successful with such a tack, getting recruits to master skills they believed were beyond them by sheer force of intimidation and repetition, and raising the recruits' self-esteem in the process. However, the judgmental approach is most likely to work when your respect is important to the other party (more than their autonomy or identity), their BATNA is weak, and they accept at some psychological level your moral authority. Such conditions are uncommon.

The second point is more telling. It may be true that there is a difference between a person's behavior and their essential character, because they could choose to act differently. Still, the behavior at issue *was* chosen and likely is reflective of the person's chosen identity and personality (at the least, by their unawareness or uncaring about its impact). So in that sense you *are* criticizing who they are, or more precisely, who they have chosen to be, and therefore should expect that pointing out the impact of their chosen behavior is likely to create some defensiveness. The respectful, side-by-side approach is probably still the most viable, but we should not expect it to eliminate all difficulty.[28]

It Sounds Simpler Than It Is
(And a Bad Effort May Be Worse Than None)

The last critique of the problem-solving approach is that it is presented as much easier to pull off and much safer to try than it really is. This critique has at least some validity.

First of all, a masterful effort can require a great deal of skill, subtlety, and technical expertise simply on the substantive level, before we get to the interpersonal. Even the concept of "interests" is much more slippery than it first appears. People actually have bundles of interests that are routinely inconsistent and the relative salience of which at any given time may change depending on the context and stimulus. Nor do people find it easy to figure out what their interests really are. We've all had the experience of asking for something, getting exactly what we asked for, and then realizing it wasn't really what we wanted after all. Interests also can be understood at different levels. On the surface, for example, I may want my view to prevail because I think it is most likely to work, but underneath there is a strong desire for vindication, and underneath that a need for recognition and acceptance. Likewise, finding the most value-creating ways to dovetail interests can require serious analytic tools and familiarity with a broad repertoire of templates. And assessing both options and alternatives typically requires the ability to think systematically about how to put an expected value on things that are probabilistically uncertain.

Second, the ability to remain respectful when you strongly disagree with another's view (and perhaps even doubt whether they believe it or even could believe it) requires a level of maturity and cognitive development greater than most people possess.[29] You have to be comfortable with a certain amount of relativism and have some awareness and acceptance of the fact that your own views are less objective than they seem. The subjective nature of our perceived "reality" is well-established by social psychologists, but an equally strong finding is people's failure to appreciate that subjectivity.[30] It may be that pursuing a problem-solving approach to negotiation furthers one's development of such awareness, but that hypothesis has not yet been tested.

Finally, it has been observed that people learning the problem-solving approach are prone to a number of characteristic errors, mostly related to the skills of combining empathy and assertiveness (or inquiry and advocacy). These errors tend to degrade the value of their outcomes. For example, when told to be firm on substance but also friendly, many negotiators in fact become more accommodating on substance, agreeing to things in essence "for the sake of the relationship."[31] Others, when told to insist on using objective criteria, use positional lock-in tactics to promote favorable but relatively unpersuasive criteria, leading to deadlock, much wasted time, and mutual frustration. Still others, working hard to make arguments in good faith, tend to interpret a lack of acquiescence by the other side as a lack of reciprocal good faith, leading to resentment that these negotiators do not know how to surface or test constructively. The tragic result is that mutual good intentions sometimes lead to an escalating cycle of hostility.[32]

In theory, these potential costs should be weighed against the likelihood of eventual benefits as the problem-solving approach is pursued more skillfully, and the cumulative expected value weighed against that of more familiar approaches. For now, this calculation is largely a matter of faith, though the potential benefits of the problem-solving approach are clearly substantial, both for individual negotiators and for society as it becomes more prevalent. If nothing else, this suggests that society would benefit from investing in systematic negotiation education. It might even make sense to offer incentives for the use of the problem-solving approach. In any event, as more and better role models develop and as the analytic insights underlying problem-solving negotiation become more generally understood and accepted, this alternative approach to negotiation will become easier to learn and master. Certainly the prevalence of a problem-solving perspective in public and private discourse about negotiation has steadily increased since the publication of *Getting to YES* in 1981.

Notes

1. This definition differs slightly from that in R. Fisher, W. Ury, and B. Patton, *Getting to YES: Negotiating Agreement Without Giving In* (2nd ed.) (New York: Penguin, 1991), p. xvii, first by including explicitly the possibility of differing—but not conflicting—interests, and second by requiring only the *possibility* of conflict. The strategic challenges in managing disclosure and other aspects of negotiation process are similar whether there is merely a possibility that interests conflict or they are known (or assumed) to do so.

2. See R. Fisher and W. Ury, with B. Patton (ed.), *Getting to YES: Negotiating Agreement Without Giving In* (New York: Houghton Mifflin, 1981).

3. See C. Menkel-Meadow, "Toward Another View of Legal Negotiation: The Structure of Problem-Solving," *UCLA Law Review,* 1984, *31,* 754–840; see also C. Menkel-Meadow, "Aha!? Is Creativity Possible in Legal Problem Solving and Teachable in Legal Education?" *Harvard Negotiation Law Review,* 2001, *6,* p. 109, n. 52. For Maslow's framework, see A. Maslow, *Motivation and Personality* (New York: HarperCollins, 1954).

4. See R. Thaler, *The Winner's Curse: Paradoxes and Anomalies of Economic Life* (New York: Free Press, 1991).

5. "Relationship" can mean many things: personal affection or antagonism, interdependence, contractual obligations, good teamwork, or an ability to resolve differences efficiently and effectively, among others. For our purposes in robustly describing the terrain of negotiation, the variable of "relationship" could include any of these that matter to one or both negotiators. In contrast, our focus narrows when we seek to advise a negotiator on tactics. A hard bargainer, for example, might be served by a relationship in which the other side feels intimidated and fearful, whereas a collaborative negotiator might seek a working relationship that can resolve differences smoothly and independent of personal affection.

6. See L. Festinger, *A Theory of Cognitive Dissonance* (Palo Alto, Calif.: Stanford University Press, 1957).

7. For an introductory discussion of the concept of identity, see D. Stone, B. Patton, and S. Heen, *Difficult Conversations: How to Discuss What Matters Most* (New York: Viking/Penguin, 1999).

8. See Fisher, Ury, and Patton, *Getting to YES,* 1991.

9. The importance of parties as a variable has been emphasized especially by Professors James Laue, Lawrence Susskind, and others who tend to focus on multiparty negotiations and public contexts in which "parties" are often not well-defined.

10. See Donald Schön, *The Reflective Practitioner* (New York: Basic Books, 1983) for a deep explanation of the concept of framing. See also Chapter Ten in this volume.

11. The role of perceptions and cognitive bias in conflict has been a major focus of social psychologists and some economists. See, for example, the work of Ralph K. White, Jeffrey Rubin, Max Bazerman, Lee Ross, Margaret Neale, and Amos Tversky and Daniel Kahneman.

12. The political consultant Tom Korologos argued at the Program on Negotiation in the early 1980s that the central task of a negotiator is to nurture doubts in the other side about the strength of their arguments.

13. See, for example, J. Camp, *Start with No* (New York: Crown Business, 2002), for the latest argument on the importance of not appearing desperate in negotiation. For similar arguments, see also H. Cohen, *You Can Negotiate Anything* (New York: Bantam, 1980); C. L. Karrass, *Give & Take: The Complete Guide to Negotiating Strategies and Tactics* (New York: Thomas Y. Crowell, 1974); and G. Nierenberg, *The Art of Negotiating* (New York: Hawthorn, 1968).

14. See R. H. Mnookin, S. R. Peppet, and A. Tulumello, *Beyond Winning: Negotiating to Create Value in Deals and Disputes* (Boston: Belknap Press of Harvard University Press, 2000).

15. Technically this is called a *pareto optimal* outcome (after the Italian economist Vilfredo Pareto) and defined as a solution in which neither party can be made better off without making the other party worse off.

16. See Fisher, Ury, and Patton, *Getting to YES,* 1991, Chapter One.

17. For an overview of research on partisan bias and cognitive distortion with implications for negotiation see E. Pronin, T. Gilovich, and L. Ross, "Objectivity in the Eye of the Beholder: Divergent Perceptions of Bias in Self Versus Others," *Psychological Review,* 2004, *111,* 791–799; M. H. Bazerman, and M. A. Neale, *Negotiating Rationally* (New York: Free Press, 1992); M. H. Bazerman, R. J. Lewicki, and B. H. Sheppard, (eds.), *Handbook of Negotiation Research* (Greenwich, Conn. and London: JAI Press, 1991); and J. Z. Rubin and B. R. Brown, *The Social Psychology of Bargaining and Negotiation* (New York: Academic Press, 1975).

18. See G. A. van Kleef, C.K.W. De Dreu, and A.S.R. Manstead, "The Interpersonal Effects of Anger and Happiness in Negotiations," *Journal of Personality and Social Psychology,* 2004, *86*(1), 57–76, for research showing that expressions of anger and frustration tend to produce concessionary behavior. More generally, see B. F. Skinner, *The Behavior of Organisms: An Experimental Analysis* (Upper Saddle River, N.J.: Prentice Hall, 1938), for ample evidence that in general, rewards increase the amount of behavior rewarded.

19. Firsthand report of interviews conducted in 1975 by Professor Roger Fisher of Harvard Law School (as reported to the author in 1977).

20. See D. Lax and J. Sebenius, *The Manager as Negotiator* (New York: Free Press, 1986).

21. See B. Patton, "Building Relationships and the Bottom Line: The Circle of Value Approach to Negotiation," *Negotiation,* 2004, *7*(4), 4–7.

22. See R. Walton and R. McKersie, *A Behavioral Theory of Labor Negotiations* (2nd ed.) (Ithaca, N.Y.: ILR Press, 1991), for an introduction to the concepts of distributive and integrative bargaining.

23. See, for example, J. J. White, "The Pros and Cons of '*Getting to YES*'," *Journal of Legal Education,* 1984, *34,* 115–124; and L. M. McCarthy, "The Role of Power and Principle in '*Getting to YES*'," *Negotiation Journal,* 1985, *1,* 59–66, for the two best-known critiques of problem solving in distributive contexts.

24. Not only do negotiators have shared interests, but where their interests differ, they tend to exaggerate the degree of conflict and difference. See R. J. Robinson, D. Keltner, A. Ward, and L. Ross, "Actual Versus Assumed Differences in Construal: 'Naïve Realism' in Intergroup Perception and Conflict," *Journal of Personality and Social Psychology,* 1995, *68,* 404–417; and R. J. Robinson and D. Keltner, "Much Ado About Nothing? Revisionists and Traditionalists Choose an Introductory English Syllabus," *Psychological Science,* 1996, *7,* 18–24.

25. See C. H. Tinsley, K. M. O'Connor, and B. A. Sullivan, "Tough Guys Finish Last: The Perils of a Distributive Reputation," *Organizational Behavior and Human Decision Processes*, 2002, *88*, 621–642; and G. Berger, M. C. Kern, and L. Thompson, *The Enlightened Negotiator: What Is the Best Type of Interaction?* paper presented at the 16th Annual IACM Conference, Melbourne, Australia, 2003 (cited with permission).

26. See Fisher, Ury, and Patton, *Getting to YES*, 1991, Chapter Two and p. 159.

27. See Edmondson, who developed the concept of psychological safety (Edmondson, A. "Psychological Safety and Learning Behavior in Work Teams." *Administrative Science Quarterly*, 1999, *44*(2), 350–383).

28. See Stone, Patton, and Heen, *Difficult Conversations*, 1999, for more detailed and realistic advice for managing such conversations.

29. See R. Keegan, *In Over Our Heads: The Mental Demands of Modern Life* (Cambridge, Mass.: Harvard University Press, 1994).

30. See Pronin, Gilovich, and Ross, "Objectivity in the Eye of the Beholder," 2004.

31. This is the phenomenon that underlies Jim Camp's critique of collaborative negotiation in Camp, *Start with No*, 2002.

32. For a fuller description of this danger see R. Fisher and S. Brown, *Getting Together: Building Relationships as We Negotiate* (New York: Penguin, 1988).

CHAPTER NINETEEN

Mediation

Kimberlee K. Kovach

Mediation is commonly defined as a process in which a third party neutral, the mediator, assists disputing parties in reaching a mutually agreeable resolution. Mediators aim to facilitate information exchange, promote understanding among the parties, and encourage the exploration of creative solutions. In other methods of dispute resolution, such as litigation or arbitration, the parties rely on a third party to make a binding determination of right or wrong. Mediation, by contrast, invites the parties to engage in a potentially creative and collaborative method of problem solving, without forcing a decision on either party.

Mediation is a flexible process, defined and re-defined by the disputants and the mediator in each case. This flexibility is one of the strengths of mediation—and it also creates considerable challenge for anyone trying to describe mediation broadly. This chapter provides a brief overview of some of the aspects of mediation that commonly cut across current variations of the process.

The chapter begins with a brief look at some of the benefits of mediation— what is it that draws disputants to this process? It then describes some of the component pieces of a typical mediation. No two mediations progress in identical ways, and yet there are some common patterns and themes in the ways that mediators conduct the process. What stages does a mediation go through? What roles might a mediator adopt? And what implications do those roles have on the practice of mediation? The chapter then highlights four current policy issues related to mediation: neutrality, confidentiality, the processes by which disputants arrive in front of mediators, and the regulation of the practice. The chapter concludes by considering the future of mediation practice—its promise and its challenges.

WHY MEDIATE?

Mediation offers a number of potential benefits that are unavailable in traditional methods of dispute resolution. Mediation's relatively informal and flexible process allows the mediator and participants to take different approaches to creative problem solving. In providing an accelerated resolution, mediation quite often saves parties time and money. Moreover, in reaching a resolution, mediation parties can often avoid much of the emotional drain from engagement in continual conflict.

Mediation also provides a different kind of forum for communication between the parties. In many cases, parties value the degree of privacy mediation affords. Those who are uncomfortable discussing personal matters in an open courtroom may be more relaxed in a private setting. In addition, the parties are not restricted by the nature of what they may say, thereby allowing for the determination and discussion of the real matters in dispute.[1]

In some circumstances, resolution may be impossible without the expression and understanding of a party's emotional needs. Mediation not only allows for the expression, understanding, and release of emotions but also can create an opportunity for relationships to be preserved. In many cases, parties involved in a conflict have a continuing relationship, whether personal or professional. Despite the dispute, continuing the relationship in one form or another may be desirable—or inevitable—for the parties.

Mediation also provides the potential for parties to exercise self-determination. In mediation, the parties are the final decision makers, whereas in adjudicative procedures, such as trial, arbitration, or administrative hearing, a third party makes the decision for them. Because of their personal involvement in the process and the resolution, the parties tend to possess a psychological ownership, making it more likely that they will comply with an agreement reached.

Finally, mediation provides an opportunity for the parties to agree to creative solutions. When disputes are resolved through court or other adjudicatory processes, the customary result is a judgment in favor of one party over another. Alternatively, through mediation parties are able to craft solutions more suitable for their particular circumstances. Mediators often encourage parties "to think outside the box" and brainstorm about potential options in order to maximize creativity.

WHAT HAPPENS IN A MEDIATION?

Every dispute is different, and every mediator is different. As a result, every mediation is at least somewhat different from every other mediation. Yet to say, "it all depends" is unhelpful for those wishing to learn more about the process. The progression of a mediation, and the roles of mediators within that progression, are important topics for exploration.

Component Pieces of a Mediation

The flexibility of mediation is one of its strengths. Still, to appreciate the complexities of mediation, it is helpful to break the process into component pieces or elements. In the section that follows, I describe mediation as having nine distinct stages, with four additional optional components. Observers of mediation vary in the way they outline the mediation process, and no consensus exists on even the number of stages involved. In many cases, mediation stages overlap or fold into one another, evidencing the fluidity of the mediation process. Indeed, resolution of a dispute may be achieved without experiencing every stage. I break mediation into these stages *not* to suggest linearity, but rather to highlight some of the important things that happen in most mediations. The thirteen stages appear in Figure 19.1.

The preliminary-arrangement stage encompasses everything that occurs prior to the actual mediation session. This includes referral to mediation, the selection of the mediator, determination of who is to attend the mediation, fees,

> Preliminary arrangements
> Mediator's introduction
> Opening remarks/Statements by parties
> Venting (optional)
> Information gathering
> Issue and interest identification
> Agenda setting (optional)
> Caucus (optional)
> Option generation
> Reality testing (optional)
> Bargaining and negotiation
> Agreement
> Closure

Figure 19.1. Possible Stages of a Mediation.

Source: Adapted principally from K. K. Kovach, *Mediation: Principles and Practice* (St. Paul, Minn.: West, 2004).

and issues regarding the allocation of settlement authority. In this initial stage, parties and the mediator often make important decisions about the parameters of the process.

The mediator's introduction may include some or all of the following: introduction of the participants, description of the mediation process, and discussion of ground rules and housekeeping matters. The mediator may also share his or her goals and objectives for the process as well as elicit the participants' expectations. In addition, the mediator may outline legal issues relevant to the mediation, such as confidentiality and settlement authority.

Following this, in the opening remarks, the parties or their representatives typically provide an uninterrupted presentation of their views of the case or dispute. These remarks provide an opportunity for the parties to express fully, in their own words, to the mediator and to each other how they view the dispute.

Information gathering follows opening remarks. During this phase, the mediator and the parties often make inquiries of one another. At times parties may also use the period after the opening remarks for a period of venting. Allowing time for the parties to address the emotions generated by the dispute is often a critical aspect of the process. As additional information is disclosed, the mediator attempts to identify exactly what issues are in dispute. This is the issue and interest identification stage.

Mediators may reframe issues in language that is more neutral and acceptable for both parties as a means of enhancing parties' understanding as well as their openness to options for resolution. At some point, the mediator may move the parties toward option generation, seeking to generate possible ideas for resolution. Mediators may facilitate the use of creative methods such as brainstorming and lateral thinking at this phase of the process.

Often during these two stages (identifying issues and interests and option generation) the mediator meets privately with each party. This is termed a caucus or private session. Some mediators use private caucuses to gain additional information from each party. The mediator's style of mediation, the mediator's approach, local practice and custom, and applicable law shape how or whether a mediator will share information gathered in caucus with the other party. As options are suggested, some mediators also engage in "reality testing" with the parties. Through the use of questioning, mediators challenge assumptions the parties (and their lawyers) may hold about the options suggested and about potential outcomes should mediation not result in resolution.

Once the potential options for settlement have been identified, the bargaining and negotiation stage often ensues. During this "give and take" part of mediation, the mediator assists the parties in achieving trade-offs. If these negotiations result in an agreement, the mediator will outline it and often draft either the complete agreement or a memorandum of settlement. This is the agreement stage of the mediation.

If no agreement is reached, the mediator will often restate where the parties stand in terms of potential settlement. The final stage of most mediations is closure, although in some models there is subsequent action on the part of the mediator with regard to follow-up and implementation of the agreement.

A Mediator's Role(s)

While mediation might be summarized as facilitating parties' negotiations, just what mediators do in terms of that assistance can be complex. A mediator's job is not merely to oversee a rigid march through the stages just listed. A mediator often assumes a number of roles in seeking to help parties reach a mutually satisfactory resolution to a dispute. These various roles include organizing the parties and information, assessing negotiation strategies, interpreting or translating information, assisting in understanding, and serving as referee, teacher, coach, coordinator, and conductor. Following are some of the most common roles a mediator may take on.

Organizer. In some cases, a mediator can help disputants enormously simply by providing administrative assistance in organizing and managing the interactions between the disputants. When will the disputants meet? What kind of information should be exchanged in advance? Who should be in the room? These and many other matters are the kinds of premediation issues that have an important effect on the eventual success of the mediation effort, and a mediator is often best positioned to be helpful on these matters.

Communication Director. During the course of a mediation, a mediator may structure how remarks are made and information is exchanged—almost assuming the role of choreographer. Many disputes arise because people do not understand or appreciate what the other has said or the perspective the other holds. By shaping the exchange of information, mediators can help parties to understand each other better. This process often requires mediators to act almost as translators or interpreters, particularly when parties arrive at the dispute with different background experiences or frames of reference. Even when communication appears otherwise satisfactory, parties who take positions and defend them often fail to reach consensus. Mediators sometimes examine what each party says and search for underlying interests as part of the translation process.

Intervenor and Guide. When disputants get stuck in stalemate or impasse, mediators can assist the parties by diagnosing the difficulties and obstacles in the parties' direct negotiations. Often mediators are able to get the negotiations back on-track. In doing so, mediators serve as teachers of negotiation and mediation. Another image of the mediator's role may be that of a conductor of the negotiation dance. The mediator may set the tone—choose the music, so to speak. When parties differ, for example, on how quickly they will dance, a mediator may serve as a timekeeper, establishing the pace. Mediators may also serve as reality testers when individuals have unrealistic expectations about the final outcome.

Encourager of Settlement. Some of the most challenging questions regarding mediators' conduct relate to mediators' stances with respect to settlement. What role should a mediator play in encouraging the parties to settle? Parties reasonably expect that the mediator will help the parties in finding a settlement—if one is possible. At the same time, however, mediators' persuasive efforts must not lapse into coercion.

Listener. Perhaps the most important role of a mediator is that of listener. Many disputants want an opportunity to be heard. By listening intently, mediators learn more about the issues in dispute and the potential interests that may assist in resolution. Mediators who actively engage in listening also may serve as a model for the parties, potentially encouraging them to listen to each other.

Why Mediators Differ

One finds variation in virtually any field of practice. Doctors do not all make decisions in the same way. Lawyers are not all the same. Yet within mediation, one finds an extraordinary diversity of approaches. Why? Part of the answer lies in the varying conceptions mediators have of their purposes and of the best approaches for attaining those purposes.

Different Views of the Purpose of Mediation. Although mediation is quite often defined as a process through which the mediator assists parties in reaching agreement or resolution to a matter, many experts differ when it comes to explicit fundamental goals or objectives of the process. Some see mediation as a process that has as its focus merely achieving a settlement of a lawsuit. In this view, mediators are primarily concerned with assisting the lawyers or parties in exchanging proposals of settlement. Others may use the process to save time and money, particularly when it is important to reach an expeditious resolution, such as during an ongoing construction project. In such a case, the mediator focuses on the immediate future, searching for ways to solve the problem promptly and efficiently.

Others employ mediation as a way to find unique and creative solutions to problems. These mediators concentrate on the use of brainstorming methods to achieve innovative resolutions. Still other mediators see the process as a means of relationship repair, with mediators working with the parties to establish direct communication between them. Adherents of the so-called "transformative" model of mediation suggest that the proper focus of the mediation is not on the dispute at all, but rather on the search for opportunities for each party to be empowered by the process and to view the dispute as a symptom of impairment of the parties' relationship.[2]

Different Views of Appropriate and Effective Behavior. A variety of factors may have an impact on the type, style, or approach of mediation employed. Mediators can be shaped by the combination of their basic personality and their initial training. Some people just lean toward one way of addressing problems.

Another key factor is the context in which the process is being adopted. Mediation appears in circumstances ranging from workplace matters, construction, civil lawsuits, family matters, and life-and-death decision making to educational matters and criminal cases, just to name a few. Each context can affect how the parties and the mediator view the process and what may be achieved through its use. For example, in cases in which ongoing relationships exist, such as workplace disputes or family law matters, mediators will commonly use a process that focuses, at least in part, on relational concerns. Techniques employed will center on the facilitation of communication between the parties and, in some cases, party empowerment and recognition. In criminal matters, particularly when the primary issue is restitution, mediation is often used to find creative options. In many jurisdictions, the use of mediation in civil lawsuits has as its basis the settlement of the matter, and legal principles are considered. In short, mediators vary, in part, because they mediate different kinds of cases.

Even in circumstances in which the disputes are relatively similar, one still finds variation in mediators' practices because mediators simply approach their jobs differently. Len Riskin describes some of the variations in mediators' orientations by suggesting, for example, that some mediators tend to define the problems before them in narrow terms (how much money is owed?), while others define the problem in broader terms (what is going on between these two former business partners?).[3] Michael Moffitt suggests that some mediators conduct themselves transparently (sharing their observations, their purposes, and their decisions with the disputants), while others maintain less transparency (conducting the mediation without revealing the mediator's inner thinking).[4] A final—and very prominent—example of differences in mediators' approaches has to do with the distinction between "facilitative" and "evaluative" practices.[5] Should a mediator share with the parties her or his assessment of what a court would likely do with the dispute in question (evaluate)? Well-educated, well-meaning mediators vary in their responses to each of these possibilities—and too many more not listed here. As a result, mediators' practices wind up looking different from each other.

DEBATES OVER MEDIATION POLICY

Given the number of contexts in which mediation is practiced, and the variety of ways in which it is practiced, it is no wonder that it has attracted the attention of policymakers. In this section, I highlight four of the important debates regarding mediation, offering a glimpse at the issues each raises.

Issues of Impartiality and Neutrality

Mediator neutrality and impartiality are two common ways to describe the principle that mediators do not favor one party over another. Although some scholars have suggested distinctions between the two terms,[6] for all intents and purposes the terms are used interchangeably to refer to the idea that mediators should be free from bias. This aspect of the process is nearly always included as an integral element in codes of ethics for mediators.

The way in which a mediator conducts a mediation has neutrality implications. In general, most scholars agree that each participant in a mediation should be provided an opportunity to be heard and a participatory role in the process. To do otherwise, they suggest, would be a breach of neutrality. In contexts in which there is a serious imbalance of power, no simple solution exists. If the mediator attempts to correct an imbalance, the mediator may be perceived as an advocate for the weaker or less able party, compromising neutrality. Yet if the mediator does nothing, the weaker party may not have the genuine ability to participate effectively, raising ethical concerns as well.

A mediator's prior relationship with one or both of the parties or with the parties' lawyers may also affect both real and perceived issues of neutrality and impartiality. Current ethical guidelines suggest that even if mediators who have had prior dealings with one party believe they can remain impartial, they still must disclose the relationship to all other parties.

A final context in which a mediator's neutrality may be challenged involves the mediator's impact or influence on the final outcome or resolution. In some instances, mediators may believe (accurately or not) that a proposed resolution is unfair to one of the disputants. Any response a mediator chooses in such a circumstance presents direct challenges to neutrality.

One school of thought regarding a mediator's roles with respect to the substance of a mediated outcome holds that mediators should not do anything to address the (perceived) imbalanced solution, especially when the parties are represented by counsel. Proponents of this view suggest that it is not the mediator's job to make a conclusion about the outcome. Underlying this view is a concern that if mediators become too influential over the outcome, the agreement may cease to be that of the parties. Some who hold this perspective also suggest that visions of fairness are often inappropriately grounded in a perception of legal rights. Mediation, they contend, offers a move away from the legal win-lose, right-wrong paradigm, changing and minimizing the role of law in the process.

Others assert that mediators do or should have a role in determining the outcome, and this approach also implicates neutrality issues. Because in many cases going to court is one of the most viable alternatives for the parties if the case does not settle, parties must be aware of potential consequences. This view places informed consent at the heart of parties' participation in mediation, making legal advice or information central to the parties' decision making in mediation. If one accepts that such information is necessary, then it follows that someone will often have to provide that information to the parties. When parties are represented, most mediators and experts agree that the responsibility for legal advice and information rests with the lawyers. If the parties are unrepresented, however, mediators face an unattractive choice: leave the parties in a position of ignorance (going against the principle of informed consent) or inform one or both of the parties about the relevant legal information (potentially going against the principle of neutrality).

Ellen Waldman has explored the mediator's role in terms of the application of social norms to the outcome. This provides yet another way to examine neutrality.[7] Mediators' influence varies contextually, depending on the need to ensure that the final agreement complies with norms. In one conception of mediation, the parties create their own norms or parameters as the basis for resolution. A competing view maintains that a mediator may have a role in informing the parties about potentially applicable norms. Some who hold this competing view go so far as to suggest that mediators may insist that any final agreement be in compliance with the stated norms.[8]

For example, in a landlord-tenant matter, there may be a landlord who is quite knowledgeable about the law and the consequences in lock-out situations. The tenant, however, is oblivious to any legal principles, including the statute that would allow damages. In a norm-generating process, the mediator remains completely neutral, saying nothing about what might be achieved through a court procedure. In a norm-educating mode, the mediator may inform the tenant (and the landlord) what the statute provides, but allows the parties to make their own final decision. Finally, some mediators, adopting a norm-advocating role, would insist that any agreement comply with what is provided by the statutory mandate.[9]

Issues of Confidentiality

In many circumstances, mediation carries a presumption of confidentiality and privacy. However, mediation confidentiality protections are never absolute, and in some contexts, the boundaries of confidentiality are unclear. These issues are particularly challenging when mediation intersects with the court system. A number of statutes, cases, rules, and ethical considerations address the nature of confidentiality in mediation. Yet this maze of regulation often leaves mediators, courts, and mediation participants without clear guidance about the extent of confidentiality in a particular case.

Those who argue in favor of confidentiality in mediation point to a number of benefits. Mirroring the confidential treatment of statements made in settlement discussions outside of the mediation context, privacy encourages the parties to disclose information they otherwise may not. This disclosure can help parties get to the real or underlying interests in a way that promotes wiser and more efficient resolutions. Maintaining confidentiality also assists in the building of trust between the mediator and participants, as well as assisting in maintaining neutrality.

At the same time, difficulties can arise from secrecy in the mediation. For example, some jurisdictions require good faith participation in mediation.[10] Confidentiality rules make it difficult for a court to ascertain what transpired during the mediation in order to determine compliance with such a requirement. If everything that occurred during mediation were to remain secret, then parties could misuse the process, and parties' ability to mislead each other might go unchecked.

Similarly, because a mediated agreement is a contract, evidence regarding the formation of the contract may affect its enforceability.[11] Yet complete confidentiality regarding the mediation proceeding would preclude evidence of contractual defenses such as fraud or duress in the creation of the agreement.

Even if mediators generally refuse to disclose voluntarily any information they gathered during a mediation, they may have an affirmative duty to disclose in certain circumstances. For example, in the context of reporting allegations of child abuse, most statutes and court rules provide that such legal requirements constitute an exception to any obligation of confidentiality. In other cases, while no requirement to report or disclose information exists, mediators may learn information that is deemed necessary to be disclosed, such as a threat of potential harm to another.

In response to extraordinary variation among states regarding confidentiality in mediation, the American Bar Association and the National Conference of Commissioners on Uniform State Laws produced a uniform statute, the Uniform Mediation Act (UMA).[12] The UMA focuses primarily on confidentiality, and some states have adopted its provisions. Still, considerable variation continues to exist, leaving the question of mediation confidentiality open and difficult.

Getting Disputes into Mediation

Once they are in a mediation session, parties retain control over the decision to settle or not. Their decision whether to participate in a mediation in the first place, however, is not always voluntary. As mediation has become more institutionalized, some disputants are in mediation because of predispute contractual commitments to mediate. Still other disputants arrive because of court rules that require participation in mediation. These methods of arriving at mediation raise important legal, policy, and practical questions.

Much debate has taken place regarding the propriety of mandatory versus voluntary mediation. On the one hand, mediation by its very nature is a voluntary process. Some view it as philosophically inconsistent, therefore, to mandate or coerce its use. On the other hand, a court mandate or contractual obligation to mediate can get reluctant or hesitant parties to the mediation table who might otherwise not consider it and who might ultimately be pleased with the result.

Despite the philosophical tension potentially created by mandatory mediation,[13] courts throughout the United States frequently direct cases to mediation, either through statute, local rule, or individual judicial determination resulting in a court order. Some jurisdictions limit mandatory participation to disputes falling within a particular subject matter, such as family law. Many mandatory mediation statutes also include requirements of attendance and good faith participation, as well as provisions that sanction noncompliance.

Because mandatory mediation takes place through the vehicle of a state entity (the court system), it presents a number of complications not present in traditional, extrajudicial, voluntary mediation. For example, who gets to serve as the mediator? When court-annexed mediation first began, some courts took an active role in the selection of mediators. This practice raised issues of favoritism and judicial ethics, however. Consequently, while many courts continue to choose the mediator in particularly complex and difficult matters, in most instances parties may select their own mediator.

Another example of the complications of mandatory mediation relates to the cost of mediation. If two disputants want to hire a mediator outside of a court case, it is of little concern to policymakers. But when the court is mandating that the parties participate, the question of "who pays" becomes significant.

The Regulation of Mediation

Beginning in the 1990s, practicing mediators have been engaged in deliberations about the issue of regulation. Regulation includes a wide range of issues such as the management of cases that use mediation, how the mediation is conducted, how mediation participants conduct themselves, and how to ensure the quality of mediators. While quality control and regulation may not be completely synonymous, the terms are used interchangeably to indicate efforts to ensure that mediators are competent and qualified. If, as many mediators contend, a new profession has evolved, then regulatory aspects of practice such as credentialing or licensing seem inevitable.

The topic of quality control is expansive, and matters of "quality" in mediation encompass many aspects of the mediator's work. The variety of forms, functions, and definitions of a mediator complicate any efforts at ensuring quality. Further complicating the picture is the range of different public, private, local, and national organizations that have undertaken quality-assurance efforts. No consistent requirements have emerged from these efforts, leaving mediation practitioners and mediation consumers with relatively little coherent guidance or assurance. If mediation were treated like certain other regulated professions, one could imagine a system of licensure that would provide consistent quality-control mechanisms. No such system currently exists, however.

The existence of ethical guidelines is often considered a hallmark of becoming a profession, and ethical standards with disciplinary consequences provide one mechanism for ensuring quality services. In the context of mediation, questions of ethics often blend with questions about effective practices. For example, issues surrounding confidentiality and neutrality are often described as ethical in nature, yet they involve more than considerations of ethics. Similarly, efforts at articulating mediator qualifications sometimes also included ethical considerations, even though the stated goal was to distinguish standards of practice and ethics from quality considerations and competency. Cross-over discussion is inevitable.

Several different ethical codes have been created by both public and private mediator organizations. While the codes vary considerably, they share several themes: competency, neutrality, confidentiality, self-determination, and quality assurance make appearances in virtually all articulations of mediator ethics.

FUTURE CONSIDERATIONS: THE POTENTIAL OF THE PROCESS

Our understanding and appropriate use of mediation is far better than it once was. Increased popular awareness, expanded knowledge, and the development of both theory and practice in the field provide grounds for celebration. Still, a number of unresolved issues invite serious consideration.

At one point, some observers legitimately wondered whether mediation was a passing fad. Few have such a concern now. Mediation has been integrated into courts, communities, companies, and contracts. Although much of this integration has been positive, institutionalization raises important questions about the nature of disputants' participation in the process and about the level of influence that other norms may have on the mediation process itself.

The use of mediation varies considerably from jurisdiction to jurisdiction within the United States as well as abroad. In some locales where mediation has been integrated within the court system for some time, it has been suggested that mediation may be fading—a victim of its own success. For a variety of reasons, the number of lawsuits that feed cases into mediation may be on the decline. In addition, due to increased education and use, lawyers who were once unfamiliar with mediation now have considerable experience with having a third party facilitate their negotiations. Perhaps these lawyers have learned through this process ways that make outside assistance less necessary. In other jurisdictions, however, reluctance to undertake the process still exists.

If mediation is to be a truly viable force in dispute resolution, then disputants need to consider mediation first, rather than the default win or lose, right or wrong paradigm. Some strides have been made in early education through peer-mediation programs in elementary, middle, and high schools. Telephone directories in metropolitan areas have a separate listing for mediation providers, though it is still dwarfed in comparison to the listings for attorneys in the same location. Still, mediation today remains the alternative, rather than the conventional method through which most disputes are resolved. Society would have much to gain if disputants engaged in collaborative problem solving and mediation before battle.

Notes

1. For more on the distinction between the legal articulation of demands and the parties' genuinely held interests, see C. Menkel-Meadow, "Toward Another View of Legal Negotiation: The Structure of Problem Solving," *University of California at Los Angeles Law Review*, 1984, *31*, 754–854; and M. L. Moffitt, "Pleadings in the Age of Settlement," *Indiana Law Journal*, 2005, *80*, 727–771.

2. The "transformative" model of mediation was most popularly articulated in R.A.B. Bush and J. P. Folger, *The Promise of Mediation: Responding to Conflict Through Empowerment and Recognition* (San Francisco: Jossey-Bass, 1994).

3. For details of Riskin's articulation of these differences, see L. Riskin, "Understanding Mediators' Orientations, Strategies, and Techniques: A Grid for the Perplexed," *Harvard Negotiation Law Review*, 1996, *1*, 7–51. See also K. K. Kovach and L. Love, "Mapping Mediation: The Risks of Riskin's Grid," *Harvard Negotiation Law Review*, 1998, *3*, 71–110.

4. See M. L. Moffitt, "Casting Light on the Black Box of Mediation: Should Mediators Make Their Conduct More Transparent?" *Ohio State Journal on Dispute Resolution*, 1997, *13*, 1–49.

5. For a brief survey of the issues raised in this debate, see J. Stulberg, "Facilitative Versus Evaluative Mediation: Piercing the 'Grid' Lock," *Florida State University Law Review*, 1997, *24*, 985–1005; L. P. Love, "The Top Ten Reasons Why Mediators Should Not Evaluate," *Florida State University Law Review*, 1997, *24*, 937–948; and Aaron, Chapter Thirteen, this volume.

6. See, for example, L. Cooks and C. Hale, "The Construction of Ethics in Mediation," *Mediation Quarterly*, 1994, *12*, 55–76.

7. See E. A. Waldman, "Identifying the Role of Social Norms in Mediation: A Multiple Model Approach," *Hastings Law Journal*, 1997, *48*, 703–769.

8. See Waldman, "Identifying the Role of Social Norms in Mediation," 1997.

9. For more on the dilemmas and dynamics of mediators facing parties with unequal information about their legal rights, see J. M. Nolan-Haley, "Court Mediation and the Search for Justice Through the Law," *Washington University Law Quarterly,* 1996, *74,* 47–102.

10. See K. K. Kovach, "Lawyer Ethics in Mediation: Time for a Requirement of Good Faith," *Dispute Resolution Magazine,* 1997, *4,* 9–13; and J. M. Lande, "Using Dispute Systems Design Methods to Promote Good-Faith Participation in Court-Connected Mediation Programs," *University of California at Los Angeles Law Review,* 2002, *50,* 69–141.

11. See E. E. Deason, "Enforcing Mediated Settlement Agreements: Contract Law Collides with Confidentiality," *University of California at Davis Law Review,* 2001, *35,* 33–102; and P. Robinson, "Centuries of Contract Common Law Can't Be All Wrong: Why the UMA's Exception to Mediation Confidentiality in Enforcement Proceedings Should Be Embraced and Broadened," *Journal of Dispute Resolution,* 2003, 135–173.

12. For more on the Uniform Mediation Act, see, generally, National Conference of Commissioners on Uniform State Laws, "Uniform Mediation Act Symposium: Uniform Mediation Act," *Journal of Dispute Resolution,* 2003, 1–60.

13. The term *mandatory* is often used in conjunction with mediation, to connote that attendance at a mediation session is required. In some instances, however, the term has been confused with a very different issue—the coercion or mandate that the parties reach some agreement or resolution at the mediation. While some confusion about the term remains, *mandatory* is used here to describe what a court, statute, or contract may require.

CHAPTER TWENTY

Arbitration

Sarah Rudolph Cole and Kristen M. Blankley

A rbitration is a process by which a private third-party neutral renders a binding determination of an issue in dispute. Like all dispute resolution processes, arbitration comes in many forms. In *contractual arbitrations,* disputants agree by contract, either before or after a dispute arises, to resolve their dispute through a final and binding arbitration. In some jurisdictions, disputants may—and sometimes must—participate in *court-annexed* or *court-ordered arbitration,* raising unique opportunities and challenges. *Labor arbitrations*—those that take place specifically in the context of collective bargaining agreements—present a third type of arbitration, raising a unique set of procedures and issues.[1] For reasons of clarity, and as a reflection of the prominence of this area of arbitration, this chapter focuses primarily on contractual arbitration.

Arbitration is a flexible process. Parties may negotiate virtually every aspect of the arbitration process, including the number of arbitrators who will hear the case; the location of the hearing; the applicable law; the availability, types, and amount of discovery; the timetable of events; the evidentiary standards; the appropriateness of expert witnesses; whether or not attorneys will represent the parties; and the use of pre- or post-hearing briefs. Arbitration's flexibility also enables parties to exercise considerable control over arbitrator selection. Thus, parties may select an arbitrator who is an expert in the field in which the dispute has arisen. Moreover, parties can and often do select arbitrators who are not lawyers. Arbitration's flexibility enables parties to tailor the arbitral process for each particular dispute.

Although it seems unlikely that anything could be described as "typical" in a process that is entirely designed by the participants, most arbitrations adhere to a fairly predictable structure. Typically, arbitration hearings are confidential. The arbitrator usually opens the arbitration with a recitation of ground rules, followed by each party's opening statement.[2] Next, each party presents witnesses and other evidence. During the hearing, an arbitrator may ask questions to clarify the evidence. Finally, the arbitrator hears closing statements. In most cases, the arbitrator allows the parties to submit post-hearing briefs that summarize each party's main arguments. The arbitrator then issues a written award, perhaps with an accompanying opinion, within the time limit that the parties set. If the parties have not indicated when the award is due, arbitrators typically issue awards within a few weeks after the hearing.

ARBITRATION COMPARED TO OTHER DISPUTE RESOLUTION PROCESSES

Arbitration shares certain qualities with mediation. Like mediation, contractual arbitration is voluntary and confidential. Furthermore, neither arbitral proceedings nor mediation proceedings may be used as evidence in a subsequent trial. Moreover, the arbitration hearing takes place in a private conference room rather than in a public courtroom. Both arbitration and mediation may save parties time and money as compared with litigation.[3] An arbitrator can be appointed and the hearing held in far less time than it would take for the same case to proceed through litigation. In addition, limited discovery makes arbitration, like mediation, a less expensive alternative to litigation.

Unlike mediation, however, arbitration is an adjudicative process. The arbitrator, like a judge, renders a decision based on the merits of the case. In arbitration, the parties do not create their own settlement. Instead, the arbitrator imposes a resolution on the parties, bounded only by the limitations articulated in the parties' agreement. Unlike in traditional litigation, the arbitrator's decision generally cannot be appealed.

Arbitration is much more flexible than litigation. In civil litigation in federal courts, the Federal Rules of Civil Procedure and Evidence govern the adjudicative process. Parties contracting for arbitration may or may not adopt formal rules of procedure or evidence to govern the arbitration. Parties may decide that a simple dispute requires only a few depositions and no pre- or post-hearing briefs, while a more complicated case may require more extensive procedures.

HISTORICAL TREATMENT OF ARBITRATION AGREEMENTS

Arbitration as we know it was developed by the merchant class in medieval Western Europe.[4] In the medieval period, merchants traveled to fairs where they could meet and conduct business with other merchants. Because these fairs occurred far from the merchants' homes, and because the merchants did not stay at any particular fair very long, it was important for the merchants to create a system to resolve the disputes that would inevitably arise from the business conducted at the fair. Unfortunately, the common law court system was not an appropriate venue for the resolution of these disputes because of its complex procedures. Moreover, the common law courts had little understanding of the customary norms the merchants followed. Merchants were interested in a system that would resolve disputes (1) quickly (so they could leave the fairs) and (2) in accordance with industry standards (to facilitate relationships among the parties).

Arbitration was developed to achieve these two goals. The arbitration system permitted parties to appoint a disinterested third party who was an industry expert to resolve the dispute quickly by applying understood customary norms. Arbitration successfully resolved mercantile disputes at least in part because informal marketplace sanctions (preserving parties' ongoing relationships and reputations within the industry) gave the parties strong incentives to abide by arbitration agreements and awards.

As the market grew wider and more impersonal, however, market sanctions became less effective and parties became more willing to simply ignore arbitral decisions that went against them, undercutting arbitration's effectiveness as a binding, final dispute resolution mechanism. As arbitration's effectiveness declined in the nineteenth century, the commercial community, both in England and in America, turned toward the courts to assist them in strengthening the enforceability of arbitration agreements and awards. Until Congress passed the Federal Arbitration Act (FAA) in 1925, this effort proved largely fruitless. American courts refused to assist the merchants in strengthening arbitration, holding instead that arbitration agreements impermissibly divested the courts of jurisdiction.

Congress, in response to merchant lobbying, designed the FAA to overcome this judicial reluctance and to place agreements to arbitrate on equal footing with other types of contracts.[5] As a result of this legislation, American courts began to recognize the legitimacy of agreements to arbitrate, at least when those agreements involved repeat players (parties who frequently negotiate arbitration agreements and participate in arbitration) and nonstatutory claims (claims arising out of contract or out of the common law). Arbitration agreements between commercial disputants, therefore, gained increasing acceptance for much of the twentieth century.

In the mid-1980s, arbitration agreements expanded beyond the context of repeat players disputing over nonstatutory claims. Contracts between a repeat player (such as a large employer or a merchant) and a one-shot player (one who rarely negotiates arbitration agreements or participates in arbitration) began to include broad arbitration clauses. Employers started including arbitration agreements in their employment contracts, and merchants started using arbitration agreements in sales to consumers. Because they perceived arbitration as potentially unfair, some one-shot players attempted to avoid enforcement of arbitration agreements. Opposition to arbitration grew also as the breadth of arbitration clauses began to include not only those disputes traditionally within the scope of arbitration (such as breach of contract) but also statutory claims (such as those arising out of antidiscrimination laws). Even in the context of one-shot disputants raising statutory claims, the Supreme Court has routinely held that these types of predispute arbitration agreements are valid, stating that there is a "federal policy favoring arbitration" when determining if arbitration is appropriate.[6] As we discuss more fully below, however, lower courts have recently revived exceptions to the general rule of enforceability.

LEGAL ISSUES IN ARBITRATION

Even though arbitration is an alternative to litigation, it must still exist within a legal framework. For instance, the Federal Arbitration Act governs the enforcement of arbitration clauses in contracts. Other legal issues that arise frequently in arbitration include the extent to which the states can regulate arbitration and what types of claims can be subject to arbitration.

Arbitration Under the Federal Arbitration Act

The FAA governs all arbitration agreements that "involve commerce."[7] The Supreme Court has held that this language indicates that Congress intended the FAA to cover all arbitration agreements falling within the scope of the Constitution's commerce clause.[8] Under the commerce clause, Congress has the power to regulate interstate commerce as well as most transactions that have substantial effect on interstate commerce. With few exceptions, Congress's ability to regulate interstate commerce extends to almost everything bought and sold within the United States, both products and services. Thus, the FAA regulates the vast majority of arbitration agreements.

The FAA's scope is limited statutorily by one exception. FAA § 1 provides that the FAA applies to all contracts except for employment contracts involving "seamen, railroad employees, or any other class of workers engaged in foreign or interstate commerce."[9] In 2001, the Supreme Court interpreted this language to exclude from the scope of the FAA only agreements to arbitrate employment disputes involving transportation workers.[10] The Court emphasized that exempting all employment disputes from FAA coverage would violate the legislative intent underlying the creation of the FAA. Thus, the FAA mandates enforcement of agreements to arbitrate disputes involving contracts to buy or sell most things in the United States, as well as almost all agreements to arbitrate employment contract disputes.

Under the FAA, court involvement occurs, if at all, in two situations: prior to the start of arbitration and after the completion of arbitration. First, pursuant to the FAA, a party with a valid arbitration agreement may obtain a stay of litigation from a court while the arbitration proceeds.[11] The judicial stay will essentially "freeze" the litigation in place until the arbitration is concluded. Second, the FAA enables enforcement of an arbitration agreement by authorizing a party to an arbitration agreement to file in federal district court a motion to compel the other party to arbitrate.[12] In other words, if one party to a dispute files a lawsuit in lieu of going to arbitration, the other party can request that the court enforce the arbitration agreement and put the litigation on hold until the arbitration is resolved. The FAA also contains provisions for limited judicial review of arbitral awards, together with provisions articulating the process for vacation or modification of arbitral awards.[13]

Federal Arbitration Law

The two primary legal concerns raised in cases involving arbitration are preemption and arbitrability. The theory of preemption is that federal laws are supreme to state laws in all areas, including state efforts to regulate arbitration. Arbitrability refers to whether or not the parties intended that a particular claim be arbitrated or litigated.

Preemption. Under federal law, contracts to arbitrate under the FAA are to be treated like any other contract. Because of the doctrine of preemption, this basic policy applies to state law and state courts as well. In other words, states cannot pass laws treating contracts to arbitrate differently than other contracts. For example, a state cannot require that an arbitration clause appear in bold print.[14] Although a company can certainly put their arbitration clause in bold type, a state cannot require this action because doing so would have the effect of treating contracts to arbitrate differently from other contracts. The FAA, which does not permit special treatment of arbitration agreements, preempts state law that provides either preferential or adverse treatment of arbitration agreements.[15]

Arbitrability. The question of arbitrability relates to whether the parties agreed to arbitrate the merits of a particular dispute. To determine whether a dispute is arbitrable, courts engage in two separate inquiries. First, the court asks whether the particular dispute falls within the category of disputes specified in the agreement to arbitrate. For example, if a contract requires arbitration of "all disputes arising out of this agreement," the question for the court is whether the dispute in question is one that arises out of the agreement. Second, a court will consider whether the agreement to arbitrate is enforceable at all. This latter inquiry involves issues of contract formation such as duress, unconscionability, fraud, mistake, and other contract defenses.

One of the first questions a court asks with respect to each of these two issues is "Who gets to decide?" That is, should a judge or an arbitrator determine, for instance, whether the dispute "arises out of" contract performance and thus falls within the terms of the agreement, or whether the parties agreed to arbitrate disputes at all. If a question arises as to the enforceability of an arbitration agreement (that is, a question of whether the parties agreed to arbitrate disputes at all), the court makes the initial determination about whether parties should arbitrate. This concept is demonstrated in *First Options of Chicago, Inc.* v. *Kaplan,* a case in which the Supreme Court held that because the parties did not sign the arbitration agreement, it was unclear whether or not the parties intended to use arbitration. In such a case, the court should make the initial determination as to the enforceability of the arbitration agreement unless the parties "clearly and unmistakably" agree that an arbitrator should resolve the arbitrability question.[16]

If the parties' *arbitration* agreement is enforceable, and there is no dispute about whether the arbitration clause applies to the particular type of controversy at issue, the court will direct the case to arbitration, in which an arbitrator decides gateway procedural questions as well as the merits of the dispute. Gateway procedural questions include, among other things, allegations of waiver, delay, violation of limitations periods, and estoppel.[17]

Another doctrine, known as the doctrine of "separability," addresses the question of whether an arbitration agreement should be enforced even when the contract that contains the arbitration agreement is arguably unenforceable. Unlike the arbitrability doctrine, the separability doctrine simply considers whether parties should resolve their disputes in arbitration in a case in which they challenge the contract that contains the arbitration agreement but do not directly challenge the arbitration agreement. For example, in *Prima Paint Corp.* v. *Flood & Conklin Mfg. Co.,* the plaintiff alleged that the defendant had fraudulently induced the plaintiff to sign a contract that contained an arbitration clause. The Supreme Court held that an arbitrator, rather than a court, should decide the merits of the plaintiff's assertion that the entire contract was fraudulently induced.[18] The *Prima Paint* Court presumed that the parties' *arbitration agreement* was valid, even though it was contained in an arguably invalid contract. As a result, the Court directed to the arbitrator the question of whether the defendant engaged in fraudulent inducement. Commentators and some courts sharply criticize the separability doctrine.[19]

Arbitration of Statutory Claims

The question of whether statutory antidiscrimination claims should be resolved in arbitration is controversial. Congress has enacted laws such as Title VII, the Americans with Disabilities Act (ADA), and the Age Discrimination in Employment Act (ADEA) to give employees who allege that their employer has discriminated against them a cause of action in the federal courts. Claims alleging a breach of one or more of these statutes are referred to as "statutory claims," and sometimes have a different structure from claims based on contractual terms or common law duties. Not all statutory claims relate to discrimination, and the courts have regularly upheld arbitration agreements covering statutory claims as diverse as the Sherman Antitrust Act, the Securities and Exchange Act, and RICO.[20] In the mid-1980s, employers began to include arbitration agreements in employees' contracts. These agreements required employees to arbitrate all claims, including statutory claims. In the seminal *Gilmer* v. *Interstate/Johnson Lane Corp.* decision, the Supreme Court unequivocally held that an arbitrator was competent to hear cases involving the ADEA. The Court reasoned that arbitration under the New York Stock Exchange (NYSE) Rules adequately protected the plaintiff's interests and that there was no reason to believe that a NYSE arbitrator was incapable of hearing and deciding a statutory claim.[21] Since *Gilmer,* the Supreme Court and lower courts have consistently upheld agreements to arbitrate statutory claims brought by employees against their employers.

ARBITRATION CLAUSES

When parties draft an agreement to resolve disputes, they consider a variety of issues, including whether arbitration should be used to resolve the dispute. Parties who choose arbitration then draft agreements covering a number of topics, the most common of which include type of dispute covered, arbitrator selection, number of arbitrators, applicable rules, type of award, available remedies, class actions, and arbitration fees and costs.

Appropriateness of Arbitration

Arbitration may be used to resolve virtually any kind of dispute; however, some disputes may be particularly well-suited to this resolution process. For instance, arbitration may provide benefits to parties who have a relationship with one another that is likely to continue after the dispute is resolved. Because arbitration is less adversarial than litigation, the process may help preserve good will between the disputants. Moreover, arbitration is usually cheaper and more efficient, enabling parties to resolve their dispute more quickly and resume their relationship. In addition, arbitration decisions bring finality to the conflict because the decisions are very difficult to appeal.

Repeat players, such as employers and big businesses, will generally benefit more from arbitration than will one-shot players, such as employees and consumers. The repeat player's greater experience, expertise, and sophistication in negotiating contracts will provide it significant advantages in interactions with one-shot players. In negotiating an arbitration agreement, for example, the repeat player is likely to have a much better understanding of the risks and benefits of the arbitral process because he or she has greater experience with it. The repeat player's greater understanding of the process and an ability to influence that process through repeated informal relations with the decision maker will also provide the repeat player considerable advantages in selecting an arbitrator and participating in the arbitration process. By contrast, a one-shot player will lack experience with the arbitration process. Thus, the one-shot player is unlikely to know how to select an arbitrator, design an arbitration hearing effectively, or make educated decisions about the arbitration process, such as whether to submit post-hearing briefs. Although the one-shot player can learn these things throughout the process, the repeat player will almost certainly have an advantage during the arbitration process.

Drafting Arbitration Clauses

Parties can draft an arbitration clause either before or after a dispute arises. If two parties have a dispute and decide to resolve it using arbitration, they can draft a stand-alone arbitration clause specifying the procedures for resolving the dispute. Parties drafting a postdispute arbitration clause typically construct an arbitral process that both suits their needs and helps them save time and money.

Parties can also draft predispute agreements to arbitrate. Such agreements usually appear in the contract governing the parties' relationship. For example, parties to a joint venture might include an arbitration procedure for resolving any disputes that arise between the business partners. When drafting a predispute arbitration agreement, the parties try to anticipate the types of disputes that might arise out of the contract and also anticipate the kind of procedure best able to resolve future disputes. Many companies include arbitration clauses in contracts governing their relationship with one-shot players, such as employees and consumers.

When drafting a pre- or postdispute resolution procedure, the drafter should remember that arbitration is only one method of dispute resolution. To create an effective dispute resolution system, a drafter might use arbitration as one of the steps in the dispute system's design process. For example, a contract could provide that good-faith negotiation, mediation, or both must occur before the parties submit their dispute to arbitration. Although arbitration is usually binding, parties who are concerned about access to the courts could create a dispute resolution procedure that includes nonbinding arbitration that can be followed by a lawsuit. Parties should try to anticipate the nature of the dispute and then create a procedure to resolve the dispute in the manner most beneficial to the parties.

Many alternative dispute resolution organizations, such as the American Arbitration Association (AAA), provide sample arbitration agreements and sample clauses.[22] These organizations also provide model language that may be relevant to a particular type of dispute, such as a construction or a financial dispute.

Arbitrator Selection

Any arbitration agreement should either designate a particular person as the arbitrator or create a process for determining who the arbitrator will be. In many postdispute agreements to arbitrate, the parties decide who will arbitrate the case and insert that person's name in the contract. Some predispute arbitration agreements also name a specific arbitrator, but this usually happens when one or both parties have a relationship with a particular arbitrator or when the arbitrator is well known in his or her field.

It is more common for an arbitration agreement to specify an arbitrator selection *method*. The selection method usually indicates that an arbitration organization, such as the AAA, will provide a list of potential arbitrators to the disputants, and the disputants will select an arbitrator from the list. Prior to making the selection, the parties review the list and investigate potential arbitrators in order to narrow the list down to one arbitrator. Some parties select an arbitrator by alternating strikes of arbitrator names until only one name is left. Other parties rank the arbitrators in order of preference. In that case, the first arbitrator chosen by both parties becomes the arbitrator for the case.

Some arbitration agreements use tripartite arbitration, also known as party-appointed arbitration. In tripartite arbitration, a panel of three arbitrators hears the case. Under this system, each party chooses one arbitrator and the two arbitrators select a third arbitrator. Presumably, an arbitrator selected by one party will have a bias toward the appointing party. The third arbitrator, by contrast, is obligated to be neutral and nonbiased. Although tripartite arbitration may substantially increase the cost of the procedure, it also allows each party to have a representative on the arbitral panel to assist the neutral decision maker after the conclusion of the hearing.

Determining Procedures

Often parties select arbitration because it affords them the opportunity to tailor a procedure that most efficiently and effectively permits them to resolve their dispute(s). Parties drafting an arbitration agreement have considerable control over the procedures governing the arbitration hearing. For instance, the parties can designate how much discovery will be allowed in the case as well as create a timetable for completing this phase of the process. Through the arbitration agreement, the parties can also, among other things, dictate whether expert or lay witnesses may be called, the order of party presentations, whether the arbitrator has subpoena powers, and whether rules of evidence or procedure will be strictly followed. Often the particular facts of the case or the dispute's complexity will affect the parties' choice of procedures.

Form of the Award

The parties to an arbitration agreement can tell the arbitrator how the award should look. Parties who value time and cost-saving procedures may request that the arbitrator issue an award that indicates only who won and how much money that person will receive, if anything. Presumably, if the arbitrator does not have to draft a written opinion, the arbitrator can make a decision quickly and notify the parties within a short period of time.

Parties can also require the arbitrator to write a reasoned opinion. A reasoned opinion usually includes a statement of the issues, a statement of the facts, the positions of the parties, the reasoning of the arbitrator, and a statement of the award. Parties who request a written opinion may benefit from understanding why the arbitrator reached a particular decision and what parts of their case were most—and least—convincing. Moreover, parties may be better able to move on with their relationship if they believe the arbitrator's decision was not arbitrary or capricious. In addition, an arbitrator required to draft a well-reasoned, written opinion may be more likely to think carefully about the case. Finally, a written opinion may be necessary if either of the parties wish to challenge the award in court.

Available Remedies

In traditional litigation, parties may only request that the court grant them monetary or injunctive relief[23] because the court does not have jurisdiction to order more creative remedies. One advantage to arbitration is that the parties can provide the arbitrator with discretion to award monetary damages, nonmonetary damages, or a combination of both. In employment disputes, for example, parties could agree that the arbitrator has the power to reinstate an employee who has been discharged, perhaps with back pay and other employment benefits. In contrast, if the same employment disputes were litigated, the court could only award money damages. A court is without authority to order a company to reinstate an employee, give employees promotions, or reinstate employee tenure or benefit packages. Thus, parties drafting an arbitration clause should consider whether they wish to authorize the arbitrator to award nonmonetary damages and, if so, consider limiting the potential scope of nonmonetary awards.

Consolidations and Class Actions

Consolidation and class action arbitration are two mechanisms by which more than one claimant can proceed against the same party in the same arbitration proceeding. When arbitration cases are consolidated, each person with a claim against the same defendant joins his or her case to the others, so that there are multiple claimants but only one defendant. In a consolidation, each affected party is a named party in the arbitration.

Class action arbitration occurs when one party brings an action against a defendant on behalf of him- or herself and all others similarly situated. As with a class action lawsuit in court, the class action arbitration can involve many people who are not named parties to the case. Unnamed parties also have an opportunity to contribute to the case and may be bound by the outcome of the proceeding.

Class action arbitrations are controversial because there are few rules governing the class action arbitration process and little guidance regarding the extent to which the courts should be involved in the proceedings.[24] If an agreement to arbitrate is valid, the arbitrator, not the court, will decide whether a class action is appropriate for the particular case.[25] In other words, if the arbitration agreement is silent on the issue of class action arbitrations, then the arbitrator will decide whether a classwide proceeding is appropriate. In contracts that specifically allow or ban class action arbitrations, the arbitrator is generally bound to respect his or her authority as defined in the contract.

Payment of Fees

Arbitration agreements typically include provisions describing the allocation of arbitration costs. Arbitration costs include filing fees, arbitrator fees, and attorney's fees. In the absence of an agreement to the contrary, the filing party pays the filing fees. Arbitrator fees are usually split evenly between the parties for two reasons: (1) this is often perceived as a fair way to split fees, and (2) equal payments help ensure that the arbitrator is not biased in favor of one party or another. The increased use of arbitration among repeat and one-shot players prompted courts to reconsider the question of who should pay filing fees and arbitrator fees. A number of courts have held that it is unconscionable to require lower-paid workers or consumers to pay filing fees or pay for the arbitrator.[26] A full discussion of unconscionable arbitration agreements will appear later in this chapter.

In arbitrations, each party typically bears his or her own attorney's fees. The parties may alter this arrangement by agreement specifying, for example, that the loser will pay the winner's attorney's fees. Attorney fee shifting clauses are more common if the arbitration involves a federal statute that would otherwise allow a successful plaintiff to recover attorney fees in court if he or she wins. Failure to shift fees in such cases may result in a finding of unconscionability if the agreement is challenged in court.

ENFORCEABILITY OF ARBITRATION AGREEMENTS

Challenges to arbitration often focus on contractual theories, particularly unconscionability. This section of the chapter explores the possible contractual challenges a party to an arbitration agreement might raise in court.

Conscionability

A court may declare an arbitration agreement void because it is unconscionable, or so one-sided that the courts refuse to enforce it. In most jurisdictions, a contract is void for reasons of unconscionability if it is both procedurally and substantively unconscionable. In some jurisdictions, however, substantive unconscionability alone may be enough to invalidate an agreement to arbitrate. Underlying the doctrine of unconscionability is the goal of preventing oppression and unfair surprise in a contract between parties with unequal bargaining power.

Procedural unconscionability may be found in an adhesion contract, that is, a contract that is presented to a person on a "take it or leave it" basis. Procedurally unconscionable contracts are most common in employment contracts and in consumer transactions. A procedurally unconscionable contract almost always involves a disparity in bargaining power between the two parties, which prevents the weaker party from successfully negotiating to change unfavorable terms. Often, courts examine the educational experience and sophistication of the party making the contract to determine if there is procedural unconscionability or undue influence.

To be unenforceable, a contract must also be substantively unconscionable. Substantively unconscionable contracts are those that contain terms that are harsh, oppressive, or unduly biased in favor of the party with greater bargaining power. When determining whether a contract is substantively unconscionable, a court will examine all of the terms contained in the arbitration agreement. From the perspective of unconscionability, certain contract provisions are more troublesome than others. Filing fee provisions often raise alarms for courts reviewing arbitration agreements between one-shot and repeat players. Contracts that require consumers and employees to pay large sums of money in order to arbitrate a dispute are generally disfavored, and some courts express concern over clauses that require these particular plaintiffs to pay anything because they would not have to pay for a decision maker if they were proceeding in court.[27] Courts also consider the adequacy of the agreement's discovery provisions because in employment and consumer cases the defendant usually has a considerable informational advantage. Whether the arbitration agreement prohibits class action arbitrations or class action lawsuits is another provision that is of particular concern to the courts. Courts also consider the accessibility of the arbitration location to assess whether it is sufficiently convenient for both parties.[28] Finally, the courts will examine the arbitrator selection process to determine whether the pool of arbitrators from which the parties will select their decision maker is biased in favor of the drafting party.[29]

Contractual Soundness

Because courts treat contracts to arbitrate just like any other contract, general contract defenses are available to challenge contracts to arbitrate. Thus, defenses such as duress, fraud, lack of consideration, illegality, and lack of capacity are available to a plaintiff when challenging an agreement in court or in front of the arbitrator. These types of defenses are generally used to challenge the validity of the contract or to prove that a contract was never formed. One must recall that the preemption doctrine prohibits states from passing laws that provide special defenses to those who are challenging the existence or validity of an agreement to arbitrate.[30]

Whether the court or the arbitrator hears these defenses is a question of arbitrability. Because courts may hear challenges to the validity of an agreement to arbitrate as well as the applicability of an agreement to arbitrate, the previously mentioned contract formation defenses are generally questions for the courts to answer. Most other defenses, such as the applicability of a statute of limitations, are reserved for the arbitrator.[31]

ARBITRATOR ETHICS

With an increasing number of disputes going to arbitration, especially disputes involving employment and consumer transactions, state legislatures and arbitral providers have begun to examine more closely the arbitrator's ethical obligations. The development and enforcement of arbitral ethical standards are ways to level the playing field, especially if the arbitration is between a repeat player and a one-shot player.

One major area of ethics reform involves arbitrator disclosure requirements. To ensure neutrality and lack of bias, a selected arbitrator must disclose any financial, professional, or social relationships the arbitrator has with the parties.[32] After full disclosure, both parties should determine if they still want that person to serve as arbitrator. If not, parties must select a different arbitrator who will also have to make preliminary disclosures. An arbitrator's obligation to disclose conflicts continues throughout the arbitration process. Thus, if the arbitrator discovers a conflict of interest in the middle of the arbitration, the arbitrator must disclose the conflict as soon as possible.[33]

Arbitrators have other ethical duties. Arbitrators should refrain from engaging in *ex parte* communications—communications with only one of the parties without the other party present—because such conduct may create an appearance of impropriety. Furthermore, the arbitrator should maintain the confidentiality of the process, run the hearing in a fair manner, and remain cognizant of any biases that he or she may develop during the process.

Arbitral providers, such as AAA, also have ethical obligations. Arbitral providers should make reasonable efforts to maximize the quality and competence of their services, provide information about their services and organization to potential clients, ensure that they administer arbitration proceedings that are "fundamentally fair and conducted in an impartial manner," provide services at a reasonable cost to low-income parties, protect the confidentiality of the proceedings, and disclose conflicts of interest "reasonably likely to affect the impartiality or independence" of the arbitral provider.[34]

ENFORCEMENT OF ARBITRAL AWARDS

Following the completion of a successful arbitration, one or more parties may petition the court to confirm the award.[35] The party seeking judicial confirmation of the award must physically take a copy of the award to the court and have it entered into the court's official record. After the award is confirmed, it can be enforced if one of the parties, usually the losing party, does not comply with its terms. A court can enforce an arbitral award in the same manner as it enforces judicial awards, through judgment liens, garnishment, or other methods.

Under limited circumstances, a party can ask a court to modify or correct an arbitration award. The FAA allows for modification or correction in three circumstances: (1) if there is a material miscalculation of an award or a material mistake in the description of anything or anyone referred to in the award, (2) if the arbitrator decided an issue that the parties did not submit to him or her and that decision affected the merits of the award, and (3) the award contains errors in its form in a way that does not affect the merits of the decision.[36] The statute notes that the award may also be corrected or modified in order to "promote justice between the parties."[37]

Judicial review of an arbitration award under the FAA is rare, and the courts are reluctant to disturb arbitration awards. The FAA allows courts to review or vacate awards on the grounds of procedural irregularity during the arbitration. The FAA authorizes judicial review to determine whether (1) the award is procured by corruption or other undue means, (2) there is evident partiality on the part of the arbitrator, (3) the arbitrator has acted in a manner that constitutes misconduct, or (4) the arbitrator exceeded his or her powers as described in the agreement to arbitrate.[38] The statute does not give any other reasons for an award to be vacated, and there is no "catchall" category for cases in which a court would prefer to review the award. Depending on the jurisdiction, a court may also review an arbitration agreement to determine, among other things, whether the arbitrator manifestly disregarded the law or was arbitrary or capricious in making his or her decision. Courts adopting these nonstatutory grounds for challenging arbitration awards still rarely overturn arbitration awards. Courts rarely vacate arbitration awards, at least in part because overturning awards undermines the finality and, consequently, the efficiency of the arbitration process.

Some arbitration consumers are dissatisfied with the limited grounds for judicial review just mentioned. These parties have attempted to contract around the FAA by adding additional grounds for review within their agreements to arbitrate. Parties often agree to expand judicial review of their arbitral award to determine whether "errors of law" appear in the arbitrator's decision. If the court finds an error of law, it would overturn the arbitral award. Whether a contractual provision that expands the bases upon which a court may review an arbitration award is enforceable remains an open question. Some courts will review agreements according to the parties' expanded standard of review while other courts refuse to vacate an award for reasons other than those specifically stated in the FAA.[39]

CONCLUSION

Arbitration is a useful process for obtaining resolution of disputes that might arise in a variety of areas including, but not limited to, commercial, construction, labor, employment, and consumer. Arbitration's flexibility enables parties to tailor a dispute resolution mechanism that suits their underlying needs and interests. Moreover, its speed, confidentiality, and finality often permit parties to preserve their existing relationship and protect their reputation within a particular industry. While concerns have been raised about the use of arbitration to resolve disputes between repeat and one-shot players, courts have limited the ability of the repeat player to exploit the one-shot player in arbitration through the application of the unconscionability doctrine. Increased attention to arbitrators' ethical obligations should also limit the ability of a repeat player to oppress a one-shot player both before and during the arbitration process.

Interest in arbitration—particularly in the business community—shows little sign of abating. While courts have used the doctrine of unconscionability to eliminate abusive arbitration agreements, they have continued to enforce fairly written arbitration agreements without hesitation. Confined by judicial decisions on the one hand and increased attention to arbitrators' and third party providers' ethical responsibilities on the other, use of arbitration will continue to grow. While the unconscionability doctrine has offered some solace to one-shot players unhappily bound to arbitrate disputes, their continued dissatisfaction with arbitration needs to be addressed. Perhaps most helpful to reverse the negative attitude of one-shot players and their representatives would be to encourage empirical research designed to determine whether one-shot players perform as well in arbitration as in litigation or have greater access to the arbitral process than to a judicial one. If such studies support the theory that arbitration is an efficient, effective mechanism for resolving disputes that does not systematically favor the repeat player, overall acceptance of arbitration will likely increase as will party satisfaction with the process.

Notes

1. This chapter will not address the topic of labor arbitration. Labor arbitration is typically governed by collective bargaining agreements between labor unions and management. Different principles and laws apply to labor arbitration than to contractual arbitration.

2. Arbitration ground rules focus on the arbitrator's personal preferences and the procedural rules that will govern the arbitration hearing. Among other issues, an arbitrator's ground rules might address introduction of documentary evidence, sequestration of witnesses, order of witness testimony, administration of witness oaths, time limitations on opening or closing statements, and length of hearing breaks. See J. W. Cooley, *The Arbitrator's Handbook* (South Bend, Ind.: National Institute for Trial Advocacy, 1998), p. 78.

3. Because arbitration is a quicker and more streamlined process, it has the potential to save both parties money. Arbitration is especially cost-effective if processes such as discovery are kept to a minimum. However, as arbitration begins to adopt more characteristics of litigation, the length and cost of the process increases. See S. J. Ware, "Paying the Price of Process: Judicial Regulation of Consumer Arbitration Agreements," *Journal of Dispute Resolution*, 2001, pp. 89–100, for a discussion on how arbitration can be either cost-effective or costly.

4. See L. W. Craig, "Some Trends and Developments in the Laws and Practice of International Commercial Arbitration," *Texas International Law Journal*, 1995, *30*, p. 5, stating that "[a]n important chapter in the development of private dispute resolution systems can be traced back to medieval Europe, when merchants and traders of different religions would assemble at markets and fairs to do business."

5. See *Gilmer* v. *Interstate/Johnson Lane Corp.*, 500 U.S. 20 (1991), p. 24, stating that the purpose of the FAA is to "reverse the long-standing judicial hostility to arbitration agreements that had existed at English common law and had been adopted by American courts, and to place arbitration agreements upon the same footing as other contracts."

6. This quotation first appeared in *Moses H. Cone Memorial Hospital* v. *Mercury Construction Corp.*, 460 U.S. 1 (1983), p. 24, and it has been cited regularly ever since. See, for example, *Howsam* v. *Dean Witter Reynolds, Inc.*, 537 U.S. 79 (2002), p. 83; *EEOC* v. *Waffle House, Inc.*, 534 U.S. 279 (2002), p. 289; *Green Tree Fin. Corp.-Alabama* v. *Randolph*, 531 U.S. 79 (2000), p. 81; and *Gilmer* v. *Interstate/Johnson Lane Corp.*, 500 U.S. 20 (1991), p. 25.

7. See Federal Arbitration Act § 2 (2003).

8. See *Circuit City Stores, Inc. v. Adams,* 352 U.S. 105 (2001), p. 112.

9. See Federal Arbitration Act § 1 (2003).

10. See *Circuit City Stores, Inc. v. Adams,* 352 U.S. 105 (2001), p. 119.

11. See Federal Arbitration Act § 3 (2003).

12. See Federal Arbitration Act § 4 (2003).

13. See Federal Arbitration Act §§ 10–12 (2003).

14. See *Doctor's Assoc., Inc. v. Cassarotto,* 517 U.S. 681 (1996), p. 687.

15. See *Volt Information Sciences, Inc. v. Bd. of Trustees of the Leland Stanford Junior Univ.,* 489 U.S. 468 (1989), pp. 446–447.

16. See *First Options of Chicago, Inc. v. Kaplan,* 514 U.S. 938 (1995), p. 946.

17. See *Howsam v. Dean Witter Reynolds, Inc.,* 537 U.S. 79 (2002), p. 86.

18. *Prima Paint Corp. v. Flood & Conklin Mfg. Co.,* 388 U.S. 395 (1967), p. 406.

19. *Shaffer v. Jeffery,* 915 P.2d 910 (Okla. 1996) (defense of fraudulent inducement of contract is for the court). See also R. C. Reuben, "First Options, Consent to Arbitration, and the Demise of Separability: Restoring Access to Justice for Contracts with Arbitration Provisions," 56 *S.M.U. L. Rev.* 819, 838–855 (2003); S. J. Ware, "Employment Arbitration and Voluntary Consent," 25 *Hofstra L. Rev.* 83, 128–138 (1996).

20. See *Rodriquez de Quijas v. Shearson/American Express, Inc.,* 490 U.S. 477 (1989) (Securities Act claim); *Shearson/American Express, Inc. v. McMahon,* 482 U.S. 220 (1987) (RICO claim); and *Mitsubishi Motors Corp., Inc. v. Soler Chrysler-Plymouth Inc.,* 473 U.S. 614 (1985) (antitrust claim).

21. See *Gilmer v. Interstate/Johnson Lane Corp.,* 500 U.S. 20 (1991), pp. 30–33.

22. See American Arbitration Association, "Drafting Dispute Resolution Clauses—A Practical Guide." [http://www.adr.org/index2.1.jsp?JSPssid = 15727&JSPsrc = upload < \\ > LIVESITE < \\ > Rules_Procedures < \\ > ADR_Guides < \\ > Current%20clausebook.html]. July 2004.

23. Examples of injunctive relief include temporary restraining orders and orders of protection.

24. See American Arbitration Association, "Supplementary Rules for Class Arbitrations," [http://www.adr.org/index2.1.jsp?JSPssid = 15747&JSPsrc = upload < \\ > LIVESITE < \\ > Rules_Procedures < \\ > National_International < \\ > . < \\ > Topics_Interest < \\ > AAAClassaction.htm]. October 2003.

25. See *Green Tree Fin. Corp. v. Bazzle,* 539 U.S. 444 (2003).

26. See *Morrison v. Circuit City Stores, Inc.,* 317 F.3d 646 (6th Cir. 2003).

27. See, for example, *Morrison v. Circuit City Stores, Inc.,* 317 F.3d 646 (6th Cir. 2003), pp. 664–665, noting that a plaintiff in court would have a free judge and a lawyer on a contingency fee basis; and *Armendariz v. Foundation Health Psychare Services, Inc.,* 6 P.3d 669 (Cal. 2000), p. 687, stating that employees cannot pay

for any "unreasonable costs or any arbitrator's fees or expenses as a condition of access to the arbitration forum."

28. See *Brower* v. *Gateway 2000*, 246 A.2d 246 (N.Y. App. Div. 1998), p. 256, holding an arbitration agreement unenforceable because it required arbitration in front of the International Chamber of Commerce in Paris, France.

29. For an example of a particularly egregious case, see *Hooters of America* v. *Phillips*, 173 F.3d 933 (4th Cir. 1999). In the *Hooters* case, the restaurant management compiled a list of potential arbitrators. Control of the list created the possibility that Hooters could "stack the deck" with favorable arbitrators.

30. See the earlier discussion on preemption in the Federal Arbitration Law section.

31. See the earlier discussion on arbitrability in the Federal Arbitration Law section.

32. See, for example, American Arbitration Association, "The Code of Ethics for Arbitrators in Commercial Disputes." [http://www.adr.org/index2.1.jsp?JSPssid = 15727&JSPsrc = upload < \\ > LIVESITE < \\ > Rules_Procedures < \\ > ADR_Guides < \\ > . < \\ > Ethics_Standards < \\ > codeofethics2004.htm], March 2004, Canon II, which states, "An arbitrator should disclose any interest or relationship likely to affect impartiality or which might create an appearance of partiality."

33. Under California law, if an arbitration provider organization, such as the AAA, supplies an arbitrator on any given case, both the arbitrator and the provider organization must disclose any conflicts of interest to the parties (California Rules of the Court, Appx, Standard 8 [2004]). Such disclosure may be burdensome for an organization such as the AAA that provides arbitrators for countless disputes across the country.

34. CPR-Georgetown Commission on Ethics and Standards of Practice in Alternative Dispute Resolution. "Principles for ADR Provider Organizations." [http://www.cpradr.org/finalProvider.pdf]. May 2002.

35. See Federal Arbitration Act § 9 (2003).

36. See Federal Arbitration Act § 11 (2003).

37. Federal Arbitration Act § 11 (2003).

38. See Federal Arbitration Act § 10 (2003).

39. Compare both *Lapine Tech. Corp* v. *Kyocera Corp.*, 130 F.3d 884 (9th Cir. 1997), in which the court enforced the party agreement to review arbitral award for errors of law, and *Gateway Tech., Inc.* v. *MCI Telecommunications Corp.*, 64 F.3d 993 (5th Cir. 1995) with *Bowen* v. *Amoco Pipeline Co.*, 254 F.3d 925 (10th Cir. 2001), in which the parties could not contractually alter the FAA standard for judicial review.

CHAPTER TWENTY-ONE

Litigation as a Dispute Resolution Alternative

Jeffrey R. Seul

The popular image of litigation has become so bleak, one can easily forget that an essential purpose of litigation is to resolve disputes, not to perpetuate them. This chapter examines the distinctive way in which civil disputes are handled through litigation before state and federal courts in the United States and assesses the merits of litigation relative to other available dispute resolution processes. Some dyed-in-the-wool trial lawyers shun arbitration, mediation, and other alternatives to litigation. Some proponents of those processes are almost dogmatically opposed to litigation as a dispute resolution alternative. Both perspectives are shortsighted. It makes little sense to ask which dispute resolution process is better in the abstract. Rather, we must consider the relative merits of each process for particular purposes, at particular moments, and in particular contexts.

This chapter has four major sections. The first section provides an overview of the typical structure of the litigation process. The second section explores—from the disputants' perspectives—some of the significant advantages and disadvantages of litigation in relation to other dispute resolution processes. The third section adopts a broader perspective—that of society generally—and briefly addresses claims that litigation is better at protecting weaker parties, produces more just outcomes, and otherwise is superior to other dispute resolution processes from a social perspective. The chapter ends with some generalizations about the circumstances in which litigation may be more desirable or effective than other dispute resolution processes from the perspective of one or more of the parties.

LITIGATION'S APPROACH TO DISPUTE RESOLUTION

In order to function, *any* dispute resolution process must answer a number of fundamental questions:

- Who will participate in the process?
- What are the basic stages of the process from beginning to final resolution?
- Where will the proceedings occur?
- Which claims and issues will be considered?
- What information will be considered and how and when will it be exchanged?
- What substantive standards will determine the outcome of the process?
- Who determines the outcome?
- What types of outcomes are possible?

I consider each of these questions in turn.

Who Will Participate in the Process?

Litigation is a dispute resolution process that typically involves many participants, supporting characters, and observers. A simple lawsuit has one "plaintiff" and one "defendant." The plaintiff is the disputant asserting some right or claim recognized by law for which the other disputant, the defendant, may be liable. Other lawsuits may have multiple plaintiffs, multiple defendants, or both.

The distinction between plaintiff and defendant becomes blurred in some lawsuits, because a defendant may assert a counterclaim against a plaintiff or a plaintiff or defendant may assert a crossclaim against another plaintiff or defendant. The number of parties also may contract or expand during the course of litigation.[1] Parties may exit the proceedings if they prevail on a pretrial motion arguing that the court has no jurisdiction over them or that there is no legal or factual basis for the claims asserted against them. Additional parties may join the litigation, either because they want to join, because they are compelled to join by an existing party, or because related lawsuits are consolidated.

In addition to the plaintiff and defendant, numerous other people play some role in the typical lawsuit. Prior to trial, the parties' attorneys and their staffs,[2] private investigators, and other consultants help prepare the case for trial. The attorneys who represent the parties provide several critical functions. They uncover evidence, and then assess, organize, and attempt to present it in ways that serve their clients' interests. They research and study the law applicable to the case and make legal arguments intended to produce favorable results for their clients. They counsel their clients regarding settlement alternatives and other critical decisions that must be made during the litigation process.

At trial, a jury or the trial judge serves as a fact-finder whose job is to determine which evidence presented by the parties is most credible.[3] The trial judge presides over the trial and determines the applicable substantive and procedural law.[4] Expert and lay witnesses may testify. Court personnel manage the court's calendar and perform other administrative functions. Appellate court judges may enter the process to decide appeals.[5] Finally, law enforcement officials may participate by enforcing the trial or appellate court's decision.

In a sense, the general public also participates in most lawsuits. Unless portions of the court record are sealed or the public and the press are excluded from all or some portion of a trial to protect a vulnerable witness (for example, a child who has been sexually abused), maintain the confidentiality of a trade secret, or serve some other compelling interest, all pretrial hearings, trials, and appellate court proceedings are open to the public, and all court documents are available for public examination.

What Are the Basic Stages of the Process from Beginning to Final Resolution?

The litigation process begins when the plaintiff files a formal, written complaint with the trial court and serves it on the defendant. A complaint summarizes the plaintiff's claims against the defendant, the plaintiff's view of the facts that give rise to the claims, and the relief that the plaintiff seeks through the lawsuit. The defendant must answer the complaint or file a motion asking the court to dismiss the lawsuit because the complaint fails to state a claim recognized by law or because the court lacks jurisdiction over the subject matter of the lawsuit or the defendant.[6] If the court denies the defendant's motion to dismiss the lawsuit, the defendant must answer the complaint, at which point the process begins to progress through various pretrial stages.

The plaintiff's ability to compel the defendant's participation in litigation is a distinctive feature of litigation as a dispute resolution process. Because of this feature, litigation is the default process for resolution of disputes recognized by law, and other dispute resolution processes typically occur in the shadow of litigation, regardless of whether a lawsuit has yet been filed. If the defendant refuses or otherwise fails to participate, the court ordinarily will issue a default judgment granting the plaintiff the relief requested in the complaint. The plaintiff can then enforce the judgment (often with the help of law enforcement authorities) by seizing the defendant's property, garnishing the defendant's wages, or taking other actions permitted by law.

During the pretrial stages of litigation, the parties engage in discovery, a process by which they gather evidence from each other and from third parties.[7] Additionally, the parties will identify witnesses, determine what they will testify about at trial, develop legal theories that support their positions, and develop a trial strategy. Finally, the parties will interact with the judge through conferences and hearings on motions to focus the claims, issues, and evidence to be considered during the trial.

The trial itself also occurs in stages. Jury trials begin with selection of the jury. Next, the parties' attorneys make opening statements that express their own partisan perspectives regarding the facts and the outcome required by applicable law. Each side then presents its case (with the plaintiff usually going first), and the other attempts to discredit that case through cross-examination of witnesses and other techniques intended to undermine evidence the other side presented. After each side has presented its case, the parties make closing arguments, and the fact finder (jury or judge) then privately takes the evidence under consideration and renders a decision.[8]

The decision does not become final until all opportunities for appeal have been exhausted, and that can take many months or years following a trial. Once all opportunities for appeal have been exhausted, the last decision of the highest court that considered the case is final and binding upon all parties, and the claims and issues presented by the case cannot be relitigated by the same parties in a new lawsuit.[9]

Overall, the process can be quite lengthy. In 2002, the median time between the filing of a complaint and commencement of trial in federal civil cases was twenty months.[10] Over 70 percent of these trials were concluded in four days.[11] It typically takes less time to reach trial in civil matters in state courts, but it almost always takes several months.[12]

Where Will the Proceedings Occur?

The main stage in any lawsuit is a courthouse. The plaintiff who initiates the suit files it with a specific court—say, the United States District Court sitting in Chicago—but that court may or may not ultimately try the case. The court selected by the plaintiff must have jurisdiction over the subject matter of the dispute and the defendant. It also must be a reasonably convenient forum for the proceeding.

Some courts have jurisdiction to resolve almost any type of civil dispute among parties. This is true of most state trial courts, which sometimes are referred to as courts of general jurisdiction. Other courts have very limited jurisdiction. For example, some states have probate courts that only hear cases involving the disposition of property under wills. Some courts have subject matter jurisdiction that overlaps with the jurisdiction of other state or federal courts, while retaining exclusive jurisdiction over particular types of cases. Federal courts, for example, have exclusive jurisdiction over copyright infringement claims.

A plaintiff's right to compel a defendant to participate in litigation in a court may have geographical limitations. Generally speaking, defendants may not be forced to appear before a court located in a state if they have not had sufficient contacts with that state to make them reasonably anticipate that they might be sued there.[13] Even in a case in which the defendant's contacts with the state are sufficient to satisfy that standard, the defendant may be successful in transferring the case to a court that is more convenient for her or him or for witnesses who will testify at trial.[14]

Which Claims and Issues Will Be Considered?

Generally speaking, courts will entertain only disputes, claims, and issues that can be expressed in terms of rights or liabilities recognized under existing law.[15] Parties are free to assert claims and theories that would require a change in existing law, but courts—and particularly trial courts, in which most litigation activity occurs—are typically reluctant to stray too far from existing legal authority.[16] Notable exceptions such as *Brown* v. *Board of Education* (which reversed the "separate but equal" doctrine enshrined in prior law, thereby catalyzing the desegregation of public schools and other institutions and establishments)[17] exist, but they are not typical of courts' treatment of novel legal arguments.

Legal disputes may be multilayered, involving a diverse set of allegations, issues, interests, and interpersonal and social considerations and dynamics. A dispute stemming from a minor auto accident may present many complex and important questions in addition to the comparatively simple questions of liability and the extent of damages on which applicable negligence law focuses. For example, should the low-income, uninsured driver who caused the accident have to take his or her child out of daycare or forfeit his or her home so that what little equity there is in it can fund the cost of repairing the other, wealthy driver's new Mercedes-Benz? Assume that the wealthy driver insulted the uninsured driver harshly, and that the uninsured driver responded with a series of racial slurs. How should either of these sets of comments be redressed, if at all?

Most courts would be unlikely to grant the negligent driver any relief from liability, since negligence law generally holds a person accountable for the full economic value of the damages he or she causes, regardless of resource disparities between the parties.[18] As a result, the relative economic impact of the outcome of the case on each of the parties almost certainly will not be considered. Similarly, the consequences of the parties' respective insults and racial slurs will be overlooked in a state that does not recognize a legal claim arising from psychological injuries unrelated to physical injuries and which does not have civil or criminal laws against racial slurs. Features of a dispute that do not fit into some established "legal category" are likely to be disregarded in litigation.

What Information Will Be Considered and How and When Will It Be Exchanged?

Only information that is relevant to a legal claim or defense and which is admissible under the rules of evidence applicable in the jurisdiction in which the court sits may be introduced at trial. Many types of information that would be considered relevant, useful, and reasonably trustworthy in other dispute resolution processes are inadmissible in litigation. For example, documents and photographs that cannot be authenticated by their creator or caretaker typically are inadmissible at trial. Likewise, testimony about what someone else said, which is known as "hearsay" testimony, is often inadmissible.[19] In a lawsuit regarding injuries arising out of a traffic accident, for instance, the plaintiff ordinarily would not be permitted to testify that a bystander said the defendant ran a red light. The plaintiff must produce the witness at trial to testify firsthand about what the witness saw. While this certainly makes the evidence more credible, it also makes the process more expensive and complicated.

As noted earlier, litigants gather and develop evidence and exchange other types of information during a pretrial phase of the litigation process called "discovery." Information gathering and exchange activities during discovery are highly formalized. They include written requests for documents, focused written questions to which another party must respond, and transcribed depositions of witnesses. During discovery, parties can seek information that would not be admissible as evidence at trial, provided the information is reasonably likely to lead to the discovery of admissible evidence.[20] The discovery phase is long, contentious, cumbersome, and expensive in many lawsuits. Information about the true interests, objectives, and preferences that underlie the position each party is attempting to advance or defend through the lawsuit may or may not be sought or disclosed prior to trial.

What Substantive Standards Will Determine the Outcome of the Process?

As indicated earlier, courts typically entertain only those claims and defenses, and grant only those types of remedies, that are recognized under current law. These legally recognized claims, defenses, and remedies are established by statutes enacted by legislative bodies, orders and regulations issued by executive officers and agencies, or the written decisions of courts.[21] They arguably embody some public authority's vision of justice regarding the subject matter of the parties' dispute, insofar as justice can be practically expressed and achieved through law and the workings of the legal system.

Law is not, however, the only source of justice principles in society. Religious, philosophical, and cultural traditions also offer norms that may dictate a different outcome in a dispute than those embodied in existing law. Whereas courts and other legal actors sometimes look to these extralegal norms for guidance when making decisions or developing new law,[22] the outcome of most lawsuits is determined through the application of legal norms for which the original rationale may now be obscure.

The outcome of a trial depends primarily upon the parties' relative success at proving their respective claims and defenses by presenting evidence and discrediting the evidence offered against them. In a civil lawsuit, the plaintiff typically has the burden of establishing that the preponderance of the evidence (that is, more than half, in terms of its persuasive value) supports his or her claim against a defendant. The defendant carries the burden of proof with respect to any legally recognized defenses on which it seeks to rely.

Who Determines the Outcome?

Litigation is designed to accomplish two primary tasks: determine the facts of a case and apply applicable law to the facts to reach a conclusion about which party will prevail and what relief the prevailing party will receive. In many cases in the United States, a citizen jury serves as the fact finder,[23] answering such questions as Did the allegedly defective toy cause the child's injuries? or What damages did the manufacturer suffer as a result of its supplier's delayed shipment? The judge determines which substantive and procedural legal principles govern the case, instructs the jury about how to apply the law to the facts, and decides all disputed questions about trial procedure and the admissibility of evidence.[24] In a trial without a jury, the judge serves both of these functions (that is, fact finding and resolving legal issues).

The decision by the fact finder provisionally resolves the legal case before the court (if not necessarily the underlying conflict). Sometimes the resolution is completely in favor of one of the parties, and sometimes it represents a compromise decision that grants each of the parties only a portion of what they sought from the court. The outcome of a trial is provisional because a party who is unhappy with it typically has the right to appeal the decision to a higher court for reconsideration. The trial typically does finalize an "official" version of the facts that gave rise to the dispute, however, because it is the only stage in litigation in which evidence is presented.

If the case is appealed, appellate courts examine the record of the trial court proceeding to determine whether the trial judge misapplied the applicable law to either the procedural or the substantive aspects of the case. If an appellate court determines that the law was misapplied, it may reverse the trial court decision or, if it finds that the trial judge excluded admissible evidence or committed some other type of procedural error, it may return the case to the trial court for further consideration or retrial. Appellate courts do not weigh evidence or make factual determinations, though they do judge whether a trial court considered all admissible evidence, excluded evidence that was inadmissible, and properly applied the law to the facts.

What Types of Outcomes Are Possible?

If a plaintiff prevails at trial, the court will grant the plaintiff some form of relief. Courts can award three principal types of relief in civil cases: money damages, equitable relief, and declaratory relief. Money damages are the most common form of relief in cases involving physical or psychological harm to persons, reputational harm to persons or corporations and other legal entities, destruction or diminution in the value of property, financial loss under contracts and other business arrangements, and other injuries for which one would expect financial compensation or for which no other form of relief can practically be provided. A court will grant "equitable" relief when money would not be adequate compensation and it can practically fashion some other adequate form of relief. For example, because plots of real estate are not fungible, courts in many jurisdictions will compel a recalcitrant seller to follow through on a sale of property rather than allowing her or him to breach the contract and pay the buyer money damages. In a child custody dispute, a divorced parent who was previously awarded physical custody of the couple's children may later be prevented from taking them to a distant state, because that would make it impractical for the other parent to exercise his or her visitation rights. Declaratory relief consists of a pronouncement by the court regarding some contested matter. In a contract dispute, for instance, the court might declare the meaning of a disputed provision, thereby clarifying the parties' respective obligations under the agreement.

Some people wrongly believe that litigation always produces "winner take all" outcomes. While it frequently does, litigation also sometimes produces outcomes that strike a balance among the parties' respective claims and interests. In a personal injury case, for example, the court might award the plaintiff only partial compensation for injuries if it determines the injuries are partially attributable to the plaintiff's own negligence. In the U.S. Supreme Court's famous *Roe* v. *Wade* decision, which established a woman's limited constitutional right to obtain an abortion, the Court struck a balance between a pregnant woman's interest in personal autonomy and the value of the life of the unborn human fetus by prohibiting late-term abortions in most circumstances.[25]

Furthermore, disputants sometimes choose to affect whether litigation will result in an all-or-nothing resolution of their dispute. Parties may agree to present only some of the issues at the core of their dispute to the court for resolution, leaving others to be resolved by agreement—or, failing that, further litigation—based upon the court's decision on the initial issues litigated. Or, parties might agree in advance what the remedy will be if a trial or appellate court determines that the defendant is liable. For example, in a class action suit initiated by older and retired I.B.M. employees who alleged that the company discriminated against them when it changed the terms of their pension plan, the parties reached a partial, post-trial settlement pursuant to which I.B.M. guaranteed the plaintiffs a minimum payment of $320 million dollars in exchange for their agreement that the company would not be required to pay more than an additional $1.4 billion if the trial court's ruling against the company was upheld on appeal.[26]

The types of relief available through litigation give courts a great deal of flexibility in shaping outcomes that redress disputants' legally recognized grievances. There are some types of relief, however, which courts either cannot grant or which are less likely to be effective if they do. Perhaps most notably, courts cannot compel unwilling parties to apologize or make other expressions of genuine regret. Imposing terms that require unwilling parties to cooperate for significant lengths of time may also prove relatively fruitless. In the end, it is possible that a party who "wins" a lawsuit will be granted some form of relief that it considers inferior to the relief it expected to obtain through another dispute resolution process (though parties typically remain free to negotiate an alternative resolution of the dispute even after a court has rendered its decision).

ADVANTAGES AND DISADVANTAGES OF LITIGATION AS A DISPUTE RESOLUTION PROCESS

Many of litigation's distinctive characteristics present both potential benefits and potential burdens relative to other available dispute resolution processes. This makes it difficult to list the pros and cons of litigation under the simple headings "advantages" and "disadvantages." Rather than attempting to do so in this section, I review some of the key characteristics of litigation that distinguish it from other dispute resolution processes and discuss the relative advantages and disadvantages of litigation in light of each.

Litigation Is a Highly Structured and Formal Process

Compared to negotiation, mediation (and other forms of facilitated negotiation), and even arbitration, litigation is a highly structured and formalized dispute resolution process. Well-established rules and procedures address nearly every detail of the process from the time a lawsuit is initiated to final appeal and enforcement of the outcome. This has the advantage of making the procedural aspects of the case reasonably predictable. The parties are aware of the basic stages of the process, the steps within them, and related deadlines at the time a lawsuit is filed, or soon thereafter.

Litigation's great emphasis on procedure, its strict adherence to formal rules of evidence, the opportunity to appeal an unfavorable outcome, and other features also make many lawsuits long and cumbersome. Advocates of alternatives to litigation frequently claim that litigation takes longer and is more expensive than other dispute resolution processes. With consensus-based processes such as negotiation and mediation, this is usually true. Arbitration, however, which can be nearly as structured and formalized as litigation, is not always speedier or cheaper.[27] Some disputants actually prefer a costly, time-consuming process, because they have greater financial resources, less need of a quick resolution, or both. They may believe these factors will cause the other party to abandon the process or settle the dispute on terms much less favorable than those the other party would expect to obtain if it could afford to continue the process.

Precisely because the litigation process is so laden with intricate rules, litigants are often tempted to engage in tactical gamesmanship to delay the process, force their adversaries to incur unnecessary costs, or gain other advantages unrelated to the merits of the case. A judge can impose penalties on a party that abuses the process, but courts are overburdened and unable to police all questionable behavior.[28]

The Outcome and Key Aspects of the Process Are in Others' Control

One of the advantages of litigation (and also arbitration, once the parties have agreed to participate) is that disputants who do not want to negotiate or otherwise cooperate with one another during the proceeding need not do so. An independent tribunal (that is, the judge or jury) will consider the dispute and render a decision that is legally binding on the parties, even if one or more of the parties is uncooperative. When one party is unwilling to deal with other parties, litigation ensures that some opportunity for redress of legally recognized claims will be available. Of course, parties who submit their dispute to a court for resolution may be disappointed by the outcome.

Decisions regarding key aspects of the process also are left to the judge. The court may compel one party to disclose information it would rather not produce, establish inconvenient dates for pretrial hearings and the trial itself, and impose other burdens to which one or more of the parties object. Once again, one of the benefits of involving a third party with the power to make decisions that are binding on the disputants is that the process progresses even when the disputants are unable or unwilling to cooperate. Each party has the potential to make the others bend to its will, provided one can persuade the court to embrace one's own perspective on a disputed procedural issue. Then again, one's opponent may persuade the court to impose requirements of which one disapproves.

One Can Compel Others to Participate, But One Cannot Always Keep Others Out

One of the clear advantages of litigation is the ability to compel others to respond to one's grievances. Unlike mediation, arbitration, and other common dispute resolution processes, litigation proceeds whether or not all participants consent to their involvement. Parties who otherwise would be content to ignore the claims against them must defend themselves or suffer the consequences of failing to do so. Litigation thus ensures that *some* resolution of a dispute will occur, provided the plaintiff's claims are recognized by law and the litigation is filed in the right court.

Once filed, however, lawsuits often have a life of their own. The initial defendant may convince the court that another party is potentially liable, or a nonparty may convince the court that it has a critical stake in the outcome and therefore must be included in the litigation. Separate lawsuits arising out of the same incident or failed transaction may be consolidated to conserve judicial resources and eliminate the possibility of inconsistent decisions. When they occur, these intrusions in a lawsuit may or may not be a bad thing; it all depends on how they affect one's case. Nonetheless, the existing participants in other dispute resolution processes generally retain greater control over the admission of new participants, and many disputants and their lawyers view this as an attractive feature of alternatives to litigation.

Lawyers Typically Dominate the Process

Because litigation is highly formalized and the law applicable to a case may be very technical and hard for a nonlawyer to research and interpret, litigants typically hire lawyers to serve as their agents during the process. Relying on lawyers has obvious benefits. Most courts demonstrate admirable patience and generosity in dealing with nonlawyers who represent themselves, but there is a limit to what a court can and will do to accommodate parties who choose to do so and who lack legal training and experience.

Though examples of lawyers complicating lawsuits (and other matters) are legion, the most significant benefit of involving lawyers in litigation may simply be the increased likelihood that the process will unfold as it should, with the right (in other words, legally recognizable) issues and claims being presented and addressed according to established procedures and protocols. Other benefits lawyers may offer their clients include knowledge of risks, opportunities, and informal norms associated with the process and substance of the lawsuit, and the judgment to use this knowledge effectively as the process unfolds (including during settlement discussions); positive preexisting relationships with court personnel, investigators, expert witnesses, and others who will be or should be involved in the process; superior advocacy and negotiation skills (and a reputation for having them); and the ability to buffer the client from some of the more unpleasant aspects of dealing with other participants in the process, including one's opponents.

Employing a lawyer as one's agent has costs, however, and they are not only financial. First, clients and their lawyers may have different interests with respect to the litigation. A client may want his lawyer to express some of the hostility he has difficulty expressing himself, and the lawyer may be unwilling to do so because of reputational or moral concerns. Second, a lawyer's and a client's respective economic incentives may be misaligned. A lawyer working for a contingency fee may encourage his or her client to accept a smaller settlement to ensure that the client gets paid, or gets paid sooner. A lawyer charging by the hour has fewer incentives to encourage early settlement of a case when that would be in the client's best interest. Finally, the flow of information between lawyer and client may be imperfect, and this could adversely affect the client's interests. These problems can be mitigated in various ways, but they cannot be eliminated.[29]

In Litigation, Some Kinds of Information Are More Reliably Exchanged, While Others Are Ignored

The rules of discovery, which courts will enforce against parties who do not voluntarily comply with them, ensure that a great deal of legally relevant information about the dispute will be exchanged among the parties. Information that would be useful to a party in advocating its perspective, and which is in the possession of another party, may or may not be obtainable in other dispute resolution processes. Even in arbitration proceedings in which discovery is permitted, discovery may have been limited in an arbitration provision to which the parties bound themselves before the dispute arose or by the rules of the organization providing arbitration services (for example, the American Arbitration Association or the International Chamber of Commerce).

While more certain access to legally relevant information is an undeniable advantage of litigation, litigation does not ensure that parties will have access to other types of information that could help them reach a favorable resolution of the dispute. For example, the parties may never learn about each other's true interests and preferences related to the dispute and its resolution or about the complementary resources each may have available for trade. A skilled mediator would elicit this information in her or his effort to help the parties explore the possibilities for creating more individual and joint value through settlement than they expect to achieve through continued litigation.

Litigation Is an Impersonal Process That Can Become Highly Acrimonious

Many of the characteristics of litigation already discussed make it a rather impersonal process for the litigants and arguably increase the odds that the dispute will escalate before it is resolved. Litigation as a social institution is sometimes referred to as the "adversary system," and its structure and many of its procedures do indeed tend to encourage competitive, rather than cooperative, behavior. In the pretrial phases of litigation, the parties and their lawyers communicate primarily through documents that are filed with the court and delivered to one another by mail. Through these documents, often burdensome and expensive fact-finding activities designed to strengthen one's own claims and weaken claims made by other disputants, and arguments made in court (when parties address the judge and jury, rather than each other), each party presents a polarized perspective on the subject matter of the dispute that emphasizes the rightness of one's own position and the folly of others' positions. Most lawsuits are analogous to debates, in which interlocutors listen to one another primarily to gather fodder for attacking the other's position or defending one's own, and not with genuine curiosity about the other's perspective or hope of finding common ground. As a result, the "tone" of a lawsuit often becomes increasingly shrill as the process unfolds.

When disputants are deeply estranged from one another or have no expectation of further interaction apart from the lawsuit, they may appreciate the fact that litigation largely spares them from having to deal with each other. When the parties will have an ongoing relationship, however—as must divorcing parents who will share custody of their children, for example—they miss an important opportunity to begin to reorient their relationship in constructive ways if they use litigation as a means of avoiding one another. Even when the parties will have no ongoing relationship after the dispute is resolved, however, the discomfort of continuing to litigate may outweigh the relatively fleeting discomfort of having to deal with other disputant(s) in the context of a negotiation or mediation process that may produce a resolution of the dispute more quickly.

The Process and the Outcome Usually Are Public

The relative openness of litigation is an advantage to parties seeking public awareness of their claims and perspectives. A plaintiff may want to turn a spotlight on the defendant's conduct to deter similar behavior in the future and put others on notice of the risks of dealing with the defendant, and the defendant may welcome the opportunity to clear his or her good name. However, one or more of the parties may prefer to resolve the dispute more discreetly, as might be the case when feuding siblings decide to dissolve a family business but are unable to reach agreement on their own. When one party wants publicity and another does not (and cannot persuade the court to limit it), litigation confers an obvious advantage on the first party.

The Outcome of a Lawsuit Is Final, Binding, and Enforceable

Once all opportunities for appeal have been exhausted, the final decision is binding upon the parties and cannot be relitigated. A plaintiff who has prevailed on her or his claims can obtain various forms of assistance from courts and law enforcement authorities to enforce the decision against a defendant who refuses to comply with it. The defendant's property may be seized and sold, his or her wages may be garnished, or other actions may be taken to satisfy the court's award to the plaintiff.

These enforcement mechanisms, however, are often time-consuming and expensive. It would be better for all concerned if the defendant were to comply with the outcome willingly. Various studies suggest that parties are more likely to comply with agreements reached through mediation than with judgments imposed through litigation.[30] One must also ask in what sense a dispute is resolved when a court imposes a decision on the parties. It certainly is resolved in the narrow sense that the parties to the lawsuit cannot bring the same claims before the court at a later date. If other, nonlegal issues are left unresolved by the litigation, however, the situation may be left ripe for further disputes. Because both legal and nonlegal issues may be addressed through negotiation and mediation, those processes arguably hold greater potential for resolving the underlying conflict that produced the dispute, to the extent the latter is a subset of the former.

Legal Norms Dictate the Outcome

The existence of legal norms that are generally known and which govern the outcome of claims recognized by law arguably protects parties against completely arbitrary outcomes in disputes that are submitted to litigation. The parties and the court quite often agree about which legal standards apply to a case. When they do not—perhaps because there are inconsistent legal precedents or because the case presents a novel issue—the standards against which the evidence presented at trial will be judged are clarified during pretrial proceedings. This relatively high degree of clarity about the substantive standards applicable to a case helps parties assess the risks of litigation and gives them a measure of confidence that their dispute will be resolved fairly (if, that is, they view the law itself as fair). However, legal norms express only one vision of fairness on a given matter. When parties allow a court to decide the outcome of their dispute, they forgo the opportunity to shape the outcome according to other values and considerations.

Lawsuits Create Legal Norms That Apply to Subsequent Disputes

The reported outcomes of lawsuits that have occurred in the past are one source of the legal norms that dictate the outcome of a pending lawsuit. Many of the final decisions of trial courts in nonjury trials, and nearly all of the decisions of appellate courts, are expressed in writing and published. Courts follow these written decisions in subsequent cases that present the same or similar facts and issues. The possibility of establishing a favorable legal norm is an important feature of litigation for many parties, because judicial precedents create rights and other types of legal "endowments" that may affect how people deal with each other in the future (including how they resolve subsequent disputes).[31]

Consider a public swimming pool being sued by an injured swimmer. If the pool can establish through litigation that its sign reading "No lifeguard on duty—Swim at your own risk" absolves it of liability for personal injuries not attributable to its own negligence, the pool will have a powerful defense against claims made by other injured swimmers in the future. The problem, of course, is that a party who litigates in hope of obtaining a favorable precedent may lose, thereby establishing an unfavorable precedent.

LITIGATION FROM A SOCIAL PERSPECTIVE

Some lawyers and legal scholars argue that litigation is superior to other dispute resolution processes because it produces more just outcomes, is better at protecting weaker parties, and is the primary means by which society's moral values are developed and articulated. Litigation, they argue, creates well-publicized norms that contribute to social stability and serve other, similarly beneficial social purposes.[32] They see consensual dispute resolution processes such as negotiation and mediation as seeking short-term peace at the expense of justice and long-term social stability. From their perspective, litigation has public-oriented, democratic virtues that other dispute resolution processes lack, and they argue that alternatives to litigation should not be encouraged for that reason. They are particularly in favor of litigating cases that present important public policy questions—cases about school prayer, abortion, affirmative action, environmental issues, and other matters involving deep moral disagreements.

Others, including myself, believe that negotiation and other consensual dispute resolution processes can be conducted in ways that enable parties to imagine and implement just outcomes that are better attuned to the context and to the parties' respective concerns and interests, that protect weaker parties and give them a greater voice than they would have in litigation, that contribute to the development of legislation and other legal and nonlegal norms regarding important moral questions, and that create important opportunities for citizen-level democratic participation.[33] Litigation and negotiation (including its facilitated variants) are complementary, mutually reinforcing social processes that each have a legitimate role to play in our nation's moral discourse. Consensual dispute resolution processes have an important and constructive role to play in the pursuit of justice, the development of social norms, and the strengthening of social bonds, even in the context of significant cases involving deep value differences.

In my view, parties to such significant cases ideally should explore the possibility of reaching a consensual resolution of their dispute through an approach to negotiation known as moral deliberation, in which parties explicitly seek mutually recognizable moral grounds on which to justify the terms of an agreement. Participants in deliberative processes seldom completely abandon their own moral perspectives for those of another party, nor should they be expected to do so. Rather, they are encouraged to seek outcomes supported by "reasons that are recognizably moral in form and mutually acceptable in content."[34] One party need not be converted to another's perspective, but each party must be able to acknowledge that every other party is defending a legitimate moral value.[35]

Collective moral deliberation is the hallmark of a concept of democracy called "deliberative democracy."[36] From a deliberative perspective, the goal of democracy is the transformation of political preferences through dialogue, rather than the mere aggregation of preferences through bargaining or voting.[37] Settlement processes that create opportunities for perspective change through collective moral deliberation can be important forums for democratic participation, particularly when they are designed to provide inputs into official policymaking processes. For example, if citizens divided over some moral issue find common ground through a deliberative dispute resolution process, they might express their agreement in draft legislation and then work with legislators in an effort to get it enacted.

Even when parties are incapable of engaging in genuine moral deliberation, however, a settlement reached through crude bargaining for strategic reasons sometimes may be a sensible alternative for parties to a significant case. One party may feel that the risk of an unfavorable ruling—one that would establish or further entrench an undesirable legal norm—is too high, perhaps because the composition of the appellate court before which the case is pending has changed or the court recently has signaled its views in a tangentially related case. A settlement offer may be attractive to the other party, in part because the outcome of litigation is never certain, and in part because the terms of the settlement address other important interests.[38]

Even when cases that present important public policy questions are settled on strategic grounds, this should not be considered deleterious from a social perspective. While such settlements represent missed opportunities to create, reinforce, or refine generally applicable legal norms, only failed efforts to resolve disputes consensually can tell us how urgently a legal norm is needed. From the public's perspective, a major potential benefit of such strategic settlements is, in a sense, delay—delay and a winnowing of the number of cases brought before courts for resolution. With time, the issues brought before courts may be further refined, and the perspective of one of the parties (or yet another perspective) on the issues may come to predominate, so that creation of a legal norm becomes unnecessary or a subsequent judicial decision on the matter, to the extent it is consistent with an emerging social consensus, may be more widely accepted. Because judge-made law is created by a very small number of public officials (that is, the trial and appellate judges who hear cases) in response to issues framed by as few as two individuals, and because judicial decisions typically go unchecked by the other branches of government, judge-made law should, in my view, be created cautiously and sparingly.

WHEN, THEN, IS LITIGATION BEST?

In the real world, the vast majority of disputes that give rise to litigation are settled through negotiation (including facilitated negotiation processes such as mediation).[39] Why, then, are lawsuits filed in the first place, and when might it make sense to litigate a case to a final decision?

When selecting a dispute resolution process, it is important to align the process with one's purposes.[40] Litigation may be an appropriate process choice in any of the following circumstances:

• *Uncooperative parties.* When other disputants are unwilling to negotiate in good faith toward a mutually beneficial resolution of the dispute, litigation may be unavoidable and an effective way to bring uncooperative parties to the bargaining table. Litigation may be particularly appropriate in situations in which the other party is uncooperative and the dispute arises out of a one-time interaction, or the parties do not otherwise expect or desire an ongoing relationship.

• *Alternative to negotiation.* When negotiation commenced before a lawsuit was filed, and one is now having difficulty achieving one's reasonable aspirations in the negotiation, it may be necessary to do more than threaten litigation. It may be necessary to file a lawsuit to develop one's alternative to a negotiated resolution of the dispute, and to demonstrate that one has confidence in that alternative.

• *Reputational effects.* A party who is subjected to multiple, dubious claims may be wise to litigate to establish a reputation for toughness that may deter some potential claimants from asserting their claims.

• *Desire for openness and publicity.* Litigation usually ensures openness of the proceedings and record, and important lawsuits often attract the public's attention. Other dispute resolution processes typically are less open and less publicly visible, though they can be conducted in ways that simulate the openness of litigation when that is the parties' preference. Where one or more of the parties has a strong desire for an open and public process, however, litigation may indeed be the best choice.

• *Legal precedent.* When establishment of a norm to which all people (or at least a significant group of people) will be legally bound is important, and when political, economic, or other factors make it impossible or impractical to establish the norm through legislation, attempting to create a judicial precedent may be one's best alternative. An insurance carrier that foresees multiple lawsuits over time regarding enforceability of an industry standard policy provision designed to exclude coverage of an unusual type of loss may wish to resolve the issue once and for all so that it can more accurately forecast its financial exposure. Parties on either side of a dispute about school prayer or another morally charged issue may be particularly eager to establish a legal precedent validating their perspective. However, parties arguably should be cautious about using litigation as a tactic for political activism when neither a majority of the members of the Supreme Court nor a substantial number of citizens currently seem to support their cause. As Jack Greenberg, former director-counsel of the NAACP Legal Defense Fund, has said, "Lawyers ought to try to avoid creating a new *Plessy* v. *Ferguson* and should apply energies where they will be most productive."[41] It may be better to accept what one may be able to achieve through other forms of political engagement than to further entrench a norm that one opposes, when the risk of creating an adverse precedent is great.

CONCLUSION

Because other approaches to dispute resolution—particularly negotiation and mediation—frequently occur against the backdrop of litigation, it is important that disputants, as well as mediators and others who hope to help parties resolve their disputes, understand the litigation process, including its relative advantages and disadvantages. Litigation is an indispensable dispute resolution alternative both for aggrieved citizens and for society, because it helps ensure that legitimate grievances are resolved, and that they are resolved relatively peacefully. It is neither better nor worse than other dispute resolution processes. While litigation should not be initiated or continued reflexively, disputants should not shy from it when it is the best approach to serving their legitimate objectives.

Notes

1. See, for example, Rules 19, 20, 22, and 24 of the Federal Rules of Civil Procedure (2003), which allow the addition and subtraction of parties in various situations.

2. It is possible to represent oneself, but, with the exception of indigent persons and prison inmates who are unable to secure counsel, relatively few people do so.

3. The number of jurors in a jury trial varies depending upon the court (state or federal) and type of case (civil or criminal), but a jury normally has between six and twelve members. See, for example, Indiana Rules of the Court, Jury Rule 16 (2004), requiring twelve jurors in a criminal trial and six jurors in a civil trial. The jury is selected by the litigants (or, rather, their attorneys) in federal trials and by either the litigants or the judge in trials before state courts.

4. See T. M. Fine, "How the U.S. Court System Functions." [http://usinfo.org/usia/usinfo.state.gov/journals/itdhr/0999/ijde/fine.htm]. Last visited September 2004.

5. See Fine, "How the U.S. Court System Functions," 2004.

6. See the section titled "Where Will the Proceedings Occur?" for a discussion of the courts' subject matter jurisdiction and personal jurisdiction.

7. See the section titled "What Information Will Be Considered and How and When Will It Be Exchanged?" for a discussion of the discovery process.

8. The defendant may file a motion at the close of the plaintiff's presentation of evidence or at the end of the evidentiary stage of the trial asking the court to dismiss the case for lack of sufficient evidence to support the plaintiff's claims. See Federal Rules of Civil Procedure, rule 50(a) (2003). Similarly, the losing party may file a motion after the jury renders its verdict, asking the court to dictate a different outcome because the jury misapplied the law to the facts of the case. See Federal Rules of Civil Procedure, rule 50(b) (2003).

9. The doctrine of *res judicata* prevents a party from litigating the same claim against the same party if there is a judgment on the merits of the case. See, for example, *Cromwell* v. *County of Sac.,* 94 U.S. 351 (1877), p. 352; and *People Who Care* v. *Rockford Board of Education,* 68 F.3d 172 (7th Cir. 1995), p. 177. Similarly, the doctrine of collateral estoppel prevents the same issues from being litigated if resolution of the issue was necessary in a prior valid judgment against the same party. See, for example, *Montana* v. *United States,* 440 U.S. 147, 153 (1979), p. 153.

10. See Figure 11 in M. Galanter, "The Vanishing Trial: An Examination of Trials and Related Matters in Federal and State Courts," *Journal of Empirical Legal Studies,* 2004, 1, 627–636.

11. See Figure 10 in Galanter, "The Vanishing Trial: An Examination of Trials and Related Matters in Federal and State Courts," 2004.

12. See M. Heise, "Justice Delayed? An Empirical Analysis of Civil Case Disposition Time," *Case Western Reserve Law Review,* 2000, *50,* 813–849, for a discussion of the average length of time it takes a civil case to go to trial and the various factors that contribute to delay.

13. See *International Shoe Company* v. *Washington,* 326 U.S. 310 (1945), p. 316, discussing the minimum contacts requirement of a court's personal jurisdiction.

14. See 28 United States Code § 1404 (2004).

15. "The judicial power shall extend to all cases, in law and equity, arising under this Constitution [and] the laws of the United States . . ." (United States Constitution, Article III, Section 2).

16. Courts typically decide cases according to precedent under the doctrine of *stare decisis,* a judicial policy that ensures predictable and consistent development of the law (*Payne* v. *Tennessee,* 501 U.S. 808 [1991], p. 827).

17. *Brown* v. *Board of Education,* 347 U.S. 483 (1954).

18. See *McCahill* v. *New York Transportation Company*, 201 N.Y. 221 (1911), in which the court adopted the eggshell plaintiff doctrine making the negligent person responsible for all direct effects of his or her actions regardless of the injured plaintiff's prior infirmity.

19. See C. B. Mueller and L. C. Kirkpatrick, *Evidence* (3rd ed.) (New York: Aspen Publishers, 2003), pp. 693–994.

20. See Federal Rules of Civil Procedure, rule 26(b)(1) (2003).

21. In cases involving events that occurred in more than one jurisdiction, or a contract that expressly adopts the substantive law of a jurisdiction other than the one in which the lawsuit is situated, complicated questions sometimes arise about which jurisdiction's law applies to the case.

22. One example is the weight given to custom among merchants in cases involving commercial disputes. See, for example, *Thomas* v. *Gusto Records, Inc.*, 939 F.2d 395 (6th Cir. 1991), p. 398, in which the court expressly recognized that New York precedent allowed custom to fill gaps in contracts.

23. Regarding the right to a jury, the 7th Amendment (which "preserves" the right to a jury trial) has been interpreted to require courts to engage in a historical examination of common law practices related to use of juries in specific circumstances prior to adoption of the Constitution. In short, the right to a jury is not absolute. In some kinds of actions, neither party can demand a jury. If no jury right exists, or if neither party requests a jury, a judge conducts all fact finding. See, for example, *Chauffeurs, Teamsters and Helpers, Local 391* v. *Terry*, 494 U.S. 558 (1990), pp. 564–565.

24. Trial judges sometimes delegate decision-making authority over certain pretrial procedural matters to a minor officer of the court known as a magistrate or special master (or some other title, depending on the jurisdiction). In such cases, the officer's rulings are subject to appeal to the trial judge.

25. *Roe* v. *Wade*, 410 U.S. 113 (1973).

26. See D. C. Johnston, "I.B.M. Makes Deal in Move to Close Big Pension Case," *New York Times*, Sept. 30, 2004, A1, reporting the terms of settlement.

27. See Public Citizen, "The Costs of Arbitration." [http://www.publiccitizen.org/publications/release.cfm?ID=7173]. Last visited October 2004.

28. See *Chambers* v. *NASCO, Inc.*, 501 U.S. 32 (1991), p. 44, for a discussion about the court's inherent power to sanction a party for abuse of the judicial process.

29. For a more complete discussion of principle-agent dynamics in dispute resolution, see Peppet, Chapter Twelve, this volume.

30. See, for example, C. McEwen and R. Maiman, "Small Claims Mediation in Maine: An Empirical Assessment," *Maine Law Review*, 1981, pp. 237–268.

31. See R. H. Mnookin and L. Kornhauser, "Bargaining in the Shadow of the Law: The Case of Divorce," *Yale Law Journal*, 1979, *88*, pp. 968–969, which argues that disputants' relative substantive and procedural rights influence negotiation behavior

and outcomes. Conversely, R. C. Ellickson, *Order Without Law: How Neighbors Settle Disputes* (Cambridge, Mass.: Harvard University Press, 1991), reports results of an empirical study of animal trespass and boundary fence dispute settlements among farmers and ranchers in Shasta County, California, in which parties based settlements on informal norms rather than on relevant legal principles, of which they were generally unaware. J. Alexander, "Do the Merits Matter? A Study of Settlements in Securities Class Actions," *Stanford Law Review*, 1991, *43*, pp. 505–568, also reports results of an empirical study of securities fraud settlements in which settlement amounts bore little or no relation to the expected value of trial outcomes.

32. See, for example, O. Fiss, "Against Settlement," *Yale Law Journal*, 1984, *93*, p. 1087; and D. Luban, "Settlements and the Erosion of the Public Realm," *Georgetown Law Journal*, 1995, *83*, 2619–2662.

33. See, for example, C. Menkel-Meadow, "Whose Dispute Is It Anyway? A Philosophical and Democratic Defense of Settlement (in Some Cases)," *Georgetown Law Journal*, 1995, *83*, 2663–2696; and J. R. Seul, "Settling Significant Cases," *Washington Law Review*, 2004, *79*, 881–968.

34. A. Guttman and D. Thompson, *Democracy and Disagreement* (Cambridge, Mass.: Harvard University Press, 1996), p. 57.

35. Theodore Benditt argues that acknowledgment of "the sincerity and earnestness of one's opponent" is a legitimate basis for compromise (Benditt, T. M. "Compromising Interests and Principles." In J. R. Pennock and J. W. Chapman (eds.), *Compromise in Ethics, Law, and Politics.* New York: New York University Press, 1979, p. 35). In my view, it is not enough to believe that one's opponent is sincere. One must also believe one's opponent's perspective is grounded in a legitimate moral perspective. Hitler no doubt sincerely believed that genocide was a justifiable means of "purifying" the German population and culture, but absolute genetic and cultural homogeneity are not morally defensible values.

36. See generally Guttman and Thompson, *Democracy and Disagreement,* 1996.

37. See J. Elster, "Introduction," in J. Elster (ed.), *Deliberative Democracy* (Cambridge, Mass.: Cambridge University Press, 1998).

38. The settlement reached on the eve of oral argument before the United States Supreme Court in the case of *United States* v. *Board of Education* provides an excellent example of the strategic settlement of a significant case: *United States* v. *Board of Education* 832 F. Supp. 836 (D.N.J. 1993), aff'd. en banc. sub nom *Taxman* v. *Board of Education*, 91 F.3d 1547 (3rd Cir. 1996) cert. granted sub nom *Piscataway Township Board of Education* v. *Taxman*, 521 U.S. 1117 (1997), cert. dismissed, 522 U.S. 1010 (1997). For an extended discussion of the settlement, see Seul, "Settling Significant Cases," 2004, p. 125ff.

39. See Galanter, "The Vanishing Trial," 2004, which charts a precipitous decline in the number of federal and state civil and criminal trials over recent decades, despite increases in the number of case filings, lawyers, and judges.

40. For a general discussion on aligning process and purposes, see F.E.A. Sander and S. B. Goldberg, "Fitting the Forum to the Fuss: A User-Friendly Guide to Selecting an ADR Procedure," *Negotiation Journal*, 1994, *10*, p. 60.

41. J. Greenberg, "Litigation for Social Change: Methods, Limits and Role in Democracy," *Record of the Association of the Bar of the City of New York*, 1974, *29*, p. 349. *Plessy* v. *Ferguson*, 163 U.S. 537 (1896) upheld a Louisiana statute requiring separate but equal railway accommodations for white and colored persons.

CHAPTER TWENTY-TWO

Consensus Building and ADR

Why They Are Not the Same Thing

Lawrence E. Susskind

My interest is in complex multiparty, multi-issue disputes—particularly those that arise in the public arena. Should there be a new oil refinery off the coast? How should a city address the problem of affordable housing? Questions like these sometimes devolve into lawsuits. Advocacy groups, developers, industry groups, individual corporations, and even governmental agencies sometimes choose to enter (or are dragged into) the realm of litigation. Yet a courtroom is usually not the right setting to bring all the relevant stakeholders together to talk through their differences on such complex issues.

What is perhaps surprising to proponents of alternative dispute resolution (ADR) is that court-connected dispute resolution efforts are not likely to represent much of an improvement over the traditional forms of litigation once complex public issues reach the courthouse. Both in litigation and in most forms of court-connected dispute resolution, participation is limited to the named parties. Courts sometimes give formal recognition or intervenor status to certain outside groups, but such groups appear at the table only if they are self-starting, self-funded, and well-organized enough to put forward a claim. Thus all the relevant stakeholders are often not at the table. Furthermore, in most forms of court-connected ADR, all parties are hyperconscious of the fact that they will be heading back to court if settlement negotiations break down. As a result, they tend to give priority to the narrow set of questions that got the case into court.[1]

Consciousness of the prospect of a return to the courthouse also tends to cause the parties to work hard to keep secret any information that might hurt them in subsequent litigation. In court-connected ADR, parties rarely demonstrate a commitment to invest in joint fact finding to establish a shared scientific basis for decision making. And because many forms of court-connected ADR offer the parties some degree of confidentiality, the process is unlikely to generate legitimacy in the public eye.

What is required in many public disputes is some other way of bringing representatives of all key groups together, in a nonpartisan, problem-solving mode, to work out an informed agreement that not only satisfies the parties but serves the public interest as well.[2] Such policy dialogues or dispute resolution efforts usually require the assistance of a highly trained mediator. In this respect, they may look, in part, like court-connected ADR. However, an ideal approach to consensus building would take place before any litigation has been filed, allowing the ultimate goal of the process to be the "best possible agreement" rather than to "do better than each side would in court." ADR as it is typically practiced is not likely to succeed in the context of complex, public disputes.

In this chapter, I will describe the key steps in consensus building and show how it works in the public disputes context. I will describe how public dispute mediation is initiated, describe why the differences between two-party and multiparty negotiation are important, and explain how and why consensus building and court-connected ADR are not the same thing.

THE ADR CONTINUUM

Many authors writing about ADR think in terms of a continuum with court at one end and negotiation at the other. At the court end, the parties give up control over both the design of the procedure for resolving their dispute and the outcome in particular applications of that procedure. At the negotiation end, the parties retain complete control over both. Mediation, in this model, falls somewhere on the negotiation side of the continuum because the parties retain the ability to make the final decision on outcome. Arbitration, with its third-party-imposed outcomes, falls closer to the court end of the continuum. Depending on their design, hybrid approaches such as the minitrial, the summary jury trial, or med-arb fall somewhere between these common ADR methods on the process continuum.[3]

This image of a process-based continuum is enticing, but inaccurate. Instead, I suggest that we should think in terms of a continuum with court-related activities on one half and non-court-related activities on the other. Mediation used in the context of court-connected dispute resolution belongs on the court half of the continuum. Mediation used before a lawsuit is even contemplated belongs on the other. As will be clear in the following, it is the reference to what will happen or might happen if a disagreement goes to court that is most important, not the choice of a dispute resolution mechanism.

THE KEY STEPS IN THE CONSENSUS-BUILDING PROCESS

Public disputes arise in several different forms. The most common are siting disputes—decisions about whether to locate facilities in particular places. For example, should there be a new wind farm in the federal waters off the coast of Massachusetts? A second type of dispute focuses on policy disagreements. For example, how should a community respond to a state mandate that municipalities take steps to ensure the affordability of housing in their area?[4] These and related disputes typically arise in response to legislative, administrative, or even judicial action. A city council might vote to rezone land so that an offshore facility has nowhere to bring its power lines ashore. A state agency might refuse to grant a license for a proposed energy facility on the grounds that it will have unacceptable impacts of various kinds. A court might declare an existing zoning or property tax system unconstitutional because it precludes equal access to the housing market for certain protected groups.

Both types of disputes—siting disputes and policy disagreements—can and sometimes do end up in court. In fact, however, they are political battles that ought to be resolved in the public policymaking arena. Framing such disputes as due process or equal protection questions that require legal adjudication side-steps the fact that any resolution will require complex political trade-offs. Such trade-offs ought not to be made by judges who do not stand for election. The perceived fairness, efficiency, stability, and wisdom of public policy choices depend more on the extent to which the stakeholders have a chance to speak their mind directly, share information, and otherwise engage in a problem-solving process than they do on the intricacies of how legal issues are resolved. Despite the numerous democratic channels through which groups can express their pleasure (or displeasure!) with the actions of their elected and appointed officials, these channels sometimes do not produce political acceptance of public policy trade-offs.

Thus, new consensus-building strategies have begun to supplement traditional representative, democratic decision-making techniques. These are not alternatives to court adjudication of disputes as much as they are methods of supplementing traditional legislative and administrative procedures. They bring specially selected representatives of all stakeholding groups together for face-to-face conversations, managed by professional neutrals who take on different roles from their counterparts in court-connected ADR systems.[5]

The goal in consensus building is to generate creative deals that allow everyone involved to come out better off than they otherwise probably would *and* that meet the broader public interest as well. Consensus-building efforts do not promise that everyone will get everything they want—that may be impossible. Instead, the objective is to bring more people into a disciplined, problem-solving process to generate trades or "packages" that create as much "value" as possible for all stakeholders and to confront difficult trade-offs in a completely transparent way.

In the following section I will use a facility-siting case to illustrate the five steps in the consensus-building process and to highlight the ways in which such efforts differ from ADR practice. The five steps are (1) *convening* all the relevant parties, (2) *clarifying the responsibilities* of the participants and the ad hoc assembly as a whole, (3) *deliberating* in a way that generates intelligently crafted "packages" that meet the needs of all the relevant stakeholders, (4) *making decisions* of a sort that generate near-unanimous agreement, and (5) *implementing agreements* on all informally negotiated commitments.

Convening

Convening occurs at the outset of a consensus-building process. Typically, a convenor—an elected or appointed official with an interest in generating an informed consensus—brings in a mediation team to prepare a written assessment. The most important product of a conflict assessment is an appraisal of the prospect of reaching agreement made by a professional neutral.[6] If the odds of reaching agreement are not high and key players are unwilling to participate, consensus building will not work. Prior to convening the parties in a consensus-building process, therefore, assessing these factors is key.

In the context of a lawsuit, getting the "right" parties to the table is a nonissue because the litigation process resolves (narrowly) the question of who is involved in the dispute. It is much more difficult to figure out who all the stakeholders are and who should represent them in an informal problem-solving forum when there is no limit on the number of parties. For this, consensus builders use a technique called conflict assessment.[7] Conflict assessment involves off-the-record interviews with widening circles of potential parties to help map the conflict. Consensus builders formulate not only a list of stakeholders who ought to be invited but also an agenda, a timeline, ground rules, and a budget.

In a facility-siting case, for example, a mediation team might meet early on with neighbors who are ardently opposed to the building of a new energy plant in their community. The conflict assessors might also fan out and try to meet with energy users who may be worried that without the new plant, energy supplies might be dangerously limited. And the assessment would not be complete until the neutrals meet with groups such as environmental advocates and fishermen concerned about the coastal impact of a new generating facility. In some cases, potential stakeholder groups might not have been paying any attention to the budding controversy. When approached, however, after considering what is at stake, these groups could become important players in a consensus-building process. Although court-connected ADR practitioners have no responsibility to seek out additional parties, conflict assessors are obligated to seek out all potential stakeholders.

Clarifying Responsibilities

Once the identified parties have agreed to participate (typically in response to a formal invitation from a convenor), their first task is usually to clarify the role and responsibilities of the ad hoc assembly of which they are a part. Consensus-building groups that operate in the public arena produce only proposals, not decisions. Groups' proposals must then be approved by those with the formal statutory power to do so. The parties, once assembled, jointly decide whether the mediator who did the assessment should stay on to assist with the process. They also begin by initialing the written timetable and ground rules. Public officials operate under "sunshine laws," meaning that in virtually all cases the public must be given notice of and access to the meetings. Although the group can go into "executive session" in the same way a public body does when contracts or personnel matters arise, a great deal of work gets done between meetings as the mediator moves back and forth among the parties, checking reactions to various proposals (using a single-text procedure).[8] Once a consensus-building process is convened, the parties jointly define the ground rules by which they will operate; clarify the scope and timing of the work they will undertake; and specify the roles and responsibilities of the neutral, the representatives of each stakeholder group, and the overall limits on the product of their collaborative efforts.

Returning to the facility-siting example, a state or regional energy regulatory body or licensing agency might invite a group of twenty-five to thirty stakeholder representatives to come together with a mediator based on the results of a conflict assessment. The role of the ad hoc assembly, clarified in the procedural ground rules each participant would sign, would be limited to producing a package of recommendations that would be passed along to the agency.

Deliberating

The main reason consensus building works is that the agenda reflects the interests of the parties. Consensus building assures parties that the issues that are most important to them will be discussed and that they will have an opportunity to make trades across issues they value differently. By exploring such trades, the parties can work until they produce a package that leaves everyone better off than they would likely be if there were no agreement. Parties engage in a face-to-face exchange of views, information, and arguments. On occasion, this exchange leads people to change their views. Because the dialogue is very public, arguments made on their merits (as opposed to self-interested demands) receive greater attention. Secret deals that cannot be justified from the standpoint of the public interest at large are not likely to win support. The product of such conversations is a written agreement, often with contingent commitments tied to certain milestones being reached or events occurring. Unlike a typical public hearing, the dialogue in a consensus-building process—managed by a trained mediator—aims to achieve a resolution. It does not, however, lead to a vote.

In a facility-siting dispute, the parties might take several months to jointly commission appropriate environmental impact or risk-assessment studies. Because these studies are produced by experts chosen collaboratively, neither side is as likely to dismiss the results. This stands in stark contrast to the manner in which parties treat each other's expert witnesses in the context of litigation. The dialogue in a consensus-building process is likely to examine alternative sites and technologies rather than focusing only on the "right" of the proponent to build the facility. It will undoubtedly explore ways in which the facility, if built, might exceed existing pollution control mandates through voluntary actions of the proponent. It might also consider compensatory payments to abutters, even if they are not required by law.

Making Decisions

While some people define consensus as unanimity, most processes of the sort I am describing aim to achieve unanimity but settle for overwhelming agreement as long as two conditions are met. First, each participant must be asked, in person and out loud, whether he or she can "live with" the draft of a final agreement generated by the mediator, in an effort to capture the key points of agreement during the deliberations. If participants say no, they must be given an opportunity to explain their opposition and to suggest further modifications that would render the agreement acceptable to them but no worse for any of the other participants. Second, all the parties must decide together that every reasonable effort has been made to meet the concerns of the "holdouts." At that point, consensus will have been reached. If a key party—one whose support is necessary for implementation—still opposes the agreement, then there is a consensus that no agreement is possible. Typically, parties are asked to sign a written document indicating their support, but only after they have had an opportunity to take the penultimate version of the agreement back to their constituency for review.

Implementing Agreements

Mediated agreements of the sort I describe here are not independently enforceable, in part because they are created by ad hoc representatives of informally organized stakeholding groups. As mentioned, the point of most consensus-building efforts in the public arena is simply to produce a clearly stated proposal that can then be submitted to the relevant elected or appointed bodies for action.

When decision-making bodies commit to the terms of a negotiated agreement, it then becomes enforceable.

Even after an ad hoc dialogue produces an agreement, a convenor may still decide to hold hearings on the group's proposal. The convenor may ultimately decide to modify the proposal, perhaps in response to concerns missed by the consensus-building group. If the convenor modifies the agreement in any substantial way, of course, the consensus may dissipate. Modifications to a consensus proposal frequently produce political backlash and often result in litigation. Alternatively, if the convenor accepts and adopts the informally negotiated agreement (pursuant to the formalities of its statutorily defined decision-making powers), it can reasonably claim to have protected the public interest.

MEDIATORS WITHIN THE CONSENSUS-BUILDING PROCESS

Mediators play a critical role in the consensus-building process, but they differ considerably from their counterparts practicing in court-connected mediation. Their roles in convening are different, and their power over the process is different. They take on different responsibilities, bring their knowledge to the table in different ways, and assume different roles during implementation. Mediators in consensus-building processes even operate with a different set of overarching duties.

Mediators in a consensus-building process play an important role in getting the "right" parties to the table. Using conflict-assessment techniques, the mediator (or mediation team) must make a judgment regarding not only who the relevant stakeholders are but also which group or individual would best represent each stakeholder. In some circumstances, a mediator may even seek to identify a surrogate of some kind to stand in for a hard-to-represent group. Mediators in court-connected processes would rarely undertake such an effort.

In the course of completing several dozen not-for-attribution interviews with potential stakeholders, the mediator(s) in a consensus-building process try to push the parties to clarify their interests; urge them to think realistically about what might happen if they fail to reach a negotiated settlement; help them contemplate the interests of the other likely stakeholders; and imagine the kinds of information that might cause them, as well as others, to alter their judgments about key questions before the group. Some mediators in court-connected ADR might do some of these things some of the time. In a consensus-building process, a mediator must do all of them all of the time (or dramatically increase the odds of failure).

The mediators in a consensus-building process influence whether the process advances to the problem-solving stage. Using the results of their conflict assessments, the mediators recommend to the convenor whether or not to proceed with the consensus-building process. Their recommendation to proceed usually hinges on the key parties having indicated that they will come to the table, reasonably good prospects of finding either common ground or mutually beneficial trades, and a sense that the parties are ready to negotiate in good faith as long as the agenda, ground rules, and behaviors of others seem reasonable. In court-connected ADR, mediators have the ability to withdraw from the mediation process, but in contrast to the consensus-building process, the decision to proceed is primarily in the hands of the disputants.

During the problem-solving stage of a consensus-building process, parties (many of whom may not be directly represented by counsel) often ask the mediator to propose possible settlements. This sometimes occurs in court-connected ADR procedures, particularly in what is called "evaluative mediation."[9] Suggesting substantive outcomes is much more complicated, however, in a multiparty situation. Further, when there are more than two parties outside a court context, coalitions almost always emerge. Depending on the decision rule chosen by the participants (for example, unanimity or overwhelming agreement), the mediator must be very careful in these situations not to interfere with the efforts of a potential "winning coalition" to build sufficient consensus for an agreement that it favors.[10] One of the key elements of consensus building that draws both powerful and relatively powerless parties to the table is the commitment to seek unanimity and the promise to settle for nothing less than overwhelming agreement. This means that weaker groups cannot be ignored or that more powerful groups cannot throw their weight around. The promise to search for consensus is what makes the entire process so appealing (even though it sometimes requires a larger commitment of time and effort than might otherwise be expected). Because mediators in court-connected contexts generally need not concern themselves with coalitional obstacles, mediators in consensus-building processes have more complicated responsibilities.

Mediators in consensus-building processes need to know a great deal about the substantive questions being discussed, if only to keep from impeding the dialogue with trivial questions or requests for explanation. The complex matters of public policy raised in these cases rarely hinge primarily on matters of legal interpretation. Instead, mediators in consensus-building processes are often selected because they have a great deal of technical knowledge about the subject of the dispute. Mediators in court-connected contexts, by contrast, are sometimes selected for their problem-solving or group-management skills.

In consensus-building situations, particularly in the public arena, mediators have responsibilities to parties who are not at the table. That is, they have a responsibility to help the stakeholders achieve an implementable agreement by taking account of the likely political reactions to whatever settlement is reached. At the same time, any agreement that fails to meet the interests of the public-at-large—at least as that is defined by the convenor or other actors with relevant interests and responsibilities—is not likely to be implemented. Thus, the mediator is often called upon to suggest ways of ensuring that negotiated agreements resulting from a consensus-building process respond to the public interest. In some instances, this requires the mediator to take the lead in meeting with the press or making public statements on behalf of the consensus-building process.[11]

There are even instances in which a mediator in a consensus-building process is called upon to help with the implementation of a negotiated agreement. In some cases, mediators will monitor the parties' ongoing performance of the agreement, gauging whether they are meeting the commitments they made during the settlement process. In other cases, mediators will reconvene the stakeholders if assumptions on which a negotiated agreement was based turn out to be wrong. Public disclosure of ongoing consensus-building efforts is important to the legitimacy of the final outcome. Thus, someone has to handle media relations. None of the parties can likely take on this role, as any party would undoubtedly be seen by the press as making comments that are self-serving. The mediator, however, can represent all the participants in a consensus-building process and take the initiative to reconvene the group if one party feels that another has not lived up to its commitments. Many consensus-building agreements address the dilemmas of implementation by including a reconvening clause. According to the terms of the clause, anyone dissatisfied with implementation is obligated to ask the mediator to reconvene the group before that party is entitled to discontinue his or her own efforts to follow though on the promises he or she made. Although similar monitoring and reconvening could be part of the scope of responsibility of neutrals involved in court-connected ADR, they rarely are.

KEY DIFFERENCES BETWEEN TWO-PARTY AND MULTIPARTY NEGOTIATIONS

I have already mentioned the importance of the coalitions and coalitional behavior that seem to take hold as soon as the number of parties involved in a settlement negotiation increases from two to three. Each side moves to find a partner (in a two-against-one game) to help him or her form a winning coalition. At the same time, each player looks for "blocking partners" to aid him or her in deflecting any agreement to which he or she is opposed.

In the context of public disputes, the number of parties can grow very large. While not as complex as global treaty negotiations (in which almost two hundred countries send large official delegations to participate in negotiations over complex documents), consensus-building efforts in the public arena often involve more than fifteen parties.[12] Add the prospect of counsel and technical advisers for each party, and the process of managing a problem-solving conversation becomes complex. Furthermore, as the number of issues (or the technical complexity of issues) increases, a mediator may be called on to summarize work done by subcommittees (between full group meetings) or by consultants to the process.[13] In sum, process management is often a major preoccupation of mediators involved in consensus-building efforts and sometimes requires a team of mediators.

In dialogues involving large numbers of participants in science-intensive policy disputes, neutrals are often called upon to facilitate joint fact finding. Consistent with the consensus-building process, independent scientific inquiries run parallel to the group's discussion of policy questions.[14] Increased scientific uncertainty may require more complex agreements that specify the obligations of each party under different sets of circumstances. Such agreements, in turn, often require a mediator to be called on to monitor events during implementation. While contingent agreements in court-connected ADR processes aim to spell out specific terms of a final settlement,[15] consensus-building proposals commonly specify a schedule of possible next steps depending on what occurs.

In multiparty agreements in the public arena, stakeholders often commit to take actions no existing rules and regulations could require them to take. For instance, in many facility-siting disputes, as mentioned earlier, the final agreement can include voluntary commitments on the part of the industry seeking to build the facility. Perhaps they will make compensatory payments to the community or install pollution-control devices that go well beyond what is mandated by law. As long as these commitments are voluntary, public agencies rarely object. The challenge with such commitments is ensuring compliance. The relevant convenor cannot insist that a regulated entity do more than the law requires. However, voluntarily negotiated commitments growing out of a public consensus-building process can be included as "orders of condition" attached to a formal license or permit issued by a regulatory agency. Implementation of the negotiated agreement thus becomes the domain of the licensing agency. Getting agreements in writing is not the end result in most consensus-building efforts. Rather, finding a way to link the informally negotiated agreement with a formal binding mechanism is necessary. In court-connected ADR efforts, the court offers a relatively simple means of redress for those who feel that the other side is not living up to the terms of a settlement. Consensus building requires a different level of creativity to design nearly self-enforcing agreements.

DESPITE THE SIMILARITIES, CONSENSUS BUILDING IS NOT ANOTHER FORM OF ADR

For the most part, consensus building does not take place "in the shadow of the law" in the same way court-connected ADR does. This makes consensus building much harder to initiate, since it is not obvious who ought to be involved and there are no a priori agreements regarding the rules of engagement. The process differences—described earlier—between consensus building and court-connected ADR suggest that the same mediator might not be appropriate in both contexts. The training, substantive background, and skills required in each setting diverge. While many successful court-connected mediators have legal training, public dispute consensus builders tend to come from the public policy or planning fields.

In a consensus-building process, the parties have to write their own rules and impose their own negotiating structure. Deciding who should be at the table in a consensus-building process is not always clear, and getting the appropriate parties to the table is not always easy. Indeed, mediators in these settings often spend a significant portion of their time at the outset of a dispute resolution effort convincing key parties that it is in their interests to participate. Parties have a clearer set of expectations about the mediation process in a court-connected ADR context, making their participation decision much more straightforward. Court-connected mediators are rarely expected to meet with a reluctant party to convince him or her to get involved. Indeed, in many court-connected circumstances, the parties do not even choose a mediator until they have all agreed to enter the process.

Consensus building, especially in the public arena, requires greater transparency than most court-related ADR procedures. Because a significant portion of the exchange among parties takes place in the public eye, the mediator is generally required to manage interactions with the public—especially the media. Operating in the public eye creates a variety of challenges. When should the mediator go into and come out of private caucuses? Which displays of emotion are genuine and which are merely efforts to play to the audience, and how should each be addressed? What and when should the press hear about the process? How can the mediator manage the process in ways that do not compromise the strategies or interests of any of the parties?

In the consensus-building context, there is a much greater burden on the parties to invent nearly self-enforcing agreements (that is, agreements that contain within them both the incentives and the mechanisms to ensure implementation). A mediator in a consensus-building process seeks out those who are implicated in the emerging agreement, working on behalf of the group to secure appropriate buy-in. Neither the participants nor the mediator in court-connected ADR have such a burden.

To ensure that the public interest is met, a mediator in a consensus-building process must worry about the interests of parties who are not at the table. Public dispute resolution is a form of public policymaking and as such, it is usually held to the same standards of openness, effectiveness, and fairness that apply to other kinds of agency decision making. Convenors, who are the ultimate decision makers, will be held accountable at the end by groups who were not represented in the consensus-building process—even if those groups chose not to participate. At the very least, therefore, consensus-building processes must take account of interests that may not be directly represented.

CONCLUSIONS

The differences between court-connected ADR and consensus building suggest several conclusions. First, moving a dispute into a court-connected ADR process may preclude the possibility of achieving the fairest, most efficient, wisest, and most stable agreement.[16] Court-connected ADR certainly offers no guarantee that the public interest will be met. Second, the neutrals involved in two-party ADR are unlikely to have the skills, experience, or substantive background needed to be effective in larger consensus-building efforts—especially those in the public arena. Finally, the implementation of consensus-based agreements requires many parties to reach near-unanimous accord on complex packages of issues, many of which are framed in nonlegal terms.

While court-connected ADR has its uses, it is not helpful to blur the distinctions between ADR and consensus building, or even worse, to think of them as the same thing. Mediation, arbitration, and other forms of dispute resolution take on a particular form in a court-related setting. In contexts when no lawsuit has yet crystallized or when picking a winner and a loser on legal grounds is inappropriate, consensus building operates quite differently. While there may be some overlap in the application of basic dispute resolution theory and methods that make them look similar, the differences between these two contexts are extremely important. Mediators in both contexts may push the parties to search for "all gain" rather than win-lose solutions, but the demands of litigation can get in the way of maximizing value creation or joint gains. Furthermore, the process management skills required in a multiparty context in which coalitional behavior is to be expected—especially when technical complexity is involved—are quite special. Thus, the idea of an ADR continuum with court at one end, negotiation at the other, and mediation in the middle is misleading. What is more useful is to think in terms of a continuum with one end labeled court-related dispute resolution mechanisms and the other titled non-court-related dispute resolution mechanisms. Mediation and related techniques should appear on both sides, but their use and the prerequisites for success should be understood as distinct.

Notes

1. For more on the mechanisms by which the litigation process narrows disputes in ways that may hinder creative problem solving, see M. L. Moffitt, "Pleadings in the Age of Settlement," *Indiana Law Journal*, 2005, *80*, 727–771.

2. See L. E. Susskind and J. Thomas-Larmer, "Conducting a Conflict Assessment," in L. E. Susskind, S. McKearnen, and J. Thomas-Larmer (eds.), *The Consensus Building Handbook* (Thousand Oaks, Calif.: Sage, 1999).

3. For more on the use and applicability of hybrid dispute resolution mechanisms, see Sander and Rozdeiczer, Chapter Twenty-Four, this volume.

4. See L. E. Susskind, *Breaking the Impasse: Consensus Building Approaches to Resolving Public Disputes* (New York: Basic Books, 1987).

5. See M.L.P. Elliott, "The Role of Facilitators, Mediators, and Other Consensus Building Practitioners," in Susskind, McKearnen, and Thomas-Larmer (eds.), *The Consensus Building Handbook,* 1999.

6. D. A. Straus, "Designing a Consensus Building Process Using a Graphic Road Map," in Susskind, McKearnen, and Thomas-Larmer (eds.), *The Consensus Building Handbook,* 1999.

7. See Susskind and Thomas-Larmer, "Conducting a Conflict Assessment," 1999.

8. See S. McKearnen and D. Fairman, "Producing Consensus," in Susskind, McKearnen, and Thomas-Larmer (eds.), *The Consensus Building Handbook,* 1999.

9. See L. L. Riskin, "Understanding Mediators' Orientations, Strategies, and Techniques: A Grid for the Perplexed," *Harvard Negotiation Law Review,* 1996, *1,* 7–42.

10. See L. E. Susskind, R. H. Mnookin, B. Fuller, and L. Rodeiczer, "Teaching Multiparty Negotiation: A Workbook," paper presented at the Teaching Multiparty Negotiation Conference, Cambridge, Massachussetts, May 2003.

11. See L. E. Susskind and P. Field, "The Media," in L. E. Susskind and P. Field, *Dealing with an Angry Public* (New York: Free Press, 1996); and L. E. Susskind, "Environmental Mediation and the Accountability Problem," *Vermont Law Review,* 1981, *6,* 1–47.

12. See L. E. Susskind, *Environmental Diplomacy: Negotiating More Effective Global Agreements* (New York: Oxford University Press, 1994).

13. See L. E. Susskind, P. F. Levy, and J. Thomas-Larmer, *Negotiating Environmental Agreements: How to Avoid Escalating Confrontation, Needless Costs, and Unnecessary Litigation* (Washington, D.C.: Island Press, 2000).

14. See J. R. Ehrmann and B. L. Stinson, "Joint Fact-Finding and the Use of Technical Experts," in Susskind, McKearnen, and Thomas-Larmer (eds.), *The Consensus Building Handbook,* 1999.

15. For more on the use of contingent agreements, see M. L. Moffitt, "Contingent Agreements, Agreeing to Disagree About the Future," *Marquette Law Review,* 2004, *87,* 691–696.

16. Susskind, *Breaking the Impasse,* 1987, p. 21.

CHAPTER TWENTY-THREE

Bargaining in the Shadow of Management

Integrated Conflict Management Systems

Howard Gadlin

The core idea of integrated conflict management systems (ICMS) is to apply the techniques and sensibility of interest-based negotiation to the identification, prevention, management, and resolution of conflict within organizations. In this chapter, I explore the basic concepts and practices of ICMS, trace their development from early experiments in mediating workplace grievances, explore the connections between ICMS and the changing nature of the workplace, and critically examine their role in transforming notions of workplace management in contemporary society.[1]

THE ELEMENTS OF ICMS

Systems for managing organizational conflict emerged in the 1990s from the infusion of alternative dispute resolution (ADR) with the principles of organizational development. In this approach, organizational policies and practices are designed to support an open and "healthy" workplace climate in which diversity flourishes and conflict is tamed. It represents a considerably more expansive orientation toward workplace management than traditional approaches, which are dominated by legal risk management and after-the-fact conflict resolution. ICMS employ a coordinated set of easily accessible organizational mechanisms to identify conflict in its earliest stages, manage it carefully to prevent escalation, and resolve it efficiently to maintain positive workplace relations. In ICMS, the resolution of individual disputes is used to identify root causes of conflict and to uncover systemic problems in an organization. Collectively, the dispute resolvers have the responsibility to inform management about systemic problems so that the practices, procedures, and policies that sustain such problems can be altered appropriately.

Those working in the field agree that there are five structural characteristics of integrated conflict management systems:[2]

- *Broad scope.* All people (managers as well as employees) within the workplace should be able to use the system to address any concern, including those for which there are not, and probably cannot be, relevant rules, policies, or laws.

- *Open culture.* The organization should welcome and support diversity of people and ideas. Difference, dissent, and disagreement are tolerated, and the organization works to resolve issues and tensions at the lowest possible level.

- *Multiple access points.* Anyone in the organization should be able to readily identify and contact a trustworthy, knowledgeable person in the organization to assist in addressing his or her concern. At least one channel within the organization ought to offer confidentiality to personnel.

- *Multiple options.* An organization should provide both rights-based and interest-based options for addressing grievances, complaints, conflicts, and problems. Formal and informal means for addressing issues ought to be complementary.

- *Coordinated support structures.* The various options and access points should be integrated and should feed back into the day-to-day management of the organization. Managerial practices ought to be informed by the same interest-based sensibility that infuses the mechanisms for addressing the ICMS.

In theory, integrated conflict management systems represent more than a complex approach to addressing grievances and conflicts within organizations; they are an expression of a very particular management philosophy and organizational vision. Central to this philosophy is a commitment to fairness, openness, and mutual accountability among all who work in an organization—managers and employees alike. The key design elements of ICMS are intended to assure employees and managers that they can raise issues or bring forth grievances without fear of reprisal or ostracism and with the realistic expectation that matters will be addressed fairly.

Toward this end, integrated conflict management systems require that

- Participation in the various conflict management processes is *voluntary.* Employees select which of multiple options, if any, they wish to pursue. These must include both rights-based and interest-based options, and there ought to be no penalty for selecting one over the other. All options should be equally well managed and have equal credibility among employees and managers.

- The overall system includes at least one *confidential* channel, to which people can come without fear that their identity will be disclosed and without worry that the issues they raise will be reported to others or acted on without their knowledge and permission. The intent is to create conditions in which people are more likely to raise issues that might never be brought to the organization's attention otherwise. Except when there is imminent risk of serious harm, there ought to be no limits to confidentiality.

- At least one option to pursue issues involves *impartial* third-party *neutrals,* whether they are identified from within or outside of the organization. Most commonly ombuds, mediators, or arbitrators play this role; some systems use more than one of these. In addition, peer panels for handling grievances or early neutral evaluation processes are used to assess complaints or conflicts.

- Organizational policies, strongly supported by top management, *prohibit* explicit or implicit *retaliation or reprisal* for good faith participation in any of the options available in the system.

It should be noted that these four requirements of ICMS supplement one another. Policies offering protection against reprisal may help overcome reluctance to come forward, but the realities of organizational life are such that in actuality it is difficult to protect people from the various ways in which managers or peers can punish someone for coming forward with a complaint, criticism, or negative information. For this reason a confidential neutral such as an ombuds can work to identify the options within an integrated conflict management system to minimize the chances of retaliation or reprisal. Ombuds are not limited to a single mode of working with those who contact them. Depending on circumstances and the preferences of the person coming forward, the ombuds might help a person assess the organization's rights-based and interest-based options for addressing the concerns, coach a person on handling a conflict in a non-adversarial way, help the individual clarify his or her real interests, serve as an informal channel of communication among parties with a damaged relationship, or mediate or facilitate a discussion between disputing parties.

Two other features of ICMS differentiate them from managerial approaches that focus only on managing legal liability or resolving conflicts to save time and money. Foremost is the idea of upward feedback. In ICMS, conflicts, concerns, grievances, and complaints that are brought forward are considered a valuable source of information about the organization. They help identify workplace climate, managerial practices, policies, or procedures that might be contributing to low morale, the generation of grievances, or the emergence of conflicts. All ICMS have mechanisms for gathering information (while protecting confidentiality) and reporting to management about areas in need for change. Indeed, to identify localized or pervasive sources of discontent and conflict within the organization and to make recommendations for addressing them is intrinsic to the ombuds role.

Almost as important in ICMS is the emphasis on proactive measures such as internal education to provide members with the skills, techniques, and motivation to reduce conflict and improve workplace relations.

THE HISTORY AND DEVELOPMENT OF ICMS

It was in the late 1950s that the idea of designing approaches for addressing conflicts and complaints within organizations began to attract attention. Writing about corporate ombuds, Isidore Silver referred to several publications on management that suggested that managerial power ought to be tempered by considerations of justice.[3] Silver argued that adaptations of the Scandinavian ombudsman role could serve as the core of a system for addressing "the 'communications gap' which creates organizational conflict." Silver maintained that employees deserve just treatment, and those then-current corporate systems for handling complaints and conflicts were neither just nor effective. By the 1980s there were recurring discussions of effective systems for managing employee concerns, especially in nonunion environments.[4] However, the term *justice* had disappeared from those discussions, which focused instead on effectiveness and cost savings.

In 1988, William Ury, Jeanne Brett, and Stephen Goldberg published *Getting Disputes Resolved*; its goal was succinctly stated in its subtitle, "Designing Systems to Cut the Costs of Conflict."[5] The authors, accomplished and respected practitioner-academics in the growing area of conflict resolution, synthesized the work and thoughts of disparate scholars, managers, and consultants who had been experimenting with new ways to address disputes in workplaces, organizations, schools, communities, and government agencies. At the core of their approach was the recognition that "traditional" approaches to addressing grievances, lawsuits, strikes, long-term animosities, and failed relationships were costly, inefficient, and frequently unsatisfying to the disputants. The approach they offered promised to reduce the costs of conflict, to transform its destructive capacity into improved relationships among disputants, and to increase productivity and performance. Key to their approach was early identification and intervention in workplace conflicts that otherwise escalate.

For many readers, their argument made enormous sense. Organizations have an impressive capacity to generate and nurture conflicts and enmity. Anyone who has worked within large organizations knows firsthand how disputes and rivalries among peers, and complaints against management, can consume significant amounts of time and energy, undermine morale, increase stress, detract from mission, and generally render an organization dysfunctional. Ironically, the formal procedures in place for addressing conflict often make matters worse. Most organizations' complaint or grievance mechanisms are distrusted by the very people encouraged or required to use them. Generally, formal procedures are excruciatingly slow and debilitating for those who use them. Often parties to a formal grievance or complaint procedure must continue to interact and work together even while they are set against each other, awaiting a decision on their dispute. Equally important, because many organizations have no mechanisms for addressing issues for which there are not and cannot be formal rules or regulations, people often have to squeeze their dissatisfactions into the formats required by formal processes just to voice their dissatisfaction. For example, in many federal workplaces employees routinely use the Equal Employment Opportunity (EEO) complaint procedure to address issues not even experienced as discrimination, simply because that is a way to get the complaint heard. Interestingly, some federal agencies adapted to this phenomenon by incorporating mediation programs into the EEO process. Originally REDRESS—the postal service's mediation program—only allowed employees to get to mediation by formulating their concern as an EEO complaint even if the issues had nothing to do with discrimination.

In *Getting Disputes Resolved,* Ury, Brett, and Goldberg differentiated among power, rights, and interests as bases for resolving disputes. They argued that structuring dispute resolution systems around the satisfaction of interests of the disputing parties could benefit both employees and managers more than could determinations of who is right or even assertions of power. The authors supported their framework by providing four criteria for comparing the three different bases for resolving disputes: transaction costs, satisfaction with outcomes, effects on the relationship, and recurrence of the dispute. Drawing from repeated successful experiences of dispute resolution consultants and practitioners, they illustrated the advantages of an interest-based approach by comparison with approaches based on power or rights.

It is worth noting that many case examples in *Getting Disputes Resolved* come from strikes and other bitter labor-management disputes; the authors described interventions that carefully balanced the concerns and perspectives of both management and labor. However, the conceptual framework of dispute systems design is formed almost exclusively around the concerns of managers: cutting costs, enhancing productivity, and containing conflict. The subtitles of a range of books about dispute resolution in organizations tell all: "Lessons from American Corporations for Managers and Dispute Resolution Professionals,"[6] "Designing Systems to Cut the Costs of Conflict,"[7] "A Guide to Creating Productive and Healthy Organizations,"[8] "Bargaining for Cooperation and Competitive Gain."[9] The title of Slaikeu and Hasson's book makes the same pitch: *Controlling the Costs of Conflict: How to Design a System for Your Organization.*[10]

The books that followed *Getting Disputes Resolved* expanded the scope of the interventions beyond the creation of interest-based programs for resolving conflicts. By the time of Costantino and Merchant's *Designing Conflict Management Systems,* writing in the field was geared toward showing managers how to create an organizational environment that guides people in the organization to assume cooperative stances, adopt problem-solving techniques, and take into account the motivations, needs, and interests of those within their organizations, even when they are in conflict. Like an advertisement that promises to transform a consumer from an unappealing misfit into the adored life of the party, integrated conflict management systems promise to transform the workplace from a dysfunctional cauldron of grief, strife, and competition into a benign workplace of cooperative employees and thoughtful managers. They offer a path to the utopian organization in which employees and managers translate potential strife into collaborative problem solving, in which managers welcome employee input and respond sensitively, and in which professional rivalries and interpersonal, racial, and gender animosities can be brought comfortably to the surface where they are skillfully managed to maintain a harmonious workplace. Ironically, the "capitulation" to a management perspective on organizational life is obscured by the emphasis, especially in recent iterations of the ICMS ideology, on voluntary choice of options, stakeholder participation, empowerment, and confidentiality, features not emphasized in *Getting Disputes Resolved.*

Starting from the observation that traditional ways of "managing" conflict— avoidance, denial, and containment—do not actually serve the managerial needs of organizations, dispute system designers argued that the key advantage to the interest-based approach was its ability to address the motivations and interests of disputing parties. Central to such an approach is the belief that for many issues, cooperative problem solving could replace formal (rights-based) and informal (power-based) fighting as a way of resolving differences. However, dispute resolution experts and consultants soon recognized that the way grievances and conflicts are handled in an organization both reflects the culture of the organization and contributes to it. With this recognition, system design grew from the application of ADR to organizational mechanisms for addressing conflict *after the fact* into an approach to addressing conflict both *before* and *after* it occurs. This approach has implications for every aspect of the way an organization is run.

Once conflict transformation was linked with the transformation of organizational cultures in the form of ICMS, the goals of dispute systems design quite naturally evolved from resolving conflict to managing and preventing conflict. Certain similarities in the dynamics of, and conditions that lead to, particular types of conflict were detected. Having identified organizational and interpersonal factors contributing to the emergence, maintenance, and escalation of conflict, many conflict resolvers quite naturally began to think about features of organizational culture that support destructive conflict. Seen from this perspective, power- and rights-based orientations reinforce competition, rivalry, and antagonism between people with differing perspectives and concerns. By comparison, an interest-based, problem-solving orientation—and the concomitant shifts it induces in how one views those with whom one differs—can help transform conflict and difference into a basis for a collaborative and collegial organizational culture.

More important, once the spotlight was turned to organizational culture, more attention was directed to all aspects of organizational life not covered by policies, grievance procedures, or even interest-based mediation programs. Under ICMS, any aspect of organizational life that could give rise to tensions, differences, or conflicts should become the focus of managerial attention. Preventing conflict, or guiding it into forums that tame it and transform differences into a resource for maintaining or increasing productivity, becomes the primary goal of the system. Resolution, while necessary and important in certain conditions, comes into play only when the benevolent, therapeutic embrace of the conflict managers and those they tutor fails to contain the disruptive forces within the organization. Within ICMS all systems are oriented toward identifying "the root causes of conflict and address[ing] them through systemic change."[11]

In 2000 a task force published design guidelines for ICMS (SPIDR).[12] Written by leading advocates and practitioners in the field, the guidelines represent a consensus about the most important principles for ICMS. The document offers aspirations for a managerial utopia sensitively responding to the concerns of everyone in the organization. It describes a workplace that "encourages," "fosters," and "welcomes" "diversity," "dissent," and "resolution."

At the core of these guidelines is the overarching and somewhat radical idea that conflict is inevitable and natural. And because it is natural it is manageable, and because it is manageable, conflict is welcome.

Most significant is the idea of integration. The various components of ICMS must be carefully integrated so that they all function to manage conflict constructively, establish norms, and shape personal and professional interactions within the organization. While the pioneers of dispute systems design promoted interest-based approaches as a superior alternative to power- and rights-based approaches, current ICMS advocates envision an organization in which the three approaches are smoothly integrated; formal and informal processes are coordinated and complement each other. In addition, the ICMS notion of integration means that the responsibilities of those whose domain is organizational compliance with laws and regulations must be integrated with the responsibilities of those who manage the informal, neutral dispute resolution programs.

In the early days of introducing ADR programs into organizations—mediation programs, ombudsman offices—the word *alternative* was key to their functioning and to whatever moral sway and influence they had. Organizational ADR programs were conceptualized as alternatives, not only to formal rights- and power-based procedures but also to management itself. These programs were concerned with procedural justice and fairness in the organization, not performance, productivity, and profits.

BEYOND IDEOLOGY: THE FUTURE OF ICMS

Thus far this chapter has explored the ideology of ICMS, the ideas and ideals that inspire most advocates and practitioners. While ICMS have gained some acceptance in some parts of the organizational world,[13] it would be wrong to assume that they are the predominant form of dispute resolution practice in organizations today. Commenting on the fact that they are not a common phenomenon, Bingham and Nabatchi observe, "most dispute systems are designed to include one or several (but not all) of the components of an integrated conflict management system."[14] Lipsky and others include thoughtful discussions of the barriers to and prospects for the implementation of these systems. They observe that there are very few companies that actually employ fully integrated conflict management systems. Those companies using ADR primarily value its potential "to save time and money."[15]

To better grasp the possible future of ICMS, it is worth asking, Why did ICMS emerge as they did and when they did? Not surprisingly, the "Guidelines for the Design of Integrated Conflict Management Systems Within Organizations" uses an evolutionary metaphor to describe the emergence of ICMS: it is the culmination of progressive development, beginning with the primitive era in which organizations simply lacked defined dispute resolution processes, moving through rights-based and then interest-based systems until achieving full development as ICMS.[16] Within this framework enlightened, employee-empowering managerial practices are applied to an increasingly complex and diverse workplace and workforce.

But in a more critical and insightful review of the development of conflict management, Lipsky, Leeber, and Fincher identify conditions to which ICMS are a partial response.[17] They see the emergent dispute systems resulting from the conflict between old ways of managing and new ways of organizing the workplace in a dynamically changing society. Using social contract theory, they locate the emergence of ICMS in the need to recalibrate the balance between individual freedoms and community needs as the United States moved from an agricultural to an industrial to a postindustrial economy. Associated with these developments are parallel changes in the family, in authority, and in underlying beliefs about the importance of individual autonomy. It is a complex picture that can only be painted in very broad strokes here but an important one because it helps us locate ICMS in a changing historical context.

Focusing on the workplace, Lipsky, Seeber, and Fincher observe that with industrialization, production moved from small shops into factories where the work of large numbers of employees required coordination and where control over the manufacturing process was transferred from skilled craftsman to managers. In the more enlightened companies, managers turned to purveyors of scientific management approaches to understand how better to organize and control the manufacturing process and the workforce. Over time, the increased power of managers was partly balanced by the emergence of unions. Still, the workplace was largely defined and controlled by managers, jobs were specialized, responsibilities were clearly defined, and the chain of command was hierarchical. In these conditions, power- and rights-based approaches to addressing conflict, and indeed to managing entire organizations, dominate.

In the last third of the twentieth century, however, technological change and globalization contributed to the deindustrialization of the U.S. economy. The production and distribution of manufactured products was supplanted by the production and distribution of information. This brought a gradual movement toward types of work that require the cooperative efforts of partly self-governing groups of people whose responsibilities change with the projects to which they are assigned. In such workplaces, social relations among employees assume an importance they lacked on the shop floor, and authority itself is transformed. Add to that the impact of other social changes, such as the legal prohibition of racial and gender discrimination, and compliance with the law provides additional incentives for managing. Inevitably peaceful negotiation of differences in the workplace becomes a requirement for everyone in the workplace.

In a provocative paper about the role of the workplace in civil society, Cynthia Estlund observed, "The workplace is the single most important site of cooperative interaction and sociability among adult citizens outside of the family. . . . Indeed, the workplace can perform one crucial function—that of fostering communication and social integration and empathy among individuals from different racial and ethnic groups in a diverse citizenry—particularly well precisely because it is subject to state regulation in the form of the employment discrimination laws."[18]

Note how the ideals of ICMS match beautifully with both the transformed nature of the workplace and the formal requirements of the antidiscrimination laws. The dilemma for management in contemporary society is that to be both productive and compliant with the law it must control aspects of the workplace that cannot be controlled directly by assertions of managerial authority—how people interact and communicate, how they negotiate differences, even how they manage and express personal likes and dislikes, values, and beliefs. In an era that valorizes autonomy, the best control is self-control. Old forms of command authority can be supplemented by new and relatively subtle forms of influence: in this case the design of systems to alter the culture of the organization so that employees and managers voluntarily conduct themselves in the way management would like them to with a minimum of surveillance or coercion, but backed up by the twin threats of discipline or social disapproval. The very idea of an organizational culture provides the framework within which new managerial disciplinary practices can be justified as improvements geared toward employee needs and interests. In *False Prophets*, a historical critique of management gurus, James Hoopes challenges the idea of corporate culture: "'[C]ulture' may be only one more device for fending off any tragic understanding of management as a necessary evil in an imperfect world. If people can be managed with culture so that internalized values drive them to act in the way management wants, there is no need for a win-lose choice between corporate prosperity and individual freedom. Managed by culture change, people freely choose to do what managers want. Employee morale rises and managers get their way without any unpleasant need to use their power."[19]

Hoopes sees the entire corps of management gurus as rationalizing and disguising managerial power. It is an old story in American history: authority reinvents itself by adapting to changed circumstances. Key to this reinvention is the coordination of authorities' interests with the needs and desires of those whom that authority would manage. When the mere assertion of power is effective, authority asserts power. When defining a "legitimate" right to control is required, authority defines its rights. When these two are challenged and self-interest and autonomy will not yield to power or honor rights, authority accommodates to self-interest and autonomy. In this way ICMS represent an interesting shift in the social meaning of dispute resolution. Ury, Brett, and Goldberg marked the beginning of a significant trend, the infiltration of the critical sensibility of ADR into mainstream managerial philosophies; ICMS represent the integration of conflict resolution techniques, separated from their critical origins, into the repertoire of methods of managerial control. The shift is a subtle one, revealed partly by the change in emphasis from appreciatively accepting conflict as an inevitable and natural consequence of social existence, and a stimulus for change and creativity, to viewing it once again as an indicator that something is wrong, that something must be tamed, managed, and eliminated.

When we examine how this new approach to managerial control has been ushered in under the banner of self-determination, participation, and democratic decision making, the significance of this shift is revealed. Many of the pioneers in conflict resolution came to the field with at least a spiritual affiliation with the values and ideologies of the 1960s movements for social justice and civil rights.[20] It was called alternative dispute resolution because it was intended to provide an alternative to formal, power- and rights-based adjudicatory systems which were criticized for being tilted in favor of the powerful and insensitive or inappropriate for the real needs of the people. ADR was seen as providing people with a voice in shaping the resolutions of their own disputes rather than their being dependent on the good judgment and fairness of powerful people such as judges and managers, whose decisions were guided by abstract general principles and rules that were not necessarily tailored to the specific circumstances and needs of the parties.

In keeping with the spirit of antiauthoritarianism, mediation allowed people to decide for themselves how to define their conflict and to determine for themselves a fair and acceptable resolution. Moreover, mediation opened up the possibility that people could find alternatives to fighting, grieving, accusing, or demonizing of the other that goes along with conflict. In this way, ADR incorporated not just antiauthoritarianism but the spirit of nonviolence as well.[21]

But a plea to switch from coercion to consent and from force to mutual interest is different when asserted by a critical reform movement seeking new ways to empower the less powerful than it is when imposed by managers who have decided that they will incorporate principles of consent and mutual interest into the management of the organization that they control. Interestingly, the idea of ICMS took hold primarily in organizations in which organized labor did not play a significant role; at times these systems were introduced as a way of resisting unionization.[22] This was aptly illustrated in 2002 when the newly formed Transportation Security Agency (TSA) announced, one day after it was decided that the employees would not be allowed to unionize, that they would be given an organizational ombudsman program through which they could address their concerns. The TSA has since implemented an integrated conflict management system, of which the ombudsman is a significant component. (It should be noted that the TSA program stands as an example of good design.) Nonetheless this program should not be seen as an autonomous expression of employee interests or needs. This skeptical view of organizational dispute systems is developed by Lauren Edelman and Mark Suchman, who argue, "Although 'have not' groups may gain some short-run advantages from the introduction of citizenship norms into the workplace, the organizational annexation of law subtly skews the balance between democratic and bureaucratic tendencies in society as a whole adding to the power and control of dominant elites."[23]

Clearly the pioneers in organizational ADR did not intend to reinforce the power and control of managers. But as is often the case with social change, differences exist between the motivations that drive reformers and the societal factors that allow their reforms to succeed. Those bringing ADR to organizations were providing effective solutions to real problems, experienced and recognized by both employees and managers. And while they may have advocated employee empowerment and democratization of the workplace, the programs and services they offered rarely address issues of power and are only superficially democratic. Even the language they use suggests a denial of differences in power: consider the term "stakeholder." When all the constituencies in an organization are lumped together and identified only as stakeholders, differences in status, power, and influence are simply hidden from sight.

Similarly, the idea of voluntary participation in dispute resolution programs cannot be taken as an expression of democratic process when employees arrive at the conflict resolution office with the announcement that they have been sent to mediation by management. Even if employees may not be ordered to mediation, often the social pressures within the organization are sufficient to compel the voluntary choice. In this way, many systems give more latitude to employees than to managers. While employees can select whichever option they prefer, managers are expected to comply with the employee's choice even when the manager believes the option is not suited to the manager's interests. Although this might make sense from the point of view of empowering employees, it blurs the difference between ADR and the other processes to which it is meant to serve as an alternative. In this way, ADR in the organizational world has followed a path similar to the one it took in the courts: from a voluntary alternative to the formal procedures of the courts to a sometimes-mandated program that is neatly integrated into the functioning of the court.

This development is not totally surprising; Mary Parker Follett, one of the inspirational voices in ADR, was also one of the pioneers of modern ideas about organizational management. While most dispute system designers see themselves as a part of the ADR movement, typically they do not recognize its origins in the movement toward systematic organizational management. This movement is usually associated with Frederick Taylor, whose time-and-motion studies around the beginning of the twentieth century reinforced direct management control of the workplace to enhance productivity and efficiency. Unlike Taylor, Follett focused on the human dimension of workplace relations. Here she followed nineteenth-century thinkers who, while certainly advocating for strong managerial control, believed very strongly that there are established principles by which one can design transformative environments. The first experiments with such design were in correctional institutions—prisons, insane asylums, orphanages, and almshouses.[24] The Boston Prison Discipline Society expounded the virtues of moral architecture—the belief that there were ways of designing buildings to improve the morals and conduct of those who resided or worked within them. Historian and medical ethicist David Rothman observes that the reformers believed they had discovered disciplinary practices that could also improve and regulate the behavior of ordinary citizens.

The transformational aspirations of today's system designers are strikingly similar to those of the nineteenth-century institutional reformers. Techniques of management control are justified in terms of their alleged responsiveness to the needs of those who are managed. Rothman cites Reverend James Finley, chaplain for the Ohio Penitentiary, who argued, "Could we all be put on prison fare, for the space of two or three generations, the world would ultimately be the better for it."[25] In many ways ICMS represent an extension of this way of thinking—in this case a vision of ideal organizations sustained by the belief that it is possible, through principles of scientific management, to transform destructive energies and enmity into constructive relations, tolerance, and cooperation.[26]

Years ago, after appreciating the role of utopian thought in opening up previously unseen possibilities, Paul Tillich warned that "[T]he unfruitfulness of utopia is that it describes impossibilities as real possibilities—and fails to see them for what they are, impossibilities."[27]

Advocates and practitioners of ICMS would do well to reflect on Tillich's discussion of utopian ideals. First, there is a danger in presenting impossibilities as possibilities: the idea that conflict can be so thoroughly tamed and managed that it supports and increases productivity may well be an impossibility. The pleasures and satisfactions that are an intrinsic part of conflict at both the individual and the organizational level are lost when conflict's energy is converted to productivity.[28] Second, there is a danger in pursuing utopian visions formulated almost exclusively from a managerial perspective; they fail to address the question of power. It is hard to imagine a comprehensive approach to understanding organizational conflict that does not reckon with power: how it is wielded and distributed. Implicit in ICMS vision is a managerial view of organizational life that overlooks a basic fact—employees are empowered individually but not collectively while managers are empowered both individually and collectively. In this way, however well intentioned they are currently, ICMS threaten to become another tool by which management wields power. So long as saving time and money are the major interests addressed by ICMS, they will remain an approach supported primarily by management, at least until the next management fad comes along. For ICMS scholars and practitioners, it is time for a critical self-evaluation.

Notes

1. See D. B. Lipsky, R. L. Seeber, and R. D. Fincher, *Emerging Systems for Managing Workplace Conflict: Lessons from American Corporations for Managers and Dispute Resolution Professionals* (San Francisco: Jossey-Bass, 2003); and L. Bingham and T. Nabatchi, "Dispute System Design in Organizations," in W. Palmer and J. Killian (eds.), *Handbook of Conflict Management* (New York: Marcel Dekker, 2003).

2. See Lipsky, Seeber, and Fincher, *Emerging Systems for Managing Workplace Conflict,* 2003; and J. Lynch and P. German, "The Emergence of Integrated Conflict Management Systems as an Organizational Development Strategy," Green College Lecture Series, University of British Columbia, October 29, 2001.

3. See I. Silver, "The Corporate Ombudsman," *Harvard Business Review,* May-June 1967, *45,* 77–87.

4. See M. Rowe and M. Baker, "Are You Hearing Enough Employee Concerns?" *Harvard Business Review,* May-June 1984, *62,* 127–135; and M. Rowe, "The Upward-Feedback, Mediation Process at Massachusetts Institute of Technology," in A. F. Westin and A. G. Feliu (eds.), *Resolving Employment Disputes Without Litigation* (Washington, D.C.: The Bureau of National Affairs, 1988), pp. 190–200.

5. W. L. Ury, J. M. Brett, and S. B. Goldberg, *Getting Disputes Resolved: Designing Systems to Cut the Costs of Conflict* (San Francisco: Jossey-Bass, 1988).

6. See Lipsky, Seeber, and Fincher, *Emerging Systems for Managing Workplace Conflict,* 2003.

7. See Ury, Brett, and Goldberg, *Getting Disputes Resolved*, 1988.

8. See C. A. Costantino and C. S. Merchant, *Designing Conflict Management Systems: A Guide to Creating Productive and Healthy Organizations* (San Francisco: Jossey-Bass, 1996).

9. See D. Lax and J. Sebenius, "Claiming Value," in D. Lax and J. Sebenius, *The Manager as Negotiator: Bargaining for Cooperation and Competitive Gain* (New York: Free Press, 1986).

10. See K. A. Slaikeu and R. H. Hasson, *Controlling the Costs of Conflict: How to Design a System for Your Organization* (San Francisco: Jossey-Bass, 1998).

11. Personal communication from C. Costantino to the author, February 21, 2005. See also Costantino and Merchant, *Designing Conflict Management Systems,* 1996.

12. M. Adams and others, *Guidelines for Design of Integrated Conflict Management Systems* (Washington, D.C.: Society for Professionals in Dispute Resolution, 2000).

13. See Lipsky, Seeber, and Fincher, *Emerging Systems for Managing Workplace Conflict,* 2003.

14. Bingham and Nabatchi, "Dispute System Design in Organizations," 2003, p. 120.

15. Lipsky, Seeber, and Fincher, *Emerging Systems for Managing Workplace Conflict,* 2003, p. 316.

16. M. Adams and others, *Guidelines for Design of Integrated Conflict Management Systems,* 2000.

17. See Lipsky, Seeber, and Fincher, *Emerging Systems for Managing Workplace Conflict,* 2003.

18. C. L. Estlund, "Working Together: The Workplace in Civil Society," Columbia Law School, Public Law and Legal Theory Working Paper No. 3, 1999, p. 4.

19. J. Hoopes, *False Prophets* (Berkeley: Perseus, 2003), p. xxvii.

20. See S. E. Merry and N. Milner, *The Possibility of Popular Justice: A Case Study of Community Mediation in the United States* (Ann Arbor, Mich.: University of Michigan Press, 1993); and B. Mayer, *Beyond Neutrality: Confronting the Crisis in Conflict Resolution* (San Francisco: Jossey-Bass, 2004).

21. That spirit is still evident in the recent writings of Bill Ury, for example: "Our challenge is to change the way we handle our most serious differences, replacing fighting, violence and war with more constructive processes such as negotiation, democracy, and non-violent action. The task is to transform the culture of conflict from coercion to consent and from force to mutual interest" (Ury, W. L. *The Third Side: Why We Fight and How We Can Stop.* New York: Penguin Putnam, 2000, p. xix).

22. See Lipsky, Seeber, and Fincher, *Emerging Systems for Managing Workplace Conflict,* 2003.

23. L. B. Edelman and M. C. Suchman, "When the 'Haves' Hold Court: Speculations in the Organizational Internalization of Law," *Law and Society Review,* 1999, *33,* p. 944.

24. See D. J. Rothman, *The Discovery of the Asylum: Social Order and Disorder in the New Republic* (Boston: Little, Brown, 1971).

25. Rothman, *The Discovery of the Asylum,* 1971, pp. 84–85.

26. See Ury, *The Third Side,* 2000.

27. P. Tillich, "Critique and Justification of Utopia," in F. E. Manuel (ed.), *Utopias and Utopian Thought: A Timely Appraisal* (Boston: Beacon Press, 1967), p. 300.

28. See H. Gadlin, "The Ombudsman: What's in a Name?" *Negotiation Journal,* 2002, *16,* 37–48.

CHAPTER TWENTY-FOUR

Selecting an Appropriate Dispute Resolution Procedure

Detailed Analysis and Simplified Solution

Frank E. A. Sander and Lukasz Rozdeiczer

W hich process or processes of dispute resolution are most appropriate for a dispute? The question of process selection presents one of the most challenging problems in the field of alternative dispute resolution (ADR). Lawyers, clients, and court officials all ask the question. Indeed, the question even extends beyond settings in which formal disputes are pending.

This chapter focuses in particular on the challenge of selecting a dispute resolution process for legal disputes. In particular, we focus on dispute resolution processes that involve the assistance of a third party. Although choosing the process remains art rather than science, we believe that both theoretical and practical indications should guide this process choice. We begin by looking at the context in which the problem of process selection commonly arises. We then describe the various responses given in the existing literature, explain why the taxonomies are difficult to compare, and demonstrate that they present at least three important, common questions which we believe are most helpful in selecting the most appropriate procedure. Finally, we suggest a simplified, user-friendly, three-step approach to choosing a dispute resolution process—one in which mediation is the default process, supplanted by another method only if certain contraindications are present.

Note: This chapter is a condensed version of a more extensive article the authors are producing for future publication.

Although in this chapter we focus on the choice of process that would best satisfy the interests of one party, it should be noted that "the most appropriate process" could also be defined as one that best satisfies the interests of both parties. This could be to create a Pareto optimal outcome or it may require some way of accommodating the goals of the other party. "The most appropriate process" can also mean the procedure that best satisfies goals of society or the state.

ISSUES SURROUNDING PROCESS SELECTION

At What Point Does Process Selection Occur?

In some contexts, parties contemplating a contractual relationship will consider the possibility of a dispute arising, and they will jointly select a dispute resolution process *before* any dispute arises. We believe that much of the advice presented in this chapter will be helpful to the parties when forming a contract and designing the dispute resolution clause. Though the parties do not know the details of the dispute, or even whether such a dispute will ever occur, the analysis presented in this chapter will help them in selecting a default procedure.

Even in cases when parties have crafted such a dispute resolution agreement ahead of time, the question of process selection remains important. An existing dispute resolution clause may not provide for a process that is appropriate for the dispute that presents itself. The parties may want to change the process at the outset of the dispute or while another procedure is pending. The analysis of the process choice at this point might be useful not only for deciding about the most appropriate procedure for the dispute but also for convincing the opponent why the new process would be superior to the status quo.

In many circumstances, the parties find themselves in the middle of a dispute without having selected a dispute resolution process ahead of time. In such a case a party should have a tool to decide whether there is any procedure more appropriate than the default procedure of going to court.

Probably the most important process choice takes place when the parties first choose their dispute resolution process. That approach, however, may not continue to be optimal. Due to possible changes of conditions throughout the dispute, and the fact that the parties and neutrals can gain a better understanding of the dispute pending its resolution, the parties could profit from changing their dispute resolution procedure during processing of the dispute. Therefore, they should question their first procedure of choice throughout the process, and keep a flexible mind attuned to a possible change or modification of the selected procedure. For example, during pre-agreed mediation of a family dispute, parties may decide that it will be more beneficial for them to use arbitration instead (perhaps because they need a definitive third-party expert opinion). Another example may be a commercial dispute in which a mediator and two mid-level managers may conclude that the desired goals may be better achieved through participation of higher-up officials of their companies who have a more free-ranging perspective. Therefore the parties could decide that a minitrial will be more appropriate than mediation.

Do the Parties Need Courts?

One of the key problems in selecting the most appropriate procedure for a case involves the choice between court-related and out-of-court processes. Although private and public processes can have identical names (such as mediation or arbitration) they may produce very different results. Therefore even if the party knows that she prefers mediation, for example, in choosing among an array of forms of mediation she needs to decide whether she wants some court connection and assistance (for example, for help with choosing a mediator, more formal discovery, enforcement, and so on). Similar links exist between court adjudication and private judging, between private arbitration and court-annexed arbitration, or between early neutral evaluation and case evaluation. Another approach to this problem is to look at critical differences in court-related and out-of-court processes in general.

Before deciding on the most appropriate option, one should determine the dispute resolution climate in the place of the dispute. Different state and federal courts offer a variety of ADR procedures from which to choose. Only when one knows what processes are available in court can one make an informed decision whether to choose a court-related or a private process.

Private and public processes are not mutually exclusive, and it is possible to combine them. For example, particularly when a factual issue needs to be established, a party may file a claim in court to go through discovery and later settle a dispute through a more facilitative and creative process such as mediation. This also brings up a strategic decision of sequencing private and public procedures. Should I sue first, and then settle? Or is it better to start with a more friendly private procedure? Or should the public and private processes proceed on parallel tracks?

How Should the Neutral Be Selected?

Another issue related to this choice is selection of a neutral. If a party wants to control the choice of the neutral he should decide for a private process. Sometimes parties have such confidence in a particular neutral that they leave the decision about process choice to that person, but usually a choice of a neutral comes after the procedure is already selected. In choosing the neutral, parties should take into account such issues as the neutral's personality and procedural and substantive expertise. In different kinds of disputes some of these elements will be relatively more important than others. For example, in a construction dispute, parties may decide that a neutral with engineering expertise is required; in a complex multiparty settlement, parties may want a neutral with particular process skills; and in an emotionally loaded divorce case they may seek a neutral with a particular personality who would be effective in such a volatile situation.

THREE IMPORTANT QUESTIONS STEMMING FROM EXISTING THEORIES FOR SELECTING A PROCESS

There have been at least four principal attempts to develop a taxonomy for deciding which process is best for a dispute. The important characteristics of each of these approaches are summarized in Table 24.1. It is difficult to compare these taxonomies, and even harder to synthesize from them the wisdom each demonstrates. The four taxonomies focus on different primary dispute resolution processes.[1] They use different categories to describe the same issue. For example, an issue may be listed under the category "impediment to the resolution of the case" under the Sander-Goldberg framework, while it is considered a "party-case characteristic" under the FJC framework, and organized under "parties' goals" in the Dauer model. The taxonomies also focus on different kinds of cases. For example, the CPR approach is designed with a focus on commercial disputes while the FJC developed its model with an emphasis on cases that go to court-annexed ADR.

Despite the difficulties in comparing taxonomies, we suggest that from this summary of approaches, three key questions emerge for those seeking to design an appropriate method for selecting a dispute resolution process.

- What are the parties' goals for the processes?
- What aspects of the dispute in question make it amenable to resolution by one or another process?
- What contributions might each process make to overcoming impediments to effective resolution?

The problem of matching the case to the process can be looked at from either end—the fuss (dispute) or the forum (processes). Early attempts to match procedures and disputes always began with describing characteristics of processes and then matching cases to them. The Sander and Goldberg article proposed an alternative analysis: that one analyze the case and then match it to an existing process or design a process that would best fit the parties' interests and case characteristics.[2]

Table 24.1. Matching Cases with Procedures: Summary of Approaches.

Author(s) of Approach	Processes Considered	Basic Question or Issue	Proposed Tools and Basis for the Results
Sander and Goldberg[1]	All (major) ADR processes Nonadjudicative processes in "impediments to settlement"	• What are the client's goals and what dispute resolution process is likely to achieve these goals? • What are the impediments to settlement, and what ADR procedure is likely to overcome those impediments?	Two grids with numeric utility of how each of the major DR processes achieves each of eight party's objectives or avoids each of ten impediments to settlement Based mostly on authors' experience, and later supported by empirical data
Dauer[2]	Not specified	• Characteristics of the case • Attributes of the parties • Features of the environment (including parties' objectives) • Barriers to Settlement	More detailed questions regarding each of the four basic questions or problems together with a commentary Example of the DC screening process presents utility value for nineteen objectives or characteristics of mediation, arbitration, and neutral case evaluation Based mostly on ADR literature and some court data
CPR[3]	Mainly mediation Particularly focuses on business disputes	• What are parties' goals for managing the dispute? • Is the dispute suitable for a problem-solving process? • What are potential benefits of mediation for the dispute in question? • Are there any "contraindications for mediation"?	Screening process consisting of ten or eleven subquestions for each of the three basic questions listed to the left. Parties or counsel choose one of three possible answers and use the key to interpreting responses and commentary to each question to provide a preliminary assessment of whether a case is appropriate for mediation Based on survey of more than six hundred corporate counsel and a study of 449 commercial dispute cases

Federal Judicial Center[4] — All major court-annexed ADR

- Is the case appropriate for ADR, based on the following?

  Parties' characteristics

  Case characteristics

- If appropriate, then, how can we best match the ADR process to the case? The two basic questions are

  Who might select the ADR process? (parties, court ADR staff, or judge)

  What criteria can the court use to match a case to an ADR process? (mediation, arbitration(s), ENE, SJT, or minitrial)

Two-stage approach:

First, detailed questions regarding parties and case characteristics that indicate whether the case is appropriate for any ADR process at all

Second, a list of examples of kinds of cases appropriate for different ADR processes

Based primarily on federal court practice and ADR theory

Sources: 1. F.E.A. Sander and S. B. Goldberg, "Fitting the Forum to the Fuss: A User-Friendly Guide to Selecting an ADR Procedure," *Negotiation Journal,* 1994, *10,* p. 49.

2. E. A. Dauer, *Manual of Dispute Resolution* (New York: Shepard's/McGraw-Hill, 1994).

3. CPR Institute for Dispute Resolution, *ADR Suitability Guide (Featuring Mediation Analysis Guide)* (New York: CPR Institute for Dispute Resolution, 2001).

4. R. J. Niemic, D. Stienstra, and R. E. Ravitz, *Guide to Judicial Management of Cases in ADR,* Federal Judicial Center, 2001, available at [http://www.fjc.gov/public/pdf.nsf/lookup/ADRGuide.pdf/$file/ADRGuide.pdf]. Oct. 2004.

Although the latter approach seems to be superior in most circumstances, in some cases, using only one kind of analysis may not be sufficient to identify all the helpful factors in choosing the most appropriate process. Therefore, in this chapter we propose to combine both approaches: In the first two questions referred to earlier (parties' goals and facilitating aspects of the case) the focus is on features of the case (fuss). In the third question (impediments), we look at the problem from the process (forum) perspective, asking how particular procedures can overcome impediments to an effective resolution.

We treat each of these questions in more detail in the following sections.

Question One: What Are the Parties' Goals?

The first question regarding the choice of the most appropriate process relates to objectives the party would like to achieve during, or at the end of, this process. In other words, this largely future-oriented approach asks: What should happen as a result of the choice of the particular dispute resolution process? As parties would usually have more than one objective, they should also try to prioritize their various goals.

Anna is going through a divorce with John. She brings her problem to you—an attorney—and asks for your advice on how to proceed. Her choice of procedure will partly depend on the goals that she wants to achieve. Does she want to preserve a workable relationship with John? Does she want John to participate in raising their children (if they have any), or, on the contrary, does she want to prevent him from seeing them? How important is it for her to maximize her monetary income from the divorce? How important is it when balanced against the relationship with John and other concerns? Does she want to keep divorce matters private? Does she have a desire for public vindication?

Before knowing what Anna really wants, it is impossible to make an informed decision about the preferable process. Table 24.2 shows some of the possible goals that Anna or other parties may want to achieve, and the degree to which various processes satisfy them.

It is very important that parties should treat the goals given in Table 24.2 just as examples among many other possible objectives. In each dispute, the parties should ask themselves about the particular goals that are salient under the circumstances. For example, in this case Anna's goal may be to prevent her children from testifying in court, and therefore she may strongly prefer mediation or other private and confidential processes.

The reader will note that some of these goals relate to a process outcome (such as privacy), and others are related to a substantive outcome (for example, to create new solutions, or to minimize or maximize recovery). The third possible sort of goals pertains to objectives that have both substantive and procedural impact (for example, to minimize costs). In looking for additional goals not listed in Table 24.2, these categories may be a helpful guide.

Table 24.2. Capacity of a Procedure to Satisfy Parties' Goals.

0 = unlikely to satisfy goal

3 = substantial chance of satisfying goal

Process[1] Goal	Mediation	Minitrial	Summary Jury Trial	ENE	Arbitration or Private Judging	Court Adjudication
1 Speed	3	2	2	3	1	0
2 Privacy	3	3	2	2	1	0
3 Public vindication	0	1	1	1	2	3
4 Neutral opinion	1	1	2	2	3	3
5 Minimize costs	3	2	2	3	$0-2^2$	0
6 Maintain or improve relationship	3	2	2	1	1	0
7 Precedent	$0-1^3$	0–1	0–1	0–1	2	3
8 Maximum or Minimum Recovery	$0\ (3)^4$	1	1	1	2	3
9 Create new solutions	3	3	1	2	1	0
10 Party control of process	3	2	1	1	$1-2^5$	0
11 Party control of outcome	3	3	1	2	1	0
12 Shift responsibility for decision to a third party	$0-1^6$	1	2	2	3	3
13 Court supervision or compulsion	$0-2^7$	0	1	1	2	3

(Continued)

Table 24.2. Capacity of a Procedure to Satisfy Parties' Goals (Continued).

0 = unlikely to satisfy goal

3 = substantial chance of satisfying goal

Process[1]	Mediation	Minitrial	Summary Jury Trial	ENE	Arbitration or Private Judging	Court Adjudication
14 Transformation of the parties	3	1	0	0	0	0
15 Other						

Source: Goals 1 through 8 were taken (after minor modification) from the table in Sander and Goldberg, "Fitting the Forum to the Fuss: A User-Friendly Guide to Selecting an ADR Procedure." *Negotiation Journal,* 1994, *10,* p. 53.

Notes: 1. The minitrial is a process invented in a complex patent and trademark dispute in 1976. It involves a hearing panel consisting of a neutral provider, flanked by a high-status settlement official from each side. Pursuant to a protocol jointly developed by the parties and the neutral, each side summarily presents the essence of its case and attempts to respond to questions from the panel and the other side. At the conclusion, the settlement officials of the two sides go off to see whether they can reach a mutually satisfactory, often interest-based, solution. If that is unsuccessful, then the neutral gives his view of the likely outcome if the case went to court, and armed with that prediction the parties again try to settle the case. The Summary Jury Trial is simply an adaptation of that process for jury cases. Here a small mock jury is assembled which, following the hearing, gives its "decision" solely for settlement purposes. ENE (early neutral evaluation) was first developed in the N.D. Cal. federal district court. Early in the case the parties appear before an experienced volunteer lawyer who seeks to help the parties to reach an amicable settlement, or, if no settlement is achieved, helps get the case ready for trial.

2. Since there are so many forms of arbitration (for example, single versus multiple arbitrators), costs will vary accordingly.

3. Although generally mediation and related processes are not good for establishing precedent for the world at large, they can serve to establish precedent for the parties involved.

4. Although, strictly speaking, mediation is not good for providing maximized gain or minimized loss, sometimes, through value creation and problem solving, one or both parties can achieve outcomes better than through adjudicative processes.

5. Ex ante, the parties have considerable freedom to select the process they want, but once they have done so, they are pretty well locked in.

6. This depends on the type of mediation being used.

7. "0" is the value for private out-of-court mediation; "2" for a court-related one.

After deciding which goals the party wants to achieve, she might be tempted to add together the values in Table 24.2 and thus "determine" which process best satisfies her objectives. Such an approach, however, assumes that all of these goals are of the same value for the party, which may not be true. A better approach would be ranking the goals and weighting them instead of adding them up. Therefore, the party could assign a weight (points) to each of her concerns, and then multiply them by the measure by which each procedure satisfies these goals (indicated in Table 24.2).

For example, Anna might decide the following: most important for her and the kids would be that she and John maintain a good relationship. In such a case she should assign the highest priority (weight of 3) to this goal. For the sake of consistency, we assume that the scale of goals' priorities is the same as the scale of processes satisfying these goals (that is, 0 to 3). It may also be very important for her to keep the procedure private. Although everybody thinks of her only as a victim now, she is convinced that had outsiders known all the facts about the breakdown of their marriage, she would have to bear part of the blame for it. Since it is less important than maintaining the relationship, she could assign a lesser weight (for example, 2) to the goal of "privacy." She is also concerned that she may not manage to be tough enough in settlement negotiations with John. Moreover, according to her lawyer, the law is on her side, and thus she has a slight preference for shifting the responsibility for decision to a third party. Her last concern is to resolve this matter at a minimal cost. Since "shifting responsibility for a decision to a third party" and "minimizing costs" are less important to her than the first two goals, which she weighted 3 and 2, she would assign weight 1 to each of them.

Assigning weights to these different goals should then be followed by multiplying assigned weight by the effectiveness of each procedure in satisfying this goal (applied from Table 24.2). For example, weight 3 for "maintaining or improving relationship" would translate to the weighted "power or strength" of 9 (3 × 3) for mediation; 6 (3 × 2) for minitrial; 6 (3 × 2) for summary jury trial; 3 (3 × 1) for early neutral evaluation; 3 (3 × 1) for arbitration; and 0 (3 × 0) for adjudication. After multiplying weights assigned to the selected goals, a party would then add up the numbers representing the strength of the weighted goals for each of the procedures. The result of this process for Anna's example is as follows: mediation = 18, minitrial = 15, summary jury trial = 14, early neutral evaluation = 12, arbitration = 9, and adjudication = 3. In this case Anna would conclude that mediation will probably best realize her objectives, and the worst choice in this case would be adjudication.

Although this example and proposed method involves a lot of counting and weighting, we still think that matching cases and procedures is more art than science. It must be remembered that the outcomes of these calculations should not be taken literally, but only as guidance for evaluating parties' goals.

It is also essential to think about the goals of the other party. Parties who have consistent goals can probably easily be convinced to use one process. However, what if the goals of the other party are inconsistent and would suggest another process? A good option might be that they would agree to start from mediation, which could help them clarify their goals and which is a "safe," no-commitment procedure for both parties, unless the case is one in which even mediation is not appropriate.

Question Two: What Aspects of the Dispute in Question Make It Amenable to Resolution by One or Another Process?

Every case has some features or dynamics that can help facilitate a good outcome for a party. A party should reflect on what attributes or features exist in his particular case. He should then consider what process is most likely to trigger or elicit these features. Certain features of the case and the parties can facilitate reaching effective resolution. However, they can only be used if triggered by an appropriate dispute resolution procedure. For example, a good relationship and trust between the parties' attorneys can facilitate their communication and therefore lead to a better settlement. However, these facilitating features would probably not come into play had the parties selected litigation. Moreover, litigation could quickly destroy a preexisting good relationship and trust, and become an impediment to the settlement later. Therefore it is crucial for the parties to recognize the attributes that may facilitate effective resolution and match them with the process that may trigger those attributes.

Generally speaking, every procedure is capable of activating some of the strengths of the case or the parties. For example, mediation and minitrial can facilitate communication and maximize parties' chances for a value-creating resolution. Summary jury trial and early neutral evaluation may give a chance for early assessment of the strengths and weaknesses of the case, thus allowing the parties to make a more informed decision about a possible settlement. Adjudication (and binding arbitration) provide certain procedural tools that can serve parties' needs, including court enforcement during the dispute resolution process and at the decision-implementation stage.

Because of the different facilitating abilities of the procedures, in Table 24.3 we divided them into problem solving (mediation and minitrial), reality checking (SJT and ENE), and adjudicating (arbitration or private judging and adjudication).

These are just some of the possible strengths or features a case might present. Parties should always be open-minded about others. This examination, however, clearly indicates that problem-solving approaches, and particularly mediation, can most efficiently trigger most of the strengths.

Table 24.3. Features of the Case That Are Likely to Encourage Resolution by One or Another Process.

0 = unlikely to trigger the "feature"

3 = most likely to trigger the "feature"

Process	Problem Solving		Reality Checking		Adjudicating	
	Mediation	Minitrial	Summary Jury Trial	ENE	Arbitration or Private Judging	Court Adjudication
Feature to Trigger[1]						
1 Good relationship between the attorneys[2]	3	2	1	1	0	0
2 Good relationship between the parties	3	2	1	1	0	0
3 Case seems apt for creative problem solving	3	2	1	1	0	0
4 One or both parties are willing to apologize	3	3	1	1	0	0
5 High rank agents are involved	2	3	2[3]	2[3]	1	1
6 Eager to settle (time is of essence)	3	2	2[3]	2[3]	0	0
7 Party would benefit from formal procedural protections	0–2[4]	1	2	1	2	3
8 Linkage to other issues in case	3	3	1	1	1	0
9 Other						

Notes: 1. Due to space limits we do not describe particular strengths here.

2. Similar effect can be achieved if a particular counsel (or party) has an excellent reputation for truth and reliability.

3. If reality checking is the problem, then SJT and ENE are fairly suitable.

4. The result might depend on whether we are dealing with in-court or out-of-court mediation.

Question Three: What Contributions Might Each Process Make to Overcoming Impediments to Effective Resolution?

In the third step of the analysis we suggest that one should focus on capacity of various procedures to overcome impediments to effective resolution. The vast majority of cases ultimately settle.[3] Even when they don't settle, most parties at least explore whether settlement is possible. In many cases, both parties perceive settlement as more beneficial than a binding win-lose decision of a third party. Therefore, considering impediments to resolution, the parties and their counsel should mainly focus on impediments to settlement, and particularly the capacity of different procedures to overcome such impediments.

Some impediments to settlement are best overcome through a problem-solving or reality-checking process. Other impediments may be best overcome by some adjudicative procedure. For that reason, and to give the parties the full spectrum of procedures to choose from, Table 24.4 includes adjudicative procedures as well.[4]

In any specific dispute parties should also look for other impediments presented by their case. If they feel that some of them are more important than others, they could utilize the procedure of weighting and adding strengths and impediments, similar to the method described in the case of parties' goals. Table 24.4 seems to suggest again that mediation is usually more efficient than other procedures in facilitating dispute resolution. This and other findings and conclusions presented so far in this chapter are summarized in the following section.

A USER-FRIENDLY, MEDIATION-CENTERED APPROACH

Step One: Assume Mediation

The combination of the theoretical examination just presented and the empirical data reviewed in creating these tables suggests that mediation is almost always a superior starting process. Even if mediation does not produce a settlement, it becomes a route leading to other processes. Trying to resolve disputes through mediation can result in one of three possible outcomes:

1. The case settles entirely.
2. The mediation resolves some of the issues, leaving others for another possibly more coercive procedure.
3. If the mediation produces no resolution, the mediator can still give an informed recommendation for another procedure.

Each of these options would make a party better off than if he or she had gone straight to litigation.

This approach is consistent with writings on dispute resolution system design, in which less invasive methods are usually preferred to more invasive ones.[5]

Table 24.4. Capacity of a Procedure to Overcome Impediments to Effective Resolution.

0 = unlikely to overcome an impediment

3 = most likely to overcome an impediment

Process	Mediation	Minitrial	SJT	ENE	Arbitration or Private Judging	Court Adjudication
Impediment						
1 Poor communication	3	2	1	1	1	0
2 Need to express emotions	3	1	1	1	1	0
3 Different view of facts	2	2	3	3	2	2
4 Different view of law	1	2	3	3	2^1	2
5 Important principle	1	0	0	0	1	3
6 Constituent pressure	3	2	2	2	0	0
7 Linkage to other disputes	2	2	1	1	1	0
8 Multiple parties	2	1	1	1	1	1
9 Different lawyer-client interests	2	1	1	1	1	1
10 Jackpot syndrome	0	1	1	1	3	3

(Continued)

Table 24.4. Capacity of a Procedure to Overcome Impediments to Effective Resolution (*Continued*).

0 = unlikely to overcome an impediment
3 = most likely to overcome an impediment

Process	Mediation	Minitrial	SJT	ENE	Arbitration or Private Judging	Court Adjudication
11 Fear of disclosing true interests (Negotiator's Dilemma)	3	2	1	1	0	0
12 Psychological barriers	2	2	1	1	0	0
13 Inability to negotiate effectively	2	2	1	1	2	2
14 Unrealistic expectations	2	2	3	3	0[2]	0
15 Disproportionate power of the parties	1	1	2	2	2	2
16 Other						

Notes: 1. Although adjudicative processes are in fact the only way to resolve the disputed question of law, sometimes the answer comes too late for the parties to use this knowledge, and they can come to a more efficient solution if they receive an informed opinion earlier in the case. For that reason we assign value 2 (not 3) to the adjudicative processes.

2. Although arbitration and litigation, in practice, most effectively can show the parties whether their expectations were realistic or not, after such binding resolution it is too late for the parties to use this knowledge to arrive at the better result. We think that the benefit for the parties of having a realistic expectation is to be able to settle rationally. An arbitration or a court award usually precludes the possibility of such later settlement.

Mediation is very flexible and can be fitted to many different contexts, and can accommodate different needs of the parties and characteristics of the case. Because mediation is more likely to produce a Pareto superior result than is adjudication, it is more likely to be responsive to the needs of both parties to the dispute. Mediation is most likely to overcome impediments to settlement, often by avoiding the need to resolve disputed questions of fact and focusing instead on a forward-looking solution. Mediation is most likely to trigger features of the case that facilitate efficient resolution of the dispute. Even when one or both parties believe they will win in litigation, mediation will still be useful by quantifying the likelihood of victory and exploring more attractive alternative solutions. Parties are more likely to comply with an agreed upon settlement as contrasted with an outcome ordered by a third party.[6] Finally, according to empirical research, practitioners and parties prefer mediation.[7]

In addition to these macrobenefits of mediation there are a number of potential microbenefits that argue for a first resort to mediation in most cases. Mediation can aid in clarifying the issues in dispute. Mediation often helps parties to channel or control anger or other negative emotions, while still giving one or both parties an opportunity to tell their stories and to be fully heard by the other side. Mediation provides an opportunity for an apology. Through mediation, parties may have access to a "reality check" from a knowledgeable intermediary regarding their legal positions or expectations. Mediation provides a confidential setting in which to explore each other's interests and needs, in which to explore the possibility for trade-offs or creative solutions, and in which to educate the decision makers on either side. Mediators sometimes make offers and counteroffers more acceptable by presenting them as their own, and mediators often reframe proposals, inject their own ideas, as appropriate, and take blame, if necessary.

Step Two: Ask Whether Mediation Would Be Inappropriate

At the outset, it should be noted that a careful study of Table 24.2 shows that mediation and adjudication have opposing strengths and weaknesses in their ability to achieve particular goals. Goals such as "improve relationship" or "minimize costs" that are highly likely to be attained through mediation (score of 3) are highly unlikely to be achieved through adjudication (score of 0–1). Similarly, goals such as obtaining a precedent are highly likely to be achieved by adjudication (score of 3) but very unlikely to be achieved through mediation (score of 0). Thus a major category of cases that are inappropriate for mediation is those cases that require adjudication.

When Mediation Is Inappropriate from the Perspective of One or Both of the Parties. As a matter of party choice, mediation may be inappropriate or insufficient for certain kinds of disputes. Such contraindications might be brought to light by the following questions:

- Does one of the parties seek an outcome that only a court or an arbitrator can provide? (For example, to set a precedent that will bind more than the immediate parties, to receive public vindication of some sort, or to maximize or minimize recovery.)

- Does one of the parties view the dispute as involving a matter of principle?

- Does one of the parties consider the claim to be wholly frivolous? (If so, a client may have a standard policy for handling the claim.)

If any of these features of a dispute is present, mediation may be inappropriate.

In other circumstances mediation is simply less likely to be successful, and other procedures may be more appropriate. These partial contraindications might be brought into light by the following questions:

- Do the parties have differing views of the relevant law? If so, litigation or some other means of clarifying legal uncertainty will be more appropriate than mediation.

- Is the outcome one that is likely to require judicial supervision? If yes, litigation may be most appropriate. (In some situations in which enforcement issues are anticipated but the case would benefit from the problem-solving feature of mediation, the resulting agreement could be embodied in a court decree.)

- Do the parties have a need to resolve their differing views of the facts? If yes, then mediation as a stand-alone procedure may be unhelpful. Mediation may still be useful after establishing these facts (for example, by a neutral third party or a panel of experts).

- Is there a significant power imbalance between the parties?

- Do the parties seek a neutral opinion on the extent of damages or on some other limited issue?

If such "contraindications" exist, the case *may* be inappropriate for mediation. These impediments should be weighed against goals of the parties, strengths of the parties and the case, and other factors that may result in mediation still being superior to its alternatives.

If this analysis results in a fifty-fifty case for mediation, then mediation should still be used because it is such a hospitable procedure. It is always easier, if necessary, to go from mediation to adjudication than would be true of the reverse course. Moreover, the case may lend itself to fragmentation, whereby one or more issues are resolved by mediation and the remainder by some other approach that is likely to suggest itself in the course of the mediation proceeding.

When Mediation Is Inappropriate from the Perspective of the Public. Some cases present circumstances that make mediation inappropriate from the perspective of the public—even if the parties themselves may be receptive to mediation. Among the most important contraindications from the public perspective is the public interest in judicial interpretation of an unclear statute or constitutional provision. Perhaps the most obvious example of such a need presented itself in *Brown* v. *Board of Education*.[8] Some cases—such as criminal cases—present a need for public sanction and may therefore be inappropriate for mediation. Finally, if the case involves recurring violations by the same party (for example, of consumer protection provisions) that militate toward a broad, injunctive remedy rather than case-by-case settlements, mediation may not serve the public interest.

Weighing the public interest in these types of cases against the parties' "freedom to settle" any particular dispute presents a difficult question—one that is beyond the scope of this chapter.

Step Three, Part One: If Mediation—What Type?

The notion of mediation as a presumed process may sound simplistic. In fact, however, a whole range of mediation processes may be applied in each case. Mediation is not a simple predetermined single process, but a range of processes. Labels describing the most important types of mediation include facilitative versus elicitive, evaluative versus directive, transformative versus problem solving, and court-annexed versus private. These approaches are not exclusive, and there is a continuum of mediators' behaviors that can be both evaluative and facilitative—"on the same issue, on different issues, simultaneously, or at different times."[9] There is also a possibility to be facilitative on substance and directive on process, as well as many other variables (such as use of caucus or not). Thus the presumption of mediation is not the end of the process; it suggests rather the need to fit a particular kind of mediation to the fuss, depending on the needs of the particular case.

The choice among the different types of mediation would depend on such facts as the nature of the dispute, the relations between the parties (both now and prospective), and what type of third-party assistance they need. For example, in a long-simmering dispute between two neighbors about a common driveway, what is needed is clarification of the cause as well as an attempt to work out a better modus operandi in the future; hence facilitative or transformative mediation seems called for. By contrast, in a large and complex commercial dispute in which the parties have attorneys but are far apart on damages, a highly experienced evaluative mediator is needed.

Step Three, Part Two: If Not Mediation—Then What?

When mediation is not appropriate, disputants should resort to the analysis presented earlier in an effort to fit the forum to the fuss. This effort includes the possibility of designing a custom-made process that responds to the needs of

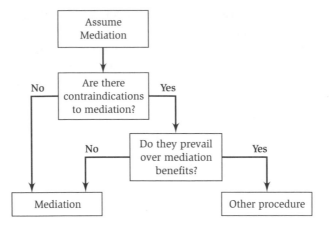

Figure 24.1. A Mediation-Centered Approach.

the parties and the characteristics of the case. But we believe that the case in which mediation is inappropriate will be relatively rare. Our thesis is that one should begin the search for the most appropriate process with automatic resort to mediation, leaving the primary task the choice of the type of mediation that is most suitable for the particular case (Figure 24.1).

CONCLUSION

Selecting an appropriate dispute resolution procedure for the effective resolution of a particular dispute is a challenging task—more art than science. It may involve a number of intangible factors, such as the ADR culture in the venue in question and the power dynamics between the parties. In this chapter we have examined the theoretical issues presented by some of the leading scholars and organizations that have looked at the problem. We have also taken into account the actual practice in the field (to the extent there exist reliable data).[10]

A preliminary conclusion of this examination is that there are no ironclad, definitive answers. However, in this chapter we tried to present several reasons for our suggested approach of normally beginning with mediation (a revealing and flexible process that readily opens the way to other processes that may be needed). The only exception to this approach comes in the limited situations in which there are contraindications to mediation. In all other situations, using some form of mediation is likely to be most productive.

Notes

1. Compare CPR Institute for Dispute Resolution, *ADR Suitability Guide (Featuring Mediation Analysis Guide)* (New York: CPR Institute for Dispute Resolution, 2001), on mediation, and E. A. Dauer, *Manual of Dispute Resolution* (New York: Shepard's/McGraw-Hill, 1994), on unspecified processes.

2. F.E.A. Sander and S. B. Goldberg, "Fitting the Forum to the Fuss: A User-Friendly Guide to Selecting an ADR Procedure," *Negotiation Journal,* 1994, *10,* 49–67.

3. According to the Administrative Office of the United States Courts, only 1.8 percent of federal civil cases were disposed of by trial. See M. Galanter, "The Vanishing Trial: An Examination of Trials and Related Matters in Federal and State Courts," *Journal of Empirical Legal Studies,* 2004, *1*(2), 627–636.

4. Impediments 1 through 10 are taken (and slightly modified) from the table in F.E.A. Sander and S. B. Goldberg, "Fitting the Forum to the Fuss: A User-Friendly Guide to Selecting an ADR Procedure," *Negotiation Journal,* 1994, *10,* p. 55.

5. See in particular W. L. Ury, J. M. Brett, and S. B. Goldberg, *Getting Disputes Resolved: Designing Systems to Cut the Costs of Conflict* (San Francisco: Jossey-Bass, 1988); C. A. Costantino and C. Sickles Merchant, *Designing Conflict Management Systems: A Guide to Creating Productive and Healthy Organizations* (San Francisco: Jossey-Bass, 1996); and D. B. Lipsky and R. L. Seeber, *The Appropriate Resolution of Corporate Disputes: A Report on the Growing Use of ADR by U.S. Corporations* (Institute of Conflict Resolution Cornell/Perc Institute on Conflict Resolution, 1998).

6. C. McEwen, "Note on Mediation Research," in S. B. Goldberg, F.E.A. Sander, N. R. Rogers, and S. R. Cole *Dispute Resolution: Negotiation, Mediation and Other Processes* (4th ed.) (New York: Aspen Law and Business, 2003).

7. See, for example, J. M. Brett, Z. I. Barsness, and S. B. Goldberg, "The Effectiveness of Mediation: An Independent Analysis of Cases Handled by Four Major Service Providers," *Negotiation Journal,* 1996, *12*(3), 259–269; American Arbitration Association, *Dispute-Wise Business Management* (New York: American Arbitration Association, 2003); and Lipsky and Seeber, *The Appropriate Resolution of Corporate Disputes,* 1998.

8. See *Brown* v. *Board of Education,* 347 U.S. 483 (1954), involving a challenge to the validity of the "separate but equal" doctrine under the equal protection clause of the U.S. Constitution.

9. See L. L. Riskin, "Who Decides What? Rethinking the Grid of Mediator Orientations," *Dispute Resolution Magazine,* Winter 2003, *9,* p. 23.

10. See, for example, J. M. Brett, Z. I. Barsness, and S. B. Goldberg, "The Effectiveness of Mediation," 1996.

Additional Resources

Bush, R.A.B., and Folger, J. P. *The Promise of Mediation: Responding to Conflict Through Empowerment and Recognition.* San Francisco: Jossey-Bass, 1994.

Bush, R.A.B., and Folger, J. P. "Transformative Mediation and Third-Party Intervention: Ten Hallmarks of a Transformative Approach to Practice." *Mediation Quarterly,* 1996, *13*(4), 263–278.

Effron, J. "Alternatives to Litigation: Factors in Choosing." *Alternatives to Litigation,* 1989, *52,* 480–497.

Goldberg, S. B., Sander, F.E.A., Rogers, N. H., and Cole, S. R. *Dispute Resolution: Negotiation, Mediation, and Other Processes* (4th ed.). New York: Aspen Law and Business, 2003.

Love, L. P. "The Top Ten Reasons Why Mediators Should Not Evaluate." *Florida State University Law Review,* 1997, *24,* 937–948.

Mnookin, R. H. "Why Negotiations Fail: An Exploration of Barriers to the Resolution of Conflict." *Ohio State Journal on Dispute Resolution,* 1993, *8*(2), 235–249.

Niemic, R. J., Stienstra, D., and Ravitz, R. R. *Guide to Judicial Management of Cases in ADR.* Federal Judicial Center, 2001, available at [http://www.fjc.gov/public/pdf.nsf/lookup/ADRGuide.pdf/$file/ADRGuide.pdf]. Oct. 2004.

Riskin, L. L. "Understanding Mediators' Orientations, Strategies and Techniques: A Grid for the Perplexed." *Harvard Negotiation Law Review,* 1996, *1,* 7–51.

Riskin, L. L. "Decisionmaking in Mediation: The New Old Grid and the New Grid System." *Notre Dame Law Review,* 2003, *79,* 1–53.

Senger, J. M. *Federal Dispute Resolution.* San Francisco: Jossey-Bass, 2004.

PART FOUR

EMERGING ISSUES
IN DISPUTE RESOLUTION

CHAPTER TWENTY-FIVE

What Could a Leader Learn from a Mediator?

Dispute Resolution Strategies
for Organizational Leadership

Hannah Riley Bowles

In the past half century a great deal has been learned about the resolving
of disputes, and leaders should familiarize themselves with it.
—John W. Gardner (1912–2002)[1]

It is hard to imagine a leadership situation that is devoid of conflict, or even what the function of leadership would be on an island of perpetual harmony where all parties shared a perfectly common vision of their objectives and how to achieve them. Many of leadership's most important challenges are born of conflict—to build coalitions among divergent interests, forge consensus from discord, and transform destructive disagreement into constructive debates.[2] We easily recognize effective leaders as expert negotiators as they confront and appeal to a multiplicity of interests to achieve their objectives.[3] We less often recognize when leaders are acting as informal mediators or arbitrators of disputes. Yet, the activities of mediators and arbitrators overlap a great deal with the skills and responsibilities of leadership.[4]

The aim of this chapter is to leverage some of the insights from the study of formal dispute resolution for the practice of leadership, and to provide organizational leaders with some new lenses through which to analyze the strategies they choose in managing disputes.[5] The chapter starts with a brief introduction to three formal dispute resolution processes: mediation, arbitration, and "med-arb" (a sequential combination of mediation and then, if necessary, arbitration). It continues with a discussion of some of the commonalities and distinctions between the roles that leaders and formal third parties play in resolving disputes. The chapter closes with an exploration of some of the advantages and disadvantages of these three dispute resolution strategies, depending on particular barriers to dispute resolution and leadership objectives.

MEDIATION, ARBITRATION, AND MED-ARB

A *mediator* is a third party who helps conflicting parties reach a voluntary agreement.[6] To do so, mediators generally convene and orchestrate a series of private and joint meetings with the conflicting parties, the purpose of which is to explore the participants' interests and options for resolving the dispute and to craft a mutually acceptable final agreement.[7] An *arbitrator* is a third party tasked with making a binding decision in order to resolve a dispute.[8] In arbitration, the third party convenes a form of hearing, at which the conflicting parties have an opportunity to explain their positions and present testimonies or other evidence supporting their cases.[9] Mediators and arbitrators both maintain considerable control over the dispute resolution process, but arbitrators are supposed to take control over the outcome of the dispute, and mediators are not.[10]

In practice, this distinction between mediators and arbitrators is sometimes blurred. There are relatively weak mediator roles, for instance, in which the third party has no particular expertise with regard to the substance of the dispute. Third parties in weaker mediator roles tend to act as neutral facilitators, employing their process skills to maintain a fair and constructive discussion and to encourage the parties to reach their own mutually beneficial solutions. There are also stronger mediator roles, in which the third party may suggest solutions or draft agreements and even pressure participants toward a particular resolution of the dispute.[11] These stronger mediators cannot dictate solutions, but they may have considerable sway over how the parties resolve the dispute.

Med-arb is a two-phase process. In the first phase, the parties attempt to reach a voluntary solution with the help of the third party acting as a mediator. If the first phase is unsuccessful, the third party shifts from the role of mediator to the role of arbitrator and issues a binding resolution to the dispute.[12] Studies have shown that mediators who have the ability to impose a solution act more like the stronger mediators described above, intervening forcefully at times and using heavy-handed tactics to pressure the parties into agreement.[13] There is also evidence to suggest that parties may be more conciliatory toward one another in med-arb processes as opposed to straight mediation—perhaps out of fear of losing control of the outcome or out of deference to an authority who can decide their fate.[14]

Mediation processes tend to have high but not perfect rates of agreement (estimated at 60 to 80 percent in some research). The greatest advantage of arbitration and med-arb processes over straight mediation is that the third party retains the right to decide the outcome of the dispute.[15] Conversely, the strongest advantage of mediation and med-arb procedures over straight arbitration is the feeling of control that the parties have over the final outcome of the dispute. Research shows that the more decision control the parties perceived themselves to have had, the more fair they judged the process and outcome to be.[16] Fair process is important to dispute resolution because it tends to enhance participants' satisfaction with the outcome, improve relations between the parties, and prevent the emergence of new problems or a recurrence of past disputes.[17] If parties do not perceive a dispute resolution process to have been fair, they are more likely to actively or passively resist the outcome.[18]

Another advantage of mediation over arbitration is the potential for enhanced information sharing and joint problem solving between the parties. The parties' principal responsibility in mediation is to reach a mutually beneficial solution with their counterpart. The parties' principal responsibility in arbitration is to persuade the third party of the correctness or righteousness of their position in the dispute. Parties in an arbitration process are likely to be more strategic in their information sharing than are parties in a mediation process, because their job is to win as opposed to collaborate to resolve the dispute. Because of this fundamental difference in the parties' perspectives, mediators tend to be in a better position than arbitrators to surface all relevant information to the dispute, identify shared or compatible interests, explore options for joint gains and, ultimately, maximize the efficiency of the dispute resolution outcome so that no value is left on the table.[19] It warrants note that one potential downside of med-arb as compared to straight mediation is that the parties may be reluctant to share information during the mediation phase, if it could reflect negatively on their case in the arbitration phase. Such strategic control of information could undermine the identification of mutually beneficial solutions.[20]

LEADERS AS MEDIATORS AND ARBITRATORS

There are some strong analogies to be drawn between these three formal dispute resolution processes (that is, mediation, med-arb, and arbitration) and the roles that leaders play. For instance, a chief executive officer (CEO) may act a lot like a mediator in managing conflicts among members of the board of directors. The CEO does not have the authority to impose a solution when disputes arise among board members (as an arbitrator would), but the CEO may play a central role in facilitating agreement on productive solutions to governance issues (as a mediator would).[21] When disputes arise between subordinates, the CEO may decide to hear out both sides and issue a decision (as an arbitrator would), or try first to help the parties to find their own solution to the problem before resorting to solving their problem for them (as would a formal third party in med-arb).[22]

However, unlike formal third parties who are assigned to mediator, med-arb, or arbitrator roles, leaders rarely benefit from clear procedural guidelines as to how they are supposed to manage disputes.[23] Leaders' enhanced discretion provides the advantage of flexibility of response, but it also creates uncertainty as to the appropriate course of action.[24] Organizational disputes are also rarely as well defined and demarcated as are the disputes assigned to formal third parties. Indeed, as Kolb and Sheppard explain, "Organizational conflicts are not conceived of as disputes but as problems . . . that are embedded in ongoing organizational activity."[25] Leaders have to interpret for themselves what the boundaries are of the problem at hand, who the appropriate parties are to involve in the problem-solving process, and what type of process strategy they should adopt in attempting to resolve the issue. Moreover, some organizational norms and cultures suppress conflict or pressure leaders to make decisions in such a way that opportunities to employ dispute resolution strategies, such as mediation, become obscured.[26]

Another factor that complicates the dispute resolution roles that leaders adopt is that leaders rarely approach disputes as fully detached and disinterested parties. Parties normally seek out the assistance of formal third parties for their independence and neutrality toward the dispute, as well as for their dispute resolution skills and expertise. Organizational leaders, in contrast, generally have ongoing relationships with the disputants and a personal stake in how the dispute is resolved.[27] Leaders have to figure into their dispute resolution strategy choices how their intervention might affect their ongoing relationship with the disputants and how options for resolving the dispute could affect their own self-interest.[28] A leader may feel compelled to play to a more directive role, for instance, when organizational members are coming to an agreement with which the leader disagrees.[29] Parties' outcome expectations are also likely to be influenced by whether they perceive the leader to be positively affiliated with their own or the other side of the dispute, and these prior expectations may color their satisfaction with the process and outcome.[30]

In sum, as compared to most formal third parties, organizational leaders tend to have more discretion in choosing their dispute resolution strategy and tend to enter the dispute resolution process with a greater stake in the dispute resolution process and outcome. These discrepancies do not obviate the potential usefulness of formal dispute strategies for organizational leadership. Indeed, as Carnevale argues, there is a strong analogy to be drawn between intervention in organizational and international disputes.[31] In respects similar to organizational leaders, international mediators enter dispute resolution processes with interests in maintaining long-term relationships with the parties and in influencing how problems between the parties are solved. As is the case with international mediators, organizational leaders have to adapt their strategies over time to the situational circumstances and their intervention objectives.

MATCHING THE PROCESS WITH THE PROBLEM

The following section outlines five barriers to organizational dispute resolution and five objectives that leaders may carry into dispute resolution efforts, and it explores some of the advantages and disadvantages of the three dispute resolution process strategies described earlier: arbitration, mediation, and med-arb. Applied to leadership situations, an arbitration strategy would involve reviewing each side's argument in the dispute and issuing a final decision as to how the problem should be resolved. A mediation strategy would involve approaching the problem with the intention of helping the parties work together to achieve a resolution to their dispute. To do this, the leader would employ process tools of mediation, such as holding private and joint meetings with the parties, probing the parties' interests, exploring options for resolving the dispute, and facilitating the crafting of an agreement between the parties that is efficient (in other words, leaves no value on the table) and sustainable. A mediation approach would require holding back from imposing a solution on the parties, but would still allow for considerable influence by the leader over the final resolution. A med-arb strategy would involve a hybrid approach. The leader would employ the tools of a mediation strategy, but would make clear to the parties that, if they cannot reach agreement, he or she will hear out each side and impose a solution. It warrants note that a pure mediation strategy is a false option if the leader has decision-making authority over the resolution of the dispute, because a pure mediation strategy would entail abdicating that responsibility. If the leader has decision-making authority, a dispute resolution strategy involving mediation is by definition a med-arb strategy.

As summarized in Tables 25.1 and 25.2, I explore the implications of each of these dispute resolution processes given a specific barrier and leadership objective and propose a suggested strategy. The list of barriers and objectives were selected for illustrative purposes; they do not exhaustively or even systematically represent the range of barriers faced or objectives pursued by organizational leaders. In proposing a suggested strategy for addressing one of these barriers or objectives, I am assuming that the leader seeks an efficient resolution to the dispute and to its antecedents (for example, relationship issues, systemic problems) to the extent that they are likely to impede sustainable resolution of the problem. I break the discussion down by individual barrier and leadership objective for expositional purposes, not to suggest that the preferred strategy given a particular barrier or objective necessarily makes it the appropriate course of action. Most organizational disputes are characterized by more than one of these (and other) barriers, and leaders often have more than one objective in resolving a dispute. The purpose of the following analysis is to illuminate some of the pros and cons of these dispute resolution processes depending on situational circumstances. Leaders should obviously weigh the importance of competing considerations and choose the approach that they deem to be the best match to the problem.

Barriers to Dispute Resolution

The five barriers to dispute resolution addressed are summarized in Table 25.1. The first is a lack of authority to impose a solution to a dispute. The second barrier

Table 25.1. Barriers to Dispute Resolution and Suggested Strategies.

Barrier	Suggested Process Strategy	Summary of Explanation
Lack of authority to impose solution	Mediation	Arbitration strategy likely to engender resistance from parties. Mediation strategy enhances influence over dispute resolution process and outcome in absence of decision-making authority.
Poor relationship between disputants	Mediation or Med-Arb[a]	Pure arbitration strategy solves substance, but not relationship problem. Mediation strategy helps parties learn to work together.
Complex multi-issue dispute	Mediation or Med-Arb	Arbitration strategy limited to presenting problem. Mediation strategy allows for more thorough problem-solving process.
Multiple stakeholders	Mediation or Med-Arb	Arbitration strategy limited to direct parties to dispute. Mediation strategy allows for broader inclusion of interested parties.
Self-serving bias	Mediation or Med-Arb	Arbitration strategy heightens bias by focusing parties on winning over compromise. Mediation encourages more perspective taking.

[a]Whether a mediation or med-arb strategy applies depends on whether the leader has decision-making authority.

is when a substantive dispute escalates into or has its roots in an interpersonal conflict that impedes the sustainable resolution of the dispute. The third potential barrier is the complexity of the problem. The fourth potential barrier is a high number of stakeholders to the dispute. The fifth is self-serving bias, an example of a psychological barrier that can lead parties to be overconfident about their positions and impede their ability to resolve their disputes.

Lack of Authority to Impose a Solution. Leaders are likely to be particularly tempted to intervene and become more directive in disputes when they are concerned about the outcome or perceive their own interests to be at stake.[32] Yet, there are many disputes that arise in organizations that leaders cannot resolve on their own because they lack the authority—formal or informal—to impose their way. Research shows that managers who lack the authority to impose a solution are more likely to fail in resolving a dispute when they attempt to tell the parties what to do as opposed to try to mediate an agreement between them.[33] The advantage of a mediation approach is that it enhances parties' sense of ownership over the problem-solving process, while still allowing the leader a great deal of influence over the substantive outcome of the dispute. Even though they do not have final decision-making authority, mediators may become deeply involved in the details of how a dispute is resolved and leverage their status, authority, and resources to influence the parties in a particular substantive direction.[34] As summarized in Table 25.1, mediation is the suggested dispute resolution process strategy when leaders seek resolutions to disputes that they do not have the formal or informal authority to resolve on their own.

Poor Relationship Between Disputants. The more acrimonious a dispute between colleagues, the less likely we are to think that a cooperative solution can be found.[35] The less potential we see for a cooperative solution between the disputants, the more tempted we are to impose our own solution to the problem.[36] If leaders make a practice of solving the problems of bickering colleagues for them (for example, by using an arbitration strategy), then those colleagues are likely to come to believe that the way to answer their problems is to appeal to the boss as opposed to trying harder to work together. Moreover, if the leader's solution to the colleagues' problem seems unfair or does not reflect an understanding of their primary concerns (for example, that the other person is really the problem), the disputants' motivation for following through on the leader's solution may be diminished. When faced with a dispute in which the parties are unable to work together constructively, it is in the long-term interest of the leader and organization to invest the time to employ a mediation or med-arb (versus arbitration) strategy that helps the parties' learn how to work through their problems and that heightens their commitment to the dispute resolution outcome.[37]

Complex Multi-Issue Dispute. Some organizational problems run deeper and are more complex than the immediate dispute might suggest. As a result, to address only the presenting problem would not prevent future eruptions over the same fundamental issues. For instance, recurrent disputes over the quality or timeliness of work products or a lack of responsiveness to e-mail and phone messages might appear on the surface to be interpersonal squabbles, but they could also reflect deeper organizational issues. Coworkers may believe they are underserved by certain colleagues, while those colleagues are simply prioritizing their work to be consistent with organizational incentives. A dispute over an employee's workload or job responsibilities may be best resolved by evaluating the alignment of his or her compensation or promotion incentives with organizational needs.

When leaders employ mediation or med-arb (versus pure arbitration) strategies, they are better positioned to diagnose the problem jointly with the parties and to enlarge the agenda in ways that facilitate a more thorough resolution of the dispute.[38] Once the parties achieve a more constructive definition of the problem and start generating options for resolving the broader issues, the leader can continue to facilitate the problem-solving process by helping the parties generate creative avenues for agreement, imposing deadlines, and ensuring faithful execution of the agreement.[39] Even if the parties clearly cannot fully resolve the problem on their own, a med-arb strategy may still be preferable to a pure arbitration strategy. This is because the leader is likely to gain a deeper grasp of the problem and of options for its resolution over the course of an initial mediation phase than could be achieved through a pure arbitration process in which parties compete to win over the leader to their starting position in the dispute. As described previously, mediation and med-arb strategies are likely to be more effective than an arbitration strategy at maximizing information sharing and joint problem solving, which are often important in resolving complex, multi-issue disputes.

Multiple Stakeholders. Multiple stakeholders can pose barriers both to the dispute resolution process and to the sustainable resolution of a dispute once agreement has been reached. Imagine, for example, that there is a dispute between the information technology (IT) group and the finance department over the timeline and process for the implementation of new accounting software. A senior manager within the organization could take an arbitration approach to the dispute between the IT manager and finance officer: hear out each side's concerns and issue a decision to resolve the dispute. However, ameliorating the friction between finance and IT might still leave unaddressed the grumbling among administrative staff about how cumbersome and confusing the software is. The administrative staff may believe that they also deserve a voice in how changes in accounting procedures are implemented and may be resistant to plans on which they have not been consulted. As mentioned already, research shows that people are more likely to go along with decisions that they believe were reached by a fair process, and people are more likely to perceive a process to be fair if they were consulted during the decision making—not simply informed of the result.[40] An arbitration strategy would not address the concerns of the administrative staff, whose cooperation would ultimately be needed to implement the new system successfully. By employing a mediation or med-arb strategy, the senior manager could construct a dispute resolution process that included consultations with administrative staff and that engendered a broader sense of ownership of the final solution. When stakeholders present a barrier to dispute resolution, a mediation or med-arb strategy enables the leader to be more inclusive in ways that facilitate the sustainable resolution of the dispute.[41]

Self-Serving Bias. The more convinced disputants are that they are in the right, the less motivated they are to make the concessions necessary to resolve their conflict. Self-serving biases contribute to disputants' sense of righteousness by focusing their attention on information that supports their point of view and by distracting them from attending to any disconfirming or contradictory information.[42] For instance, one study of teacher contract negotiations found that teachers focused on compensation comparisons with districts where teachers were higher paid, and school boards focused on comparisons with districts where teachers were lower paid.[43] This phenomenon might appear at first blush to be a simple case of strategic behavior. However, research has shown that parties are not easily dislodged from these self-serving viewpoints. Even when researchers reward disputants with extra money for accuracy, each side remains convinced that a neutral third party would tend to resolve the dispute in their favor.[44] One debiasing intervention that researchers have shown to be effective in helping parties overcome self-serving biases involves asking each party to write down all of the weaknesses in their own case. In this way, disputants are prompted to consider information that works against them as well as in their favor, and they develop a more balanced perspective of the problem.[45] Self-serving biases are likely to be more acute when subordinates expect the leader to use an arbitration (versus mediation) strategy to resolve their dispute, because they are more focused on winning their case than on finding a compromise solution. A mediation approach, in contrast, places responsibility on the parties to cooperate with one another and enables the leader to work with the parties to broaden their perspectives on the dispute and on options for its resolution. A mediation or med-arb strategy is suggested for helping parties to overcome the self-serving biases that impede their ability to resolve their own disputes.

Leadership Objectives

Five leadership objectives are summarized in Table 25.2. The first is maximizing the perceived fairness of the process and outcome of the dispute. The second is maximizing the efficiency of the outcome of the dispute in terms of creating the most value possible from the perspective of the organization, the parties, and the leader. The third is to minimize the time costs of the dispute

Table 25.2. Leadership Objectives and Suggested Strategies.

Leadership Objective	Suggested Process Strategy	Summary of Explanation
Maximize fairness of process and outcome	Mediation or Med-Arb[a]	Parties tend to perceive mediation and med-arb processes to be more fair than arbitration processes.
Maximize efficiency of solution	Mediation or Med-Arb	Arbitration invites strategic information revelation. Mediation encourages more information sharing and joint problem solving.
Minimize time costs of process	Arbitration	Mediation and med-arb processes tend to be time-consuming. Arbitration strategy minimizes time costs to decision maker.
Establish policy or precedent	Arbitration	Arbitration strategy more appropriate for leader establishing policy or precedent. Mediation gives decision-making authority to parties to solve their own circumscribed problem.
Redress an ethical problem	Arbitration	Arbitration strategy more appropriate when ethical issues arise between disputants. Mediation outcomes may not be valid if not conducted in good faith or if there is a power imbalance between parties.

[a]Whether a mediation or med-arb strategy applies depends on whether the leader has decision-making authority.

resolution process. The fourth is to establish a policy or precedent. The fifth is to redress an ethical violation or power imbalance.

Maximize Fairness of Process and Outcome. Because they have ongoing relationships with the disputants and, generally, some stake in the outcome of the dispute resolution process, leaders may be more at risk of having their impartiality questioned than would most formal third parties. Perceived fairness, as explained earlier, has a significant effect on parties' satisfaction with and commitment to dispute resolution outcomes.[46] Research suggests that informal third parties (such as organizational leaders) who are more concerned about fairness tend to take more control in the early stages of the dispute resolution process— presumably out of a sense of responsibility or belief in their ability to ensure a fair solution.[47] Contrary to this intuition, however, disputants tend to judge processes that grant *them* greater process and decision control to be fairer than those that do not. To maximize the perceived fairness of the dispute resolution process and outcome, researchers of dispute resolution in organizations strongly advise mediation or med-arb strategies over an arbitration approach.[48]

Maximize Efficiency of Solution. As described in the section "Mediation, Arbitration, and Med-Arb," mediation processes tend to be superior to arbitration processes in terms of maximizing the flow of information about key interests underlying the conflict and the options for resolving the dispute in a mutually beneficial manner. Through a mediation (versus arbitration) strategy, leaders have a greater opportunity to work with the parties to develop creative solutions to the problems at hand. Howard Raiffa proposes, for instance, that informal mediators adopt the role of "contract embellishers" who use their privileged knowledge of the parties' beliefs, interests, and values to propose mutually beneficial improvements on the final agreement.[49] By working jointly and individually with the parties to understand the problem and their concerns and to explore the trade-offs associated with various potential solutions, the leader can use a mediation or med-arb approach to maximize the value to be gained by all from the problem-solving process. As summarized in Table 25.2, a mediation or med-arb strategy is suggested for maximizing the efficiency of the dispute resolution outcome.

Minimize Time Costs of Process. As indicated in Tables 25.1 and 25.2, mediation or med-arb strategies have been the favored strategies for dealing with the barriers listed and for maximizing the perceived fairness and thoroughness of the dispute resolution process. Mediation and med-arb approaches have strong advantages in terms of the potential for confidence building and inclusiveness, information sharing and perspective taking, procedural justice, and outcome efficiency, but they are likely to carry substantially greater time costs for organizational leaders than would an arbitration strategy. Leaders need to consider whether the time investment required for a mediation or med-arb strategy is warranted given the scale and implications of the dispute.[50] Moreover, there are many circumstances under which the speed and certainty of an arbitration strategy will outweigh the risks with regard to the disputants' satisfaction and relationship and the potential for dispute recurrence.[51] For instance, disputes that arise in the midst of an impending work delivery deadline may necessitate quick and decisive resolution. An arbitration strategy is suggested in cases in which the leader seeks to minimize the time costs of the dispute resolution process.

Establish Policy or Precedent. The leader must also consider whether the organizational interest is best served by resolving the details of the particular dispute or raising the issue to a policy level.[52] Consider a dispute between a salesperson and her manager over the salesperson's end-of-year bonus. If the dispute is kicked up to the department head, the department head could employ a mediation or med-arb strategy to help the salesperson and manager improve their working relationship and to identify a creative solution to the problem. But the department head might also determine that the interests of the department and organization would be would better served if the bonus issue were not addressed as a stand-alone case for this one salesperson but rather as a performance incentive issue for the department. If the department head perceives a need for a broader policy, it would make more sense for him or her to use an arbitration-type strategy in which all sides of the issues were presented and management made a policy decision. An arbitration strategy is likely to be more appropriate than a mediation or med-arb strategy for situations in which the leader intends to use the dispute resolution process to establish a policy or precedent.

Redress an Ethical Problem. Finally, there are certain cases in which it is the leader's responsibility to intervene in the dispute in such a way as to correct or prevent unethical behavior or to support a disempowered party. Under these circumstances, there are three main limitations to mediation strategies. First, a mediation strategy, by definition, hands control over the decision-making process to the parties themselves. In the case of an ethical violation, this would be akin to including the fox in decision making over the security of the hen house. A mediation strategy could reward unethical behavior and do a disservice to the organization. Second, mediation is basically a form of assisted negotiation. If one party's ability to negotiate for his or her own interests is impaired or compromised, then that undermines the legitimacy of the mediation process and outcome. Finally, mediation helps to resolve the problems of a particular set of parties. As in the situation when the leader's objective is to make a policy decision, it may be more appropriate to sanction offenses publicly and categorically than to work out private solutions to the problem.[53] For these reasons, an arbitration strategy is strongly suggested over a mediation or med-arb strategy when the leader aims to redress an ethical violation or power imbalance.

CONCLUSION

Mediation, med-arb, and arbitration are three dispute resolution strategies that are applicable to the challenges of leadership in organizational contexts. Each strategy has advantages and disadvantages, depending on certain barriers to agreement and leadership objectives. The analogy between formal third parties and the informal roles that leaders play is not perfect. The roles for leaders as third parties are much more open to interpretation and improvisation than are the roles for formal third parties. Still, the study of alternative dispute resolution processes offers leaders a great deal as they strategize about how to manage their own organizational problems. More work should be done to investigate the relevance and limitations of formal alternative dispute resolution processes for leadership, and to reverse the flow of insight so that dispute resolution professionals can learn more from how organizational leaders resolve disputes.

Notes

1. J. W. Gardner, *On Leadership* (New York: Free Press, 1990), p. 104. John W. Gardner was the author of multiple books on public affairs and leadership and served in leadership positions ranging from Marines captain to U.S. Secretary of Health, Education, and Welfare to president of the Carnegie Corporation of New York. In 1964 he was awarded the highest civilian honor in the United States, the Presidential Medal of Freedom.

2. See J. M. Burns, *Leadership* (New York: Harpertorch Books, 1978); Gardner, *On Leadership,* 1990; and P. Selznick, *Leadership in Administration* (New York: HarperCollins, 1957).

3. See D. Lax and J. Sebenius, *The Manager as Negotiator: Bargaining for Cooperation and Competitive Gain* (New York: Free Press, 1986); R. E. Neustadt, *Presidential Power and the Modern Presidents: The Politics of Leadership from Roosevelt to Reagan* (New York: Free Press, 1990); and H. Raiffa, *The Art and Science of Negotiation* (Cambridge, Mass.: Belknap Press of Harvard University Press, 1982).

4. See H. Raiffa, "Mediation of Conflicts," *American Behavioral Scientist,* 1983, *27*(2), 195–210.

5. For the purposes of this chapter, I use the term *organizational leader* in the broad sense of someone assigned to a position of authority (for example, plant manager, department head, director, or executive) or someone who has emerged through informal interaction with organizational members to be mutually recognized to be in a position of authority regardless of formal title. See P. G. Northouse, *Leadership: Theory and Practice* (2nd ed.) (Thousand Oaks, Calif.; Sage, 2001), pp. 2–6.

6. D. G. Pruitt and J. Z. Rubin, *Social Conflict: Escalation, Stalemate, and Settlement* (New York: Random House, 1986), p. 203.

7. See B. G. Picker, *Mediation Practice Guide: A Handbook for Resolving Business Disputes* (2nd ed.) (Washington, D.C.: American Bar Association, 2003); K. Duffy,

J. Grosch, and P. Olczak, *Community Mediation: A Handbook for Practitioners and Researchers* (New York: Guilford Press, 1991); and J. E. Beer and E. Stief, *The Mediator's Handbook* (Gabriola Island, B.C.: New Society Publishers, 1997).

8. See D. E. Conlon, "The Mediation-Intravention Discussion: Toward an Integrative Perspective," *Negotiation Journal,* 1988, *2,* 143–148; and Pruitt and Rubin, *Social Conflict,* 1986.

9. W. H. Ross and D. E. Conlon, "Hybrid Forms of Third-Party Dispute Resolution: Theoretical Implications of Combining Mediation and Arbitration," *Academy of Management Review,* 2000, *25*(2), p. 417.

10. See Conlon, "The Mediation-Intravention Discussion," 1988; and B. H. Sheppard, "Third Party Conflict Intervention: A Procedural Framework," in B. M. Staw and L. L. Cummings (eds.), *Research in Organizational Behavior* (Greenwich, Conn.: JAI Press, 1984).

11. See Raiffa, "Mediation of Conflicts," 1983. For descriptions of a range of mediator tactics and strategies, see, for example, Pruitt and Rubin, *Social Conflict,* 1986; D. M. Kolb, "Roles Mediators Play: Orchestrator and Dealmakers," in *The Mediators* (Cambridge, Mass.: MIT Press, 1985); and P. J. Carnevale, "Mediating Dispute and Decisions in Organizations," in M. H. Bazerman, R. Lewicki, and B. Sheppard (eds.), *Research on Negotiation in Organizations* (Greenwich, Conn.: JAI Press, 1986).

12. See Ross and Conlon, "Hybrid Forms of Third-Party Dispute Resolution," 2000. In some med-arb cases the mediator and arbitrator are different people, but research suggests that having the same person fulfill the mediator and arbitrator roles is as, if not more, effective than having two people split the mediation and arbitration functions. For the purposes of this chapter, we will discuss the med-arb model in which one person fulfills both roles.

13. See D. E. Conlon, P. J. Carnevale, and J. K. Murnighan, "Intravention: Third-Party Intervention with Clout," *Organizational Behavior and Human Decision Processes,* 1994, *57,* 387–410; and N. B. McGillicuddy, G. L. Welton, and D. G. Pruitt, "Third-Party Intervention: A Field Experiment Comparing Three Different Models," *Journal of Personality and Social Psychology,* 1987, *53*(1), 104–112.

14. See McGillicuddy, Welton, and Pruitt, "Third-Party Intervention," 1987.

15. See Ross and Conlon, "Hybrid Forms of Third-Party Dispute Resolution," 2000.

16. See D. E. Conlon and W. H. Ross, "Influence of Movement Toward Agreement and Third Party Intervention on Negotiator Fairness Judgments," *The International Journal of Conflict Management,* 1992, *3*(3), 207–221; J. M. Brett and S. B. Goldberg, "Grievance Mediation in the Coal Industry: A Field Experiment," *Industrial and Labor Relations Review,* 1983, *37,* 49–69; and D. L. Shapiro and J. M. Brett, "Comparing Three Processes Underlying Judgments of Procedural Justice: A Field Study of Mediation and Arbitration," *Journal of Personality and Social Psychology,* 1993, *65*(6), 1167–1177.

17. See D. G. Pruitt, R. S. Peirce, N. B. McGillicuddy, and G. L. Welton, "Long-Term Success in Mediation," *Law and Human Behavior,* 1993, *17*(3), 313–330; Shapiro and Brett, "Comparing Three Processes Underlying Judgments of Procedural

Justice," 1993; R. Karambayya and J. M. Brett, "Managers Handling Disputes: Third-Party Roles and Perceptions of Fairness," *Academy of Management Journal,* 1989, *32*(4), 687–704; R. Karambayya, J. M. Brett, and A. Lytle, "Effects of Formal Authority and Experience on Third-Party Roles, Outcomes, and Perceptions of Fairness," *Academy of Management Journal,* 1992, *35*(2), 426–438; E. A. Lind and T. R. Tyler, *The Social Psychology Of Procedural Justice* (New York: Plenum Press, 1988); and J. Thibaut and L. Walker, *Procedural Justice: A Psychological Analysis* (Hillsdale, N.J.: Erlbaum, 1975).

18. See Pruitt, Peirce, McGillicuddy, and Welton, "Long-Term Success in Mediation," 1993; and Ross and Conlon, "Hybrid Forms of Third-Party Dispute Resolution," 2000.

19. See Raiffa, "Mediation of Conflicts," 1983; Pruitt and Rubin, *Social Conflict,* 1986; and Ross and Conlon, "Hybrid Forms of Third-Party Dispute Resolution," 2000.

20. See Ross and Conlon, "Hybrid Forms of Third-Party Dispute Resolution," 2000.

21. See Raiffa, "Mediation of Conflicts," 1983, pp. 203–207.

22. See Raiffa, "Mediation of Conflicts," 1983; and Ross and Conlon, "Hybrid Forms of Third-Party Dispute Resolution," 2000.

23. See Karambayya and Brett, "Managers Handling Disputes," 1989; and D. M. Kolb and B. H. Sheppard, "Do Managers Mediate, or Even Arbitrate?" *Negotiation Journal,* 1985, *3,* 379–388.

24. See Conlon, Carnevale, and Murnighan, "Intravention," 1994.

25. Kolb and Sheppard, "Do Managers Mediate, or Even Arbitrate?" 1985, p. 385.

26. See Kolb and Sheppard, "Do Managers Mediate, or Even Arbitrate?" 1985.

27. See Kolb and Sheppard, "Do Managers Mediate, or Even Arbitrate?" 1985; and Carnevale, "Mediating Dispute and Decisions in Organizations," 1986.

28. See Conlon, Carnevale, and Murnighan, "Intravention," 1994; and Carnevale, "Mediating Dispute and Decisions in Organizations," 1986.

29. Conlon, Carnevale, and Murnighan, "Intravention," 1994, p. 408.

30. See D. E. Conlon, "The Effects of Partisan Third Parties on Negotiator Behavior and Outcome Perceptions," *Journal of Applied Psychology,* 1993, *78*(2), 280–290.

31. See Carnevale, "Mediating Dispute and Decisions in Organizations," 1986.

32. See Conlon, Carnevale, and Murnighan, "Intravention," 1994.

33. See Karambayya, Brett, and Lytle, "Effects of Formal Authority and Experience on Third-Party Roles, Outcomes, and Perceptions of Fairness," 1992.

34. See Pruitt and Rubin, *Social Conflict,* 1986; and Carnevale, "Mediating Dispute and Decisions in Organizations," 1986.

35. See L. Thompson and P. H. Kim, "How the Quality of Third Parties' Settlement Solutions Is Affected by the Relationship Between Negotiators," *Journal of Experimental Psychology,* 2000, *6*(1), 3–14.

36. Conlon, Carnevale, and Murnighan, "Intravention," 1994, p. 406.

37. See Karambayya and Brett, "Managers Handling Disputes," 1989; Pruitt, Peirce, McGillicuddy, and Welton, "Long-Term Success in Mediation," 1993; and

F.E.A. Sander and S. B. Goldberg, "Fitting the Forum to the Fuss: A User-Friendly Guide to Selecting an ADR Procedure," *Negotiation Journal,* 1994, *10,* 49–67.

38. See Sander and Goldberg, "Fitting the Forum to the Fuss," 1994.

39. Raiffa, "Mediation of Conflicts," 1983, pp. 202–203.

40. See T. R. Tyler, "The Psychology of Procedural Justice: A Test of the Group-Value Model," *Journal of Personality and Social Psychology,* 1989, *57*(5), 830–838.

41. See Sander and Goldberg, "Fitting the Forum to the Fuss," 1994.

42. See L. Babcock and G. Loewenstein, "Explaining Bargaining Impasse: The Role of Self-Serving Biases," *Journal of Economic Perspectives,* 1997, *11*(1), 109–126; and L. Babcock, G. Loewenstein, S. Issacharoff, and C. Camerer, "Biased Judgments of Fairness in Bargaining," *American Economic Review,* 1995, *85*(5), 1337–1343.

43. See L. Babcock, X. H. Wang, and G. Loewenstein, "Choosing the Wrong Pond: Social Comparisons in Negotiations That Reflect a Self-Serving Bias," *Quarterly Journal of Economics,* 1996, *111*(1), 1–19.

44. See Babcock, Loewenstein, Issacharoff, and Camerer, "Biased Judgments of Fairness in Bargaining," 1995; Babcock and Loewenstein, "Explaining Bargaining Impasse," 1997; and G. S. Loewenstein, C. C. Issacharoff, and L. Babcock, "Self-Serving Assessments of Fairness and Pretrial Bargaining," *Journal of Legal Studies,* 1993, *22*(1), 135–159.

45. See Babcock and Loewenstein, "Explaining Bargaining Impasse," 1997.

46. See Karambayya and Brett, "Managers Handling Disputes," 1989; Karambayya, Brett, and Lytle, "Effects of Formal Authority and Experience on Third-Party Roles, Outcomes, and Perceptions of Fairness," 1992; T. R. Tyler, "Procedural Justice in Organizations," in R. J. Lewicki, B. H. Sheppard, and M. H. Bazerman (eds.), *Research on Negotiation in Organizations* (Greenwich, Conn.: JAI Press, 1986); and Pruitt, Peirce, McGillicuddy, and Welton, "Long-Term Success in Mediation," 1993.

47. See B. H. Sheppard, D. M. Saunders, and J. W. Minton, "Procedural Justice from the Third-Party Perspective," *Journal of Personality and Social Psychology,* 1988, *54*(4), 629–637.

48. See Lind and Tyler, *The Social Psychology of Procedural Justice,* 1988; Karambayya and Brett, "Managers Handling Disputes," 1989; Karambayya, Brett, and Lytle, "Effects of Formal Authority and Experience on Third-Party Roles, Outcomes, and Perceptions of Fairness," 1992; Shapiro and Brett, "Comparing Three Processes Underlying Judgments of Procedural Justice," 1993; and Brett and Goldberg, "Grievance Mediation in the Coal Industry," 1983.

49. See Raiffa, "Mediation of Conflicts," 1983.

50. See Carnevale, "Mediating Dispute and Decisions in Organizations," 1986.

51. See Karambayya, Brett, and Lytle, "Effects of Formal Authority and Experience on Third-Party Roles, Outcomes, and Perceptions of Fairness," 1992.

52. See Sander and Goldberg, "Fitting the Forum to the Fuss," 1994.

53. See Sander and Goldberg, "Fitting the Forum to the Fuss," 1994.

CHAPTER TWENTY-SIX

Online Dispute Resolution

Ethan Katsh

O nline dispute resolution (ODR) applies the tools and resources of cyberspace to the goals and processes of dispute resolution. ODR uses high-speed computer networks and powerful information-processing machines to deliver both expertise and information from afar. ODR's initial efforts were focused on disputes arising out of online activities. The lessons learned in that environment are now being applied to enhance dispute resolution efforts that involve face-to-face interactions and offline disputes.

ODR is based on the premise that every model of dispute resolution—from the simplest to the most complex, both in and out of court—involves generating, communicating, evaluating, processing, and managing information. ODR will become increasingly valuable in both online and offline disputes as applications are designed that efficiently and effectively meet the information processing and communication needs of disputants and third parties. The use of ODR, and the range of disputing contexts in which it is used, will likely increase as ODR software becomes more powerful and accessible.

ODR draws many themes and concepts from dispute resolution processes such as negotiation, mediation, and arbitration. ODR gives the parties a medium for communicating when they have not planned to meet face-to-face, or cannot do so. As software is added to communication, even software as simple as a Website, capabilities for managing and shaping information are added to the capabilities for communicating information. Such software adds to the array of resources and tools that a third party or the disputants themselves can employ.

In describing ODR, some commentators have begun to describe the role of technology as that of a "fourth party."[1] This concept recognizes the role and value of software as the network is used as more than a simple conduit. The fourth-party concept suggests that software aids or collaborates with a third party, but does not generally replace it. A fourth-party tool, for example, might allow parties to clarify issues before a face-to-face session or help to identify party priorities during a meeting. In essence, software and mediators are involved in a similar task, namely the management of information and communication. The third party has skills and capabilities that may be more useful than what a fourth party can provide, but some tools embedded in software can be more powerful or more efficiently applied by machine than by a person. Traditionally, third parties have used a variety of communication tools, such as colored markers and charts, but the fourth party concept suggests the emergence of an online resource that collaborates with third parties and that is different from those traditional tools.

People most frequently think of the Internet as an environment in which to search for information or communicate with others. ODR involves these activities, but also uses software to coordinate and manage various informational activities. In recent years, many processes have been put online in arenas as diverse as banking, investing, shopping, gambling, and teaching. Dispute resolution may be more complex than some of these processes, but all share the task of managing information. Online banking, shopping, and gaming are familiar and easy to use, but were cumbersome and had far fewer features when they were first introduced. The more people used the Internet, the more refinements were made, leading to even greater Internet usage. If ODR has limitations today, both its capabilities and use will increase as more powerful and more refined versions replace old ones.

A BRIEF HISTORY OF ODR

Although the Internet began in 1969, a need for ODR did not emerge until the early 1990s. For its first two decades, the Internet was used by a limited number of people in a limited number of ways. Those with Internet access were associated either with the military or with academic institutions, and even in those environments, relatively few computers had Internet access.[2] While screens with images and e-mail with advertisements are commonplace today, they were unknown at that time. The World Wide Web was not invented until 1989, and, perhaps even more significantly, the National Science Foundation banned commercial activity from the Internet until 1992.[3]

In the early 1990s, groups used listservs to communicate, and this form of online discussion soon generated "flaming" and violations of "netiquette," personal attacks that violated generally accepted norms for online discussions.[4] Disputes also arose involving participants in role-playing games that allowed one to create an online identity and interact with others in a virtual "space."[5] Various online mechanisms were employed to deal with these conflicts, but there were no organized dispute resolution institutions devoted specifically to ODR. Indeed, the acronym *ODR* had not yet been invented.

The decision by the National Science Foundation in 1992 to lift its ban on Internet-based commercial activity was highly controversial and enormously significant. After the ban's removal, disputes related to online commerce began to surface. In 1994, for example, the first commercial spam occurred when two lawyers tried to recruit clients to participate in an immigration scam.[6] A few months later, the U.S. Federal Trade Commission filed its first case alleging online fraud.[7] The case involved an AmericaOnline subscriber who advertised the following: "FOR JUST $99.00 WE WILL SHOW YOU HOW TO CREATE A BRAND NEW CREDIT FILE AT ALL 3 OF THE MAJOR CREDIT BUREAUS . . . 100% LEGAL AND 200% GUARANTEED." The FTC did not consider the process to be legal or guaranteed. As a result of the FTC action, the subscriber agreed to stop advertising credit repair programs and to provide compensation to consumers.

The idea for online dispute resolution emerged from the recognition that the number of disputes would grow as the range of online activities grew. The origins of ODR, therefore, are traceable to a simple insight: the more transactions and interactions there are online, the more disputes there will be. In addition, people understood that the Internet was an information resource that should be able to support information-dependent activities such as dispute resolution.[8] In other words, the Internet was part of the problem because it generated disputes, but it was also part of the solution because it might have resources to respond to disputes.

The National Center for Automated Information Research (NCAIR) sponsored a conference on online dispute resolution in 1996. The conference was the most significant ODR development during the mid-1990s, as it led to the funding of three experimental ODR projects. The Virtual Magistrate project aimed at resolving disputes between Internet service providers and users.[9] The University of Massachusetts Online Ombuds Office hoped to facilitate dispute resolution on the Internet generally. Finally, the University of Maryland wanted to see if ODR could be employed in family disputes in which parents were located at a distance.

The years from 1996 on have been a period of significant activity and notable achievement for ODR.[10] The United Nations now holds an annual ODR conference and has formed an Expert Group on ODR.[11] ODR has become accepted as a necessary process, one that can even be used to resolve traditional disputes originating offline. The key questions concerning ODR now involve the design, testing, and adoption of new tools and systems, not viability or value.

TWO EXAMPLES OF ODR

The two most widely known and used ODR venues in cyberspace-related disputes are the online auction site eBay and the domain name dispute resolution process designed by the Internet Corporation for Assigned Names and Numbers (ICANN). Since March 2000, an Internet start-up, SquareTrade.com, has handled over two million disputes, mostly related to eBay transactions, wholly through online processes of negotiation and mediation. SquareTrade is probably the largest private dispute resolution provider in the world. Approximately eight thousand domain name disputes between trademark owners and domain name holders have been resolved through ICANN's Uniform Dispute Resolution Policy, a nonbinding arbitration process.[12]

EBay: Assisted Negotiation, Then Mediation

EBay is an online auction site that makes it possible for sellers and buyers located anywhere to deal with one another. The service has over ninety-two million registered users and lists over fourteen million items for sale each day. EBay itself is not a party to any transaction and, in general, assumes no responsibility for problems that arise between buyers and sellers. In 1999, eBay decided that having a dispute resolution process might strengthen trust between buyers and sellers. After a pilot project conducted by the Center for Information Technology and Dispute Resolution mediated over two hundred disputes, eBay selected an Internet start-up, SquareTrade, to be its dispute resolution provider.[13] Before providing a human mediator, SquareTrade uses a technology-supported negotiation process in which parties try to resolve the dispute themselves before requesting a mediator. SquareTrade also uses the Web, rather than e-mail, as the means for communicating and working with disputants.

SquareTrade's use of the Web illustrates how relatively small changes in communication can have large consequences. Most who file complaints with SquareTrade have already tried to negotiate via e-mail and have reached an impasse. Not only do parties seem more willing to negotiate via the Web than through e-mail, but the negotiations are more frequently successful.[14] Square-Trade's Website provides a more structured set of exchanges than does e-mail. SquareTrade recognized that almost all eBay disputes fall into eight to ten categories, allowing it to create forms that clarify and highlight both the parties' disagreements and their desired solutions. While parties have an opportunity to describe concerns in their own words, the forms and the form summaries they receive reduce the amount of free text complaining and demanding, and thus lower the amount of anger and hostility between them.

Negotiation, as classically defined, takes place between the disputants, without the presence of third parties. SquareTrade's use of the Web in negotiations adds a novel element to traditional negotiation, a kind of "virtual presence." The Website frames the parties' communication and provides some of the value traditionally provided by a mediator. Perhaps as parties increase their use of technology in negotiation, the distinction between negotiation and mediation will become less stark.

When Web-based negotiation fails, SquareTrade provides a human mediator for a modest fee. The conversation is facilitated by a third-party neutral using the Web interface. Because the parties are using the Web, they do not all need to participate at the same time.

ODR and Arbitration: ICANN and Domain Name Disputes

The demand for domain names grew as commercial activity on the Internet grew and as businesses wanted potential customers to have an easy way to find them. The domain name system had been designed before commercial activity was permitted on the Internet. No one had anticipated that many businesses with similar names might want the same domain name, or that owners of trademarks would be upset if someone registered a domain name that was similar to a trademark. The combination of domain name scarcity and the concerns of trademark holders led to disputes over domain names.

In 1998, the U.S. government agreed to allow a new organization, ICANN, to manage the domain name system. One of the first things ICANN did was enact the Uniform Dispute Resolution Policy (UDRP), establishing both a process and a set of rules for deciding domain name disputes.[15] Both the modified arbitration process ICANN chose and the systems which have implemented this approach represent another step in moving dispute resolution online.

UDRP dispute resolution occurs without face-to-face meetings and, except in rare instances, without telephone communication. The process employed by the two most active current dispute resolution providers, the National Arbitration Forum (NAF) and the World Intellectual Property Organization (WIPO), is dispute resolution at a distance but involves only limited use of the Internet. Both current providers have online systems that could be used, and probably will be in the future. Parties submit online filings with increasing frequency, and sometimes parties use e-mail. Unlike the eBay mediations, however, NAF and WIPO do not use the Web for their dispute resolution sessions.

The UDRP is not classic arbitration because the decisions are not binding or enforceable in court.[16] UDRP arbitrators are called "panelists," since the word "arbitrator" denotes someone who can make a decision enforceable in court. When parties register for a domain name, they agree to terms in a contract that empower UDRP panelists to make decisions. The panelists' decisions are enforced by changes entered in the domain name registry. The UDRP created an efficient, unorthodox, yet controversial process whose fairness has been challenged.[17]

ODR FOR OFFLINE DISPUTES: ENHANCING ADR
AND UNBUNDLING ODR

The SquareTrade and ICANN processes involve no face-to-face meetings. They are conducted wholly at a distance. The need for ODR with no physical meetings is most obvious in cases that arise online and when, because of distance, it is not feasible to meet face-to-face or go to court. It is not surprising that ODR was first directed at such disputes as well. ODR has grown in part because it is valuable for resolving traditional offline disputes. SquareTrade, for example, now resolves real estate disputes between home buyers and sellers. When the power of the computer to process information is added to the power of the network to transmit information the result is an array of dispute resolution processes that can be employed in any dispute, whether it arises, or is handled, online or offline.

A Simple Example: Automated Blind Bidding Processes

Blind bidding systems allow disputing parties to submit settlement offers to a computer and, if the offers are within a certain range, often thirty percent of each other, to split the difference. Blind bidding is attractive because if the parties do not reach settlement, the offers are never revealed. This practice encourages parties to be more truthful about their "bottom line."

Blind bidding is a negotiation tool, a technique that, if done offline and without a computer, would be cumbersome. The efficiency of blind bidding is that the computer transmits and receives information, processes it, and makes distinctions between what is private and public. If the offers are within the thirty percent range, for example, the parties are informed that there is a settlement. If not, no information about the offer is revealed to the parties. As Internet users come to understand how encryption and other techniques can protect confidentiality, trust in such systems and use of such systems will increase.

Thus far, blind bidding has been employed mainly in claims against insurance companies. These are claims that are generally settled at some point through negotiation. The traditional process of resolution in such cases, involving personal injury lawyers and insurance claim adjusters, is often lengthy and inefficient. There are problems with the parties and their representatives playing phone tag and posturing in ways that often take up time. A human third party could accept offers in a manner similar to the way a computer accepts offers in a blind bidding system, but could never do so as efficiently.

Blind bidding systems are both efficient and simple to use. They are also extremely limited, since they work only with disputes in which a single variable is contested. This variable must involve numbers so that the machine can make the necessary calculations. The insurance context is a fitting first arena for blind bidding because such differences often focus exclusively on money and the existing dispute resolution system is both expensive and inefficient.

The future of blind bidding will inevitably broaden beyond insurance company disputes. In many mediations or arbitrations, there are initially numerous differences, but ultimately only a monetary issue. Blind bidding technology could be helpful in such situations. In other situations, blind bidding might be an option before beginning a lengthier process. Blind bidding is a tool that can be added at any phase of a dispute resolution process.

Blind bidding also raises the question of what else a network-connected computer can do to assist parties involved in a dispute. Blind bidding is such a simple tool that it could easily be taken for granted if viewed only as a merging of a calculator with the network. Computers, however, are much more than calculators, and systems can be built to process and evaluate qualitative information.

A More Complex Example: SmartSettle

SmartSettle[18] is much more sophisticated negotiation software than the blind bidding systems. It is intended for use in a range of disputes—simple or complex, single-issue or multi-issue, two-party or multiparty, comprising quantitative or qualitative issues, of short or long duration, or involving interdependent factors and issues. SmartSettle will never be as easy to use as blind bidding, and may not be needed for common and relatively simple disputes. However, experience with the software has demonstrated that network-connected computers can bring solutions that may not have been apparent to disputing parties.

SmartSettle moves disputants through several stages that clarify the issues in dispute, how strongly the parties feel about these issues, and the range of acceptable outcomes. In the early phases, SmartSettle provides a structure to clarify and assess issues that, by itself, can help parties reach consensus. What is most novel about SmartSettle, however, is that it can take a tentative agreement and suggest alternative approaches that may give each party a more favorable outcome.

While blind bidding involves only one quantifiable issue, SmartSettle may involve many issues. At the beginning of negotiations, parties are asked to place values on their different interests and demands. A family dispute, for example, may include issues of child support, the division of assets, care and custody schedules, and other relationship issues. A successful end result will involve trade-offs by each party. SmartSettle works to combine interests and issues into packages or groups so that the parties can see the impact of various decisions, enabling them to reach an end result that meets their needs. With SmartSettle, the computer not only stores the users' information and transmits it electronically, but also makes suggestions that will provide the parties with an attractive combination of settlement options.

THE "FOURTH" PARTY

E-mail negotiations simply have people at two ends of a network, thus allowing quick communication among parties who might not have been able otherwise to communicate. Negotiation with almost no overhead may be the most common method for attempting or beginning online negotiation. What the Web permits, and what blind bidding, SmartSettle, and SquareTrade demonstrate, is that there can be value in adding computer-processing capabilities to the people at the ends of the network.

The fourth-party metaphor alludes more to software such as SmartSettle than to blind bidding, more to something that is an influence on the process of negotiation and something that adds value to the third-party roles of mediator or arbitrator. This fourth party can alter the role(s) of a third party, since the third party will increasingly be working with an electronic ally.

The fourth party enhances the process and does more than simply deliver information across the network. For example, blind bidding is a system that involves communicating, calculating, evaluating, and applying a set of rules to the results of the calculation. Similarly, SmartSettle takes data that has been entered and, using more sophisticated algorithms, evaluates and then responds to offers. The fourth-party approach assumes that although face-to-face encounters provide a rich and flexible opportunity for communication, they are neither perfect nor complete. The fourth party will grow more useful and the network more valuable in dispute resolution as we gain experience using information management and processing tools.

Efficient information management and organization, including effective displays of information for disputants, allows SquareTrade to process a large number of disputes. Thus an important difference between e-mail negotiation and SquareTrade's Web-based negotiation is that SquareTrade provides a much higher level of information management. SquareTrade does not evaluate positions and recommend solutions but instead clarifies issues and presents information on-screen that highlights areas of agreement and difference. Like a mediator, the software maintains a respectful discourse between the parties until the contours of a solution appear.

The challenge for ODR is to facilitate information processing along with efficiencies in transmission. In the past, many inefficiencies arising from the distance between the parties were considered "tolerated inefficiencies"[19] in that nothing could be done to bridge distance and time constraints. The network, however, significantly changes disputants' ability to overcome these tolerated inefficiencies. As we grow more comfortable with the network, we realize that certain parts of how third parties handle disputes need to be reevaluated. For example, we have new tools for communicating with parties in between face-to-face sessions. Should we do so? For this and other instances of tolerated inefficiencies, we need to decide whether what we are accustomed to is still appropriate given the new tools we are acquiring that allow us to change how and where interactions with parties might take place.

E-GOVERNMENT AND ODR: FROM CONSUMER TO MULTIPARTY PUBLIC DISPUTES

One of the functions of government agencies is the resolution of disputes between citizens and government, or among citizens. In addition, many governmental functions, such as rule making, strive for consensus among interested parties. Increasing efforts in e-government and e-democracy are focusing attention on the value of ODR. ODR is also of interest because of the growing use of ADR by federal agencies.[20] ODR becomes more relevant as the government uses technology not only to provide information to citizens but to allow them to engage in processes.[21]

Most e-commerce disputes involving consumers are fairly simple since they usually concern two parties and a limited set of issues. The same problems recur, usually involving money, transaction terms, or delivery problems. Government agencies handle disputes ranging from simple and relatively straightforward to highly complex. Increasingly, ODR tools have the capacity to facilitate resolution in complex disputes. In the multiparty context, technology can help with information flow, making it easier to disseminate announcements, revise proposals, and track versions of documents.

When information management tools are linked together, even face-to-face meetings might be enhanced. For example, wirelessly networked handhelds might be used to collect two hundred key issues from thirty participants in five minutes, which the participants can then rate by importance. Thus, with the click of a mouse the top twenty topics can quickly be up on a screen in the front of the room. What would have taken three hours with a pen and a flipchart is done in fifteen minutes. With another click, all of the flipcharts and slideshows can be sent to the participants by e-mail. Documents can be dynamically edited by the group on-screen, and consensus evaluation can take place confidentially and continuously.

Complexity in dispute resolution processes often increases exponentially whenever an additional disputant is added to the process. Handling multiparty cases is work-intensive for the facilitator, as each participant needs to feel that he or she is being heard in the process. As a result, multiparty processes are often more complicated than two- or three-party dispute resolution processes. The tools ODR provides to neutrals may prove most useful in large, public cases because there are many individual communication channels to manage.

Public disputes are disputes in which the government is involved, either as a facilitator or as a stakeholder, and in which the public as a whole has an interest in the outcome of the matter. Zoning disputes are a familiar example of a public dispute. For example, a developer might apply to build a new mall on a vacant lot of land in a suburban community. It may be that the matter technically involves only a few parties directly, such as the developer, the landowner, and perhaps a few local merchants. But the public as a whole is indirectly involved as well, because of traffic, environmental, and property value concerns. There might be thousands of individuals who would be affected by the outcome of the zoning process. It would be impossible (or at least highly impractical) to get every one of the stakeholders into a single room to debate the issues. Increasingly, online tools can be employed in such situations.

There are strong incentives to use dispute resolution, rather than courts, in multiparty situations. Courts may be appropriate when it is necessary to make findings of who between two parties is right and wrong, but they are not as efficient at sorting out matters when there might be dozens of involved parties. ADR is more effective in these situations because mediators can act as conveners and facilitators, working to build consensus behind a particular resolution as opposed to finding fault.

The integration of ODR into public dispute resolution processes will bring many benefits. Online technology can help with many of the key tasks in such processes, such as circulating agendas and draft revisions, setting up meeting times and places, and tracking contact information for participants. Facilitators can spend an inordinate amount of time coordinating the process, which is distinct from the actual work of making progress toward a resolution to the dispute. ODR can help to streamline these tasks, freeing facilitators to focus on the more substantive issues that need to be addressed.

For many multiparty processes the ultimate goal is to generate a document that all of the participants are willing to support. The drafting and redrafting in the creation of these documents is often complex, involving the synthesis of myriad comments from many participants. Facilitators may be challenged to keep track of the suggested changes and integrate them into a coherent document. Online technology can help to organize the drafting process without relying on the facilitator to shuttle every proposed change among the parties. Because the deliberative process itself is text-based, it is easier to translate the discussion into text that will likely satisfy all of the participants.

One of the issues in multiparty disputes is the degree to which communications between the facilitator and the participants is public. In a large group meeting it is difficult for the mediator to speak one-on-one with any of the participants because the group as a whole needs to keep moving forward. If the facilitator wants to evaluate the group's progress toward reaching agreement on a particular point, online tools make it easier to poll participants, share large quantities of information, and jointly edit documents. The facilitator also has the ability to be in multiple conversations and workgroups at once, as she or he has access to all the electronic conversations going on, unlike the procedure common in physical meetings.

Online communication can also open the door to input from people normally excluded from face-to-face deliberative discussions. Group discussions are often dominated by a handful of participants while others, perhaps even the majority, stay silent. Certain individuals are more comfortable expressing their opinions forcefully in public situations, whereas others are less so. Online communication may reduce barriers for participants who would not contribute in a face-to-face meeting, allowing a different group of people to express their opinions. In addition to providing important information to the facilitator, the result is a much richer process for all involved.

CONCLUSION

As of this writing, the World Wide Web is only fifteen years old and yet has already touched every important societal institution. Dispute resolution has felt the impact of the Web both in the generation of disputes and in the building of systems to respond to disputes. Yet, what has occurred is only a beginning.

While impressive, online dispute resolution has handled mainly disputes that would be relatively easy to settle face-to-face, if the parties were able to meet face-to-face. Mediation is a very complex interaction, potentially involving many parties, many issues, significant consequences, and very angry people. Cases that are difficult to resolve in a face-to-face setting should be a reminder that ODR will not soon be a substitute for such sessions, although ODR may reduce the need for such sessions and may provide new tools for use in such meetings. Looked at in this way, ODR is an asset that mediators will be expected to use rather than a threat to or replacement of an existing process.

Cyberspace is, increasingly, a place where there are *processes* available to users as well as *information*. This should not be surprising since processes are sets of informational transactions and exchanges. What makes building processes out of informational transactions challenging is structuring and regulating the flow of information and the numerous informational exchanges among the parties. What makes building processes interesting, and what makes ODR a field with an exciting future, are innovations in software design and advances in the ability of software to manage complex interactions. ODR will grow in importance as offline activities migrate to the Web. The growth of ODR is partly a recognition that disputing is a kind of growth industry on the Internet. ODR is also, however, a sign or indicator that cyberspace is maturing. Many of the same tools that built such online venues as auctions, stores, and casinos can contribute to building online civic institutions such as courts and dispute resolution systems.

Notes

1. See, for example, E. Katsh and J. Rifkin, *Online Dispute Resolution: Resolving Conflicts in Cyberspace* (San Francisco: Jossey-Bass, 2001).

2. A history of the Internet can be found at B. Stewart, *Living Internet.* [http://livinginternet.com/?i/ii_nsfnet.htm]. Last updated July 7, 2004.

3. See J. P. Kesan and R. C. Shah, "Fool Us Once Shame on You—Fool Us Twice Shame on Us: What We Can Learn from the Privatizations of the Internet Backbone Network and the Domain Name System," *Washington University Law Quarterly,* 2001, *79,* 89–220.

4. See V. Shea, *Netiquette* (San Francisco: Albion Books, 1997).

5. For one account, see J. Dibble, "A Rape in Cyberspace," *The Village Voice,* Dec. 23, 1993. [http://www.juliandibbell.com/texts/bungle.html].

6. See R. E. Church, "The Spam That Started It All," April 1999. [http://www.wired.com/news/politics/0,1283,19098,00.html].

7. See Federal Trade Commission, "FTC Targets Advertising on 'Information Superhighway': Credit Repair Co. Urged Consumers to Falsify Data, FTC Charged," September 1994. [http://www.ftc.gov/opa/predawn/F95/chaseconsultin.htm].

8. See C. Rule, *Online Dispute Resolution for Businesses* (San Francisco: Jossey-Bass, 2002).

9. See R. Gellman, "A Brief History of the Virtual Magistrate Project: The Early Months," May 1996. [http://www.odr.info/ncair/gellman.htm].

10. See M. Conley Tyler and D. Bretherton, "Seventy-Six and Counting: An Analysis of ODR Sites," July 2003. [http://www.odr.info/unece2003/pdf/Tyler.pdf]; and T. Schultz, G. Kaufmann-Kohler, D. Langer, and V. Bonnet, "Online Disputes Resolution: The State of the Art and the Issues," *Report of the E-Commerce Research Project of the University of Geneva,* 2001. [http://www.online-adr.org/publications.htm].

11. See, for example, the homepage for the United Nations' 2003 Forum on ODR. E. Katsh and D. Choi, "Online Dispute Resolution (ODR): Technology as the Fourth Party: Papers and Proceedings of the 2003 United Nations Forum on ODR," June 2003. [http://www.odr.info/unece2003].

12. See Internet Corporation for Assigned Names and Numbers (ICANN), "Domain Name Dispute Resolution Policies." [http://www.icann.org/udrp]. Last modified January 2004.

13. See E. Katsh, J. Rifkin, and A. Gaitenby, "E-Commerce, E-Disputes, and E-Dispute Resolution: In the Shadow of 'eBay Law'," *Ohio State Journal on Dispute Resolution,* 2000, *15,* 705–734.

14. See S. Abernathy, "Building Large-Scale Online Dispute Resolution & Trustmark Systems," July 2003. [http://www.odr.info/unece2003/pdf/Abernethy.pdf].

15. See ICANN, "Domain Name Dispute Resolution Policies," 2004.

16. See E. G. Thornburg, "Going Private: Technology, Due Process, and Internet Dispute Resolution," *U.C. Davis Law Review,* 2000, *34,* 151–220.

17. See M. Mueller, *Ruling the Root: Internet Governance and the Taming of Cyberspace* (Cambridge, Mass.: MIT Press, 2002); and M. Geist, "Fair.com?: An Examination of the Allegations of Systemic Unfairness in ICANN UDRP," August 2001. [http://www.udrpinfo.com].

18. Information on SmartSettle can be found at http://www.smartsettle.com (last visited September 2004).

19. See E. Katsh, "Online Dispute Resolution: The Next Phase," Spring 2002. [http://www.lex-electronica.org/articles/v7–2/katsh.htm].

20. See J. Senger, *Federal Dispute Resolution: Using ADR with the United States Government* (San Francisco: Jossey-Bass, 2004).

21. An ambitious experiment in ODR is currently being undertaken by the National Mediation Board, the agency responsible for labor disputes in the transportation industry, the National Science Foundation, and the University of Massachusetts Center for Information Technology and Dispute Resolution. See National Mediation Board, "Online Dispute Resolution Project." [http://www.nmb.gov/adrservices/odr-statement.pdf]. Last visited September 2004.

CHAPTER TWENTY-SEVEN

Public and Private International Dispute Resolution

Andrea Kupfer Schneider

C onflict resolution is neither new nor uniquely American. People have been using forms of negotiation, mediation, and arbitration since they started living together in groups. As both domestic and international dispute resolution processes have evolved to meet changing needs, information exchange between the two disciplines can better inform practitioners and theorists in both areas. Each dispute resolution process operates differently among various countries, in diverse contexts. This chapter will highlight some of the developments in each of the international dispute resolution processes and identify interesting parallels between domestic and international controversies over where, how, and when to use dispute resolution.

Public international dispute resolution traditionally refers to disputes among countries, for example, between the United States and Iraq. Private international dispute resolution, in contrast, applies in the context of disputes among individuals or companies from different countries, for example, between U.S.-based Kodak and Japan-based Fuji over ownership of intellectual property. For the purpose of organization, this chapter divides disputes between those that are public and those that are private. As a descriptive matter, however, this simplistic division no longer captures fully the reality of modern disputes. Many disputes are neither wholly public nor wholly private. As companies invest in foreign countries at an increasing rate, there are now direct disputes between these companies and the governments of the countries. Nongovernmental organizations (NGOs), such as Amnesty International or the World Wildlife

Foundation, have entered the fray of international disputes and often negotiate directly with governments for policy changes. Finally, within intergovernmental organizations such as the European Union (EU) and the World Trade Organization (WTO), individuals, countries, and the organization itself can all be involved in a dispute. Traditional modes of dispute resolution have evolved to take note of these new parties involved in international disputes and to provide stimulating models for comparison with the evolution in domestic dispute resolution.

At the same time, some of the theories and models used in domestic dispute resolution offer useful insights into international negotiations. For example, much as labor negotiators in the United States must adopt strategies for dealing with their constituencies, so must diplomats concern themselves with domestic interest groups. Other theories drawn from domestic dispute resolution may need to be modified to take account of the international parties at the table. For example, some of our most cherished beliefs in domestic processes (such as the neutrality of the mediator) are either diluted or nonexistent in many international mediations.

INTERNATIONAL NEGOTIATION

The next section discusses both private and public international negotiation. In the private arena, globalization has had a great impact on standardizing certain terms of negotiation and facilitating private international negotiations. At the same time, globalization has required the consideration of a broader constituency in public negotiations.

Private International Negotiations: Individual to Individual

Cultural differences are perhaps the most salient issues raised in negotiations between individuals from different countries, even in diplomatic negotiations. U.S. Trade Representative Charlene Barshefsky's experiences negotiating with the Chinese Trade Minister turned as much on the cultural differences of negotiating with the Chinese as they did on the policy differences between the United States and China.[1]

Less experienced negotiators often make the mistake of focusing on those similarities and differences they can see between themselves and the negotiator on the other side. They focus, for example, on things such as race, gender, and culture, rather than on less visible characteristics such as education, negotiation style, experience, level of preparation, or negotiation authority and parameters.[2] Researchers have found that personality, negotiation style, or professional training could have just as much influence on negotiation behavior as does culture. While it is important to be aware of potential cultural differences (and avoid behavior that would be perceived as insulting), negotiators also need to be wary of assuming that every difference derives from culture.[3]

In addition to highlighting cultural differences, international negotiations raise heightened concerns about clear communication. Terms that mean one thing in one country may not mean the same thing in other countries. Governing law and enforcement in the event of a breach of contract are also more complicated in international negotiations than in domestic negotiations. Addressing a breach of contract is typically easier in a context involving only domestic parties than if one or more of the parties to the contract is located abroad. Negotiations within a single country benefit from having one set of laws that apply to contracts and a court system well-versed in contract interpretation according to that law. No single court system interprets private law at the international level.

As the world has become more interdependent, however, and these issues arise repeatedly, some of them have become much easier to manage. For example, international treaties now govern issues of contract interpretation and terms across many countries.[4] Furthermore, while enforcement of a contract in another country's court system would have been quite difficult years ago, the growth of international arbitration and treaties concerning judicial cooperation make both arbitration and litigation easier. In many other respects, private international negotiations and domestic negotiations operate similarly.[5]

Public International Negotiation: Country to Country

The studies of international diplomacy, international relations, and foreign affairs all primarily relate to the issue of how governments communicate with one another about a variety of issues. In the domestic realm, some theorists have divided negotiation into *dispute settlement negotiation* versus *deal-making negotiation*.[6] These theorists suggest that the negotiation might be conducted differently in one context versus the other. Similarly, in the international context, sometimes countries engage in deal-making negotiations—for example, to craft the terms of a treaty regarding trade practices such as the negotiation among Mexico, Canada, and the United States regarding the North American Free Trade Agreement (NAFTA). At other times, countries must deal with the aftermath of a dispute (dispute settlement negotiation)—for example, when one country arrests the citizen of another country.

This domestic division between disputes and deals, however, often is too simplistic for international negotiations for two reasons. First, as discussed earlier, domestic dispute settlement has the backdrop of a single court system and governing law. If the parties do not reach agreement, they can turn to the courts to resolve the issue. At the international level, one country does not usually have the ability to sue another in an international court because countries do not grant these courts jurisdiction. (Some famous exceptions exist—for example, Nicaragua brought a case in the International Court of Justice (ICJ) against the United States in the mid-1980s for violating Nicaraguan sovereignty with the U.S. naval blockade.[7] This, of course, raises the issue of enforcement, since the ICJ relies on voluntary compliance with its rulings.)

Second, many disputes that reach the U.S. court system are between parties that do not need to work with each other in the future unless they choose. In international relations, few countries can exist without engaging in relations with other countries on a regular basis. The future relationship is not optional for countries that expect to be involved in most important international issues. Even with those countries with whom the United States has no official relationship, such as Cuba, ongoing communication and negotiation continues through multiple unofficial channels.

Historically, the focus in international negotiations has been on the diplomat or leader who conducts the negotiation. The importance of diplomats and their ability to negotiate has long been recognized by international law. Some of the earliest treaties on record deal with diplomatic immunity and the freedom of messengers to travel even in wartime.[8] Perhaps one of the most famous political science treatises ever, *The Prince*, is primarily a book of negotiation advice to the Florentine leader on how he should deal with the populace and with other countries.[9] Much analysis of international negotiation continues to give diplomats advice on conducting negotiations.

Advice to international negotiators often resembles generalized negotiation advice, and, as with most forms of advice, different schools of thought have developed. Much like the difference between an adversarial and problem-solving approach in any negotiation, different political science schools—realist, regime theory, public choice, liberal international relations—provide different approaches on how a country should determine its interests and, by implication, how these interests should be pursued.[10] Much of the advice for individual diplomats, whose long-term relationships and reputation are a key measure of their worth, more clearly reflects what we would call a problem-solving approach.[11] A diplomat should be trustworthy (although not completely trusting), clear in communication (with extra attention paid to the potential for miscommunication through translation), flexible, and concerned with the interests of the other side.[12]

More recently, the focus on the individual leader or diplomat has been supplemented by the study of the interaction between the leader and his or her constituency. In nondemocratic forms of government, leaders might not take the interests and opinions of a broad citizenry into account when formulating policy and negotiating with other countries. In democracies, however, a leader can rarely ignore the public. A democratic leader who wants to be a statesman on the international scene is first and foremost an elected politician and, probably, a politician facing reelection at some point. This means that in

Figure 27.1. Two-Level Negotiation.

international negotiations there are actually two levels of negotiations happening at once (Figure 27.1). The first negotiation is between the two leaders, X and Y. Each of those leaders, however, must negotiate with their domestic constituencies (x and y) to back their international policy.

The discussion of such multiple negotiations is called "Two-Level Games."[13] The impact of multiple negotiations clearly complicates the original negotiation between leaders. A domestic constituency can tie the hands of a leader—for example by threatening to vote the leader out of office. This can make it difficult for the negotiators to reach and sustain agreement. Conversely, a belligerent constituency can help lend credence to the argument that it is the other side that must concede, implying to them that "your hands are tied." Just as we might use an analysis of a bargaining zone to see if two individuals can reach an agreement in a domestic negotiation, the impact of two-level diplomacy can either expand or narrow the range of agreements as well as help determine which party gets more of the surplus good.

A final issue in international negotiation is whether one should negotiate at all. Are there parties with whom we should not negotiate? The old saying is that if you are going to sup with the devil, use a long spoon. Sometimes, leaders believe that no spoon is long enough to make negotiating appropriate. Winston Churchill refused to negotiate with Hitler because Churchill felt it would give Hitler respect he did not deserve. Some U.S. leaders explain their refusal to negotiate with Cuba in similar terms. Many countries refuse to negotiate with terrorists out of fear of setting a precedent of negotiation or conferring legitimacy on the terrorists. Should the United States have negotiated with the Taliban rather than invading Afghanistan? Should the United States have negotiated with Saddam Hussein rather than invading Iraq? Are there any circumstances in which we should negotiate with terrorists?[14] Experts on terrorism argue that any negotiation strategy must take into account the type of terrorist. An "absolutist" terrorist is someone whose goal is complete anarchy and destruction of the political system.[15] Many people would put Osama bin Laden in this category and argue that negotiation with him would be fruitless and immoral. At the other end of the spectrum is the hostage-taker with an agenda (much like a domestic hostage-taker), looking for specific action or money. With this type of terrorist—for example, kidnappers in

Columbia—negotiation can be helpful.[16] In the vast middle, of course, falls the terrorist-or-freedom-fighter distinction in which some would label the actor as a terrorist and others would argue that the terrorist actions stem from a goal of political change. Examples of this type of terrorists would include the IRA, the PLO, and Chechen separatists. Negotiation with such groups may bring results, as in Northern Ireland, but many people would worry about the precedent set by negotiating, the morality of negotiating and, of course, whether any negotiation would actually bring peace.[17]

INTERNATIONAL MEDIATION

Adding a neutral party to the negotiation to facilitate the conversation among the disputants shifts the negotiation to a mediation. In this section on international mediation, I examine the increasing use of mediation in private international commercial disputes as well as the key issues of who, when, and how third party intervention should occur in public international disputes.

Private Mediation

Mediation between individuals or companies from different countries has increased dramatically in the past several years. While international arbitration has long historic roots, international mediation among private parties is a more recent development. This growth in international private mediation is primarily due to the popularity and growth of mediation within countries more generally. Companies that engage in domestic mediation to solve problems want the same options for dispute resolution with overseas customers or clients.

Many international disputes arise between private disputants who have important ongoing relationships. Suppliers and distributors, shippers and receivers, and many other international business partners face the same range and number of disputes as one would expect to see in domestic business relationships. Mediation offers an opportunity to resolve disputes without damaging the parties' long-term ability to work together. Other advantages of mediation, including speed, cost-efficiency, and party control of outcome, are often highlighted against the choice of litigation. In the international arena, litigation is an even less attractive alternative (at least for one party), since one party will have to litigate in the "home state" of the other disputant. The time, energy, expense, and expertise required for litigation is greater in a foreign country, giving companies in private international disputes even more reason to prefer mediation. Finally, foreign judgments sometimes pose enforcement challenges, risking yet another round of litigation.

International mediation raises important legal and procedural issues in addition to those already discussed regarding negotiation. How will the mediation agreement be enforced? Under what law should it be interpreted? Different countries may have different laws concerning the confidentiality of mediation and any privileges for the mediator. These legal issues should be clarified prior to the mediation. Procedural issues for the mediation process, such as choosing the mediator and location, are the same as in domestic mediations, though the concern with mediator neutrality and appearances of bias may be highlighted in a cross-cultural setting. Parties must decide whether the mediator should be from a country different from the participants or whether the location should be in a third country. Furthermore, the mediator may also need to handle communication or translation issues. Setting up an international mediation has become easier in recent years as mediation providers globalize their services and as international arbitration providers add mediation to their services.[18]

International Public Mediation: Intervening in Country-to-Country Disputes

International mediation, like international negotiation, has a long history in international relations. World leaders, such as the pope or the Holy Roman Emperor, tried to mediate disputes among other world leaders to end war and reach agreements. The Treaty of Westphalia in 1648, known for establishing the concept of sovereignty as we know it today, explicitly thanks the Ambassador of the Republic of Venice for his long efforts in mediating the end of the Thirty Years War. With the creation of international organizations such as the United Nations, mediation has become even more institutionalized and promoted as an alternative to warfare. This section will discuss three primary issues in international mediation: how to decide who acts as the mediator, how to determine when mediation might work, and how the mediation or intervention should actually occur.

Historically, mediators in international disputes were world leaders who brought the stature and power of their office or their country to the mediation table. For example, the mediator could be the pope or a representative of the pope's office, who would urge the two Catholic countries to end their dispute. One example of this was the pope's mediation in the late 1970s between Argentina and Chile over maritime rights near the Beagle Channel. The Beagle Channel was home to three barren islands near the southern tips of each country. Sovereignty over the islands could determine fishing and oil exploration rights. Both international arbitration and direct negotiation had failed, and the countries were preparing for military action when the Vatican intervened to mediate a peaceful end of the dispute. The United Nations today also serves as the secular equivalent of the pope's role in intervening in international conflicts.

The mediator can also come from a country with an interest in the dispute or in the parties, such as the United States trying to resolve a dispute between two U.S. allies. Alexander Haig's attempt to avert the Falklands War between Great Britain and Argentina is an example of an unsuccessful mediation; Jimmy Carter's mediation between Israel and Egypt at Camp David or, more recently, Richard Holbrooke's mediation to the end of the Bosnian conflict through the Dayton Accords are quintessential examples of success. Mediators have also come from neighboring countries who want to see the conflict on their borders ended and demonstrate regional leadership. Costa Rica's mediation of the El Salvadoran civil war (which involved Nicaragua and Honduras as well) is one example; South Africa's ongoing mediation effort toward resolving the wars in the Congo is another.

Unlike domestic mediators, international mediators cannot possibly be neutral, objective, or disinterested because the mediator has a distinct interest in the outcome of the mediation. This is particularly true when the alternative is violence. When a neighbor intervenes (as in El Salvador), the fear of violence spilling over, regional destabilization, and refugee issues are sufficient to make the dispute a national interest. Similarly, in many of the disputes in which the United States engages, it prefers to be involved and to receive credit for working out the dispute.[19] For example, even though bilateral negotiations between Egypt and Israel were progressing without U.S. involvement at the end of the 1973 Arab-Israeli war, Secretary of State Henry Kissinger forced an end to bilateral negotiations and insisted on mediating the dispute. One could also argue that the United States pushed the Bosnian Muslims to accept a settlement in the Dayton Accords, when a better offer might have been available at a later date, in order to be able to announce the resolution of the dispute. Furthermore, international country-to-country mediation is public, implicating the reputation of the mediating party even more clearly than in a domestic mediation context.

Another issue in international mediation is the determination of *when* it makes sense to intervene in a conflict. If the parties ask for help, then the answer is relatively straightforward. Other times, however, the mediator steps forward on behalf of the world community to try to end the conflict. Some theorists have argued that a situation needs to be "ripe"—having deteriorated sufficiently for the parties to view mediation as an attractive alternative.[20] For example, if one party is convinced that military force will prevail or that the conflict is not that painful, then that party will have little incentive to resolve the dispute through mediation. Some theorists argue that the parties will only participate in real mediation when military force is not successful or the situation has devolved into a "mutually hurting stalemate."[21] An example of a stalemate that was ready for mediation might be Northern Ireland and George Mitchell's successfully mediated Good Friday Accords. Other theorists disagree with this assessment and argue that international mediation is not like picking ripe apples but rather is more like cultivation, in which a mediator needs to work with the parties over time to develop both the relationship and the possible solution.[22] Long-term mediation efforts by both intergovernmental and nongovernmental organizations between Armenia and Azerbaijan over territorial disputes could be an example of relationship cultivation.

Finally, intervention in international disputes is also broader than just the mediation process. As more NGOs become involved in conflict resolution, interventions have become multifaceted. Years ago, intervention meant the traditional shuttle diplomacy among high-level diplomats, but today intervention can come in multiple forms, including community-building activities between disputing groups led by an NGO such as Search for Common Ground or Mercy Corps, humanitarian efforts led by Doctors Without Borders, and focused peacemaking efforts led by the United Nations or regional intergovernmental organizations. These efforts are known as multitrack diplomacy, involving citizens in different parts of society. Part of the ongoing task for those involved in international conflict is to coordinate these activities so that the mediation at the diplomatic level works in conjunction with the humanitarian efforts at the local level, building on existing peacemaking efforts.[23]

INTERNATIONAL ARBITRATION AND HYBRID PROCESSES

This section reviews the history of how international commercial arbitration became so widespread and then discusses the use of arbitration and hybrid processes to resolve disputes among countries.

Private International Arbitration

Arbitration has its roots in international commercial dispute resolution. Merchant guilds in Europe developed arbitration as a swift and fair method for dealing with commercial disputes across borders when domestic laws were varying and unclear. The popularity and ease of international commercial arbitration persists today. Much like domestic arbitration, international arbitration can offer the advantages of speed, cost-efficiency, finality, and subject-matter expertise of the arbitrator. In addition, avoiding litigation in foreign courts remains a significant advantage.

Countries have encouraged the use of arbitration to resolve commercial disputes by committing to enforce arbitration awards. As of this writing, 134 countries have signed the New York Convention on the Recognition and Enforcement of Foreign Arbitral Awards (1958).[24] This treaty provides that enforcement of arbitral awards among the signatory countries shall be virtually automatic—much faster than the process required to enforce a foreign court judgment. Under the New York Convention, there are very few reasons for a court to set aside an arbitration award. These limited grounds for setting aside or refusing recognition of an award include procedural defects such as improper notice of hearings, inappropriate composition of the arbitral panel under various rules and doctrines, or failure of the arbitration award to be within the contemplated agreement of parties. An award can also be set aside in some limited cases when recognition or enforcement of the award would be contrary to public policy of the enforcing country.

Responding to the proliferation of international arbitration, international arbitration centers worldwide have developed arbitral rules and procedures based on legal and cultural differences. These centers offer disputants a choice in location, rules, and underlying law, making international arbitration even more popular. Some of these arbitration centers include the London Court of International Arbitration, the American Arbitration Association, the Center for Public Resources in New York, and the International Chamber of Commerce in Paris, as well as centers in Stockholm, Hong Kong, and the Middle East. Centers such as these start by providing a basic set of procedures and can also help choose and appoint the arbitrators, organize the logistics of the arbitration, and coordinate the exchange of documents, reports, and experts.

Public International Arbitration and Mixed Processes

Arbitration between countries was rare historically. Countries usually want to resolve disputes among themselves and not have a third party impose a decision on them. For example, the Permanent Court of Arbitration, created in 1899 to voluntarily resolve disputes between countries, has heard only forty-seven cases. One famous arbitration in U.S. history was the *Alabama* arbitration case between the United States and Great Britain growing out of the U.S. Civil War. The United States accused Great Britain of helping the South in violation of its obligation as a neutral under international law; rather than negotiate the claims or resort to force, both countries agreed to arbitration. An arbitration panel agreed with the United States and awarded it over $15 million in damages.[25]

In the late twentieth century, more countries started to turn to arbitration for a number of reasons. First, the International Court of Justice (ICJ), created in 1945, has had great success in acting as an arbiter between countries over issues such as boundaries, territorial disputes, and fishing rights. Using the ICJ is most attractive for countries in contexts in which the dispute is law-based, the issue is politically sensitive enough that compromise would be difficult, and the stakes are low enough that the use of force would be absurd. For example, the United States and Canada could not reach a negotiated agreement over fishing rights in the Gulf of Maine. Compromising for either country would have been politically difficult with important domestic constituencies involved. The countries submitted the case to the ICJ and used a panel process by which the parties agreed to five judges with maritime expertise. This process, which looked much like arbitration, successfully resolved the case between the two neighbors.[26]

The second reason for the expansion of arbitration between countries is the creation of new forums to handle disputes. For example, the WTO was created in 1994 with a separate dispute settlement body to arbitrate trade cases between countries. The disputes are heard by rotating panels of arbitrators with expertise in trade law. More recently, the United Nations established a tribunal to hear disputes arising under the Law of the Sea Convention.[27]

A third reason that arbitration has expanded internationally is that countries are often involved in disputes with private parties rather than with another country. Neither the ICJ nor the WTO process is available to private parties to pursue their investment disputes with countries. Domestic courts are also not available because countries often have sovereign immunity both at home and in foreign courts. Therefore, the International Centre for the Settlement of Investment Disputes (ICSID), established under the World Bank, was created to handle disputes between countries and private parties to facilitate investment and development. Most of the United States's bilateral investment treaties around the world, as well as NAFTA, refer any dispute arising under the treaty to ICSID or ad hoc arbitration rules created by the United Nations Commission on International Trade Law (UNCITRAL). An example of this type of dispute would be one well-known case under NAFTA involving a Canadian company arbitrating against the United States for an unfair state jury trial outcome.[28] These public-private disputes have been growing dramatically as foreign investment grows.

The expansion of arbitration has also led to the development of mixed processes to deal with different types of disputes and parties. The development of international hybrid processes responds to the varying needs of the states for control over the outcome, level of enforcement desired, different parties involved, and underlying international law. For example, as discussed earlier, Chapter Eleven of NAFTA deals with disputes between private investors and the host country, using and enforcing arbitration under the New York Convention rules. Other provisions of NAFTA permit arbitration only between the member countries rather than arbitration with private companies.[29] Another variation is found at the WTO, where the panel process between states alone is supplemented by the right of appeal. WTO member countries wanted to ensure that the international trade law is applied consistently and narrowly across cases. Enforcement under the WTO, however, remains with each country's executive branch rather than its court system.

Table 27.1 outlines the different types of international regimes available for resolving disputes and examines different factors that make up these regimes. The first factor, "direct effect," refers to whether the settlement is immediately enforceable as a matter of domestic law, or whether a separate domestic proceeding must occur. Second, "standing" indicates whether only countries

Table 27.1. International Dispute Resolution Regimes and Their Different Factors.

Factors / Regimes	Direct Effect	Standing for Private Actors	Supremacy	Transparency	Enforcement
Negotiation	No	No	None	Optional	Negotiation
Investment arbitration	Yes	Yes	Only as to that award	Optional	Likely
International adjudication	No	No	Supreme, but not integrated into domestic law	Yes	Varying: None (NAFTA) to Retaliation (WTO)
Supranational Court	Yes	Yes, directly and indirectly	Supreme and integrated	Yes	Fines and damages; domestic remedies also

Source: "Getting Along: The Evolution of Dispute Resolution Regimes in International Trade Organizations," *Michigan Journal of International Law*, 1999, *20*, 697. Reprinted with permission of Andrea K. Schneider.

or also individuals can bring a case. The third column, "supremacy," shows whether a ruling is supreme and trumps domestic law. If the ruling is not supreme, then countries are not required to follow it. Transparency is the issue of how open and understandable the process is. Are the opinions published? Does the public have access to the oral arguments and briefs? If the process is transparent, more parties are likely to use the process as well as grant it legitimacy. The final factor is enforcement and punishment; whether there are ramifications for ignoring a ruling. For example, the European Court of Justice can award damages to an individual harmed by lack of action on the part of a country, and these awards are enforceable in the country's domestic courts.

International Regimes Available for Resolving Disputes

The challenge moving forward in international dispute resolution is to be creative and flexible in developing institutions to resolve disputes. The Internet Corporation for Assigned Names and Numbers (ICANN) is an example of such a creative institution. Any party who believes that a domain name should belong to him or her can lodge a complaint with ICANN under its dispute settlement procedures. For example, Harvard University could file a complaint with ICANN to settle a dispute over ownership of a Website at Harvard.com.[30] Serving both private and public parties, ICANN uses arbitration to resolve these disputes in a timely and fair fashion.[31]

PARALLEL ISSUES IN DOMESTIC AND INTERNATIONAL DISPUTE RESOLUTION

There are many interesting and evolving parallel questions in domestic and international dispute resolution. The most striking difference between the two is the question of mediator neutrality. In the domestic context, most scholars and commentators have argued that mediators ought to remain neutral.[32] In the international context, however, such a concern is virtually unheard of—perhaps because the concept of neutrality holds such a different meaning in the international arena.

There are also two intriguing parallels—the question of representing a constituency in a negotiation leading to "two-level" diplomacy and the evolution of arbitration and adjudication processes to meet the changing needs of the parties and disputes.

Three additional parallel debates are interesting to examine. First, both domestic and international mediation practitioners often debate the appropriateness of different approaches to mediation. For example, domestic mediators disagree over the primacy of the so-called "transformative" approach to mediation. This approach emphasizes how disputants deal with one another, with the particular resolution of a specific dispute a secondary purpose. While some mediators prefer this practice, others worry that the transformative approach is either unnecessary or harmful when the real point of the mediation is to resolve the dispute. This debate is mirrored in the ongoing debates about how to intervene in international disputes. Some theorists argue, much like transformative mediation practitioners, that long-term international dispute resolution is only possible with the transformation of the relationship between the factions. Other theorists argue that solving the problem and ending the violence must take priority over retraining the parties to think differently about the conflict and each other. These theorists might agree, for example, that rewriting textbooks in an effort to change underlying mind-sets may be a noble cause. In the face of costly, ongoing conflict, however, they would argue that an immediate goal of relationship-building and cultural change is too remote.

A second debate concerns which disputes should be settled by a court versus which should employ some other dispute resolution process. Domestically, this debate has continued with the growth of ADR as some theorists argue that settlement is bad for the justice system.[33] There has also been some debate about the merits of diplomacy versus the judicialization of international disputes.[34] Is it better for the United States and the European Union to negotiate disputes over tariffs that favor certain former European colonies, or is it better for the WTO to resolve the disputes?[35] Some international relations experts lament the loss of diplomatic flexibility that accompanies judicialization, while others laud the creation of international courts as the true sign of progress in relations between countries.

Finally, the use of mandatory arbitration for consumer disputes remains very controversial in the academic literature on arbitration (although quite settled in the courts at the moment).[36] Those who disfavor mandatory arbitration argue that arbitration is the wrong process for the uninformed and obligated public who buy a computer, apply for a credit card, or use the hospital emergency room. Similarly, there is some debate about what cases the WTO should hear. While the WTO may be a suitable process for trade disputes, critics argue that too many other disputes are being swept into WTO jurisdiction under the rubric of trade. These critics argue that environmental and human rights cases were not meant to be decided under trade law by a group of trade experts.[37] Others argue that the expansion of the WTO process is a positive development that allows more cases to be uniformly decided.

CONCLUSION

Understanding how international dispute resolution operates can help us understand where dispute resolution started, how it has developed, and what international and domestic dispute resolution contexts can take from each other in order to work best. It is important to recognize that much of mediation has its roots in native practices from around the world, while domestic arbitration's roots are a history of successful international commercial cases. As international interactions developed and changed, so have dispute resolution processes changed to meet these needs in a variety of ways that should inspire ongoing domestic experimentation. Finally, debates about with whom to negotiate, mediator neutrality, and appropriate subject matter for dispute resolution can provide interesting reflections and counterparts to evolving domestic discussions.

Notes

1. See E. Walsh, "The Negotiator," *The New Yorker*, March 18, 1996, pp. 86–97.

2. See J. Z. Rubin and F.E.A. Sander, "Culture, Negotiation, and the Eye of the Beholder," *Negotiation Journal*, 1991, *7*, 249–254.

3. See J. K. Sebenius, "Caveats for Cross-Border Negotiations," *Negotiation Journal*, 2002, *14*, pp. 121–134; and J. W. Salacuse, "Ten Ways That Culture Affects Negotiating Style: Some Survey Results," *Negotiation Journal*, 1998, *14*, 221–240.

4. See *United Nations Convention on Contracts for the International Sale of Goods*, April 10, 1980, S. Treaty Doc. No. 98–99.

5. See, for example, *Hague Convention on the Recognition and Enforcement of Foreign Judgments in Civil and Commercial* Matters, 144 United Nations Treaty Series 249, February 1, 1971.

6. See F.E.A. Sander and J. Rubin, "The Janus Quality of Negotiation: Dealmaking and Dispute Settlement," *Negotiation Journal,* 1988, *4,* 109–113.

7. See *Military and Paramilitary Activities in and Against Nicaragua (Nicaragua* v. *United States),* 1986 International Court of Justice 14 (June 27, 1986).

8. See, for example, Sir Ernest Mason Satow, *Satow's Guide to Diplomatic Practice,* ed. Lord Gore-Booth (London: Longman, 1979). An early example of a mutual defense is the treaty between the Jews and Romans, circa 160 B.C. See M. W. Janis and J. E. Noyes, *International Law Cases and Commentary* (St. Paul, Minn.: West Publishing Company, 2001).

9. See N. Machiavelli, *The Prince* (2nd ed.), trans. H. Mansfield (Chicago: University of Chicago Press, 1998).

10. See, for example, A. Slaughter, "International Law and International Relations Theory: A Dual Agenda," *American Journal of International Law,* 1993, *87,* 205–244.

11. See I. W. Zartman and M. R. Berman, *The Practical Negotiator* (New Haven, Conn.: Yale University Press, 1982).

12. See R. Fisher, E. Kopelman, and A. K. Schneider, *Beyond Machiavelli: Tools for Coping with Conflict* (Cambridge, Mass.: Harvard University Press, 1994).

13. See R. D. Putnam, "Diplomacy and Domestic Politics: The Logic of Two-Level Games," in P. Evans, H. Jacobson, and R. Putnam (eds.), *Double-Edge Diplomacy: International Bargaining and Domestic Politics* (Berkeley, Calif.: University of California Press, 1993), pp. 431–468.

14. See R. H. Mnookin, "When Not to Negotiate: A Negotiation Imperialist Reflects on Appropriate Limits," *University of Colorado Law Review,* 2003, *74,* pp. 1077–1097.

15. See R. E. Hayes, S. R. Kaminski, and S. M. Beres, "Negotiating the Non-Negotiable: Dealing with Absolutist Terrorists," *International Negotiation,* 2003, *8,* 451–467.

16. See G. O. Faure, "Negotiating with Terrorists: The Hostage Case," *International Negotiation,* 2003, *8,* 469–494.

17. See "Negotiating with Terrorists and Non-State Actors: The Journey to World Peace," Symposium 4, *The Cardozo Journal of Conflict Resolution,* 2003.

18. For example, the American Arbitration Association has both expanded overseas and expanded into offering mediation services (American Arbitration Association, "International Centre for Dispute Resolution"). [http://www.adr.org/index2.1.jsp?JSPssid=15732]; and [http://www.adr.org/index2.1.jsp?JSPssid = 15732& JSPsrc=upload < \\ > LIVESITE < \\ > focusArea < \\ > international < \\ > AAA175 current.htm]. Last visited October 2004.

19. See M. A. Levitt, "Kilometer 101: Oasis or Mirage? An Analysis of Third-Party Self-Interest in International Mediation," *Mediation Quarterly,* 1997, *15,* 155–176.

20. See I. W. Zartman, "The Timing of Peace Initiatives: Hurting Stalemates and Ripe Moments," in J. Darby and R. M. Ginty (eds.), *Contemporary Peacemaking: Conflict, Violence and Peace Processes,* Vol. 19 (New York: Palgrave Macmillan, 2003).

21. Zartman, "The Timing of Peace Initiatives," 2003, p. 19.

22. See J. P. Lederach, "Cultivating Peace: A Practitioner's View of Deadly Conflict and Negotiation," in J. Darby and R. M. Ginty (eds.), *Contemporary Peacemaking: Conflict, Violence and Peace Processes,* Vol. 33 (New York: Palgrave Macmillan, 2003).

23. See R. Ricigliano, "Networks of Effective Action: Implementing an Integrated Approach to Peacebuilding," *Security Dialogue,* 2003, *34*(4), 445–462.

24. See United Nations, New York Convention on the Recognition and Enforcement of Foreign Arbitral Awards, New York, June 1958.

25. See M. W. Janis, *An Introduction to International Law* (New York: Aspen Publishers, 2003).

26. See *Case Concerning Delimitation of the Maritime Boundary in the Gulf of Maine Area,* 1984 International Court of Justice 246 (Oct. 12, 1984).

27. See http://www.un.org/Depts/los/index.htm for a description of the tribunal.

28. See *Loewen Group, Inc. and Loewen* v. *United States,* Case No. ARB (AF)/98/3 (2003).

29. See, for example, *Cross-border Trucking Services,* NAFTA Ch. 20 Arb. Trib., February 6, 2001. [http://www.worldtradelaw.net/nafta20/truckingservices.pdf]. Last visited October 2004.

30. See Internet Corporation for Assigned Names and Numbers (ICANN). [http://www.icann.org/dndr/udrp/policy.htm]. Last visited September 2004.

31. See E. Katsh, J. Rifkin, and A. Gaitenby, "E-Commerce, E-Disputes, and E-Dispute Resolution: In the Shadow of E-Bay Law," *Ohio State Journal on Dispute Resolution,* 2000, *15,* 705–727.

32. For a different view of mediator responsibility, see L. Susskind, "Environmental Mediation and the Accountability Problem," *Vermont Law Review,* 1981, *6,* 1–47.

33. See O. Fiss, "Against Settlement," *Yale Law Journal,* 1984, *93,* 1073–1090.

34. See, for example, E. Petersmann, "Constitutionalism and International Organizations," *Northwestern Journal of International Law & Business,* 1966–1967, *17,* 398–451.

35. See, for example, J. L. Dunoff, S. R. Ratner, and D. Wippman, *International Law Norms, Actors, Process* (New York: Aspen Law & Business, 2002), discussing the Banana Wars between the United States and the European Union at the World Trade Organization.

36. See J. R. Sternlight, "Rethinking the Constitutionality of the Supreme Court's Preference for Binding Arbitration: A Fresh Assessment of Jury Trial, Separation of Powers, and Due Process Concerns," *Tulane Law Review,* 1997, *72,* 1–99; and

J. R. Sternlight, "Panacea or Corporate Tool? Debunking the Supreme Court's Preference for Binding Arbitration," *Washington University Law Quarterly,* 1996, *74,* 1–11.

37. See G. C. Shaffer, "The World Trade Organization Under Challenge: Democracy and the Law and Politics of the WTO's Treatment of Trade and Environment Matters," *Harvard Environmental Law Review,* 2001, *25,* 1–92; and J. Atik, "Identifying Antidemocratic Outcomes: Authenticity, Self-Sacrifice, and International Trade," *University of Pennsylvania Journal of International Economic Law,* 1998, *19,* 229–253.

CHAPTER TWENTY-EIGHT

Victim Offender Mediation

Evidence-Based Practice Over Three Decades

Mark S. Umbreit, Robert B. Coates, and Betty Vos

Rich Jenks, a seventeen-year-old young man, was out drinking with some friends and ran out of money. His friends convinced him to break into a house to find some. Although Rich was nervous when he entered the house through a broken window and stole about $200 and a television, it didn't seem like a big deal to him, since these people probably had insurance anyway. His friends waited in a car and were never caught by the police. Rich, however, was apprehended.

When Rich was approached about the possibility of meeting the victim, in the presence of a trained mediator, he was nervous and unsure what to make of it, but also glad to hear that he had some choice in the matter. Eventually he agreed to the mediation session.

Sarah Andrew, the victim, was upset about the financial loss. She was also emotionally shaken, feeling a heightened sense of vulnerability. Sarah felt as if she had been personally assaulted. While Sarah was initially hesitant about the idea of mediation, she ultimately decided it might be helpful.

In the mediation session, Sarah told Rich how the break-in affected her. Meeting the victim in person had a profound impact on Rich, particularly after learning about the huge emotional impact the break-in had had on her. Rich offered a sincere apology. The two later discussed Sarah's actual losses from the break-in, and they worked out a restitution agreement in which Rich agreed to pay $200 over a six-month period.

Both Rich and Sarah felt that the restitution plan they developed together was fair, and they both expressed gratitude that the courts had referred their case to victim offender mediation. Sarah left the mediation feeling less vulnerable. And

Rich had a clearer realization that victims are people and families to be respected, not objects to abuse.

Victim offender mediation (VOM) is a process that provides interested victims and offenders an opportunity to meet in a safe and structured setting with a trained mediator. VOM aims to hold the offender directly accountable for his or her behavior while also providing assistance and compensation to the victim.[1] Most commonly, the crimes involved are property crimes and minor assaults, and the mediators are often community volunteers. With the assistance of a trained mediator, the victim is able to let the offender know how the crime affected him or her, receive answers to questions he or she may have, and be directly involved in developing a restitution plan for the offender to be accountable for the losses the victim incurred. The offender is able to take direct responsibility for his or her behavior, learn the full impact of what he or she did, and develop a plan for making amends to the victim. VOM offers opportunities for both parties to come together in a controlled setting to share the anger and pain of being victimized, as well as to answer questions of why and how. This personalization of the consequences of crime enhances satisfaction levels with the entire justice process.

While many other types of mediation are largely "settlement driven," VOM is primarily "dialogue driven," with the emphasis upon victim healing, offender accountability, and restoration of losses. Contrary to many other applications of mediation in which the mediator first meets the parties during the joint mediation session, most VOM programs use a different process that is based upon a humanistic model of mediation.[2] A humanistic model of mediation involves reframing the role of the mediator from encourager of settlement to facilitator of dialogue and mutual aid. This includes scheduling separate premediation sessions with each party, connecting with the parties through building rapport and trust (though remaining impartial), and identifying the strengths of each party. Within the humanistic model, the mediator uses a nondirective style of mediation that creates a safe space for dialogue and accesses the strengths of participants. Mediators are also trained to recognize and use the power of silence. Mediators using a humanistic approach typically say very little in the mediation session and intentionally try to get out of the way so that the involved parties can speak directly with each other.

Most VOM sessions result in a signed restitution agreement. Within VOM theory, however, reaching an agreement is secondary to the importance of the initial dialogue between the parties that addresses emotional and informational needs of victims. This dialogue is central to victim healing and to development of victim empathy in the offender, which can lead to less criminal behavior in the future. Studies have consistently found that the restitution agreement is less important to crime victims than the opportunity to talk directly with the offender about how they felt about the crime.[3]

Victim offender mediation is the most widely used and researched form of restorative justice in the world.[4] More than fifteen hundred VOM programs in seventeen countries have been developed in the past three decades, and more than fifty empirical studies of VOM have been conducted in five different countries.[5] The VOM process can be summarized by four distinct phases: (1) referral and intake, (2) preparation for mediation, (3) mediation, and (4) follow-up. Each raises important issues of policy, practice, and implementation, and we survey each in the following sections. We also offer brief summaries of what the research demonstrates regarding participant characteristics, participant satisfaction, restitution, recidivism, cost, and the more recent use of VOM in crimes of severe violence.

REFERRAL AND INTAKE PHASE

The VOM process begins when offenders are referred to a program by a criminal justice agency, most frequently the probation office. Most programs accept referrals after a formal admission of guilt has been entered with a court. Some programs accept cases that are referred prior to a formal admission of guilt as part of a deferred prosecution effort.

The most common types of offenses that are referred for VOM include property offenses such as residential burglary, commercial burglary, theft, vandalism, and those involving individuals or small businesses. Certain crimes against persons, such as common assault, are also referred for VOM. Most programs use a similar set of criteria to determine which referrals to accept. They are most likely to consider a case appropriate for VOM if there is an identifiable loss and need for restitution and if the offender has admitted guilt, has no more than two prior convictions, has no major mental health problems, and has no major active substance abuse problems.

PREPARATION FOR THE MEDIATION PHASE

The preparation for the mediation phase begins with the assignment of the case to a case manager and ends with the beginning of the first joint mediation session. The quality of work done during this phase has a significant impact upon the actual mediation session. Unless the mediator effectively establishes rapport and trust with both the victim and offender, it is difficult to proceed to a mediation session. Most problems that occur later in the mediation session result from failure to complete this essential VOM phase thoroughly.

Careful preparation of participants is one of the hallmarks of the victim offender mediation movement. In general, preparation meetings consist of face-to-face contact between the mediator and the participants, though meetings are sometimes carried out via telephone. In some programs the offenders are more likely than the victims to have received their preparation in face-to-face meetings, although this practice is not encouraged.

The mediator's first task during preparation is to explain the process to the offender and prepare the offender for participation in the mediation process. This requires listening to the offender's story, explaining the program and potential benefits, encouraging the offender's participation, and assessing his or her ability to pay restitution, do work for the victim, or do community service.

The rhetoric of much of the literature in the field implies that offender participation in the mediation process is voluntary. Actual practice in the field suggests something quite different. The state exercises a significant amount of coercion when offenders are referred to mediation by the court via probation or are diverted from prosecution if they complete the program. Most programs attempt to temper this by trying to get referrals in the least coercive manner possible, by allowing offenders to choose not to participate if they are either strongly opposed to participation or deemed to be inappropriate candidates for VOM. If an offender denies significant involvement in the crime, requiring participation risks revictimizing the victim, rather than contributing to the victim's healing.

The mediator's second task in preparing for mediation is to contact and interview the victim to secure his or her consent to participate. This involves calling the victim to schedule an individual meeting, meeting with the victim to listen to his or her story, explaining the program and its potential benefits, encouraging the victim's participation, and making clear that participation in the program is voluntary. It can often be helpful for a mediator to share with the victim some of what he or she learned about the offender during the initial meeting. The mediator makes every effort to avoid having to "sell" the program to the victim over the phone during the initial call. Rather, the mediator attempts to obtain a commitment from the victim to meet in order to listen to the victim's version of the offense and the concerns the victim may have about VOM. At that meeting the victim will decide if he or she wants to participate in VOM.

Preparation usually gets high marks from both offenders and victims. Across six empirical studies, the proportion of victims feeling adequately prepared to meet the offender ranged from 68 percent to 98 percent.[6] Only three studies reported offender opinions of their preparation for mediation, with offender satisfaction with preparation ranging from 89 percent to 93 percent.[7]

MEDIATION PHASE

If, after the initial separate contact, both parties express a willingness to proceed, the mediator schedules a face-to-face meeting between the victim and offender. The meeting typically begins with the mediator explaining his or her role, identifying the agenda, and stating the ground rules. The first part of the meeting focuses upon a discussion of the impact of the crime on both parties. Victims are given the unique opportunity to express their feelings directly to the offender, as well as to receive answers to many lingering questions such as "Why me?" or "How did you get into our house?" or "Were you stalking us and planning on coming back?" Victims are often relieved to finally see the offender, who usually bears little resemblance to the frightening character they may have conjured up in their minds.

The expression of feelings by the victim is not typically highly emotional and rarely rises to the level of verbal violence. Some of the initial anger is dissipated through the preliminary meeting with the mediator. Yet, it is often important that some of this intensity of feeling be recalled and expressed directly to the offender during the joint meeting. During the meeting, offenders must face the person they violated, giving them a chance to display the human dimension of their character and even to express remorse. Through open discussion of their feelings, both victim and offender deal with each other as people rather than as stereotypes or objects.

Following this sharing of each other's stories or perspectives, the second part of the meeting focuses on a discussion of losses and the negotiation of a mutually acceptable restitution agreement. This agreement serves as a tangible symbol of conflict resolution and a focal point for accountability. If the victim and offender are unable to agree upon the amount or form of restitution, the case is referred back to the referral source (sometimes a sentencing judge), with a good likelihood that the offender will be placed in a different program. Mediators do not impose a restitution settlement. In more than 95 percent of all meetings, a written restitution agreement is negotiated and signed at the end of the meeting by the victim and offender.[8]

However, rather than focus primarily on restitution, most VOM programs emphasize the importance of allowing enough time to address the real emotional and practical effects the crime has had on the lives of both victims and offenders.

The mediation session is designed to address the needs of both victims and offenders in a manner that personalizes the process of justice by facilitating the empowerment of both parties to resolve the conflict at a community level. It is not meant to be primarily a victim assistance or offender rehabilitation process. Attempting to address some of the needs of both parties does not mean that they are treated as if they have both equally contributed to the conflict. To the contrary, since the issue of guilt is not at question, the mediator must exercise special sensitivity when working with the victim. Victims must be presented with choices, rather than judgmental statements.

While VOM is not meant for all victims and offenders, the theory of the program is that the conflict between those victims and offenders who participate in mediation can be humanized, stereotypes of each other lessened, and fear reduced. The mediation process thereby consistently offers a more satisfactory experience of justice for both the victim and the offender than the traditional criminal justice process and has a positive impact on reducing further criminal behavior.[9]

FOLLOW-UP PHASE

Many VOM practitioners believe that close monitoring and follow-up of cases is needed. This often involves periodic phone contact with the victim to monitor fulfillment of the restitution agreement. Follow-up may also include the scheduling of additional victim-offender meetings when appropriate. One or more follow-up meetings between the victim and the offender can play a significant role in strengthening the personal accountability of the offender to the victim. These follow-up meetings, briefer and less structured than the initial VOM session, provide an informal opportunity to review the implementation of the restitution agreement and discuss any problems that may have arisen related to the payment schedule. The meetings can also be a time for the victim and offender to simply share small talk if they feel so moved.

The need for and willingness to have follow-up meetings is tempered by the amount of restitution to be paid. If only a small amount of restitution is owed, a follow-up meeting might not be appropriate. Conversely, if a larger amount is due, brief follow-up sessions (mid-contract and "close-out" meetings) can be quite helpful. Only a small proportion of VOM cases include follow-up victim-offender meetings.

WHO PARTICIPATES IN VOM AND WHY

Across a range of programs, about 40 to 60 percent of victims referred to VOM participate.[10] Victim willingness to participate is driven by a desire to receive restitution, hold the offender accountable, and learn more about why the offender committed the crime. Victims also typically want to share their pain with the offender, avoid court processing, or help the offender change behavior. In three studies, the top-ranked victim reason for choosing to participate was to help the offender.[11] Offenders choosing to participate often want to take direct responsibility for their own actions, pay back the victim, apologize for the harm they caused, and get the experience behind them.

Less is known about why some persons who are referred to VOM elect not to participate. Only a handful of studies have interviewed such persons to examine their choice not to participate. Among victims, refusals typically come from persons who believe the crime to be too trivial to merit the time required.[12]

Others fear meeting the offender, want the offender to have a harsher punishment, or feel that there had been too much time delay between the incident and the proposed mediation.[13] Additional victim concerns include worries about personal safety, pressure from family or friends not to participate, and not wanting to help the offender.[14] Even less attention has been given to offender reasons for nonparticipation. In one study, offenders reported that they were sometimes advised by lawyers not to participate.[15] Others simply did not want "to be bothered."[16]

The seriousness of the offense is not an accurate predictor of participation rates. One study found that victims were more likely to participate if the offense were a misdemeanor rather than a felony.[17] Another found that property offense cases were more likely to be mediated than personal offense cases.[18] This study also found that the time lapse between the crime and the referral was correlated differently with participation rates by type of offense.[19] Longer time lapses for property cases resulted in fewer mediations, while longer time lapses in personal offenses resulted in more mediations.[20]

PARTICIPANT SATISFACTION

Victims and offenders across sites, cultures, and seriousness of offenses consistently express high levels of satisfaction with VOM. However, the voluntary nature of participating in VOM is a self-selection factor overlaying the findings reported. The high levels of satisfaction may have something to do with the opportunity to choose. Perhaps those who are able to choose among justice options are more satisfied with their experiences.

Typically, eight or nine out of ten respondents who have participated in mediation are satisfied with the process and the resulting agreement.[21] Even in a study based in England that yielded some of the lowest satisfaction scores among the studies reviewed, 84 percent of those victims who participated in VOM were satisfied with the outcome.[22] Victims frequently report satisfaction with the opportunity to share their stories and the pain resulting from the crime event. One victim stated she had wanted to "let the kid know he hurt me personally, not just the money . . . I felt raped."[23] Some pointed to their role in the process with satisfaction. One commented, "We were both allowed to speak . . . he (the mediator) didn't put words into anybody's mouth."[24] Another female victim indicated, "I felt a little better that I [had a] stake in punishment."[25] Another indicated that "it was important to find out what happened, to hear his story, and why he did it and how."[26]

Of course not all victims are satisfied with the process. A male victim complained: "It's like being hit by a car and having to get out and help the other driver when all you were doing was minding your own business."[27] Another stated, "Mediation process was not satisfactory, especially the outcome. I was not repaid for damages or given compensation one year later. Offender has not been adequately dealt with. I don't feel I was properly compensated."[28]

Offenders generally report surprise about having positive experiences. As one youth offender said, "He understood the mistake I made, and I really did appreciate him for it."[29] Some reported changes: "After meeting the victim I now realize that I hurt them a lot . . . to understand how the victim feels, makes me different."[30] One offender stated the reason for his satisfaction quite succinctly, "Without mediation I would have been convicted."[31] Some offenders feel that victims occasionally abuse the process, "We didn't take half the stuff she said we did; she either didn't have the stuff or someone else broke in too."[32]

The question of fairness is related to satisfaction. Not surprising, given the high levels of satisfaction, the vast majority of VOM participants (typically over 80 percent) across setting, cultures, and types of offenses report the process and the agreement as fair to both sides.[33] When comparison groups were employed, those individuals exposed to mediation report feeling treated more fairly than those going through the traditional court proceedings.[34]

These high levels of satisfaction with VOM also translated into relatively high levels of satisfaction with the criminal justice system. Victims and offenders going through mediation indicated more satisfaction with the criminal justice system as a whole than did those going through traditional court proceedings.[35]

RESTITUTION

In VOM, restitution may take many forms, including direct compensation to the victim, community service, work for the victim, and sometimes creative paybacks devised between victim and offender. Restitution was regarded by many early VOM program advocates as a secondary yet important by-product of bringing offender and victim together in a face-to-face meeting. Today, however, some jurisdictions see VOM as a promising vehicle for achieving restitution for the victim. This tendency is reflected in what victims report as their initial motivation for participation: securing restitution. Following participation, however, victims frequently report that what they appreciated most about the program was the opportunity to talk with the offender.[36]

VOM often results in restitution. About half the studies under review looked at restitution as an outcome of mediation.[37] Typically, 90 percent of those cases that included a face-to-face meeting between victim and offender resulted in an agreement of some sort. Restitution of one form or another (monetary, community service, or direct service to the victim) was part of the vast majority of these agreements. In one study, youths who participated in VOM had a much higher rate of fulfilling their restitution agreement (81 percent) than those who did not participate in VOM (57 percent).[38]

RECIDIVISM

Recidivism is frequently used to evaluate the long-term impact of justice programs. One of the first comparative studies to report VOM's effect on recidivism was part of a much larger research project regarding restitution programs.[39] Youths randomly assigned to a Washington, D.C., VOM program were less likely to have subsequent offenses resulting in referral to a juvenile or adult court than youths in a comparison probation group.[40] These youths were tracked for over thirty months.[41]

A study based in Kettering, England, compared recidivism data on the VOM offenders who went through face-to-face mediation with those who were exposed only to "shuttle mediation."[42] The recidivism rate of the former group was lower than the latter, 15.4 percent compared with 21.6 percent.[43] As with the satisfaction measures reported earlier, face-to-face mediation seems to generate better results both in the short run and in the longer run than the less personal indirect mediation.

In a study of youths participating in VOM programs in four states, youths in mediation had lower recidivism rates after a year than did a matched comparison group of youths who did not go through mediation.[44] Overall, across sites, eighteen percent of the program youths reoffended, compared with 27 percent for the comparison youths.[45] Also, program youths tended to reappear in court for less serious charges than those of their comparison counterparts.[46]

Eighty percent of the youths processed through Resolutions Northwest's Victim-Offender Mediation Program in Multnomah County, Oregon, did not recidivate during a one-year follow-up period, while 58 percent of the comparison group did not reoffend during a year of follow-up.[47]

In a Lane County, Oregon, study, 150 youths referred to VOM from July of 1996 to November 1998 in that county were also followed for a year after referral.[48] Comparing their referral frequencies the year prior to the referral to VOM with the year after, all referred youths had 65 percent fewer referrals to the system in the subsequent year.[49] Juveniles referred to VOM but refusing to participate had 32 percent fewer referrals; youths who met with their victims had 81 percent fewer referrals than the preceding year; and juveniles who fully completed their agreements had 76 percent fewer referrals compared with 54 percent fewer referrals for those youths who did not complete any part of the agreement.[50]

Recidivism data was gathered on VOM programs in two additional Oregon counties in a study conducted by the authors.[51] These data reflect one year before intervention comparisons of number of offense with one year after.[52] For the group of youths in the Deschutes County program, there was a 77 percent overall reduction in reoffending.[53] Similarly, for the group of juveniles going through the victim-offender program in Jackson County there was an overall 68 percent reduction in recidivism.[54]

COSTS

The relative costs of correctional programs are difficult to assess. Cost per unit case is influenced by the number of cases handled and the amount of time devoted to each case. The results of a detailed cost analysis in a Scottish study were mixed.[55] Given the relatively small number of cases many of the programs handled, it is difficult to assess the prospect of economies of scale in program administration. Evaluation of a large-scale VOM program in California revealed that the cost per case was reduced dramatically as the program grew in size and could capture economies of scale.[56]

An alternative way of considering the cost impact of VOM is to consider broader system impact. Reduction of incarceration time served can yield considerable savings to a state or county.[57] Reduction of trials such as in Henderson County, North Carolina, where trials were reduced by two-thirds, produces a tremendous cost savings.[58] Researchers evaluating a VOM program in Cobb County, Georgia, point out that the time required to process mediated cases was only a third of that needed for nonmediated cases.[59]

The potential cost savings of VOM programs when they are employed as true alternatives rather than as showcase add-ons is significant. Yet like any other program option, these programs can be swamped with cases to the point at which their quality is compromised. In the search for savings there is the temptation to expand the eligibility criteria to include individuals who would not be suitable for mediation.

CRIMES OF SEVERE VIOLENCE

Increasingly over the past two decades, victims of serious and violent crimes such as assault and homicide have been seeking to meet with the offenders who harmed them or their loved ones. Texas and Ohio were the first two states to develop and offer statewide programs for victim-offender dialogue in serious and violent crimes for victims who desire such a meeting.[60]

One recent study focused on these two pioneering programs and their early participants.[61] The study interviewed victims and offenders who participated in mediation or dialogue sessions regarding serious and violent crimes. Exactly half of the crimes were murder or manslaughter, and the remaining crimes included sexual assault, felony assault or attempted murder, and theft or burglary. The interviews covered the participants' experiences of the crime, their reasons for seeking or agreeing to meet, their preparations for the meeting, their evaluations of their preparation, their dialogue meetings and their mediators or facilitators, their experiences of the dialogue meeting, and their assessments of its impact on their lives. The three most frequent reasons victims sought to meet were to seek information, to show offenders the impact of their actions, and to have some form of human contact with the person responsible for the crime. Offenders focused primarily on benefits to victims, such as the opportunity to give an apology or to help the victims heal. Offenders also often hoped that participation in VOM would contribute to their own rehabilitation or that it might change how their victims viewed them. Many also reported spiritual reasons for wanting to meet with their victims.

Both victims and offenders gave overwhelmingly positive evaluations of their preparations, their dialogue meetings, and their mediators or facilitators. The vast majority of the research participants reported that their participation in the mediation or dialogue program had a profound effect on their lives. Victims, family members, and offenders alike reported feeling more at peace and better able to cope with their lives.

CONCLUSION

The process of victim offender mediation is certainly not meant for all victims and offenders. Nor should VOM be seen as diminishing the fine work being done by the many other important programs serving the needs of victims or offenders. Rather, the theory underlying victim offender mediation complements that which already exists in the broader fields of alternative dispute resolution and criminal justice.

The research on victim offender mediation strongly indicates that this theory is supported in practice. Thousands of VOM cases take place every year, and empirical evidence from the past twenty-five years across many sites in numerous countries demonstrates its contributions. VOM improves victims' involvement and healing. It increases the extent to which offenders take responsibility for their behaviors and learn from their experience. VOM offers community members a role in shaping a just response to law violation, and it contributes to a more positive public attitude toward juvenile and criminal courts.

Notes

1. See M. S. Umbreit, *The Handbook of Victim Offender Mediation: An Essential Guide to Practice and Research* (San Francisco: Jossey-Bass, 2001).

2. See Umbreit, *The Handbook of Victim Offender Mediation,* 2001; M. S. Umbreit, "Humanistic Mediation: A Transformative Journey of Peacemaking," *Mediation Quarterly,* 1997, *14,* 201–213; and M. S. Umbreit, *Mediation of Criminal Conflict: An Assessment of Programs in Four Canadian Provinces* (St. Paul, Minn.: Center for Restorative Justice and Peacemaking, 1995).

3. See R. Coates and J. Gehm, "An Empirical Assessment," in M. Wright and B. Galaway (eds.), *Mediation and Criminal Justice* (London: Sage, 1989), pp. 251–263; M. S. Umbreit and R. Coates, "Cross-Site Analysis of Victim-Offender Mediation in Four States," *Crime and Delinquency,* 1993, *39,* 565–585; and M. S. Umbreit, "Restorative Justice Through Mediation: The Impact of Offenders Facing Their Victims in Oakland," *Journal of Law and Social Work,* 1995, *5,* 1–13.

4. See G. Bazemore and M. S. Umbreit, "Rethinking the Sanctioning Function in Juvenile Court: Retributive or Restorative Responses to Youth Crime," *Crime and Delinquency,* 1995, *41*(3), 296–316; D. Van Ness and K. Heetderks, *Restoring Justice* (2nd ed.) (Cincinnati: Anderson Publishing Company, 2002); H. Zehr, *Changing Lenses: A New Focus for Crime and Justice* (Scottsdale, Pa.: Herald Press, 1990); and H. Zehr, *The Little Book of Restorative Justice* (Intercourse, Pa.: Good Books, 2002).

5. See M. S. Umbreit, R. Coates, and B. Vos, *Juvenile Victim Offender Mediation in Six Oregon Counties* (Salem, Ore.: Oregon Dispute Resolution Commission, 2001); and M. S. Umbreit, R. B. Coates, and B. Vos, "The Impact of Restorative Justice Conferencing: A Multi-National Perspective," *British Journal of Community Justice,* 2002, *1*(2), 21–48.

6. See J. P. Collins, *Final Evaluation Report on the Grande Prairie Community Reconciliation Project for Young Offenders* (Ottawa: Ministry of the Solicitor General of Canada, Consultation Centre (Prairies), 1984); C. Fercello and M. S. Umbreit, *Client Satisfaction with Victim Offender Conferences in Dakota County, Minnesota* (St. Paul, Minn.: Center for Restorative Justice and Peacemaking, 1999); L. Roberts, *Victim Offender Mediation: An Evaluation of the Pima County Juvenile Court Center's Victim Offender Mediation Program (VOMP),* masters thesis, Tucson, Ariz.: Department of Communications, University of Arizona, 1998; E. Strode, *Victims of Property Crime Meet Their Juvenile Offenders: Victim Participants' Evaluation of the Dakota County (MN) Community Corrections Victim Offender Meeting Program,* masters thesis, Northampton, Mass.: Smith College of Social Work, 1997; Umbreit, *Mediation of Criminal Conflict,* 1995; and M. S. Umbreit, R. Coates, and B. Vos, "The Impact of Victim Offender Mediation: Two Decades of Research," *Federal Probation,* December 2001, pp. 29–35.

7. See Fercello and Umbreit, *Client Satisfaction with Victim Offender Conferences in Dakota County, Minnesota,* 1999; Roberts, *Victim Offender Mediation,* 1998; and Umbreit, Coates, and Vos, "The Impact of Victim Offender Mediation," 2001.

8. Umbreit, Coates, and Vos, "The Impact of Victim Offender Mediation," 2001.

9. See M. S. Umbreit, *Victim Meets Offender* (Monsey, N.Y.: Criminal Justice Press, 1994); M. S. Umbreit, "Restorative Justice Through Mediation: The Impact of Programs in Four Canadian Provinces," in B. Galaway, and J. Hudson (eds.), *Restorative Justice: International Perspectives* (Monsey, N.Y.: Criminal Justice Press, 1996); and Umbreit, *The Handbook of Victim-Offender Mediation,* 2001.

10. Umbreit, Coates, and Vos, "The Impact of Victim Offender Mediation," 2001.

11. See R. Coates, H. Burns, and M. S. Umbreit, *Victim Participation in Victim Offender Conferencing: Washington County, Minnesota Community Justice Program* (St. Paul, Minn.: Center for Restorative Justice and Peacemaking, 2002); J. Gehm, "Mediated Victim-Offender Restitution Agreements: An Exploratory Analysis of Factors Related to Victim Participation," in B. Galaway, and J. Hudson (eds.), *Criminal Justice, Restitution, and Reconciliation* (Monsey, N.Y.: Criminal Justice Press, 1990), pp. 177–182; and P. Wyrick and M. Costanzo, "Predictors of Client Participation in Victim-Offender Mediation," *Mediation Quarterly,* 1999, *16,* 253–257.

12. See R. Coates and J. Gehm, *Victim Meets Offender: An Evaluation of Victim-Offender Reconciliation Programs* (Valparaiso, Ind.: PACT Institute of Justice, 1985); and Umbreit, "Restorative Justice Through Mediation," 1995.

13. See Coates and Gehm, *Victim Meets Offender,* 1985; and Umbreit, "Restorative Justice Through Mediation," 1995.

14. See Coates, Burns, and Umbreit, *Victim Participation in Victim Offender Conferencing,* 2002.

15. See A. Schneider, "Restitution and Recidivism Rates of Juvenile Offenders: Results from Four Experimental Studies," *Criminology,* 1986, *24,* 533–552.

16. See Coates and Gehm, *Victim Meets Offender,* 1985.

17. See Gehm, "Mediated Victim-Offender Restitution Agreements," 1990.

18. See Wyrick and Costanzo, "Predictors of Client Participation in Victim-Offender Mediation," 1999.

19. See Wyrick and Costanzo, "Predictors of Client Participation in Victim-Offender Mediation," 1999.

20. See Wyrick and Costanzo, "Predictors of Client Participation in Victim-Offender Mediation," 1999.

21. See R. Davis, M. Tichane, and D. Grayson, *Mediation and Arbitration as Alternatives to Prosecution in Felony Arrest Cases: An Evaluation of the Brooklyn Dispute Resolution Center* (New York: VERA Institute of Justice, 1980); Coates and Gehm, *Victim Meets Offender,* 1985; L. Perry, T. Lajeunesse, and A. Woods, *Mediation Services: An Evaluation* (Winnipeg, Manitoba: Research, Planning and Evaluation Office of the Attorney General, 1987); T. Marshall, "Results of Research from British Experiments in Restorative Justice," in B. Galaway and J. Hudson (eds.), *Criminal Justice, Restitution, and Reconciliation* (Monsey, N.Y.: Criminal Justice Press, 1990), pp. 83–107; M. S. Umbreit, "Minnesota Mediation Center Produces Positive Results," *Corrections Today,* 1991, *53*(5), 194–197; M. S. Umbreit and R. Coates, *Victim Offender Mediation: An Analysis of Programs in Four States of the U.S.* (St. Paul, Minn.: Center for Restorative Justice and Peacemaking, 1992); S. Warner, *Making Amends: Justice for Victims and Offenders* (Aldershot, U.K.: Avebury, 1992); M. S. Umbreit, "Juvenile Offenders Meet Their Victims: The Impact of Mediation in Albuquerque, New Mexico," *Family and Conciliation*

Courts Review, 1993, *31,* 90–100; Umbreit and Coates, "Cross-Site Analysis of Victim-Offender Mediation in Four States," 1993; M. S. Umbreit, "Crime Victims Confront Their Offenders: The Impact of a Minneapolis Mediation Program," *Research on Social Work Practice,* 1994, *4,* 436–447; Umbreit, *Victim Meets Offender,* 1994; T. Roberts, *Evaluation of the Victim Offender Mediation Project, Langley, B.C.: Final Report* (Victoria, B.C.: Focus Consultants, 1995); C. Carr, *VORS Program Evaluation Report* (Inglewood, Calif.: Centenela Valley Juvenile Diversion Project, 1998); Roberts, *Victim-Offender Mediation,* 1998; M. S. Umbreit, "Restorative Justice Through Victim-Offender Mediation: A Multi-Site Assessment," *Western Criminology Review,* 1998, *1* [http://wcr.sonoma.edu/v1n1/umbreit. html]; A. Evje and R. Cushman, *A Summary of the Evaluations of Six California Victim-Offender Reconciliation Programs* (San Francisco: Judicial Council of California, Administrative Office of the Courts, 2000); and Umbreit, Coates, and Vos, "The Impact of Victim-Offender Mediation."

22. See M. S. Umbreit and A. W. Roberts, *Mediation of Criminal Conflict in England: An Assessment of Services in Coventry and Leeds* (St. Paul, Minn.: Center for Restorative Justice and Peacemaking, 1996).

23. M. S. Umbreit, "Violent Offenders and Their Victims," in M. Wright and B. Galaway (eds.), *Mediation and Criminal Justice* (London, U.K.: Sage, 1989).

24. M. S. Umbreit, "Mediation of Victim Offender Conflict," *Journal of Dispute Resolution,* 1988, *35,* 85–105.

25. Coates and Gehm, *Victim Meets Offender,* 1985, pp. 1–44.

26. Umbreit and Coates, *Victim-Offender Mediation,* 1992, p. 106.

27. Coates and Gehm, *Victim Meets Offender,* 1985, pp. 1–44.

28. Umbreit, *Mediation of Criminal Conflict,* 1995, p. 162.

29. Umbreit, "Minnesota Mediation Center Produces Positive Results," 1991.

30. Umbreit and Coates, *Victim-Offender Mediation,* 1992, p. 18.

31. Umbreit, *Mediation of Criminal Conflict,* 1995, p. 144.

32. Coates and Gehm, *Victim Meets Offender,* 1985, p. 12.

33. See Umbreit, Coates, and Vos, "The Impact of Victim-Offender Mediation," 2001.

34. See M. S. Umbreit, "Crime Victims Seeking Fairness, Not Revenge: Toward Restorative Justice," *Federal Probation,* 1989, *53*(3), 52–57.

35. See Umbreit and Coates, *Victim-Offender Mediation,* 1992; and Umbreit, *Mediation of Criminal Conflict,* 1995.

36. See Coates and Gehm, *Victim Meets Offender,* 1985; and Umbreit and Coates, *Victim-Offender Mediation,* 1992.

37. See Collins, *Final Evaluation Report on the Grande Prairie Community Reconciliation Project for Young Offenders,* 1984; Coates and Gehm, *Victim Meets Offender,* 1985; Perry, Lajeunesse, and Woods, *Mediation Services,* 1987; Umbreit, "Mediation of

Victim-Offender Conflict," 1988; B. Galaway, "Informal Justice: Mediation Between Offenders and Victims," in P. Albrecht and O. Backes (eds.), *Crime Prevention and Intervention: Legal and Ethical Problems* (New York: Walter de Gruyter, 1989), pp. 103–116; Umbreit, "Minnesota Mediation Center Produces Positive Results," 1991; Umbreit and Coates, *Victim-Offender Mediation,* 1992; Warner, *Making Amends,* 1992; S. Roy, "Two Types of Juvenile Restitution Programs in Two Midwestern Counties: A Comparative Study," *Federal Probation,* 1993, *57*(4), 48–53; Evje and Cushman, *A Summary of the Evaluations of Six California Victim-Offender Reconciliation Programs,* 2000; and Umbreit, Coates, and Vos, *Victim-Offender Mediation,* 2001.

38. See Umbreit and Coates, *Victim-Offender Mediation,* 1992.

39. See Schneider, "Restitution and Recidivism Rates of Juvenile Offenders," 1986.

40. See Schneider, "Restitution and Recidivism Rates of Juvenile Offenders," 1986.

41. See Schneider, "Restitution and Recidivism Rates of Juvenile Offenders," 1986.

42. See J. Dignan, *Repairing the Damage: An Evaluation of an Experimental Adult Reparation Scheme in Kettering, Northamptonshire* (Sheffield, U.K.: Centre for Criminological Legal Research, Faculty of Law, University of Sheffield, 1990).

43. See Dignan, *Repairing the Damage,* 1990.

44. See Umbreit and Coates, *Victim-Offender Mediation,* 1992.

45. See Umbreit and Coates, *Victim-Offender Mediation,* 1992.

46. See Umbreit and Coates, *Victim-Offender Mediation,* 1992.

47. See K. Stone, *An Evaluation of Recidivism Rates for Resolutions Northwest's Victim-Offender Mediation Program,* masters thesis, Portland, Ore.: Portland State University, 2000.

48. See S. Nelson, *Evaluation of the Restorative Justice Program* (Eugene, Ore.: Lane County Department of Youth Services, 2000).

49. See Nelson, *Evaluation of the Restorative Justice Program,* 2000.

50. See Nelson, *Evaluation of the Restorative Justice Program,* 2000.

51. See Umbreit, Coates, and Vos, *Victim-Offender Mediation,* 2001.

52. See Umbreit, Coates, and Vos, *Victim-Offender Mediation,* 2001.

53. See Umbreit, Coates, and Vos, *Victim-Offender Mediation,* 2001.

54. See Umbreit, Coates, and Vos, *Victim-Offender Mediation,* 2001.

55. See Warner, *Making Amends,* 1992.

56. See M. Niemeyer and D. Shichor, "A Preliminary Study of a Large Victim/Offender Reconciliation Program," *Federal Probation,* 1996, *60*(3), 30–34.

57. See Coates and Gehm, *Victim Meets Offender,* 1985.

58. See S. Clarke, E. Valente, and R. Mace, *Mediation of Interpersonal Disputes: An Evaluation of North Carolina's Programs* (Chapel Hill, N.C.: Institute of Government, University of North Carolina, 1992).

59. See S. Stone, W. Helms, and P. Edgeworth, *Cobb County [Georgia] Juvenile Court Mediation Program Evaluation* (Carrolton, Ga.: State University of West Georgia, 1998).

60. See M. S. Umbreit, B. Vos, R. B. Coates, and K. Brown, *Facing Violence: The Path of Restorative Justice and Dialogue* (Monsey, N.Y.: Criminal Justice Press, 2003).

61. See Umbreit, Vos, Coates, and Brown, *Facing Violence,* 2003.

CHAPTER TWENTY-NINE

Youths, Education, and Dispute Resolution

Donna K. Crawford and Richard J. Bodine

Conflict resolution education is designed to provide youths with the ability and the propensity to engage in constructive, creative, collaborative problem solving to reconcile personal differences with others. Conflict resolution education has three components: a set of problem-solving principles, a structured problem-solving process, and the skills for creative cooperation between individuals and among groups. Certain precepts underlie conflict resolution education:

- Conflict is natural and normal.
- Differences can be acknowledged and appreciated.
- Conflict, when viewed as a solution-building opportunity, can lead to positive change.
- When conflicting parties build on one another's strengths to find solutions, the resulting climate nurtures individual self-worth and opportunities for fulfillment of each individual's needs.[1]

Conflict resolution education embraces the "principled negotiation" elements: separating people from the problem, focusing on interests not positions, inventing options for mutual gain, and using objective criteria. The foundation abilities of conflict resolution, presented later in this chapter, indicate specific learnings necessary to employ these four principles within a structured problem-solving process.

Conflict resolution education employs three problem-solving processes—negotiation, mediation, and group problem solving (referred to in some of the literature as consensus decision making). "*Negotiation* is problem solving in which the two parties in the dispute meet face-to-face to work together, unassisted, to resolve the dispute. *Mediation* is problem solving in which the two parties in the dispute meet face-to-face to work together, assisted by a neutral third party called the mediator, to resolve the dispute. *Group problem solving* is problem solving in which all parties of the dispute meet in collaboration to resolve the dispute by crafting a plan of action that all parties can and will support. This process may or may not be facilitated by a neutral third party."[2]

The use of any of these processes is characterized by consensual participation of the antagonists in collaborative problem solving. The six basic steps in each conflict resolution problem-solving process are (1) set the stage, (2) gather perspectives, (3) identify interests, (4) create options, (5) evaluate options, and (6) generate agreement. Conflict resolution education provides extensive training and practice in the use of these steps.

FOUNDATION ABILITIES FOR CONFLICT RESOLUTION

Effective implementation of problem-solving processes requires a particular set of attitudes, understandings, and skills. We refer to these as six "foundation abilities" of conflict resolution:

Orientation Abilities. Orientation abilities encompass values, beliefs, attitudes, and propensities that are compatible with effective conflict resolution. Orientation abilities include nonviolence, compassion and empathy, fairness, trust, justice, tolerance, self-respect, respect for others, celebration of diversity, and appreciation for controversy.

Perception Abilities. Perception abilities encompass the understanding that conflict lies not in objective reality but in how individuals perceive that reality. Perception abilities include empathizing in order to see the situation as the other side sees it, self-evaluating to recognize personal fears and assumptions, suspending judgment and blame to facilitate a free exchange of views, and reframing solutions to allow for face saving and to preserve self-respect and self-image.

Emotional Abilities. Emotional abilities encompass behaviors to manage anger, frustration, fear, and other emotions effectively. Emotional abilities include learning language for communicating emotions effectively, developing the courage to make emotions explicit, expressing emotions in nonaggressive, noninflammatory ways, and exercising self-control so as to not react to the emotional outbursts of others.

Communication Abilities. Communication abilities encompass behaviors of listening and speaking that allow for the effective exchange of facts and feelings. Communication abilities include using active listening behaviors to understand, speaking to be understood, and reframing emotionally charged statements into neutral, less emotional terms.

Creative Thinking Abilities. Creative thinking abilities encompass behaviors that enable individuals to be innovative in defining problems and making decisions. Creative thinking abilities include contemplating the problem from a variety of perspectives, approaching the problem-solving task as a mutual pursuit of possibilities, and brainstorming to create, elaborate, and enhance a variety of options.

Critical Thinking Abilities. Critical thinking abilities encompass the behaviors of analyzing, hypothesizing, predicting, strategizing, comparing and contrasting, and evaluating. Critical thinking abilities include recognizing existing criteria and making them explicit, establishing objective criteria, applying criteria as the basis for choosing options, and planning future behaviors.

Successful implementation of problem-solving processes of conflict resolution requires each of these skills. Yet an effective curriculum must contain more than these foundational skills. Conflict resolution education must include the application of these abilities to one or more of the problem-solving processes. For example, it is true that conflict resolution rarely happens if the disputants do not communicate with each other, but it is generally not enough to just talk and listen in order to resolve conflicts. Communication needs the kinds of purpose and direction that problem-solving processes provide.

APPROACHES TO CONFLICT RESOLUTION EDUCATION

Four basic approaches to conflict resolution education are prominent across the country: the mediation approach, the peaceable classroom approach, the process curriculum approach, and the peaceable school approach. In actuality, the lines dividing these four are sometimes difficult to draw, yet the categories can be useful in describing the focus of each approach. The strength of each approach lies in its application of problem-solving processes. Some of the best conflict resolution implementation examples have evolved in schools where the principles and problem-solving processes of conflict resolution allowed for gradual expansion from one approach to another.

Mediation Approach

The mediation approach in conflict resolution education provides training for a cadre of students and staff in the principles of conflict resolution, in the foundation abilities described above, and in the mediation process. This cadre of mediators provides neutral third-party facilitation to assist those in conflict to reach a resolution. The whole school often participates in orientation sessions designed to develop a shared understanding of conflict and how conflicts are resolved through mediation.

Within this approach to conflict resolution education, mediation is offered as a tool to help manage and resolve conflicts between young people, between young people and adults, and between adults. Adults at the school who receive mediation training are most commonly called on to assist in disputes that involve at least one other adult. For example, an adult mediator may assist in resolving conflicts such as work problems between staff members, disciplinary actions disputed by parents, and disputes over the development of appropriate programs for children with special needs. Students trained as mediators may be called on to help resolve disputes between peers involving jealousies, rumors, misunderstandings, fights, personal property, and damaged friendships. In addition, youths and adults may co-mediate conflicts such as personality clashes, issues of respect and behavior, and other conflicts that damage youth-adult relationships. Youth-adult mediations are usually an outgrowth of established peer mediation programs or adult mediation programs.

Peer mediation is among the most widely chosen types of conflict resolution approaches used in schools, and it can be highly effective in dealing with disputes among students. Young people are often effective mediators because they understand their peers, make the process age appropriate, empower their peers and command their respect, and normalize the conflict resolution process.[3] Young people connect with their peers in ways that adults cannot. Peer mediators are capable of framing disputes using the perspective, language, and attitudes of youth. Young people perceive peer mediation as a way to talk out problems without the fear of an adult judging their behavior, thoughts, or feelings. Peer mediators are respected because they uphold the problem-solving process and honor the disputants in the way they conduct the mediation sessions. The self-empowering process appeals to youths, fostering self-esteem and self-discipline. When young people solve their own problems, they feel they are in control and can make a commitment to the solutions they have created.

Any discussion of peer mediation must include at least two important caveats. First, a student who violates rules does not avoid appropriate consequences simply by participating in mediation. Mediation is most effectively used as a vehicle for planning more constructive future behavior. As such, it may be used to augment disciplinary action, in concert with school discipline policies. Second, peer mediation is not always an appropriate process for addressing all student conflicts. For example, victims of bullying are not able generally to advocate for themselves, and some bullies may not be able to empathize, feel compassion, and take responsibility for their actions.[4] Peer mediation is an appropriate intervention only when there is a more symmetrical balance of power between parties. Such a balance can only result from adult intervention to address the bully's behavior.

In schoolwide peer mediation programs, a cadre of students is trained in conflict resolution. Student mediation training requires twelve to twenty hours of basic training and may involve twelve to twenty hours of additional advanced training as mediators gain experience. Basic training activities include understanding conflict, responding to conflict, understanding sources of conflict, learning communication skills, learning the role of the mediator, and engaging in the mediation process. Advanced training activities include developing bias awareness, appreciating sociocultural diversity, using advanced communication, uncovering hidden interests, dealing with anger, caucusing, negotiating, and group problem solving. Students who complete the basic training are able to mediate most disputes between peers with ongoing supervision and support. The advanced training strengthens their abilities to use the mediation process and expands their understanding of diversity with regard to conflict resolution.[5] Peer mediation training can be flexible, accommodating the school's schedule and resources and the developmental level of the students involved. For example, training for elementary students might be conducted in two-hour sessions over several weeks, whereas training for high school students might be done in full-day sessions.

Peaceable Classroom Approach

The peaceable classroom approach is a whole-classroom methodology that includes teaching students the foundation abilities, the principles of conflict resolution, and one or more of the three problem-solving processes of conflict resolution. The peaceable classroom approach integrates conflict resolution into the curriculum, infuses conflict resolution into the management of the classroom, and uses the instructional methods of cooperative learning and academic controversy.

Curriculum integration occurs when the skills and concepts needed to resolve conflicts constructively are incorporated into core subject areas. Teachers who integrate conflict resolution into their curriculums help create classroom environments that support conflict resolution and prosocial behavior. William J. Kreidler, a pioneer of the peaceable classroom, describes the peaceable classroom as a caring and respectful community having five qualities: cooperation, communication, emotional expression, appreciation for diversity, and conflict resolution.[6] Peaceable classrooms incorporate learning activities and teachable moments that encourage youths to recognize and choose nonviolent options in conflict situations, meet the needs of the individuals involved, and improve relationships.

Teachers in peaceable classrooms rely extensively on the cooperative learning and academic controversy methods developed by David Johnson and Roger Johnson. In cooperative learning, students work in small groups to accomplish shared learning goals. Students have the responsibility to learn the assigned material and to ensure that other group members learn it.[7] Academic controversy methods are used when one student's ideas, information, conclusions, theories, and opinions are incompatible with those of another, and the two seek to reach an agreement. Controversies are resolved through deliberate discourse—the discussion of the advantages and disadvantages of proposed actions. Such discussion is aimed at creative problem solving by synthesizing novel solutions.[8]

In peaceable classrooms, youths learn to take responsibility for their actions and develop a sense of connectedness to others and their environment. Peaceable classrooms build the capacity of youths to manage and resolve conflict on their own by learning to understand and analyze conflict, to understand peace and peacemaking, to recognize the role of perceptions and biases, to identify feelings, to identify factors that cause escalation, to handle anger and other feelings appropriately, to improve listening skills, to improve verbal communication skills, and to identify common interests. Students in peaceable classrooms also build their capacity by learning to brainstorm about multiple options that address interests, evaluate the consequences of different options, and create a win-win agreement.

"Partners in Learning: From Conflict to Collaboration in Secondary Classrooms," published by the Educators for Social Responsibility (ESR),[9] offers examples for incorporating conflict resolution into primary and supplementary lessons for the secondary level. For example, ESR recommends teaching literature by exploring the concept of conflict escalation in novels and short stories, or by reading selections about American and global peacemakers whose life work has made a positive difference for others—for example, Eleanor Roosevelt, Cesar Chavez, Mary McLeod Bethune, Ralph Bunche, and Jane Addams. Science classes might explore the concept of global ecology by examining environmental problems that require international cooperation. Civics classes might examine legislation or policies on controversial issues at the state, federal, or international level. In geography classes, students can compare different nations to identify how geographic features influence economy and quality of life. The key to integrating conflict resolution into classroom studies is the recognition that conflict is an integral part of every curricular area. Examining the curricular content as conflict often makes the subject matter seem more relevant to learners, and focusing on the natural conflicts of the area of study reinforces the learnings about conflict.

Process Curriculum Approach

The process curriculum approach is characterized by devoting a specific time to teaching about conflict resolution. In a separate course, distinct curriculum, daily lesson plan, or technology-based independent learning activity, students explore the foundation abilities, principles of conflict resolution, and one or more of the problem-solving processes of conflict resolution. The lessons are unified in scope and sequence, taking place through structured activities such as simulations, role plays, group discussions, and cooperative-learning activities.

The structure chosen for the process curriculum approach depends, in part, on the age of the students in question. The daily lesson method is most often part of elementary school offerings. Middle and high schools may also use daily lessons over the length of a semester, though many instead run a series of workshops.

It is important to remind those interested in the process curriculum approach that youths receive more powerful messages from what teachers actually do than from what educators say or teach. Carol Lieber reminds us, "How and when adults model conflict resolution skills themselves and provide opportunities for student[s] to practice them in meaningful ways will, in large part, determine how often and how well student[s] actually use these skills in the classroom, in the hallways, or at home—and even how well kids act as models for each other."[10] Effective implementation of the process curriculum approach requires time not only for teaching the concepts and skills of conflict resolution but also for ongoing opportunities to practice.

Peaceable School Approach

The peaceable school approach is a comprehensive, whole-school methodology that infuses conflict resolution as a system of operation into the school as well as the classroom. It assimilates the peaceable classroom, mediation, and process curriculum approaches. Every member of the school community learns and uses conflict resolution concepts and skills. The peaceable classroom is the unit block of the peaceable school because the classroom is where students gain the knowledge and skills needed to resolve conflicts creatively. The classroom is also where the majority of conflicts are addressed.[11] By incorporating the other three approaches, the peaceable school approach appears to maximize the likelihood that students will develop sustainable life skills of conflict resolution.

Peaceable school climates aim to reflect caring, honesty, cooperation, and appreciation for diversity. As ongoing, comprehensive, whole school processes, peaceable school approaches incorporate cooperative learning environments, direct instruction and practice of conflict resolution skills and processes, noncoercive school and classroom management systems, and integration of conflict resolution concepts and skills into the curriculum.

Peaceable schools challenge youths and adults to believe that a nonviolent, diverse society is a realistic and desirable goal. Peaceable schools value and encourage diversity and promote peacemaking as the normative behavior of adults and students. Participants in the peaceable school apply conflict resolution skills to address interpersonal and intergroup problems. Issues that confront students, faculty, administrators, and parents all fall within the scope of the peaceable school approach.

Peaceable school programs offer training in consensus decision making and negotiation to all members of the school community. Peer mediation in the classroom aims primarily to facilitate problem solving between students from that classroom. Peer mediation, used as a schoolwide intervention, not only provides a service to resolve disputes between students but also sometimes assists with disputes between students and adults. Peaceable school programs incorporate conflict resolution into the school's operations, affecting relationships between all members of the school community, including parents. Effective conflict resolution behavior requires participants to develop mutual appreciation and respect for differences. The successful development of conflict resolution skills depends above all on the absence of coercion.[12]

The peaceable school approach supports the school community in addressing specific elements that will transform the school. These elements are not a developmental sequence but entry points to initiating the peaceable school approach. The peaceable school emerges in phases, coming to fruition once all transformations have taken place. The elements of transformation include instituting conflict resolution training for adults in the school, designing behavior expectations and management systems in concert with conflict resolution theory, building cooperation by incorporating cooperative learning and interaction activities into the classroom, and developing the scope and sequence of conflict resolution skills taught to students.

The peaceable school approach provides learning experiences for an age-appropriate understanding of conflict, including definitions, origins, choices for response, consequences of choices, and potential opportunities that may be gained from conflict. It also provides opportunities for an age-appropriate understanding of the value and behaviors of peace and peacemaking. Integral to the transformation into a peaceable school is age-appropriate understanding of the principles of conflict resolution. The transformation to a peaceable school occurs when students have opportunities to learn and practice problem-solving strategies of negotiation and consensus decision making within the classroom. Similarly, schools seeking to transform into peaceable schools provide mediation training for those who want to become mediators in the schoolwide program, and schools provide students with the opportunity to serve as peer mediators in their classrooms. Ideally, these schools also develop an evaluation process to support and expand learning and to assess progress toward achieving a peaceable school.

Discipline and Peaceable Schools

Typical school academic and disciplinary policies and practices often contradict the peaceful resolution of conflicts. Peaceable schools have reviewed and rethought such operations. Unless the operation of the system corresponds to the desired behavior of the individuals within the system, the contradictory messages will result in confusion and unclear expectations. As David Johnson and Roger Johnson, codirectors of the Conflict Resolution and Cooperative Learning Center of the University of Minnesota, point out, "It makes no sense to talk of constructive conflict management in schools structured competitively. The first step in teaching students the procedures for managing conflicts, therefore, is creating a cooperative context in which conflicts are defined as mutual problems to be resolved in ways that benefit everyone involved."[13] In competitive systems, individuals usually focus on short-term self-interests and try to maximize their own goals at the expense of others. In cooperative systems, individuals focus on long-term, mutual interests and try to maximize joint solutions. When cooperation is promoted throughout the school, the problem-solving processes of conflict resolution seem natural, logical, and desirable. Cooperative systems create a context in which conflicts can be resolved constructively and reduce the factors that place individuals at risk for using violence.

Many schools adopt methods of behavior management that are based on punishment rather than discipline. Such programs gain student compliance through externally imposed behavior expectations that are enforced through coercion. This approach appears contrary to conflict resolution principles such as respect, tolerance, and appreciation of differences. Gisela Konopka argues, "Obedience is demanded to achieve a person with discipline, but this is a discipline that comes from the outside and works only when one is afraid of someone who is stronger than oneself. We do need discipline, an inner discipline to order our life. What is inner discipline? To my thinking it is the opposite of blind obedience. It is the development of a sense of values."[14] Table 29.1 contrasts the differences in the practices of punishment-driven programs and the practices of discipline-driven programs.

The goal of the peaceable school is to create a schoolwide discipline program focused on empowering students to regulate and control their own behavior. The program allows educators to model an orderly, productive system accomplished through cooperation and persistent pursuit of constructive behavior. Students are provided ways to think, behave, and self-evaluate as opposed to just being told to refrain from, or to employ, a particular behavior. The

Table 29.1. Punishment Versus Discipline.

Punishment	*Discipline*
Expresses power of an authority; usually causes pain to the recipient; is based upon retribution or revenge; is concerned with what has happened (the past)	Is based on logical or natural consequences that embody the reality of a social order (rules that one must learn and accept to function adequately and productively in society); is concerned with what is happening now (the present)
Is arbitrary—probably applied inconsistently and unconditionally; does not accept or acknowledge exceptions or mitigating circumstances	Is consistent—accepts that the behaving individual is doing the best he or she can do for now
Is imposed by an authority (done to someone), with responsibility assumed by the one administering the punishment and the behaving individual avoiding responsibility	Comes from within, with responsibility assumed by the behaving individual and the behaving individual desiring responsibility; presumes that conscience is internal
Closes options for the individual who must pay for a behavior that has already occurred	Opens options for the individual who can choose a new behavior
As a teaching process, usually reinforces a failure identity; is essentially negative and short term, without sustained personal involvement of either teacher or learner	As a teaching process, is active and involves close, sustained personal involvement of both teacher and learner; emphasizes developing ways to act that will result in more successful behavior
Is characterized by open or concealed anger; is a poor model of the expectations of quality	Is friendly and supportive; provides a model of quality behavior
Is easy and expedient	Is difficult and time-consuming
Focuses on strategies intended to control the behavior of the learner	Focuses on the learner's behavior and the consequences of that behavior
Rarely results in positive changes in behavior; may increase subversiveness or result in temporary suppression of behavior; at best, produces compliance	Usually results in a change in behavior that is more successful, acceptable, and responsible; develops the capacity for self-evaluation of behavior

Source: R. D. Bodine and D. K. Crawford, *Developing Emotional Intelligence: A Guide to Behavior Management and Conflict Resolution in Schools* (Champaign, Ill.: Research Press, 1999), p. 98. Reprinted with permission of the authors and Research Press.

problem-solving processes of conflict resolution enable students to achieve principled responses.

CONFLICT RESOLUTION EDUCATION RESEARCH

"Literally hundreds of studies have evaluated the impact of conflict resolution education on students' knowledge, attitudes, and behavior. The results have been positive far more often than not, providing an extensive literature of support for conflict reduction and/or constructive conflict resolution behavior brought about by conflict resolution education programs."[15] As an education innovation, conflict resolution education is relatively young and research to inform the practice is evolving, but "[t]here is enough credible evidence to indicate conflict resolution training can have positive effects."[16]

Results of conflict resolution education research studies provide valuable information about the need for conflict resolution education and about the impact of conflict resolution training on students' ability to manage their conflicts constructively. In addition, these studies move us beyond the narrow view of prescribing a curriculum toward a broader understanding of the components of the conflict resolution education approaches. These studies also provide insight into the variety of practices that may allow educators to respond effectively to varying institutional circumstances.

Johnson and Johnson Studies

David Johnson and Roger Johnson report the results of seventeen studies they completed between 1988 and 2000.[17] These studies were designed to examine students' ability to manage conflict before and after training in the Teaching Students to Be Peacemakers program.[18] Their research is highly relevant because their curriculum is based upon the theories of integrative bargaining,[19] perspective reversal,[20] and constructive conflict.[21] These same theories pervade most of the quality conflict resolution education programs in operation within schools today. The Teaching Students to Be Peacemakers curriculum is used to support conflict resolution education in both peaceable classroom and peaceable school approaches.

The findings from the Johnson and Johnson research indicate that students learn conflict resolution procedures, retain their knowledge throughout the school year, apply conflict resolution procedures to actual conflicts, transfer the procedures to nonclassroom and nonschool settings, and use the procedures similarly in family and school settings. When given the option, students trained in this program tend to engage in problem-solving rather than win-lose negotiations. The results further demonstrate that conflict resolution procedures can be taught in a way that increases academic achievement. Finally, in schools that adopt this training, adults in the school generally perceive the conflict resolution program to be constructive and helpful.

The Johnson and Johnson research demonstrated that even young children can be taught how to negotiate and mediate—a finding that is important for a number of reasons. First, skill in negotiation and mediation empowers students to regulate their own behavior. Self-regulation is the ability to act in socially approved ways in the absence of monitoring by others. It is a central and significant hallmark of cognitive and social development. Frequently, adults act as referees and judges in the lives of children. When they take on these roles, adults place children in a dependent position and deprive them of opportunities to learn valuable social skills. Second, children who are able to negotiate and mediate have a developmental advantage over children without these skills. The researchers hypothesize that children who use their own competencies to resolve conflicts constructively increase both their strength and ability to cope with stress and adversity and their ability to build and maintain high-quality relationships with peers.

Comprehensive Peer Mediation Evaluation Project

The Comprehensive Peer Mediation Evaluation Project (CPMEP), conducted by Tricia Jones and the CPMEP research team from Temple University, investigated the impacts of various programs on students' conflict attitudes and behaviors, on school climate, and on the use of mediation as a dispute resolution process. Some schools in the study had peer mediation only (cadre programs); some had whole-school programs; and some schools had no peer mediation program.[22] Jones's research clearly establishes the efficacy of peer mediation training and the peer mediation approach in conflict resolution education. It suggests a number of implications that inform development of peer mediation programs:

- Peer mediation programs yield significant benefit in developing constructive social and conflict behavior in children at all educational levels. Students who are direct recipients of program training receive the most impact; however, students without direct training also benefit. Youths trained as peer mediators are able to enact and use the behavioral skills taught in training in life situations as well as in formal mediation settings.

- Peer mediation programs had a significant and sustained impact on teacher and staff perceptions of school climate. Elements of climate most notably affected were the development of a productive learning environment, maintenance of high standards, the creation of a supportive and friendly environment, and the development of a positive overall climate.

- Peer mediation effectively handles peer disputes, demonstrating a very high rate of agreement and high mediator and disputant satisfaction. However, the number of cases documented suggests that mediation may be underused in comparison to its potential benefits.

- Both cadre and whole-school programs yield significant benefits. Cadre programs yield better individual outcomes, while whole-school programs yield better climate outcomes. Those few individuals trained under the cadre approach usually receive more intensive training and more support. They, therefore, usually are more adept at transferring their learning to other life contexts. Alternatively, the whole-school approach provides universal training so that nearly all students can practice constructive conflict resolution which has a greater impact on the overall school climate. Students exposed to conflict resolution under both the cadre and whole-school approaches reduced their personal conflicts; increased their prosocial values, perspective-taking, and conflict-competence skills; and experienced a decrease in aggressiveness.
- Peer mediation programs are effective at all educational levels. The programs have significant positive effects at the elementary, middle, and high school levels.
- Race and gender differences do not affect program efficacy. Peer mediation programs are beneficial for diverse populations.[23]

The Comprehensive Peer Mediation Evaluation Project provides information that clearly supports the impact of peer mediation programs on the development of positive individual and school outcomes. The results consistently demonstrate that both cadre and whole school programs can have significant impacts on students' conflict attitudes and behavior and on school climate. Further, the data confirm that mediation is an effective means of handling peer disputes.

Teachers College Columbia University Early Childhood Study

Recent scientific work in neurology and childhood development has concluded that early childhood is the optimal time for instilling social-emotional skills that become lifelong habitual responses to problem solving and interpersonal situations. If a child experiences difficulties with relationships early in life, chemicals in the brain normally devoted to cognitive development may be diverted to dealing with stress. Children learn how to react to hundreds of situations with parents in the first year. In this, parental modeling plays a large role. The response to children's inherited temperamental differences will shape a large part of the child's future.

Sandra V. Sandy and Susan K. Boardman from Columbia University led a scientific evaluation of the early childhood component of Peaceful Kids ECSEL (Educating Communities in Social Emotional Learning). Their research demonstrated that children who participated in the Peaceful Kids ECSEL program with their parents and teachers demonstrated significant increases in assertive behavior, cooperative behavior, and self-control compared to control groups. Children's aggressive (fighting, hitting, verbal insults) and socially withdrawn behavior (shyness) decreased significantly in post-test measures of social-emotional competence. Given conflict resolution education, parents' behavior changed from permissive or authoritarian to a more authoritative approach in which children were given specific rules but also opportunities to negotiate in a variety of family decision-making areas. The evaluation strongly supported the need for a systemswide approach to achieving social-emotional learning and conflict resolution skills in young children.[24]

Teachers College Columbia University Alternative High School Study

The International Center for Cooperation and Conflict Resolution (ICCCR) at Columbia University initiated a conflict resolution project at an alternative high school (AHS) in New York City.[25] The goal of the project was to determine the effects of cooperative learning and conflict resolution training on AHS students. This AHS was established in 1971 as part of a network of alternative high schools in New York City. It has approximately 180 students and fourteen teachers, including a site coordinator, at each of its four campuses. Anyone under the age of nineteen living anywhere in New York City may apply to any campus of the school. Students may be admitted to the AHS in several ways. Students who have already dropped out or are at risk of dropping out of another school may apply voluntarily, while others are referred by high school counselors or the court system.

The results of the ICCCR project indicate positive effects on students trained in conflict resolution and cooperative learning. Students who received training demonstrated improved conflict management, greater social support, and fewer feelings of victimization. As their relations with others improved, these youths experienced increased self-esteem, decreased feelings of anxiety and depression, and more frequent positive feelings of well-being. Greater self-esteem produced a greater sense of control over their fate, which in turn led to higher academic performance. Indirect evidence indicated that the students' work readiness and performance also improved.

The ICCCR project was initiated with the strong support of the principal and assistant principal and the voluntary cooperation of the staff. The conflict resolution training combined resources from a number of curriculums to address the needs of the student population. This project was successfully conducted under considerably more problematic conditions than those most schools experience. The students at this AHS were significantly at-risk and faced more difficult life circumstances, and their teachers worked in an extremely challenging environment, often within older buildings equipped with fewer resources. The positive results produced by the training under these conditions indicate the significance of administrative support, voluntary cooperation, and relevant learning experiences. These results also suggest that cooperative learning and conflict resolution training are valuable in a wide range of settings.

CONCLUSION

Effective conflict resolution education is based on proven integrative negotiation theory. The underlying theory must be operationalized into instructional procedures that educators can be trained to use and that students can use to resolve their own conflicts. The demonstrated theory base and the pragmatic delivery system are the critical benchmarks of quality conflict resolution education.

Conflict resolution education produces a positive moral climate in schools and reduces reliance on authoritarian approaches to conflict resolution. It enables students to negotiate and mediate solutions and to regulate their actions. Students who receive conflict resolution education have improved attendance and academic achievement, fewer suspensions, better peer relationships, and a greater interest in learning. In short, conflict resolution education has positive effects for students—it works.

Notes

1. Bulleted list from R. D. Bodine and D. K. Crawford, *The Handbook of Conflict Resolution Education: A Guide to Building Quality Programs in Schools* (San Francisco: Jossey-Bass, 1998), p. 47.

2. See R. D. Bodine and D. K. Crawford, *Developing Emotional Intelligence: A Guide to Behavior Management and Conflict Resolution in Schools* (Champaign, Ill.: Research Press, 1999), pp. 174–175.

3. See R. Cohen, *Students Resolving Conflict: Peer Mediation in Schools* (Glenview, Ill.: Good Year Books, 1995).

4. See R. Cohen, "Stop Mediating These Conflicts Now," *The School Mediator Newsletter.* School Mediation Associates, Watertown, Mass., 2002.

5. See F. Schrumpf, D. K. Crawford, and R. D. Bodine, *Peer Mediation: Conflict Resolution in Schools* (rev. ed.) (Champaign, Ill.: Research Press, Inc., 1996).

6. See W. Kreidler, *Elementary Perspectives I: Teaching Concepts of Peace and Conflict* (Cambridge, Mass.: Educators for Social Responsibility, 1990).

7. See D. W. Johnson and R. T. Johnson, *Reducing School Violence Through Conflict Resolution* (Alexandria, Va.: Association for Supervisors and Curriculum Development, 1995).

8. See Johnson and Johnson, *Reducing School Violence Through Conflict Resolution,* 1995.

9. See C. M. Lieber, "Partners in Learning: From Conflict to Collaboration in Secondary Classrooms" (Cambridge, Mass.: Educators for Social Responsibility, 2002).

10. C. M. Lieber, "Laying a Solid Foundation: Practices That Support Conflict Resolution Education," in T. Jones and R. Compton (eds.), *Kids Working It Out:*

Stories and Strategies for Making Peace in Our School (San Francisco: Jossey-Bass, 2002), p. 53.

11. See R. D. Bodine, D. K. Crawford, and F. Schrumpf, *Creating the Peaceable School: A Comprehensive Program for Teaching Conflict Resolution* (2nd ed.) (Champaign, Ill.: Research Press, 2003), p. 3.

12. See Bodine, Crawford, and Schrumpf, *Creating the Peaceable School,* 2003.

13. D. W. Johnson and R. T. Johnson, "Cooperative Learning and Conflict Resolution," *The Fourth R,* 1993, *42,* p. 8.

14. G. Konopka, "A Renewed Look at Human Development, Human Needs, and Human Services," paper presented at the Proceedings of the Annual Gisela Konopka Lectureship (St. Paul, Minn.: University of Minnesota Center for Youth Development and Research, 1985), p. 186.

15. S. V. Sandy, S. Bailey, and V. Sloane-Akwara, "Impact on Students: Conflict Resolution Education's Proven Benefits for Students," in T. Jones and D. Kmitta (eds.), *Does It Work? The Case for Conflict Resolution Education in Our Nation's Schools* (Washington, D.C.: Conflict Resolution Education Network, 2000), p. 15.

16. M. Deutsch and P. Coleman, *The Handbook of Conflict Resolution* (San Francisco: Jossey Bass, 2000), p. 575.

17. See D. W. Johnson and R. T. Johnson, *Teaching Students to Be Peacemakers: Results of Twelve Years of Research.* [http://www.co-operation.org/pages/peace-meta.html]. October 2004.

18. See D. W. Johnson and R. T. Johnson, *Teaching Students to Be Peacemakers* (4th ed.) (Edina, Minn.: Interaction Book Company, 1995).

19. See D. Pruitt, *Negotiation Behavior* (New York: Academic Press, 1981).

20. See D. W. Johnson, "Role Reversal: A Summary and Review of the Research," *International Journal of Group Tensions,* 1971, *1,* 318–334.

21. See M. Deutsch, *The Resolution of Conflict: Constructive and Destructive Processes* (New Haven, Conn.: Yale University Press, 1973).

22. See T. S. Jones, A. Bodtker, J. Jameson, I. Kusztal, B. Vegso, and D. Kmitta, *Comprehensive Peer Mediation Evaluation Project: Preliminary Final Report,* Report for the William and Flora Hewlett Foundation (Philadelphia, Pa.: Temple University, College of Allied Health Professions, 1997).

23. See T. S. Jones, "Research Supports Effectiveness of Peer Mediation," *The Fourth R,* 1998, *82,* 1, 10–12, 18, 21, 25, 27.

24. See S. V. Sandy and S. K. Boardman, "The Peaceful Kids Conflict Resolution Program," *The International Journal of Conflict Management,* 2000, *11*(4), 337–357.

25. See M. Deutsch, V. Mitchell, Q. Zhang, N. Khattri, L. Tepavac, E. A. Weitzman, and R. Lynch, *The Effects of Training in Cooperative Learning and Conflict Resolution in an Alternative High School* (New York: Columbia University, 1992).

CHAPTER THIRTY

Institutionalization and Professionalization

Nancy A. Welsh

Within the past couple of decades, a remarkably large and diverse range of institutions has embraced alternative dispute resolution (ADR) processes. Arbitration, mediation, ombuds services, and dispute system design are just some of the innovative processes that are now used regularly—in other words, "institutionalized"—in the public, private, and nonprofit sectors. ADR processes are now so common that some commentators have begun to urge that the "A" in "ADR" should stand for *appropriate*, rather than *alternative*, dispute resolution.[1]

This institutionalization has been marked by dramatic diversity and little consistency or predictability. The "look" of each of the dispute resolution processes described in this book is strongly influenced by the context and culture within which the process operates. The process of mediation, for example, has changed as it has moved from neighborhood dispute resolution to the courthouse. Debates currently rage regarding the forms and goals that should characterize various ADR processes. The lack of consensus on these issues presents challenges for the development of recognizable dispute resolution "professionals." Nonetheless, the very fact of widespread and successful institutionalization has led to the pursuit of professionalization.

This chapter will provide examples of the successful institutionalization of several dispute resolution processes—specifically arbitration, mediation, ombuds services, and dispute system design—and will demonstrate the influence of context upon these processes. The chapter will then turn to the topic of professionalization and explore what is generally required before a practice area can claim status as a profession. These requirements—a shared body of knowledge, shared performance standards to permit self-regulation, and shared social norms—will be applied to the current mediation "professionalism project." Ultimately, this chapter suggests that the flexibility and adaptability that are often celebrated in ADR processes may make professionalization quite difficult.

EXAMPLES OF SUCCESSFUL INSTITUTIONALIZATION OF ADR

Arbitration, mediation, and ombuds services have all been successfully incorporated into a variety of institutions. In the United States, arbitration was the pioneer among dispute resolution processes in many ways. For much of the twentieth century, arbitration was used primarily to resolve commercial disputes between businesses, to assist management and unionized labor in averting strikes, and to deal with construction-related conflicts.[2] Today, in contrast, arbitration is used to address a wide variety of disputes, and arbitration clauses are ubiquitous. Often without realizing it, consumers agree to resolve their disputes through arbitration when they purchase computers, open bank accounts, take out loans, become the clients of brokerage firms, enter nursing homes, or even purchase telephone cards.[3] Similarly, employees who sign employment application forms or who receive personnel policies often find later that they agreed to arbitrate any and all employment-related issues that might arise.[4] Some courts now offer arbitration themselves as a means to enable litigants to resolve their cases without going to trial.[5] Even national governments are turning more frequently to arbitration to resolve international public disputes governed by treaties. The North American Free Trade Agreement, for example, provides for arbitration between nations and disgruntled private investors.[6]

Mediation has also enjoyed considerable growth as an ADR practice. What emerged as an "alternative" to the traditional litigation process in the 1960s and 1970s is now an integral part of the civil litigation system.[7] The process is used to resolve personal injury, contract, employment, divorce, child custody, and myriad other civil matters.[8] Many state courts mandate parties' participation in mediation or require attorneys to consult with their clients and advise judges regarding the appropriateness of the process.[9] Congress has required all federal courts to institute ADR programs,[10] and many of those programs feature mediation.[11] Even many appellate courts now funnel cases to mediation, with substantial rates of settlement.[12]

In addition to court systems, an increasing number of public agencies have also embraced the mediation process. At the state level, departments charged with protection of the environment, human rights, farming interests, and transportation offer mediation services or regularly agree to participate in mediation processes.[13] Within the federal government, the United States Postal Service (USPS) resolved over seventeen thousand workplace disputes in 2000–2001 through its REDRESS mediation program.[14] Over the past several years, the Equal Employment Opportunity Commission (EEOC) has also experimented with mediation, mediating seven thousand cases in 2001.[15] The Department of Health and Human Services, the United States Air Force, and the Environmental Protection Agency have also made significant use of mediation to resolve disputes over contract matters, employment, and site cleanup.[16]

Finally, corporate disputants express great support for mediation as a means to save the time and money required by litigation, preserve valuable business relationships, and achieve more satisfactory results.[17] An impressive 87 percent of the Fortune 1000 corporate counsel responding to a recent survey indicated that their companies had recently used mediation, and a majority also overwhelmingly preferred mediation for future disputes.[18] Many well-known corporations—Motorola, Toro, General Mills, Bank of America, Shell International, American Airlines, Coca-Cola Enterprises, Aetna, and CIGNA, to name just a few—have adopted ADR programs or strategies that feature mediation. The most effective of these programs has been undertaken as part of company-wide efforts to understand and manage disputing.[19] Motorola, for example, requires its in-house counsel to evaluate all sorts of damage claims for their ADR potential. If outside counsel fees in a case reach a particular monetary threshold, Motorola has actually established a *presumption* that ADR—most frequently mediation—will be used.[20] Motorola also encourages early settlement by enabling easy, computerized litigation risk analysis,[21] offering incentives for attorneys' fulfillment of ADR objectives,[22] educating internal "clients" regarding litigation's costs and ADR's potential,[23] and even participating in premediation educational sessions with opposing parties who have expressed reluctance to try the process.[24] Motorola has claimed litigation cost reductions of more than 75 percent as a result of its commitment to ADR and early case assessment.[25]

Ombuds services have also been adopted by a wide range of institutions. Many federal agencies, including the National Institute of Health, the Small Business Administration, the Federal Deposit Insurance Corporation, the Internal Revenue Service, and the Department of Homeland Security, now have ombuds.[26] Additionally, Congress has directed states to offer ombuds services in certain federally funded areas such as long-term elder care pursuant to the Older Americans Act.[27] Within state government, meanwhile, officials have chosen to establish ombuds within the legislative branch, administrative agencies, and even a few court systems.[28] Outside the governmental context, ombuds can also be found on the staffs of many universities and newspapers, as well as some private corporations.[29]

Governmental agencies and corporations increasingly turn to consultants for assistance in determining which processes to institutionalize, for which disputes, and at what points in the evolution of those disputes. Thus far, the most substantial use of "dispute system design," or DSD, seems to be in the resolution of internal disputes, such as those involving interdepartmental or employment-related issues.[30] Market forces may trigger further expansion in this corporate use of DSD: "As entities become larger and larger in the wake of mergers, disputes which used to take place among independent companies doing business with each other now tend to arise more frequently within the same organization."[31] Several federal agencies, meanwhile, have turned to DSD to comply responsibly with executive orders directing them to make greater use of ADR.[32] Some have even proposed that courts should incorporate DSD principles to develop local rules.[33]

These are only some of the many ways in which ADR processes have been integrated into many sectors of government and business. Other processes, such as summary jury trial, early neutral evaluation, and private judging, have been institutionalized on a more limited basis.[34] However, a simple description of the successful institutionalization of ADR processes does not tell the entire story. Context also plays a critical role.

THE INFLUENCE OF CONTEXT

Each of the dispute resolution processes included in the previous discussion is influenced by the context in which it is practiced. The format of each process, its underlying goals, and the role of the neutral can vary dramatically, depending on where the process occurs.

For example, though traditional arbitration is a binding process, arbitral decisions issued in court-connected programs generally are *not* binding. Court rules permit litigants to reject an arbitrator's decision and request trial *de novo,* though courts also may impose sanctions upon those litigants who proceed to trial and fail to improve significantly upon the arbitral award. In some contexts, disputants generally submit their cases to a single impartial arbitrator. In other contexts, three-member panels preside over arbitration hearings, with only one of the three arbitrators expected to be fully impartial. Context also determines the usual length and formality of the arbitration process.[35] Will the arbitrator adhere to the rules of evidence? Will the parties be permitted to conduct discovery? Will the arbitrator issue a written opinion? The questions—and answers—are many and varied.

However, arbitration appears predictable in comparison with the "enormous variation in their duties and structures" that characterize ombuds offices.[36] Some ombuds wield substantial authority, with responsibility for assisting legislatures or agencies in holding entities or particular programs accountable.[37] Some ombuds have less coercive power, and are instead responsible for working collaboratively with officials to improve programs' performances based on complaints received from internal or external constituents.[38] Still other ombuds focus on conducting inquiries to address problems presented by employees, members, or contractors. These ombuds may also choose to "advocate for modifications in policies or procedures."[39] Perhaps most interestingly, some ombuds are authorized to "advocate on behalf of individuals or groups found to be aggrieved."[40] Depending upon the scope of their authority and responsibilities, different ombuds may employ very different techniques, including

> conducting an inquiry; investigating and reporting findings; developing, evaluating, and discussing the options that may be available for remedies or redress; facilitating, negotiating, or mediating; making recommendations for the resolution of an individual complaint or a systemic problem to those persons who have authority to act on them; identifying complaint patterns and trends; . . . educating . . . [and] advocat[ing] on behalf of affected individuals or groups when authorized by the charter and the situation warrants that action.[41]

Thus, though all of the different categories of ombuds share the same process title, their implementation of the process can vary dramatically, depending on the needs of the organization that established the office.

Context-driven differences also are becoming quite clear in the field of mediation. Traditionally, mediation was described by some as a facilitative process designed to help parties reach resolution of their dispute, a process in which the mediator's role is to enable the parties' exercise of self-determination. Within this vision of mediation, a mediator helps parties to communicate with each other, explore their underlying interests, select the norms that will guide them, generate options, and ultimately reach their own customized, and perhaps creative, resolution. The parties themselves are the key players in this vision. They determine the content of their discussion and any resolution. The mediator plays a supporting role. A growing body of research demonstrates, however, that institutionalized mediation often diverges from this facilitative, party-directed, resolution-oriented model.

In the court-connected context, mediation programs have evolved to reflect the needs and preferences of the professionals who dominate litigation: judges and attorneys. Court-connected mediators are more likely than those outside of court systems to view their role as evaluative, contributing their own assessment of possible legal outcomes and settlement options. In the family area, for example, while the parties are encouraged to express their feelings and develop their own settlement agreements, courts often limit the time that parties can spend in mediation and make mediators directly responsible for the quality of the agreements, particularly for those terms relevant to the protection of children's best interests. As a result, many mediators become quite directive in shaping mediated outcomes.[42] Attorneys who attend family mediation sessions also often rely upon mediators to offer their assessments regarding likely outcomes if the case goes before the judge,[43] thus helping to reconcile unhappy parties to working within the "shadow of [the] law."[44]

The mediation process in nonfamily court-connected civil cases, such as personal injury, contract, employment, property damage, and medical malpractice cases, often diverges even further from a party-oriented, facilitative model. Generally, attorneys dominate these sessions, with parties playing minimal roles. In fact, defendants in personal injury and medical malpractice cases are not even likely to attend. Mediators in this context typically spend little time in joint session encouraging face-to-face communication between the parties. Instead, they move quickly to caucuses, case evaluation, and bargaining.[45] At least part of the explanation for this approach stems from the expectations and preferences of the professionals who dominate this context. Attorneys are generally responsible for selecting mediators, and they prefer experienced litigators who have the substantive knowledge that will permit them to understand the parties' legal arguments, assess the merits of their cases, and even opine regarding settlement ranges.[46] Attorneys value these mediator interventions because they view mediation primarily as an efficient settlement tool that can provide opposing counsel and their own clients with a needed "reality check."[47] Few attorneys in nonfamily civil litigation appear to choose mediation because they perceive that their clients might like it or experience greater satisfaction or control or be more creative.[48] Meanwhile, many courts have promulgated ethical codes for court-connected mediators that permit mediators to engage in the evaluative functions that attorneys seek.[49] Ultimately, attorneys and the courts favor approaches to mediation that move parties toward settlement of their lawsuits. Mediator evaluation appears quite effective in reaching that goal,[50] and, therefore, court-connected mediation is characterized by caucus, evaluative interventions, and bargaining.

Another large institution, with a more complex set of goals, has produced a quite different implementation of mediation. In 1994, the U.S. Postal Service (USPS) instituted a mediation program called Resolve Employment Disputes, Reach Equitable Solutions Swiftly (REDRESS), that is based on the "transformative" model of mediation. It uses techniques aimed at supporting parties in the presentation of their views and in their deliberation and decision making. The REDRESS mediators also encourage parties to "recognize"—or consider and empathize with—each other's views.[51] Settlement is specifically excluded as a goal of transformative mediation; and evaluation is excluded as a mediator intervention.[52]

USPS officials' institutionalization of the transformative model of mediation can be traced to the distinct needs and culture of the agency.[53] The USPS instituted REDRESS as part of the settlement of a race discrimination class action. Though one goal of the program was to reduce the number of formal EEO complaints,[54] other goals included improving communication between employees and supervisors and establishing more effective conflict management skills in the workplace.[55] The USPS decided to make participation in a REDRESS mediation session voluntary for the employees bringing informal EEO complaints but mandatory for the respondent supervisors.[56] Aware that the USPS prevails in 90 to 95 percent of all EEO claims filed against it, the agency's officials were concerned that permitting mediators to evaluate might discourage employees from electing to participate in the REDRESS program:

> [I]n ninety to ninety-five percent of . . . evaluative mediation sessions, the mediator would be telling employees that they have no case or that they will probably not prevail on the merits . . . [and, if using] a narrow focus, he or she will steer the parties away from discussing issues unless they are directly related to a legal cause of action. . . . A program with this system design would probably fail. . . . As the mediators advised complainants they have no case, the first employees would come back to the workroom floor complaining that the mediator spent all her time explaining why management was right, and that the mediator was biased. Soon no one would bother to use the system.[57]

Institutionalization of the transformative mediation model at the USPS thus reflects the sponsoring agency's preferences for widespread voluntary usage and enhanced employee relations.[58]

USPS officials undertook a series of measures to ensure mediators' compliance with the transformative model. All REDRESS mediators are required to participate in free training sessions, in which they are directed to focus on "support[ing] and facilitat[ing] parties' efforts to shift their conflict interaction" by using "the opportunities for empowerment and recognition that arise as a conflict unfolds."[59] Transformative mediators are reassured that the achievement of "constructive conflict interaction (increased personal clarity, decision-making and interpersonal understanding)" is their mission, while resolution is viewed "more as a by-product" of that interaction.[60] The USPS has a corps of trained ADR Specialists who observe mediators and judge whether their performance conforms to the theory of transformative mediation.[61] Finally, the USPS monitors the REDRESS program for quality, voluntary usage rate, and settlement rate. (Resolution of EEO complaints remains an important program goal, and the use of transformative mediation has resulted in an 81 percent rate of case closure.[62])

These examples of ADR processes' adaptation to their environments illustrate how institutional and professional interests currently drive the goals and techniques that characterize ADR processes in different settings. Thus, even though these processes have attained substantial institutionalization, there is neither uniformity nor universal agreement regarding the fundamental meaning of each of the processes.

PROFESSIONALIZATION OF ADR

A profession is characterized by a number of factors. Professions have a shared body of knowledge, often imparted in an institutional setting that certifies competence and quality. Entry into professions is conditioned upon the demonstration of sufficient skill in applying the core knowledge, and professions self-regulate to ensure competent and ethical performance.[63] Terence Johnson describes the concept of profession as "a method of controlling work, one in which an occupation, rather than individual consumers or an agent or agency mediating between occupation and consumer, exercises control over its work."[64] Societies grant such autonomy to professions in recognition of their value in assisting members of society with risky physical and moral problems[65] and the scarcity of the profession's special knowledge and skills in providing such assistance.[66]

To determine whether an occupation can achieve the status of a profession, many scholars place particular emphasis on the existence of a distinct knowledge system that binds together the members of the profession and serves as the basis for their practical techniques. In a sense, the shared knowledge base or cognitive structure serves as a conceptual map that distinguishes the members of the profession, "fram[ing] the professionals' approach to classifying social problems, to reasoning about them, and to acting upon them."[67] Members of a profession share a commitment to their particular knowledge base, consequent performance standards, and particular social norms that may be either explicit or embedded within the knowledge base and performance standards. This shared sense of professional identity enables the profession to determine appropriate mechanisms for training, regulation of entry, and enforcement of ethical and competent practice.

As ADR processes have become institutionalized, with the neutrals generally paid for their services either by the parties or sponsoring organizations, there are increasing references to "dispute *professionals*" or "*professional* mediators."[68] Indeed, particular segments of the ADR field have adopted, or more accurately have attempted to adopt, many of the characteristics that distinguish professions from mere occupations. This has been particularly true for mediators, who have pointed to the need to ensure the quality of mediation services, protect mediation from bureaucratization or incursions by already-established professionals, protect the public (and the reputation of all mediators) from incompetent or unethical practitioners, and encourage public confidence.[69] But the current lack of clarity regarding the forms, goals, and interventions that should characterize mediation and other ADR processes poses challenges for the drive to professionalize.

Even a cursory examination of the mediation "professionalism project"[70] reveals many actions taken by mediators in their drive for social recognition and professionalization. Mediators, at times in combination with other dispute resolution professionals, have established professional organizations at national, regional, and state levels. National organizations include the Association for Conflict Resolution (ACR), the National Association for Community Mediation (NAFCM), and the Center for Alternative Dispute Resolution in Education (CADRE). These organizations are vibrant, with well-attended annual conferences and regular publications. The national organizations have collaborated to develop an ethical code applicable to all mediators. In 1994, the Society of Professionals in Dispute Resolution (ACR's predecessor), the American Arbitration Association (AAA), and the American Bar Association (ABA) created the Model Standards for the Conduct of Mediators. The Model Standards have served as the template for many organizations' and states' ethics codes for mediators. (ACR, AAA, and ABA currently are working together again to revise the Model Standards.) Mediation training programs abound: the curricula at colleges and universities regularly include dispute resolution and mediation courses, and several institutions of higher education now offer graduate programs in dispute resolution. Court-connected, agency-connected, and private mediation programs generally require individuals to meet certain knowledge, training, or practice requirements before they are accepted as mediators. Some state courts and private organizations have even established certification programs for mediators.[71] These developments suggest that professionalization of mediation is well under way. And the recent decision of the National Conference of Commissioners on Uniform State Laws to adopt a Uniform Mediation Act—which, among other things, defines the process and provides mediators with their own privilege to protect against disclosure of mediation communications—provides evidence of mediators' increasing legitimacy and social recognition.

Mediators' bustle of activity and progress in the "professionalization project," however, should not obscure two central problems. First, there is no consensus regarding the approach, skills, and norms that mediators should share. Second, there is no agreement regarding a systematic body of esoteric, abstract knowledge upon which the work of mediation is based.[72] As a result, it is not clear that mediation represents such an innovative and unique way of understanding and handling social problems that a new profession, as distinct from the retooling of existing professions, is required.[73] As noted earlier, the most extensive institutionalization of mediation, in courts and public agencies, has resulted in a process that has adapted to the norms and needs of the professionals and officials who already dominate those institutions.

The lack of consensus regarding the approach, skills, and norms that should characterize mediation and the lack of a foundational body of mediation knowledge are intertwined issues. For example, though most court-connected, agency-connected, and private mediation programs require training, there is little professionwide agreement regarding the extent and content of the training that is essential. As a result, these program requirements vary significantly. Some court-connected programs require thirty to forty hours of training; others require twenty hours or much less.[74] Court- and agency-connected programs often focus on developing mediators' skills. Other programs, such as those in family and education law, also require training in substantive issues.[75] Transformative mediation training programs, in contrast, do not incorporate substantive issues and instead concentrate on teaching skills that improve parties' conflict interaction. Clearly, there is no agreed upon mediation training standard.

Even to the extent that there is some overlap in mediation training programs, the field is driven by practice and not grounded in its own unique and abstract knowledge.[76] To date, mediators' knowledge base and skills are largely available to others, making mediators' claims to special authority or the need for protection constantly vulnerable to challenge. Lack of a unique and shared understanding of theoretical underpinnings creates a situation in which there is no clear foundation from which qualifications can emerge.[77] Indeed, depending on the context within which they practice, mediators are likely to borrow heavily from the theories and knowledge base primarily associated with *other* disciplines, such as law, psychology, and social work.[78] It is difficult to build a sense of identity, or profession, from such fundamental diversity.

The same fundamental diversity currently bedevils certification efforts. For example, both the Florida Supreme Court and Family Mediation Canada (FMC) have established programs for certifying family mediators. A superficial analysis suggests general consistency between the programs: both are voluntary; neither requires certification to serve as a party-selected mediator (though Florida courts will only make direct judicial referrals to certified mediators); both programs include training and supervision. Beyond these similarities, however, the two programs' requirements are quite different.

Florida demands that its certified mediators have an advanced educational degree and substantial professional experience ("a master's degree or doctorate in social work, mental health, or behavioral or social sciences; a physician certified to practice adult or child psychiatry; or an attorney or a certified public accountant . . . and have at least four years practical experience in one of the aforementioned fields").[79] Florida also requires certified mediators to complete forty hours of training, observe two family mediation sessions conducted by a certified family mediator, and conduct two family mediation sessions under the supervision and observation of a certified family mediator.[80] No guidance is provided to the already-certified mediators responsible for observation and supervision, and there is no requirement of satisfactory performance. (As this book went to press, the Florida Supreme Court Committee on Alternative Dispute Resolution Rules and Policy was considering comments regarding proposed modifications to the certification requirements. These proposed modifications would allow substantial mediation experience to substitute for advanced educational degrees and would increase the supervision and observation requirements. Further, an applicant would receive credit for participating in a "supervised" mediation only if the mentoring mediator determined that the applicant "had a significant impact on the outcome" or "made a substantial contribution to the mediation." The proposed modifications do not, however, provide guidance to mentoring mediators regarding the behavior that would satisfy these performance standards.[81])

Canada's FMC certification process, in contrast, requires much more extensive training (180 hours of training for family relations or financial mediators and 230 hours for "comprehensive" mediators). FMC also demands substantial mediation practice experience, participation in a supervised practicum, satisfactory performance on a four-hour substantive-knowledge written exam, client evaluations, and a self-assessment. In addition, FMC requires satisfactory performance based on a videotaped mediation session that is assessed by two FMC evaluators.[82] The "skills assessment tool" used by the FMC evaluators is designed to reflect what the organization's mediators have identified as "the fundamental values and principles of the [mediation] discipline."[83] Among other things, mediators are expected to "promote clients' cooperative efforts and mutual understanding," "facilitate opportunities for full participation," and "attend to and explore participants' interests."[84]

The differences between the Florida and Canada FMC requirements illustrate the lack of consensus on the "core knowledge" that ought to be included in mediator certification. Florida relies heavily on the substantive knowledge of other, already-established professions. Even though there is a requirement of skills training, mediators are not required to demonstrate any particular skills before they may begin practicing as certified mediators. Florida is not unique in this respect. Canada FMC, meanwhile, has built its certification process quite intentionally around "human interdependence" and the "interpersonal principles of respect, caring, and procedural fairness."[85] Unless mediators can demonstrate mastery of these principles, they will not be certified. Canada FMC's "clear and cohesive definition of what mediation does or does not entail"[86] contrasts quite markedly with the Florida courts' lack of clarity regarding the principles and practices that should distinguish its certified mediators. The contrast also reveals the current absence of consensus regarding mediators' core knowledge.

Attempts to develop broad-based evaluation tools have been beleaguered by similar challenges presented by the diversity of mediation practices. The Hewlett-sponsored Test Design Project intended to develop one tool that could serve as a model for the entire mediation field. Ultimately, however, the project published three different tools in response to concerns raised by mediators with very different philosophies and practices.[87] Even the Model Standards of Conduct for Mediators, which have been so influential in the development of states' and organizations' codes of ethics and "provide a useful starting point for the basic principles of good mediation" have been criticized as "vague" and "not provid[ing] adequate guidance in particular settings."[88]

Though many mediators seek professionalization, and the rewards that flow from social legitimacy and the grant of a monopoly, the professionalization project is clearly hampered by the lack of agreement regarding the unique knowledge, norms, and practices that should be shared by mediators. The same fundamental void and internal confusion seem likely to afflict the professional aspirations of other ADR practitioners whose claims to expertise are grounded more in process skills than in unique substantive knowledge (for example, ombuds services).

The current state of confusion should not be surprising. Throughout history, people have used various approaches to help other people resolve their disputes peaceably. As an organized field, ADR has given names to some of these different approaches, but viewed with a historical perspective, this effort is relatively recent. Professionalization can require decades and even centuries. For example, the "first statutory recognition [in England] of the medical profession was in 1512 but it did not achieve . . . market closure until 1858."[89] The prospect of professionalization also threatens many ADR neutrals. Mediators, for example, currently ask, Which models of mediation will be adopted, and which will be disapproved and excluded? Will individual mediators' creativity and innovation be stifled? Which mediators will be discounted as "amateurs" because they lack the education or experience now deemed essential? How will it be proven that the mediators designated as "professional" truly deserve the special privileges that result from their designation?[90] It is no wonder that ADR neutrals with these questions are wary—sometimes reluctant—participants in the drive for professionalization.

CONCLUSION

The dramatic institutionalization of ADR represents a tremendous success for the field's visionaries and advocates. Indeed, institutionalization has helped to create the momentum for professionalization. If ADR neutrals want to be recognized as self-autonomous professionals, however, they must reach consensus regarding the forms, goals, and interventions that should characterize their processes. They must also identify the unique and abstract knowledge that serves as the basis for such practice and norms. Without consensus on these issues, it is likely that the institutions that have adopted ADR will also define and ultimately contain it.

Notes

1. See C. Menkel-Meadow, "When Dispute Resolution Begets Disputes of Its Own," *U.C.L.A. Law Review*, 1997, *44*, 1871–1934.

2. See Cole and Blankley, Chapter Twenty, this volume.

3. See J. R. Sternlight, "The Rise and Spread of Mandatory Arbitration as a Substitute for the Jury Trial," *University of San Francisco Law Review*, 2003, *38*, 17–38.

4. See P. D. Hardin, "Sacrificing Statutory Rights on the Altar of Pre-Dispute Employment Agreements Mandating Arbitration," *Capital University Law Review*, 2000, *28*, 469–470.

5. See L. V. Katz, "Compulsory Alternative Dispute Resolution and Voluntarism: Two-Headed Monster or Two Sides of the Coin?" *Journal of Dispute Resolution*, 1993, *1993*(1), 1–55.

6. See C. D. Hansen, "*Mondev International Ltd.* v. *United States*: A Case Study of the Political Risks of NAFTA's Ever-Expanding Arbitration Provisions," *North Carolina Journal of International Law and Commercial Regulation*, 2003, *29*, 351–387.

7. See N. A. Welsh, "The Thinning Vision of Self-Determination in Court-Connected Mediation: The Inevitable Price of Institutionalization?" *Harvard Negotiation Law Review*, 2001, *6*, 1–96.

8. See, for example, E. Plapinger and D. Stienstra, *ADR and Settlement in the Federal District Courts: A Sourcebook for Judges & Lawyers* (Washington, D.C.: Federal Judicial Center and CPR Institute for Dispute Resolution, 1996), describing mediation as "the primary ADR process in the federal district courts"; B. McAdoo, "A Report to the Minnesota Supreme Court: The Impact of Rule 114 on Civil Litigation Practice in Minnesota," *Hamline Law Review*, 2002, *25*, 401–477, describing Minnesota state courts' institutionalization of mediation and other ADR processes; B. McAdoo and A. Hinshaw, "The Challenge of Institutionalizing Alternative Dispute Resolution: Attorney Perspectives on the Effect of Rule 17 on Civil Litigation in Missouri," *Missouri Law Review*, 2002, *67*, 473–593, describing Missouri state courts' institutionalization of mediation and other ADR processes; and S. Press, "Institutionalization: Savior or Saboteur of Mediation?" *Florida State University Law Review*, 1997, *24*, 903–917, describing Florida's court-connected dispute resolution program.

9. See A. S. Rau, E. Sherman, and S. Peppet, *Processes of Dispute Resolution: The Role of Lawyers* (New York: Foundation Press, 2002).

10. See *U.S.C. 28* § 651(b) (1998).

11. See *U.S.C. 28* § 651(a) (1998), allowing for mediation as a form of ADR; and Plapinger and Stienstra, *ADR and Settlement in the Federal District Courts*, 1996, p. 4, describing mediation as "the primary ADR process in the federal district courts."

12. See C. Menkel-Meadow, "When Litigation Is Not the Only Way: Consensus Building and Mediation as Public Interest Lawyering," *Washington University Journal of Law and Policy*, 2002, *10*, 37–61. Also see, generally, R. J. Niemic, *Mediation & Conference Programs in the Federal Courts of Appeals: A Sourcebook for Judges and Lawyers* (Washington, D.C.: Federal Judicial Center, 1997).

13. See Policy Consensus Institute, Directory of DR Programs [http://www.policyconsensus.org/directories/statedirectories.html] (October 2004), which provides an online list and brief description of dispute resolution programs that

have been established by state courts and agencies. The list is maintained by the Policy Consensus Initiative, a nonprofit organization that helps state governments to establish and evaluate such programs.

14. See United States Postal Service, REDRESS Research [www.usps.com/redress/_pdf/MediationChart.pdf] (October 2004); and also D. Marcus and J. M. Senger, "ADR and the Federal Government: Not Such Strange Bedfellows After All," *Missouri Law Review,* 2001, *66,* 709–723, describing the Post Office mediation program.

15. See M. B. Manzo, "A Guide to EEOC Mediations," *Illinois Bar Journal,* 2002, *90,* 607–612.

16. See Marcus and Senger, "ADR and the Federal Government," 2001.

17. See J. Lande, "Getting the Faith: Why Business Lawyers and Executives Believe in Mediation," *Harvard Negotiation Law Review,* 2000, *5,* 137–231; and C. A. McEwen, "Managing Corporate Disputing: Overcoming Barriers to the Effective Use of Mediation for Reducing the Cost and Time of Litigation," *Ohio State Journal on Dispute Resolution,* 1998, *14,* 1–27, concluding that in disputes involving corporate disputants, issues of "time and cost appear to be tightly interwoven with issues of quality"; C. Cronin-Harris and P. H. Kaskell, "How ADR Finds a Home in Corporate Law Departments," *Alternatives to High Cost of Litigation,* 1997, *15,* 169–171, finding that corporate law departments viewed top benefits of mediation as costs savings, savings of lawyers and executives' time, faster results, and preservation of business relationships; and D. B. Lipsky and R. Seeber, "In Search of Control: The Corporate Embrace of ADR," *University of Pennsylvania Journal of Labor & Employment Law,* 1998, *1,* 133–157, describing a Cornell/PERC Institute on Conflict Resolution survey of the corporate counsel of the one thousand largest U.S.-based corporations, which found that they perceived mediation as saving time and money, providing control over outcomes, offering a more satisfactory process than litigation, and resulting in more satisfactory settlement.

18. See D. B. Lipsky and R. Seeber, "Patterns of ADR Use in Corporate Disputes," *Dispute Resolution Journal,* 1999, *54,* 66–71.

19. See McEwen, "Managing Corporate Disputing," 1998.

20. See C. Cronin-Harris, "Mainstreaming: Systematizing Corporate Use of ADR," *Albany Law Review,* 1996, *59,* 847–879.

21. See Cronin-Harris, "Mainstreaming," 1996.

22. See Cronin-Harris, "Mainstreaming," 1996.

23. See L. Smith, "ADR Profile: Motorola's Mighty Commitment Continues," *Of Counsel,* 1991, *18,* 18–19.

24. See Cronin-Harris, "Mainstreaming," 1996.

25. See K. A. Slaikeu and D. W. Slaikeu, "Medispute: Resolving Health Care Conflicts: Confidential from General Counsel to CEO: 'I'm Fed Up, and We're Not Going to Take This Anymore!'" *Journal of Health Care Law & Policy,* 2002, *5,* 335–355.

26. See J. S. Lubbers, "Ombudsman Offices in the Federal Government: An Emerging Trend," *Administrative and Regulatory Law News*, 1997, *22*, 6–7.

27. See E. B. Herrington, "Strengthening the Older Americans Act's Long-Term Care Protection Provisions: A Call for Further Improvement of Important State Ombudsman Programs," *Elder Law Journal*, 1997, *5*, 321–357.

28. See J. J. Brearton, K. Hinck, E. Lott, and S. Nazario, "Section 44: State Public Advocate," *American Jurisprudence* (2nd ed.) (Rochester, N.Y.: Lawyers Cooperative Publishing, May 2003); and M. Bertran, "Judiciary Ombudsman: Solving Problems in the Courts," *Fordham Urban Law Journal*, 2002, *29*, 2101–2102.

29. See D. L. Meltzer, "The Federal Workplace Ombuds," *Ohio State Journal on Dispute Resolution*, 1998, *13*, pp. 554–557.

30. See L. B. Bingham, "Self-Determination in Dispute System Design and Employment Arbitration," *University of Miami Law Review*, 2002, *56*, 873–908. Also see, generally, C. A. Costantino and C. S. Merchant, *Designing Conflict Management Systems: A Guide to Creating Productive and Healthy Organizations* (San Francisco: Jossey-Bass, 1996); and W. L. Ury, J. M. Brett, and S. B. Goldberg, *Getting Disputes Resolved: Designing Systems to Cut the Costs of Conflict* (San Francisco: Jossey-Bass, 1988).

31. C. Duve, "Dispute Resolution in Globalization Context," *New York Law Journal*, April 12, 1999, p. 9.

32. See S. G. Dick, "ADR at the Crossroads," *Dispute Resolution Journal*, 1994, *49*, 47–60; N. J. Manring, "Dispute Systems Design and the U.S. Forest Service," *Negotiation Journal*, 1993, *9*, 13–21; and Dispute System Design Working Group, *Performance Indicators for ADR Program Evaluation* (Washington D.C.: Administrative Conference, November 1993).

33. See J. Lande, "Using Dispute System Design Methods to Promote Good-Faith Participation in Court-Connected Mediation Programs," *U.C.L.A. Law Review*, 2002, *50*, 69–141.

34. See McAdoo, "A Report to the Minnesota Supreme Court," 2002, pp. 447–457; McAdoo and Hinshaw, "The Challenge of Institutionalizing Alternative Dispute Resolution," 2002; and Plapinger and Stienstra, *ADR and Settlement in the Federal District Courts*, 1996.

35. See T. E. Carbonneau, *Cases and Materials on the Law and Practice of Arbitration* (New York: Juris Publishing, 2004).

36. American Bar Association, "Sections of Administrative Law and Regulatory Practice, Business Law, Dispute Resolution and Individual Rights and Responsibilities," report by member groups presented to the House of Delegates on Standards for the Establishment and Operation of Ombudsman Offices, San Antonio, February 2004, p. 2.

37. See American Bar Association, "Sections of Administrative Law and Regulatory Practice . . . ," 2004.

38. See American Bar Association, "Sections of Administrative Law and Regulatory Practice . . . ," 2004.

39. See American Bar Association, "Sections of Administrative Law and Regulatory Practice . . . ," 2004, p. 12.

40. See American Bar Association, "Sections of Administrative Law and Regulatory Practice . . . ," 2004, p. 2.

41. See American Bar Association, "Sections of Administrative Law and Regulatory Practice . . . ," 2004, p. 4.

42. See N. A. Burrell, W. A. Donohue, and M. Allen, "The Impact of Disputants' Expectations on Mediation: Testing an Interventionist Model," *Human Communication Research*, 1990, *17*, 108–109, describing research in divorce and community mediation showing that mediators using a more directive, more structured, and more control-oriented model—including intervening after periods of high conflict, providing orientation information, directing topics, enforcing rules, and keeping disputants focused on interests and away from past relationship-related concerns—achieved more cooperation between the parties and a better discussion of the issues. Also see J. Pearson and N. Thoennes, "Divorce Mediation: Reflections on a Decade of Research," in K. Kressel and D. Pruitt (eds.), *Mediation Research: The Process and Effectiveness of Third-Party Intervention* (San Francisco: Jossey-Bass, 1989), observing that mediators are "responsible for making the most of the proposed solutions"; and N. A. Welsh, "Reconciling Self-Determination, Coercion and Settlement," in J. Folberg, A. Milne, and P. Salem (eds.), *Divorce Mediation: Current Practices and Applications* (New York: Guilford Press, 2004).

43. See Welsh, "Reconciling Self-Determination, Coercion and Settlement," 2004.

44. See R. Mnookin and L. Kornhauser, "Bargaining in the Shadow of the Law: The Case of Divorce," *Yale Law Journal*, 1979, *88*, p. 997. See also D. Golann, "Is Legal Mediation a Process of Repair—or Separation? An Empirical Study and Its Implications," *Harvard Negotiation Law Review*, 2002, *7*, 301–336.

45. See N. A. Welsh, "Making Deals in Court-Connected Mediation: What's Justice Got to Do with It?" *Washington University Law Quarterly*, 2001, *79*, 801–813, describing the evolution of court-connected civil nonfamily mediation, particularly regarding the reduced role of the disputants, the marginalization of joint session, and the rise of evaluative interventions. Contrast that with J. Macfarlane, "Culture Change? A Tale of Two Cities and Mandatory Court-Connected Mediation," *Journal of Dispute Resolution*, 2002, *2002*, 309–313, urging that court-connected mediation has resulted in "some convergence between the structure and actions of mediation and traditional litigation."

46. See, for example, J. J. Alfini, "Trashing, Bashing, and Hashing It Out: Is This the End of Good Mediation?" *Florida State University Law Review*, 1991, *19*, 47–75, describing "trashers" and "bashers"; E. Gordon, "Why Attorneys Support Mandatory Mediation," *Judicature*, 1999, *82*(5), 224–231, noting that attorneys prefer mediators who are experienced trial lawyers; and McAdoo, "A Report to the Minnesota Supreme Court," 2002, pp. 429–430, reporting that the top factors motivating lawyers to choose mediation include saving expenses, making settlement more likely, and providing a reality check for opposing counsel and own client. When asked about important mediator qualifications, 87 percent of

lawyers responded "Mediator knows how to value case," and 83 percent responded "Mediator should be a litigator." See also McAdoo and Hinshaw, "The Challenge of Institutionalizing Alternative Dispute Resolution," 2002, reporting that the top factors motivating lawyers to choose mediation include saving litigation expense, speeding settlement, providing a needed reality check for opposing counsel and party and own client, making settlement more likely, and helping everyone value the case. Lawyers' selection of mediation is infrequently motivated by evidence that clients like mediation, increased potential for creative solutions, or preservation of relationships. See also B. McAdoo and N. Welsh, "Does ADR Really Have a Place on the Lawyer's Philosophical Map?" *Hamline Journal of Public Law and Policy*, 1997, *18*, 376–393, noting that Hennepin County lawyers said that they wanted mediators to give their view of settlement ranges; T. Metzloff, "Empirical Perspectives on Mediation and Malpractice," *Law & Contemporary Problems*, 1997, *60*, 107–152, reporting that almost 70 percent of attorneys want mediators to provide opinions on the merits of cases and that attorneys highly valued the mediator's substantive expertise; and R. L. Wissler, *An Evaluation of the Common Pleas Court Civil Pilot Mediation Project*, Feb. 2000 (unpublished manuscript, on file with author), p. ix, reporting that "[a]ttorneys had more favorable assessments of the [mediation] process and mediator and analyzed mediation was more helpful in achieving case objectives if the mediator evaluated the merits of the case and suggested settlement options."

47. See McAdoo, "A Report to the Minnesota Supreme Court," 2002, reporting that the top factors motivating lawyers to voluntarily choose mediation include saving litigation expenses (67.9 percent), making settlement more likely (57.4 percent), providing a needed reality check for opposing counsel or party (52.2 percent), and providing a needed reality check for own client (47.7 percent); and B. McAdoo and A. Hinshaw, "The Challenge of Institutionalizing Alternative Dispute Resolution," 2002, reporting that top factors motivating lawyers to choose mediation are saving litigation expenses (85 percent), speeding settlement (76 percent), providing a needed reality check for opposing counsel or party (69 percent), making settlement more likely (69 percent), helping everyone value the case (69 percent), and providing a needed reality check for own client (67 percent). See also E. Gordon, "Attorneys' Negotiation Strategies in Mediation: Business as Usual?" *Mediation Quarterly*, 2000, *17*, p. 387, reporting that attorneys who are not also mediators perceive that the "mediator's primary duty is to act as referee between opposing sides or to convey offers and counteroffers"; and Macfarlane, "Culture Change?" 2002, describing both attorneys' appreciation of mediators' evaluation and their perceptions regarding the limits of such interventions.

48. See McAdoo, "A Report to the Minnesota Supreme Court," 2002, reporting that the top factors motivating lawyers to choose mediation include saving expenses, making settlement more likely, and providing a reality check for opposing counsel and own client. Lawyers' selection of mediation is rarely motivated by the increased potential for creative solutions, preservation of parties' relationships, or evidence that clients "like" mediation. Few attorneys analyzed that mediation has the effect of either "providing greater client satisfaction" or "providing greater client control."

49. See Welsh, "The Thinning Vision of Self-Determination in Court-Connected Mediation," 2001, pp. 50–52, 56–57, describing Florida's and Minnesota's ethical rules for mediators regarding the propriety of evaluative interventions.

50. See R. L. Wissler, "Court-Connected Mediation in General Civil Cases: What We Know from Empirical Research," *Ohio State Journal on Dispute Resolution*, 2002, *17*, 679–680, reporting that cases were more likely to settle if mediators evaluated the merits of cases or assisted parties in evaluating cases' value.

51. See R. A. Bush and J. Folger, *The Promise of Mediation: Responding to Conflict Through Empowerment and Recognition* (San Francisco: Jossey-Bass, 1994); and R. A. Bush, "'What Do We Need a Mediator For?': Mediation's 'Value-Added' for Negotiators," *Ohio State Journal on Dispute Resolution*, 1996, *12*, 1–36.

52. See Bush and Folger, *The Promise of Mediation*, 1994; and Bush, "'What Do We Need a Mediator For?'" 1996.

53. See L. B. Bingham, "Why Suppose? Let's Find Out: A Public Policy Research Program on Dispute Resolution," *Journal of Dispute Resolution*, 2002, *2002*(1), pp. 112–113.

54. See L. B. Bingham, "Mediating Employment Disputes: Perceptions of Redress at the United States Postal Service," *Review of Public Personnel Administration*, 1997, *17*, 20–21, describing the point at which mediation is introduced to try to reach resolution before the filing of a formal complaint; and Bingham, "Why Suppose? Let's Find Out," 2002, pp. 115–118, observing that the Postal Service sought "effect on dispute processing efficiency" and that formal EEO complaints have dropped significantly since implementation of REDRESS.

55. See Bingham, "Why Suppose? Let's Find Out," 2002.

56. See Bingham, "Why Suppose? Let's Find Out," 2002.

57. Bingham, "Why Suppose? Let's Find Out," 2002, pp. 114–115.

58. See Bingham, "Mediating Employment Disputes," 1997.

59. J. R. Antes, J. P. Folger, and D. J. Della Noce, "Transforming Conflict Interactions in the Workplace: Documented Effects of the USPS REDRESS™ Program," *Hofstra Labor and Employment Law Journal*, 2001, *18*, pp. 430–431.

60. D. Della Noce, "Microfocus: The Process and Practice of Transformative Mediation," Workshop Materials: Advanced Level, New York: Institute for the Study of Conflict Transformation, April 2002, p. 14.

61. See T. Nabatchi and L. B. Bingham, "Transformative Mediation in the USPS REDRESS™ Program: Observations of ADR Specialists," *Hofstra Labor & Employment Law Journal*, 2001, *18*, 404–405.

62. See L. B. Bingham and M. C. Novac, "Mediation's Impact on Formal Discrimination Filing: Before and After the REDRESS™ Program at the U.S. Postal Service," *Review of Public Personnel Administration*, 2001, *21*, 308–331.

63. See J. Birkhoff, "Mediators' Perspectives on Power: A Window into a Profession?" Unpublished doctoral dissertation, George Mason University, 2000; A. Abbott, *The System of Professions: An Essay on the Division of Expert Labor* (Chicago: University

of Chicago Press, 1988); and G. L. Geison, *Professions and Professional Ideologies in America* (Chapel Hill, N.C.: University of North Carolina Press, 1983).

64. Birkhoff, "Mediators' Perspectives on Power" 2000, p. 20; quoting T. Johnson, *Professions and Power* (London: Macmillan, 1972), p. 106.

65. See R. Dingwall and P. Lewis, *The Sociology of the Professions: Lawyers, Doctors and Others* (London: MacMillan, 1983).

66. See M. Larson, *The Rise of Professionalism: A Sociological Analysis* (Berkeley, Calif.: University of California Press, 1977).

67. Birkhoff, "Mediators' Perspectives on Power" 2000, p. 23; quoting Abbott, *The System of Professions,* 1988, p. 40.

68. See, for example, R. Creo, "Mediation 2004: The Art and the Artist," *Penn State Law Review,* 2004, *108*; and Menkel-Meadow, "When Dispute Resolution Begets Disputes of Its Own," 1997.

69. See F. Mosten, "Institutionalization of Mediation," *Family Court Review,* 2004, *42*, 292–303; and P. English and L. Neilson, "Certifying Mediators," in J. Folberg, A. Milne, and P. Salem (eds.), *Divorce and Family Mediation* (New York: Guilford Press, 2004).

70. Larson, *The Rise of Professionalism,* 1977, p. xvi.

71. See E. Waldman, "Credentializing Approaches: The Slow Movement Toward Skills-Based Testing Continues," *Dispute Resolution Magazine,* 2001, *8*, 14–16.

72. See C. Picard, "The Emergence of Mediation as a Profession," in C. Morris and A. Pirie (eds.), *Qualifications for Dispute Resolution: Perspectives on the Debate* (Victoria, B.C.: University of Victoria Institute for Dispute Resolution, 1994).

73. See Abbott, *The System of Professions,* 1988.

74. See B. McAdoo and N. Welsh, "Court-Connected General Civil ADR Programs: Aiming for Institutionalization, Efficient Resolution and the Experience of Justice," in D. Stienstra and S. Yates (eds.), *ADR Handbook for Judges* (New York: American Bar Association Section of Dispute Resolution, 2004).

75. See E. Waldman, "Identifying the Role of Social Norms in Mediation: A Multiple Model Approach," *Hastings Law Journal,* 1997, *48*, 761–764.

76. See Picard, "The Emergence of Mediation as a Profession," 1994.

77. See M. L. Duryea, "The Quest for Qualifications: A Quick Trip Without a Good Map," in C. Morris and A. Pirie (eds.), *Qualifications for Dispute Resolution: Perspectives on the Debate* (Victoria, B.C.: University of Victoria Institute for Dispute Resolution, 1994).

78. See Picard, "The Emergence of Mediation as a Profession," 1994.

79. Florida Rules for Certified and Court-Appointed Mediators, Rule 10.100(b) (2004).

80. See Florida Rules for Certified and Court-Appointed Mediators, Rule 10.100(b) (2004).

81. S. Press, "Proposed Revisions to Mediator Certification Qualifications," *The Resolution Report,* October 2004, *19*(2), pp. 1, 13–23. Quotes are from page 17.

82. See English and Neilson, "Certifying Mediators," 2004.

83. English and Neilson, "Certifying Mediators," 2004, p. 484.

84. See English and Neilson, "Certifying Mediators," 2004, pp. 492–498.

85. English and Neilson, "Certifying Mediators," 2004, pp. 484–485.

86. Waldman, "Credentialing Approaches," 2001, p. 16.

87. See The Test Design Project, *Performance-Based Assessment: A Methodology for Use in Selecting, Training and Evaluating Mediators* (Washington, D.C.: National Institute for Dispute Resolution, 1995).

88. Menkel-Meadow, "When Dispute Resolution Begets Disputes of Its Own," 1997, p. 1912.

89. R. Dingwall, "Divorce Mediation, Market Failure and Regulatory Capture," in G. Hanlon and S. Halpern (eds.), *Liberating Professions, Shifting Boundaries* (Institute for the Study of the Legal Profession, Sheffield, U.K.: University of Sheffield, 1997), p. 43.

90. See Mosten, "Institutionalization of Mediation," 2004; and English and Neilsen, "Certifying Mediators," 2004.

CHAPTER THIRTY-ONE

The Next Thirty Years

Directions and Challenges in Dispute Resolution

Robert C. Bordone, Michael L. Moffitt, and Frank E. A. Sander

As Carrie Menkel-Meadow observed in her chapter in this volume, disputes are as old as humankind and dispute resolution is only a bit younger.[1] Yet dispute resolution has only recently become the focus of formal academic and professional exploration. Thirty years ago, virtually no law schools, business schools, or policy schools offered classes in mediation or negotiation. One could find no centers for the study of conflict management and no degree programs in peace studies or dispute resolution. Indeed, few courts encouraged the use of nonlitigious forms of dispute resolution or had programs to support them.

Just thirty years after Frank Sander proposed the multidoor courthouse at the Pound Conference,[2] the landscape for dispute resolution has changed dramatically. Today, dispute resolution courses are offered in virtually all professional schools. Research centers at major universities now facilitate the development of knowledge and the application of knowledge to real-world problems. A substantial and growing number of undergraduate and professional schools now offer separate degrees focused on dispute resolution and conflict management. And more than thirty states have established separate offices of dispute resolution.[3] Given the tremendous growth of dispute resolution as a field during recent decades, there is much to celebrate.

At the same time, dispute resolution's evolution as a field is far from complete. Its reach into the worlds of practice and education is still incomplete. Advances in our understanding of dispute resolution have not reached as broad an audience as they should. Most students navigate their educational careers—from elementary school right through graduate and professional degree programs—without ever receiving formal training in dispute resolution. Those who do study dispute resolution, and who wish to pursue it as a career, continue to find that there are few entry points into the field and even fewer full-time job possibilities.

Furthermore, as an academic discipline, dispute resolution is at something of a crossroads. The "intellectual founders" of the modern dispute resolution movement are no longer the only voices in the field. The moment when inspirational founders of a movement or institution pass their work, energy, ideas, and vision to others is critical. It is a moment of testing: Has a new and legitimate movement or field emerged? Or was the excitement misplaced, a fortuitous but coincidental confluence of charismatic individuals postulating attractive ideas at a ripe moment in history? Will the addition of new voices build upon, strengthen, and broaden the initial endeavor? Or will the founders' visions slowly ossify, lose energy, and fade?

We have great hope that dispute resolution—both as an academic discipline *and* as a growing career opportunity for professionals—is here to stay. The work encapsulated in this volume represents more than a mere blip on the intellectual radar screen. And yet, the field's evolution is not complete. Over the next thirty years, important opportunities and challenges are sure to arise. In this chapter, we survey four questions that we expect will drive much of the agenda for those in the dispute resolution field:

- *How can we best respond to those who have voiced concerns with the application of dispute resolution principles?* Not everyone is enthusiastic about the recent expansion of dispute resolution. Consistent with the very principles underlying the effective management of differences, we need to understand better their concerns and develop appropriate responses.

- *How can we best address private resistance to dispute resolution in the world of practice?* For dispute resolution to fulfill its promise, scholars, practitioners, disputants, and the general public must benefit from effective transfer of knowledge. We must also identify and overcome the obstacles facing those who seek to apply the ideas in practice.

- *How can we build bridges between the various disciplines working on questions of dispute resolution?* The field is interdisciplinary by nature, and many of the most promising developments demand greater cross-disciplinary collaboration and greater cross-disciplinary utilization of knowledge and resources.

- *How can we develop new knowledge about dispute resolution processes?* Dispute resolution rests on an important set of hypotheses about how disputants, dispute contexts, and various dispute resolution mechanisms interact. Yet we know less about each of these than we would prefer.

Many professionals ought to have a deep understanding of dispute resolution—but only some have such an understanding. Despite the advances of dispute resolution over the past thirty years, most lawyers, businesspersons, and government officials still have no formal exposure to or understanding of the various processes of dispute resolution. In the face of conflict, these individuals, depending on the context, are apt to choose between lumping it, litigating it, or fighting it out. How many corporate executives understand disputants' cognitive biases? How many lawyers can nimbly apply problem-solving approaches to create value? How many government leaders appreciate the panoply of processes for managing differences?

A scan of the newspapers shows workers and managers locked in escalating battles over diminishing resources, lawyers doggedly pursuing scorched-earth litigation tactics in the face of overwhelming pressures to settle, and politicians promising not to negotiate with their enemies. Indeed journalists have an incessant tendency to characterize disputes in binary, win-lose terms in ways that cloud dispute resolution opportunities. There is much evidence that dispute resolution has not taken hold as broadly as some in the field would prefer.

Why not? And what can be done about it?

CHALLENGE ONE: RESPONDING TO THOSE WHO HAVE VOICED CONCERN WITH DISPUTE RESOLUTION

Not all observers applaud the recent "successes" of dispute resolution. For example, there are some who worry that the growth of mediation and other nonpublic dispute resolution processes wrongly privatizes disputing. They argue that the increase in settlement rates prevents courts from serving important functions, including the adjudication of rights and the articulation of legal norms.[4] Some have criticized "negotiated rulemaking" (a process by which stakeholders in the promulgation of a federal rulemaking come together to negotiate the terms of a federal regulation). These critics worry that government officials may fail to protect zealously the public interest as they negotiate collaboratively with the very corporate interests that they are charged with regulating. This dynamic is called "agency capture."[5] Still others worry that dispute resolution processes might be applied in contexts in which they are inappropriate. For example, some have voiced concerns that mediation in certain contexts of power imbalance may fail to protect against unjust or even exploitative outcomes.[6] Others have criticized the expansion of arbitration beyond its traditional boundaries into areas of questionable consent.[7] Still others have argued that the use of mediation in sexual harassment cases in the workplace is inappropriate because it risks trivializing the seriousness of the violation.[8] Finally, some have voiced concerns that informal dispute resolution processes may disadvantage minority participants and others who hold less structural power.[9]

For the most part, we concur with the basic spirit of these concerns. We believe dispute resolution processes must be tailored to the nature of the dispute. And we would say the same about all dispute resolution processes—whether adjudicative or not.

We do not count ourselves as unqualified dispute resolution imperialists. Some in our field seem to insist that all disputes should be resolved through consensual means without resort to litigation. We think this misunderstands the promise of appropriate dispute resolution. Those who overpromise when "selling" dispute resolution decrease its legitimacy. Those who march forward with particular processes, even when contraindications against their use are present, do a disservice to the field.

At the same time, we believe that those who have written against the dispute resolution movement have often overstated their arguments. In most cases, they reflect an oversimplified understanding of the application of dispute resolution principles to complex problems.

Part of what we need is an improved dialogue about dispute resolution processes, their promise, and their pitfalls. We need conversations, rather than polemics. We need nuanced analyses, careful examinations of real-world experiences, and a welcoming of a range of perspectives into what should be an ongoing collective effort to find the best ways to manage our differences. And we see signs of hope that these conversations are beginning.[10]

Another piece of the puzzle lies with educators. Quality instruction about dispute resolution processes must also include an appreciation for how one *diagnoses* a dispute. A surgeon who knows how to operate on kidney stones, but who cannot diagnose when this surgery is appropriate, is more dangerous than helpful.

We should situate our field, working to clarify that dispute resolution is an umbrella that encompasses the full range of mechanisms for resolving differences. A thorough study of dispute resolution must include an appreciation for traditional rights-based models (such as litigation or arbitration) in addition to models focused on nonadversarial approaches. And it should recognize that disputes do not take place against a blank slate. It is not enough to imagine what processes *should* exist, if no background processes were already in place. Early efforts simply to graft dispute resolution onto existing rights-based structures have produced as many challenges as successes. These challenges mount as one considers the myriad cultures and contexts into which dispute resolution mechanisms have been thrust. A complete understanding of dispute resolution requires knowing what processes work best *in the context* faced by the disputants.

CHALLENGE TWO: ADDRESSING PRIVATE RESISTANCE

Not all who resist dispute resolution do so through open, principled opposition to one or more of its foundational ideas. Instead, many engage in what we term "private" resistance. Many in this category publicly support various forms of collaborative dispute resolution, while at the same time they privately fail to modify behavior or take steps to ensure that wise processes are applied in each dispute.

The reasons for such resistance are many and varied. For some, the invitation to act beyond the comfort zones of their traditional practice feels threatening; for others high-quality training programs are not readily available; still others may think that learning about dispute resolution processes is a good idea, but because of hectic schedules, it never becomes a priority that they can get around to.

In some cases, parties' private resistance to dispute resolution ideas stems from their perceptions about what they stand to gain. A company believes it is relatively "powerful" and can extract concessions out of a counterpart by engaging in adversarial tactics. Why should it refrain from doing so? Unless it believes that it stands to gain even more by expanding the value to be divided, the company is likely to resist any adaptation in the process by which it seeks to resolve the dispute. This dynamic is exacerbated when one introduces agents into the equation—agents who may have interests that are well-served in the existing dispute resolution mechanisms. And agency problems are not limited to outside professionals such as lawyers. In many companies a settlement is charged to the budget of that division, but litigation costs are not charged to the department. This creates an incentive to division managers to litigate even if it makes no sense from a larger corporate perspective.[11] In short, if disputants do not see value in the change, they will not change—even if they would not admit it publicly.

Part of the answer to this dilemma lies in education. Training in dispute resolution should be commonplace—if not mandatory—in professional schools. The decision makers of tomorrow should make dispute resolution choices based on a thorough understanding of their options. Moreover, dispute resolution education should not be limited to professional academies. Dispute resolution programs in elementary and high schools are particularly promising. Such programs give students skills that are transferable from the school to a whole host of other critical contexts. Indeed, the skills and insights embedded in quality dispute resolution programs may be of even more use to those who are not destined to occupy the positions of greatest authority.

Another piece of the response to this challenge ought to rest in a more compelling, effective set of stories and images. Popular perceptions are more frequently shaped by vivid accounts of a single transaction than by broad empirical surveys. As it now stands, stories of war, of intense litigation, and of winner-take-all showdowns saturate the media.[12] With rare exceptions (for example, Ken Feinberg's work administering the 9/11 Fund), stories of successful problem-solving dispute resolution are covered, if at all, only on the back pages of the *New York Law Journal*. For dispute resolution to gain traction outside the academy, we must identify and publicize stories in which organizations and individuals chose wise dispute resolution strategies. We need stories in which parties with apparent "power" realized even greater value through creative problem solving than they would have through traditional means of dispute resolution. Examples are out there. Companies such as Toro Motors, Johnson & Johnson, E.I. du Pont de Nemours and Co., Georgia-Pacific Corp., Bridgestone/Firestone, General Electric Co., and Motorola[13] have adopted settlement-friendly dispute resolution programs that save them millions of dollars each year.[14] If we are to succeed in efforts to reduce resistance to dispute resolution, our field must make more concerted efforts to promote stories of effective, wise dispute resolution.

The field will also continue to need intellectual leaders at prominent institutions. At least part of the credibility of the early claims regarding dispute resolution stemmed from the sources of the ideas. Leadership from high-profile professors at leading universities was critical to attracting the attention of practitioners, corporations, funders, and policymakers. These institutions are uniquely placed to disseminate knowledge more broadly to the outside world of practice. If dispute resolution is to succeed in disseminating information to the broader community, prominent civic institutions must remain the centers of thinking and research in dispute resolution. Part of the challenge, therefore, lies with these institutions, in figuring out how to build and maintain such efforts. And part of the challenge lies with the field, in figuring out how to persuade these prominent institutions of the need for such endeavors. The 2003 decision of the Hewlett Foundation to cease its funding of dispute resolution theory centers at prominent American universities only adds to the urgency of those in the field to promote the need for continued funding and research.[15]

Similarly, dispute resolution will be enhanced enormously when we begin to see scholars from the field ascend to positions of importance in their educational institutions. Consider the exciting opportunities a law school might create for faculty and students if it appointed a dean with a background in *multiple* forms of dispute resolution. If the chair of a department were trained in dispute resolution, what rich interdisciplinary opportunities would she or he be likely to create for younger colleagues and students?

Finally, just as dispute resolution will need intellectual champions from within the academic community, it will need prominent figures from within the world of practice to encourage its continued growth.[16] Organizations such as the CPR Institute for Dispute Resolution, the ABA Section on Dispute Resolution, and business groups have an opportunity to educate a broader audience than do most academics. Prominent judges can educate members of the bar and the public in unique and important ways.[17] Government officials and policymakers can shape the environment in which disputes are addressed.[18] Legislators, civic leaders, clergy, and a host of other figures are poised to improve the lives of so many, through the application of wise dispute resolution principles.

CHALLENGE THREE: BRIDGING THE CROSS-DISCIPLINARY GAP

One of the greatest attractions of dispute resolution as a field is its interdisciplinary nature. No single discipline has a lock on or monopoly in the field.[19] The contributions in this volume serve to bring home this point. Unfortunately, more often than not, theorists and researchers are unaware of each other's work. A 2004 report commissioned by The William and Flora Hewlett Foundation by Robert A. Baruch Bush found that even scholars working along related lines in the same institution or field often were completely unaware of each other's work.[20] Indeed, every contributor to this volume is virtually certain to find brand new ideas in these pages—ideas captured by others in other disciplines. Opportunities for cross-disciplinary fertilization are still too rare in our field.[21]

Cross-disciplinary work is not easy. Established academic disciplines such as economics, psychology, sociology, and law have each contributed to our understanding of dispute resolution. Yet each has its own highly specialized terminology, peer review standards, and research traditions. This challenge is exacerbated by structural limitations within most universities that speak glowingly of cross-disciplinary collaboration, only to enact policies and procedures that fail to encourage it.

In very few institutions, for example, would an untenured professor in one department or school be encouraged to undertake joint work with a faculty member in another discipline. Not only would the resulting work be coauthored (a negative in many academic settings), but also it would invariably have at least some of the scholarly trappings of the "other" discipline. For relatively junior academics, therefore, cross-disciplinary work is a challenge. And the challenge is not limited to those facing the prospect of tenure review. Departments, schools, universities, and the broader academic community are accustomed to rewarding a particular vein of specialized research. Cross-disciplinary work has a hard time fitting into that model.

Many of the most important advances in our field have come through the collaborative efforts of individuals who came to dispute resolution through different avenues. Cross-disciplinary work involving law, economics, psychology, organizational behavior, and sociology has been invaluable. And much more can be done within each of these fields. However, if dispute resolution is to make the impact it should, dispute resolution theorists will need to follow their own advice and capitalize on their own differences in resources and capabilities by forging productive working relationships.

One important development toward this end has been the establishment of university research centers or projects for the study of negotiation and dispute resolution. These research centers are no panacea, yet they have been instrumental in bridging the gap between disciplines. With strong faculty leadership from various departments and schools within a university, research centers can provide forums to expose faculties to the work of their colleagues. Moreover, such centers can fund cutting-edge collaborative work by those who aspire to study and teach dispute resolution. Finally, the existence of such programs helps to facilitate fortuitous meetings of faculty who may not ever otherwise meet each other. These meetings can result in spontaneous collaborations between colleagues who do similar work in parallel, nonintersecting disciplines.

An even more promising development is found in the emergence of degree programs in dispute resolution, peace studies, or conflict management. The faculty for such programs is now drawn from other academic departments. One need not imagine this as a permanent condition, however. Perhaps we are not so far removed from the day when universities will have faculties in Dispute Resolution Studies. Perhaps one day the home department for these faculty members will be Dispute Resolution, rather than Economics, or Psychology, or Law. The tenure review process in such a department would probably *demand* (rather than merely tolerate) cross-disciplinary work.

Needless to say, those in the field of dispute resolution ought not to hold their collective breath for such developments within the academy. It may be many years before these developments come to fruition. It may be multiple generations. And it may never come to pass in the form we have described. What is important is that we consider ways to encourage the kinds of cross-disciplinary collaboration that are so critical to the continued development of our field.

CHALLENGE FOUR: DEVELOPING NEW KNOWLEDGE

We know more than we used to about dispute resolution—and we know less than we need to.

There seem to be almost limitless areas in which we need further research. No one could hope to provide an exhaustive list of topics worthy of further study. Our ignorance is so profound that we probably do not even know what we do not know. In this section, we identify a few of the research areas we think are most promising—areas in which dispute resolution scholars and practitioners have the most to gain from one another.

Quantification of the Costs and Benefits of Dispute Resolution

One of the foremost challenges for dispute resolution researchers in the years ahead will be to quantify the costs and benefits of various approaches to dispute resolution. Funding for dispute resolution programs is down significantly across the nation.[22] In an age of cost-cutting, companies are reevaluating high-priced internal training programs. More and more, those who advocate for dispute resolution programs are being asked to defend continued funding by showing actual cost savings and value. Unfortunately, there is a serious dearth of rigorous evaluative data.[23] As we move forward, anecdotal data and interesting stories will be insufficient to win funding in an age of ever-growing demand for resources.

Multiparty Dispute Resolution

There is an enormous amount of work to be done with respect to building a robust theory and practice of multiparty dispute resolution. Few disputes in modern days involve only two parties, yet very little empirical research has been done relating to multiparty disputes. As Howard Raiffa observed in *The Art and Science of Negotiation*, "There is a vast difference between conflicts involving two disputants and those involving more than two disputants."[24] During the past few years several law schools, including Harvard, Georgetown, and Stanford, have begun to offer advanced classes on multiparty negotiation. While some scholarly work has been done in this area, we still do not have a parsimonious and useful model for understanding multiparty disputes.[25]

Role of Culture

As Anthony Wanis-St. John appropriately asserts in his chapter on culture in this volume, researchers in dispute resolution have largely downplayed the role of culture in the resolution of disputes.[26] Understanding how cultural differences influence disputes—and how they can be used to improve the processes of dispute resolution—has become even riper for research in the post-9/11 world. As it now stands, the role of culture as a construct and influence in conflict, though recognized as important, is virtually unexplored.[27]

Role(s) of Emotions

No one with experience in dispute resolution would deny that emotion plays a role. Yet until very recently, scholars have offered relatively little helpful advice to those who engage in dispute resolution regarding the roles of emotion.[28] The best answer surely is not "Don't get emotional," nor is it to say simply, "Manage your emotions." We hope that with time, researchers will develop a richer understanding of the ways that shame, anger, hope, and fear affect disputants. And we hope that scholars will find vehicles for translating these findings into advice that will be useful to practitioners.

Effective Teaching Pedagogies

Because dispute resolution is essentially interdisciplinary in nature, the challenge for an instructor teaching dispute resolution is enormous. Effective teachers of dispute resolution in professional programs need to have a basic level of proficiency in many areas in order to teach dispute resolution successfully. Despite the tremendous growth in the number and type of dispute resolution classes, we have relatively little information about the kinds of pedagogies that are most likely to result in students actually developing transferable dispute resolution skills. Some negotiation scholars have begun to study empirically the kinds of negotiation teaching pedagogies that are most effective in the teaching of dispute resolution.[29] As the demand for dispute resolution instruction explodes, both in professional schools and in the professional world, the field needs to learn what teaching pedagogies and styles are most effective in helping learners transfer theoretical knowledge to practice.

CONCLUSION

We admit that we are not neutral observers of this field. And still, we believe that dispute resolution may be the most exciting place to be right now.

The field is at a crossroads, providing fertile opportunity for those who seize it to shape the course of its development. Dispute resolution is in the midst of an enormous exploration of the possibilities and limits of translating theory into practice—and practice into theory. The field calls, therefore, for ambassadors in the world of government, business, and civil society who can advocate for the principles of dispute resolution and who can effectively spread the word about the effectiveness of dispute resolution in resolving disputes and better managing conflict. Paradoxically, as the field becomes more institutionalized, it must simultaneously guard against a dilution of the idealism, vibrancy, and flexibility that inspired its birth and initial attraction.

Dispute resolution faces the unique challenge of creating an independent space for itself alongside traditional academic disciplines such as economics, psychology, and sociology. At the same time, the field itself must bridge the cultural and language gaps that exist between these fields and develop its own, unique, and crosscutting disciplinary language.

To these elements that make ours a most exciting and dynamic field, we add a final element: urgency. At the start of the twenty-first century, the question of how we human beings manage and resolve our differences—how we manage and resolve our disputes—is of central importance. The need for the work of dispute resolution scholars and practitioners in all sectors of society has never been greater. Force and the threat of force are the least elegant, most destructive, most costly, and most alienating of dispute resolution mechanisms. And yet the use of force is becoming more commonplace on both the international and domestic fronts. Even when force is averted, there is an increasing tendency toward polarized, zero-sum rhetoric regarding some of our most important differences. Technology and the realities of modern life bring us into more frequent contact with those from whom we are different, either by virtue of race, culture, creed, education, class, or viewpoint. To survive, we must manage those differences with skill.

Our field has an urgent mandate. If we act with congruence—walking the talk—we have an opportunity to learn from each other, to teach each other, and to improve the ways in which those with differences interact.

Notes

1. See Menkel-Meadow, Chapter Two, this volume.

2. See F.E.A. Sander, "Varieties of Dispute Processing," *Federal Rules Decisions,* 1976, *77,* 111–123.

3. See L. P. Senft and C. A. Savage, "ADR In the Courts: Progress, Problems, and Possibilities," *Penn State Law Review,* 2003, *108,* 327–348.

4. See O. Fiss, "Against Settlement," *Yale Law Journal,* 1984, *93,* 1073–1090; J. Resnik, "Many Doors? Closing Doors? Alternative Dispute Resolution and Adjudication," *Ohio State Journal On Dispute Resolution,* 1995, *10,* 211–265; and L. Nader, "Controlling Processes in the Practice of Law: Hierarchy and Pacification in the Movement to Re-Form Dispute Ideology," *Ohio State Journal on Dispute Resolution,* 1993, *9*(1), 1–26.

5. S. Rose-Ackerman, "Consensus Versus Incentives: A Skeptical Look at Regulatory Negotiation," *Duke Law Journal,* 1994, *43,* p. 1216.

6. See, for example, T. Grillo, "The Mediation Alternative: Process Dangers for Women," *Yale Law Journal,* 1991, *100*(6), 1545–1610.

7. Jean Sternlight has written extensively on the perils associated with the rise of arbitration. See J. Sternlight, "Mandatory Binding Arbitration and the Demise of the Seventh Amendment Right to a Jury Trial," *Ohio State Journal on Dispute Resolution,* 2001, *16,* 669–733.

8. See M. Irvine, "Mediation: Is It Appropriate for Sexual Harassment Grievances?" *Ohio State Journal on Dispute Resolution,* 1993, *9,* 27–52.

9. Ian Ayres has conducted some of the most interesting research on this topic. See, for example, I. Ayres, "Further Evidence of Discrimination in New Car Negotiations and Estimates of Its Cause," *Michigan Law Review,* 1995, *94,* 109–147; and I. Ayres, "Fair Driving: Gender and Race Discrimination in Retail Car Negotiations," *Harvard Law Review,* 1991, *104,* 817–872.

10. See, for example, C. Menkel-Meadow, "When Litigation Is Not the Only Way: Consensus Building and Mediation in Public Interest Lawyering," *Washington University Journal of Law and Policy,* 2002, *10,* 37–61; and J. Seul, "Settling Significant Cases," *Washington Law Review,* 2004, *79,* 881–967.

11. See F.E.A. Sander, "The Future of ADR," *Journal of Dispute Resolution,* 2000, pp. 3–10.

12. See Sander, "The Future of ADR," 2000.

13. See, for example, R. H. Wiese, "The ADR Program at Motorola," *Negotiation Journal,* 1989, *5,* 381–394.

14. See A. Jones, "Bullish on Settling." [http://www.law.com/jsp/article.jsp?id = 1095434457836]. September 24, 2004.

15. See Hewlett Foundation. [http://www.hewlett.org/Programs/ConflictResolution/preslettcr.htm]. October 2004.

16. See F.E.A. Sander, "Some Concluding Thoughts," *Journal of Legal Education,* 2004, *54,* 115–118.

17. U.S. Magistrate Judge Wayne Brazil and Ohio Supreme Court Justice Tom Moyer provide two examples of the opportunity for innovative contributions from the bench. Judge Brazil, a magistrate judge in the Northern District of California, was instrumental in developing and overseeing the multi-option justice program in that court and is a nationally recognized leader in the speaking and writing about court-connected ADR. Thomas Moyer was an early proponent of ADR who promoted a statewide program of court ADR in Ohio, for which he was awarded the James Henry Award by the CPR Institute for Dispute Resolution in 2004.

18. For example, Janet Reno's efforts within the Department of Justice have had a pronounced effect on the integration of dispute resolution into the government's litigation practices.

19. See R. H. Mnookin, "Strategic Barriers to Dispute Resolution: A Comparison of Bilateral and Multilateral Negotiations," *Harvard Negotiation Law Review,* 2003, *8*(1), 1–27.

20. See R.A.B. Bush, "The Knowledge Gaps Project: Scholarly Views on the Unanswered Questions in Conflict Resolution," *Conflict Resolution Quarterly,* forthcoming.

21. But compare K. Arrow, R. H. Mnookin, L. Ross, A. Tversky, and R. Wilson (eds.), *Barriers to Conflict Resolution* (Cambridge, Mass.: PON Books, 1999).

22. See G. T. Jones, "Fighting Capitulation: A Research Agenda for the Future of Dispute Resolution," *Penn State Law Review,* 2003, *108,* 277–308.

23. See Sander, "The Future of ADR," 2000.

24. H. Raiffa, *The Art and Science of Negotiation* (Cambridge, Mass.: Belknap Press of Harvard University Press, 1982), p. 11. For further observations, see also W. Zartman, *International Multilateral Negotiation Approaches to the Management of Complexity* (San Francisco: Jossey-Bass, 1994).

25. See, for example, D. A. Lax and J. K. Sebenius, "Thinking Coalitionally: Party Arithmetic, Process Opportunism, and Strategic Sequencing," in H. P. Young (ed.), *Negotiation Analysis* (Ann Arbor, Mich.: University of Michigan Press, 1991); and L. Susskind, S. McKearnan, and J. Thomas-Larmer (eds.), *The Consensus Building Handbook* (Thousand Oaks, Calif.: Sage, 1999).

26. See Wanis-St. John, Chapter Eight, this volume.

27. See Bush, "The Knowledge Gaps Project," forthcoming.

28. Roger Fisher and Dan Shapiro, both of Harvard Law School, are among those dispute resolution scholars who have begun to study and write about the role of emotion in negotiation and dispute resolution. See also Shapiro, Chapter Five, this volume.

29. See J. Nadler, L. Thompson, and L. Van Boven, "Learning Negotiation Skills: Four Models of Knowledge Creation and Transfer," *Management Science*, 2003, *49*, 529–540.

ABOUT THE EDITORS

Michael L. Moffitt is an associate professor and the associate director of the Appropriate Dispute Resolution Program at the University of Oregon School of Law. He was formerly a lecturer on law at Harvard Law School, served as the clinical supervisor of the Harvard Mediation Program, and was a visiting professor at the Ohio State University College of Law. Moffitt was also a senior consultant with Conflict Management Group, designing and delivering mediation services, negotiation coaching, and training workshops around the world. His clients have ranged from senior judges to tribal leaders, from unionized prison guards to accountants, from railroad officials to diplomatic academy trainees. Moffitt has published more than a dozen academic articles on negotiation and dispute resolution. Since arriving at Oregon, he has received awards for outstanding teaching from both the law school and the university. He served as law clerk to United States District Judge Ann Aldrich, and is a graduate of Marietta College and Harvard Law School.

Robert C. Bordone is the Thaddeus R. Beal Lecturer on Law at Harvard Law School and the deputy director of the Harvard Negotiation Research Project, where he teaches several courses on negotiation and dispute resolution. Bordone is also an adjunct professor of law at Georgetown University Law Center. He has written numerous articles and role simulations on negotiation and dispute resolution in journals such as the *Harvard Negotiation Law Review* and *Negotiation Journal*. His research interests include negotiation ethics, the role of leadership in negotiation, and the design and implementation of organizational dispute systems. In addition to his academic work, Bordone consults and teaches for a wide range of corporate, government, and nonprofit clients. Before coming to Harvard, he clerked for United States District Judge George A. O'Toole Jr. and worked for law firms in New York City and Washington, D.C., as well as for CBS News and the Boston Consulting Group. Bordone is a graduate of Dartmouth College and Harvard Law School.

ABOUT THE CONTRIBUTORS

Marjorie Corman Aaron is the executive director of the Center for Practice in Negotiation and Problem Solving at the University of Cincinnati College of Law, where she teaches mediation, negotiation, ADR, and interviewing and counseling. Aaron is an active mediator, arbitrator, and trainer. She is a mediator panelist and ADR training faculty member of the CPR Institute for Dispute Resolution, has served as a panelist for the Merrill Lynch Claims Resolution Process, and is vice chair of the Ohio Commission on Dispute Resolution and Conflict Management. Aaron is the former executive director of the Program on Negotiation at Harvard Law School and was also a vice president at Endispute, Inc. and a mediator for the Middlesex Multi-Door Courthouse. Aaron has mediated a wide variety of commercial legal disputes. She also designs and teaches workshops on mediation, negotiation, ADR, and decision analysis.

Keith G. Allred is an associate professor at Harvard's Kennedy School of Government, where he teaches and conducts research on negotiation and conflict resolution. During 2004-2005 he was the Frank Church Distinguished Professor at Boise State University in his home state of Idaho. An internationally recognized scholar in negotiation and conflict resolution, he has significant experience in applying his scholarly knowledge to real-world challenges. As a professional mediator, he has helped manage and resolve many disputes, particularly focusing on conflicts in the American West. He is also the founder of TheCommonInterest.org, a grassroots political organization that works across party lines to improve policy.

Max H. Bazerman is the Jesse Isidor Straus Professor of Business Administration at the Harvard Business School. Prior to joining the Harvard faculty in 2000, he was on the faculty of the Kellogg Graduate School of Management of Northwestern University for fifteen years. He is affiliated with Harvard's Kennedy School of Government and its Psychology Department, and is a member of the executive committee of the Program on Negotiation at Harvard Law School. Bazerman's research focuses on decision making, negotiation, creating joint gains in society, and the natural environment. He is the author or coauthor of over 150 research articles and chapters, and the author, coauthor, or coeditor of eleven books, including *Predictable Surprises* (2004, with Michael Watkins), *Smart Money Decisions* (1999), *Judgment in Managerial Decision Making* (2005, now in its sixth edition), and *Negotiating Rationally* (1992, with M. Neale). He is a member of many editorial boards, including those of the *Journal of Behavioral Decision Making,* the *International Journal of Conflict Management,* and the *Negotiation Journal.*

Corinne Bendersky is an assistant professor at the UCLA Anderson School of Management. Her research is on how characteristics of organizations affect individuals' interpretations of, behaviors in, and evaluations of conflict. Bendersky also studies social psychological mechanisms underlying negotiator behaviors—in particular, the reduction of cognitive dissonance for offers a person proposes during negotiations. Bendersky received her Ph.D. from the MIT Sloan School of Management and her B.A. with honors from Oberlin College. She teaches in the UCLA Anderson School's full-time and fully employed MBA programs, and in many of its executive education programs. Prior to graduate school, Bendersky was a negotiation and mediation trainer and consultant in Boston, Massachusetts.

Kristen M. Blankley is a 2004 graduate of The Ohio State University Moritz College of Law, where she earned her Certificate in Dispute Resolution. She has published two articles on the issue of class action arbitration, and she recently won first prize in the James Boskey ADR Writing Competition, law division, for her paper on mediation confidentiality. Currently, she is working as a law clerk for a judge on the Sixth Circuit Court of Appeals.

Richard J. Bodine is a cofounder of the National Center for Conflict Resolution Education, serving as training director since 1997 and consultant for the Illinois Institute for Dispute Resolution since 1992. Bodine has trained over three thousand adults and over one thousand youths in conflict resolution processes. He holds training certificates from CDR Associates of Boulder, Colorado, for Mediation, for Dispute Management Systems Design, and for Conflict Resolution in Organizations. He is coauthor of the following books: *The School for Quality*

Learning: Managing the School and the Classroom the Deming Way (1993); *Creating the Peaceable School* (1994, 2002 [2nd ed.]); *Peer Mediation: Conflict Resolution in Schools, Revised* (1997); *Conflict Resolution Education: A Guide to Implementing Programs in Schools* (1996, 2001 [revised ed.]); *The Handbook for Conflict Resolution Education* (1998); and *Developing Emotional Intelligence: A Guide to Behavior Management and Conflict Resolution in Schools* (1999).

Hannah Riley Bowles is an assistant professor of public policy at the Kennedy School of Government, Harvard University. She is engaged in research on negotiation and leadership, and is interested in how people negotiate for resources and opportunities to advance into leadership positions and under what conditions gender affects negotiation. Bowles teaches and has conducted case research on leadership in crisis and complex multiparty conflict. Earlier in her career, she worked for Conflict Management Group and the Costa Rican Ministry of Natural Resources, Energy & Mines. She was a fellow at the Argentinean National Institute of Public Administration, the West German Parliament, and Oxford University's Forestry Institute. She has a D.B.A. from the Harvard Business School, an M.P.P. from the Kennedy School, and an A.B. from Smith College.

Robert B. Coates is currently part-time senior research associate with the Center for Restorative Justice and Peacemaking. He has held positions as associate director, Harvard Center for Criminal Justice; associate professor, University of Chicago School of Social Service Administration; and professor of social work, University of Utah Graduate School of Social Work. Coates has also spent a dozen years serving churches as a pastor. He has authored numerous publications on deinstitutionalization, community-based services, system change, and restorative justice.

Jonathan R. Cohen is associate professor of law and associate director of the Institute for Dispute Resolution at the University of Florida Levin College of Law. He received his J.D. and Ph.D. in economics from Harvard University. Cohen's research focuses on the intersection between dispute resolution and ethics. In recent years, he has written articles addressing the role of apology in legal disputes, the ethics of respect in negotiation, and the moral requirement that injurers take, rather than deny, responsibility for harms they commit.

Sarah Rudolph Cole, professor of law at the Moritz College of Law, Ohio State University, received her J.D. with honors from the University of Chicago Law School. After clerking on the Ninth Circuit for the Honorable Eugene Wright, Cole practiced labor and employment law at law firms in Seattle and Chicago. Cole was a member of the faculty at Creighton University School of Law and at the University of Oklahoma College of Law prior to joining the Moritz College of Law in 1998. She is coauthor, with Nancy H. Rogers and Craig A. McEwen, of *Mediation: Law, Policy and Practice* and of *Dispute Resolution: Negotiation, Mediation and Other Processes* with Nancy H. Rogers, Stephen Goldberg, and Frank E. A. Sander. She writes, teaches, and speaks on a variety of alternative dispute resolution topics, particularly mediation and arbitration.

Donna K. Crawford is a cofounder of the Illinois Institute for Dispute Resolution and the National Center for Conflict Resolution Education, serving as executive director since 1992. She is an experienced mediator, reality therapist, and dispute resolution trainer. Her training in alternative dispute resolution methods includes the Justice Center of Atlanta, Georgia, the Illinois State Board of Education Department of Specialized Services, and the Harvard University Law School. Donna coauthored the following publications: *Peer Mediation: Conflict Resolution in Schools* (1991, 1997 [revised ed.]); *The School for Quality Learning: Managing the School and the Classroom the Deming Way* (1993); *Creating the Peaceable School* (1994, 2002 [2nd ed.]); *Conflict Resolution Education: A Guide to Implementing Programs in Schools* (1996, 2001 [revised ed.]); *The Handbook for Conflict Resolution Education* (1998); *Developing Emotional Intelligence: A Guide to Behavior Management and Conflict Resolution in Schools* (1999); and *Take a Stand: Stop the Violence* Multimedia CD-ROM and Video (1999).

Clark Freshman received his B.A. from Harvard College, his B.A. from University College, Oxford (where he was a Marshall Scholar), and his J.D. from Stanford Law School. He clerked for Judge William Norris of the Ninth Circuit and practiced litigation in Los Angeles for several years. He is currently a professor of law at the University of Miami, and, for 2004–2005, a visiting professor at Santa Clara University Law School. He is also a mediator, negotiation trainer, and expert witness on arbitration. He has been an invited speaker on negotiation at many law schools, including Harvard, Yale, and UCLA, and his work has appeared in law reviews at Harvard, Stanford, Cornell, and elsewhere. In collaboration with Adele Hayes, a psychology professor and internationally recognized expert on depression, he has studied emotion and success at negotiation and law school in a series of theoretical and quantitative studies.

Howard Gadlin has been ombudsman and director of the Center for Cooperative Resolution at the National Institutes of Health since the beginning of 1999. Before that, from 1992 through 1998, he was university ombudsperson and adjunct professor of education at UCLA. He was also director of the UCLA Conflict Mediation Program and codirector of the Center for the Study and Resolution of Interethnic/Interracial Conflict. While in Los Angeles, he served as consulting ombudsman to the Los Angeles County Museum of Art. Prior to moving to Los Angeles, Gadlin was ombudsperson and professor of psychology at the University of Massachusetts, Amherst. He currently serves as chair of the Coalition of Federal Ombudsmen. Gadlin is past president of the University and College Ombuds Association and of The Ombudsman Association.

Chris Guthrie is the associate dean for academic affairs and a professor of law at Vanderbilt University Law School. A graduate of Stanford University (B.A.), the Harvard Graduate School of Education (M.Ed.), and Stanford Law School (J.D.), Guthrie began his academic career at the University of Missouri School of Law and has served as a visiting professor at Northwestern, the University of Alabama, and Washington University. Guthrie has received multiple prizes for his teaching and research, including the CPR Institute for Dispute Resolution Professional Article prize in 2001 and 2003 and the Outstanding First Year Professor Award at Northwestern in 2004.

Sheila Heen is a partner at Triad Consulting in Cambridge, Massachusetts, and has been teaching negotiation as a lecturer on law at Harvard Law School for a decade. She is a coauthor of *Difficult Conversations: How to Discuss What Matters Most* (1999), which grew out of ten years of work at the Harvard Negotiation Project. At Triad, Sheila works with corporate clients such as Citigroup, Merck, IBM, and Shell and on nonprofit projects with the New England Organ Bank, The Citadel, and Greek and Turkish Cypriots in Cyprus. Triad helps executives and communities improve the way they navigate decision making and handle their most challenging conversations.

Ethan Katsh is professor of legal studies and director of the Center for Information Technology and Dispute Resolution at the University of Massachusetts at Amherst. He is the author of *Online Dispute Resolution: Resolving Conflicts in Cyberspace* (2001) and *Law in a Digital World* (1995). He has been visiting professor of law and cyberspace at Brandeis University, is chair of the UN Economic Commission for Europe Expert Group on ODR, and cochair of the Association of Conflict Resolution Section of Online Dispute Resolution. He is currently principal investigator for a National Science Foundation project involving the use of online dispute resolution in federal administrative agencies. His e-mail is katsh@legal.umass.edu; Website: http://www.odr.info.

Deborah M. Kolb is professor of management at Simmons School of Management and at the Center for Gender in Organizations there. From 1991 through 1994, Kolb was executive director of the Program on Negotiation at Harvard Law School. She is currently a senior fellow at the Program, where she codirects The Negotiations in the Workplace Project. Dr. Kolb is a principal in The Shadow

Negotiation, LLC., an e-learning company that provides negotiation training specially designed for women. Kolb (with Judith Williams) is the author of *Everyday Negotiation: Navigating the Hidden Agendas of Bargaining* (Jossey-Bass/John Wiley, 2003). Under its original title, *The Shadow Negotiation*, the book was named by *Harvard Business Review* as one of the ten best business books of 2000, and it received the best-book award from the International Association of Conflict Management at its meetings in Paris in 2001. Kolb is currently working on a new book, *Taking the Lead: Negotiating the Challenges of Leadership Success*. Other books that Kolb has authored or edited include *The Mediators; Hidden Conflict in Organizations: Uncovering Behind-the-Scenes Disputes; Making Talk Work: Profiles of Mediators;* and *Negotiation Eclectics: Essays in Memory of Jeffrey Z. Rubin*. Kolb is on the editorial boards of the *Negotiation Journal* and the *Journal of Conflict Resolution*.

Russell Korobkin is professor of law at the University of California, Los Angeles (UCLA), where he teaches negotiation, contracts, and health care law. He also conducts negotiation training workshops for lawyers and other professionals and provides mediation services. Prior to joining the UCLA faculty in 2001, he taught at the University of Illinois and the University of Texas. Korobkin is the author of the textbook *Negotiation Theory and Strategy* (2002), as well as more than thirty scholarly articles on negotiating in the transactional and dispute resolution contexts and other topics that combine law, economics, and psychology. Before entering law teaching, Korobkin received his B.A. and J.D. from Stanford University, clerked for the Honorable James L. Buckley of the U.S. Court of Appeals for the District of Columbia Circuit, and worked as an associate at the law firm of Covington and Burling.

Kimberlee K. Kovach has more than twenty-five years' experience in mediation and has spent the past fifteen years teaching in the field of alternative dispute resolution. She is a past chair of the American Bar Association Section of Dispute Resolution as well as the State Bar of Texas ADR Section. Kovach is the author of a textbook for law school use, *Mediation: Principles and Practice* (3rd ed., 2004), as well as of *Mediation in a Nutshell* (2003). She has also written several law review articles along with shorter commentaries on topics surrounding mediation use. Kovach has lectured throughout the United States and abroad and serves as a mediator, arbitrator, and ADR trainer. She is currently the distinguished lecturer in dispute resolution at South Texas College of Law.

Carrie Menkel-Meadow is the A. B. Chettle Jr. Professor of Dispute Resolution and Civil Procedure and director of the Hewlett-Georgetown Program in Conflict Resolution and Legal Problem Solving at Georgetown University Law Center. She is also chair of the Georgetown-CPR Commission on Ethics and

Standards in ADR. She is the editor of *Mediation: Theory, Policy and Practice* (2000) and author of *Dispute Processing and Conflict Resolution: Theory, Policy and Practice* (2003), and coauthor of *What's Fair: Ethics for Negotiators* (2004, with Michael Wheeler) and *Dispute Resolution: Beyond the Adversarial Model* (2004, with Lela Love, Andrea Schneider, and Jean Sternlight), as well as the author of over one hundred academic articles. She has won the CPR Institute for Dispute Resolution First Prize for Scholarship in ADR three times (1983, 1991, 1998) and the Rutter Prize for Excellence in Teaching at UCLA Law School. She currently serves as coeditor–in-chief of the *Journal of Legal Education* and the *International Journal of Law in Context,* and as associate editor of the *Negotiation Journal,* published by the Harvard Program on Negotiation.

Bruce Patton is deputy director of the Harvard Negotiation Project, which he cofounded with Roger Fisher and William Ury in 1979, and a founder and director of Vantage Partners, LLC., a consulting firm that helps organizations manage critical negotiations and relationships. From 1985 through 1999 Patton was Thaddeus R. Beal Lecturer on Law at Harvard Law School, where he continues to teach part-time. Patton's experience includes training the white cabinet and the A.N.C. Negotiating Committee in South Africa before the constitutional talks that ended apartheid, mediating at the behest of both governments in the 1980 U.S.-Iranian hostage conflict, and working with Oscar Arias on Central American peace. His clients are among the world's best-known corporations. Patton is coauthor with Fisher and Ury of *Getting to YES: Negotiating Agreement Without Giving In* (2nd ed., 1991) and with Stone and Heen of *Difficult Conversations: How to Discuss What Matters Most* (1999).

Scott R. Peppet is an associate professor of law at the University of Colorado School of Law in Boulder, Colorado, where he specializes in legal ethics and alternative dispute resolution and negotiation. He is the coauthor of *Beyond Winning: Negotiating to Create Value in Deals and Disputes* (2000, with Mnookin and Tulumello), which received the CPR Institute for Dispute Resolution Award for best new book in 2000. He has also authored various articles on legal negotiation and dispute resolution. These include "Lawyers' Bargaining Ethics, Contract, and Collaboration: The End of the Legal Profession and the Beginning of Professional Pluralism" (*Iowa Law Review,* 2005); "Contract Formation in Imperfect Markets: Should We Use Mediators in Deals?" (*Ohio State Journal on Dispute Resolution,* 2004); and "Contractarian Economics and Mediation Ethics: The Case for Contingent Fee Mediation" (*Texas Law Review,* 2003).

Linda L. Putnam is professor of organizational communication in the Department of Communication at Texas A & M University. Her current research interests include negotiation, organizational conflict, gender and negotiation, and language analysis in organizations. Putnam received her Ph.D. from the University of Minnesota. She is the coeditor of four books, including *Communication and Negotiation* (1992). She is a past president of the International Communication Association, a past president of the International Association of Conflict Management, and a past board member-at-large of the Academy of Management. She is a fellow of the International Communication Association and a distinguished scholar of the National Communication Association.

John Richardson is a Ph.D. candidate in the Organization Studies Department at Boston College. His research focuses on the effect that a negotiator's choice of distribution method has on integrative outcomes and the relationship between negotiators, and on how criteria spread through social networks. Before starting on his doctorate, John was a lawyer at Anderson Kill Olick and Oshinsky and a lecturer on law at Harvard Law School. He is a coauthor, with Howard Raiffa and David Metcalfe, of *Negotiation Analysis: The Science and Art of Collaborative Decision Making*; and with Roger Fisher and Alan Sharpe of *Getting It Done: How to Lead When You Are Not in Charge.*

Lukasz Rozdeiczer holds a law degree from the Warsaw University, a diploma in British and European legal studies from Cambridge and Warsaw Universities, and an LL.M. from Harvard Law School. He is currently a visiting scholar at Georgetown University Law Center and an associate of the Dispute Resolution Program at the Program on Negotiation at Harvard Law School. Lukasz's current research focuses on mediation in commercial disputes and transactions, including corporate reorganization and international transactions. He is writing his Ph.D. thesis at Warsaw University on introducing commercial mediation to the Polish Legal System (Code of Civil Procedure). Before coming to the United States, Lukasz practiced law in international law firms in Warsaw, and was adviser to the secretary of state of the Republic of Poland. He currently lives in Washington, D.C., where he continues his research at Georgetown Law Center and works as a consultant for the World Bank. While writing his chapter in this volume he was a Senior Hewlett Fellow on Law and Negotiation at the Program on Negotiation, Harvard Law School.

Frank E. A. Sander is Bussey Professor at Harvard Law School. He was born in Stuttgart, Germany, and received his A.B. and LL.B. from Harvard. Following graduation, he served as law clerk to Chief Judge Calvert Magruder of the U.S. Court of Appeals for the First Circuit (1952–1953) and Justice Felix Frankfurter of the U.S. Supreme Court (1953–1954). After brief stints with the U.S. Justice Department in Washington and Hill and Barlow in Boston, he began teaching at Harvard Law School in 1959, specializing initially in taxation and family law, and, since 1975, in dispute resolution. In 1976 at the Pound Conference he delivered a seminal paper titled "Varieties of Dispute Processing" that put forth the notion of the Multidoor Courthouse. He was a member of the ABA Standing Committee on Dispute Resolution from 1976 to 1989. He has written and lectured extensively on various aspects of ADR; *Dispute Resolution: Negotiation, Mediation, and Other Processes,* the textbook he coauthored, won the CPR Prize in 1985 for the best book on ADR published that year.

Andrea Kupfer Schneider joined the faculty of Marquette Law School in 1996. She is the author of *Creating the Musée d'Orsay: The Politics of Culture in France* (1998) and is also a coauthor of two additional books, *Beyond Machiavelli. Tools for Coping with Conflict* (1994) and *Coping with International Conflict* (1997). Schneider has published numerous articles on negotiation and international law, including articles in the *Harvard Negotiation Law Review,* the *Michigan Journal of International Law,* the *University of Pennsylvania Journal of International Economic Law,* and the *Negotiation Journal.* Schneider received her A.B. *cum laude* from the Woodrow Wilson School of International Affairs and Public Policy at Princeton University and her J.D. *cum laude* from Harvard Law School. She also received a Diploma from the Academy of European Law in Florence, Italy.

Jeffrey R. Seul is vice president, general counsel, and secretary of Groove Networks, Inc., a Boston-based software company, and a lecturer on law at Harvard Law School, where he teaches negotiation. Jeff was a senior associate of the Program on International Conflict Analysis and Resolution at Harvard's Weatherhead Center for International Affairs from 1996 to 2000. He has served as a mediator, facilitator, arbitrator, or consultant in a wide range of conflicts and negotiations in both the public and private sectors. His articles on negotiation and conflict resolution have appeared in the *Journal of Peace Research,* the *Ohio State Journal of Dispute Resolution, Washington Law Review,* and other publications.

Daniel L. Shapiro is associate director of the Harvard Negotiation Project. He also is on the faculty at Harvard Law School and the Psychiatry Department at Harvard Medical School/McLean Hospital. With a background in clinical psychology, Shapiro researches psychological dimensions of conflict management. He focuses particular attention on causes and prescriptive strategies for dealing with the psychological complexities of ethnopolitical conflict. To these ends, he provides negotiation consultation for governments and, starting in 1991, initiated a conflict management program across Eastern and Central Europe that now reaches close to one million people in twenty-one countries.

Katie Shonk is a research associate at Harvard Business School and the editor of Harvard Business School Publishing and the Program on Negotiation's monthly newsletter, *Negotiation*. She is the coauthor of *"You Can't Enlarge the Pie": Six Barriers to Effective Government* (with Max H. Bazerman and Jon Baron) and the author of *The Red Passport,* a short-story collection set in contemporary Russia.

Douglas Stone is a partner at Triad Consulting Group and a lecturer on law at Harvard Law School, where he teaches negotiation. Through Triad, he consults to a wide range of organizations, including Fidelity, Shell, Honda, the Boston Area Rape Crisis Center, and the World Health Organization. He has worked with mediators and journalists in South Africa, Greek and Turkish community leaders in Cyprus, and diplomats at the Organization of African Unity in Ethiopia. Doug is a coauthor of *Difficult Conversations* (1999) and *Real College* (2004), and was for many years associate director of the Harvard Negotiation Project.

Lawrence E. Susskind is Ford Professor of Urban and Environmental Planning at the Massachusetts Institute of Technology, where he has taught for more than thirty years. He is also visiting professor of law at Harvard Law School, where he helped to found the Program on Negotiation. In 1993, Susskind created the Consensus Building Institute, a not-for-profit provider of mediation and dispute resolution services. Through CBI (www.cbuilding.org) he has helped to mediate more than fifty complex disputes around the world. Susskind is coauthor of the award-winning *Consensus Building Handbook* (1999), as well as thirteen other books.

Mark S. Umbreit is a professor and founding director of the Center for Restorative Justice & Peacemaking at the University of Minnesota, School of Social Work. He serves as a fellow of the International Centre for Healing and the Law in Kalamazoo, Michigan. He is an internationally recognized practitioner and scholar with more than thirty-three years of experience as a mediator, trainer, researcher, and author of six books and more than 130 articles, book chapters, and monographs in the fields of restorative justice, mediation, and peacemaking. His most recent book, *Facing Violence: The Path of Restorative Justice & Dialogue,* reports on the first multisite study of victim offender mediation and dialogue in crimes of severe violence, primarily homicide. Umbreit has conducted research, training seminars, and lectures throughout the world. As a practitioner, he specializes in facilitating a dialogue between victims or family survivors of severe violence, primarily homicide, and the offender.

Betty Vos, a social work practitioner for over thirty years, served as assistant professor of social work at Valparaiso University and the University of Utah before joining the Center for Restorative Justice & Peacemaking, where she is a part-time senior research associate. Her recent research and publications have focused on restorative justice dialogue in bias-motivated crimes, victim offender dialogue in serious and violent crime, juvenile victim offender mediation, and peacemaking circles.

Anthony Wanis-St. John is a research associate at the Center on International Conflict Resolution at Columbia University. He earned his Ph.D. (2001) and M.A. (1996) from the Fletcher School, Tufts University, and was a doctoral fellow at Harvard Law School's Program on Negotiation. His research appears in periodicals such as *Negotiation Journal* and *Harvard Negotiation Law Review.* He facilitates organizational alliances and mediates corporate and labor-management disputes. He provides negotiation training to Fortune 1000 companies and consults with the World Bank on judicial modernization projects in Guatemala, Venezuela, El Salvador, and Mexico. He speaks fluent Spanish and French as well as basic Arabic. He was born in 1965 in Egypt of Lebanese and Palestinian families and emigrated to the United States in 1968.

Nancy A. Welsh is professor of law and associate director of the Center for Dispute Resolution at the Dickinson School of Law of the Pennsylvania State University. Her scholarship, which has appeared in journals including the *Washington University Law Quarterly,* the *Harvard Negotiation Law Review,* and the *Ohio State Journal of Dispute Resolution,* focuses on the institutionalization of court-connected and agency-sponsored mediation and the procedural justice offered by the mediation process. Before joining Penn State, Welsh was executive director of the nonprofit Mediation Center and served on the Minnesota ADR Review Board, which developed and implemented rules governing ADR in the state's courts. She is a graduate of Allegheny College and Harvard Law School.

NAME INDEX

SUBJECT INDEX

A

Accuser bias, 85–88

Action Science school of thought (Argyris), 40

Adjectival ambiguities, 204–205

Adjudication rules: and admission of settlement discussions, 269–270; and fee-shifting and offer of settlement rules, 267–269; and judicial review of settlement terms, 270–271

Aetna, 489

Affective satisfaction, 71–73

Affirmative misrepresentation, 257–260

Afghanistan, 442

African Americans, 104–105

African National Congress, 66, 67, 79

Age Discrimination in Employment Act (ADEA), 324

Agency capture, 509

Alabama arbitration, 447

Alaska Supreme Court, 266

Alternative dispute resolution: *versus* consensus building, 358–369; continuum, 358–360; and influence of context, 490–493; professionalization of, 494–498; successful institutionalization of, 488–490

American Airlines, 59, 489

American Arbitration Association (AAA), 20, 324, 331, 347, 447, 495

American Bar Association (ABA), 19, 259, 313, 495; Section on Dispute Resolution, 23, 513

American rule, 267

Americans with Disabilities Act (ADA), 324

AmericaOnline, 427

Amnesty International, 438–439

Arab-Israeli War (1973), 445

Arbitrability, 322–324

Arbitration: appropriateness of, 324–325; and arbitrator selection, 326; clauses, 324–328; compared to other dispute resolution processes, 319; determining procedures for, 326–327; under Federal Arbitration Act, 321–322; and federal arbitration law, 322–324; history of, 320–321; legal issues in, 321–324; of statutory claims, 324

Arbitrator: ethics, 330–331; selection, 326

Argentina, 444, 445

Armenia, 446

Army Corps of Engineers, 22

Art and Science of Negotiation (Raiffa), 52, 62, 125, 515

Assessment Center (CIA/OSS), 45, 46

Association for Conflict Resolution (ACR), 23, 493, 495. *See also* Society for Professionals in Dispute Resolution

AT&T, 45

Automated blind bidding processes, 430–431

Award: enforcement of arbitral, 331–332; form of, 327
Azerbaijan, 446

B

Bank of America, 489
Bargaining behavior, law of: and affirmative misrepresentation, 257–260; and coercion, 264–267; and mediation context, 263–264; and nondisclosure, 260–263
Bargaining, positional, 288–290
BATNA (Best Alternative To a Negotiated Agreement), 74, 142, 175, 283–285, 287–289, 292, 294, 295, 299
Beagle Channel, 444
Belief: and emotional escalator, 107; identity and, 102–104; in storytelling, 164; strategies for managing, 108–109
Beyond Winning: Negotiating to Create Value in Deals and Disputes (Mnookin, Peppet, and Tulumello), 180, 219
Big Five personality taxonomy, 37, 40; and agreeableness, 42; and conscientiousness, 42; and emotional stability, 42–43; and extraversion, 41–42; methodology, 41–43; and openness to experience, 43
Board of Education, Brown v., 340, 403
Bosnia, 445
Boston Prison Discipline Society, 383
Bridgestone/Firestone, 512
Brown v. Board of Education, 340, 403
Buddhist psychology, 103

C

California, 21
California Supreme Court, 264
Camp David Accords, 185, 186, 445
Canada, 440, 447, 448
Center for Alternative Dispute Resolution in Education (CADRE), 495
Center for Information Technology and Dispute Resolution, 428
Center for Public Resources, 20, 447
Chechen separatists, 443
Chicken, game of, 291–292
Chile, 444
China, 439
CIA, 45, 57
CIGNA, 489
Cobb County, Georgia, 464
Coca-Cola Enterprises, 489
Coercion, 264–267
Cold War, 17, 54
Collaborative law, 21, 196, 197

Collectivism, *versus* individualism, 121–122
Colombia, 442, 443
Columbia University, 483, 484
Commitments, 284
Communication, as element of negotiation, 284–285
Community Relations Service (United States Department of Justice), 19–20
Comprehensive Peer Mediation Evaluation Project (CPMEP), 482, 483
Concessions, 288–290
Confidentiality, issues of, 312–313
Confirmatory bias, 84–85
Conflict, dispute *versus*, 2–3
Conflict Management Group (CMG), 4, 158
Conflict Management, Inc., 295
Conflict resolution education: approaches to, 473–481; and Comprehensive Peer Mediation Evaluation Project (CPMEP), 482–483; discipline and peaceable schools in, 479–481; foundation abilities for, 472–473; Johnson and Johnson studies in, 481–482; mediation approach to, 474–475; peaceable classroom approach to, 475–476; peaceable school approach to, 477–479; process curriculum approach to, 477; research, 481–485; and Teachers College Columbia Alternative High School Study, 484; and Teachers College Columbia University Early Childhood Study, 483–484
Congo, 445
Conscionability, 329–330
Consensus building: *versus* alternative dispute resolution, 358–369; clarifying responsibilities for, 362; convening, 361–362; deliberating in, 362–363; and differences between two-party and multiparty negotiations, 364–366; implementing agreements in, 363–364; key steps in, 360–364; and making decisions, 363; mediators within process of, 364–366
Consistency Bias, 160
Context, influence of, 490
Contractual soundness, 330
Controlling the Costs of Conflict (Slaikeu and Hasson), 376
Cosmopolitan magazine, 36
Costa Rica, 445
CPR Institute for Dispute Resolution, 389, 390, 513
Cross-disciplinary gap, 513–514
Cuba, 441, 442
Cultural negotiation preference template, 130

Social position, 139–140
Society for Professionals in Dispute
  Resolution, 23, 495. *See also* Association
  for Conflict Resolution
South Africa, 66, 78, 445
Spaulding v. *Zimmerman*, 263
SquareTrade.com, 22, 428, 430, 432
Stanford Center on Conflict and Negotiation
  (SCCN), 23
Stanford University, 23, 515
Stare v. *Tate*, 263
State University of New York, 43
Stories: assumptions and implicit rules in,
  162–164; building, 152–153; causation and
  blame in, 156–158; characters in, 154–156;
  crucial role of frames in, 160–165; data
  for, 151–152; elements of, 154–160; and
  emotion, 164–165; impact of strong emotions
  on, 154; and labels, 161; and metaphor,
  161–162; personal experiences, values, and
  beliefs in, 164; and reinforcing existing
  storylines, 153–154; timelines in, 158–160
Swedish ombudsman, 22–23
Syria, 126

T
Tate, Stare v., 263
Teaching pedagogies, 516
Teaching Students to Be Peacemakers
  program, 481
Test Design Project (Hewlett Foundation), 497
Texas, 464
Thematic Apperception Test (TAT), 160
Theory centers (Hewlett Foundation), 23
Thirty Years War, 444
Thomas-Kilmann styles inventory, 102
Toro Motors, 489, 512
Transformative outcomes, 142–144, 309–310
Transportation Security Agency (TSA), 381
Treaty of Ghent, 260
Treaty of Westphalia (1648), 444
Turkey, 105
Turkish Cypriots, 126, 159
Two-level games, 442

U
Uncertainty avoidance, 122
Uniform Commercial Code, 16–17
Uniform Mediation Act (UMA), 245, 313
United Airlines, 59
United Kingdom, 96
United Nations, 427, 444, 446, 448;
  Commission on International Trade Law
  (UNCITRAL), 448

United States Air Force, 489
United States Department of Health and
  Human Services, 489
United States Department of Homeland
  Security, 489
United States Department of Justice,
  20, 271
United States Federal Trade Commission, 427
United States Postal Service (USPS), 489,
  492, 493
United States Supreme Court, 321, 343
University of Chicago, 106
University of Maryland, 427
University of Massachusetts Online Ombuds
  Office, 427
University of Minnesota Conflict Resolution
  and Cooperative Learning Center, 479
University of Washington, Seattle, 71
USAir, 59
USPS. *See* United States Postal Service

V
Value creation: and assumptions about value
  in disputes, 174–176; and differences in
  capabilities, 180–181; and differences in
  prediction, 179; and differences in priorities,
  178; and differences in risk tolerance, 180;
  and differences in timeframe, 178–179;
  disputes as opportunities for, 173–186;
  negotiating behavior leading to, 181–186;
  and reducing implementation problems,
  178; and reducing transaction costs, 177;
  and shared interests, 176–177
Vantage Partners, LLC., 295
"Varieties of Dispute Processing" (Sander), 19
Victim offender mediation (VOM), 21; costs,
  464; and crimes of severe violence, 464–465;
  and follow-up phase, 460; mediation phase,
  458–460; overview, 455–457; and participant
  satisfaction, 461–462; participants in,
  460–461; and preparation for mediation
  phase, 457–458; and recidivism, 463;
  referral and intake phase, 457; and
  restitution, 462
Victim-Offender Mediation Program
  (Resolutions Northwest), 463
Violent crime, 464–465. *See also* Victim
  offender mediation (VOM)
Vividness bias, 60

W
Wade, Roe v., 343
War of 1812, 260
Washington, D.C., 463